Cracking the

ACT*

2009 Edition

The Princeton Review

Cracking the
ACT*

2009 Edition

Geoff Martz, Kim Magloire, and
Theodore Silver

PrincetonReview.com

Random House, Inc. New York

The Princeton Review, Inc.
2315 Broadway
New York, NY 10024
E-mail: editorialsupport@review.com

Library of Congress Cataloging-in-Publication Data

ISBN 978-0-375-42899-9
ISSN 1030-5507

ACT is a registered trademark of ACT, Inc.

Editor: Rebecca Lessem
Production Coordinator: Kim Howie
Production Editor: Meave Shelton

Printed in the United States of America.

10 9 8 7 6 5 4 3 2 1

2009 Edition

Acknowledgments

A test-preparation course is much more than clever techniques and powerful computer score reports; the reason our results are so great is that our teachers really care. Eleven years ago, a small group of Princeton Review instructors enthusiastically created a program to prepare students for the previous version of the ACT. We would like to thank John Cauman, Judy Moreland, Bill Lindsley, and Jim Reynolds for their commitment to the original ACT project.

The completion of this book would not have been possible without the help and dedication of several individuals. We would like to thank Melissa Hendrix, Krista Prouty, and Jonah Firestone for their work on this edition. Thanks also to those who have updated previous editions. Special thanks to Adam Robinson, who conceived of and perfected the Joe Bloggs approach to standardized tests and many other successful techniques used by The Princeton Review.

Contents

Foreword

In 2008, a record number of high school students took the ACT. This is a good trend. The ACT is a better test than the SAT, and since every four-year college and university now accepts either, there's no reason to take that other test.

More students are prepping for the ACT as well, and scores are up for the third time in the last five years. I'm glad you've chosen this book to prepare and hope you are too. We've always tried—in our tutoring, online courses, classroom programs, and books—to be effective and efficient. We know the key to raising your ACT score does not lie in memorizing dozens of math theorems, the periodic table of elements, and the complete rules of English grammar. The information needed to do well on the ACT is surprisingly limited, and we'll concentrate on a small number of crucial concepts.

If you feel that standardized test scores don't reflect your high school grades, you might suspect that there's more to mastering this test than just honing math, verbal, and science skills. At its root, this test is trying to measure your reasoning. The test writers do this by leading you to wrong answers (called, fittingly, distracters). Some of our techniques address distracters; I think you'll find them fun and useful on every standardized test you take.

Despite the strength of our approach, a book can't mold itself around your strengths and weaknesses. We've set up an array of online tools that you can access at **PrincetonReview.com** once you register the serial number at the back of your book. We'll be adding new tools and lessons throughout the year, so check back from time to time.

Good luck on the ACT! And if you need more help, or just want to find the right college or the best way to pay for it, please stop by **PrincetonReview.com** or call us at 800-2Review.

John Katzman
Chairman and Founder

...So Much More Online!

More Lessons...

- Step-by-step guide to solving difficult problems
- Tutorials that put our strategies into action
- Interactive, click-through learning for English, Math, Reading, and Science
- Overview of the question types you will find on the ACT

More Practice...

- Reading Drill with passages, questions, and hints
- English Drill on Grammar, Sentence Structure, and Punctuation
- Full-length practice test

More Scores...

- Automatic scoring for online test
- Instant scoring and analysis for your book tests
- Optional essay scoring with our LiveGrader℠ service
- Performance analysis to tell you which topics you need to review

More Good Stuff...

- Sign up for e-mail tips and tricks
- Chat with other ACT students

...then College!

- Detailed profiles for hundreds of colleges help you find the school that is right for you
- Information about financial aid and scholarships
- Dozens of Top 10 ranking lists including Quality of Professors, Worst Campus Food, Most Beautiful Campus, Party Schools, Diverse Student Population, and tons more

princetonreview.com/cracking

Getting The Most Out Of Your Princeton Review Materials

1 Register

Go to PrincetonReview.com/cracking. You'll see a Welcome page where you should register your book using the serial number. What's a serial number, you ask? Flip to the back of your book and you'll see a bunch of letters and numbers printed on the inside back cover. Type this into the window, dashes included. Next you will see a Sign Up/Sign In page where you will type in your e-mail address (username) and choose a password. Now you're good to go!

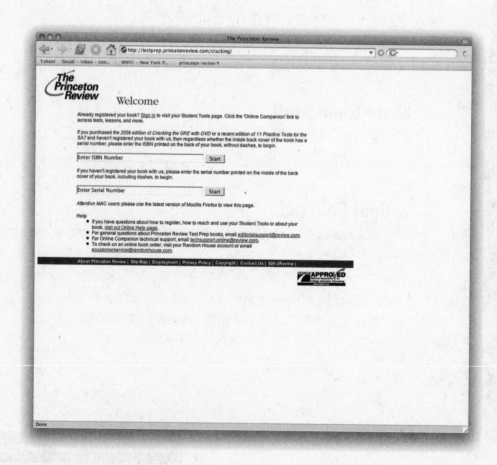

2 Check Out Your Student Tools

Once you are logged in and registered, click on "Your Student Tools." From there, you can access practice tests, online course demos, class information (for current students), important dates and more. Check out the "Advice Library" and "What's New" for additional information. But first, look under "Your Course Tools" and click on the name of your book. Be sure to enable pop-ups! The window that will pop-up when you click on your book is called the dashboard and it will lead you to tons of helpful online components.

3 Make Use of the Dashboard

The dashboard has 5 buttons displayed vertically. Click on each of these buttons to explore your options. There's a lot of fantastic online content, including drills, problem-solving strategies worked out in examples, a full practice test with automatic grading, discussion area, and more.

Find the college that is right for you with our ranking lists. See which school has the best cafeteria food, the best dorms, the most red-tape and lines, the worst library, the best parties, and many more categories. Sign up for email tips about the ACT and check out the vocabulary "Word du Jour" for a new word each day. Our website is your resource for tons of practice exercises and college information.

Part I
Orientation

Chapter 1
Introduction to the ACT

So, you have to take the ACT? What will you need to do first? This chapter presents an overview of the ACT as a whole and discusses registration requirements, when to take the test, how to have your scores reported to colleges (or how not to), and the ways in which colleges use your scores.

THE ACT

The Princeton Review has a reputation for test bashing that is richly deserved. In general, we don't have many nice things to say about the tests we tackle or the organizations that write them. So it's a pleasure to take on what we feel is (by comparison) a fair and good-hearted test, written by intelligent people.

The ACT measures what it says it does—academic achievement. It doesn't pretend to measure your analytic ability or your intelligence. The people at ACT admit that you can increase your score by preparing for the test. They even put out their own coaching book.

So if we ever seem to be poking fun at the test or the people who write it, we want you to remember that it does not lessen our underlying affection and respect for the exam and its authors.

If there is any flaw in the ACT, it is that, in its attempt to be fair, it has become a little, well, predictable. Of course, when we say that the ACT is a completely predictable test, we mean it in the nicest possible way. We *like* predictable tests, and so should you.

The ACT Is a ~~Standardized~~ *Predictable* Test

From now on, whenever you see the word *standardized*, think *predictable* instead. The ACT tests the same information the same way, year after year. For example, there are always 14 plane geometry questions on the ACT, not 13, not 15, exactly 14. There are exactly 10 questions on punctuation. You can count on it. Even the way the test asks the questions is predictable, based on the need for a standardized product.

The review in this book is based on the very specific knowledge you need to do well on this test. The test-taking strategies we have developed are designed to take advantage of the ACT's predictability.

Do I Need to Prepare if I Have Good Grades?

Let's take the hypothetical case of Sid. Sid is valedictorian of his class, editor of the school paper, and the only teenager ever to win the Nobel Prize. To support his widowed mother, he sold more seeds from the back of comic books than any other person in recorded history. He speaks eight languages in addition to being able to communicate with dolphins and wolves. He has recommendations from Colin Powell *and* Bill Gates. So if Sid had a bad day when he took the ACT (the plane bringing him back from his Medal of Freedom award presentation was late), we are pretty sure that he is going to be just fine anyway. But Sid wants to ensure that when his colleges look at his ACT score, they see the same high-caliber student they see when they look at the rest of his application, so he carefully reviews the types of questions asked and learns some useful test-taking strategies.

I Have Lousy Grades in School. Is There Any Hope?

Let's take the case of Tom. Tom didn't do particularly well in high school. In fact, he has been on academic probation since kindergarten. He has caused four of his teachers to give up teaching as a profession, and he prides himself on his perfect homework record: He's never done any, not ever. But if Tom aces his ACT, a college might decide that he is actually a misunderstood genius and give him a full scholarship. Tom decides to learn as much as he can about the ACT.

Most of us, of course, fall between these two extremes. So is it important to prepare for the ACT?

If you were to look in the information bulletin of any of the colleges in which you are interested, we can pretty much guarantee that somewhere you would find the following paragraph:

> Many factors go into the acceptance of a student by a college. Test scores are *only one* of these factors. Grades in high school, extracurricular activities, essays, and recommendations are also important and may in some cases outweigh test scores.

> (2008 University of Anywhere Bulletin)

Truer words were never spoken. In our opinion, just about *every* other element in your application "package" is more important than your test scores. The Princeton Review (among other organizations) has been telling colleges for years that scores on the ACT or the SAT are pretty incomplete measures of a student's overall academic abilities. Some colleges have stopped looking at test scores entirely, and others are downplaying their importance.

So Why Should You Spend Any Time Preparing for the ACT?

Out of all the elements in your application "package," your ACT score is the easiest to *change*. The grades you've received up to now are written in stone. You aren't going to become captain of the football team or editor of the school paper overnight. Your essays will be only as good as you can write them, and recommendations are only as good as your teachers' memories of you.

On the contrary, in a few weeks you can substantially change your score on the ACT (and the way colleges look at your applications). The test does not pretend to measure analytic ability or intelligence. It measures your knowledge of specific skills such as grammar, algebra, and reading comprehension. Mostly, it measures how good you are at taking this test.

Size Matters
Large schools process more applications, so they rely heavily on standardized test scores. Small schools have the time to read the rest of your application.

When It Comes to the ACT, *Nothing* Is Written in Stone

It doesn't matter how well you've done in school up to now. Good grades are not a guarantee that you will do well on the ACT. It doesn't matter if you've always been bad at taking standardized tests. Colleges aren't going to see any of your scores from earlier standardized tests. It doesn't matter if you hate math in general or English in general or science in general. The ACT doesn't measure math in general. It measures the math that is on the ACT.

By reviewing the very specific knowledge that the people who write the ACT think is important and by learning good test-taking strategies, you should be able to increase your ACT score significantly. This is not just our opinion. Even the people who write the test agree.

What Is the ACT?

The ACT is a multiple-choice standardized exam that is supposed to measure your knowledge of some of the subjects taught in high school. The ACT takes about three and a half hours and has one break. It is divided into four tests, which are always given in the same order. (ACT calls them tests, but we may also use the term "sections" in this book to avoid confusion.)

1. English Test (45 minutes—75 questions)

In this section, you will see 5 essays on the left side of the page. Some words or phrases will be underlined. On the right side of the page, you will be asked whether the underlined portion is correct as written or whether one of the three alternatives listed would be better. This is a test of grammar, punctuation, sentence structure, and rhetorical skills. Throughout each essay, commonly known as a "passage," there will also be questions about overall organization and style or perhaps about how the writing could be revised or strengthened.

2. Math Test (60 minutes—60 questions)

These are the regular, multiple-choice math questions you've been doing all your life. The easier questions, which test basic math proficiency, *tend* to come first, but the folks at the ACT try to mix in easy, medium, and difficult problems throughout the Math Test. A good third of the test covers pre-algebra and elementary algebra. Slightly less than a third covers intermediate algebra and coordinate geometry (graphing). Regular geometry accounts for less than a quarter of the questions, and there are four questions that cover trigonometry.

Power Booking
If you were getting ready to take a history test, you'd study history. If you were preparing for a basketball game, you'd practice basketball. So if you're preparing for the ACT, study the ACT!

3. Reading Test (35 minutes—40 questions)

In this test, there will be 4 reading passages of about 750 words each—the average length of a *People* magazine article but maybe not as interesting. There is always one prose fiction passage, one social science passage, one humanities passage, and one natural science passage, and they are always in that order. After reading each passage, you have to answer 10 questions.

4. Science Reasoning Test (35 minutes—40 questions)

No specific scientific knowledge is necessary for the Science Reasoning Test. You won't need to know the chemical makeup of hydrochloric acid or any formulas. Instead, you will be asked to understand six sets of scientific information presented in graphs, charts, tables, and research summaries, and you will have to make sense of one disagreement between two or three scientists. (Occasionally, there are more than three scientists).

There may be one additional section on the ACT. During this section, you will pay for the privilege of being a guinea pig while the test writers at ACT try out some experimental questions on you. This section typically comes at the end of the test and is usually very easy to recognize, as it is much shorter than a regular section—just 10 to 15 minutes long. In other words, it's not a big deal. This section usually shows up on the June exam, and it won't count toward your score.

5. Optional Writing Test (30 minutes)

The ACT contains an "optional" writing test featuring a single essay. We recommend you take the "ACT Plus Writing," version of the test because some schools require it. While on test day you may think you don't need it, you might later decide to apply to a school that requires a writing score. The last thing you want is to be forced into taking the whole ACT all over again… this time *with* the writing test. The essay consists of a prompt "relevant" to high school students on which you will be asked to write an essay stating your position on the prompt. Two people will then grade your essay on a scale of 1 to 6 for a total score of 2 to 12. In this book, we will teach you how to write the best possible essay for the ACT.

**More great titles by
The Princeton Review**
Word Smart

Where Does the ACT Come From?

The ACT is written by a company that used to call itself American College Testing but now just calls itself ACT. The company's main offices are in Iowa City, Iowa. The people at ACT have been writing a version of this test since 1959. Even if you aren't looking forward to taking the ACT this year, you would probably prefer it to the version they used to give. In the old days, the test included detailed questions about topics like the Constitution of the United States, electrostatic forces, and planets in the solar system.

The people at ACT also write a number of other tests, including a test for professional golfers and a test for dieticians. They provide a broad range of services to educational agencies and business institutions.

How Is the ACT Scored?

Scores for each of the four tests are reported on a scale of 1 to 36 (36 being the highest score possible). The four scores are averaged to yield your composite score, which is the score colleges and universities primarily use to determine admission. Next to each score is a percentile ranking. Percentile ranking refers to how you performed on the test relative to other people who took it at the same time. For instance, a percentile ranking of 87 indicates that you scored higher than 87 percent of the people who took the test and 13 percent scored higher than you.

Closed Loop
The ACT tests how well
you take the ACT.

Some of the scores have subcategories. English is broken down into Usage/ Mechanics and Rhetorical Skills. The subcategories may be of some marginal use to colleges; they are much more useful to you if you decide to take the test again, because they pinpoint your strengths and weaknesses. In these subcategories, scores are reported on a scale of 1 to 18 (18 being the highest score possible). They are also reported as percentiles.

If you decide to take the ACT Plus Writing Test, you will receive standard ACT scores plus two additional scores. One will be a scaled score from 1 to 36, which combines your performance on the Writing test and the English Test. The other will be a subscore, ranging from 2 to 12, which reflects how you did on your essay. Neither score contributes to your composite score. The Writing Test costs an additional $14.50, which you will be charged when you sign up for the ACT. The ACT with the Essay section is more expensive than the ACT without the Essay section. Check **www.act.org** for costs.

Three to seven weeks after you take the ACT, you and the colleges you have selected, if any, will receive your ACT scores in the mail. If you want, you can pay to see your scores a bit earlier (about 10 to 14 days after your test date).

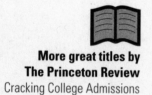

**More great titles by
The Princeton Review**
Cracking College Admissions

Who Actually Receives the Scores?

You might think that your scores will be mailed directly to your home, but this is not always the case. If you take the June administration of the test, scores are mailed to colleges and to you. For all other administrations, scores are sent to colleges and to your high school counselor, not directly to you, unless your high school has given ACT permission to send them to you. You then get the scores from the counselor. We've checked with ACT, and the people we talked to there said that if you choose not to provide a High School Code, your scores simply won't be sent to your high school. So, if you want your scores sent to your home (and not your high school), leave the High School Code blank. All colleges you list will get copies of your score regardless of whether you leave the High School Code blank.

There is one potential downside to not reporting your scores to your high school: If you're likely to receive a state-awarded scholarship on the basis of your ACT score, such a score is usually reported to the state's scholarship-awarding entity through—you guessed it—the high school. If you anticipate receiving such a score and are counting on such a scholarship (taking at least one test as a reality check is a good idea), go ahead and provide your High School Code. As the owners of your transcript, you and your parents can go to your high school and have a score removed from it later if you feel the score doesn't reflect your abilities. In any event, because ACT allows score choice (sending scores from just one testing date to colleges), the test scores on your high school transcript ultimately don't matter that much.

When Should You Take the ACT?

The test is given four times each year in New York and five times each year in most of the rest of the country, usually at 8:00 A.M. on a Saturday morning. In some states, there are six administrations each year (they include a September test date as well). Most students take the ACT in the spring of their junior year or in the fall of senior year. Check out **www.act.org** to determine which administrations are best for you. A good case can be made for taking it at the earlier date. For one thing, you'll have a better idea of where you stand. If your score is about what you want, you can spend the summer visiting colleges or getting started on your applications. If your score is lower than you want, you can use the summer to prepare to take the test again in the fall.

The cost of the ACT changes from time to time and depends on whether you decide to take the Writing Test. Currently, the test without the writing portion is $30.00 and $44.50 with it. You can obtain a registration packet for the ACT at your high school guidance office, online at **www.actstudent.org/forms/stud_req.html**, or by writing or calling ACT at the address and phone number below.

ACT Registration
P.O. Box 414
Iowa City, IA 52243
319-337-1270

You can also register directly online via ACT's website at **www.actstudent.org**. But before you decide on a test date, there are other things that you should know.

Special Considerations

The ACT offers accommodations to students with special needs, learning or otherwise. You cannot, however, get accommodations without prior arrangement with ACT. A detailed description of the types of special accommodations available and of ACT's documentation requirements is available at **www.act.org/aap/disab**.

Some ACT Test Dates Are Better Than Others

On certain dates, the ACT offers what it calls "Test Information Release." If you take the ACT on one of these dates, you can, for $15.00 (at press time), receive a copy of the test that you took and a photocopy of your actual answer sheet. We strongly advise that you take the test on one of these dates. It is not unheard of for ACT to make a mistake when scoring. You certainly won't find out about this un-less you can see the test you took and your own answers. For example, it is possible to fill in an oval on the answer sheet darkly enough for the human eye to see, but not darkly enough for the machine that scores the test to read. In this case, if you point it out to them and pay another small, additional fee, the people at ACT will hand-score your test and change your grade if they indeed made a mistake.

What If I've Already Taken the ACT Once Before?

The nice folks at ACT allow you to decide which of your ACT scores they report to colleges. If you want to have full control over this, it is a good idea *not* to take advantage of the four free score reports ACT offers to send to colleges directly after the test. Why send colleges scores you might not want them to see? While it costs a few extra dollars to get ACT to send scores to schools later, it is well worth being able to send the colleges your best results.

How to Prepare for the ACT

The Princeton Review materials and test-taking techniques contained in this book should give you all the information you need to improve your score on the ACT.

Other popular coaching books contain several complete practice ACT exams. We strongly advise you *not* to waste your time taking these tests. In some cases, the questions in these books are not modeled on real ACT questions. Some of them cover material that is not even on the real ACT. Others give the impression that the ACT is much easier or more difficult than it really is. Taking the practice tests offered in these books could actually hurt your score.

One reason these coaching books do not use real ACT questions is that the folks at ACT won't let them. They have refused to let anyone (including us) license ac-tual questions from old tests. You may have chosen our book because it contains two practice ACT exams. Rest assured that these tests are *modeled very closely after actual ACT exams*, with the proper balance of questions reflective of what the ACT actually tests.

Cynics might suggest that no one else can license ACT exams because ACT sells its own review book called *The Real ACT Prep Guide*. Although *The Real ACT* doesn't contain a very full review section and offers only limited test-taking strategies (after all, no one wants to rob his or her own house), we think ACT's book is well worth the price just for the three real tests it contains. We recommend that you either buy the book or ask your high school to send away to ACT for actual ACT Tests. You can also buy real ACT Tests on **www.act.org**. You should get a copy of *Preparing for the ACT Assessment* from your counselor. It's free, and it contains a complete, real ACT. The same test can be downloaded for free from ACT's website.

While we advise you to obtain these practice tests to further your preparation for the ACT, it is important that you use them properly. Many students like to think that they can prepare by simply taking test after test until they get the scores they want. Unfortunately, this doesn't work all that well. Why? Well, in many instances, repetitive test taking only reinforces some of the bad test-taking habits that we address in this book. You should use practice tests for the following three key purposes:

- to build up familiarity with the exam
- to learn how to avoid the types of mistakes you are currently making
- to master our techniques and strategies so you can save time and earn more points

The ACT vs. the SAT

You may have to take the ACT anyway, but most of the schools in which you're interested also accept the SAT. We think the SAT is nowhere near as fair a test as the ACT. Whereas the ACT says it measures "achievement" (which we believe *can* be measured), the SAT says it measures "ability" (which we don't think can be measured at all; and if it can, the SAT sure isn't doing it).

**More great titles by
The Princeton Review**
Crash Course for the ACT,
Cracking the SAT

What Exactly Are the Differences?

The SAT tends to be less time-pressured than the ACT. However, many of the questions on the SAT are trickier than those on the ACT. The SAT Verbal sections have a stronger emphasis on vocabulary than do the ACT English and Reading Tests. The SAT Math section Tests primarily algebra and plane geometry and includes no trigonometry at all.

Both tests include an Essay section, although ACT has made this new essay optional because some colleges require it while others do not. ACT doesn't want to force students to take (and pay for) a test they don't need. The implication then is that many students can ignore the new Writing Test altogether depending on what the schools to which they are applying require.

To find out if the schools in which you are interested require the ACT essay, visit the ACT writing test page at **www.actstudent.org/writing** or contact the schools directly.

While we are obviously not tremendously fond of the SAT, you should know that some students end up scoring substantially higher on the SAT than they do on the ACT and vice versa. It may be to your advantage to take a practice test for each one and see which is more likely to get you a better score.

What Is The Princeton Review?

The Princeton Review is the world's leading test-preparation and educational services company. We run courses at hundreds of locations worldwide and offer web-based instruction at **PrincetonReview.com**. Our test-taking techniques and review strategies are unique and powerful. We developed them after studying all the real ACTs on which we could get our hands and analyzing them with the most sophisticated software available. For more information about our programs and services, feel free to call us at **800-2Review**.

A Final Thought Before You Begin

The ACT does not measure intelligence, nor does it predict your ultimate success or failure as a human being. No matter how high or how low you score on this test initially, and no matter how much you may increase your score through preparation, you should *never* consider the score you receive on this or any other test a final judgment of your abilities.

Chapter 2
Triage

The ACT is a time-limited test. You can develop strategies to help you use the time you are given to your advantage. One simple strategy is to prioritize the questions rather than answer them in the order in which they appear. In this chapter, you'll learn how to use a two-pass, or triage, system for approaching the ACT efficiently and effectively.

How Questions Are Organized

Wouldn't it be great if all the questions on the ACT were arranged in order of difficulty? Then you could do the easiest questions first and move on from there. That way you wouldn't waste a lot of time trying to answer difficult questions before you had answered all the easy questions, which count for the same number of points anyway.

Unfortunately, the ACT is not organized that way.

According to the ACT writers we interviewed, the English section of the test is not in any order of difficulty. In the Math Test, according to ACT literature, "most people find the first questions on the test easier...than the ones that come later," but these are only very rough guidelines. Many Princeton Review students find that some questions toward the end of the test are easier than many of the questions in the beginning.

Equality
Remember that easy questions are worth just as much as difficult questions, so do the easy ones first!

Oh. But What If…

But what if the Science Reasoning and Reading *passages* were arranged in order of difficulty? Some of the other test-preparation books maintain that they are. According to one ACT writer, this is true, "…only in an average sense. We believe in the philosophy that if students are running out of time, the questions they don't get to should be ones they would have difficulty with anyway. But students will find plenty of exceptions." So by its own admission, ACT does not use a definite order of difficulty in the Science Reasoning or Reading Tests.

Oh. But…

But nothing! On the ACT, if you want to do the easy questions first, you're going to have to find them for yourself. We have a good way to think about this. We call it "triage."

TRIAGE

Triage is the medical term that describes the technique used by emergency-room doctors when they have several emergencies at the same time. To save the most lives, doctors separate patients into three groups: those who will die regardless of intervention, those who require immediate medical attention, and those who can afford to wait a little while. The routine patients are left until last.

In ACT triage, you adapt this strategy somewhat. See that really tough algebra problem sitting over there? Forget it; it's a goner. How about that problem on frequency and amplitude? That would take far too long, and even if you got it right, it would still only be worth one point. Now this problem involving basic arithmetic—this is something different altogether. It's an easy question, so you should do it right away.

See that tough, horrible-looking passage about European authoritarianism during the nineteenth century? Let's see if it's still breathing after we finish the one about Ronald Reagan's election in 1980.

Just One More Minute…

If you find yourself stuck on a question, waiting for divine inspiration, it's time to move on to another, easier problem. Save your time and live to fight another day (or question, that is). The temptation to get stubborn and stay with a particular problem can be very strong, especially when you've already invested some time on it. Nonetheless, you need to move on. Why stick with a question that's giving you problems when there are easier questions to be answered?

For more help check out our academic tutoring offers at PrincetonReview.com

"Oh, Yeah!"

We've all had the experience of riding home in the car and suddenly slapping our hand to our forehead as we finally realized exactly how to do question number five. By using triage, you can sometimes have this sudden revelation *before* the test is over, when you can still do something about it. So how does triage work exactly?

Now, Later, Never

Do you want to do the problem *now*? That is the question you should constantly be asking yourself during the exam. If you finish reading a problem and immediately know how to solve it, then of course you should do it right away.

But what if you finish reading a problem and you aren't really certain how to begin? If you think you might be able to figure it out on your second pass, circle the question number and move on. This might seem hard to do at first, but it is one of the central tenets of good test taking, and it gets easier with practice. You aren't necessarily skipping the problem forever. You're just putting it at the back of the line.

However, if the problem is a goner and you're sure you'll never figure it out, fill in your guess answer and forget it. There are other problems out there waiting for you; don't worry about the ones you just *can't* do.

Two Passes

First Pass, Second Pass
On the first pass, do the questions you know how to do and guess on the questions that you have no idea how to do. On the second pass, answer all the questions that are doable but likely to take you more time.

We want you to do each section in two passes. During the first pass, the object is to nail every single question you can answer. By answering all the questions of which you're sure, you will never have to hear the words, "Okay, pencils down," and know that there were several more questions you could have done if only there had been more time. You will have already done them.

What Happens if I Think I Know How to Do It, but then I Realize I Was Wrong?

Nobody's right all the time. As soon as you realize you're stuck, you should put a big circle around the question and move on. This is the time when people tend to get stubborn. They think, "But I've already spent so much time on this question. It would be a waste to skip it now."

You Haven't Wasted the Time; You've Invested It

When you come back to this question on the second pass, you won't be starting from scratch. You'll already have read the question once. You may have made some notes in the margin. Perhaps reading it again will make you realize an important point you missed the first time. If not, throw it to the back of the line and count your blessings: You could still be back there working on question number five!

The Second Pass

After you've finished everything you can do on the first pass and bubbled in your Letter of the Day on all questions that you're sure you can't do, come back to the questions you circled for a second pass. Again, think ACT triage. Most of the "patients" in your emergency room have now been handled. Look over the remaining problems and ask yourself the same question: Which one do I want to do *now*? Obviously, none of them struck you as easy the first time or you would have answered on the first pass. On the contrary, among the remaining problems, some are probably more likely bets than others.

Sometimes when you read a question again, you suddenly realize what the point of the question really is. This will save you from having that "Oh, yeah!" revelation on the car ride home. But other times when you re-read a question, you suddenly realize that you will hate this question for the rest of your life and you never, ever want to see it again. Fine. Throw it to the back of the list and keep looking. These are "never" questions: Do them only if you have time to spare.

Sometimes you reject a question initially because you think it will take too much time. Well, now you have time. You've already locked in all the sure points, so maybe this is the question to do now.

Scoring More Points with ACT Triage

Deciding whether you will do a question *now*, *later*, or *never* is a crucial part of improving your results on the ACT. The whole point of ACT triage is to help you invest your time more profitably. By utilizing the two-pass approach and the concept of triage, you will, unlike most test takers, spend the majority of your time working on questions that seem easy or at least doable. As a result, you will score more points.

I've Done All the Questions I Know How to Do and All the Questions I Think I Know How to Do. Now What?

You guess. Guessing on the ACT is so important that we've given it its own chapter.

Time to Spare
Let's face it—the ACT is designed to be difficult to finish in the time given. Most students are not going to finish early. But what if you do? Do you lay your head down and catch a few z's? No way! Go back to the problems that you skipped the first time through or that you wondered if you'd done right. There's always something to check!

Chapter 3
Guessing and POE

There is no penalty for guessing on the ACT, so it is to your advantage to fill in an answer for every question. In this chapter, you'll learn how to take advantage of the multiple-choice nature of the ACT and get more points by understanding and using the Process of Elimination.

NO PENALTY FOR GUESSING

Imagine for a moment that you are a game show contestant. It's the final, big deal of the day. The host asks you, "Do you want curtain number one, curtain number two, or curtain number three?" As you carefully weigh your options, the members of the audience are screaming out their suggestions, but you can bet there is one suggestion no one in the audience is going to shout at you.

"Skip the question!"

Be Test Smart
Many students with good grades get below-average scores because they refuse to guess.

It wouldn't make sense. You have a one-in-three shot of winning, and there is no penalty for guessing wrong. (Okay, you might have to cart home a lifetime supply of toilet paper.)

On the ACT, you don't even have to worry about the toilet paper because there is no guessing penalty at all.

You Must Fill in an Answer for Every Single Question on the ACT

There are 215 questions on the ACT. If you went into the test room, filled out your name, and then went to sleep for the entire test, your composite score would be just about what you might expect: 0.

If, however, you went into the test room, filled out your name, went to sleep for most of the time, then woke up and picked answer choice (B) or (G) 215 times, your composite score would be a 12!

We would not recommend random guessing as an overall strategy (unless all you need is a 12, and that's only the first percentile), but you can see that it is in your interest to guess on every question you either can't answer or don't get to in time.

Ah, but there's guessing, and then there's *guessing*.

How to Score Higher on the ACT

Try the following question:

Multiple Choice
The ACT is a multiple-choice test. This means you don't have to come up with an answer; you just have to identify the correct one from among the four or five choices provided.

1. What is the French word for "eggplant"?

What? You don't know? Well then, you'd better guess at random. (By the way, there are no questions about vegetables, French or otherwise, on the ACT. We're just using this question to make a point.)

If you really don't know the answer to a question, of course, you should always guess. But before you choose an answer at random, take a look at the problem the way you would see it on the ACT.

1. What is the French word for "eggplant?"

    A. のみもの
    B. すきやき
    C. Aubergine
    D. デザート

Suddenly the question looks a lot easier, doesn't it? You may not have known the correct answer to this question, but you certainly knew three answers that were incorrect.

POE

The Process of Elimination (POE for short) enables you to make your guesses really count. Incorrect answer choices are often easier to spot than correct ones. Sometimes they are logically absurd; sometimes they are the opposite of the correct answer. If you find a wrong answer, eliminate it. While you will rarely be able to eliminate all of the incorrect answer choices, it is often possible to eliminate one or two, and each time you can eliminate an answer choice, your odds of guessing correctly get better.

Try another question.

1. What is the capital of Malawi?

    A. New York
    B. Lilongwe
    C. Paris
    D. Kinshasa

This time you could probably eliminate only two of the answer choices. However, that meant you were down to a fifty-fifty guess—much better than random guessing.

The Process of Elimination is a tremendously powerful tool. We refer to it in every single chapter of this book, and explain how to use it on a variety of specific types of questions.

Letter of the Day

Which makes more sense—guessing the same letter every time or switching around? If you think you're better off switching around, think again. As counterintuitive as it may seem, you will pick up more points consistently if you always guess the same letter. Sure, you won't get all of your random guesses correct, but you'll get some points. On the contrary, if you vary your guess answer, you might get some correct, but you might miss all of them just as easily.

It doesn't matter what letter you pick as your Letter of the Day. Contrary to popular opinion, you won't get more questions right if you guess (C) rather than any other choice. Go crazy, guess (A) or (F) on the next ACT you take. Just be consistent.

What if someone approached you moments before the ACT began and offered to give you the answers to the test? You'd be SHOCKED, right? But what if we told you that the person making the offer was the proctor running the test? The fact is that every student who takes the test gets to see all the answers ahead of time; they're printed in the test booklet, right underneath each question.

Chapter 4
Taking the ACT

Preparing yourself mentally and physically to take the ACT are both important. This chapter helps you learn exactly what you're in for, so you can plan ahead and be as comfortable as possible on test day. We not only talk about what to do but also what *not* to do.

PREPARING FOR THE ACT

The best way to prepare for any test is to find out exactly what is going to be on it. This book provides you with just that information. In the following chapters, you will find a comprehensive review of all the question types on the ACT, complete information on all the subjects covered by the ACT, and some powerful test-taking strategies developed specifically for the ACT.

To take full advantage of the review and techniques, you should practice on the tests in this book as well as on real ACT questions. We've already told you how to obtain copies of real ACT exams. Taking full practice exams allows you to chart your progress (with accurate scores for each test), gives you confidence in our techniques, and develops your stamina.

The Night Before the Test

Unless you are the kind of person who remains calm only by staying up all night to do last-minute studying, we recommend that you take the evening off. Go see a movie or read a good book (besides this one), and make sure you get to bed at a normal hour. No final, frantically memorized math formula or grammatical rule is going to make or break your score. A positive mental attitude comes from treating yourself decently. If you've prepared over the last several weeks or months, then you're ready.

If you haven't really prepared, there will be other opportunities to take the test, so get some rest and do the best you can. Remember, colleges will see only the score you choose to let them see. No *single* ACT is going to be crucial. We don't think night-before-the-test cramming is very effective. For example, we would not recommend that you try going through this book in one night.

On the Day of the Test

It's important that you eat a real breakfast, even if you normally don't. We find that about two-thirds of the way through the test, people who didn't eat something beforehand suddenly lose their will to live. Equally important, bring a snack to the test center. You will get a break during which food is allowed. Some people spend the break out in the hallways comparing answers and getting upset when their answers don't match. Ignore the people around you and eat your snack. Why assume they know any more than you do?

Don't Leave Home Without 'Em
Here are some items you'll want to have on test day.
- admissions ticket
- photo ID or letter of identification
- plenty of sharpened No. 2 pencils
- a watch
- an acceptable calculator with new batteries

Warming Up

While you're having breakfast, do a couple of questions from an ACT on which you've already worked to get your mind going. You don't want to use the first test on the real exam to warm up. And please don't try a hard question you've never done before. If you miss it, your confidence will be diminished, and that's not something you want on the day of the test.

At the test center, you'll be asked to show some form of picture ID or provide a note from your school—on school stationery—describing what you look like. The time or time remaining is often *not* announced during the test sections, so you should also bring a reliable watch—not the beeping kind—and, of course, several No. 2 pencils, an eraser, and a calculator. Check **www.actstudent.org/faq** to see if your calculator model is permitted. If you haven't changed the batteries recently (or ever), you should do that before the test or bring a back-up calculator.

When you get into the actual room in which you'll be taking the exam, make sure you're comfortable. Is there enough light? Is your desk sturdy? Don't be afraid to speak up; after all, you're going to be spending three and a half hours at that desk. And it's not a bad idea to go to the bathroom *before* you get to the room. It's a long haul to that first break.

ZEN AND THE ART OF TEST TAKING

Once the exam begins, tune out the rest of the world. That girl with the annoying cough in the next row? You don't hear her. That guy who is fidgeting in the seat ahead of you? You don't see him. It's just you and the exam. Everything else should be a blur.

As soon as one test ends, erase it completely from your mind. It no longer exists. The only test that counts is the one you are taking right now. Even if you are upset about a particular test, erase it from your mind. If you are busy thinking about the last test, you cannot focus on the one on which you are currently working, and that's a surefire way to make costly mistakes. Most people aren't very good at assessing how they performed on a given section of the exam, especially while they're still taking it, so don't waste your time and energy trying.

Some Things to Remember
- Make sure you know where the test center is located and where you need to go once you are at the test center.
- Show up early; you can't show up right when the test is scheduled to begin and expect to get in.
- Lay out your pencils, calculator, watch, admission ticket, and photo identification the night before the test. The last thing you want to be doing on the morning of the test is running around looking for a calculator. Also, it's important to have your own watch because there's no requirement that the room you're in have a working clock.
- Bring a snack and a bottle of water just in case you get hungry. There's nothing worse than testing on an empty stomach.

Keep Your Answers to Yourself

Please don't let anyone cheat off you. Test companies have developed sophisticated anti-cheating measures that go way beyond having a proctor walk around the room. We know of one test company that gets seating charts of each testing room. Its computers scan the score sheets of people sitting in the immediate vicinity for correlations of wrong answer choices. Innocent and guilty are invited to take the exam over again, and their scores from the first exam are invalidated.

Beware of Misbubbling Your Answer Sheet

Probably the most painful kind of mistake you can make on the ACT is to bubble in (A) with your pencil when you really mean (B), or to have your answers be one question number off (perhaps because you skipped one question on the test but forgot to skip it on the answer sheet). Aargh! The proctor isn't allowed to let you change your answers after a section is over, so it is critical that you either catch yourself before a test section ends or—even better—that you don't make a mistake in the first place.

Write Now
Feel free to write all over your test booklet. Don't do computations in your head. Put them in the booklet; you paid for it. Go nuts!

We suggest to our students that they write down their answers in their test booklets. This way, whenever you finish a page of questions in the test booklet, you can transfer all your answers from that page in a group. We find that this method minimizes the possibility of misbubbling and it also saves time. Of course, as you get near the end of a test, you should go back to bubbling question by question.

If you get back your ACT scores and they seem completely out of line, you can ask the ACT examiners to look over your answer sheet for what are called "gridding errors." If you want to, you can even be there while they look. If it is clear that there has been an error, ACT will change your score. An example of a gridding error would be a test in which, if you moved all the responses over by one, they would suddenly all be correct.

Should I Ever Cancel My Scores?

We recommend against canceling your scores, even if you feel you've done poorly. If you have registered as we recommended and not sent the scores to any colleges and possibly not to your high school, then the score you receive won't go anywhere unless you send it on later. There is no need to panic and cancel your score without knowing what it is if no one will ever see it. You never know—perhaps you did better than you think. Furthermore, if you've taken the ACT two or more times (something we heartily recommend), you can choose which score you want colleges to see when you request reports from ACT.

If you do decide to cancel your scores, ACT allows you to do it only at the test center itself. However, you can stop scores from reaching colleges if you call ACT by 12:00 P.M., Central Time on the *Thursday* following the test. The number to call is 319-337-1270.

Part II
How to Crack the ACT English Test

Chapter 5
Introduction to the
ACT English Test

The English test does not test how well you write. It tests how well you know and can apply the rules of standard written English. The ACT is a standardized test, so it always tests the same basic concepts. If you don't know what the question is testing, you can look at the answers for clues. In this chapter, you'll learn how you can find these clues and use them along with test strategy to get a higher English score.

What's Good Writing?

Deciding what constitutes good writing is difficult. So much depends on the context, on what the writer is trying to accomplish, and on who is doing the deciding.

Call Us Ignorant, but We Prefer "Four Score and Seven"

These days, there are computer programs that are supposed to fix our writing. Mike Royko, the national columnist, once decided to try out one of these computer programs on Abraham Lincoln's Gettysburg Address, with predictably humorous results. "Four score and seven years ago" became "eighty-seven years ago" and it went downhill from there, turning a moving document of history into trite, conventional, standard written English.

What the English Test Tests

The English test measures how well you understand "the conventions of standard written English." There are 5 passages to read. Portions of each passage will be underlined, and you must decide whether these portions are correct as written or whether one of the other answer choices is better.

Some questions are designed to measure your knowledge of punctuation, grammar, and sentence structure. Other questions are designed to see if you know how to revise and strengthen a passage, how to change particular words for style or clarity, or how to "explain or support a point of view [more] clearly and effectively." There are a total of 75 questions to answer in 45 minutes.

For more great titles by The Princeton Review:
Grammar Smart, Cracking AP Literature Exam

On Your Mark...
You have 45 minutes for 75 questions.

What Your Score Means

Good writing is, to some extent, a matter of opinion. No matter how well or how poorly you do on the English test, you should not feel that your ACT English score truly represents your ability to write. A good score does not make you the next Jane Austen; a bad score does not make you the next Bart Simpson.

We don't mean to imply that ACT is doing a bad job. It's tough to measure English skills, and we think the test writers have constructed a fair test. In the end, however, what the ACT English test measures is how well you take the ACT English test.

Remember, This Is a Standardized Test

Every time the ACT is given, it tests the same things in the same way. You don't need to be a strong writer to do well on this test. You *do* need to know what types of errors crop up again and again and how to fix them. By going into the exam armed with this knowledge, you can more easily identify both the intentional errors and the correct answers for these questions.

We are going to review all punctuation, grammar, sentence structure, and rhetorical skills that are tested on this exam.

Early Decision
Many selective colleges commit more than half of their admissions spots to Early Decision applicants. To take this route, you must file your application in early November. By mid-December, you'll find out whether you got in, but there's a catch. If you're accepted Early Decision to a college, you must withdraw all applications to other colleges.
Source: *Best 366 Colleges,* 2008 Edition

What Do the Passages Look Like?

Here is part of a sample passage.

[1]

When studying a foreign language, <u>its</u>
₁

helpful to have a grasp <u>with</u> other foreign
₂

<u>languages, if only</u> because one has already
₃
learned what things are most important to
know how to say first.

[2]

[1] I am proud to tell you that I can ask, "Where is the bathroom?" in four different languages. [2] We both, however, admire the accomplishments of my clumsy friend, Al. [3] He can <u>says</u> he is sorry in fourteen
₄

different languages. [5]

1. A. NO CHANGE
   B. its'
   C. it's
   D. it, is

2. F. NO CHANGE
   G. of
   H. to
   J. OMIT the underlined portion

3. A. NO CHANGE
   B. languages. Only
   C. languages, only if
   D. language: only if

4. F. NO CHANGE
   G. say
   H. said
   J. says that

5. Suppose the author wants to add the following sentence to paragraph 2:

   My friend Alice can ask for directions in five different languages.

   The best place to insert this sentence would be:

   A. Before sentence 1
   B. Before sentence 2
   C. Before sentence 3
   D. After sentence 3

Item 6 asks about the preceding passage as a whole.

6. Suppose the author had chosen to write a short essay on the value of studying Japanese. Would this essay successfully fulfill the writer's goal?

   F. No, because the writer is speaking about the general experience of learning a language.

   G. No, because the writer fails to mention which languages are the easiest to learn.

   H. Yes, because the writer explains how to learn additional languages.

   J. Yes, because the writer offers such facts as how to say "Where is the bathroom?"

Most of the questions refer to individual words or phrases in the passage; these words are underlined and numbered. A few of the questions (such as question 5) ask you about the organization of a paragraph. You can tell what paragraphs they ask about by looking for the question number in a box at the end of a paragraph. (See the number 5 in a box at the end of the passage?) You will also see a few questions (such as question 6) that ask you about the passage as a whole. By the way, the answers are 1. (C), 2. (G), 3. (A), 4. (G), 5. (B), and 6. (F).

TRIAGE

In Chapter 1, we introduced you to the concept of triage and told you that it would be useful on every test on this exam. In the English test, the ACT writers have concocted their own brand of triage so that the specific questions (on subjects such as punctuation, grammar, and sentence structure) tend to come earlier in each passage. Usually there will be one or two questions about style or rhetoric at the end of each passage, dealing with the passage as a whole.

Some rhetorical questions are sprinkled throughout the passages, and just because a question is at the beginning of a passage or only deals with a small mistake in grammar doesn't mean that you will necessarily spot the correct answer right away. If you are not sure what point of grammar, punctuation, or sentence structure is being tested, you should probably use POE (Process of Elimination) and move on: If you can eliminate any of the answer choices because you are sure they are wrong, you should cross out those choices and guess from what is left. You get the most out of your ability when you really attack the answer choices.

First Pass, Second Pass

On your first pass, answer all the questions that you know you can answer quickly and confidently. On your second pass, answer the questions that require more thought or that you skipped the first time through. Use POE to help you get rid of wrong answers.

In our students' experience, the format of this test—passages side by side with the questions—tends to make them want to guess too quickly. The impulse to pick the first answer that sounds good is sometimes very strong. After all, this *is* English, which for many of us is our first language.

The problem is, of course, that it is *not* the English we speak every day.

ACT Island

The Laws of ACT Island
Don't just rely on what sounds incorrect: Look for specific errors.

Imagine that a bunch of ACT writers were shipwrecked on a desert island about 20 years ago. Not having much to do, they continued to write tests, which they slipped into empty bottles and cast into the sea. The tests regularly wash up on the coast of Iowa (yes, we know that Iowa is landlocked), where the national headquarters of ACT is located. The company is grateful and uses the tests regularly.

The only problem is that, after 20 years, the test writers' English is feeling a little old-fashioned and stilted. Still, the company feels a lot of loyalty to these shipwrecked grammarians and wouldn't dream of changing their tests.

If you make a lot of mistakes in this test, it is probably because you are relying on your ear, which is used to hearing a less formal English than is tested on the ACT. Moreover, English is a funny language—lots of things that sound all right are grammatically incorrect, while other things that sound incorrect are perfectly fine. A much better way to approach this test is to look for the specific errors that appear on the test all the time. By looking for these errors, you can take the guesswork out of your approach to the ACT English test.

Looking for Clues

For more great titles by The Princeton Review:
Reading Smart, Word Smart

One of the best ways to look for errors is to search the answer choices for clues. The underlined portions are very short—usually only a few words—so it's easy to see how each choice is different from the others. These differences offer a strong indication of what is on the minds of the ACT writers.

Look at the following example:

27. **A.** NO CHANGE
    B. one goes
    C. you go
    D. he goes

Clearly, this question is about pronouns. Even if you do not spot something wrong with the underlined portion of the passage as you read it, the answer choices are telling you to check to see which of these pronouns agrees with the noun referred to in the passage. (Don't worry if you are rusty on pronouns; we'll cover them in detail later in this section.)

In the sections that follow, we show you the key elements for which to look in the passages and in the answer choices.

What If There Is More Than One Thing Wrong?

There is often more than one error in the underlined portion of a sentence. The best way to approach these questions, however, is not to try to see everything at once. Find *one* error. Eliminate the answer choices that contain the same error, then compare the remaining answer choices. Regardless of the number of errors you find in the question, keep your focus on the *differences* in the answer choices.

POE

You've probably already noticed that sometimes, even though you're not sure what the right answer is, you're *certain* that some of the answers are WRONG. Whenever you know an answer is wrong, cross it out. That's called POE (Process of Elimination), and it's a powerful tool for raising your score on the ACT.

When you come across an English question you're not sure how to answer, don't immediately circle it for later consideration and move on. First, take a look at the answers and see if there are any obvious mistakes in them. If there are, use POE. Cross out the wrong answers and guess from what's left. You should still circle the question and come back to it later if you have the time, but this way, you're getting the most out of the passage right as you're doing it. By crossing out the wrong answers and guessing now, you're preventing yourself from accidentally picking an answer you *know* is wrong when you use your Letter of the Day.

What's Wrong?
About 25 percent of the time…absolutely *nothing*.

No Change

Many of the questions in this test have NO CHANGE as the first of the answer choices. Just because this is a test is no reason to assume that there is always something wrong. NO CHANGE turns out to be the correct answer a little less than a quarter of the time it is offered. So don't be afraid to select it.

OMIT the Underlined Portion

A few of the questions in this test will have "OMIT the underlined portion" as the last of the four answer choices. When this choice is offered, it has a high probability of being correct—better than half the time on some recent tests. Unfortunately, a couple of recent tests we've seen had OMIT as the correct choice *less* than half the time, so you can't just choose it every time you see it.

It is worth noting that when you see OMIT, you should examine it very carefully.

What If Time Is Running Out?
Remember that as good as the techniques in the next chapters are, this is still a timed test. What should you do if you are running out of time? First, fill in every question with your guess answer. That way, if the proctor calls time, you at least have something filled in. Then go to the questions you haven't done and see which look like they would be the fastest to do. Usually, these are the questions with the shortest answer choices, not the longer rhetorical skills questions. Do as many of these as you can, changing the answers that you've already bubbled in as you go.

A Warning

To forestall the objections of the expert grammarians out there, let us say at the outset that this discussion is not designed to be an exhaustive discourse on English grammar and usage. You are reading this chapter to do well on the English test of the ACT. Thus, if we seem to oversimplify a point or ignore an arcane exception to a rule, it's because we feel no further detail is warranted. A rule is unlikely to be tested if it is obscure or controversial.

Before We Begin, Some Terminology

The ACT is not going to ask you to identify parts of speech or diagram a sentence, but it will be helpful for the following discussion if you know some basic definitions. Here's a simple sentence.

> *Tom broke the vase.*

This sentence is made up of two nouns, a verb, and an article.

- A **noun** is a word used to name a person, a place, a thing, or an idea.
- A **verb** is a word that expresses action.
- An **article** is a word that modifies or limits a noun.

In the sentence above, *Tom* and *vase* are both nouns. *The* is an article. *Broke* is a verb. *Tom* is the **subject** of the sentence because it is the person, place, or thing that is "doing" the action (the passive voice is an exception and will be discussed later). *Vase* is the **object** of the sentence because it receives the action of the verb (again, the passive voice is an exception).

Here's a more complex version of the same sentence.

> *Tom accidentally broke the big vase of flowers.*

We've added an adverb, an adjective, and a prepositional phrase to the original sentence.

- An **adverb** is a word that modifies a verb, an adjective, or another adverb.
- An **adjective** is a word that modifies a noun.
- A **preposition** is a word that notes the relation of a noun to an action or a thing.
- A **phrase** is a group of words that acts as a single part of speech. A phrase is missing either a subject, a verb, or both.
- A **prepositional phrase** is a group of words beginning with a preposition.

In the sentence above, *accidentally* is an adverb modifying the verb *broke*. *Big* is an adjective modifying the noun *vase*. *Of* is a preposition because it shows a relationship between *vase* and *flowers*. *Of flowers* is a prepositional phrase that acts like an adjective by modifying *vase*.

Here's an even more complex version of the same sentence.

As he ran across the room, Tom accidentally broke the big vase of flowers.

Now we've added to the original sentence a secondary clause containing a pronoun.

- A **pronoun** is a word that takes the place of a noun.
- A **clause** is a group of words that contains a subject and a verb.

Tom accidentally broke the big vase of flowers is considered the **independent clause** in this sentence because it contains the main idea of the sentence and could stand by itself. *As he ran across the room* is also a **clause** (it contains a subject and a verb), but because it is not a complete thought, it is called a **dependent clause**. In this clause, *he* is a pronoun taking the place of *Tom*.

Summary

- Do the questions in order, leaving only tougher rhetorical questions for the end. If you're having trouble with a particular question, leave it and come back. Often a later question will help you with an earlier one.

- Search the answer choices for clues. Focus on the differences between the answer choices, and use that information to determine the error(s) being tested.

- Look for one error at a time. It is a good idea to start by narrowing down the choices on the basis of errors in sentence structure and grammar, and then use punctuation to make your selection between the remaining choices. For instance, if the choices offer you a list of items or actions, first check for parallel construction and then look for correct use of serial commas.

- Don't forget that NO CHANGE is correct a little less than a quarter of the time. If you can't find anything wrong with the underlined portion, it may be correct as written.

Chapter 6
Sentence Structure and Punctuation

The ACT English test contains a number of questions that test sentence-structure issues and punctuation errors. This chapter takes a look at the primary errors in sentence structure: sentence fragments, comma splices and run-ons, misplaced modifiers, and non-parallel construction. It also covers the basics of how and when to use certain punctuation marks. Often, a sentence-structure and punctuation questions can be spotted by looking at the variations in the answer choices.

THE BASICS OF SENTENCE STRUCTURE

Good sentence structure is about putting together words, phrases, and clauses—the essential building blocks of sentences—in logical ways. Before we talk about the *errors* of sentence structure, let's spend a moment talking about correct structure. Here is that example again.

> *As he ran across the room, Tom broke the vase.*

This sentence consists of two clauses. Each clause has a subject and a verb. The second clause ("Tom broke the vase") is considered the main clause and is independent because it can stand alone. The first clause ("As he ran across the room,") is called dependent because it cannot stand alone.

You can easily change a dependent clause into an independent clause and vice versa. Often, all it takes is a single word.

> *He ran across the room.*

By removing "as" from the dependent clause, we suddenly have a sentence that can stand on its own. By adding an "as" to the second clause, we can instantly change it into a dependent clause.

> *As Tom broke the vase,…*

If we stuck these two new clauses together now, the meaning of the sentence would be very different. Could we have kept the meaning more or less the same and still made the first clause independent? Sure. Try this

> *Tom ran across the room, breaking the vase.*

Now the first half of the sentence contains the main independent clause. We had to change "he" to "Tom" so that the reader would know about whom the sentence was talking. We also had to change the second half of the sentence from a clause into a modifying phrase. **While a clause has a subject and a verb, a phrase is missing at least one of these.**

PUTTING THE PIECES TOGETHER

Proficient writers use a mixture of dependent clauses, independent clauses, phrases, and varied punctuation to add variety to their writing and to create emphasis. By combining these building blocks in different ways, writers create a rhythm and show readers which thoughts are most important.

Here are the most often used structures.

- Independent clause (period) new independent clause (period)
  Jane lit the campfire. Frank set up the tent.

- Independent clause (comma plus conjunction) independent clause (period)
  Jane lit the campfire, and Frank set up the tent.

- Independent clause (semicolon) independent clause (period)
  Jane lit the campfire; Frank set up the tent.

- Independent clause (comma) dependent clause (period)
  Jane lit the campfire, while Frank set up the tent.

- Dependent clause (comma) independent clause (period)
  As Jane lit the campfire, Frank set up the tent.

All of these examples are correct. A writer might choose one over another to emphasize one thought over another. For example, in the last sentence, the writer is choosing to make "setting up the tent" the focus. Perhaps in the next sentence the tent is going to collapse with Frank inside it.

THE GLUE

Punctuation serves as the glue that holds the pieces of our sentences together. It's important to use the correct punctuation; otherwise, the pieces of a sentence won't form a coherent sentence.

There are several types of punctuation that are used in different ways. Some types, such as the period, are only used in one way (to end a sentence). Other types, such as the apostrophe, can be used in many situations (denoting contractions or possession, for example). If that sounds confusing, don't worry—we'll go through each type and explain how it works and affects sentence structure.

As you saw previously, there are many different ways to combine clauses and phrases. Now let's see how punctuation works in these scenarios.

Two Independent Clauses

> *Mary wondered why there was a bird in the classroom and she decided to ask the teacher what the bird was doing indoors.*

When two independent clauses appear in the same sentence, they are usually joined by a conjunction (a word like *and, or, but, for, nor,* or *yet*). Thus, the two independent clauses above are: "Mary wondered why there was a bird in the classroom" and "she decided to ask the teacher what the bird was doing indoors." A comma belongs before the conjunction that joins the two independent clauses.

> *Mary wondered why there was a bird in the classroom, and she decided to ask the teacher what the bird was doing indoors.*

Alternatively, you could separate the two clauses with a period or a semicolon. To do that, you would also need to remove the conjunction *and*.

> *Mary wondered why there was a bird in the classroom. She decided to ask the teacher what the bird was doing indoors.*

Or:

> *Mary wondered why there was a bird in the classroom; she decided to ask the teacher what the bird was doing indoors.*

The first example using a period separates the two clauses completely. A semicolon, the other hand, indicates that the two clauses are related. However, the ACT doesn't tend to differentiate between the two.

You can also use a colon to connect two independent clauses if the second is an expansion or explanation of the first clause. Let's look at an example.

> *I didn't know what to do: I could either go camping or stay home and study for the ACT.*

An Independent Clause and a Dependent Clause

Check for Commas
Look out for
  • words and phrases in a series
  • introductory phrases and words
  • mid-sentence phrases that are not essential to the sentence

Commas are also used to separate independent clauses from dependent clauses. You'll remember that a dependent clause is one that cannot stand on its own as a sentence. Identify the dependent clause in the sentence below.

> *Before Mary could reach the teacher she saw the woman offer the bird part of the bagel.*

The first clause, "Before Mary could reach the teacher," cannot stand by itself and therefore is a dependent clause. "She saw the woman offer the bird part of the bagel" can stand by itself, so it is an independent clause. Here, the two must be separated by a comma.

> *Before Mary could reach the teacher, she saw the woman offer the bird part of the bagel.*

An Independent Clause and a Modifying Phrase

Commas are also used to separate independent clauses from modifying phrases of more than just a couple of words. A modifying phrase modifies or describes something else, usually a noun. Identify the modifying phrase in the sentence below.

Hungry and excited the bird snapped up the bagel.

"Hungry and excited" is a modifying phrase (it modifies the noun "bird"). "The bird snapped up the bagel" is an independent clause. The two must be separated by a comma.

Hungry and excited, the bird snapped up the bagel.

Additional Information Within an Independent Clause

You might decide to include some extra information or details in your independent clause. You can set that information apart from the rest of the sentence by using commas or dashes. You can also use a colon to add a list of related details.

Josh, who needed to stock up for the party, went to the store to buy the necessary supplies: soda, chips, balloons, and weasels.

Commas

Commas can change restrictive clauses or phrases to being nonrestrictive. What does that mean?

A "restrictive" clause or phrase is essential to the meaning of a sentence, and it should not be separated from the rest of the sentence by commas.

People who snore are advised to sleep on their sides.

"Who snore" is essential to the meaning of this sentence. The sentence is not saying that *all* people should sleep on their sides, just the ones who snore.

A "nonrestrictive" clause or phrase is not essential to the meaning of a sentence. It merely adds a parenthetical thought, and therefore, it needs to be separated from the rest of the sentence by commas.

My father, who snores loudly, always sleeps in his long johns.

Identify the nonrestrictive clause in the sentence below.

Mary who by now was very confused stopped in front of the woman.

The nonrestrictive clause is "who by now was very confused." This clause modifies the noun that precedes it—in this case, "Mary"—but is not essential to the meaning of the sentence. "Mary stopped in front of the woman" does not need the clause in order to make sense as a sentence. To set off the clause from the rest of the sentence, you need to surround it with a *pair* of commas.

> *Mary, who by now was very confused, stopped in front of the woman.*

Identify the restrictive clause in the sentence below.

> *"Only a person who is a little peculiar would feed a bagel to a bird!" thought Mary.*

"Who is a little peculiar" is a restrictive clause because it adds essential information to the sentence. Thus, it does *not* require separation by commas.

How Do You Spot Restrictive/Nonrestrictive Comma Errors?

As always, the answer choices provide you with a very small menu of options from which to choose. If you see differences in punctuation among the choices, check to see whether the underlined portion of the sentence is part of a restrictive or nonrestrictive phrase or clause.

Dashes

Dashes Often Travel in Pairs

Dashes (like parentheses) are used to set off a phrase that is not essential to the meaning of the sentence

Dashes (—) separate a word or group of words from the rest of the sentence. Dashes are used either to indicate an abrupt break in thought or to introduce an explanation or afterthought.

In the example below, which group of words should be separated from the rest of the sentence?

> *I tried to express my gratitude not that any words could be adequate but she just nodded and walked away.*

The clause "not that any words could be adequate" must be isolated from the rest of the sentence.

> *I tried to express my gratitude—not that any words could be adequate—but she just nodded and walked away.*

When the group of words that needs isolating is in the middle of a sentence, dashes function as a pair of less formal parentheses. However, when the phrase that needs isolating is at the end of the sentence instead, only one dash is required.

> *Just outside the door to the cabin we heard the howling of wolves—a sound that made our hair stand on end.*

How Do You Spot Dash Errors?

If the underlined portion *or any of the answer choices* contains a dash, compare the dash to the punctuation marks available in the other answer choices. Also check the non-underlined portion of the passage for dashes that might be linking up with this one to isolate a clause or phrase. Ask yourself whether the sentence contains a sudden break in thought, an explanation, or an afterthought.

Remember that if the group of words that needs isolating is in the middle of the sentence, there should be a *pair* of dashes. If the group of words is at the end of the sentence, there should be only one.

Colons

Colons are usually used after a complete statement to introduce a list of related details. The list can have many items or just one. In the following sentence, try to decide where the statement ends and the details begin.

> *Maria just purchased all the camping supplies for our trip, a backpack, a sleeping bag, and a pair of hiking boots.*

"Maria just purchased all the camping supplies for our trip" is the complete statement in the sentence above. "A backpack, a sleeping bag, and a pair of hiking boots" are the related details. A colon belongs between the two.

> *Maria just purchased all the camping supplies for our trip: a backpack, a sleeping bag, and a pair of hiking boots.*

How Do You Spot Colon Errors?

If the underlined phrase *or any of the answer choices* contains a colon, you should ask yourself the following question:

Is a list of some kind introduced by an independent clause?

If so, a colon preceding the list or statement is correct. If not, a colon is probably incorrect.

One of ACT's favorite tricks is to write a sentence that utilizes a colon to introduce a list but to do so incorrectly because it follows an incomplete thought. Look out for colons that follow the verb *including* or the phrase *such as*.

> *Maria just purchased all the camping supplies for our trip, including: a backpack, a sleeping bag, and a pair of hiking boots.*

In this example, the colon is used improperly. By adding the word "including," the part of the sentence preceding the colon is no longer an independent clause, and therefore, the sentence, as written, is incorrect.

Check for Colons
Look out for
- an underlined phrase that contains a list

To make a sentence more complex, you can always add more clauses and phrases (with the appropriate punctuation, of course), but those are the basic building blocks. Now that we know how to put these pieces together, let's look at some of the ways the ACT tests sentence structure errors.

AVOID THESE COMMON ERRORS IN SENTENCE STRUCTURE

There are four main types of errors in sentence structure.

1.   sentence fragments
2.   run-ons and comma splices
3.   misplaced modifiers
4.   non-parallel construction

All of these errors are the result of incorrect placement of the building blocks that make up sentences. Sentence structure on the ACT is closely tied to punctuation. The two are related because sentence structure errors can often be fixed by using the appropriate punctuation. In fact, you will find that by using punctuation clues from the answer choices, you will often be able to zero in on sentence structure errors in the passages.

Error #1: Sentence Fragments

A complete sentence must have a subject and a verb, and it must be able to stand alone. In other words, it must be or contain an independent clause. Remember the very first example in this chapter?

> *Tom broke the vase.*

This is an independent clause. We can change it into a dependent clause by adding just one word.

> *When Tom broke the vase,...*

Even though it still has a subject and a verb, this clause can no longer stand alone. It is now waiting for an independent clause to finish the sentence.

> *When Tom broke the vase, Sid ran to tell their aunt Sally.*

You can turn any independent clause into a dependent clause by *adding* one of the words in the box below to the beginning of the clause.

Fragments
The ACT always contains.
A few sentence fragments.
Like these.

Check for Sentence Fragments
Look out for
- a dependent clause by itself
- punctuation changes in the answer choices

> when, where, why, how, if, as, because,
>
> although, while, despite, that, who, what

(You may see these words referred to in *The Real ACT* or in grammar books as sub-ordinating conjunctions, relative pronouns, or prepositions, but these terms are not important.)

By the same token, you can turn most dependent clauses into independent clauses by *taking away* these words.

The First Type of Sentence Fragment

There are two kinds of sentence fragments. The first is just a dependent clause waiting for a second half that isn't there. Here's an example.

The bride and groom drove away in their

car. As the children ran behind, shouting and
[1]
laughing.

1. A. NO CHANGE
   B. While the
   C. During which the
   D. The

Here's How to Crack It

The second "sentence" in the example isn't a sentence at all; it is a dependent clause Answer choices (B) and (C) repeat the error. The only answer that makes the clause independent is (D).

Could we have combined the second "sentence" with the first to make a correct sentence? Yes, but in this case, ACT doesn't give us that option: The period at the end of the first sentence isn't underlined, so we can't change it.

The Second Type of Sentence Fragment

In the second type of sentence fragment question, the ACT writers ask you to *incorporate* the sentence fragment into the complete sentence coming immediately before or after the fragment through the use of different punctuation marks. In the example that follows, notice that the underlining extends from the end of one sentence through the beginning of the next sentence, so it includes the punctuation as well.

Although it will always be associated with Shakespeare's famous literary character. The castle at Elsinore was never home to Hamlet.

2. **F.** NO CHANGE
   G. character, the
   H. character; the
   J. character. A

Here's How to Crack It

The underlined portion of this passage includes pieces of two sentences and the punctuation in between. We have to check both "sentences" to make sure they are complete. Let's check the first "sentence" first. Can it stand on its own? No. It's a dependent clause. Aha! This is the error. Could we have removed the "Although" at the beginning to create an independent clause? Sure, but that isn't an option in this case because "Although" isn't underlined.

This time, the only way to fix the passage is to combine the dependent clause with the independent clause to form one big sentence. As we mentioned earlier in the chapter, you need a comma between a dependent and an independent clause. The only answer choice that contains a comma is (G). This must be the correct answer.

How Do You Spot Sentence Fragments?

You will often be able to spot this type of error as you read the passage itself, now that you know to look for a dependent clause all by itself. If you don't see the error as you read the passage the first time, however, don't despair. There are three terrific clues waiting for you—the three remaining answer choices after NO CHANGE.

The Answer Choices Contain Valuable Clues

If you're having trouble deciding whether a passage has a sentence-construction error, it helps to look at the answer choices. They often contain great clues as to what is going on in the minds of the test writers. In the last question, for example, it may have helped to look at the differences in *punctuation* among the answer choices. Some of the choices break the two clauses into two sentences. Others combine them. This should make you ask, "Why would ACT give me this choice? Maybe this question is about sentence construction. Would it be better to combine the two clauses? Hmm. Let me check for sentence fragments."

Sometimes, of course, there will be no need to change the sentence at all. Remember, the answer NO CHANGE is correct slightly less than a quarter of the time. However, the flip side of this is that NO CHANGE is wrong slightly more than three-quarters of the time.

Error #2: Comma Splices and Run-Ons

In a comma splice, two independent clauses are jammed together into one sentence, with only a comma to try to hold them together.

> *Aunt Sally ran into the room, Tom was already gone.*

There are several ways to fix this sentence. The easiest way would be to break it up into two sentences.

> *Aunt Sally ran into the room. Tom was already gone.*

If there is a clear reason that one clause might be connected to the other (for example, if Tom has just broken Aunt Sally's vase), you can also fix it by putting a **conjunction** (such as "and" or "but") between the two thoughts.

> *Aunt Sally ran into the room, but Tom was already gone.*

You can also break up the two thoughts with a semicolon instead of a period.

> *Aunt Sally arrived home several hours later; Tom was already gone.*

Conjunctions

Conjunctions plus commas can be used to link two independent clauses.

> *Mary wondered why there was a bird in the classroom, and she decided to ask the teacher what the bird was doing indoors.*

You will also see conjunctions linking dependent clauses to independent clauses, as in this example.

> *Susie was sick because she ate seven hamburgers.*

The first part of the sentence does give a complete thought, but the "because" in the second part means that clause cannot stand on its own. The "because" is a conjunction, however, and links the dependent clause to the independent clause.

A **run-on** sentence is the same thing as a comma splice but without the comma.

> *Aunt Sally swept up the shards of glass she was furious.*

Again, the easiest way to solve the problem is to break up the sentence into two new sentences.

> *Aunt Sally swept up the shards of glass. She was furious.*

A run-on sentence is often much longer than our example, running on and on, you might actually run out of breath if you read it out loud and then wonder whether perhaps it would have been better to split it up into more than one sentence. That last sentence, of course, was a run-on as well.

Check for Comma
Splice
Look out for
- punctuation
changes in the
answer choices

Here's How They Look on the ACT

Here's how a comma splice or run-on might look on the ACT.

―――――――――○――――――――――

There is not much difference between the decision to enter politics and the decision to jump into a pit full of <u>rattlesnakes, in fact,</u>₃ you might find a friendlier environment in the snake pit	3. A. <u>NO CHANGE</u> B. rattlesnakes. In fact, C. ~~rattlesnakes in fact~~ D. rattlesnakes, in fact

Here's How to Crack It

Check the punctuation. As soon as you see that one or more of the answer choices gives you the option of breaking up the sentence into two pieces, you should immediately consider that there might be a comma splice or a run-on problem. Are the two clauses surrounding the punctuation both independent? Yes! This is probably a comma splice error. Now the question is how to fix it. Only one of the answer choices breaks the long sentence into two smaller ones. Answer choice (B) is probably correct. Remember, however, that there are other ways to fix a comma splice; to be certain, try out the other answer choices in the sentence. Perhaps one of them will use a conjunction to bridge the two clauses. Is that the case here? No. Therefore, the correct answer is (B).

―――――――――○――――――――――

―――――――――○――――――――――

The college's plans for expansion included a new science building and a new <u>dormitory if the funding drive is successful,</u>₄ there will be enough money for both.	4. F. NO CHANGE G. dormitory, if H. dormitory; if, J. dormitory. If

Here's How to Crack It

If you could start from scratch, there would be many different ways of expressing the thoughts in this passage. However, as always, you must find the way that the ACT writers decided to use.

Again, the answer choices provide immediate clues. In some, the sentence is broken up into two smaller sentences. Check to see if there are independent clauses on either side of the punctuation. Bingo: This is a run-on sentence. Which choices can we eliminate? (F) and (G) bite the dust. Both (H) and (J) successfully break up the two clauses. (Remember, a semicolon will often do the trick if the subjects of the two clauses are related.)

Is there anything else wrong with either of them? Come to think of it, the comma at the end of (H) is unnecessary. The correct answer is (J).

Error #3: Misplaced Modifiers

A modifying phrase needs to be near what it is modifying. If it gets too far away, it can get misplaced.

> *Sweeping up the shards of glass, the missing key to the jewelry box was found by Aunt Sally.*

As written, this sentence gives the impression that the *missing key* was sweeping up the shards of glass. When a sentence begins with a **modifying phrase** (a group of words without a subject), the noun being modified must follow the phrase. *Who* was sweeping up the shards of glass? Aunt Sally, of course. The correct version of this sentence would be:

> *Sweeping up the shards of glass, Aunt Sally found the missing key to her jewelry box.*

A more subtle version of the same type of error

> *Ecstatic and happy, Aunt Sally's key opened the jewelry box for the first time in weeks.*

At first glance, it looks like the modifying phrase "ecstatic and happy" is modifying Aunt Sally. However, what is the real subject of this sentence, as written? The key. "Aunt Sally's" is actually modifying the key. A correct version of this sentence would be

> *Ecstatic and happy, Aunt Sally used her key to open the jewelry box for the first time in weeks.*

Check for Misplaced Modifiers
Look out for
- modifying phrases followed by commas. Do the nouns being modified appear right after the modifiers?

Here's How They Look on the ACT.

Here's how a misplaced modifier might look on the ACT.

Walking to the pawnshop, <u>Bob's watch dropped into the sewer.</u>₅

5. **A.** NO CHANGE
 B. <u>Bob's watch dropped in the sewer</u>
 C. Bob dropped his watch into the sewer
 D. Bob's dropped watch into the sewer

Here's How to Crack It
Bob's watch may have dropped into the sewer, but it certainly isn't walking to the pawnshop. We've got to get Bob closer to the comma so it's clear that the modifying phrase in the first half of the sentence refers to him. Only (C) does that.

How Do You Spot Misplaced Modifiers?
That's easy! If the underlined portion of the sentence is part of a modifying phrase, check to make sure it modifies the correct noun. If the underlined portion of the sentence includes the noun that is supposed to be modified, check to make sure it is the correct noun.

Construction Shifts
A related type of error is what the ACT writers call a construction shift. These resemble misplaced modifiers in that the modifier is in the wrong place, but construction shifts require no words to be changed. Instead, the modifying word or phrase simply has to be moved over slightly.

Check for Construction Shifts
Look out for
- shifting phrases in the answer choices

Stepping to avoid the large puddle,

I carefully tripped and fell.
 6

6. F. NO CHANGE
   G. (Place after *Stepping*)
   H. (Place after *and*)
   J. (Place after *fell*)

Need more Grammar help?
Check out Grammar Smart

Here's How to Crack It

These questions require just a little common sense. "Carefully" is an adverb. It must modify a verb. The only question for us is, which verb? Only a stunt man trips or falls "carefully." This effectively disposes of answer choices (F), (H), and (J). If we put "carefully" after "stepping," does the sentence make sense? Yes, so the answer is (G).

How Do You Spot Construction Shifts?

That's easy. The answer choices in construction shifts are either presented as shown above, or as follows:

Stepping to avoid the large puddle, I
 7

carefully tripped and fell.
 7

7. A. NO CHANGE
   B. Stepping carefully over the puddle, I tripped and fell.
   C. Stepping over the puddle, I tripped and carefully fell.
   D. Stepping over the puddle, I tripped and fell carefully.

Here's How to Crack it

In either case, it is easy to see that the only difference in each of the answer choices is the position of the word "carefully." This should alert you to consider the position of the modifier. Once again, you must keep your focus on the differences among the answers.

Error #4: Non-Parallel Construction

There are two major types of parallel construction errors tested on the ACT. They both involve some kind of list. You might see a list of verbs.

> When Tom finally came home, Aunt Sally _kissed_ him, _hugged_ him, and _gives_ him his favorite dessert after dinner.

The sentence above has an error because all of the items on the list must be in the same tense. The first two verbs in the example above ("kissed" and "hugged") are in the past tense, but the third verb ("gives") is in the present tense. It is not "parallel" with the other two. The correct sentence should read

> When Tom finally came home, Aunt Sally _kissed_ him, _hugged_ him, and _gave_ him his favorite dessert after dinner.

You also might see a list of nouns.

Check for Non-Parallel Construction
Look out for
- a series of nouns or verbs

The Serial Comma

Commas are used to separate items in a series. Let's look at an example.

> When Mary walked into the classroom, she saw a school teacher, a doctor, a woman eating a bagel and a bird.

A comma should be placed after each item in a series. Thus, we need a comma after the phrase "a woman eating a bagel." As this sentence stands, you might get the impression that the woman was eating the bird as well.

In some writing, it is acceptable to omit the comma before the "and" in a series of three or more items. However, the ACT test writers prefer a more formal version of English (no surprise there), so use a comma to separate every item in a series, including the last one.

Three explanations for Sid's locking himself in his room were a desire to do his homework, a sense that he needed to hone his college essays, and disliking his brother Tom, who always got away with murder.

The sentence above is wrong because while "a desire" and "a sense" are both nouns, "disliking" is a gerund, or a verb functioning as a noun. Is there a more noun-like way to say the same thing? If you said "a dislike of," you are absolutely right. Now the sentence is parallel. Here's the corrected version.

Three explanations for Sid's locking himself in his room were a desire to do his homework, a sense that he needed to hone his college essays, and a dislike of his brother Tom, who always got away with murder.

The lists do not have to have _three_ nouns or _three_ verbs. Sometimes there are only two.

To see the beauty of a sunset in Venice is experiencing perfection.

This is wrong because if the first half of the sentence begins with the infinitive "to see," the second half of the sentence must also begin with an infinitive.

To see the beauty of a sunset in Venice is to experience perfection.

Reminder
Don't forget that some of the punctuation questions will be correct _as is_. Many punctuation questions on the ACT concern commas.

How Do You Spot Parallel-Construction Problems?

That's easy. First, as you read the passage, be on the lookout for a series of actions or nouns. Now that you know what to look for, you may spot an error even without having to go to the answer choices. Second, look for changes in verb tense or the way in which nouns are set up among the answer choices.

"Just the Punctuation, Ma'am"

The ACT also likes to test one kind of punctuation all by itself: the apostrophe. These errors aren't related to sentence structure, but they are fairly common.

Apostrophes

An apostrophe is used either to indicate possession or to mark missing letters in a word.

When it is used to indicate possession, it appears either right before or right after the *s* at the end of the possessive noun.

> *Peter's new car is extremely expensive.*
> *Women's issues will be important in the next election.*
> *The girls' room will be renovated this summer.*

The apostrophe tells us that the car belongs to Peter. If the noun in possession is singular—as in the case of Peter—the apostrophe falls before the "s." If the noun in possession is singular and ends in "s"—such as "boss"—add an apostrophe and an "s" *if* the possessive form would be pronounced as would the plural form (in this case, "boss's" is pronounced "bosses"). The ACT does not test the few exceptions to this rule.

If it is plural and it doesn't end in "s"—as in the case of women—the apostrophe falls before the "s." If it is plural and it ends in "s"—as in the case of "girls"—the apostrophe falls after the "s." Note: Don't worry too much about the plural nouns. ACT seems more interested in your ability to form singular possessives correctly.

The ACT folks also seem very interested in whether you know when an apostrophe is *unnecessary*; some apostrophe questions require you to *drop* an apostrophe. Remember, for the apostrophe to be correct when forming a possessive, the noun containing it must be followed by another noun or an adjective and a noun.

> *Peter's new car*
> *Women's issues*
> *Girls' room*

The apostrophe is also used to indicate missing letters in a word.

I'm sorry. I couldn't make it to your party.

In the sentences above, the apostrophe takes the place of "a" (*I'm* instead of *I am*) and the place of "o" (*couldn't* instead of *could not*). Words that use apostrophes in this way are called **contractions**. Common contractions include *don't, isn't, won't,* and *can't.*

Its/It's/Its'

The most common apostrophe error you'll see tested on the ACT is misuse of *it's* and *its,* which have their own special rules.

The word "it's"—with an apostrophe—is used only when you want to say "it is" or "it has."

> *It's important.* (It is important.)
> *It's been nice talking to you.* (It has been nice talking to you.)

The word "its"—without an apostrophe—is (in this case only) the possessive form of the word "it."

> *The baby bear could not find its mother.*

Pronouns Most Frequently Misused
The ACT test writers will sometimes try to confuse you by presenting both a possessive pronoun and the same pronoun in a contraction as answer choices. Do you know the difference between these words: *whose, who's, its, it's?*

We realize this is a little confusing because you usually use an apostrophe to form the possessive. The ACT writers realize this is confusing, too; that's why this error is on the test. Possessive pronouns (such as *his, her, your, our*) NEVER take apostrophes.

The word *its'* isn't a word at all. That doesn't stop ACT from throwing it on the test to try to trip you up. Most ACT English tests have at least one made-up word on them somewhere.

How Do You Spot Apostrophe Errors?

If a word in the underlined portion *or any of the answer choices* contains an apostrophe, you should ask yourself whether the apostrophe is meant to form a contraction or to make a noun possessive and which you need for the sentence. When the word(s) *it's* or *it is* is in the underlined portion *or any of the answer choices*, use the special rules we just discussed.

What About !(")*?

It seems that the ACT test writers just aren't that interested in whether you know how to use exclamation points, parentheses, asterisks, and question marks correctly. They mention in their guide that the ACT tests some of these points, but not one of the ACTs in *The Real ACT Prep Guide* contains any such questions.

Quotation marks sometimes surround words in the underlined portion and the answer choices, but when they do appear, they show up in every answer choice (you aren't given the option of removing them) and seem intended to distract you from some other error.

As a result, we think you're safe spending your time worrying about other kinds of punctuation. The most common punctuation errors on the ACT deal with commas, semicolons, colons, dashes, and apostrophes. Learn how to use these correctly, and you should be covered.

PUTTING IT ALL TOGETHER

How Do You Spot Punctuation Errors?

That's easy. Look for changes in punctuation among the answer choices. These changes tell you what the ACT writers are up to.

Look at the following example:

    A. NO CHANGE
    B. cities environmental problems
    C. city's environmental problems
    D. citys' environmental problems

Clearly, this question is about proper use of the apostrophe. Read the entire sentence and use the rules you've learned in this chapter to pick the best answer.

One Last Note

There are some forms of punctuation that can be used interchangeably. As we stated above, a semicolon can sometimes take the place of a period. Dashes can sometimes be used instead of parentheses. Sometimes a colon can be replaced by a dash. We haven't discussed these possibilities at length because on the ACT, you will never be asked to make a decision between two correct alternatives.

If two kinds of punctuation can both be considered correct, only one will appear among the answer choices. After all, questions can't have two right answers, can they?

For more practice, go online!
If you haven't registered yet, go to PrincetonReview.com/cracking

Sentence Structure and Punctuation Drill

In the drill below, you will find only questions that focus on sentence construction. Before you start, take a few moments to go back over the review material and techniques. If you don't spot an error as you read, remember that the answer choices may help to suggest an error for which you should look. Answers in Part VII.

When you see the gingerbread houses of Roskilde with their neatly thatched roofs, the gardens filled with flowers, blooms, and the happy smiles on the fresh-faced inhabitants, it is difficult to believe that this town was once the home of a more warlike people—the Vikings. Roskilde's main museum is devoted to those early inhabitants, the Vikings once wandered throughout Europe, and by some reports, may have travel all the way to North America as well. The museum sits on a site at the edge of Roskilde fiord. Where the Viking ships were once launched on voyages of conquest and plunder. Until 20 years ago used only by the fishermen who still ply their trade in the fiord, tourists now arrive in buses at the craggy shoreline to watch local artisans build the Viking ships in the traditional manner.

High above the fiord is Roskilde Cathedral, built by the famous Viking King Harold Blue-toothe in the 1200s the king is said to have converted to Christianity when a visiting priest was able to cure his toothache.

In one corner of the cathedral is a column on which the heights of some other famous historical figures who visited the cathedral are recorded. The tallest (more than seven feet tall, if the markings are to be believed) was Peter the Great; the shortest was a king of Siam; who one hopes was only a boy at the time.

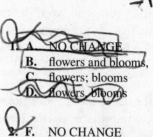

1. A. NO CHANGE
   B. flowers and blooms,
   C. flowers; blooms
   D. flowers blooms

2. F. NO CHANGE
   G. inhabitants the Vikings
   H. inhabitants. The Vikings
   J. inhabitants, the Vikings,

3. A. NO CHANGE
   B. travels
   C. traveled
   D. had traveled

4. F. NO CHANGE
   G. fiord. Where,
   H. fiord, where
   J. fiord; where

5. A. NO CHANGE
   B. the craggy shoreline must now be shared with tourists who arrive in buses
   C. tourists now arrive at the craggy shoreline in buses
   D. the craggy shoreline must now share itself with tourists who arrive in buses

6. F. NO CHANGE
   G. (Place after artisans)
   H. (Place after build)
   J. (Place after watch)

7. A. NO CHANGE
   B. in the 1200s. The king
   C. in the 1200s, the king
   D. in the 1200s, the king,

8. F. NO CHANGE
   G. Siam. Who
   H. Siam, whom
   J. Siam, who

My most memorable vacation as a child was a trip I took to

the Grand Canyon with my grandfather. I was only eleven at

the time; and I'd never been outside the city of Boston. My
<u>   </u>
9

grandfather, a true adventurer, decided that it was time for me to
<u>   </u>
10

discover the great West. My romantic picture of the

West complete with cowboys and Indians was a little out of
<u>   </u>
11

date, but the incredible scenery took my breath away.

On our first day we decided that the best way to explore the
<u>   </u>
12

vast beauty of the canyon would be to take a mule-packed trip

down one of the trails. As I rode along on my mules back, I
<u>   </u>
13

noticed that each rock stratum displayed a distinctive

hue; gray and violet in some places, dark brown and green in
<u>   </u>
14

others. The rock layers of the Grand Canyon are mostly made of

limestone, freshwater shale and sandstone. The Grand Canyon
<u>   </u>
15

was truly magnificent. As I looked up from the floor of the

canyon, it's imposing peaks made me realize how small I really
<u>   </u>
16

was.

9. **A.** NO CHANGE
   B. at the time and
   C. at the time, and
   D. at the time. And

10. **F.** NO CHANGE
   G. grandfather, a true, adventurer,
   H. grandfather: a true adventurer
   J. grandfather, a true adventurer

11. **A.** NO CHANGE
   B. West—complete with cowboys and Indians—
   C. West—complete with cowboys and Indians
   D. West; complete with cowboys and Indians,

12. **F.** NO CHANGE
   G. On our first day we,
   H. On our first day, we
   J. On, our first day, we

13. **A.** NO CHANGE
   B. on my mules' back
   C. on our mules' back
   D. on my mule's back

14. **F.** NO CHANGE
   G. hue. Gray
   H. hue, gray
   J. hue: gray

15. **A.** NO CHANGE
   B. limestone, freshwater, shale, and sandstone.
   C. limestone, freshwater shale, and sandstone.
   D. limestone freshwater shale and sandstone.

16. **F.** NO CHANGE
   G. its imposing
   H. its' imposing
   J. its, imposing

Summary

- ACT writers like to test your knowledge of whether sentences are put together and punctuated correctly.

- Watch for sentence fragments, run-ons and comma splices, serial commas, restrictive/nonrestrictive clause separation errors, misplaced modifiers, and non-parallel construction.

- ACT test writers also like to test semicolon usage. Semicolons should be used to connect two related yet independent clauses.

- You might also see colons being used in sentences. A colon typically introduces a list that follows an independent clause.

- Dashes can be used to separate a word or group of words from the rest of a sentence, but a dash cannot be combined with a comma. Dashes typically come in pairs unless the isolated group of words is at the end of the sentence.

- Watch for apostrophes. They can either indicate possessives or contractions.

- *It's* can be used only to replace *it is* or *it has*. *Its* is the possessive form of the word *it*. *Its'* is not a word.

- If you are not sure what the question is asking you to do, check the answer choices. The differences among the answer choices can provide clues to what the ACT is testing.

Chapter 7
Grammar and Usage

The ACT heavily tests grammar and usage. The test writers focus on pronoun and verb questions, with particular emphasis on agreement issues. The ACT test writers like to include lots of extra language to hide these errors and lure students into picking the wrong answer. In addition to the pronoun and verb questions, there are many questions that involve adjectives, adverbs, and idioms. This chapter will help you learn the rules you need to crack these questions on the English test.

PRONOUNS

Pronouns—words such as *he*, *she*, *it*, and *they*—are used to replace nouns. The ACT writers like to see if you understand the rules of pronouns. There will probably be several pronoun questions on the test you take.

The First Pronoun Rule: Agreement

A pronoun must always agree with the noun to which it refers. Sound straightforward? Try to spot the error in the sentence below.

> *Any young boy who watched the first moon landing probably spent the next few years wishing that they could become an astronaut.*

In spoken English, people make pronoun agreement errors all the time. In written English, you have to be precise. As you look at the sentence above, try to decide which noun is being referred to by the word "they." If you decided that "they" was referring to "boy," you were absolutely correct. However, because "boy" is singular, the pronoun referring to "boy" has to be singular as well. "He" correctly refers back to "boy."

> *Any young boy who watched the first moon landing probably spent the next few years wishing that he could become an astronaut.*

The charts below contain some commonly used singular and plural pronouns.

Singular Pronouns		
Subject	**Object**	**Possessive**
I	me	my, mine
you	you	you, yours
he	him	his

Singular Pronouns		
she	her	hers
it	it	its

Plural Pronouns		
Subject	**Object**	**Possessive**
we	us	our, ours
you	you	you, yours
they	them	their, theirs

Be Familiar with the Rules of Pronouns
Agreement—
singular/plural
Case—
subject/object

Here's another example.

> *Neither of the two young girls with whom I watched the first moon landing expressed their feelings out loud, but I knew that all three of us wanted to be astronauts.*

Neither and *either* are considered singular. Therefore, in this sentence, it is incorrect to use the possessive pronoun "their." We should use "her" instead.

> *Neither of the two young girls with whom I watched the first moon landing expressed her feelings out loud, but I knew that all three of us wanted to be astronauts.*

The following indefinite pronouns are all singular.

anybody	each	somebody
anyone	everybody	someone
either	everyone	nobody

Let's look at an example in ACT format:

Although the American bald eagle has

been on the endangered species list for years,

<u>they have been</u> sighted in wildlife preserves
₁

much more frequently during the past two

years.

1. **A.** NO CHANGE
   B. they are
   C. it can be
   D. it has been

Here's How to Crack It

As you read the sentence, look to see if there is a pronoun in the underlined portion. If you find one, check to make sure the pronoun agrees with the noun to which it refers. What does "they" refer to here? Obviously, it must refer to "the American bald eagle." Although the sentence is clearly talking about the American bald eagle in its *general* sense, we need to use a singular pronoun to agree with the singular noun. Thus, we can eliminate (A) and (B). Choices (C) and (D) both

That's an Error?

Remember ACT Island? It takes the writers of the ACT a while to catch up to the way we use English. For example, your English teacher at school may think it's okay to use "they" to replace a singular noun, although technically it is not. We get so used to using language incorrectly that when the ACT comes along and tests the formal rules of pronoun usage, the right answers sound wrong even though they are grammatically correct. This is one place where you really can't use your ear. You need to learn the pronoun rules.

contain the correct pronoun, "it." How do we decide which one to pick? Note the difference between (C) and (D). Choice (C) uses the present tense, while (D) uses a type of past tense. According to the sentence, when were these birds sighted? "In the past two years." Which answer do you want to pick? If you said choice (D), you were absolutely correct.

Even if you missed the pronoun as you read the sentence, you almost certainly would have noticed that the *answer choices* offered you two different pronouns. The answer choices are always great clues to what might have been going on in the ACT writers' minds. Don't forget to use your answer choices as clues if you can't find the error on your own.

The Second Pronoun Rule: Case

Check for Pronouns
Look out for
*   **pronouns in the answer choices.** Should the pronoun be singular or plural? Is the pronoun being used as a subject or an object?

If a pronoun is the subject of a sentence, it must be expressed as a subject. Subject pronouns include *I, we, you, he, she, it, they,* and *who.* If a pronoun is the object of a sentence, or the object of a preposition, it must be expressed as an object. Object pronouns include *me, us, you, him, her, it, them,* and *whom.*

Which choice best fits the sentence below?

>   (She/her) bought a souvenir NASA sweatshirt.

Because the person who buys the shirt is the subject of the sentence, the correct pronoun is "she."

>   Jane bought a souvenir NASA sweatshirt for (he/him).

Because the person who receives the shirt is the object of the preposition "for," the correct pronoun is "him."

ACT's favorite pronoun case errors involve the use of *who* and *whom,* both of which are called relative pronouns. Let's look at a correct example first.

>   *The TV announcer, who was quite an expert, told us many interesting facts about the lunar mission.*

The group of words "who was quite an expert" is functioning here as an adjective describing the TV announcer. Is this group of words a phrase or a clause? You may remember that a phrase often does not contain a subject, but a clause must contain both a subject and a verb. In this group of words, the relative pronoun "who" functions as a subject, which means that this group of words is a clause. You should always use "who" when the relative pronoun is functioning as the subject of a clause or as the subject of the entire sentence. The phrase "… whom was quite an expert" would be wrong here.

Now try an incorrect example.

> *Before the moon landing, the TV announcer gave some additional background on the astronauts, about who we were all quite interested.*

If you spot *who* following a preposition (in this case, "who" follows the word "about") on the ACT, it will almost certainly turn out to be incorrect. A pronoun following a preposition is supposed to be the object of that preposition. The sentence should read

> *Before the moon landing, the TV announcer gave some additional background on the astronauts, about whom we were all quite interested.*

Let's try an example in ACT format.

The students, who had been studying the
                                        2
space program, were thrilled to witness the
               2
lunar landing.

2. **F.** NO CHANGE
  G. about whom had been studying the space program,
  H. whom had been studying the space program,
  J. who had been studying the space program

Here's How to Crack It

The group of words "who had been studying the space program" functions as an adjective clause describing the students. Is "who" the subject of this adjective clause? Yes, it is, so we are down to (F) (NO CHANGE) and (J), both of which contain the correct form of the pronoun—"who." How do the two remaining choices differ? Answer choice (F) contains a comma after "program" while choice (J) does not. Is the comma necessary? We look back at the passage and see that a comma precedes the clause, which is a nonrestrictive clause. "The students were thrilled to witness the lunar landing" would be perfectly acceptable in this example. Nonrestrictive clauses require commas on either side of them, so (F), NO CHANGE, is correct.

How Do You Spot Pronoun Errors?

Look for pronouns! Whenever you see a pronoun in the underlined portion of the sentence or in the answer choices, you must first determine which noun the pronoun is replacing. If the pronoun is replacing a singular noun, it must be singular; if it is replacing a plural noun, it must be plural.

If the pronoun is being used as a subject, it must be in its subject form. If the pronoun is being used as an object, it must be in its object form.

If *who* or *whom* appears in the underlined portion of the passage or in the answer choices, you must determine whether the pronoun is the subject or the object of the clause in which it appears. If it is the subject, *who* is correct. If it is the object, *whom* is correct. Generally, if the relative pronoun follows a preposition, the correct form will be "whom."

SUBJECT-VERB AGREEMENT

The verb of a sentence must always agree with its subject. If a sentence contains a singular subject, the verb that goes with it must also be singular. If a sentence contains a plural subject, then the verb that goes with it must also be plural.

Check for Subject-Verb Agreement
Look out for

- **a verb in the underlined portion of the sentence.** Do the answer choices contain different forms of the verb?

Let's look at an example.

> The best moment during a broadcast filled with many great moments
> was ~~were~~ when the astronaut stepped out of the lunar lander and bounced
> on the moon.

The subject of this sentence is "moment," which is singular. See if you can find the main verb of the sentence. If you said "were," you were absolutely correct. But because the subject is singular, the verb should also be singular. The correct form of the verb is "was."

> The best moment during a broadcast filled with many great moments
> was when the astronaut stepped out of the lunar lander and bounced
> on the moon.

Now, if the original sentence had been written like this

> was
> The best moment ~~were~~ when the astronaut stepped out of the lunar
> lander and bounced on the moon.

the error would have been a *lot* easier to spot.

ACT writers like to stick many modifying phrases and clauses between the subject and the verb in the hope that you will forget what the subject was by the time you get to the verb. The best way to check subject-verb agreement is to cross out all the words between the subject and the verb so that you can see if the subject and verb really agree.

PRONOUN-VERB AGREEMENT

Sometimes, the subject of a sentence turns out to be a pronoun; don't let that throw you. The verb must still agree with the subject, even if the subject is just a pronoun. Let's look at an example.

> *has*
>
> *Each of these moments ~~have~~ played in my mind again and again as I try to recapture the excitement of that momentous day in June.*

The subject of this sentence is "each," which you'll recall is singular (along with *either, neither, anyone, everybody,* and *everyone*). The verb is "have played," which is plural. The subject (in this case a pronoun) and the verb don't agree. How do you fix the sentence?

> *Each of these moments has played in my mind again and again as I try to recapture the excitement of that momentous day in June.*

Sounds awkward, doesn't it? It's correct, though. This is a great example of an instance in which knowing and applying the rules leads you to the correct answer while using your ear may not.

How Do You Spot Subject-Verb Agreement Errors?

That's easy. Isolate the subject and the verb of the sentence. To see the relationship between the subject and the verb, try drawing a line through any words, phrases, or clauses in between them. As always, remember that the answer choices themselves can provide valuable clues. If the underlined portion of a sentence contains a verb, you should check to see whether the answer choices contain different forms of that verb. If they do, you have a potential subject-verb agreement error.

Check for Verb Agreement

Look out for

- **a verb in the underlined portion of the sentence.** Does it agree with the subject? Is the verb's tense consistent with the other verbs in the sentence?

More Great Titles From The Princeton Review
Grammar Smart

VERB TENSE

Verb tense tells us when the action of the sentence is taking place—in the past, in the present, or in the future. Let's review the different verb tenses.

The **present tense** indicates an action that is happening right now.

> *He runs the 440 in 50 seconds.*

The simple **past tense** indicates an action that took place entirely in the past.

> *He ran the 440 in 50 seconds last week.*

The **future tense** indicates an action that will take place at some point down the road.

> *He will run the race next Saturday.*

The **present perfect tense** indicates an action that started in the past but that may continue into the present.

> *He has run the 440 in under 50 seconds in the last four races.*

The **past perfect tense** indicates an action that happened in the past and that preceded another action also in the past.

> *He had run 100 yards of the race when he twisted his ankle.*

The **future perfect tense** indicates that an action will be completed by a definite time in the future.

> *He will have finished the race by next Sunday.*

How Does the ACT Test Verb Tense?

The ACT writers don't care whether you know the names of the verb tenses or sometimes even whether you know in which tense a particular passage should be written.

What the ACT writers want to see is whether you can spot *inconsistencies* in verb tense (they are testing a form of agreement here). If a verb in a non-underlined portion of the sentence is in one tense, the verb in the underlined portion tends to be in the same tense. What's wrong with the following sentence?

> *Sam is walking down the street when he* <u>found</u> *a large suitcase.*

The verbs "is walking" and "found" are in two different tenses. "Is walking" is in the present tense and "found" is in the past tense. One or the other has to change.

The new sentence can read either.

> *Sam is walking down the street when he finds a large suitcase.*

> or

> *Sam was walking down the street when he found a large suitcase.*

On the ACT, you generally will not be asked to make a decision as to which tense (in this case, past or present) would be most appropriate for the sentence. Only one of the verbs will be underlined, and it will be up to you to look at the other verb in the sentence or the verbs in surrounding sentences to decide how to change the underlined verb.

Look at underlined verbs in the "–ing" form very carefully. This is especially true when the sentence uses the verbs "having" and "being," which are almost always used improperly.

How Do You Spot Verb Tense Agreement Errors?

That's easy. If you see a verb in the underlined portion of the sentence or in any of the answer choices, you should immediately anticipate that the error could be one of two types: subject-verb agreement (about which we've already spoken) or tense.

You should begin by asking yourself whether the verb agrees with its subject. If that is not the problem, then ask yourself whether the verb's tense is consistent with the tense of other verbs in the sentence or in surrounding sentences. If there is an inconsistency, then you've probably spotted the error.

Be careful, though, because sometimes a verb-tense change within a sentence is correct. For instance

> *Once he has finished reading, he will set the table.*

This sentence actually requires a change from present to future tense.

One More ACT Verb Error

Sometimes, ACT will put together two perfectly fine past tense verbs to create a past tense construction that does not work. For example

> *Mike ~~has~~ ate all the cookies in the cookie jar.*

In this sentence, either "ate" or "has eaten" would be correct, but "has ate" is incorrect.

ADJECTIVES AND ADVERBS

Adjectives modify nouns. Adverbs modify everything else—verbs, adjectives, and other adverbs. The ACT sometimes tests to see whether you know the difference between adjectives and adverbs. You may remember from grade school a method that often helps to decide if a word is an adjective—simply put the word you aren't sure about into the following sentence: "He (or she or it) is very _____ ." If the word fits the blank, then the word is an adjective. Let's try it out.

> *He is very <u>intelligent</u>.*

> *He is very <u>intelligently</u>.*

Intelligent fits the blank in the first sentence, so *intelligent* must be an adjective. *Intelligently* does not fit the blank in the second sentence. In fact, *intelligently* is an adverb. You can often recognize an adverb by the "–ly" at the end of the word.

> *She thinks intelligently.*

A comparative adjective is often used when a sentence is comparing two things.

> *Juanita is taller than Jane.*

> *("Taller" is a comparative adjective.)*

In general, if an adjective has only one syllable, you can make it comparative by adding an "–er" to the end of the word. If an adjective has more than one syllable, you can usually make it comparative by adding a "more" or a "less" in front of the adjective.

> *Sid is more careful than Tom.*

> *Tom is less careful than Sid.*

A comparative adverb is often used when a sentence is comparing two actions.

> *Juanita dances more gracefully than Jane.*

> *("More gracefully" is a comparative adverb.)*

Adjectives and Adverbs

Adjectives and adverbs can usually be distinguished from each other by the "He is very—" test (if the word fits, it's probably an adjective) or by their form (most adverbs end in "–ly").

To make most adverbs comparative, you also need to add a "more" or "less" in front of the adverb.

> *Sid behaves more politely than Tom does.*

> *Tom behaves less politely than Sid does.*

When more than two things are being compared, a sentence needs a superlative adjective.

> *Of the many men in the room, John is the strongest.*

> *("Strongest" is a superlative adjective.)*

To make a comparison among three or more people or things, add "–est" to the adjective. When more than two actions are being compared, a sentence often needs a superlative adverb.

> *Compared with the other boys in the school, Sid behaves the most politely.*

> *("Most politely" is a superlative adverb.)*

IDIOMATIC EXPRESSIONS

Why do we say, "I am in love *with* you," instead of, "I am in love *for* you?" The answer is,

> *"Well, just because!"*

Each idiomatic expression is a law unto itself. There are no general rules to go by. Of course, it would be difficult to memorize every single idiom in the English language, at least on short notice. Fortunately, it turns out that you already know most of the idioms that come up on the ACT. Here's an example.

> *My sculpture is based after Rodin's Thinker.*

Do you base something "after?" No; the correct expression is

> *My sculpture is based on Rodin's Thinker.*

Idioms

Idioms are expressions that require the use of a specific preposition. Fortunately, you'll be familiar with many of the idioms on the test. The best way to spot them is to look for prepositions in the answer choices.

How Do You Spot Idiomatic Errors?

You already know most of the idiomatic expressions likely to appear on the ACT. The only problem will be spotting the error in the first place. As always, the answer choices provide excellent clues. Let's see how that last example would have looked on the ACT.

My sculpture is based after Rodin's
Thinker.

3. **A.** NO CHANGE
    B. is based over
    C. is based on
    D. based on

Here's How to Crack It

Even if you didn't spot the error as you read the sentence, when you went to the answer choices, you would have noticed that the question seemed to be mostly concerned with the preposition that followed the word "based."

The best way to check out a potential idiom error is to try making up your own sentence using the idiomatic expression.

> _My term paper is based after the discoveries of Edison._

Does that sound correct? No! We need to say "is based on..." Answer choice (D), while it uses the correct idiomatic expression, creates a sentence fragment. Thus, the best answer is choice (C).

Grammar Drill

In the drill below, you will find questions focusing only on grammar. Before you start, take a few moments to go back over the review material and techniques. If you don't see an error as you read, examine the answer choices for clues as to the errors for which you should look.

Have you ever had a day when you realized in retrospect that it would have been better if one had stayed in
<u>bed? Yesterday was one of those days. I woke up at 10:30 to

find that my alarm clock <u>has failed</u> to go off. I was already an
2
hour and a half late for work. I jumped into my clothes and ran to my car, only to discover that I had left the lights
<u>on the previously evening</u> and the car wouldn't start. Each of
3

the first three taxis I saw <u>were</u> too far away to hail. The taxi
4

driver <u>who finally picked</u> me up didn't have change for a ten
5

dollar bill. When I finally arrived at the office, my boss was not only furious that I was late, <u>and she</u> was also mad that I had for-
6

gotten to bring the report I had been preparing at home. Of all the bad days I have experienced in my life, this <u>was the worse.</u>
7

1. **A.** NO CHANGE
   B. if you had
   C. if you has
   D. had one

2. **F.** NO CHANGE
   G. have failed
   H. had failed
   J. having failed

3. **A.** NO CHANGE
   B. on the evening previously
   C. on the evening previous
   D. on the previous evening

4. **F.** NO CHANGE
   G. was
   H. are
   J. is

5. **A.** NO CHANGE
   B. whom finally picked me up
   C. whom picked me up finally
   D. who finally picks me up

6. **F.** NO CHANGE
   G. and her
   H. but her
   J. but she

7. **A.** NO CHANGE
   B. was the more worse
   C. was the worst
   D. was the worser

Summary

○ Many ACT questions include pronoun errors, subject-verb agreement errors, and other grammatical mistakes.

○ If a verb is underlined, check for subject-verb agreement, verb tense errors, and verb parallelism.

○ If a pronoun is underlined, check for noun-pronoun agreement, pronoun-verb agreement, and pronoun case (subject or object).

○ ACT test writers like to mix up adjectives and adverbs. Be careful that you are using the correct type of modifier for what is being modified.

○ Idioms are expressions that require the use of a specific preposition. If you know the correct idiom, great. If not, just guess.

○ If you are not sure what the question is asking you to do, check the answer choices. The differences among the answer choices can provide clues to what the ACT is testing.

Chapter 8
Rhetorical Skills

In the ACT English test, 35 of the 75 questions are designed to test what the ACT test writers call rhetorical skills. These questions include strategy, transition, organization, and style questions. You may be asked to reorder sentences or paragraphs, to reword something, or to evaluate whether the writer of a passage has satisfied a particular assignment. Rhetorical skills questions vary more widely than grammar and usage questions, and we'll talk about the best strategies to get you through them.

Questions that test your rhetorical skills are not necessarily harder than the types we've been discussing up to now; they're just different. Rather than asking you about specific points of grammar, rhetorical skills questions get into the realm of style and editing. A few will concern the passage as a whole; save these for last. For the most part, the test writers have placed those at the end of the passage anyway.

The Real ACT Prep Guide suggests two strategies for rhetorical skills questions with which, frankly, we disagree.

First, *The Real ACT* (we're going to stick with the abbreviated name from now on) suggests that you read or skim the entire passage quickly for content and then start answering the questions. We think this is a waste of time. You don't get any points for *reading* these passages. The proctor is not going to walk around the room saying, "Ah, excellent reading form there. Five points." You get points for *answering questions* correctly. Because most of the questions (including many of the rhetorical skills questions) can be answered just by looking at the particular sentence that contains the underlined portion related to that question, you may as well wade in there and start racking up points.

Second, *The Real ACT* suggests that it might be a good idea to answer the general rhetoric questions first. *The Real ACT* points out that if a general question asks you to rearrange the order of paragraphs, your new order will make it easier for you to answer other questions. Unfortunately, we think it's equally distracting to try to read a passage for content when every other sentence has something grammatically wrong with it.

The ACT writers break down rhetorical skills into three subcategories: strategy, organization, and style.

No Points for Reading!
You get points only for answering questions.

STRATEGY QUESTIONS

Among the strategy questions, many concern **transitions** of ideas. Transition questions pop up throughout the passage, not just at the end. They are probably the easiest of the rhetorical skills questions.

A transition is sometimes needed at the *beginning* of a clause, sentence, or paragraph, as the writer attempts to move smoothly from one thought to another. Writers use what are called sentence connectors to get from one thought to the next. There are only three main types of sentence connectors in the world: *but, also,* and *therefore.* Try filling in each of the blanks below with one of these three words.

> Fred and Sue were looking forward to going to dinner at a Chinese restaurant with their friends, ~~but~~ their friends wanted to go to an Italian restaurant.
>
> When European children hear the word *Chicago*, the first thing they think of is gangsters. ~~therefore~~ it must be a disappointment to them when they get off the plane and see that no one is wearing spats or carrying a tommy gun.
>
> The campers were very tired. ~~Also~~ they were very hungry.

There's a food fight brewing in the first sentence. To indicate that the friends are in disagreement with Fred and Sue, we need a word implying *contradiction*. That word is *but*.

In the second sentence, we want to imply a *cause-and-effect* relationship. The first part of the sentence is meant to cause the second half. The word that suggests this relationship is *therefore*.

The third example connects two sentences. Surely the two are related but much less directly than in either of the first two examples. Our transition word needs to stress that the second idea is an addition to the first. The word to use here is *also*.

Of course, there are many different ways of saying *but*, *therefore*, and *also*. Here's a partial list.

> **but (contradiction)**—*however, quite the contrary, despite, rather, notwithstanding, contrarily, on the other hand, on the contrary, although, yet, nevertheless*
>
> **therefore (cause and effect)**—*hence, and so, thus, consequently, for example, because of, finally, in conclusion*
>
> **also (in addition)**—*in addition, for example, furthermore, another, and, first, second, moreover, by the same token, besides, so too, similarly*

The Big Three Transitions
but, also, therefore

Each of these words has a slightly different shade of meaning. We don't mean to imply that all the "but" words, for example, are interchangeable. However, the answer choices in a transition question generally won't give you a choice among four different kinds of *but*s. Often, your choice will be between a *but* and three *also*s, or a *therefore* and three *but*s.

How Do You Spot Transition Questions?

The underlined portion in a transition question is almost always at the *beginning* of a new clause, sentence, or paragraph.

The answer choices themselves will help you to spot transition questions. They are invariably made up of different sentence connectors from the list we just gave you. You have to decide which sentence connector is appropriate.

Now go back to the passage. Think *but, therefore,* or *also*. Which type of sentence connector would be most appropriate to express the transition from one thought to the other? Look at the answer choices again to see which version of the sentence connector you want is available to you this time. Here's an example.

Funds provided by the Stafford program are not considered scholarships; so too, they are part of the extended student loan system.

1. A. NO CHANGE
   B. in addition,
   C. rather
   D. moreover

Here's How to Crack It

There are two clues that might immediately point you in the right direction on this question: The underlined portion is at the *beginning* of a new clause; it also contains one of the sentence connectors we just listed. If you still aren't sure what type of question this is, look at the other answer choices. What do you see? More sentence connectors. This is a transition question.

Check for Transitions
Look out for
- underlining at the *beginning* of sentences

As the passage stands, what type of transition is being used? "So too" is an *also*. Is this what we need? No. The next clause is not an *additional* thought but rather a contrary thought. If we eliminate any answer choices that contain *also*s, (A), (B), and (D) all bite the dust. The answer must be (C).

Note that in this case, it might have been harder to decide among the answer choices if one of them had been a *therefore*. Fortunately, that was not an option.

The Other Strategy Questions

Other strategy questions involve *improving* the passage rather than fixing errors. Many of these questions require you to choose a correct answer based on the purpose of a sentence or the effect of the passage on the reader.

Let's see some examples.

Many dog owners turn to animal trainers when they find they can no longer control their pets. Most experts find that a poorly trained dog has received plenty of affection but not enough discipline or exercise. [2]

2. Which of the following sentences provides new, specific guidelines about the proper training of a dog?

F. Behavior that was cute in a twenty-pound puppy is alarming in a one hundred-pound adult dog.

G. Would-be dog owners should consider their own lifestyles and the temperament of a specific breed before adopting the animal.

H. Dogs should be walked at least three times a day and should never be given a treat without first obeying a command.

J. Small children should never be left unsupervised with a dog.

Here's How to Crack It

Pay careful attention to the question itself when confronted with strategy questions. Not only do we have an actual question, as opposed to just answer choices, but the text in the question also provides a valuable clue. According to the question, one of these choices *provides new, specific guidance about the proper training of a dog*. We don't even need to go back into the passage. Find an answer choice that fulfills the purpose. Answer choices (F), (G), and (J) all may be true, but they do not offer any specific information about training a dog. Only (H) does that, and it is our correct answer.

ORGANIZATION QUESTIONS

There are three kinds of organization questions.

- The first asks you to check the placement of an underlined word or a phrase in a sentence and possibly relocate it, according to what the underlined word or phrase should logically modify.
- The second asks you to reorder sentences within a paragraph.
- The third asks you to reorder paragraphs within the passage as a whole.

Let's talk about sentences within a paragraph first. Here's an example.

**More great titles by
The Princeton Review**
Grammar Smart

[1] Particularly in his later paintings, van Gogh creates thick swirls of paint that perhaps mirror the emotional storm raging within. [2] DuFevre piles the paint onto the canvas in thick swatches that rise off the canvas by a good half inch at times. [3] Perhaps the most telling similarity between van Gogh and DuFevre, the little-known modern surrealist, lies in their use of brushstrokes. [4] It is almost as if he is challenging van Gogh to a contest to determine who was more emotionally disturbed.

3. Which of the following ordering of sentences will make the paragraph most logical?

A. NO CHANGE
B. 1, 3, 2, 4
C. 1, 4, 3, 2
D. 3, 1, 2, 4

Here's How to Crack It

Although you might not think so at first, organization questions are actually easier when they ask you to reorder all of the sentences in the paragraph, as they do in this example. The trick is to figure out which of the sentences should come *first*.

Look at the answer choices to see which sentences you have to consider as contenders for the first slot. In this case, the options are Sentence 1 and Sentence 3. You don't have to consider the other sentences yet. You should look for any obvious transition words, especially those that suggest either the introduction of the paragraph or its conclusion. This should eliminate several of the answer choices and make your job much easier.

In this case, the word "perhaps" is used to set up our story, which talks about the similarities between van Gogh and DuFevre.

The third sentence suggests a similarity between two painters that is explained and amplified in the other sentences. Which of the answer choices has Sentence 3 in the lead-off position? Only one. The answer must be (D). In this case, you are done!

If you can't decide which of the choices comes first, another trick is to pair sentences that you can connect in some way. For example, in the paragraph on the previous page, you may have looked at Sentence 4 and noticed that the pronoun "he" could refer only to DuFevre. This implies that Sentence 4 comes right after Sentence 2. This would eliminate (A) and (C). This technique is also useful for ordering the remaining sentences.

Check for Organization
Look out for
• words like *ordering*, *organize*, and *summary*

Ordering Whole Paragraphs

When the ACT writers ask you to reorganize the paragraphs in a passage, they always position the question at the end of the passage after all the other specific questions. That's exactly where this question belongs. Don't spend large amounts of time re-reading the entire passage. If you are struck by something strange in the ordering of paragraphs during the first read, go back and look at that place; otherwise, do some quick elimination and guess.

Again, you don't need to be sure of the position of *all* the paragraphs to do some quick elimination. Look for either the first paragraph or a pair of paragraphs that you are pretty sure go together, and use POE.

Here's a small-scale example. Let's assume that you've worked a passage and summarized each of the paragraphs in your head. Here are the summaries.

Summary of Paragraph 1   Most people believe eating healthy, nutritious food is good for you.

Summary of Paragraph 2   Carrying the heavy boxes home, I pulled a muscle.

Summary of Paragraph 3   I recently went to the health food store and bought big boxes of wheat germ, carrot juice, and tofu.

Summary of Paragraph 4   But you can take this health kick too far, as I discovered.

4. Which of the following ordering of paragraphs best organizes this passage?

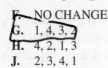

F. NO CHANGE
G. 1, 4, 3, 2
H. 4, 2, 1, 3
J. 2, 3, 4, 1

Here's How to Crack It

There are several ways to approach this question. You could look for the first paragraph of the passage. (In this case, we have a choice of four paragraphs, so this won't be as easy as the last question.) You could try to establish some relationship between any two of the paragraphs. You could try to spot the last paragraph of the passage.

Let's begin by trying to establish some relationship between any two paragraphs. In this passage, is there any observable cause and effect going on? Yes. Lifting the boxes caused a pulled muscle in the narrator. He couldn't pull the muscle until after he bought the boxes, which means Paragraph 2 must come after Paragraph 3. This option exists in only one of the answer choices. It begins to look as if (G) must be correct.

To check, we can look to see what (G) offers us as the beginning and end paragraphs. However, bear in mind that you don't want to spend too much time on any one question. Reading an entire passage again with a new beginning is a laborious task. Bubble in (G) on your answer sheet and move on.

STYLE QUESTIONS

The largest number of style errors stems from **redundancy.** Put simply, redundancy means saying the same thing twice.

How Do You Spot Redundancy?

Some redundancy errors are easier to see than others. Here are a couple of easy examples.

Cheap and inexpensive gifts can be found in the shopping district.

Weak and without strength, the old car could not make it up the hill.

In both of the examples above, two adjectives are saying exactly the same thing. Because there is really no need for both, the best way to correct the sentences would be to remove one of the superfluous adjectives.

> *Inexpensive gifts can be found in the shopping district. The weak, old car could not make it up the hill.*

Slightly more difficult

> *After birth, the newborn babies are weighed by a nurse. In the year 1992…*

These examples would be perfectly acceptable in normal speech. However, newborn babies have obviously just been born, and 1992 is already a year. To fix these sentences, simply remove one of the superfluous items.

> *After birth, the babies are weighed by a nurse. In 1992…*

A comprehensive list of all the possible redundancies would be too long to do you any good. All you have to do in questions like these is spot the redundancy, and that's easy enough. Look for repetition in the underlined portion of the sentence or among the answer choices. When you see it, expunge it ruthlessly.

The Vietnam veterans were recently <u>memorialized by a memorial sculpture</u> in Washington.

5. **A.** NO CHANGE
   B. memorialized by a
   C. memorialized with a new memoria
   D. memorialized in a recent

Here's How to Crack It

This is an obvious case of redundancy. We need to find an answer choice that does not repeat itself. Choice (D) seems possible until we realize that "recently memorialized in a recent sculpture" merely makes the same error with another word, "recently." The only possible answer is (B).

The Other Style Questions

A small number of style questions relate to the overall tone of the passage and to the suitability of individual words. Some deal with issues of irrelevancy, wordiness, or slang. Remember, ACT prefers formal English. There are relatively few of these questions, and because many of the answer choices are extreme or clearly do not conform to ACT's formal style, you can use POE with relative ease.

Check for Redundancy
Look out for
- **redundancy**
  Oh, and check for sentences that say the same thing twice too.

Rhetorical Skills Drill

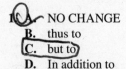

[1]

The golden age of television means many things to many people, and to the small band of actors, writers, and directors who
                                    ___
                                     1

would rise to prominence in the late 50s and early 60s, without a
                _____
                     2

doubt it meant the "live" television shows such as *Playhouse 90,*

where many of them initially worked for the first time.
                   _____
                                 3

[2]

[1] Each week, a new "teleplay" was created from scratch—written, cast, rehearsed, and performed. [2] *Playhouse 90* was truly a remarkable training ground for the young talents. [3] Such future luminaries as Paddy Chayefsky, Marlon Brando, and Patricia Neal worked long hours honing to a knife edge their craft.
                                               _____
                                                       4

[4] In some cases, when there were problems with the censors, it would have to be created twice. ⬚5

[3]

Despite the frantic pace, accidents happened frequently.
_____
   6

David Niven once revealed that, during an early show, he inadvertently locked his costume in his dressing room two minutes before air time. As the announcer read the opening credits, the sound of axes splintering the door to Niven's dressing room could be heard in the background. ⬚7

1. **A.** NO CHANGE
   B. thus to
   C. but to
   D. In addition to

2. **F.** NO CHANGE
   G. prominent famousness
   H. famous prominence
   J. famousness

3. **A.** NO CHANGE
   B. initially for the first time worked.
   C. for the first time worked initially.
   D. worked for the first time.

4. **F.** NO CHANGE
   G. to an edge
   H. edges
   J. OMIT the underlined portion.

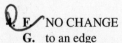

5. Which of the following sequences would best organize the sentences in Paragraph 2?
   A. NO CHANGE
   B. 1, 2, 4, 3
   C. 2, 1, 4, 3
   D. 2, 3, 1, 4

6. **F.** NO CHANGE
   G. Due to
   H. In spite of
   J. Thus

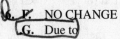

7. If the writer wished to make the tone of Paragraph 3 more lighthearted, she could change the word "accidents" to
   A. NO CHANGE
   B. casualties
   C. mishaps
   D. grave errors

Questions 8 and 9 ask questions about the preceding passage as a whole.

8. Which of the following would best summarize the passage as a whole?
   F. The golden age of television meant many things to many different people.
   G. Early television shows such as *Playhouse 90* provided the training ground where talented new entertainers could learn their craft.
   H. The golden age of television had many amusing moments.
   J. The rise of Paddy Chayefsky, Marlon Brando, and Patricia Neal helped to make *Playhouse 90* a success.

9. Which of the following sequences of paragraphs would make the structure of the passage as a whole the most logical?
   A. NO CHANGE
   B. 3, 2, 1
   C. 3, 1, 2
   D. 2, 3, 1

Summary

- Do the questions in order. However, if you're having trouble with a particular question, or if it seems to be taking too much time, circle the question number, leave it, and come back on your second pass. Often a later question will help you with an earlier one.

- Search the answer choices for clues. Focus on the differences between the answer choices, and use that information to determine the error(s) being tested.

- Look for one error at a time. Eliminate all answers that do not correct the first error you spotted. Compare the remaining answers and choose the most concise answer choice free of any additional errors.

- Don't forget that NO CHANGE is correct a little less than a quarter of the time. If you can't find anything wrong with the underlined portion, it may be correct as written.

- Remember to look very carefully at any question with OMIT as an answer. If you can OMIT and the passage/sentence is still correct, then do so.

Part III
How to Crack the ACT Mathematics Test

Chapter 9
Introduction to the
ACT Mathematics Test

The second section of the ACT will always be the Math test. To perform your best, you'll need to become familiar with the structure and strategy of the ACT Math test. In this chapter, we discuss the types of questions you can expect to see and how you can use organizational strategy, estimation, and elimination skills to improve your Math score.

WHAT TO EXPECT ON THE MATH TEST

You will have 60 minutes to answer 60 multiple-choice questions based on "...topics covered in typical high school classes." For those of you who aren't sure if you went to a typical high school, these questions break down into rather precise areas of knowledge.

There are usually

33 Algebra questions
- 14 pre-algebra questions based on math terminology (integers, prime numbers, etc.), basic number theory (rules of zero, order of operations etc.), and manipulation of fractions and decimals
- 10 elementary algebra questions based on inequalities, linear equations, ratios, percents, and averages
- 9 intermediate algebra questions based on exponents, roots, simultaneous equations, and quadratic equations

23 Geometry questions
- 14 plane geometry questions based on angles, lengths, triangles, quadrilaterals, circles, perimeter, area, and volume
- 9 coordinate geometry questions based on slope, distance, midpoint, parallel and perpendicular lines, points of intersection, and graphing

4 Trigonometry questions
- 4 questions based on basic sine, cosine, and tangent functions, trig identities, and graphing

What Not to Expect on the Math Test

Because the ACT test writers care more about your math skills than do the SAT test writers, the ACT does not provide any formulas at the beginning of the Math test. Before you panic, take a second look at the chart on the previous page. Because the ACT is so specific about the types of questions it expects you to answer, preparing to tackle ACT Math takes a few simple steps.

THE PRINCETON REVIEW APPROACH

Because the test is so predictable, the best way to prepare for ACT Math is with

1. a thorough review of the very specific information and question types that come up repeatedly
2. an understanding of The Princeton Review's test-taking strategies and techniques

In each chapter of the Math test, you'll find a mixture of review and technique, with a sprinkling of ACT-like problems. At the end of each chapter, there is a summary of the chapter and a drill designed to pinpoint your math test-taking strengths and weaknesses. In addition to working through the problems in this book, we strongly suggest you practice our techniques on some real ACT practice tests. Let's begin with some general strategies.

Easy, Medium, Difficult

You get 60 minutes for 60 questions. This seems fairly straightforward, but don't let the symmetry of these two numbers fool you; some problems will take much less than a minute, and others could take forever if you let them.

The first few questions are designed to be easier than the rest of the test, then the questions get a bit tougher for the remainder of the test—at least, this is ACT's intention. However, what the people at ACT think is easy may not strike you the same way. Similarly, you may find some of the problems in the middle or end of the test to be a piece of cake.

In fact, if you took a room full of high school students and asked them to vote on which type of ACT math question they would prefer to do, you would almost certainly get different answers: While one student may prefer algebra questions, another student would choose geometry questions instead. Is one of the students more justified in his or her selection? Absolutely not. On the ACT, establishing an order of difficulty for the questions is a *personal* process. Only you can determine which questions are most worth your time investment. Again, we can use triage to help plan our math strategy.

MATH TRIAGE

In Chapter 2, we introduced the concept of triage. Let's apply this concept to ACT Math. Here's a problem.

1. Cynthia, Peter, Nancy, and Kevin are all carpenters. Last week, each built the following number of chairs:

   Cynthia–36   Peter–45   Nancy–74   Kevin–13

   What was the average number of chairs each carpenter built last week?

   A. 39
   B. 42
   C. 55
   D. 59
   E. 63

First Pass

Do the problems you're *sure* you know how to do.

Second Pass

Do the problems you *think* you know how to do. For seemingly impossible questions, pick a Letter of the Day and move on.

Now, Later, Never

When the average test taker begins the ACT Math test, what do you think the person's first instinct is? If you said, "Work questions 1 through 60 as quickly as possible until time runs out," you're 100 percent correct. After all, isn't that what we do on our high school math tests?

The problem with taking such an approach on the ACT is that you are probably robbing yourself of points. Instead of starting with question 1 and finishing with question 60 (if you even make it that far), use the triage approach to actively seek out questions that fit your Personal Order of Difficulty. If question 5 is about a topic with which you're not comfortable, mark it for review and see what else lies ahead. The next page may have several questions that are more worthy of your immediate attention. Attempting easier questions on your "first pass" will guarantee that your time investment actually yields points. As you consistently identify and attempt questions that fit your first pass criteria, your confidence will increase as well; you'll be surprised by how much easier the second pass questions will seem once you've established a successful pattern. Don't get caught up in the psychology of the test. Use your practice time to study ACT's question types and categorize them according to your Personal Order of Difficulty.

I'm Almost Done...

The temptation to get stubborn and stay with a particular problem can be very strong. But if it takes you four minutes to solve question 5, then it might mean that you don't have the time to do several problems later on that you may have found easier. As we mentioned in Chapter 2, you might have the "oh, yeah!" revelation on this problem before you finish the test.

That Was an Easy One

Of course, to solve the problem about the four carpenters, you were probably not going to have to depend on a revelation. Did you want to do it right away? Sure. It's a moderately easy average problem.

An Easy Problem
has one or two steps.

Here's How to Crack It

To find the average of a group of numbers, add the numbers together and divide by the number of terms.

$$\frac{\text{sum of everything}}{\text{number of things}} = \text{average}$$

In this case, the thing we don't know is the average, but we do know everything else, so let's put the numbers into our formula.

$$\frac{36+45+74+13}{4} = \text{average}$$

(By the way, we cover average problems more fully in Chapter 11. The answer to this question is (B).)

You distinguish an easy problem from a tough one in part by deciding whether it can be done in one or two steps or whether it will require three or more steps.

Here's a Medium ACT Problem

22. Four carpenters built an average of 42 chairs each last week. If Cynthia built 36 chairs, Nancy built 74 chairs, and Kevin built 13 chairs, how many chairs did Peter build?

    F.   24
    G.   37
    H.   45
    J.   53
    K.   67

$$\frac{36 + 74 + 13 + x}{4} = 42 \cdot 4$$

$$123 + x = 168$$
$$-123$$

$$45$$

A Medium Problem
has two or three steps.

This is still an average problem, but it is less straightforward and requires an extra step to get the final answer.

Here's How to Crack It

Let's put the information we have into the same formula we used before.

$$\frac{36 + 74 + 13 + \text{Peter}}{4} = 42$$

You might want to substitute the variable x for Peter. Medium and difficult average problems often give you the number of terms and the average. What they don't give you—and the important thing to figure out—is the sum of the numbers to be averaged.

If we multiply both sides by 4, we get the sum of all four numbers.

$$36 + 74 + 13 + \text{Peter} = 168$$

To find out Peter's number of chairs, we just have to add the other numbers and subtract from 168. $168 - 123 = 45$. The answer is (H).

Here's a Hard ACT Problem

A Difficult Problem

has more than three steps.

41. Four carpenters each built an average of 42 chairs last week. If no chairs were left uncompleted, and if Peter, who built 50 chairs, built the greatest number of chairs, what is the **least** number of chairs one of the carpenters could have built, if no carpenter built a fractional number of chairs?

A. 18
B. 19
C. 20
D. 39.33
E. 51

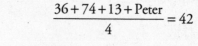

The concept behind this question is really no more difficult than either of the first two problems. It is still about averages. But now there are several more steps involved, including a small leap of faith. You can tell it's more difficult than the first two questions partly because of the language it uses: "If no chairs were left uncompleted" is closing a potential loophole. Easy problems are usually too simple to have loopholes. "What is the **least**" implies the need for reflection.

Here's How to Crack It

Let's put what we know into the same formula we have used twice already.

$$\frac{50 + x + y + z}{4} = 42$$

The only individual about whom we know something specific is Peter. We've represented the other three carpenters as x, y, and z. Because the sum of all four carpenters' chairs adds up to 168, we now have

$$50 + x + y + z = 168$$

By itself, an equation with three variables can't be solved, so unless we can glean a little more information from the problem, we're stuck, and it's time to put a circle around the problem and move on.

Let's assume you skipped the problem temporarily, and you have now come back to it after completing all the problems you thought were easier.

The problem asks for the *least* number of chairs one carpenter could have built. To figure this out, let's have the other two carpenters build the *most* number of chairs they could build. According to the problem, Peter constructed 50, and no one else built as many as he did. So let's say two of the other carpenters constructed 49 each—the largest possible amount they could build and still have built fewer than Peter. By making carpenters x and y construct as many chairs as possible, we can find out the *minimum* number of chairs carpenter z would have to make.

Now the problem looks like this:

$$50 + 49 + 49 + z = 168$$

If we add $50 + 49 + 49$ and subtract it from 168, then $z = 20$, and the correct answer is (C).

———————————◯———————————

Least Happy Students
1. State University of New York—Stonybrook University
2. New Mexico Institute of Mining
3. United States Mercant Marine Academy
4. University of Hawaii—Manoa
5. New Jersey Institute of Technology
6. Fisk University
7. Illinois Institute of Technology
8. Clarkson University
9. Tuskegee University
10. Albion College
Source: *Best 366 Colleges*, 2008 Edition

USE PROCESS OF ELIMINATION (POE)

Even if you weren't sure how to do that last problem, you may have been able to eliminate two answer choices right away using the major technique we introduced in Chapter 3: POE. Remember, ACT doesn't take away any points for wrong answers, so it is in your interest to guess on every question you can't solve using other methods. But your guesses will be much more valuable if you can eliminate some of the answer choices first. The problem said Peter built the greatest number of chairs—50 of them. Therefore, could any of the other carpenters have built *more* than that? No, so (E) doesn't make sense. And because no carpenter built a fractional number of chairs, (D) doesn't make sense, either.

At this point, you're down to three answer choices. But before you guess, you can try a few more tactics. What if you decide to try (A)? If (A) is the correct answer choice, then one carpenter (the one who made the least number of chairs) produced 18 chairs. So what do you do now? Well, that would leave 100 chairs for the other two carpenters, which either means that both of them made 50 chairs or one made more than 50. However, that can't be true because Peter, who made the most chairs, made only 50. So (A) is eliminated. If you try (B), you'll find that the same holds true, and thus, only (C) remains.

Cross Out the Crazy Answers

What's the average of 100 and 200?

A. ~~500~~
B. 150
C. ~~a billion~~

BALLPARK

You can frequently get rid of several answer choices in an ACT math problem without doing any complicated math. Narrow down the choices by estimating your answer. We call this ballparking. Let's look at an example:

---

3. There are 600 school children in the Lakeville district. If 54 of them are high school seniors, what is the percentage of high school seniors in the Lakeville district?

   A.   .9%
   B.   2.32%
   C.   9%
   D.   11%
   E.   90%

Here's How to Crack It

This is not an advanced problem. ACT wants us to write a simple equation, and we will review just how to do that in the arithmetic chapter. But before we do any heavy math, let's see if we can get rid of some answer choices by ballparking.

The question asks us to find a percentage of 600. Just to get a rough fix on where we are, what is 10 percent of 600? If you said 60, you are right. To find 10 percent of anything, you simply move the decimal point over one place to the left. If 60 is

10 percent, then 54 must be slightly less than 10 percent. Which answer choices don't make sense? Choices (D) and (E) don't work because we need something less than 10 percent. On the contrary, we need something only *slightly* less than 10 percent. Could the answer be (A) or (B)? No. On this problem, it is just as easy to eliminate wrong answers as it is to solve for the right answer. The answer is (C).

Of course, your calculator is certainly handy for narrowing down the answer choices on questions like this. If you were to enter 54/600 and press $\boxed{\text{ENTER}}$, you would know exactly which numbers should appear in the answer choices. After you eliminate the answers that don't match, it's just a matter of taking your result and multiplying by 100 to determine the percentage. We will discuss accurate calculator methods in detail later in this chapter, but the process is as simple as typing (54/600) * 100 and hitting $\boxed{\text{ENTER}}$.

───────────────○───────────────

On most ACT problems, you will be able to eliminate only one or two answer choices by ballparking, but it's still vital that you always think about what a reasonable answer might be for a particular problem *before* you solve it mathematically. This is because the ACT has some trap answers waiting for you.

AVOID PARTIAL ANSWERS

Sometimes students think they have completed a problem before the problem is actually done. The test writers at ACT like to include trap answer choices for these students. Here's an example.

───────────────○───────────────

4. A bus line charges $5 each way to ferry a passenger between the hotel and an archaeological dig. On a given day, the bus line has a capacity to carry 255 passengers from the hotel to the dig and back. If the bus line runs at 90% of capacity, how much money did the bus line take in that day?

229.5

F. $1,147.50
G. $1,275
H. $2,295
J. $2,550
K. $2,625

Here's How to Crack It

The first step in this problem is to determine how much money the line would make if it ran at total capacity. If there were 255 passengers, each of whom paid $10 (remember, the bus company charges $5 each way), that would be $2,550.

If you were in a hurry, you might decide at this point that you were already done and go straight to the answer choices. And there is (J), beckoning seductively. Unfortunately, of course, (J) is not the right answer. The bus line is running at only 90 percent of capacity. To get the real answer, we have to find 90 percent of $2,550.

You also may have missed, or put aside temporarily, the information that each passenger has to pay coming *and* going, in which case you may have multiplied 255 by 5 to get $1,275, and then found 90 percent of that, $1,147.50, which just happens to be (F).

Both (F) and (J) were partial answers. Students who picked one of these answers did not make a mistake in their math, nor did they misunderstand the overall concept of the problem; they simply stopped before they were finished. All you had to do to $1,147.50 to get the right answer was double it so that you included both trips. All you had to do to $2,550 to get the right answer was to take 90 percent of it. The answer is (H).

Are Partial Answers Fair?

You may decide that it is not very sporting of ACT to try to trip up students with partial answer choices. However, if this had been a short-answer test, students might well have made exactly the same mistake on their own. Besides, if partial answers represent the downside of multiple-choice testing, there is a tremendous upside as well: Let's see how taking bite-size pieces can help us on long word problems.

Taking Bite-Size Pieces

As you have probably noticed by now, difficulty on many ACT questions is directly related to the number of steps required to determine the correct answer. To avoid partial answers on multistep problems, break down lengthy questions into manageable steps. You can chew on one bite-size piece at a time. Let's walk through an example.

Pop Quiz

Q: What percent of the ACT Math tests trigonometry?

8. Each member in a club had to choose an activity for a day of volunteer work. $\frac{1}{3}$ of the members chose to pick up trash. $\frac{1}{4}$ of the remaining members chose to paint fences. $\frac{5}{6}$ of the members still without tasks chose to clean school buses. The rest of the members chose to plant trees. If the club has 36 members, how many of the members chose to plant trees?

    F.   3
    G.   6
    H.   9
    J.   12
    K.   15

Here's How to Crack It

Although your gut reaction may be to jam everything into your calculator and circle whatever pops up on the screen, think about how neatly the information is divided. If you were to translate each part of the question into math language and write each step in your test booklet, wouldn't you be less likely to make a mistake? Try this.

1. Because the question is dealing with fractions, we'll need to start with the number of members in the club. Write "36 members" down in your scratch work area.

2. Now, let's work the question in steps. The first thing we read is "$\frac{1}{3}$ of the members chose to pick up trash." We'll just need to take $\frac{1}{3}$ of 36, so write the equation down before completing it or entering it into your calculator. After you find out that 12 people picked up trash, be sure to label the information so you don't forget what the number is.

3. The next thing we read is "$\frac{1}{4}$ of the remaining members chose to paint fences." Be careful here—we want to take $\frac{1}{4}$ of the *remaining* members, not of the original 36. If 12 people are already picking up trash, we know there are 24 people remaining. Write down the proper equation to express this: $\frac{1}{4} \times 24 = 6$ people. Again, be sure to note that 6 is the number of people painting fences.

4. What's next? We see a line saying, "$\frac{5}{6}$ of the members still without tasks chose to clean school buses." In the last step, we were down to 24 members; if 6 are painting fences, how many are left over? 18. The answer is 18. Use this to write your next equation: $\frac{5}{6} \times 18 = 15$ people. We now know that 15 people are cleaning school buses.

How to Avoid Partial Answers

You can prevent yourself from picking partial answers by doing the following three things:

1. Slow down. It isn't going to help to do a problem so quickly that you miss important information and get the question wrong.
2. Once you've read the question, underline what it's really asking. Now go back and do the question piece by piece. If you find yourself reading the whole question over again, STOP! You're not going to do the whole problem all at once, and if you did, you'd probably make a mistake. So just take it one step at a time.
3. When you finish the problem, re-read what you underlined to make sure you've answered the question that was asked by the ACT test writer.

Pop Quiz

A: 4 questions out of 60 is equal to roughly 6.67%.

5. Almost there…the next line says, "All of the remaining members chose to plant trees." We don't need to do much math here. If 15 out of 18 people ended up cleaning school buses, then we know there are only 3 people left. Those 3 are planting trees.

6. Finally, we arrive at what the question is asking. Now that all the math involved is nicely mapped out and labeled, we should have no problem finding the answer. The question asks, "How many of the members chose to plant trees?" If we refer to our scratch work, we see that 3 people planted trees. We can safely pick answer choice (F) and move on. Your scratch work for this problem should look something like this.

$$36 \text{ members}$$

$$\frac{1}{3} \times 12 = 12 \text{ (trash)}$$

$$24 \text{ remaining}$$

$$\frac{1}{4} \times 24 = 6 \text{ (fences)}$$

$$18 \text{ remaining}$$

$$\frac{5}{6} \times 18 = 15 \text{ (buses)}$$

$$3 \text{ remaining (trees)}$$

By taking a more manageable approach, you can guarantee that you won't pick any of the distracter answers. To illustrate the point, take a look at the steps above and compare them with the answer choices. Notice anything? (J) was the number of people picking up trash. Similarly, (G) was the number of people painting fences, and (K) was the number of people cleaning school buses. As you can see, being too quick on the draw can get you into trouble on multistep word problems. If you take bite-size pieces of word problems, you'll be able to move many of them into your first-pass question group.

CAN I USE MY CALCULATOR?

You sure can, and you should. Although the folks who write the ACT state that none of the math questions requires a calculator, the fact is the math on the test has become steadily more complex since calculators were first allowed. The test writers clearly expect you to have a calculator.

Furthermore, there are plenty of questions on the test that will go much more quickly and smoothly if you know how to use your calculator properly. As we go through the math in this book, we'll be pointing out which questions are particularly calculator-friendly and telling you just what to do with your calculator to succeed. The key, of course, is that you need to know how to use your calculator before the test begins. So when we tell you to make sure you can do a certain type of operation on your calculator, be sure to check right away.

Throughout the rest of the Math chapters, we discuss ways to solve calculator-friendly questions in an accurate and manageable way. Because TI-89 and TI-92 calculators are not allowed on the ACT, we will show you how to solve problems on the TI-83. If you don't plan to use a TI-83 on the test, we recommend that you make sure your calculator is acceptable for use on the test and that it can do the following:

- handle positive, negative, and fractional exponents
- use parentheses
- graph simple functions
- convert fractions to decimals and vice versa
- change a linear equation into $y = mx + b$ form

Pop Quiz

A: 0 is neither positive nor negative, but it is an even number

RED HERRINGS

Of the 60 problems in the Math section, several will contain extra information that is not, strictly speaking, necessary to solve the problems. The test writers want to see if you can distinguish important information from filler. Because there are so few of these questions, it isn't necessary to examine each new piece of information with a magnifying glass to see if it might be a red herring. In almost every problem on the ACT, you will need *all* the information given to solve it. However, if you're staring at a particular number that doesn't seem to have anything to do with the solution of the question you're doing, it might be a red herring. Here's an example.

5. Susan's take-home pay is $300 per week, of which she spends $80 on food and $150 on rent. What fraction of her take-home pay does she spend on food?

A. $\dfrac{2}{75}$

B. $\dfrac{4}{15}$

C. $\dfrac{1}{2}$

D. $\dfrac{23}{30}$

E. $\dfrac{29}{30}$

$\dfrac{8}{30}$

Here's How to Crack It

The last line tells us what we need to do. A fraction is a part over a whole. In this case, the whole is $300. The part is the amount of money spent on food.

$$\frac{\$80}{\$300} \text{ which reduces to } \frac{4}{15}$$

Where does the $150 fit in? It doesn't. The question isn't asking about rent. The test writers just threw that in to confuse you. Note that if you got confused and found the fraction of the take-home salary that was paid in rent, $150/$300, you would pick (C). The correct answer is (B).

Thinking About College
The key question for students and parents researching colleges shouldn't be *"What college is best, academically?"* .... It's not hard to find academically great schools in this country.... The key question...is *"What is the best college for me?"*
Source: *Best 366 Colleges*, 2008 Edition

Summary

o   On the ACT Math test, you have 60 minutes to attempt 60 questions. The questions fall into the following categories:

- 33 Algebra questions (14 pre-algebra, 10 elementary algebra, 9 intermediate algebra)
- 23 Geometry questions (14 plane geometry, 9 coordinate geometry)
- 4 Trigonometry questions

o   Use triage and your Personal Order of Difficulty to establish a two-pass system.

- On the first pass, actively search for questions that require only a few steps and/or deal with topics you find manageable.
- Save any multistep, unfamiliar, or difficult questions for your second pass. As time runs out, or if a question seems exceedingly difficult, pick a Letter of the Day and invest your time in something more worthwhile.

o   You can use POE to cancel out wrong answer choices. Sometimes it is easier to get rid of wrong answers than to find the correct answer.

- Incorrect answers are sometimes partial answers—answers you arrive at on the way to the final solution if you quit before you are really done.
- Incorrect answers sometimes don't really make sense if you look at them in the cold light of day. Frequently, you can eliminate answer choices because they are nowhere near what common sense says the answer would have to be.
- Incorrect answers are sometimes based on red herrings—pieces of information that are not really necessary to solve the problem.

o   Take bite-size pieces of questions with multiple steps. Use the space in your test booklet to translate each sentence into its math equivalent, and be sure to label your information to avoid confusion.

o   Be sure you put an answer down for every question—even the ones you don't have time to do. There's no penalty for wrong answers.

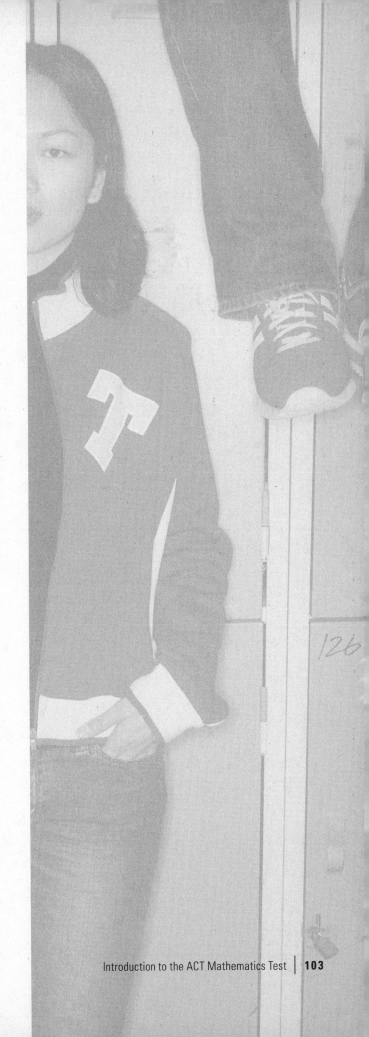

Chapter 10
Basics

To successfully tackle the questions you'll encounter on the ACT Math test, you must have a strong command of mathematical nuts and bolts. In this chapter, we'll discuss math terminology, properties of numbers, basic operations, and processes involving exponents and roots.

Look at the following problem:

1. How many even prime numbers are there between 0 and 100 ?
   A. 0
   B. 1
   C. 2
   D. 3
   E. 4

If you know what the terms *even* and *prime* mean, this problem is a snap. Without a knowledge of these terms, the problem is impossible. Let's begin our math review by going over all the basic math terms and operations covered on the ACT. By the way, the answer to the question is (B).

BASIC TERMS

Real Numbers

Real numbers are all the numbers you think of when you think of numbers: 5, $\frac{1}{4}$, 7.9, 100, –43, $\sqrt{2}$, etc. They include everything *except* imaginary numbers, which appear only occasionally on the ACT. An example of an imaginary number is *i*, which is the square root of –1.

Rational Numbers

Any number that can be written as a whole number, a fraction (an integer over another integer), or as a repeating decimal is a rational number. This means that 5, $\frac{1}{5}$, and $.33\overline{3}$ are rational numbers. In fact, most of the numbers you'll see on the ACT are rational numbers.

Irrational Numbers

An irrational number cannot be written as an integer over another integer. π is irrational. Like other irrational numbers, it goes on forever. While you may think of π as 3.14, it can be written out to as many decimal places as you feel like writing down—3.141592, etc.—and as many places as you take it, you will never find a repeating pattern.

Pop Quiz

Q: Is 0 even or odd?

Q: Is 0 a prime number?

Other irrational numbers? Any square root of a number that does not have a perfect square root. For example, $\sqrt{3}$ or $\sqrt{2}$. By contrast, $\sqrt{4}$, which simplifies to 2, is a rational number.

Integers

Integers include everything *except* what we normally think of as fractions or decimals: 2, 134, −56, 0, and 7 are all integers. $\frac{1}{2}$, 6.7, and $\frac{-31}{2}$ are not.

Positive and Negative

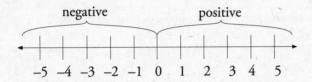

Positive numbers are to the right of the 0 on the number line above. Negative numbers are to the left of zero on the number line above. Zero itself is neither negative nor positive.

Note that positive numbers get bigger as they move away from 0. Negative numbers get smaller. For example, −3 is smaller than −1.

There are three rules regarding the multiplication of positive and negative numbers. They are

> positive × positive = positive
>
> positive × negative = negative
>
> negative × negative = positive

When you add a positive number and a negative number, you're subtracting the number with the negative sign in front of it from the positive number.

$$5 + (-3) = 2$$

When you add two negative numbers, you're adding the two numbers as if they were positive and then putting a negative sign in front of the sum. In the process, you are going farther away from zero.

$$-3 + -4 = -7$$

When entering negative numbers into your calculator, use the negative key (–) rather than the subtraction key. This will ensure that you don't end up with the incorrect answer by entering too many or too few operands.

Even and Odd Numbers

Even numbers are integers that can be divided evenly by 2 (leaving no remainder.)

$$-4, -2, 0, 2, 4, 6, \text{etc.}$$

Odd numbers are integers that cannot be divided evenly by 2.

$$-5, -3, -1, 1, 3, 5, \text{etc.}$$

Note that 0 is even. There are several rules regarding multiplication and addition of even and odd numbers. They are

$$\text{even} \times \text{even} = \text{even}$$

$$\text{odd} \times \text{odd} = \text{odd}$$

$$\text{even} \times \text{odd} = \text{even}$$

$$\text{even} + \text{even} = \text{even}$$

$$\text{odd} + \text{odd} = \text{even}$$

$$\text{even} + \text{odd} = \text{odd}$$

Pop Quiz

Q: What's the only even prime?

Digits

There are ten digits: 0, 1, 2, 3, 4, 5, 6, 7, 8, 9.

The number 364 has three digits—3, 6, and 4. In this number, the 4 is called the **ones** digit, or **units** digit. The 6 is called the **tens** digit. The 3 is called the **hundreds** digit.

The number 4.56 has three digits—4, 5, and 6. The 4 is called the ones digit or units digit. The 5 is called the **tenths** digit, and the 6 is called the **hundredths** digit.

Prime Numbers

A prime number can be divided evenly by two and only two distinct factors—1 and itself. Thus, 2, 3, 5, 7, 11, and 13 are all prime numbers. The number 2 is the only even prime number. Neither 0 nor 1 is a prime number. There are no negative prime numbers.

For more help, check out our ACT Academic Tutoring options at our website, PrincetonReview.com.

Absolute Value

The absolute value of a number is the distance between that number and 0 on the number line. The absolute value of 6 is expressed as $|6|$.

$$|6| = 6$$

$$|-6| = 6$$

Variables and Coefficients

In the expression $3x + 4y$, x and y are called **variables** because we don't know what they are. 3 and 4 are called **coefficients** because you multiply the variables by them.

BASIC OPERATIONS

Divisibility Rules

If a number can be divided evenly by another number, it is said to be divisible by that number. A good way to save time dividing is to know the rules of divisibility for some common numbers. The rules are as follows:

1. A number is divisible by 2 if its units digit can be divided evenly by 2 (in other words, if it is even). 46 is divisible by 2. So is 3,574.
2. A number is divisible by 3 if the sum of its digits can be divided evenly by 3. We can quickly determine that 216 is divisible by 3 because the sum of the digits (2 + 1 + 6) is divisible by 3.

Pop Quiz

A: 2. (It's also the smallest prime number. That's right: 1 is *not* prime.)

3. A number is divisible by 4 if the number formed by its last two digits (tens digit and units digit) is also divisible by 4. Thus, 316 is divisible by 4 because 16 is divisible by 4. 728 is also divisible by 4 because 28 is divisible by 4.

4. A number is divisible by 5 if its last digit (units place) is either 0 or 5. For example, 60, 85, and 15 are all divisible by 5.

5. A number is divisible by 6 if it is also divisible by the factors of 6, which are 2 and 3. For example, 228 is divisible by 6 because it is even (divisible by 2) and the sum of its digits is divisible by 3.

6. A number is divisible by 8 if the number formed by its last three digits (hundreds, tens, and unit digits) is also divisible by 8. Thus, 9,128 is divisible by 8 because 128 is divisible by 8.

7. A number is divisible by 9 if the sum of its digits can be divided evenly by 9. For example, 873 is divisible by 9 because the sum of the digits (8 + 7 + 3) is divisible by 9.

The Four Horsemen

Make sure you can identify terms that invoke the four basic operations.

- **Sum** is the result of addition.
  The sum of 3 and 4 is 7.
- **Product** is the result of multiplication.
  The product of 5 and 2 is 10.
- **Difference** is the result of subtraction.
  The difference between 7 and 3 is 4.
- **Quotient** is the result of division.
  If you divide 14 by 7, the quotient is 2.

Pop Quiz

Q: If a number is divisible by 2 and by 3, it's also divisible by…

Factors and Multiples

A number is a **factor** of another number if it can be divided evenly *into* that number. Is 3 a factor of 15? Yes, because 3 can be divided evenly into 15. The complete list of factors of 15 is 1, 3, 5, and 15.

A number is a **multiple** of another number if it can be divided evenly *by* that number. For example, multiples of 15 include 15, 30, 45, and 60.

All integers have a limited number of factors and an infinite number of multiples. You can remember this with the following mnemonic: Factors, Few; Multiples, Many.

What is the only factor of 15 that is also a multiple of 15? 15.

STANDARD SYMBOLS

Symbol	Meaning
=	is equal to
≠	is not equal to
<	is less than
>	is greater than
≤	is less than or equal to
≥	is greater than or equal to

EXPONENTS

An exponent is a short way of writing the value of a number multiplied several times by itself. $4 \times 4 \times 4 \times 4 \times 4$ can also be written as 4^5. This is expressed aloud as "4 to the fifth power." The lower and larger number (4) is called the **base**, and the upper number (5) is called the **exponent**. There are several rules to remember about exponents.

Multiplying Numbers with the Same Base

When you multiply numbers that have the same base, you simply add the exponents.

$$6^2 \times 6^3 = 6^{(2+3)} = 6^5 \qquad \left(y^2\right)\left(y^3\right) = y^{(2+3)} = y^5$$

Pop Quiz

A: 6

Dividing Numbers with the Same Base

When you divide numbers that have the same base, you simply subtract the bottom exponent from the top exponent.

$$\frac{4^7}{4^2} = 4^5 \qquad \frac{x^7}{x^2} = x^5 \qquad \frac{y^3}{y^5} = \frac{1}{y^2} = y^{-2}$$

Negative Powers

In that last example, we also wrote the result as y^{-2}. A negative power is simply the reciprocal of a positive power. (The reciprocal of 3 is $\frac{1}{3}$.)

$$3^{-1} = \frac{1}{3} \qquad 3^{-2} = \frac{1}{9} \qquad 3^{-3} = \frac{1}{27}$$

Fractional Powers

When a number is raised to a fractional power, the **numerator** (the number above the line in a fraction) functions like a real exponent, while the **denominator** (the number below the line in a fraction) tells you what power radical to make the number. (Radicals will be defined on page 114.)

$$9^{\frac{1}{2}} = \sqrt{9} = 3 \qquad 8^{\frac{2}{3}} = \sqrt[3]{8^2}$$

Raising a Power to a Power

When you raise a power to a power, you simply multiply the exponents.

$$(4^2)^6 = 4^{(2 \cdot 6)} = 4^{12} \qquad (y^3)^2 = y^{(3 \cdot 2)} = y^6$$

Pop Quiz

Q: What number is both a factor and multiple of 21?

The Zero Power

Anything to the zero power is 1.

$$4^0 = 1 \qquad x^0 = 1$$

The First Power

Anything to the power of 1 is itself.

$$5^1 = 5 \qquad y^1 = y$$

Distributing Exponents

When several numbers are inside parentheses, the exponent outside the parentheses must be distributed to all of the numbers within.

$$(4y)^2 = 4^2 y^2 = 16y^2$$

But Watch Out For...

Exponents are shorthand for multiplication, so the rules apply only when you multiply or divide the same base.

$$\text{Does } x^2 + x^3 = x^5 \,? \text{ NO!}$$

$$\text{Does } x^4 - x^2 = x^2 \,? \text{ NO!}$$

$$\text{Does } \frac{x^2 + y^3 + z^4}{x^2 + y^3} = z^4 \text{ NO!}$$

You would expect that raising a number to a power would increase that number, and usually it does, but there are exceptions.

- If you raise a positive fraction of less than 1 to a power, it gets smaller.

$$\left(\frac{1}{2}\right)^2 = \frac{1^2}{2^2} = \frac{1}{4}$$

- If you raise a negative number to an odd power, the number gets smaller (unless it is between 0 and –1).

$$(-3)^3 = (-3)(-3)(-3) = -27$$

(Remember, –27 is smaller than –3.)

- If you raise a negative number to an even power, the number becomes positive.

$$(-3)^2 = (-3)(-3) = 9$$

RADICALS

The **square root** of a positive number x is the number that, when squared, equals x. For example, the square root of 16 equals 4 because $4 \times 4 = 16$. On the ACT, you will not have to worry about negative square roots; for ACT purposes, the square root of 16 is just 4.

The symbol for a positive square root is $\sqrt{}$. The symbol $\sqrt{}$ is also called a **radical**.

$$\sqrt{16} = 4$$
$$\sqrt{9} = 3$$

The **cube root** of a positive number x is the number that, when cubed, equals x. For example, the cube root of 8 equals 2 because $2 \times 2 \times 2$ equals 8.

$$\sqrt[3]{8} = 2$$
$$\sqrt[3]{27} = 3$$

Be sure that you know how to use your calculator to find more than just square roots and simple exponents like 4^2. The ACT is going to have fractional exponents, negative exponents, and all sorts of weird roots, and you'll need to be able to solve them quickly and accurately. Can you do the two examples above on your calculator? What about questions 4 and 5 in the drill at the end of this chapter? If you can't, be sure to learn how.

Rules to Remember About Radicals

- $\sqrt{x} + \sqrt{x} = 2\sqrt{x}$

    For example, $2\sqrt{5} + 20\sqrt{5} = 22\sqrt{5}$

- $\sqrt{x} \cdot \sqrt{y} = \sqrt{xy}$

    For example, $\left(\sqrt{12}\right)\left(\sqrt{3}\right) = \sqrt{36}$, or 6.

    $3\sqrt{5} \cdot 6\sqrt{2} = 18\sqrt{10}$

- $$\sqrt{\dfrac{x}{y}} = \dfrac{\sqrt{x}}{\sqrt{y}}$$

  For example, $\sqrt{\dfrac{3}{16}} = \dfrac{\sqrt{3}}{\sqrt{16}} = \dfrac{\sqrt{3}}{4}$

- To simplify a radical, try factoring. Look for a perfect square to factor out.

  $$\sqrt{32} = \sqrt{16}\sqrt{2} = 4\sqrt{2}$$
  $$2\sqrt{5} + 4\sqrt{125} = 2\sqrt{5} + 4\left(\sqrt{25}\right)\left(\sqrt{5}\right) =$$
  $$2\sqrt{5} + (4)(5)\left(\sqrt{5}\right) = 22\sqrt{5}$$

- The square root of a positive fraction less than 1 is actually larger than the original fraction.

  For example, $\sqrt{\dfrac{1}{4}} = \dfrac{1}{2}$

- Always try to have a ballpark idea of how large the number you are dealing with actually is. $\sqrt{63}$ is a bit less than $\sqrt{64}$ or 8. $\sqrt[3]{9}$ is a bit more than $\sqrt[3]{8}$ or 2. Some good approximations to memorize and helpful hints to remember them are as follows:

  $\sqrt{2} \approx 1.4$ (Valentine's Day is 2/14.)
  $\sqrt{3} \approx 1.7$ (St. Patrick's Day is 3/17.)

- Your calculator can make working with radicals even easier. Choose $\boxed{2^{\text{nd}}}$, then $\boxed{x^2}$ for square roots.

- For cube roots, hit $\boxed{\text{MATH}}$ and choose $\left[4 : \sqrt[3]{(}\;\right]$.

- For all roots, always remember to close the parentheses after you enter your number.

Basics Drill

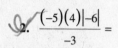

1. Which of the following expresses the prime factorization of 54 ?

   A. 9×6
   B. $3 \times 3 \times 6$
   C. $3 \times 3 \times 2$
   D. $3 \times 3 \times 3 \times 2$
   E. 5.4×10

2. $\dfrac{(-5)(4)|-6|}{-3} =$

   F. -120
   G. -40
   H. 40
   J. 60
   K. 120

3. The number 1,134 is divisible by all of the following except

   A. 3
   B. 6
   C. 9
   D. 12
   E. 14

4. $(-2)^3 + (3)^{-2} + \dfrac{8}{9} =$

   F. -7
   G. $-1\dfrac{7}{9}$
   H. $\dfrac{8}{9}$
   J. $1\dfrac{7}{9}$
   K. 12

5. $27^{\frac{2}{3}}$

   A. -9
   B. -4
   C. 9
   D. 18
   E. 81^3

6. For all $x \neq 0$, $y \neq 0$, $\dfrac{(xy)^3 z^0}{x^3 y^4} =$

   F. $\dfrac{1}{y}$
   G. $\dfrac{z}{y}$
   H. z
   J. xy
   K. xyz

7. When is $\dfrac{11-a}{2}$ an integer?

   A. Only when a is negative
   B. Only when a is positive
   C. Only when a is odd
   D. Only when a equals 0
   E. Only when a is even

8. How many even integers are there between -4 and 4 ?

   F. 1
   G. 3
   H. 4
   J. 5
   K. 7

9. If the four-digit number 47W6 is divisible by 6 (W represents the tens digit), which of the following could be the value of W ?

   A. 2
   B. 3
   C. 4
   D. 6
   E. 8

10. If $9^x = \dfrac{1}{3}$, then $x =$

    F. -3
    G. -2
    H. -1
    J. $-\dfrac{1}{2}$
    K. $-\dfrac{1}{3}$

Summary

o Make sure you are familiar with math terminology. Many partial answers rely on the misinterpretation of key terms; don't be a victim.

o Knowing the rules of divisibility can be very useful on the ACT. In case you forget the rules, you can also test divisibility by entering the numbers into your calculator. If you get an integer result, the number is divisible by its factor.

o For any given number, the factors and multiples are *always* distinct, with one exception—the number itself. The number 10, for instance, is both a factor and a multiple of itself.

o Know the rules for multiplying and dividing exponents, raising a power to a power, and expressing fractional and negative exponents.

o On the ACT, square roots must be positive. However, exponents have both positive and negative roots.

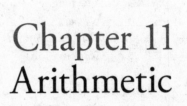

Chapter 11
Arithmetic

Most of the arithmetic operations you'll come across on the ACT will seem like ancient history. While some questions will deal with only your ability to follow the correct order of operations, others will ask you to apply the same rules to a problem involving exponents and fractions. What do all these questions have in common? Getting them correct hinges on your command of basic arithmetic topics. In this chapter, we show you how to identify and attack questions that deal with the types of numbers and operations we commonly see in arithmetic questions.

Pay close attention to questions that deal only with arithmetic and do them first. Remember the concept of triage? These are exactly the type of questions that are points ready for the taking, so make sure you work them out carefully and get them right.

Here are the specific arithmetic (and related) topics tested on the ACT.

1. Order of operations
2. Fractions
3. Decimals
4. Ratios
5. Percentages
6. Averages
7. Charts and graphs
8. Combinations

First, let's discuss the fundamentals of each topic before we show you how ACT constructs questions based on those fundamentals.

Calculators

Students are permitted (but not required) to use calculators on the ACT. You should definitely bring a calculator to the test. Remember: We'll point out the calculator-friendly questions and tell you what you need to be able to do with your calculator on the ACT. Be sure to confirm that you can do each of the operations we mention. If it's been awhile since you used your calculator to figure out material tested on the ACT, put it through its paces again.

ORDER OF OPERATIONS

For problems that involve several different operations, you must perform the operations in a particular order. Here's an easy way to remember the order of operations.

Please Excuse My Dear Aunt Sally

First, you do operations enclosed in Parentheses; then you take care of Exponents; then you Multiply, Divide, Add, and Subtract, working from left to right. Most calculators follow the correct order of operations, but you have to be sure to enter the equations into your calculator correctly. Now's the time to test your calculator's ability to handle order of operations (and your ability to push tiny buttons properly).

Try this one.

$(-1)^2$

$$\left((-5)+4\right)^2\left(\frac{8}{2}\right)+4-8=$$

$4 \cdot 4 - 8$
$8 - 8 = 0$

Now try this one.

$$(-8)+\left(\frac{8}{2}\right)(4-5)^2+4=$$

$-8 + 4 \cdot 4 = 0$

If your calculator follows order of operations, then you should have gotten the same answer both times: 0.

The Associative Law: When adding a string of numbers, you can add them in any order you like. The same thing is true when multiplying a string of numbers.

> 5 + 6 + 7 is the same as 7 + 6 + 5
>
> $2 \times 3 \times 4$ is the same as $3 \times 4 \times 2$

The Distributive Law: Some combinations of addition and multiplication can be written in two different formats, which often proves extremely useful in finding ACT answers. The distributive law states that

> $$a(b + c) = ab + ac$$
>
> and that
>
> $$a(b - c) = ab - ac$$

What Comes First?
Perform all operations within parentheses first. The distributive law is something of an exception; it gives you two ways to get the same result.

If a problem gives you information in factored format, which is $a(b + c)$, you should distribute it immediately. If the information is given in distributed form, which is $ab + ac$, you should factor it. An ACT problem might look like this.

1. For all $x \neq -2$, $\dfrac{2x+4}{x+2} = ?$

   A. $x + 2$
   B. x
   C. 2
   D. $x + 4$
   E. 4

$$\frac{2(x+2)}{x+2}$$

Here's How to Crack It
Let's use the distributive property on the numerator of this fraction and rewrite it in factored form.

$$\frac{2(x+2)}{(x+2)}$$

$\dfrac{(x+2)}{(x+2)}$ equals just 1. Therefore, we can cancel out both terms and the answer must be (C).

FRACTIONS

Calculators and Fractions

Your calculator is an excellent tool to perform many of the basic operations concerning fractions. Many of the common calculator errors, however, involve fractions. We have found that the best way to avoid these errors is to know how to perform basic operations on fractions by hand. Even if you use a TI-83/84 on the ACT, the next few pages will provide you with an understanding of what fractions are and how they work.

Fractions can be thought of in two ways. A fraction is just another way of expressing division. The expression $\frac{1}{2}$ means 1 divided by 2. $\frac{x}{y}$ is nothing more than x divided by y. A fraction is made up of a numerator and a denominator. The numerator is on top; the denominator is on the bottom. Just think, *denominator* starts with "d," just like *downstairs*.

$$\frac{1}{2} \quad \frac{\text{numerator}}{\text{denominator}}$$

The other way to think of a fraction is as a part over a whole.

$$\frac{1}{2} \quad \frac{\text{part}}{\text{whole}}$$

In the fraction $\frac{1}{2}$, we have one part out of a total of two parts.

In the fraction $\frac{3}{7}$, we have three parts out of a total of seven parts.

Reducing Fractions

To reduce a fraction, see if the numerator and the denominator have a common factor. It may save time to find the largest factor they share, but getting this information isn't crucial. Whatever factor they share can now be canceled. Let's take the fraction $\frac{6}{8}$. Is there a common factor? Yes: 2.

Fraction Reduction
In any fraction involving large numbers, try to reduce the fractions before you do anything else.

$$\frac{6}{8} = \frac{\cancel{2} \times 3}{\cancel{2} \times 4} = \frac{3}{4}$$

Get used to reducing all fractions (if they can be reduced) before you do any work with them. It saves a lot of time and prevents errors that crop up when you try to work with large numbers. Use your calculator's [FRAC] function under the MATH menu to reduce as well.

Comparing Fractions

Sometimes a problem will involve deciding which of two fractions is larger. If your calculator can convert fractions to decimals at the touch of a button, that's the way to compare them. If not, keep reading, and we'll explain how to do it by hand.

Which is larger, $\frac{2}{5}$ or $\frac{4}{5}$? Think of these as parts of a whole. Which is bigger, two parts out of five or four parts out of five? $\frac{4}{5}$ is clearly larger. In this case, it was easy to tell because they both had the same whole, or the same denominator.

Try this one. Which is larger, $\frac{2}{3}$ or $\frac{3}{7}$? To decide, we need to find a common whole, or denominator. You change the denominator of a fraction by multiplying it by another number. To keep the entire fraction the same, however, you must multiply the numerator by the same number.

Let's change the denominator of $\frac{2}{3}$ into 21.

$$\frac{2 \times 7}{3 \times 7} = \frac{14}{21}$$

$\frac{14}{21}$ still has the same value as $\frac{2}{3}$ (it would reduce to $\frac{2}{3}$) because we multiplied the fraction by $\frac{7}{7}$, or one.

Let's change the denominator of $\frac{3}{7}$ into 21 as well.

$$\frac{3 \times 3}{7 \times 3} = \frac{9}{21}$$

$\frac{9}{21}$ still has the same value as $\frac{3}{7}$ (it would reduce to $\frac{3}{7}$) because we multiplied the fraction by $\frac{3}{3}$, or one.

Now we can compare the two fractions. Which is larger, $\frac{14}{21}$ or $\frac{9}{21}$? Clearly, $\frac{14}{21}$ (or $\frac{2}{3}$) is bigger than $\frac{9}{21}$ (or $\frac{3}{7}$). Why did we decide on 21 as our common denominator? The easiest way to get a common denominator is to multiply the denominators of the two fractions you wish to compare: $7 \times 3 = 21$.

Let's do it again. Which is largest?

$$\frac{2}{3} \text{ or } \frac{4}{7} \text{ or } \frac{3}{5}?$$

To compare these fractions directly, you need a common denominator, but finding a common denominator that works for all three fractions would be complicated and time-consuming. It makes more sense to compare these fractions two at a time. Let's start with $\frac{2}{3}$ and $\frac{4}{7}$. An easy common denominator is 21.

$$\frac{2}{3} \qquad\qquad \frac{4}{7}$$

$$\frac{2 \times 7}{3 \times 7} = \frac{14}{21} \qquad\qquad \frac{4}{7} \times \frac{3}{3} = \frac{12}{21}$$

Because $\frac{2}{3}$ is larger, let's compare it with $\frac{3}{5}$. This time, the easiest common denominator is 15.

$$\frac{2}{3} \qquad\qquad \frac{3}{5}$$

$$\frac{2}{3} \times \frac{5}{5} = \frac{10}{15} \qquad\qquad \frac{3}{5} \times \frac{3}{3} = \frac{9}{15}$$

So $\frac{2}{3}$ is larger than $\frac{3}{5}$, which means it's also the biggest of the three.

Using the Bowtie

A more streamlined way to do this is to use the **Bowtie**. Let's compare the last two fractions again. We get the common denominator by multiplying the two denominators together.

$$\frac{2}{3} \rightarrow \frac{3}{5} = \frac{}{15}$$

We get the new numerators by multiplying as shown below.

$$\overset{\texttextcircled{10}}{} \quad \overset{\textcircled{9}}{}$$
$$\frac{2}{3} \bowtie \frac{3}{5} = \frac{}{15}$$

So $\frac{2}{3}$ is larger.

Easiest Common Denominator

Your teachers wanted you to calculate the Least Common Denominator (LCD) of a fraction. They even made you "show your work." The ACT doesn't care. This gives you the luxury of finding the Easiest Common Denominator by using the Bowtie.

Adding and Subtracting Fractions

Now that we've reviewed finding a common denominator, adding and subtracting fractions is simple. Let's use the Bowtie to add $\frac{2}{5}$ and $\frac{1}{4}$.

$$\frac{8}{20} \quad \frac{5}{20}$$

$$\overset{\textcircled{8}}{} \quad \overset{\textcircled{5}}{}$$
$$\frac{2}{5} \bowtie \frac{1}{4} \rightarrow \frac{8+5}{20} = \frac{13}{20}$$

Let's use the Bowtie to subtract $\frac{2}{3}$ from $\frac{5}{6}$.

$$\overset{\textcircled{15}}{} \quad \overset{\textcircled{12}}{}$$
$$\frac{5}{6} \bowtie \frac{2}{3} \rightarrow \frac{15-12}{18} = \frac{3}{18} \text{ or } \frac{1}{6}$$

Multiplying Fractions

To multiply fractions, line them up and multiply straight across.

$$\frac{5}{6} \times \frac{4}{5} = \frac{20}{30} = \frac{2}{3}$$

Was there anything we could have canceled or reduced *before* we multiplied? Yes.

We could cancel the 5 on top and the 5 on the bottom. What's left is $\frac{4}{6}$, which reduces to $\frac{2}{3}$.

Sometimes students whose math skills are a bit rusty think they can cancel or reduce in the same fashion *across an equal sign*.

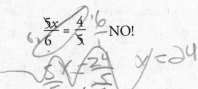

$$\frac{5x}{6} = \frac{4}{5} \quad \text{NO!}$$

You *cannot* cancel the 5s or reduce the $\frac{4}{6}$ in this case. When there is an equal sign, you have to cross-multiply, which yields $25x = 24$, so x in this case would equal $\frac{24}{25}$.

Dividing Fractions

To divide one fraction by another, just invert the second fraction and multiply.

$$\frac{2}{3} \div \frac{3}{4} \text{ is the same thing as } \frac{2}{3} \times \frac{4}{3} = \frac{8}{9}$$

You may see this same operation written like this.

$$\frac{\frac{2}{3}}{\frac{3}{4}}$$

Again, just invert and multiply. Try the next example.

$$\frac{6}{1} \cdot \frac{3}{2} \quad \frac{18}{2} = \frac{6}{\frac{2}{3}}$$

$$9$$

Think of 6 as $\frac{6}{1}$ and do the same thing.

$$\frac{6}{1} \times \frac{3}{2} = \frac{18}{2} = 9$$

Converting to Fractions

An integer can always be expressed as a fraction by making the integer the numerator and 1 the denominator. $8 = \frac{8}{1}$.

Sometimes the ACT gives you numbers that are mixtures of integers and fractions (e.g., $3\frac{1}{2}$). It is often easier to work with these numbers by converting them completely into fractions. Because the fraction is being expressed in halves, let's convert the integer into halves as well. $3 = \frac{6}{2}$. Now just add the $\frac{1}{2}$ to the $\frac{6}{2}$. $3\frac{1}{2} = \frac{7}{2}$.

Now How Does the ACT Test Fractions?

An ACT fraction problem combines several of the elements we've just discussed. Here's a typical problem.

---

1. After $\dfrac{4\frac{1}{3}}{2\frac{3}{5}}$ has been simplified to a single fraction in lowest terms, what is the denominator?

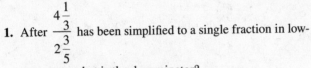

   A. 2
   B. 3
   C. 5
   D. 9
   E. 13

Here's How to Crack It

First, let's convert the mixture of integers and fractions into fractions. $4\frac{1}{3} = \frac{13}{3}$, $2\frac{3}{5} = \frac{13}{5}$. Remember, to divide fractions, simply flip and multiply $\frac{13}{3} \times \frac{5}{13}$. The 13s cancel, leaving $\frac{5}{3}$. The answer is (B).

More complicated fraction problems might test your ability to recognize that every fraction implies another fraction—what's left over. If a glass is $\frac{3}{5}$ full, what part of the glass is empty? $\frac{2}{5}$.

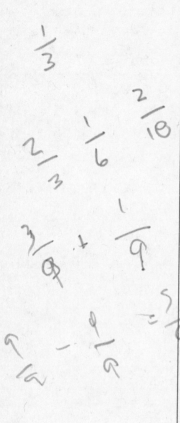

2. On Friday, Jane does one-third of her homework. On Saturday, she does one-sixth of the remainder. What fraction of her homework is still left to be done?

F. $\frac{4}{9}$

G. $\frac{1}{2}$

H. $\frac{5}{9}$

J. $\frac{5}{6}$

K. $\frac{7}{12}$

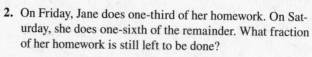

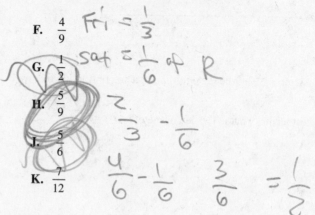

Here's How to Crack It

Jane did $\frac{1}{3}$ on Friday. How much is still left to be done? That's right: $\frac{2}{3}$. On Saturday she did $\frac{1}{6}$ *of the remainder.* In math, the word "of" always means multiply, so let's set it up.

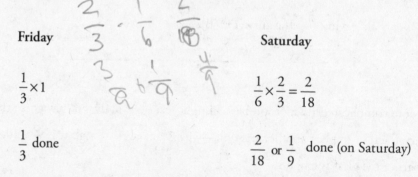

Friday

$\frac{1}{3} \times 1$

$\frac{1}{3}$ done

Saturday

$\frac{1}{6} \times \frac{2}{3} = \frac{2}{18}$

$\frac{2}{18}$ or $\frac{1}{9}$ done (on Saturday)

If we find a common denominator, we can add up what she's done. Then we get

$$\frac{3}{9} + \frac{1}{9} = \frac{4}{9}$$

Altogether, she has done $\frac{4}{9}$ of the assignment. If you thought you were done at this point, you may have picked (F), but the question doesn't ask how much was done but rather how much remained *undone.* How much is left? $\frac{5}{9}$. The answer is (H).

POE Pointers

In that last problem, (F) was a *partial* answer designed to catch people who thought they were done before they really were. Choice (G), on the contrary, was designed to catch people who slightly misunderstood the question. If you missed the words "of the remainder" as you read the question, you probably added $\frac{1}{6}$ to $\frac{1}{3}$ and got $\frac{1}{2}$.

DECIMALS

Most simple decimal problems are easier to figure out on a calculator than on paper. However, unless you understand the theory behind them, it is easy to make a mistake.

A fraction can be written as a decimal and vice versa. Take the fraction $\frac{3}{5}$. Remember what we said before: A fraction is just another form of division.

$$\frac{3}{5} = 3 \div 5 = .6 \qquad \qquad 5\overline{)3.0}^{\,.6}$$

You can also express any decimal as a fraction.

$$.4 = \frac{4}{10} = \frac{2}{5} \qquad\qquad .03 = \frac{3}{100}$$

The test writers frequently ask questions using decimals but want answers as fractions, or vice versa, so the ability to go back and forth between the two is essential to succeeding on the test. If your calculator can do this for you, be sure you know how to use that function.

Adding and Subtracting Decimals

To add or subtract decimals, just line up the decimal points and proceed as if it were regular addition or subtraction. To add 9.25, 3.2, and 8.567

$$
\begin{array}{r}
9.250 \\
3.200 \\
+\ 8.567 \\
\hline
21.017
\end{array}
$$

It helps to add zeros to fill out the decimal places of the numbers with fewer digits. 3.2 is the same as 3.200.

Stay in Line
When adding or subtracting decimals, keep all decimal points lined up.

Multiplying Decimals

To multiply decimals, simply ignore the decimal points and multiply your numbers. When you've finished, count all the digits to the right of the decimal points in the original numbers you multiplied. Now place the decimal point in your answer so that there are the same number of digits to the right of it.

Here's an example.

$$\begin{array}{r} 2.32 \\ \times\,.03 \\ \hline .0696 \end{array}$$

$3 \times 232 = 696$. There are a total of four digits to the right of the decimal point in the original numbers. Therefore, we now place the decimal so that there are four digits to the right in the answer.

Dividing Decimals

Place Value

Compare decimals place-by-place, going from left to right.

The best way to divide one decimal by another is to convert the number you are dividing *by* (in mathematical terminology, the **divisor**) into a whole number. You do this simply by moving the decimal point as many places as necessary.

This works as long as you also remember to move the decimal point in the number that you are dividing (in mathematical terminology, the **dividend**) the same number of spaces.

To divide 12 by .6, set it up the way you would an ordinary division problem.

$$.6\overline{)\ 12}$$

To convert .6 into a whole number, move the decimal point over one place to the right. Now you must move the decimal point in 12 one place as well. The operation looks like this:

$$6\overline{)120} \qquad 6\overline{)\overset{20}{120}}$$

SCIENTIFIC NOTATION

The purpose of scientific notation is to express very large numbers or very small numbers without endless strings of zeros.

$$3.24 \times 10^2$$

All you have to do to simplify this expression is move the decimal point over to the right by the same number as the power of ten—in this case, two places. If the power of ten is negative, you move the decimal point to the left instead.

$$3.24 \times 10^3 = 3{,}240$$

$$3.24 \times 10^2 = 324$$

$$3.24 \times 10^{-1} = .324$$

$$3.24 \times 10^{-2} = .0324$$

An ACT scientific notation problem might look like this.

───────────○───────────

1. $\left(9 \times 10^{-3}\right) - \left(2 \times 10^{-2}\right) = ?$
   A. −0.007
   B. −0.07
   C. −0.011
   D. −0.11
   E. 0.11

(handwritten: .009 − .02)

Here's How to Crack It

$$9 \times 10^{-3} = .009$$

$$2 \times 10^{-2} = .02$$
$$
\begin{array}{r}
.009 \\
-.02 \\
\hline
-.011
\end{array}
$$

The answer is (C).

───────────○───────────

There are relatively few ratio problems on the ACT. The important thing to remember is the difference between a ratio and a fraction. While a fraction is a $\frac{\text{part}}{\text{whole}}$, a ratio is a $\frac{\text{part}}{\text{part}}$.

Take the ratio of $\frac{4 \text{ cats}}{3 \text{ dogs}}$. What is the whole of this ratio? If you said the total number of animals, or 7, you are absolutely correct. So what fractional part of the animals is dogs? Let's change the ratio $\left(\frac{\text{part}}{\text{part}} \right)$ into a fraction $\left(\frac{\text{part}}{\text{whole}} \right)$. The part made up of dogs is 3. The whole is 7. Thus, the fractional part of the animals that is dogs is $\frac{3}{7}$.

Ratio problems don't often need to be converted to fractions, but knowing what a ratio is is important.

———————————————○———————————————

1. If the ratio of $2x$ to $5y$ is $\frac{1}{20}$, what is the ratio of x to y?

   A. $\frac{1}{40}$
   B. $\frac{1}{20}$
   C. $\frac{1}{10}$
   D. $\frac{1}{8}$
   E. $\frac{1}{4}$

   $\dfrac{2x}{5y} = \dfrac{1}{20}$

   $40x = \dfrac{5y}{5}$

   $40x = 5y$

Here's How to Crack It

$$\frac{2x}{5y} = \frac{1}{20}$$

To isolate $\frac{x}{y}$ on the left side of this equation, what do we have to do to it? Let's multiply both sides by $\frac{5}{2}$.

$$\frac{5}{2} \times \frac{2x}{5y} = \frac{1}{20} \times \frac{5}{2}$$

$$\frac{x}{y} = \frac{5}{40}$$

$\frac{5}{40}$ reduces to $\frac{1}{8}$. The answer is (D).

PERCENTAGES

A percentage is a fraction in which the denominator equals 100. In literal terms, the word *percent* means "divided by 100," so any time you see a percentage in an ACT question, you can punch it into your calculator quite easily. If a question asks for 40 percent of something, for instance, you can express the percentage as a fraction: $\frac{40}{100}$. Any time you are looking for a percent, you can use your calculator to find the decimal equivalent and multiply the result by 100. If four out of five dentists recommend a particular brand of toothpaste, you can quickly determine the percent of doctors who recommend it by typing $\frac{4}{5} \times 100$ and hitting the ENTER key. The resulting "80" just needs a percent sign tacked onto it. To properly translate all percent questions, it is helpful to have a decoding table for the various terms you'll come across.

English	Math Equivalent
percent	/100
of	multiplication ($\times$)
what	variable (y, z)
is, are, were	=
what percent	$\frac{y}{100}$

Using the above table, let's say you had a word problem in which you had to translate the following sentence into math terms: "What percent of 7 is 14?" Word for word, substitute the math terms above in the appropriate places. You should end up with

$$\frac{y}{100} \times 7 = 14$$

Now, solve for y to arrive at 200. Tack on your percent sign and call it a day.

Percentage Shortcuts

In the last problem, we could have saved a little time if we had realized that $\frac{1}{5} = 20$ percent. Therefore, $\frac{4}{5}$ would be 4×20 percent or 80 percent. Below are some fractions and decimals whose percent equivalents you should know.

Another fast way to do percents is to move the decimal place. To find 10 percent of any number, move the decimal point of that number over one place to the left.

10% of 500 = 50

10% of 50 = 5

10% of 5 = .5

To find 1 percent of a number, move the decimal point of that number over two places to the left.

1% of 500 = 5

1% of 50 = .5

1% of 5 = .05

You can use a combination of these last two techniques to find even very complicated percentages by breaking them down into easy-to-find chunks.

- 20% of 500: 10% of 500 = 50, so 20% is twice 50, or 100.
- 30% of 70: 10% of 70 = 7, so 30% is three times 7, or 21.
- 32% of 400: 10% of 400 = 40, so 30% is three times 40, or 120.
- 1% of 400 = 4, so 2% is two times 4, or 8.

Therefore, 32 percent of 400 = 120 + 8 = 128

You may also have to convert a decimal into a percentage. This is similar to converting a fraction to a percentage, which we just reviewed. Remember the dentists? We turned four out of five dentists into a fraction, but we could have turned it into a decimal as well. If you divide four by five, you get .8. To turn that into a percentage, take it to two decimal places and then put it over 100 (removing the decimal point).

$$.8 = .80 = \frac{80}{100}$$

That's the same as 80 percent, which is the same answer we got before (good thing).

Here's what an ACT percentage problem might look like.

1. At a restaurant, diners enjoy an "early bird" discount of 10% off their bill. If a diner orders a meal regularly priced at $18 and leaves a tip of 15% of the discounted meal, how much does he pay in total?

   A. $13.50
   B. $16.20
   C. $18.63
   D. $18.90
   E. $20.70

   18 − 1.8
   16.2 × .15

Here's How to Crack It

A combination of bite-size pieces, percent translation, and calculator work will make this problem easy to tackle. When we take fractions or percentages of something, we need to start with the original number. The first thing we'll have to do is figure out how much the discounted meal costs. Write out the steps.

$$\text{Discount taken: } \left(\frac{10}{100}\right) \times 18 = \$1.80$$

Discounted meal price: $18 − $1.80 = $16.20

$$\text{Tip paid for meal: } \left(\frac{15}{100}\right) \times 16.20 = \$2.43$$

Total meal price: $16.20 + $2.43 = $18.63

Circle (C). Take your time and make it painless.

POE Pointers

Even before you began this problem, you could have eliminated one answer choice through POE. Did you spot it? Answer choice A was way too small. The diner is getting a discount of only 10 percent off the $18 and he must still pay the tip, which will add a bit more money. Could the answer be as low as $13.50? Nope. Cross off answer choice A.

Even if you didn't notice that answer choice A was too small, once you figured out that 10 percent of $18 was $16.20, you could have eliminated choices A and B because there was still the tip to pay, so the total had to be larger than $16.20.

AVERAGES

There are only three parts to any average question. Fortunately for you, the ACT must give you two of these parts, which are all you need to find the third. The average pie is an easy way to keep track of the information you get from questions dealing with averages. If you have the total, you can always divide by either the average or the number of things in the set (whichever you are given) to find the missing piece of the pie. Similarly, if you have the number of things and the average, you can multiple the two together to arrive at the total (the sum of all the items in the set).

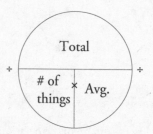

For example, if you want to find the average of 9, 12, and 6 using the average pie, you know you have 3 items with a total of 27. Dividing the total, 27, by the number of things, 3, will yield the average, 9. Your pie looks like this:

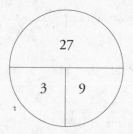

Although you probably could have done that without the average pie, more difficult average questions involve multiple calculations and lend themselves particularly well to using the pie. Let's take a look at one:

3. Over 9 games, a baseball team had an average of 8 runs per game. If the average number of runs for the first 7 games was 6 runs per game, and the same number of runs was scored in each of the last 2 games, how many runs did the team score during the last game?

A. 5
B. 15
C. 26
D. 30
E. 46

Here's How to Crack It

Let's use bite-size pieces to put the information from the first line of this problem into our trusty average pie.

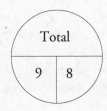

What is the sum of everything for these 9 games? 9×8, or 72.

Now let's put the information from the second line into the average equation.

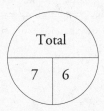

What is the sum of everything for these 7 games? 7×6, or 42.

If all 9 games added up to 72, and 7 of these games added up to 42, then the remaining 2 games added up to $72 - 42$, or 30. In case you are feeling smug about getting this far, the ACT writers made 30 the answer for (D).

But of course, if you read the last line, you know that they only want the runs they scored in the last game. Because the same number of runs was scored in each of the last two games, the answer is $\frac{30}{2}$ or 15, (B).

The Weighted Average

ACT writers have a particular fondness for "weighted average" problems. First, let's look at a regular unweighted average question.

If Sally received a grade of 90 on a test last week and a grade of 100 on a test this week, what is her average for the two tests?

Piece of cake, right? The answer is 95. You added the scores and divided by 2. Now let's turn the same question into a weighted average question.

If Sally's average for the entire year last year was 90, and her average for the entire year this year was 100, is her average for the two years combined equal to 95?

The answer is "not necessarily." If Sally took the same number of courses in both years, then yes, her average is 95. But what if last year she took 6 courses while this year she took only 2 courses? Can you compare the two years equally? ACT likes to test your answer to this question. Here's an example.

1. The starting team of a baseball club has 9 members who have an average of 12 home runs apiece for the season. The second-string team for the baseball club has 7 members who have an average of 8 home runs apiece for the season. What is the average number of home runs for the starting team and the second-string team combined?

   A. 7.5
   B. 8
   C. 10
   D. 10.25
   E. 14.2

   $12 \times 9 + 7 \times 8 =$

Here's How to Crack It

The ACT test writers want to see whether you spot this as a weighted average problem. If you thought the first-string team was exactly equivalent to the second-string team, then you merely had to take the average of the two averages, 12 and 8, to get 10. In weighted average problems, the ACT test writers always include the average of the two averages among the answer choices, and it is always wrong. 10 is (C). Cross off (C).

The two teams are not equivalent because there are different numbers of players on each team. To get the true average, we'll have to find the total number of home runs and divide by the total number of players. How do we do this? By going to the trusty average formula as usual. The first line of the problem says that the 9 members on the first team have an average of 12 runs apiece.

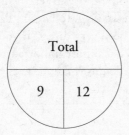

So the sum of everything is 9 × 12, or 108.

The second sentence says that the 7 members of the second team have an average of 8 runs each.

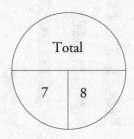

So the total is 7 × 8, or 56.

Now we can find the true average. Add all the runs scored by the first team to all the runs scored by the second team: 108 + 56 = 164. This is the true total. We divide it by the total number of players (9 + 7 = 16).

The answer is 10.25, or (D).

The Missing Number
The ACT loves to leave out totals on average problems. You aren't done until you've found it.

POE Pointers

Although we could eliminate (C) in that last problem because it represented the "unweighted" average, there were several other answers we might have eliminated through POE. If the average of the first team was 12 and the average of the second team was 8, it stood to reason that the correct answer would be somewhere between those two numbers. Could the answer really have been higher than 12? Answer choice (E) bites the dust. Could the answer really have been equal to or lower than 8? Answer choices (A) and (B) also fall by the wayside.

CHARTS AND GRAPHS

Since calculators were added to the arsenal you're allowed to bring with you when you take the ACT, more and more of the test has been composed of questions on which calculators are of little or no use, such as questions based on charts and graphs. On this type of question, your math skills aren't really being tested at all; what ACT is interested in is your ability to read a simple graph (not unlike on the Science Reasoning test, which we'll get to later in Part V). All of the questions we have seen in this format have been very direct. If you can read a simple graph, you can always get them right. What's most important on questions like these is paying attention to the labels on the information. Let's take a look at a graph.

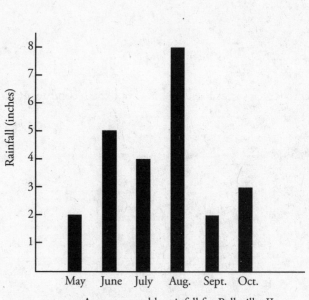

Average monthly rainfall for Belleville, IL.

3. Between which two months was the change in total rainfall the greatest?

   A. May and June
   B. June and July
   C. July and August
   D. August and September
   E. September and October

Here's How to Crack It

The ACT test writers want to see if you can decipher the information presented in the graph. Before you read the question then, you need to take a look at the graph. What is measured here? It says on the bottom: Average monthly rainfall in Belleville, IL. You should look at the values along the left side and bottom of the graph as well. When you do, you'll see that the rain is measured in inches (left-hand side), and the measurements were made each month (bottom).

Now for the question. To determine which two months had the greatest change, we need to compare the change between each pair of months, discarding the smaller ones until we have only one left. The difference from May to June is about 3, and that's larger than June to July and September to October, so (B) and (E) are out. July to August is larger still, though, so (A) is out, leaving only (C) and (D). It should be pretty apparent that the August to September change is larger than the July to August change, though, so the correct answer must be (D).

Although most questions involving graphs on the Math test are this simple, you may see slightly more complicated variations. Here's another question based on the same bar graph.

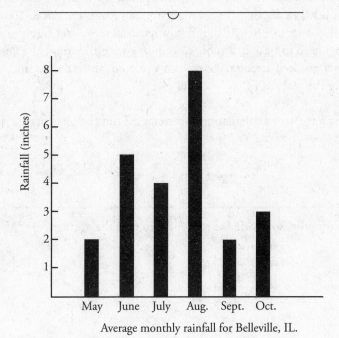

Average monthly rainfall for Belleville, IL.

24. Based on the information presented in the graph above, what is the approximate average monthly rainfall in Belleville, IL, for the period given?

   F. 2
   G. 3
   H. 4
   J. 5
   K. 8

Here's How to Crack It

As with the last question, the first thing you want to do is examine the graph and figure out what information is being given to you and how it is being presented. Because you already did that for this graph, we'll skip that step on this one.

This question combines graph reading with average calculation, so the next thing you'll have to do is estimate the rainfall for each month. Because the question uses the word *approximate*, you don't have to worry too much about making super-exact measurements of the heights of the bar graphs. Eyeballing it and rounding to the closest value given on the left-hand side will be good enough to get you the right answer. Do that now before you read the next sentence.

To us, it looks like about 2 inches fell in May and September, and around 3 fell in October. July saw about 4, June roughly 5, and August about 8. Your estimates should be the same as ours. If they're not, go back now and figure out why not. You probably need to be a little more careful in your estimating. Use another piece of paper as a guide if necessary (you can use your answer sheet in this manner when taking the real ACT).

Now it's just a matter of calculating the average. Find the total first.

$$2 + 2 + 3 + 4 + 5 + 8 = 24$$

There are 6 months, so divide the total by 6 to find the average.

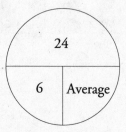

So the answer is 4, or (H).

COMBINATIONS

Combination problems ask you how many different ways a number of things could be chosen or combined. The rule for combination problems on the ACT is straightforward.

> The number of combinations is the **product** of the number of things of each type from which you have to choose.

Here's an example.

---

4. At the school cafeteria, students can choose from 3 different salads, 5 different main dishes, and 2 different desserts. If Isabel chooses one salad, one main dish, and one dessert for lunch, how many different lunches could she choose?

   F. 10
   G. 15
   H. 25
   J. 30
   K. 50

   $3 \times 5 \times 2$

Here's How to Crack It

Isabel is going to choose her lunch by choosing one of each of the items. The numbers of items she has to choose from for each type of dish are 3, 5, and 2. The number of possible combinations she could choose from is always the product of the number of things of each type she can choose from, so there are $3 \times 5 \times 2 = 30$ possible lunch combinations. Therefore, the answer is (J).

On a more difficult problem, you may run into a combination with more restricted elements. Just be sure to read the problem carefully before attempting it; if the question makes your head spin, pick your Letter of the Day and return to it later.

College Lingo

Direct Loan Program: With this federal educational loan program, funds are lent directly by the U.S. government through the school's financial aid office, with no need of a private lender or bank.
Source: *Best 366 Colleges,* 2008 Edition

55. At the school cafeteria, 2 boys and 4 girls are forming a lunch line. If the boys must stand in the first and last places in line, how many different lines can be formed?

A. 2
B. 6
C. 48
D. 360
E. 720

Here's How to Crack It

Let's think about the restricted spots first. If only boys can stand in the first spot, how many people in the question can be first in line? Because there are only 2 boys available, there are only two options for spot #1. Now, what about the last spot in line? Again, if only boys can stand there, and if one of the boys is going to have to stand in the first spot, there is only 1 boy left to fill the position. The spots in the middle must go to the girls. Because the question does not set any additional limits on the girls, we can assume they can be placed in any of the 4 remaining spots. Thus, any of the 4 girls can stand in spot #2, leaving 3 girls to stand in spot #3, 2 girls to stand in spot #4, and the last girl to stand in spot #5. Now all we need to do is multiply all the possibilities together. If you drew a picture of the line and wrote in the above arrangements, it should look like this.

$$\frac{2}{B} \times \frac{4}{G} \times \frac{3}{G} \times \frac{2}{G} \times \frac{1}{G} \times \frac{1}{B}$$

When you multiply everything, you'll get 48, which is answer choice (C).

Arithmetic Drill

(handwritten at top: $\frac{4}{5}$ $\frac{x}{27}$ 4 9 56 $5x =$ -1)

1. The ratio of boys to girls at the Milwood School is 4 to 5. If there are a total of 27 children at the school, how many boys attend the Milwood School?

A. 4
B. 9
C. 12
D. 14
E. 17

(handwritten: $5 \cdot \frac{4}{5} \times x = 27$ $\frac{4}{9} \cdot \frac{x}{25}$ $4:5$ 4)

2. Linda computed the average of her six biology test scores by mistakenly adding the totals of five scores and dividing by five, giving her an average score of 88. When Linda realized her error, she recalculated and included the sixth test score of 82. What is the average of Linda's six biology tests?

F. 82
G. 85
H. 86
J. 87
K. 88

3. In the process of milling grain, 3% of the original is lost because of spillage, and another 5% of the original is lost because of mildew. If the mill starts out with 490 tons of grain, how much (in tons) remains to be sold after milling?

A. 425
B. 426
C. 420.5
D. 440
E. 450.8

(handwritten: $14.7 +$)

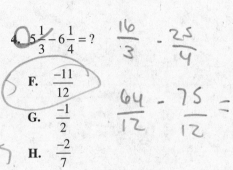

4. $5\frac{1}{3} - 6\frac{1}{4} = ?$ *(handwritten: $\frac{16}{3} - \frac{25}{4}$)*

F. $\frac{-11}{12}$
G. $\frac{-1}{2}$
H. $\frac{-2}{7}$
J. $\frac{1}{2}$
K. $\frac{9}{12}$

(handwritten: $\frac{64}{12} - \frac{75}{12} = \frac{-11}{12}$)

5. $1,245 \div .05 = ?$

A. 200
B. 2,490
C. 2,500
D. 24,900
E. 25,000

Summary

o   The eight main topics of arithmetic are
  - order of operations
  - fractions
  - decimals
  - percentages
  - ratios
  - averages
  - charts and graphs
  - combinations

o   Your calculator can be an extremely powerful tool on the ACT. Having command of 9 or 10 simple operations on the calculator will raise your score and lower your blood pressure significantly.

o   Arithmetic operations must be performed in a particular order. Here's an easy way to remember the order of operations: **Please Excuse My Dear Aunt Sally.** First, you do operations enclosed in **p**arentheses; then you take care of **e**xponents; then you **m**ultiply, **d**ivide, **a**dd, and **s**ubtract.

o   When you add or multiply a group of numbers, you can put them in any order that suits you. This is called the associative law.

o   The distributive law states that $a(b + c) = ab + ac$ and that $a(b - c) = ab - ac$. On the ACT, if you see a problem in one form, you will make the problem much easier by immediately putting it in the other form.

o   A fraction can be thought of as a $\dfrac{\text{part}}{\text{whole}}$.

o   You must know how to reduce, multiply, divide, compare, add, and subtract fractions. The Bowtie is a great method for doing the last three items mentioned, but your calculator is even better—if you know how to use it.

- Every fraction implies another fraction—what is left over. If a glass is $\frac{3}{5}$ empty, it is $\frac{2}{5}$ full.

- A decimal is just another way to express a fraction.

- You must know how to add, subtract, multiply, and divide decimals as well as be familiar with scientific notation.

- A ratio is different in one respect from a fraction: A ratio is a $\frac{\text{part}}{\text{part}}$. If the ratio of cats to dogs is $\frac{3}{4}$, the whole is 7.

- A percentage is just a fraction in which the denominator is equal to 100. Most percentage problems can be set up to look like this: $\frac{\text{part}}{\text{whole}} = \frac{x}{100}$.

- On word problems dealing with percentages, you can use the percent translation table to create a calculator-friendly equation.

- In average questions, you should immediately think

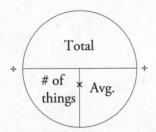

- The ACT has a particular fondness for weighted averages. Be on the lookout for them.

- The number of possible combinations is the product of the number of things of each type from which you have to choose.

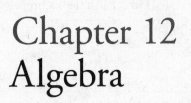

Chapter 12
Algebra

Algebra is all about solving for an unknown quantity. In this chapter, we'll take a look at the different ways you will see algebra on the ACT and give you some strategies to tackle it. You'll get plenty of practice with these techniques while you brush up on topics such as factoring, quadratic equations, simultaneous equations, inequalities, and logarithms.

Algebra is all about solving for an unknown quantity. The unknown is usually represented by a variable such as x or y. There are two general kinds of algebra questions on the ACT. The first kind asks you to solve for a particular x. The second kind asks you to solve for a more cosmic x (don't worry, we'll explain). Let's begin with the particular.

WHEN *X* HAS A PARTICULAR VALUE: THE BASIC EQUATION

Here is a simple example of a basic equation.

$$3x + 7 = 28$$

There is only one number in the world that will satisfy this equation. To find it, we need to isolate x on one side of the equation and get all of the numbers on the other side. To get rid of the 7 that is being added on the left side, we must do the opposite of addition and subtract 7 from the left side. However, to avoid changing the entire equation, we also have to subtract 7 from the right side. Whatever is done to one side must also be done to the other.

$$\begin{array}{r} 3x + 7 = 28 \\ -7 \quad -7 \\ \hline 3x = 21 \end{array}$$

To get rid of the 3 that is being multiplied on the left side, we must do the opposite of multiplication and divide the left side by 3. If we are dividing the left side by 3, we must also divide the right side by 3.

$$\frac{3x}{3} = \frac{21}{3} = 7$$

$$x = 7$$

But in this last problem, we left out one very important thing: ACT questions always have multiple-choice answers. Let's look at this question the way it would have appeared on the actual test.

1. If $3x + 7 = 28$, what is x ?
   A. 4
   B. 5
   C. 6
   D. 7
   E. 8

You might say, "Well, what's the difference? It's the same problem." But in fact, it's not the same problem at all.

Most Particular *X* Problems Can Also Be Solved *Backward*

Algebra is a wonderful discipline, and we do want you to be able to solve problems like the one above algebraically, particularly when they are easy. However, there is another way to do most particular x problems—a way that can, in some cases, save you huge amounts of time and trouble. It's called "Working Backward."

If we asked you to *guess* the value of *x* in this question, it might take you a long, long time. After all, there's only going to be one number in the whole world that satisfies this equation, and there is a limitless supply of numbers from which to choose. Or is there?

In fact, on the ACT there are always just five—the five possible answer choices—and one of them has to be the correct answer. Let's try doing the problem backward. To do this, you take the answer choices one at a time and put them into the equation to see which one makes the equation work. With which choice should we begin?

The one in the middle. Numeric answers are always presented in order on this test, from least to greatest. There are three steps to **Working Backward**.

---

1. Start with the middle answer—(C) or (H).
2. If it's too big, go to the next smaller choice.
3. If it's too small, go to the next larger choice.

Here's the problem again.

1. If $3x + 7 = 28$, what is *x* ?
   A. 4
   B. 5
   C. 6
   D. 7
   E. 8

Here's How to Crack It

Let's start with (C): 3(6) + 7 equals only 25. Could this be the right answer? No, it's supposed to equal 28. Do we need a smaller or a larger *x*? Because we need a larger number, we can immediately knock out (A) and (B). Let's try (D). 3 times (7) + 7 = 28. Bingo! We have our answer.

Note that if (D) had still been too small, the only possible answer would have been (E), and you would not have had to check it. Remember, if you've eliminated 4 wrong answers, what's left *must* be right. One of the great things about Working Backward is that you will usually have to do only two actual calculations. You start with (C). If (C) is correct, you're done. If (C) is too big, then you're down to (A) and (B). Now you try (B). If (B) is correct, you're done. If it isn't, you're still done. The answer must be the only remaining choice: (A).

Now we know that many of you are thinking, "This technique is a waste of time. It would have been way easier to just solve for *x*." You know what? You're right. On this example, solving for *x* would have been easier, but if you don't learn how to do the Working Backward technique on easy questions, you won't be able to do it effectively on more complex questions (and believe us, the questions get *much* more complex). So do yourself a favor and use Working Backward on these easy questions so that you have a good feel for it when it's time to do the tough ones.

Let's Do It Again
Here's another problem.

---

2. If $600 was deposited in a bank account for one year and earned interest of $42, what was the interest rate?

   F. 6.26%
   G. 7.00%
   H. 8.00%
   J. 9.00%
   K. 9.50%

Which Way?
Sometimes, it's hard to tell which way to work backward after eliminating (C). Should you go higher or lower? Don't fret; just pick a direction and try. Find a choice with an easy-to-manipulate number. It may turn out to be wrong, but it won't take long to find out. It may also tell you whether to go higher or lower.

Here's How to Crack It
Of course, we could write an equation. On the contrary, one of these answer choices is correct, and all we have to do is find out which one it is. Why not work backward?

We'll start, as always, in the middle, this time with (H). If the interest rate is 8 percent, then 8 percent of 600 should equal 42. Use percent translation (and your calculator) to check the equation: Does $\frac{8}{100} \times 600 = 42$? Nope—it equals 48, which means our percentage is too large. Eliminate (H), (J), and (K), and try (G).

Does $\frac{7}{100} \times 600 = 42$? It does, so we circle (G) and continue on to the next problem.

———————————○———————————

The Reverse Question
Sometimes the ACT test writers will make your job even easier by giving you the value for the variable within the question itself.

———————————○———————————

How Do You Know When to Work Backward?
You can *always* work backward when you see numbers in the answer choices and when the question asked in the last line of the problem is relatively straightforward. For example, if there are numbers in the answer choices and the question asks, "What is *x*?" you can work backward.

However, if the question asks instead, "What is the difference between *x* and *y*?" then you probably don't want to work backward. In this case, the answers won't give us a value to try for either *x* or *y*.

1. What is the value of $3x^2 + 5x - 7$ when $x = -1$?
   - A.   −15
   - B.   −9
   - C.   −1
   - D.   5
   - E.   15

$3 - 5 - 7$

Here's How to Crack It
There is still only one number in the world that will satisfy this question, and in this case, you know what *x* is supposed to be. This time the ACT test writers ask you to find the value of the entire polynomial. (A **polynomial** is a type of equation.) These problems are about as easy as this test gets.

Note that it would be pointless to work backward on this problem, because the answer choices don't give you possible values for *x* but rather for the entire polynomial. Simply plug −1 into the polynomial and solve.

$$3(-1)^2 + 5(-1) - 7 =$$
$$3 - 5 - 7 = -9$$

Choice (B) is the correct answer.

———————————○———————————

Now There's a Choice

When you are asked to find a particular value for x, you have a choice: You can solve for x or you can work backward. There are times when one technique is more suitable than the other, but as we cover different algebra topics in this chapter—factoring, quadratics, inequalities—we will keep returning to the concept of Working Backward. You will find it extremely useful, particularly on the more difficult questions that you might not want to take the time to solve the old-fashioned way. That's why we now want you to practice Working Backward on the easier questions.

WHEN *X* HAS NO PARTICULAR VALUE: THE COSMIC EQUATION

Now let's look at the following problem:

1. What is 5 more than the product of 4 and a certain number x?

A. $4x - 5$
B. $4x$
C. $-x$
D. $5x - 4$
E. $4x + 5$

In this problem, there is *no* one value for x. The variable x could be 5 or 105 or −317. In fact, the ACT test writers are asking you to create an expression that will answer this question no matter what the "certain number" is.

In other words, this is a cosmic problem. The correct answer choice will be correct *for any value of x*. There are two methods for approaching cosmic problems.

Translation Revisited

On the ACT, many word problems require you to translate English terms into their math equivalents. In Chapter 11, we discussed using translation to tackle word problems dealing with percentages; on many of the algebraic problems you're tasked with, you'll want to use the same method. We've expanded the percent translation table to include some of the common phrases you'll find in algebra questions.

ACT English ⟶	ACT Math
is (any form of the verb "be") *is the same as*	=
of *product* *times*	× (multiplication)
what *a certain number*	*x, y, z* (your favorite variable)
percent	100 (Alternatively, we could use "over 100.")
30 percent	$\dfrac{30}{100}$
what percent	$\dfrac{x}{100}$
more than	+ (addition)
less than	− (subtraction)

Let's translate the problem word for word.

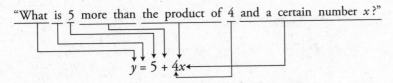

Does this look like any of the answer choices? Yes—(E).

While translation is a fine way to solve this problem, we want you to try thinking about cosmic problems in a slightly different way. If a problem is truly cosmic—if the correct answer is correct for *every* value of "a certain number"—then it should be correct for *any* value you can think of, right?

A Few More Translations/Math Terms

English	Math
more than	+ (addition)
the sum of	+ (addition)
increased by	+ (addition)
is added to	+ (addition)

The Other Method Is Plugging In

Why don't we pick our own value? Let's make $x = 7$. (Why? Why not? We could just as easily have chosen 5 or 12 or whatever you like. Try it and see.) The advantage of using a specific number is that our minds do not think naturally in terms of variables. We don't go into a store and ask for an x-pack of soda. We have a specific number in mind. There are three steps involved in **Plugging In**.

1. Pick numbers for the variables in the problem (and write them down).
2. Using your numbers, find an answer to the problem.
3. Plug your numbers into the answer choices to see which choice equals the answer you found in step 2.

Here's the problem again.

1. What is 5 more than the product of 4 and a certain number x ?

    A. $4x - 5$
    B. $4x$
    C. $-x$
    D. $5x - 4$
    E. $4x + 5$

Here's How to Crack It

Let's make $x = 7$. In the space over the x in the problem above, write down "7." Now, let's figure it out. Reread the question with "7" for the x. The product of 4 and 7 is 28. 5 more than 28 is 33. So, if $x = 7$, then the answer to the question is 33. We're done. All we have to do now is check to see which of the answer choices equals 33.

- Let's start with (A). Because $x = 7$, $4(7) - 5 = 23$. Not the answer.
- Let's look at (E). Because $x = 7$, $4(7) + 5 = 33$. The answer is (E).

You might be thinking, "Wait a minute. It was easier to solve this problem algebraically. Why should I plug in?" There are a couple of reasons.

- This was an easy problem. Plugging In makes even difficult problems easy, so you should learn how to do it by practicing on the easy ones, just as we advised with the Working Backward technique for particular x problems.
- The ACT test writers try to anticipate how you might mess up this problem using algebra. If you make one of these common mistakes, your answer will be among the answer choices; you will pick it and get it wrong.

Get Real
There's nothing abstract about the ACT. So if a problem says Tina is x years old, why not plug in your own age? That's real enough. You don't have to change your name to Tina.

How Do You Spot a Cosmic Problem?

Any problem with variables in the answer choices is a cosmic problem. You may not choose to plug in on every one of these, but you *could* plug in on *all* of them. However, there are also some cosmic problems that do *not* have variables in the answer choices. For example,

16. A number q has a remainder of 5 when divided by 6. What is the remainder when $3q$ is divided by 6 ?

    F. 0
    G. 1
    H. 3
    J. 4
    K. 15

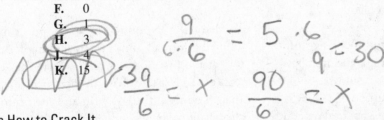

Here's How to Crack It

In this case, the unknown is very explicitly stated, so we can go ahead and think of a number that fits the bill. First and foremost, we must choose a number that satisfies the restrictions imposed by the question. When we divide q by 6, we must have 5 left over. Could we make $q = 12$? Definitely not, because it would divide evenly and leave 0 as the remainder. We could, however, make q equal to 17; if we divided $\frac{17}{6}$, we would be able to divide evenly only twice (giving us 12). What's the remainder? $17 - 12$ would leave us with 5, so we know our numbers work.

Let's move to the second step in the problem: What would the remainder be if $3q$ were divided by 6? In our scenario, $3q$ would equal 51. How many times can we divide 6 into 51? Only 8 times, because $6 \times 8 = 48$. How much is left over before we get to 51? Only 3. Thus, our answer is (H).

So Now There's Another Choice

When x has *no* particular value, you also have a choice: You can translate or you can plug in. There are times when one technique is more suitable than the other. As we cover the different algebra topics in this chapter, we will keep returning to the concept of Plugging In.

FACTORING

Many ACT problems involve factoring of one kind or another. Here is the most basic kind of factoring problem.

$$x^2 + 7x + 12 = ?$$

If your calculator can solve quadratics, now's the time to make sure you know how to put it through its paces.

To factor this expression by hand, put it into the following format, and start by looking for the factors of the first and last terms. Note that the factors for the last term have to meet two conditions: Their product is the last term and their sum is the coefficient of the second term.

$$x^2 + 7x + 12 =$$
$$(\quad)(\quad) =$$
$$(x\quad)(x\quad) =$$
$$(x\quad 3)(x\quad 4) =$$
$$(x + 3)(x + 4) =$$

Some Numbers Are Better than Others

In that last problem, only certain numbers could be plugged in for q—numbers that agreed with the conditions set forth in the problem.

In most cosmic problems, you can pick any number you like. However, there are some numbers that work better than others. In general, you might want to stick to small numbers just because they're easier to work with. If a problem is about days and weeks, 7 might be a particularly good number. If the problem is about percents, 100 is probably a good number.

Some numbers to avoid are 0, 1, and numbers that are already being used in the problem. Why? If you plug in one of these numbers, you may find that more than one answer choice appears to be correct.

To ensure that you've factored correctly, you can also use the FOIL (First, Outer, Inner, Last) method to check your math. Let's try it on the above polynomial.

1. First—multiply the first two terms in each polynomial: $(x)(x)$. The result should equal the first term of your quadratic expression: x^2.

2. Outer/Inner—multiply the outer terms from each polynomial: $(x)(4)$. Do the same with the inner terms: $(3)(x)$. Add the two terms to arrive at the middle term of your quadratic expression: $3x + 4x = 7x$.

3. Last—multiply the last terms in each polynomial: $(3)(4)$. This should be equal to the last term in your quadratic expression: 12.

4. When you add your First, Outer, Inner, and Last terms together, you get back to where you started.

$$x^2 + 7x + 12$$

The ACT test writers might use that last expression to make a problem like this.

1. If $\dfrac{x^2 + 7x + 12}{(x+4)} = 5$, for $x \neq -4$ then $x = ?$

   A. 1
   B. 2
   C. 3
   D. 5
   E. 6

$$\frac{(x+4)(x+3)}{(x+4)}$$

$$x + 3 = 5$$
$$-3 \quad -3$$
$$x = 2$$

Here's How to Crack It

This is a specific x question. If we factor the top expression as we did a moment ago, we get.

$$\frac{(x+3)(x+4)}{(x+4)} = 5$$

Now we can cancel the $(x + 4)$s, with the result that $x + 3 = 5$. To get rid of the 3, we subtract it from both sides. Now $x = 2$, and the answer is (B).

POE Pointers

1. Note that, like all specific x problems, this could also have been solved by Working Backward.

2. If there isn't an obvious clue, try thinking of factors of the last term (2 and 6; 3 and 4) and then checking if their sum matches the coefficient of the middle term.

3. If you were having trouble factoring $x^2 + 7x + 12$, it may have helped to wonder why—of all the numbers in the world—ACT picked $(x + 4)$ as the denominator of its problem. It was almost bound to be one of the factors of the polynomial in the numerator. Always look for clues in the question itself or in the answer choices when dealing with factoring questions.

---

1. If $\dfrac{x^2 + 7x + 12}{(x + 4)} = 5$, then $x = ?$

   A. 1
   B. 2
   C. 3
   D. 5
   E. 6

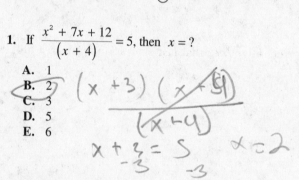

Here's How to Crack It

The question asks, "What is x?" Let's start with 3—(C).

$$\frac{(3)^2 + 7(3) + 12}{(3 + 4)}$$

$$= \frac{9 + 21 + 12}{7}$$

$$= \frac{42}{7}$$

$$= 6$$

Because the answer was supposed to be 5, we know that we need a smaller x. Eliminate answer choices (C), (D), and (E). Let's try 2.

$$\frac{(2)^2 + 7(2) + 12}{(2+4)}$$

$$= \frac{4+14+12}{6}$$

$$= 5$$

Again, the answer is (B).

———————○———————

The same kind of equation could have been used in a cosmic problem.

———————○———————

1. For all $x \neq -3$, which of the following is equivalent to the expression $\dfrac{x^2 - x - 12}{x + 3}$?

A. $x - 4$
B. $x - 2$
C. $x + 2$
D. $x + 4$
E. $x + 6$

Here's How to Crack It
Again, we could solve this by factoring.

$$x^2 - x - 12 =$$

$$(\quad)(\quad)$$
$$(x\quad)(x\quad)$$
$$(x\quad 4)(x\quad 3)$$
$$(x-4)(x+3)$$

Therefore, we can write the problem as $\dfrac{(x-4)(x+3)}{(x+3)}$.

The $(x+3)$s cancel and we get $(x-4)$, or (A).

———————○———————

POE Pointers

1. As in the preceding problem, if you were having trouble factoring $x^2 - x - 12$, it may have helped to wonder why—of all the numbers in the world—ACT picked $(x+3)$ as the denominator of its problem. It was almost bound to be one of the factors of the polynomial in the numerator.
2. Because this was a cosmic problem (variables in the answer choices), we also could have done this problem by Plugging In.

Here's how. Let's choose a value for x. How about 3?

$$\frac{(3)^2 - (3) - 12}{(3+3)}$$

$$= \frac{9 - 3 - 12}{6}$$

$$= \frac{-6}{6}$$

$$= -1$$

Now all we have to do is plug 3 (our value for x) into the answer choices to see which one gets us the answer -1. Let's try (F), $x - 4$. Bingo.

$$3 - 4 = -1$$

Factoring: Advanced Principles

More advanced factoring problems set a factorable expression equal to zero. This is called a **quadratic equation**.

$$x^2 + 7x + 6 =$$
$$(\quad)(\quad) =$$
$$(x\quad)(x\quad) =$$
$$(x\ \ 6)(x\ \ 1) =$$
$$(x+6)(x+1) =$$

Quadratic equations often have two values that solve the equation. In this example, x could be either -6 or -1. These two solutions are sometimes called the **roots** or **zeros** of the equation. Let's try an ACT-type quadratic equation.

1. What is the positive value of x in the equation
$2x^2 - 4x - 6 = 0$?

   A. −1
   B. 2
   C. 3
   D. 4
   E. 6

[handwritten: $x(x+1)$ $-3(x+1)$ $x-3$ $x^2 - 2x - 3$ $3 \cdot 3 \quad 1$ $x^2 + x - 3x - 3$]

Here's How to Crack It

Before we can factor the expression the way we did in the previous problems, we need to reduce it. Look to see if all of the terms have any factor in common. Yes, each of the terms can be divided by 2.

$$\frac{2x^2}{2} - \frac{4x}{2} - \frac{6}{2} = \frac{0}{2}$$

Let's rewrite the equation.

$$2\left(x^2 - 2x - 3\right) = 0$$

Now we can factor. The expression becomes.

$$2(x+1)(x-3) = 0$$

x could equal −1 or 3. Unfortunately, both our values are among the answer choices. Which one is correct? If we reread the question, we realize that we were asked to find the *positive* value of x. Therefore, the answer is 3, (C).

POE Pointers

1. Because the problem asked us for a *positive* value, we should have crossed out (A) even before we factored the expression. If we had done this, we would not have been tempted by it when we finished factoring and discovered it was one of the solutions to the problem.

2. This was a particular *x* problem. That's right; you could have worked backward. Start with (C) and put it back into the equation. Does $2(3)^2 - 4(3) - 6 = 0$? It sure does. The answer must be (C).

A warning: When you work backward with a quadratic problem, remember that there may be two solutions. The problem will usually find a way to ask you for only one of them, but sometimes the ACT test writers will ask you for the *sum* or the *product* of the two solutions. Remember what we said before: If a question asks, "What is *x*?" you can work backward; if a question asks, "What is *x* + *y*?" then you probably can't.

The ACT's Three Favorite Quadratics

The test writers are really fond of three quadratic equations in particular. The first is called the difference of perfect squares (although the name isn't important).

$$x^2 - y^2 = (x + y)(x - y)$$

For some reason, they use this one all the time. You should just memorize it. The idea is that whenever you see this expression in the form on the left, you should immediately put it into the form on the right. If you see it in the form on the right, you should immediately put it into the form on the left. That's all there is to it. Here's an example.

The ACT's Favorite Factors

Train yourself to recognize these quadratic expressions instantly in both factored and unfactored form:

$$x^2 - y^2 = (x + y)(x - y)$$
$$x^2 + 2xy + y^2 = (x + y)^2$$
$$x^2 - 2xy + y^2 = (x - y)^2$$

Learn them, love them. Better yet, if your calculator can factor quadratics, use these to make sure you know how to use that function.

1. If for all $x \neq -3$, $\dfrac{x^2 - 9}{x + 3} = 12$, then $x = ?$

   A. 10
   B. 15
   C. 17
   D. 19
   E. 20

Here's How to Crack It

Do you recognize the form of the numerator? Great, so let's factor it.

$$\frac{(x+3)(x-3)}{(x+3)} = 12$$

Now we can cancel the $(x + 3)$ terms and are left with $(x - 3)$. The answer is 15, or (B).

POE Pointers

Could you have worked backward to solve this problem? Yes, although it wouldn't have been much fun squaring those large numbers. In this case, it was definitely faster to solve by factoring if you recognized the difference of perfect squares.

The two other quadratic equations ACT test writers are fond of are these.

$$x^2 + 2xy + y^2 = (x + y)^2$$

$$x^2 - 2xy + y^2 = (x - y)^2$$

As with the difference of perfect squares, the important thing is to recognize the two forms that each of these equations takes. Whichever form is used in the problem, the solution lies in immediately putting it into its *other* form. Memorize both forms and look for them on the test.

SIMULTANEOUS EQUATIONS

If you see one equation with two variables, can you solve for either variable? For example, if $x + y = 4$, do we know exactly what x and y equal? No. If x is 2, then y is 2, but if x is 3, then y is 1. You can *never* solve one equation with two variables. However, if there are *two* equations, each of which contains the same two variables, then you can solve it using a process known as simultaneous equations. An easy problem might look like the problem on the following page.

If $4x + 2y = 5$ and $6x - 2y = 15$, then what is x?

To solve, set one equation above the other and add or subtract one equation to or from the other so that one of the variables disappears.

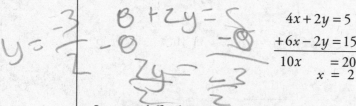

$$4x + 2y = 5$$
$$\underline{+6x - 2y = 15}$$
$$10x \quad\quad = 20$$
$$x = 2$$

In more difficult simultaneous equations, you'll find that neither of the variables will disappear when you try to add or subtract the two equations. In such cases, you must multiply both sides of one of the equations by some number to get the coefficient in front of the variable you want to disappear to be the same in both equations.

This sounds more complicated than it really is. A difficult problem might look like this:

1. What is the value of y in the system of equations below?

$$3x + 4y = 5 \qquad 6x + 2y = 2$$

A. $\dfrac{4}{3}$

B. $\dfrac{8}{3}$

C. 6

D. 7

E. 9

Here's How to Crack It

Line up the two equations.

$$3x + 4y = 5$$

$$6x + 2y = 2$$

Because we want to end up with a value for y, we need to make x disappear. To do this, let's multiply the entire top equation by 2.

$$6x + 8y = 10$$
$$6x + 2y = 2$$

When we subtract one equation from the other, all the x's will disappear.

$$6x + 8y = 10$$
$$\underline{-6x + 2y = 2}$$
$$6y = 8$$

$y = \dfrac{8}{6}$ or $\dfrac{4}{3}$, and the answer is (A).

INEQUALITIES

There is one difference between an inequality and an equality. You solve both in exactly the same way, except that when you multiply or divide both sides of an inequality by a negative number, the direction of the inequality sign flips. Here's an example.

Warning!
When you multiply or divide an inequality by a negative number, you must reverse the inequality sign.

$$
\begin{array}{ll}
3x + 7 > 28 & \quad -3x + 7 > 28 \\
\underline{-7 \quad -7} & \quad \underline{-7 \quad -7} \\
3x > 21 & \quad -3x > 21 \\
\dfrac{3x}{3} > \dfrac{21}{3} & \quad \dfrac{-3x}{-3} < \dfrac{21}{-3} \\
x > 7 & \quad x < -7
\end{array}
$$

Because most inequalities on the ACT involve graphing, we will be discussing them in more detail in the Graphing and Coordinate Geometry chapter.

LOGARITHMS

$$\log_x y = z \text{ means } x^z = y$$

Logarithm questions are not too common on the ACT (at most, one per test), but they *do* come up, and they're not too tough once you understand how they work. Logarithms are just another form of notation for exponents, and you know how to deal with exponents, right?

Take a look at the formula above. Let's work it from right to left, because the stuff on the right is that with which people are most familiar.

As you know, $5^2 = 25$. Well, as a logarithm, you'd write that as $\log_5 25 = 2$. Compare that with the formula on the previous page and you'll see how to go from one to the other. Now if ACT were to give you $\log_5 25 = x$ and ask what x was, you'd know that it's 2 because you have to raise 5 to the 2nd power to get 25.

Try this one.

---

41. If $\log_x 32 = 5$, what is the value of x ?

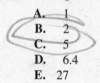

- A. 1
- B. 2
- C. 5
- D. 6.4
- E. 27

Here's How to Crack It

Use the formula in the box above to rewrite this in simple exponential form and you'll be on the way to the answer.

According to your formula, $\log_x 32 = 5$ is the same as $x^5 = 32$.

So you can plug in the answers and see which one works here.

Let's start in the middle with (C). If $x = 5$, then we've got $5^5 = 32$, but that's not right because $5^5 = 3,125$, not 32. (C) is clearly way too big, so we can eliminate it, as well as (D) and (E), and move on to something smaller.

So let's try (B). If $x = 2$, we have $2^5 = 32$. Yep, that's right, so we're done. The answer is (B).

Algebra Drill

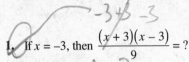

(handwritten: $9 - 9 + -9 - 9$ over 9, $= -1$)

1. If $x = -3$, then $\dfrac{(x+3)(x-3)}{9} = ?$

(handwritten: $-3+3 \quad -3$)

- **A.** 0
- **B.** 1
- **C.** 3
- **D.** 5
- **E.** 6

(handwritten: $\dfrac{-3-3}{-6}{9}$, $\dfrac{-2}{3}$, $\dfrac{x^2 - 3x + 3x - 9}{9}$)

2. What is the largest value of x that solves the equation $x^2 - 4x + 3 = 0$?

- **F.** 1
- **G.** 2
- **H.** 3
- **J.** 4
- **K.** 5

(handwritten: $x + 2y = 8$, $x - 2y = 20$)

3. If $x + 2y = 8$ and $\dfrac{x}{2} - y = 10$, then $x = ?$

- **A.** −7
- **B.** 0
- **C.** 10
- **D.** 14
- **E.** 28

(handwritten: $x + 2y = 8$, $\dfrac{2x}{2} = \dfrac{28}{2}$, $x = 14$, $\left(\dfrac{x}{2} - y = 10\right)$)

4. For all $x \neq -9$, $\dfrac{x^2 + 6x - 27}{(x+9)} = ?$

- **F.** $x + 9$
- **G.** $x - 3$
- **H.** $x + 3$
- **J.** $2x - 4$
- **K.** $2x + 3$

(handwritten: 27, $9 \quad -3$)

$$x^2 + 9x \mid -3x - 27$$
$$x(x+9) \qquad -3(x+9)$$
$$\dfrac{(x-3)(x+9)}{x+9}$$
$$x - 3$$

5. If 2 less than 3 times a certain number is the same as 4 more than the product of 5 and 3, what is the number?

- **A.** 7
- **B.** 10
- **C.** 11
- **D.** 14
- **E.** 15

(handwritten: $3x - 2 = 4 + 15$, $3x - 2 = 19 \quad 3x = 21$, $+2 \quad +2$)

6. A certain number of books are to be given away at a promotion. If $\dfrac{2}{5}$ of the books are distributed in the morning and $\dfrac{1}{3}$ of the remaining books are distributed in the afternoon, what fraction of the books remains to be distributed the next day?

- **F.** $\dfrac{1}{5}$
- **G.** $\dfrac{2}{5}$
- **H.** $\dfrac{1}{3}$
- **J.** $\dfrac{5}{7}$
- **K.** $\dfrac{8}{9}$

(handwritten: $\dfrac{3}{5} \cdot \dfrac{1}{3}$, $\dfrac{3}{15}$, $\dfrac{6}{15}$, $\dfrac{12}{15}$, $\dfrac{3}{5} \times \dfrac{2}{5}$, $\dfrac{4}{5}$, $\dfrac{1}{5}$)

Summary

- There are two main types of algebra questions on the ACT: particular value questions, which ask you to solve for a particular x, and no particular value questions, otherwise known as cosmic problems.

- On particular value questions, you can use algebra or you can work backward from the answer choices. Working Backward is frequently easier. When you work backward, begin with the middle answer choice to see whether you need a larger number or a smaller number. You can always work backward if you see specific numbers in the answer choices and the question in the last line is relatively straightforward.

- On cosmic problems, you can use algebra or you can plug in. Plugging In is frequently easier. You can always plug in if you see variables in the answer choices or if the problem itself does not depend on specific numbers.

- You must know how to factor quadratic equations. ACT's favorites are $x^2 + 2xy + y^2 = (x + y)^2$, $x^2 - 2xy + y^2 = (x - y)^2$, and $x^2 - y^2 = (x + y)(x - y)$. Remember that many quadratic problems can be solved by Working Backward, Plugging In, or using FOIL.

- In solving simultaneous equations, add or subtract one equation to or from another so that one of the two variables disappears. You can also Work Backward if you're having trouble solving the equation.

- When you solve an inequality, remember that if you multiply or divide by a negative number, the sign flips.

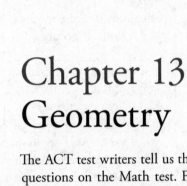

Chapter 13
Geometry

The ACT test writers tell us there will be 23 geometry questions on the Math test. Fortunately, the types of geometry questions you'll see won't deal with proofs, theorems, or complex three-dimensional figures. Instead, you'll need to focus on a small cross-section of very commonly tested formulas and concepts. This chapter primarily deals with plane geometry, which appears in 14 questions on the ACT Math test.

Even if geometry was your least favorite subject in school, you should count on getting most of the ACT geometry questions correct after you've finished reading this chapter. They are trickier than they are difficult, as long as you know your rules.

PRELIMINARY TIPS ON CRACKING ACT GEOMETRY

Before we begin our review, however, ask yourself the following important questions:

To Scale or Not to Scale?

That is the question. In the instructions to the Math portion of the ACT, the test writers say that the diagrams are "NOT necessarily drawn to scale." On the contrary, in the ACT's own *The Real ACT,* one of the suggested strategies is to use the diagrams to estimate the correct answer. The book says that "some of the figures are reasonably accurate."

We didn't think measuring the diagrams would be a very successful strategy if some of them were accurate and some of them weren't. So we carefully measured the diagrams on every geometry problem of every ACT test we could get our hands on. The results? EVERY diagram was drawn EXACTLY to scale. When we asked an ACT spokesperson about this, he said that ACT diagrams were never intended to be misleading, but that there might be rare instances in which it was impossible to draw a problem to scale. Because we couldn't find a single one of these problems, you should consider it a very rare possibility indeed.

POE and Crazy Answers

In the previous chapters, you've seen how POE can be used to prevent picking careless or partial answers when you know how to do a problem. You've also seen how POE can narrow down the range of reasonable answers when you *don't* know how to do a problem and just need to guess.

In geometry, because the problems are *always* drawn to scale, it will be possible to get very close approximations of the correct answers *before you even do the problems.*

How Big Is Angle *NLM*?

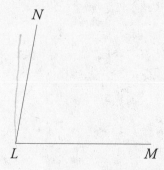

All a Matter of Degree	
Degrees in a circle:	360
Degrees in a line:	180
Degrees in a perpendicular angle:	90
Degrees in a triangle:	180
Degrees in a quadrilateral:	360

Obviously, you don't know exactly how big this angle is, but it would be easy to compare it with an angle whose measure you *do* know exactly. Let's compare it with a 90-degree angle.

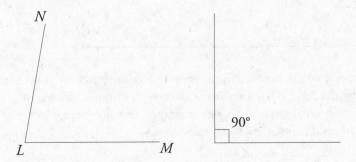

Angle *NLM* is clearly a bit less than 90°. Now look at the following problem, which asks about the same angle *NLM*.

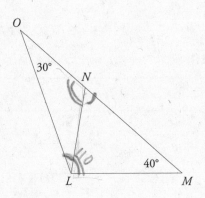

1. In the figure above, *O*, *N*, and *M* are collinear. If the lengths of $\overline{ON}$ and $\overline{NL}$ are the same, and the measure of angle *LON* is 30° and angle *LMN* is 40°, what is the measure of angle *NLM* ?

    A.   40
    B.   80
    C.   90
    D.   120
    E.   150

Here's How to Crack It

This is a relatively easy problem, and we will show you its geometric solution later in the chapter (as well as explaining terms like "collinear" and which angle is meant by angle *LON*).

For now, however, let's focus on eliminating answer choices that don't make sense. We've already decided that ∠NLM is a little less than 90°, which means we can eliminate (C), (D), and (E). How much less than 90°? 40° is less than half of 90°. Could angle NLM be that small? Of course not. The answer to this question must be (B).

In this case, it wasn't necessary to do any real geometry at all to get the question right. Why did the ACT writers make the other answers so crazy? They wanted to include some partial answers for people who tried to do the problem geometrically but who stopped before they were really done.

For example, students who used the information that segments $\overline{ON}$ and $\overline{NL}$ were the same may have realized that triangle ONL is isosceles (has two equal sides) and that ∠ONL is equal to 120°. This was a possible first step to getting the correct answer geometrically. However, if they felt carried away with their own brilliance at getting this far and looked straight to the answers, the folks at ACT wanted 120° to be one of the possible answer choices.

Let's Do It Again

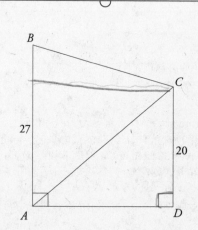

2. In the figure above, if $\overline{AB} = 27, \overline{CD} = 20$, and the area of triangle ADC = 240, what is the area of polygon ABCD ?

F. ~~420~~
G. ~~480~~
H. 540
J. 564
K. 1,128

Here's How to Crack It

Again, we will solve this problem using geometry a little later in the chapter. For now, let's concentrate on eliminating crazy answers. This polygon is not a conventional figure, but if we had to choose one figure that the polygon resembled, we might pick a rectangle. Try drawing a line at a right angle from the line segment $\overline{AB}$ so that it touches point C, thus creating a rectangle. It should look like this

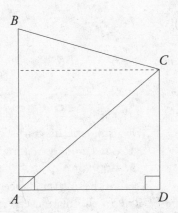

The area of polygon $ABCD$ is equal to the area of the rectangle you've just formed, plus a little bit at the top. The problem tells you that the area of triangle ADC is 240. What is the area of the rectangle you just created? If you said 480, you are exactly right, whether you knew the geometric rules that applied or whether you just measured it with your eyes.

So the area of the rectangle is 480. Roughly speaking, then, what should the area of the polygon be? A little more. Let's look at the answer choices. (F) and (G) are either less than or equal to 480; get rid of them. Choices (H) and (J) both seem possible; they are both a little more than 480; let's hold on to them. Answer choice (K) seems pretty crazy. We want more than 480, but 1,128 is ridiculous.

Thus, on this problem, which was of medium difficulty, we were able to eliminate three of the five answer choices without doing any real geometry. Now what should you do? If you know how to do the problem, you do it. If you don't or if you are running out of time, you guess and move on.

Important Approximations

In some cases, you may want to estimate problems that contain answer choices with radicals or π. Here are some useful approximations.

$$\sqrt{2} \approx 1.4$$
$$\sqrt{3} \approx 1.7$$
$$\pi \approx 3+$$

What Should I Do if There Is No Diagram?

Draw one! It's always easier to understand a problem when you can see it in front of you. If possible, draw your figure to scale so that you can estimate the answer as well.

GEOMETRY REVIEW

By using the diagrams ACT has so thoughtfully provided, and by making your own diagrams when they are not provided, you can often eliminate several of the answer choices. In some cases, you'll be able to eliminate every choice but one. Of course, you will also need to know the actual geometry concepts that ACT is testing. We've divided our review into the following four topics:

1. Angles and lines
2. Triangles
3. Four-sided figures
4. Circles

ANGLES AND LINES

Here is a line.

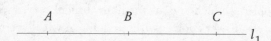

A line extends forever in either direction. This line, called l_1, has three points on it: *A*, *B*, and *C*. These three points are said to be **collinear** because they are all on the same line. The piece of the line in between points *A* and *B* is called a line **segment**. ACT will refer to it as segment *AB* or simply $\overline{AB}$. *A* and *B* are the **endpoints** of segment *AB*.

A line forms an angle of 180°. If that line is cut by another line, it divides that 180° into two pieces that together add up to 180°.

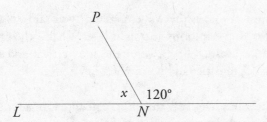

In the above diagram, what is the value of *x*? If you said 60°, you are correct. To find ∠*x*, just subtract 120° from 180°.

An angle can also be described by points on the lines that intersect to form the angle and the point of intersection itself, with the middle letter corresponding to the point of intersection. For example, in the previous diagram, ∠*x* could also be described as ∠*LNP*. On the ACT, instead of writing out "angle *LNP*," they'll use math shorthand and put ∠*LNP* instead. So "angle *x*" becomes ∠*x*.

If there are 180° above a line, there are also 180° below the line, for a total of 360°.

When two lines intersect, they form four angles, represented below by letters *A*, *B*, *C*, and *D*. ∠*A* and ∠*B* together form a straight line, so they add up to 180°.

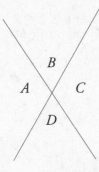

Angles that add up to 180° are called **supplementary** angles. ∠*A* and ∠*C* are opposite from each other and always equal each other, as do ∠*B* and ∠*D*. Angles like these are called **vertical** angles.

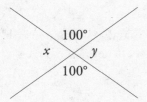

In the previous figure, what is the value of ∠x? If you said 80°, you're right. Together with the 100° angle, x forms a straight line. What is the value of ∠y? If you said 80°, you're right again. These two angles are vertical and must equal each other. The four angles together add up to 360°.

When two lines meet in such a way that 90° angles are formed, the lines are called **perpendicular**. The little box at the point of the intersection of the two lines below indicates that they are perpendicular. It stands to reason that all four of these angles have a value of 90°.

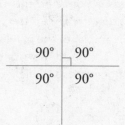

When two lines in the same plane are drawn so that they could extend into infinity without ever meeting, they are called **parallel**. In the figure below, l_1 is parallel to l_2. The symbol for parallel is $||$.

When two parallel lines are cut by a third line, eight angles are formed, but in fact, there are really only two—a big one and a little one. Look at the diagram below.

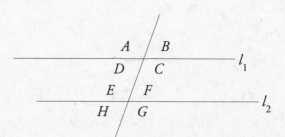

If ∠A = 110°, then ∠B must equal 70° (together they form a straight line). ∠D is vertical to ∠B, which means that it must also equal 70°. ∠C is vertical to ∠A, so it must equal 110°.

The four angles ∠E, ∠F, ∠G, and ∠H are in exactly the same proportion as the angles above. The little angles are both 70°. The big angles are both 110°.

Try the following problem.

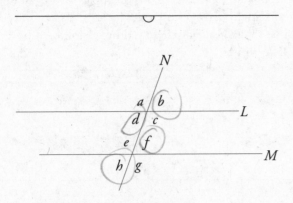

1. In the figure above, line *L* is parallel to line *M*. Line *N*
    intersects both *L* and *M*, with angles *a*, *b*, *c*, *d*, *e*, *f*, *g*, and
    h as shown. Which of the following lists includes all the
    angles that are supplementary to ∠*a* ?

    A. Angles *b*, *d*, *f*, and *h*
    B. Angles *c*, *e*, and *g*
    C. Angles *b*, *d*, and *c*
    D. Angles *e*, *f*, *g*, and *h*
    E. Angles *d*, *c*, *h*, and *g*

Here's How to Crack It

An angle is supplementary to another angle if the two angles together add up to
180°. Because ∠*a* is one of the eight angles formed by the intersection of a line
with two parallel lines, we know that there are really only two angles: a big one
and a little one. ∠*a* is a big one. Thus only the small angles would be supplementary to it. Which angles are those? The correct answer is (A). By the way, if you
think back to the last chapter and apply what you learned there, could you have
plugged in on this problem? Of course you could have. After all, there are variables in the answer choices. Sometimes it is easier to see the correct answer if you
substitute real values for the angles instead of just looking at them as a series of
variables. Just because a problem involves geometry doesn't mean that you can't
plug in on it.

$$a = 100° \quad b = 80°$$
$$d = 80° \quad c = 100° \qquad L$$

$$e = 100° \quad f = 80°$$
$$h = 80° \quad g = 100° \qquad M$$

TRIANGLES

A triangle is a three-sided figure whose inside angles always add up to 180°. The largest angle of a triangle is always opposite its largest side. Thus, in triangle *xyz* below, *xy* would be the largest side, followed by *yz*, followed by *xz*. On the ACT, "triangle *xyz*" will be written as Δ*xyz*.

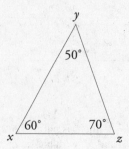

The ACT likes to ask about certain kinds of triangles in particular.

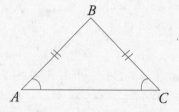

An **isosceles** triangle has two equal sides. The angles opposite those sides are also equal. In the isosceles triangle above, if ∠*A* = 50°, then so does ∠*C*. If $\overline{AB}$ = 6, then so does $\overline{BC}$.

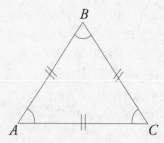

An **equilateral** triangle has three equal sides and three equal angles. Because the three equal angles must add up to 180°, all three angles of an equilateral triangle are always equal to 60°.

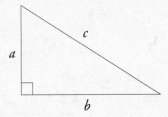

A **right triangle** has one inside angle that is equal to 90°. The longest side of a right triangle (the one opposite the 90° angle) is called the **hypotenuse**.

Pythagoras, a Greek mathematician, discovered that the sides of a right triangle are always in a particular proportion, which can be expressed by the formula $a^2 + b^2 = c^2$, where a and b are the shorter sides of the triangle, and c is the hypotenuse. This formula is called the **Pythagorean theorem**.

There are certain right triangles that the test writers at ACT find endlessly fascinating. Let's test out the Pythagorean theorem on the first of these.

$$3^2 + 4^2 = c^2$$
$$9 + 16 = 25$$
$$c^2 = 25, \text{ so } c = 5$$

The ACT writers adore the 3-4-5 triangle and use it frequently, along with its multiples, such as the 6-8-10 triangle and the 9-12-15 triangle. Of course, you can always use the Pythagorean theorem to figure out the third side of a right triangle, as long as you have the other two sides, but because ACT problems almost invariably use "triples" like the ones we've just mentioned, it makes sense just to memorize them.

The ACT has three commonly used right-triangle triples.

3-4-5 (and its multiples)

5-12-13 (and its multiples)

7-24-25 (not as common as the other two)

Don't Get Snared

- Is this a 3-4-5 triangle?

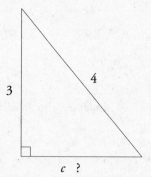

No, because the hypotenuse of a right triangle must be its *longest* side—the one opposite the 90° angle. In this case, we must use the Pythagorean theorem to discover side c: $3^2 + c^2 = 16$. $c = \sqrt{7}$.

- Is this a 5-12-13 triangle?

No, because the Pythagorean theorem—and triples—apply only to *right* triangles. We can't determine definitively the third side of this triangle based on the angles.

The Isosceles Right Triangle

As fond as the ACT test writers are of triples, they are even fonder of two other right triangles. The first is called the **isosceles right triangle**. The sides and angles of the isosceles right triangle are always in a particular proportion.

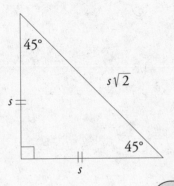

You could use the Pythagorean theorem to prove this (or you could just take our word for it). Whatever the value of the two equal sides of the isosceles right triangle, the hypotenuse is always equal to one of those sides times $\sqrt{2}$. Here are two examples.

Be on the Lookout…

for problems in which the application of the Pythagorean theorem is not obvious. For example, every rectangle contains two right triangles. That means that if you know the length and width of the rectangle, you also know the length of the diagonal, which is the hypotenuse of both triangles created by the diagonal.

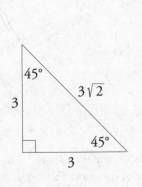

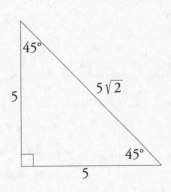

The 30-60-90 Triangle

The other right triangle tested frequently on the ACT is the **30-60-90 triangle**, which also always has the same proportions.

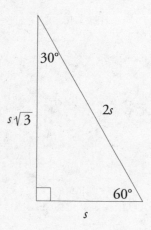

You can use the Pythagorean theorem to prove this (or you can just take our word for it). Whatever the value of the short side of the 30-60-90 triangle, the hypotenuse is always twice as large. The medium side is always equal to the short side times $\sqrt{3}$. Here are two examples.

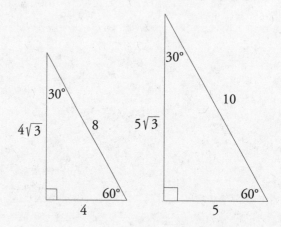

Because these triangles are tested so frequently, it makes sense to memorize the proportions, rather than waste time deriving them each time they appear.

Don't Get Snared

- In the isosceles right triangle below, are the sides equal to $3\sqrt{2}$?

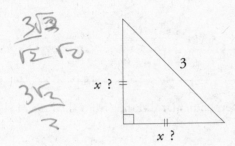

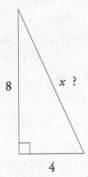

No. Remember, in an isosceles right triangle, hypotenuse = the side $\times \sqrt{2}$. In this case, $3 =$ the side $\times \sqrt{2}$. If we solve for the side, we get $\dfrac{3}{\sqrt{2}} =$ the side.

For arcane mathematical reasons, we are not supposed to leave a radical in the denominator, but we can multiply top and bottom by $\sqrt{2}$ to get $\dfrac{3\sqrt{2}}{2}$.

- In the right triangle below, is x equal to $4\sqrt{3}$?

No. Even though it is one of ACT's favorites, you have to be careful not to see a 30-60-90 where none exists. In the triangle above, the short side is half of the *medium* side, not half of the hypotenuse. This is some sort of right triangle all right, but it is not a 30-60-90. The hypotenuse, in case you're curious, is really $4\sqrt{5}$.

Area

The **area** of a triangle can be found using the following formula:

$$\text{area} = \frac{\text{base} \times \text{height}}{2}$$

Height is measured as the perpendicular distance from the base of the triangle to its highest point.

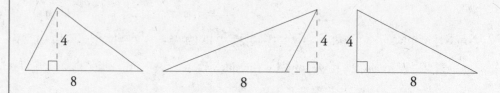

In all three of the above triangles, the area is

$$\frac{8 \times 4}{2} = 16$$

Don't Get Snared

- Sometimes the height of a triangle can be *outside* the triangle itself, as we just saw in the second example.
- In a right triangle, the height of the triangle can also be one of the sides of the triangle, as we just saw in the third example. However, be careful when finding the area of a *non-right* triangle. Simply because you know two sides of the triangle does not mean that you have the height of the triangle.

Similar Triangles

Two triangles are called similar if their angles have the same degree measures. This means their sides will be in proportion. For example, the two triangles below are similar.

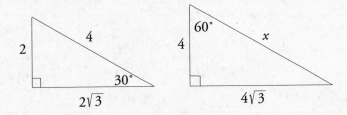

Because the sides of the two triangles are in the same proportion, you can find the missing side, x, by setting up a proportion equation.

$$\frac{\text{short leg}}{\text{hypotenuse}} \quad \overset{\text{small triangle}}{\frac{2}{4}} = \overset{\text{big triangle}}{\frac{4}{x}}$$

$$x = 8$$

ACT Triangle Problems

Most of the triangle problems on the ACT combine *several* of the triangle concepts we've just reviewed. Be flexible, and look for clues as to which concepts are being tested. See the next page for some triangle problems as they might appear on the ACT.

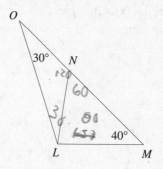

1. In the figure above, *O*, *N*, and *M* are colinear. If the length of $\overline{ON}$ and $\overline{NL}$ are the same, and the measure of ∠*LON* is 30° and ∠*LMN* is 40°, what is the measure of ∠*NLM* ?

A. 40°
B. 80°
C. 90°
D. 120°
E. 150°

Third Side Rule

It is impossible for the third side of a triangle to be longer than the total of the other two sides. Nor can the third side of a triangle be shorter than the difference between the other two sides. Imagine a triangle with sides *a*, *b*, and *c*. $c < a + b$ and $c > a - b$.

Here's How to Crack It

We saw this problem at the beginning of the chapter and managed to solve it without using any geometry. Now let's solve it geometrically. Because $\overline{ON}$ is equal to $\overline{NL}$, we know that Δ*ONL* is isosceles. If ∠*O* = 30°, then so does ∠*OLN*, and therefore ∠*ONL* is equal to 120°. Because this angle and ∠*LNM* add up to a straight line, ∠*LNM* must be equal to 60°. ∠*LNM* plus ∠*LMN* add up to 100°, meaning that the angle we are looking for (*NLM*) is equal to 80° and the answer is B. Alternatively, in Δ*OLM*, ∠*OLM* must equal 110°, and ∠*OLN* makes up 30°, leaving 80° for ∠*NLM*. The answer is (B).

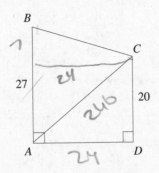

2. In the figure above, if $\overline{AB} = 27, \overline{CD} = 20$, and the area of
   $\triangle ADC = 240$, what is the area of polygon $ABCD$?

   F. 420
   G. 480
   H. 540
   J. 564
   K. 1,128

Here's How to Crack It

Again, we saw this problem at the beginning of the chapter and managed to eliminate three of the five answer choices by using POE. Now let's solve it geometrically. The polygon in question is made up of two triangles. We are told that the
area of $\triangle ADC$ is 240.

> The formula for the area of a triangle $= \dfrac{\text{base} \times \text{height}}{2}$

We don't know the base of this triangle, but we do know the height and the total
area. Can we figure out the base? Of course.

$$\frac{(b)(20)}{2} = 240$$

$$b = 24$$

Now let's look at the other triangle. We need to find its area because the sum of
the areas of the two triangles equals the area of the polygon for which we are looking. If we turn the polygon on its side so that $\overline{BA}$ is on the bottom, we have the
base of the $\triangle ABC$. Do we know the height? Yes! The base of $\triangle ADC$ also happens
to be equal to the height of $\triangle ABC$: 24.

All that's left is to plug the base and height into the area formula to get the area of △ABC.

$$\frac{(27)(24)}{2} = 324$$

The area of the polygon is 324 + 240 = 564, or (J).

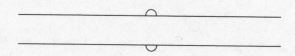

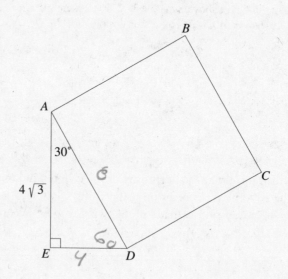

3. In the figure above, square *ABCD* is attached to △*ADE* as shown. If ∠*EAD* is equal to 30° and $\overline{AE}$ is equal to $4\sqrt{3}$, then what is the area of square *ABCD* ?

   A. $8\sqrt{3}$

   B. 16

   C. 64

   D. 72

   E. $64\sqrt{2}$

Here's How to Crack It

The triangle in this diagram is a 30-60-90. Because angle *A* is the short angle, the side opposite that angle is equal to 4 and the hypotenuse is equal to 8. Because that hypotenuse is also the side of the square, the area of the square must be 8 times 8, or 64. This is (C). If you forgot the ratio of the sides of a 30-60-90 triangle, go back and review it. You'll need it.

POE Pointers

If you didn't remember the ratio of the sides of a 30-60-90 triangle, could you have eliminated some answers using POE? Of course. Let's see if we can use the diagram to eliminate some answer choices.

The diagram tells us that $\overline{AE}$ has length $4\sqrt{3}$. Remember the important approximations we gave you earlier in the chapter? A good approximation for $\sqrt{3}$ is 1.7. So $4\sqrt{3}$ = approximately 6.8. We can now use this to estimate the sides of square $ABCD$. Just using your eyes, would you say that $\overline{AD}$ is longer or shorter than $\overline{AE}$? Of course it's a bit longer; it's the hypotenuse of $\triangle ADE$. You decide and write down what you think it might be. To find the area of the square, simply square whatever value you decided the side equaled. This is your answer.

Now all you have to do is see which of the answer choices still makes sense. Could the answer be (A)? $8\sqrt{3}$ equals roughly 13.6. Is this close to your answer? No way. Could the answer be (B), which is 16? Still much too small. Could the answer be (C), which is 64? Quite possibly. Could the answer be 72? It might be. Could the correct answer be $64\sqrt{2}$? An approximation of radical 2 = 1.4, so $64\sqrt{2}$ equals 89.6. This seems rather large. Thus, on this problem, by using POE we could eliminate (A), (B), and (E).

FOUR-SIDED FIGURES

The interior angles of any four-sided figure (also known as a quadrilateral) add up to 360°. The most common four-sided figures on the ACT are the rectangle and the square, with the parallelogram and the trapezoid coming in a far distant third and fourth.

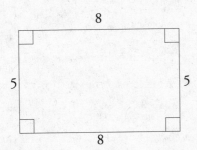

A **rectangle** is a four-sided figure whose four interior angles are each equal to 90°. The area of a rectangle is *base* × *height*. Therefore, the area of the rectangle above is 8 (*base*) × 5 (*height*) = 40. The perimeter of a rectangle is the sum of all four of its sides. The perimeter of the rectangle above is 8 + 8 + 5 + 5 = 26.

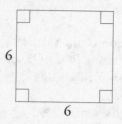

A **square** is a rectangle whose four sides are all equal in length. You can think of the area of a square, therefore, as **side squared**. The area of the above square is 6 (*base*) × 6 (*height*) = 36. The perimeter is 24, or *4s*.

A **parallelogram** is a four-sided figure made up of two sets of parallel lines. We said earlier that when parallel lines are crossed by a third line, eight angles are formed but that in reality there are only two—the big one and the little one. In a parallelogram, 16 angles are formed, but there are still, in reality, only two.

The area of a parallelogram is also *base* × *height*, but because of the shape of the figure, the height of a parallelogram is not necessarily equal to one of its sides. Height is measured by a perpendicular line drawn from the base to the top of the figure. The area of the parallelogram above is 9 × 5 = 45.

A **trapezoid** is a four-sided figure in which two sides are parallel. Both of the figures above are trapezoids. The area of a trapezoid is the *average of the two parallel sides × the height*, or $\frac{1}{2}$ (*base* 1 + *base* 2)(*height*), but on ACT problems involving trapezoids, there is almost always some easy way to find the area without knowing the formula (for example, by dividing the trapezoid into two triangles and a rectangle). In both trapezoids above, the area is 27.

CIRCLES

The distance from the center of a circle to any point on the circle is called the **radius**. The distance from one point on a circle through the center of the circle to another point on the circle is called the **diameter**. The diameter is always equal to twice the radius. In the circle on the left below, AB is called a **chord**. CD is called a **tangent** to the circle.

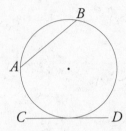 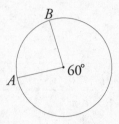

The curved portion of the right-hand circle between points A and B is called an **arc**. The angle formed by drawing lines from the center of the circle to points A and B is said to be **subtended** by the arc. There are 360° in a circle, so that if the angle we just mentioned equaled 60°, it would take up $\frac{60}{360}$ or $\frac{1}{6}$ of the degrees in the entire circle. It would also take up $\frac{1}{6}$ of the area of the circle and $\frac{1}{6}$ of the outer perimeter of the circle, called the **circumference**.

> The formula for the **area** of a circle is πr^2.
>
> The formula for the **circumference** is $2\pi r$.

In the circle below, if the radius is 4, then the area is 16π, and the circumference is 8π.

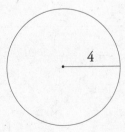

The key to circle problems on the ACT is to look for the word or phrase that tells you what to do. If you see the word *circumference*, immediately write down the formula for circumference, and plug in any numbers the problem has given you. By solving for whatever quantity is still unknown, you have probably already answered the problem. Another tip is to find the radius. The radius is the key to many circle problems.

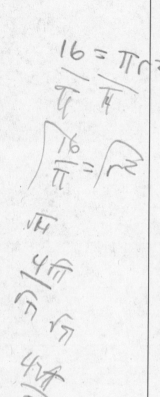

1. If the area of a circle is 16 meters, what is its radius in meters?

   A. $\dfrac{8}{\pi}$

   B. 12π

   C. $\dfrac{4\sqrt{\pi}}{\pi}$

   D. $\dfrac{16}{\pi}$

   E. $144\pi^2$

Here's How to Crack It

As soon as you see the word *area*, start thinking $\pi r^2 = 16$. The problem is asking for the radius, so you have to solve for r. If you divide both sides by π, you get

$$r^2 = \frac{16}{\pi}$$

$$r = \sqrt{\frac{16}{\pi}}$$

$$= \frac{4}{\sqrt{\pi}}$$

$$= \frac{4\sqrt{\pi}}{\pi}$$

The correct answer is (C).

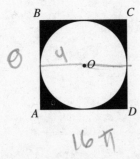

0 *4* *.0*

16π

2. In the figure above, the circle with center *0* is inscribed inside square *ABCD* as shown. If a side of the square measures 8 units, what is the area of the shaded region?

64 − 16π

F. $8 - 16\pi$
G. 8π
H. 16π
J. $64 - 16\pi$
K. 64π

Geometry Hint
If there isn't a diagram, draw one yourself.

Here's How to Crack It

Because the side of the square measures 8 units, the area of the square is 64 square units. Hold that thought.

Before we do any more real math, let's take a moment to look at the diagram. What portion of the entire square would you say is shaded? Could it be as much as $\frac{1}{2}$? No, so we're looking for an answer that is less than half of 64—in other words, less than 32. Most of the answer choices are in terms of π, but a rough approximation of π is 3. Let's go through the choices and see if there are any we can eliminate.

F. $8 - 16(3) = -40$. This is clearly crazy. You can't have a negative area.
G. $8(3) = 24$. Let's hold onto this one.
H. $16(3) = 48$. No, we need an answer less than 32.
J. $64 - 16(3) = 16$. Let's hold onto this one, too.
K. $64(3) = 192$. This is larger than the entire square. No way.

You can use POE to eliminate three of the choices. If you're running out of time, or don't remember how to do the problem geometrically, guess and move on.

To solve the problem the way ACT expects you to, you must find the area of the circle and subtract it from the area of the square. What is left over is the shaded region. The formula for the area of a circle is πr^2. Do we know the radius of this circle? Sure. Because the circle is inscribed in the square, the side of the square has the same measure as the diameter of the circle. In other words, the radius of the circle is 4, and the area of the circle is 16π. Subtracting the area of the circle from the area of the square, we get $64 - 16\pi$, which is (J).

Geometry Drill

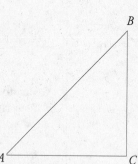

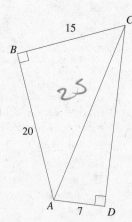

1. In $\triangle ABC$ above, $\angle A = \angle B$, and $\angle C$ is twice the measure of $\angle B$. What is the measure, in degrees, of $\angle A$?

A. 30
B. 45
C. 50
D. 75
E. 90

3. In the figure above, right triangles ABC and ACD are drawn as shown. If $\overline{AB} = 20$, $\overline{BC} = 15$, and $\overline{AD} = 7$, then $\overline{CD} = ?$

A. 21
B. 22
C. 23
D. 24
E. 25

4. If the area of circle A is 16π, then what is the circumference of circle B if its radius is $\dfrac{1}{2}$ that of circle A ?

F. 2π
G. 4π
H. 6π
J. 8π
K. 16π

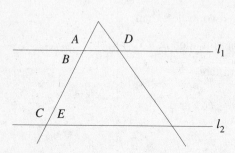

2. In the figure above, $l_1 \parallel l_2$. Which of the labeled angles must be equal to each other?

F. A and C
G. D and E
H. A and B
J. D and B
K. C and B

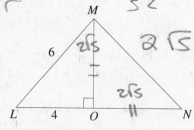

5. In the figure above, $\overline{MO}$ is perpendicular to $\overline{LN}$, $\overline{LO}$ is equal to 4, $\overline{MO}$ is equal to $\overline{ON}$, and $\overline{LM}$ is equal to 6. What is $\overline{MN}$?

A. $2\sqrt{10}$
B. $3\sqrt{5}$
C. $4\sqrt{5}$
D. $3\sqrt{10}$
E. $6\sqrt{4}$

Summary

o If there is no diagram included in a problem, you should draw your own.

o There are several things to know about angles and lines.
   - A line is a 180° angle.
   - When two lines intersect, four angles are formed, but in reality there are only two distinct measures.
   - When two parallel lines are cut by a third line, eight angles are formed, but in reality there are still only two (a large one and a small one).

o There are several things to know about triangles.
   - A triangle has three sides and three angles; the sum of the angles equals 180°.
   - An isosceles triangle has two equal sides and two equal angles opposite those sides.
   - An equilateral triangle has three equal sides and three equal angles; each angle equals 60°.
   - A right triangle has one 90° angle. In a right triangle problem you can use the Pythagorean theorem to find the lengths of sides.
   - Some common right triangles are 3-4-5, 6-8-10, 5-12-13, and 7-24-25.
   - ACT test writers also like the isosceles right triangle, in which the sides are always in the ratio $s : s : s\sqrt{2}$, and the 30-60-90 triangle, in which the sides are always in the ratio $s : s\sqrt{3} : 2s$.
   - Similar triangles have the same angle measurements and sides that are in the same proportion.
   - The area of a triangle is equal to $\dfrac{(\text{base} \times \text{height})}{2}$, with height measured perpendicular to the base.

o Four-sided objects are called quadrilaterals and have four angles, which add up to 360°. There are several important things to remember.

- The area of a rectangle, a square, or a parallelogram can be found using the formula *base × height = area,* with height measured perpendicular to the base.

- The perimeter of any object is the sum of the lengths of its sides.

- The area of a trapezoid is equal to the average of the two bases times the height.

o For any circle problem, you need to know four basic things:

- radius
- diameter
- area (πr^2)
- circumference (πd or $2\pi r$)

o Don't forget that you can plug in on geometry questions that have variables in the answer choices.

Chapter 14
Graphing and Coordinate Geometry

Out of the 23 geometry questions you can expect to see on the ACT Math test, 9 deal with coordinate geometry. Many of these questions will involve visualizing points on a line or within the coordinate plane; luckily for us, our graphing calculators can handle most of the work. While we discuss how to mathematically attack all the coordinate geometry problems the Math test will throw at us, we also show you how to use your calculator to simplify your approach.

GRAPHING REVIEW

Graphing Inequalities

Here's a simple inequality

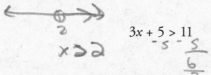

$$3x + 5 > 11$$

As you know from reading the algebra chapter of this book, you solve an inequality the same way that you solve an equality. By subtracting 5 from both sides and then dividing both sides by 3, you get the expression

$$x > 2$$

An Open Circle
On the number line, a hollow circle means that point is *not* included in the graph.

This can be represented on a number line as shown below.

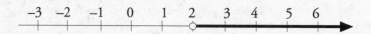

The open circle at 2 indicates that x can include every number greater than 2, but not 2 itself or anything less than 2.

A Solid Dot
On the number line, a solid dot means that point is included in the graph.

If we had wanted to graph $x \geq 2$, the circle would have to be filled in, indicating that our graph includes 2 as well.

An ACT graphing problem might look like the one on the following page.

1. Which of the following represents the range of solutions for inequality $-5x - 7 < x + 5$?

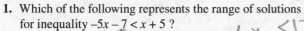

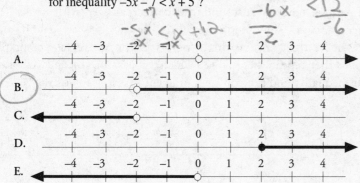

A.

B.

C.

D.

E.

Here's How to Crack It

The ACT test writers want you first to simplify the inequality and then figure out which of the answer choices represents a graph of the solution set of the inequality. To simplify, isolate x on one side of the inequality.

$$
\begin{array}{rcl}
-5x - 7 & < & x + 5 \\
-x & & -x \\
\hline
-6x - 7 & < & 5 \\
+7 & & +7 \\
\hline
-6x & < & 12
\end{array}
$$

Now divide both sides by -6. Remember that when you multiply or divide an inequality by a negative, the sign flips over.

$$
\frac{-6x}{-6} < \frac{12}{-6}
$$
$$
x > -2
$$

Which of the choices answers the question? If you chose (B), you're right.

Flip Flop
Remember that when you multiply or divide an inequality by a negative, the sign flips.

POE Pointers

You could have done this (and most other inequality graphing problems) just as easily by Working Backward. Look at the possible answer choices. The ACT test writers tend to surround the correct answer with at least one *almost* correct answer. Why don't we begin by checking to see if any numbers appear more than once as origin points in the answer choice graphs? The only number that repeats here is –2, which appears in (B) and (C). Let's plug –2 into our inequality and pretend for a moment that it is an equality.

$$\text{Does} -5(-2) - 7 = (-2) + 5?$$
$$10 - 7 = 3?$$

Yes. Now, to decide whether the answer is (B) or (C), just pick a number that is in one answer but not the other. For example, in (C), –4 is part of the solution set but is not included in (B). By plugging –4 into the inequality, we will see if (C) is correct. If it isn't, then the answer is (B).

$$-5(-4) - 7 < (-4) + 5$$
$$20 - 7 < 1$$
$$13 < 1$$

Is this true? No, so the answer must be (B).

Graphing in Two Dimensions

More complicated graphing questions concern equations with two variables, usually designated x and y. These equations can be graphed on a Cartesian grid, which looks like this.

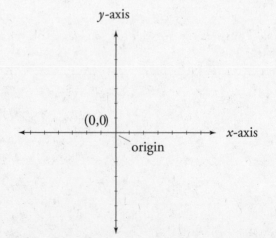

College Lingo

Merit-based grant: A scholarship (not necessarily covering the full cost of tuition) given to students because of some special talent or attribute.
Source: *Best 366 Colleges*, 2008 Edition

Every point (*x,y*) has a place on this grid. For example, the point *A* (3,4) can be found by counting over on the *x*-axis 3 places to the right of (0,0)—known as the **origin**—and then counting on the *y*-axis 4 places up from the origin, as shown below. Point *B* (5,–2) can be found by counting 5 places to the right on the *x*-axis and then down 2 places on the *y*-axis. Point *C* (–4,–1) can be found by counting 4 places to the left of the origin on the *x*-axis and then 1 place down on the *y*-axis.

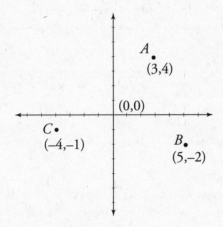

The grid is divided into four quadrants, which go counterclockwise.

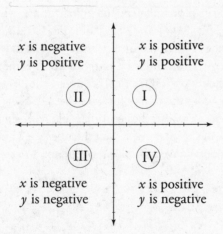

- In the first quadrant, *x* and *y* are both positive.
- In the second quadrant, *x* is negative but *y* is positive.
- In the third quadrant, *x* and *y* are both negative.
- In the fourth quadrant, *x* is positive but *y* is negative.

Note: This is when your graphing calculator (if you have one) will really get a chance to shine. Practice doing all the ACT coordinate geometry questions on your calculator now and you'll blow them away when you actually take the test.

Graphic Guesstimation

A few questions on the ACT might involve actual graphing, but it is more likely that you will be able to make use of graphing to *estimate* the answers to questions that the ACT test writers think are more complicated.

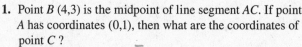

1. Point *B* (4,3) is the midpoint of line segment *AC*. If point *A* has coordinates (0,1), then what are the coordinates of point *C* ?

   A. (−4,−1)
   B. (4,1)
   C. (4,4)
   D. (8,5)
   E. (8,9)

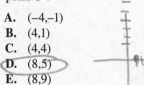

Here's How to Crack It

You may or may not remember the midpoint formula: The ACT test writers expect you to use it to solve this problem. We'll go over it in a moment, along with the other formulas you'll need to solve coordinate geometry questions. However, it is worth noting that by drawing a rough graph of this problem, you can get the correct answer without the formula.

On your TI-83, you can plot independent points to see what the graph should look like. To do this, hit $\boxed{\text{STAT}}$ and select option [1: Edit]. Enter the *x*- and *y*-coordinate points in the first two columns; use [L1] for your *x*-coordinates and [L2] for the *y*-coordinates. After you enter the endpoints of the line, hit $\boxed{\text{2nd}}\boxed{\text{Y=}}$ to access the [STAT PLOT] menu. Select option [1: Plot1]. Change the [OFF] status to $\boxed{\text{ON}}$ and hit $\boxed{\text{GRAPH}}$. You should now see the two points you entered. Now you can ballpark the answers based on where they are in the coordinate plane. Keep in mind that you can also plot all the points in the answers as well. Just be sure you keep track of all the *x*- and *y*-values. If you don't have a graphing calculator, use the grid we've provided on the next page.

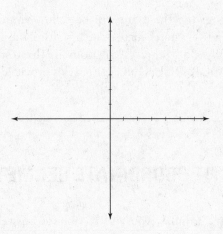

College Lingo

Need-based grant: A scholarship (not necessarily covering the full cost of tuition) given to students because they would otherwise be unable to afford college.
Source: *Best 366 Colleges,* 2008
     Edition

B is supposed to be the midpoint of a line segment *AC*. Draw a line through the two points you've just plotted and extend it upward until *B* is the midpoint of the line segment. It should look like this:

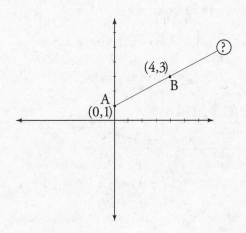

The place where you stopped drawing is the approximate location of point *C*. Now let's look at the answer choices to see if any of them are in the ballpark.

A.   (−4,−1): These coordinates are in the wrong quadrant.
B.   (4,1): This point is way below where it should be.
C.   (4,4): This point does not extend enough to the right.
D.   (8,5): Definitely in the ballpark. Hold on to this answer choice.
E.   (8,9): Possible, although the *y*-coordinate seems a little high.

Which answer choice do you want to pick? If you said (D), you are right.

By the way, the folks giving the exam will not allow you to bring graphing paper (or any other kind of scratch paper) with you to the real test, so get used to making your graphs and other calculations in the test booklet. A full column, labeled "DO YOUR FIGURING HERE," is provided on every page of the Mathematics test.

THE IMPORTANT COORDINATE GEOMETRY FORMULAS

By memorizing a few formulas, you will be able to answer virtually all of the coordinate geometry questions on this test. Remember, too, that in coordinate geometry you almost *always* have a fallback—just graph it out.

And always keep your graphing calculator handy on these types of problems. Graphing calculators are great for solving line equations and giving you graphs you can use to ballpark. Be sure you know how to solve and graph an equation for a line on your calculator before you take the ACT.

The following formulas are listed in order of importance:

The *y*-Intercept Formula

$$y = mx + b$$

To Find the *x*-intercept

Set *y* equal to zero and solve for *x*.

By putting (x,y) equations into the formula above, you can find two pieces of information that ACT likes to test: the **slope** and the *y*-intercept. Most graphing calculators will put an equation into *y*-intercept form at the touch of a button.

The **slope** is a number that tells you how sharply a line is inclining, and it is equivalent to the variable *m* in the equation above. For example, in the equation $y = 3x + 4$, the number 3 (think of it as $\frac{3}{1}$) tells us that from any point on the line, we can find another point on the line by going up 3 and over to the right 1.

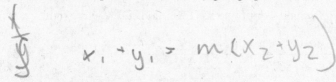

In the equation $y = -\frac{4}{5}x - 7$, the slope of $-\frac{4}{5}$ tells us that from any point on the line, we can find another point on the line by going up 4 and over 5 to the left.

The **y-intercept**, equivalent to the variable **b** in the equation above, is the point at which the line intercepts the y-axis. For example, in the equation $y = 3x + 4$, the line will strike the y-axis at a point 4 above the origin. In the equation $y = 2x - 7$, the line will strike the y-axis at a point 7 below the origin. A typical ACT $y = mx + b$ question might give you an equation in another form and ask you to find either the slope or the y-intercept. Simply put the equation into the form we've just shown you.

---

1. What is the slope of the line based on the equation
   $5x - y = 7x + 6$?

   A. −2
   B. 0
   C. 2
   D. 6
   E. −6

Here's How to Crack It
Isolate y on the left side of the equation. You can have your graphing calculator do this for you, or you can do it by hand by subtracting $5x$ from both sides.

$$
\begin{array}{rcrl}
5x - y &=& 7x & + 6 \\
-5x & & -5x & \\
\hline
-y &=& 2x & + 6
\end{array}
$$

We aren't quite done. The format we want is $y = mx + b$, not $-y = mx + b$. Let's multiply both sides by -1.

$$(-1)(-y) = (2x + 6)(-1)$$
$$y = -2x - 6$$

The slope of this line is −2, so the answer is (A).

The Slope Formula

You can find the slope of a line, even if all you have are two points on that line, by using the slope formula.

$$\text{slope} = \frac{\text{change in } y}{\text{change in } x} \quad \text{or} \quad \frac{y_1 - y_2}{x_1 - x_2}$$

---

1. What is the slope of the straight line passing through the points (–2,5) and (6,4) ?

   A. $-\dfrac{1}{16}$

   B. $-\dfrac{1}{8}$

   C. $\dfrac{1}{5}$

   D. $\dfrac{2}{9}$

   E. $\dfrac{4}{9}$

[handwritten notes: $\frac{5-4}{-2-6}$ and $\frac{1}{-8}$]

Here's How to Crack It

Find the change in y and put it over the change in x. The change in y is the first y-coordinate minus the second y-coordinate. (It doesn't matter which point is first and which is second.) The change in x is the first x minus the second x.

$$\begin{array}{ll} y_1 - y_2 & 5 - 4 = 1 \\ x_1 - x_2 & -2 - 6 = -8 \end{array}$$

The correct answer is (B).

If you take a look at the formula for finding slope, you'll see that the part on top ("change in y") is how much the line is rising (or falling, if the line points down and has a negative slope). That change in position on the y-axis is called the *rise*. The part on the bottom ("change in x") is how far along the x-axis you move and called the *run*. So the slope of a line is sometimes referred to as "rise over run."

In the question we just did, then, the rise was 1 and the run was −8, giving us the slope $-\frac{1}{8}$. Same answer, different terminology.

Midpoint Formula

If you have the two endpoints of a line segment, you can find the midpoint of the segment by using the midpoint formula.

$$\left(x[m], y[m]\right) = \left(\frac{x_1 + x_2}{2}, \frac{y_1 + y_2}{2}\right)$$

It looks much more intimidating than it really is.

To find the midpoint of a line, just take the *average* of the two x-coordinates and the *average* of the two y-coordinates. For example, the midpoint of the line segment formed by the coordinates (3,4) and (9,2) is just

$$\frac{(3+9)}{2} = 6 \text{ and } \frac{(4+2)}{2} = 3$$

$$\text{or} \left(6,3\right)$$

Remember the first midpoint problem we did? Here it is again.

1. Point B (4,3) is the midpoint of line segment AC. If point A has coordinates (0,1), then what are the coordinates of point C ?

   A. (−4,−1)
   B. (4,1)
   C. (4,4)
   D. (8,5)
   E. (8,9)

The Shortest Distance Between Two Points Is…a Calculator?

If you want to draw a line between two points on your TI-83, you can use the Line function. To access this, you'll want to press [2nd] [PRGM] to access the [DRAW] menu. From there, select option [2: Line]. The format of the line function is Line (X1, Y1, X2, Y2); for example, if you wanted to view the line that passes through the points (−2, 5) and (6,4), you would enter Line (−2, 5, 6, 4). Hit [ENTER] to see your line.

Here's How to Crack It

You'll remember that it was perfectly possible to solve this problem just by drawing a quick graph of what it ought to look like. However, to find the correct answer using the midpoint formula, we first have to realize that, in this case, we already *have* the midpoint. We are asked to find one of the endpoints.

The midpoint is (4,3). This represents the average of the two endpoints. The endpoint we know about is (0,1). Let's do the *x*-coordinate first. The average of the *x*-coordinates of the two endpoints equals the *x*-coordinate of the midpoint. So $\frac{(0+?)}{2} = 4$. What is the missing *x*-coordinate? 8. Now let's do the *y*-coordinate. $\frac{(1+?)}{2} = 3$. What is the missing *y*-coordinate? 5. The answer is (D).

If you had trouble following that last explanation, just remember that you already understood this problem (and got the answer) using graphing. Never be intimidated by formulas on the ACT. There is usually another way to do the problem.

The Distance Formula

We hate the distance formula. We keep forgetting it, and even when we remember it, we feel like fools for using it because there are much easier ways to find the distance between two points. We aren't even going to tell you what the distance formula is. If you need to know the distance between two points, you can always think of that distance as being the hypotenuse of a right triangle. Here's an example.

---

1. What is the distance between points *A* (2,2) and *B* (5,6) ?

   A. 3
   B. 4
   C. 5
   D. 6
   E. 7

Let's make a quick graph of what this ought to look like.

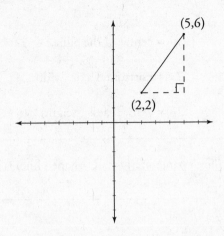

If we extend lines from the two points to form a right triangle under the line segment *AB*, we can use the Pythagorean theorem to get the distance between the two points. What is the length of the base of the triangle? It's 3. What is the length of the height of the triangle? It's 4. So what is the length of the hypotenuse? It's 5. Of course, as usual, it is one of the triples of which ACT is so fond. The answer is (C). You could also have popped the points into your calculator and had it calculate the distance for you.

Circles, Ellipses, and Parabolas, Oh My!

You should probably have a *vague* idea of what the equations for these figures look like; just remember that there are very few questions concerning these figures, and when they do come up, you can almost always figure them out by graphing.

The standard equation for a circle is shown below.

$$(x - h)^2 + (y - k)^2 = r^2$$

(h,k) = center of the circle

r = radius

The standard equation for an ellipse (just a squat-looking circle) is shown on the next page.

$$(x - h)^2 + (y - k)^2 = r^2$$

$$\frac{(x-h)^2}{a^2} + \frac{(y-k)^2}{b^2} = 1$$

(h,k) = center of the ellipse

$2a$ = horizontal axis (width)

$2b$ = vertical axis (height)

The standard equation for a parabola (just a U-shaped line) is shown below.

$$y = x^2$$

1. If the equation $x^2 = 1 - y^2$ were graphed in the standard (x,y) coordinate plane, the graph would represent which of the following geometric figures?

   A. square
   B. straight line
   C. circle
   D. triangle
   E. parabola

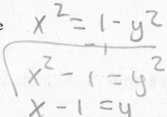

Graphing Circles on Your Calculator

To draw a circle on your TI-83, you first need to alter the Zoom settings. Press [ZOOM] and select option [5: ZSquare]. Next, hit [2nd] [PRGM] to access the [DRAW] menu. Select option [9: Circle]. All you need to do is enter the coordinates of the circle's center and the value of its radius. If, for instance, you were trying to graph a circle with a center of (2,3) and a radius of 5, your screen would say the following: Circle (2,3,5). Hit [ENTER] to see the resulting graph. You can draw as many circles as you like, but to clear the graph you need to press [2nd][DRAW] and select option [1: ClrDraw].

Here's How to Crack It

If you're familiar with what the equations of the various elements in the answer choices are supposed to look like, you may be able to figure out the problem without graphing at all. (However, that's why you bought a graphing calculator in the first place....) Let's consider what we know about the equations of geometric figures. If an equation has only x and y, we know that the graph of the equation is a straight line. (Think back to the $y = mx + b$ problems we did earlier.) However, in this equation, both x and y are squared, so we can rule out (B). There is no equation for a square, so we can rule out (A). Similarly, there's no equation for a triangle, so (D) is out. If only one of the variables were squared, this might be a parabola, but in this problem both are squared, which means we can eliminate (E). We are left with (C).

Estimating Note

Of course, we could also just plug some numbers into the equation and plot them out on a homemade (x,y) axis in the scratchwork column of the test booklet. Let's try this on the grid below.

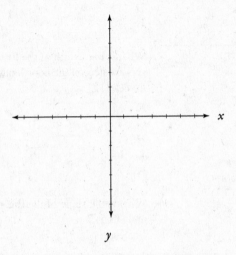

The easiest way to start is to let one of the variables equal 0. If $x = 0$, then y must equal 1. So one point of this equation is $(0,1)$. If we let $y = 0$, then x must equal 1. So another point of this equation is $(1,0)$. Plot out some other points of the equation. How about $(-1,0)$ and $(0,-1)$? What kind of geometric figure does it appear that we have? If you said a circle, you are correct.

Graphing and Coordinate Geometry Drill

1. Which of the following represents the solution of the inequality $-3x - 6 > 9$?

   $\dfrac{-3x}{-3} > \dfrac{15}{-3}$ $x < -5$ $+6 \ +6$

   A.

   B.

   C.

   D.

   E.

2. What is the midpoint of the line segment whose endpoints are represented on the coordinate axis by the points (3,5) and (–4,3) ?

   F. (–2,–5)

   G. $(-\frac{1}{2},4)$

   H. (1,8)

   J. $(4,-\frac{1}{2})$

   K. (3,3)

   $\dfrac{-1}{2} , \ 4$)

3. What is the slope of the line represented by the equation $10x + 2x = y + 6$?

   A. 10 $12x = y + 6$
   B. 12
   C. 14 $-y = -12x + 6$
   D. 15
   E. 16 $y = 12x - 6$

4. What is the length of the line segment whose endpoints are represented on the coordinate axis by the points (–2,–1) and (1,3) ?

   F. 3
   G. 4 $(-2-1)^2 + (-1-3)^2$
   H. 5
   J. 6 $(-3)^2 + (-4)^2$
   K. 7

5. What is the slope of the line that contains the points (6,4) and (13,5) ?

   $9 + 16$

   A. $-\dfrac{1}{8}$

   B. $-\dfrac{1}{9}$ $\dfrac{4-5}{6-13}$ $\dfrac{-1}{-7}$

   C. $\dfrac{1}{7}$

   D. 1

   E. 7

Summary

o   In graphing an inequality, solve for the variable and look for the number-line graph that expresses the equation. Remember, you can often work backward on inequality graphing questions. Remember to flip the inequality when you divide or multiply by a negative.

o   Graphing on an (x,y) axis is most useful as a way to estimate the correct answers to coordinate geometry questions.

o   Most coordinate geometry questions can be solved by putting them into the format $y = mx + b$, where m is the slope of the line and b is the y-intercept.

o   Some coordinate geometry questions can be solved by using the slope formula.

$$\text{slope} = \frac{\text{change in } y}{\text{change in } x}$$

o   Other coordinate geometry questions can be solved using the midpoint formula.

$$\left(x[m], y[m]\right) = \frac{x_1 + x_2}{2}, \frac{y_1 + y_2}{2}$$

o   You can always find the distance between two points by drawing a line between them and making it the hypotenuse of a right triangle.

o   Every once in a while, ACT asks a question based on the equations of circles, ellipses, and parabolas. If you need a very high score, it might help to memorize these equations, but remember, these questions can frequently be done by using graphing to estimate the correct answer.

Chapter 15
Trigonometry

How much does ACT care about trigonometry? Because only four of the questions on the ACT Math test deal with trig, it doesn't seem to be all that important. Still, we'll spend some time reviewing what little content you need to ace these questions. You can expect two of the trigonometry questions on the test to be straightforward, so we'll start with the basic trig relationships. From there, we'll move on to the content that is likely to appear on any tougher trig questions.

SIDES OF A RIGHT TRIANGLE—RELATIONSHIPS

The easier trigonometry questions on this test involve the relationships between the sides of a right triangle. In the right triangle below, the angle *x* can be expressed in terms of the ratios of different sides of the triangle.

SOH CAH TOA

sin x =

$\frac{O}{H}$

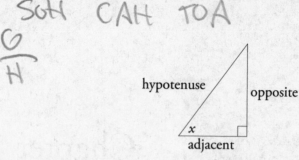

The **sine** of angle $x = \dfrac{\text{length of side opposite angle } x}{\text{length of hypotenuse}}$

The **cosine** of angle $x = \dfrac{\text{length of side adjacent angle } x}{\text{length of hypotenuse}}$

The **tangent** of angle $x = \dfrac{\text{length of side opposite angle } x}{\text{length of side adjacent angle } x}$

There is a very handy acronym to remember all this.

SOHCAHTOA

Sine is **O**pposite over **H**ypotenuse. Cosine is **A**djacent over **H**ypotenuse. Tangent is **O**pposite over **A**djacent. So in the triangle on next page, the sine of angle θ [*theta*, a Greek letter] would be $\frac{4}{5}$. The cosine of angle θ would be $\frac{3}{5}$. The tangent of angle θ would be $\frac{4}{3}$.

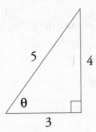

Sine, cosine, and tangent are often abbreviated as sin, cos, and tan, respectively.

YOU'RE ALMOST DONE

There are three more relationships to memorize. They involve the reciprocals of the previous three.

$$\text{The cosecant} = \frac{1}{\text{sine}}$$

$$\text{The secant} = \frac{1}{\text{cosine}}$$

$$\text{The cotangent} = \frac{1}{\text{tangent}}$$

Let's try a few problems.

TOA

31. What is $\sin \theta$, if $\tan \theta = \frac{4}{3}$?

A. $\frac{3}{4}$

B. $\frac{4}{5}$

C. $\frac{5}{4}$

D. $\frac{5}{3}$

E. $\frac{7}{3}$

$$\frac{\sin \theta}{\cos \theta} = \frac{4}{3}$$

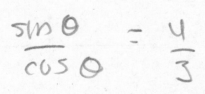

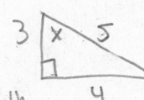

> **Helpful Trig Identities**
>
> $\sin^2 \theta + \cos^2 \theta = 1$
>
> $\frac{\sin \theta}{\cos \theta} = \tan \theta$

Here's How to Crack It

It helps to sketch out the right triangle and fill in the information we know.

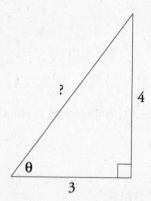

What kind of right triangle is this? That's right—a 3-4-5. Now, we need to know the sine of angle θ: opposite over hypotenuse, or $\dfrac{4}{5}$, which is (B).

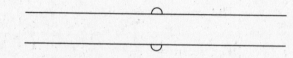

43. For all θ, $\dfrac{\cos\ \theta}{\sin^2\theta + \cos^2\theta} =$

   A. $\sin\theta$
   B. $\csc\theta$
   C. $\cot\theta$
   D. $\cos\theta$
   E. $\tan\theta$

Here's How to Crack It

$\sin^2\theta + \cos^2\theta$ always equals 1. $\dfrac{\cos\theta}{1} = \cos\theta$. The answer is (D).

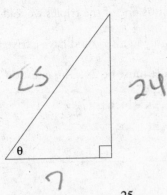

50. In a right triangle shown above, sec θ is $\frac{25}{7}$. What is sin θ ?

$\frac{7}{25}$ ¬CAH

F. $\frac{3}{25}$

G. $\frac{5}{25}$

H. $\frac{7}{25}$ SOH

J. $\frac{24}{25}$ $\frac{24}{25}$

K. $\frac{25}{7}$

Here's How to Crack It

The secant of any angle is the reciprocal of the cosine, which is just another way of saying that the cosine of angle θ is $\frac{7}{25}$.

Secant θ = $\frac{1}{\cos θ}$, so $\frac{1}{\cos θ} = \frac{25}{7}$, which means that cos θ = $\frac{7}{25}$. Are you done? No! Cross off (H) because you know it's not the answer.

Cosine means adjacent over hypotenuse. Let's sketch it.

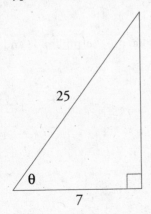

As you can see, we now have two sides of a right triangle. Can we find the third side? If you said this was one of the triples we told you about before, you are absolutely correct, although you also could have derived this by using the Pythagorean theorem. The third side must be 24. The question asks for sin θ. Sine = opposite over hypotenuse, or $\dfrac{24}{25}$, which is (J).

HARDER TRIGONOMETRY

When graphing a trig function, such as sine, there are two important **coefficients**, A and B: A{*sin* (Bθ)}.

The two coefficients A and B govern the **amplitude** of the graph (how tall it is) and the **period** of the graph (how long it takes to get through a complete cycle), respectively. If there are no coefficients, then that means A = 1 and B = 1 and the graph is the same as what you'd get when you graph it on your calculator.

- Increases in A increase the amplitude of the graph. It's a direct relationship.

That means if A = 2, then the amplitude is doubled. If A = $\dfrac{1}{2}$, then the amplitude is cut in half.

- Increases in B decrease the period of the graph. It's an inverse relationship.

That means if B = 2, then the period is cut in half, which is to say the graph completes a full cycle faster than usual. If B = $\dfrac{1}{2}$, then the period is doubled.

You can add to or subtract from the function as a whole, and also to or from the variable, but neither of those actions changes the shape of the graph, only its position and starting place.

Here's the graph of sin *x*. What are the amplitude and period?

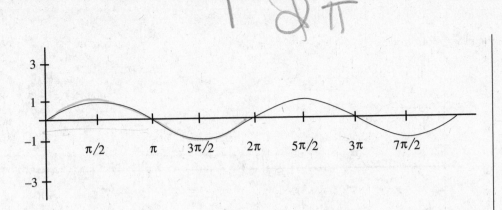

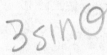

The simple function sin θ goes from –1 to 1 on the *y*-axis, so the amplitude is 1, while its period is 2π, which means that every 2π on the graph (as you go from side to side) it completes a full cycle. That's what you see in the graph above.

The graph below is also a sine function, but it's been changed. What is the function graphed here?

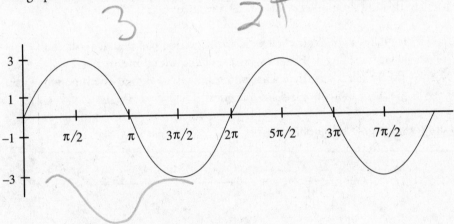

You have three things to check when looking at this graph: Is it sin or cos, is the period changed, and is the amplitude changed?

- This is a sin graph because it has a value of 0 at 0. Cos has a value of 1 at 0.
- It makes a complete cycle in 2π, so the period isn't changed. In other words, B = 1.
- The amplitude is triple what it normally is, so A = 3. The function graphed, therefore, is 3 sin θ.

3 sin θ

How about here? $3\sin\frac{1}{2}\theta$

$3\sin2\theta$

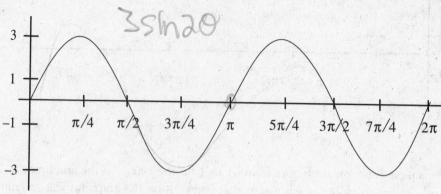

Once again, there are three things to check.

- This is a sin graph because it has a value of 0 at 0. Cos has a value of 1 at 0.
- It makes a complete cycle in π, so the period has changed—it's half of what it usually is. B has an inverse effect, which means B = 2.
- The amplitude is triple what it normally is, so A = 3. The function graphed, therefore, is 3 sin 2θ.

Let's try some practice questions.

49. As compared with the graph of $y = \overset{3}{\cancel{}}\cos x$, which of the following has the same period and three times the amplitude?

A. $y = \cos 3x$

B. $y = \cos \frac{1}{2}(x + 3)$

C. $y = 3 \cos \frac{1}{2}x$

D. $y = 1 + 3 \cos x$

E. $y = 3 + \cos x$

Here's How to Crack It

Recall that the coefficient on the outside of the function changes the amplitude and the one on the inside changes the period. Because the question states that the period isn't changed, you can eliminate (A), (B), and (C). The amplitude is three times greater, you're told; because there's a direct relationship between (A) and amplitude, you want to have a 3 multiplying the outside of the function. That leaves only (D) as a possibility.

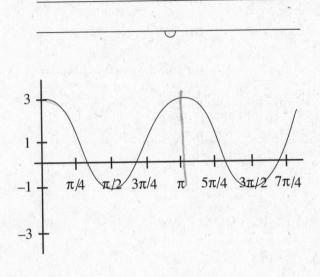

52. Which of the following equations describes the equation graphed above?

   F. $2 \cos x$ 3+cos2x
   G. $1 + 2 \cos x$
   H. $\cos 2x$
   J. $1 + \cos 2x$
   K. $1 + 2 \cos 2x$

   2cos 2x +1

Here's How to Crack It

At first it looks like this graph has an amplitude of 3, but if you look closer, you'll see that though the top value is 3, the bottom value is –1, which means that the whole graph has been shifted up. Because (F) and (H) don't add anything to the function (which is how you move a graph up and down), they're out. The period of this graph is half of what it usually is, so B = 2, which eliminates (G). Because the amplitude is changed also, you can eliminate (J). The answer is (K).

Trigonometry Drill

1. In $\triangle ABC$ below, the tan θ equals

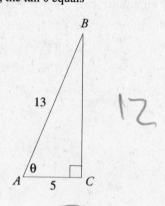

A. $\dfrac{5}{12}$

B. $\dfrac{12}{13}$

C. $\dfrac{17}{12}$

D. $\dfrac{12}{5}$

E. 3

Handwritten: 12   TOA $\dfrac{12}{5}$

2. If the cotangent of an angle θ is 1, then the tangent of angle θ is

F. −1

G. 0

H. 1

J. 2

K. 3

Handwritten: $\dfrac{1}{1}$ 1

3. If $x + \sin^2\theta + \cos^2\theta = 4$, then $x = ?$

A. 1

B. 2

C. 3

D. 4

E. 5

Handwritten: $x + 1 = 4$ $-1 \quad -1$ $x = 3$

Summary

o There are only four trigonometry questions on the ACT. At least two will deal with right triangles, and they are relatively easy if you know a few formulas.

o SOHCAHTOA will help you remember most of the formulas.

$$\text{sine} = \frac{\text{opposite}}{\text{hypotenuse}}; \text{cosine} = \frac{\text{adjacent}}{\text{hypotenuse}};$$

$$\text{tangent} = \frac{\text{opposite}}{\text{adjacent}}$$

o The cosecant $= \dfrac{1}{\text{sine}}$, the secant $= \dfrac{1}{\text{cosine}}$, and the cotangent $= \dfrac{1}{\text{tangent}}$.

o $\sin^2 \theta + \cos^2 \theta = 1$.

o $\dfrac{\sin \theta}{\cos \theta} = \tan \theta$.

o For trig graphs, focus on the amplitude and the period: A{*sin* (Bθ)}. The amplitude is directly related to the size of A, while the period is inversely related to the size of B.

Part IV
How to Crack the ACT Reading Test

Chapter 16
Introduction to the ACT Reading Test

Reading on the ACT is not the same as reading for school. When you're reading for school, you have to *understand* what you've read and be able to discuss it. On the ACT, you only have to understand enough of the passage to answer the questions. You don't need to discuss the passage later. In fact, you'll just forget it. Therefore, rather than reading to remember, you'll want to direct your reading to find the right answers. This chapter shows you how to do just that.

OVERVIEW: CRACKING AND PACING THE READING TEST

The ACT Reading Test Format
You read 4 passages and answer 40 questions in 35 minutes.

The ACT Reading test presents 4 passages with 10 questions each. That's 40 questions total. You get 35 minutes for the whole section, which means you have about 9 minutes to cover each passage and the questions that follow it, *if* your pacing strategy requires you to work all 4 passages

The passages are edited pieces of books and magazines, and according to ACT, they're "typical of what a college freshman might be required to read...." And the questions? ACT says they test your ability to "understand" the passages.

But That's Not Really True

No one ever achieved a great insight by spending eight or nine pressured minutes reading an isolated fragment of a book or an article. Serious writers don't intend their works to be read in fragments or in so hurried a fashion as reading tests require. (Imagine that you were asked to read a *fragment* of the history of the relations between the United States, Germany, and Japan during the twentieth century. Suppose, in particular, that you're asked to read only about their cooperative relations in the years 1985–1990. You'd be missing the history of their relationships during the years 1940–1945—World War II—which means you'd be missing a rather important piece of the story.)

Furthermore, serious readers take time to think about the things they read. How far would Albert Einstein have gotten if someone had interrupted his reading after 35 minutes to announce that he should "close his book because time is up"? As a college student, you'll be asked not only to read but also to think about what you read—and then to reread—and then to think some more. Any professor will tell you that understanding takes thought, and thought usually takes time.

When you take the ACT Reading test, you're not asked to understand. You're not asked to do anything you'll ever do in college. You're just asked to take a "reading test."

The ACT Reading Test: Cracking the System

You'll raise your reading score if you're "wise" to the test and if you think strategically. We're first going to show you how ACT reading questions are built. Then we'll show you how to use that knowledge to select correct answers. You'll learn to implement the techniques covered on the next page.

1. Attack the passages in the order that best suits you.
2. See through the camouflage that hides correct answer choices.
3. Identify incorrect answer choices and eliminate them quickly.
4. Answer questions without really reading the passage.
5. Put all of these techniques together to approach every passage and question with a step-by-step strategy that leads systematically to the correct answers.

READING TEST TRIAGE: ORDERING THE PASSAGES

The Reading test has four passages, one each from the following fields:

- Prose Fiction (excerpts from short stories and novels)
- Social Sciences (history, economics, psychology, political sciences, and anthropology)
- Humanities (art, music, architecture, and dance)
- Natural Sciences (biology, chemistry, physics, and physical sciences)

Students differ in their abilities to tackle these different passage types, and it's important that you decide which passages are easiest and hardest for you. That way you can decide which passages to do first (the easier ones) and which to do last or never (the harder ones). The passages are always in the same order.

Prose Fiction Passages

The prose fiction passage is almost the opposite of the natural science passage. It tells a fictitious story and is supposed to be packed with hints and suggestions about characters and their motivations.

> Allen's grandmother was readying herself to leave. She was, in fact, putting the final touches on her makeup which, as always, looked to Allen as though someone had thrown it on her face with a shovel. As Mrs. Mandale placed her newly purchased bracelet over her wrist, a look of troubled ambivalence came over her. "Perhaps this bracelet isn't right for me," she said. "I won't wear it."
>
> Waiting now for 30 minutes, Allen tried to be tolerant. "It is right for you," he said. "It matches your personality. Wear it." The bracelet was a remarkable illustration of poor taste. Its colors were vulgar and the structure lacked any sign of thoughtful design. The truth is, it did match his grandmother's personality. All that she did and enjoyed was tasteless and induced in Allen a quiet hopelessness.

Fiction Passages

Most prose fiction passages are primarily concerned with the following five things:
- Who
- What
- When
- Where
- Why

Prose fiction questions often require that you "read between the lines" and draw inferences about the way characters feel or behave.

1. Allen most likely encouraged his grandmother to wear her bracelet because he:

   A. found it colorful and approved of its appearance.
   B. found its appearance pathetic and wished his grandmother to look pretty.
   C. was impatient with his grandmother for spending time worrying about the bracelet.
   D. felt the bracelet matched his grandmother's bright personality.

Some people have an ability for these kinds of passages and questions. Others find them unclear and confusing. If you find literature passages easiest, do them first. If you find them most difficult, do them last or never.

For the record, the answer is (C). Allen has been waiting and is trying "to be tolerant."

Social Science and Humanities Passages

Social science and humanities passages are sort of a cross between natural science and prose fiction. Often, the author has views about the subject he or she is discussing, and you might be asked to draw inferences about them. You might also be asked questions about details.

Religion is so fundamental a part of human existence that one might easily forget to ask how it started. Yet it had to start somewhere and there had to be a time when human beings or their apelike ancestors did not entertain notions of the supernatural. Hence the historian should want to probe the origins of religious belief.

It is doubtful that morality played a part in the beginnings of religious belief. Rather, religion is traceable to a far more fundamental human and animal characteristic. Storms, floods, famine, and other adversities inspired *fear* in the hearts of primitive peoples as well they should have. Curiously, humankind early took the position that it might somehow subject such catastrophes to its control. Specifically, it believed it might control them by obedience and submission and by conforming its behavior to their mandates. Worship, ritual, sacrifice of life, and property became means through which early peoples sought to cajole the powers and avoid the blights and miseries the peoples dreaded. As Petronius, in Lucretius's tradition remarked, "It was fear that first made the gods."

11. According to the passage, natural disasters contributed to the development of religion by:

    A. motivating human beings to acquire some command over their environment.
    B. making human beings distinguish themselves from animals.
    C. causing human beings to sacrifice their lives and goods.
    D. providing a need for ritual and tradition.

12. The author believes that the origins of religion:

    F. are extremely easy to ascertain and understand.
    G. should not be questioned by historians because religion is fundamental to civilized life.
    H. are directly tied to apelike subhuman species.
    J. should be the subject of serious historical inquiry.

The correct answer to 11 is (A) and the answer to 12 is (J).

Mark Twain had magnificent style, and with *The Adventures of Huckleberry Finn*, he built the gateway to American fiction. *Huckleberry Finn* treats extraordinarily serious themes, and it reflects the author's coming of age. Although they don't represent truly mature works, other Twain Mississippi River stories, published before Huck Finn, afford Americans a clear, collective picture of pre–Civil War life in the Mississippi Valley.

With the coming and going of the Civil War, however, Twain adopted a revised agenda, which was reflected in the style and subject matter of his writing. The postwar era demanded that he address himself to the nation's social squalor. His work was more intellectualized, artificial, and at times angry. The author himself had faced several personal tragedies in series, and these too might have contributed to the metamorphosis.

21. According to the passage, which of the following statements is true of *The Adventures of Huckleberry Finn*?

    A. It appeared after the publication of other Mark Twain stories describing life on the Mississippi River.
    B. It was the first full-length book that Mark Twain published.
    C. It would have been quite different if Mark Twain had not suffered personal tragedy.
    D. It had no serious themes and addressed no serious issues.

22. In the author's opinion, *The Adventures of Huckleberry Finn*:

    F. should not be read by children.
    G. contributed less to American literature than did Twain's postwar writings.
    H. is less adult in its subject matter than were Twain's postwar writings.
    J. reveals that Mark Twain had grown since writing his early Mississippi River stories.

Our answers here are (A) for 21 and (J) for 22.

Natural Science Passages

Natural science passages are filled with lots of details and technical descriptions.

> It is further noteworthy that the terrestrial vertebrate's most significant muscles of movement are no longer located lateral to the vertebral column as they are in the fish but rather in ventral and dorsal relation to it. This trend in terrestrial evolution is highly significant and means that the terrestrial vertebrate's principal movements are fore and back, not side to side. The trend is well documented in the whale, an aquatic animal whose ancestors are terrestrial quadrupeds. The whale, in other words, has "returned" to the sea secondarily after an ancestral stage on the land. Unlike the fish, and in accordance with its ancestry, it propels itself by moving the tail up and down, not side to side. In a sense, the whale moves itself by bending up and down at the waist. Indeed, that very analogy is recalled by the mythical mermaid figure who seems to represent a humanlike line returned to the water secondarily like the whale.

The questions usually track the text pretty closely and require you to make few inferences.

31. Which of the following best represents a general trend associated with mammalian evolution?

    A. Enhancement of bodily movement from right to left and left to right
    B. Minimization of muscle groups oriented lateral to the vertebral column
    C. The development of propulsive fins from paired limbs
    D. Secondary return to the sea

Some people have a flair for the ACT's natural science passages, and some people find them extremely tedious and difficult. (And, by the way, it isn't necessarily good science students who do well with these passages nor poor science students who have trouble with them.) If among all of the passage types you find natural science the easiest, you should make it a rule to address the natural science passage first. If you find natural science passages the most difficult, however, save them for last.

The answer to 31 is (B).

Reading Test Triage
If you have a knack for particular passage types, great. Do them first. If not, look at the topics, as well as the questions and answer choices. Some will be straightforward, while others will look more complicated. Use your time wisely.

TIME, TIME AGAIN

After working through the chapters in this book, you will have a good idea of which types of passages are easiest for you and which are hardest. When you take the Reading test, you should do the easiest (for you) passages first. Why? Because many people run out of time on the ACT Reading test. It's better to run out of time and have to guess on the passages that are the most difficult. You'll get more points at the beginning by working the easier passages first, and you'll lose fewer points by guessing on the hardest passage as time runs out.

For more great titles by The Princeton Review
Reading Smart

How to Tell Which Passages You Find Easy and Hard

What do you do if you dislike all of the passages equally or show no particular—or, for that matter, consistent—knack for certain passage types? The subject matter of the passages may be dull, but in the end, you should base your ordering of the passages on

- **the user-friendliness of the topics themselves**
  "Wait a minute!" you say. "I thought you said that if I show no particular knack for certain passage types…" True, but…
  Let's say you notice that a social science or humanities passage is historical in nature. Chances are that events will be presented in chronological order, making the passage easy to navigate. Or let's say you've recently learned about lasers in physics class and, lo and behold, the natural sciences passage is about lasers. Chances are that you'll be able to eliminate answers or even answer some of the questions based on what you've learned. You don't have to love a topic to take advantage of familiarity with it. In fact, being too enamored of a topic can work against you. Remember, you get points for answering questions correctly, not for understanding the passages, and certainly not for reading over them with great interest.

- **the user-friendliness of the questions and answer choices**
  Many students who dislike all the passages find this an especially helpful guideline. Look at the questions. Do many of them direct you to particular lines in the passage, refer to dates, refer to proper nouns, or refer to italicized words? If so, a passage with several such questions will usually be much easier to manage. Look at the answer choices. Are they relatively straightforward, or do they resemble miniature novels? A passage with several longwinded questions and/or answer choices will always take more time to complete.

Take a quick look at the Reading in practice test 1. Try glancing at each passage—looking at either the topic or the questions and answer choices—and ask yourself which one looks easiest to you and which one you definitely want to leave for last. Ordering passages takes a little time at the beginning, but it can save you a lot of time (and gain you points) in the end.

Now that we've talked about the ordering of the passages and questions, let's talk about the whole point of this book—finding right answers.

THE RIGHT ANSWER MIGHT BE CAMOUFLAGED

Look at these two phrases.

"rationally conceived idea"

"concept born of reason"

The two phrases don't have a single word in common, but if you think about it, you'll probably agree that they mean the same thing. Lots of ACT reading questions test your ability to see that one sentence or phrase means more or less the same as another even though the wording is quite different. They test whether you can see that a sentence has been *paraphrased*, which means reworded.

Correct Answer Choices May Be Disguised
Look for answer choices that reword parts of the passage.

Read This Passage; It's Very Short

> Regardless of personal religious belief, no true student of history can emerge from study without a scholarly appreciation for the significant role of religion in the development of human civilization.

Now that you've read the passage, answer this question.

11. Which of the following represents the author's belief regarding religion and the study of history?

   A. Many historians develop a deep suspicion of totalitarian societies and the way in which they abuse human rights.
   B. Most historians have a profound distaste for ancient documents and torn papers.
   C. True historians develop an appreciation for the role of religion in the course of human development.
   D. Few historians develop insight into the manner in which political leaders gain power.

It's pretty easy to see that (C) is right, and that (A), (B), and (D) are wrong. Choice (C) features the author's words and accurately reflects his meaning. Choices (A), (B), and (D) are extreme and have nothing whatsoever to do with anything in the passage. This question is pretty straightforward. The wrong answers are clearly wrong, and the right answer is clearly right.

Many ACT Questions Aren't so Easy

ACT questions won't always provide you with a correct answer that reprints the author's own words. Instead, the author's statements will be camouflaged by *rewording*. That means you must be on the lookout for answer choices that don't seem right because the author's sentences have been reworded. Let's take the question we just answered and turn it into an ACT question by rewriting the answer choices.

11. Which of the following represents the author's belief regarding the role of religion in the study of history?

   A. Few historians have gained a complete appreciation for the development of religion.

   B. Historians should not allow their personal religious beliefs to affect the historical conclusions with which they emerge.

   C. Serious historians regard religious belief as an important force in man's social evolution.

   D. A true student of religious history should not ignore a general study of human development.

Answer choice (C) is still the correct answer, but that's not so easy to spot anymore. Unless you're on the lookout for camouflage, you might not appreciate the similarity between these two statements:

1. …no true student of history can emerge from study without a scholarly appreciation for the significant role of religion in the development of human civilization.	*and*	2. Serious historians regard religious belief as an important force in man's social evolution.

These two statements don't have a single word in common. Yet, when you think about it,

"serious historians"	*is camouflage for*	"true student of history"
"important force"	*is camouflage for*	"significant role"
"man's social evolution"	*is camouflage for*	"development of human civilization"

Answer choice (C) presents the author's statements—camouflaged.

See Through the Camouflage

You'll raise your ACT score if you learn first to recognize camouflage and then to see through it. So let's practice. Each of the very short readings below comes from an ACT-type passage. We want you to

- read each one
- think carefully about what it means
- *with that meaning in mind* consider the meaning of each answer choice
- determine which one constitutes the author's statements, camouflaged

Let's try one.

    The human condition is unequal, distributing its gifts and penalties according to a wildly haphazard scheme. A person is not what he deserves to be but simply what he is.

12. According to the passage, it is true that the human condition:

    F. is a precious gift and should not be treated haphazardly.
    G. does not allocate its burdens and benefits according to merit.
    H. will become more predictable as human beings learn to appreciate it.
    J. is sometimes unjust due to fundamental aspects of human nature.

Here's How to Crack It

What does the author say? The author says that life's pleasures and hardships are not given out fairly—according to what people deserve. Instead, they're given out randomly. The author is saying that you don't get what you deserve. You just get what you get.

With that in mind, let's look at the answer options and see which one makes the same statement in a different way.

What do the choices mean?

Answer choice (A) means that life is a very valuable thing and that people should not be careless with it. That's not what we're looking for.

Answer choice (B) says just what the author has said—in different words. Think about it.

"allocate"	*is camouflage for*	"distributing"
"burdens and benefits"	*is camouflage for*	"gifts and penalties"
"merit"	*is camouflage for*	"deserves"

Answer choice (C) means that people who appreciate life will find that it offers fewer surprises. The author did not say that.

Answer choice (D) means that human nature is the cause of life's unfairness. Interesting, but that's not what the author wrote.

Only (B) comes close to expressing the author's meaning. That's why it's right.

Try another.

Poverty, deformity, illness, loss, weakness, and mistreatment impose themselves relentlessly on individual lives. That circumstance begs the historian to ask why humans have for the most part accepted the situation so peaceably.

13. The passage indicates that persistent poverty and illness:

   A. are caused partially by humanity's overriding concern with acceptance and peace.
   B. are due in some part to a faulty understanding of history.
   C. should make historians question the role of the individual in human affairs.
   D. should provoke historical inquiry into humanity's willingness to tolerate adversity.

Here's How to Crack It

What does the author say? The author says, first of all, that people have always had a lot of trouble in their lives. He then says that historians should try to figure out why they're so willing to put up with it.

What do the choices mean?

Answer choice (A) means that people have trouble because they're too concerned with peace. Ridiculous, but more important, it's not what the author wrote.

Answer choice (B) means that people have trouble because they don't understand history. Not so ridiculous, but the author made no such statement.

Answer choice (C) means that all of this trouble should make historians try to figure out the place of individuals in society. Whatever that means, it's not what we're looking for.

Now look at answer choice D. It's just what the doctor ordered. It's the author's statement—camouflaged. Think about it.

"should provoke historical inquiry"	*is camouflage for*	"begs the historian to ask"
"willingness to tolerate adversity"	*is camouflage for*	"why humans…accepted the situation so peaceably"

So answer choice (D) is right.

Here's another one.

> Religious belief allows the unlucky, on some very important level, to treat their misery as insignificant in the grand scheme of things, for they look to something higher: the approval of their god and the faith that they will not in the end be forsaken.

14. The passage states that religious belief helps people by:

   F. allowing them to accept the idea that they have been forsaken.

   G. providing them with faith that they will overcome their difficulties.

   H. diminishing the importance they might place on their day-to-day pain.

   J. emphasizing that spiritual strength is more significant than luck.

Here's How to Crack It

What does the author say? The author says that religious belief helps people whose lives are difficult. It causes them to focus on the wish to please their god, which means that they place relatively little importance on the troubles they face in their lives.

What do the choices mean?

Answer choice (A) means that religious believers don't mind being forsaken. Sorry, not what we're looking for.

Answer choice (B) means that religion helps people believe they'll get over their problems. Sounds good, but it's not the meaning we're after.

Answer choice (C) means that religious believers don't think their troubles are so important. That's what the author said! Choice (C) represents the author's statements camouflaged. Think about it:

"diminishing the importance"	*is camouflage for*	"treat…as insignificant"
"pain"	*is camouflage for*	"misery"

Answer choice (D) means that religious believers think spiritual strength is more important than luck. The author doesn't say anything like that. Only (C) reflects the author's meaning. That's why it's right.

Summary

- There are always 4 passages and 40 questions on the ACT Reading test. The passages are always in this order: prose fiction, social science, humanities, and natural science.

- Spend the first minute of the test determining which passage will be hardest for you—this is the one to leave until last. Playing to your strengths early in the test will gain you the most points.

- Be wary of camouflaged answers. ACT test writers rarely use a direct quote from the passage in the correct answer.

- Don't forget to always guess your Letter of the Day if there are questions that you can't answer or don't get to in time.

Chapter 17
Distracters

The ACT test writers are good at writing wrong answers that look right. To get you to pick these wrong answers, they utilize certain distracting techniques. This chapter shows you how to be on the lookout for deceptive answers that track the language of the passage very closely, for switches that say the opposite of the correct answer, for extreme answer choices, and for answers that sound too nice. They are usually incorrect.

GET WISE TO DISTRACTERS: USE PROCESS OF ELIMINATION

You'll raise your ACT Reading score if you're good at spotting not only right answers but also the wrong ones. In the standardized test business, wrong answers are called "distracters," and that's a perfect name for them. Distracters are designed to misdirect your thinking—to break your concentration, distract you, and throw you off course. Even if you have a pretty good grasp of the passage and the question you're trying to answer, distracters can make you lose sight of both. But if you're wise to distracters, you can quickly eliminate them and rapidly make your way to the right answer.

FOUR KINDS OF DISTRACTERS

You should know about the four kinds of distracters that show up on the ACT Reading test. We're going to show you how each one operates so you'll know how to use them to your advantage.

Distracter 1: Deceptive Answers

Many distracters steal words directly from the passages and use them to create a statement that does *not* reflect the content of the passages. These distracters use the authors' words but distort their meanings, so we call them *deceptive answers*.

Read this statement.

> *Tom loves going to the movies with Mary.*

It's easy to write a bunch of sentences that do not reflect the statement's meaning, even though they use the words "Tom," "love," "movies," and "Mary." For example, consider this

> *Tom fell in love with Mary at the movies.*

or this

> *Tom and Mary love movies.*

or this

> *Tom and Mary generally enjoy seeing movies about love.*

If you think about *meaning*, not one of these statements resembles the one with which we started. Each distorts the original by taking its words and rearranging them. Yet they all sort of "sound like" the original because they use the same words.

Each one of the deceptive answers we just read would make a good ACT distracter. Suppose you've just read an ACT passage that contains the statement we worked with: "Tom loves going to the movies with Mary." Now imagine that you get a question like this

1. According to the passage, which of the following statements is true regarding Tom and Mary?

   A. Tom fell in love with Mary at the movies.
   B. Tom enjoys viewing motion pictures with Mary as his companion.
   C. Tom and Mary generally enjoy seeing movies about love.
   D. Both Tom and Mary love going to the movies.

Notice that (A), (C), and (D) use words that come straight from the passage. *They're all wrong.* Which one is right? Answer choice (B): It presents the author's meaning—in camouflage.

Don't Let Deceptive Answers Snare You

Don't be fooled by answer choices that misuse words and phrases from the passage.

Look at these four excerpts from ACT-like passages. Each one is followed by five statements. Three of the five are deceptive answer distracters. The other two accurately reflect the author's meaning; they *don't* distort. For each passage, decide which three statements are deceptive answers and which two are not.

Read this natural science excerpt.

As an explanation for the age and origin of the solar system, the nebular hypothesis lost ground at the turn of the twentieth century over questions about the distribution of angular momentum.

What does the author say?

- The nebular hypothesis was intended to explain the age and origin of the solar system.
- It lost influence at the beginning of the twentieth century.
- It happened because people raised questions about the distribution of angular momentum, and the nebular hypothesis did not provide adequate answers.

Use Process of Elimination (POE)

Look for the following four types of distracters on the ACT Reading test:
- deceptive answers
- the switch
- extremes
- answer choices that sound too nice

Now evaluate these statements.

	Deceptive Answer	Not a Deceptive Answer
31. According to the nebular hypothesis, the solar system was created by distributions of angular momentum.	✓	
32. The nebular hypothesis came under question at the beginning of the twentieth century.		✓
33. The nebular hypothesis was challenged because of issues related to angular momentum.		✓
34. Knowledge about the solar system's angular momentum was first distributed in the twentieth century.	✓	
35. The nebular hypothesis was poorly understood until the twentieth century, when theories of angular momentum gained ground.	✓	

Important
Distortions are often words in the passage that are used out of context. Eliminate them.

Statements 31, 34, and 35 are deceptive. They distort the author's meaning. The words come straight from the passage, but the meanings definitely do not. The author does not say

- the nebular hypothesis states that distributions of angular momentum created the solar system
- someone first distributed knowledge about angular momentum in the twentieth century
- people didn't understand the nebular hypothesis until the twentieth century

Statements 32 and 33 are not deceptive answers. They do not distort. The author does say

- the nebular hypothesis was questioned (lost ground) at the beginning of the twentieth century
- the nebular hypothesis was questioned because of concerns relating to angular momentum

Read this social science excerpt.

> With revolutionary improvements in health care technologies, modern medicine's expansive arsenal has undoubtedly created an improved state of national health. Although the incidence of degenerative disease is on the rise, that is primarily because degenerative diseases are characteristic of old age and the population is living, on average, longer than did its parents and grandparents.

What does the author say?
- There has been great progress in medicine.
- It's true that there's more degenerative disease around than there used to be.
- That's because degenerative diseases usually affect the elderly, and people are living long enough to *get* these diseases.

Now evaluate these statements.	Deceptive Answer	Not a Deceptive Answer
11. Modern medicine has increased the individual's average life span.	☒	☑
12. Revolutionary health care techniques have produced degeneration in the state of national health.	☑	☒
13. Few people doubt that degenerative disease tends to increase longevity.	☑	☐
14. Today's health care technologies have bettered the national health.	☐	☑
15. With today's tools and techniques the physician can cure degenerative diseases that once caused early death.	☑	☐

Statements 12, 13, and 15 are deceptive answers. They distort the author's meaning. The words are familiar, but they've been rearranged to say something that has nothing to do with the passage. The author does not say

- modern medicine has had a negative effect on health care
- most people think degenerative disease makes for longer life
- modern medicine allows physicians to cure degenerative diseases

Statements 11 and 14 are not deceptive answers. They do not distort. The author does say

- modern medicine has increased the average life span
- modern medicine has improved the national health

Read this prose fiction excerpt.

Mrs. Mandale's physician repeatedly reminded his patient of her diabetes and had ordered her on several occasions to lose weight. Hence, Allen found himself taking his grandmother once each week to her weight-watching group.

Mrs. Mandale was not among the heavier women in her group. She never announced her weight, however, because, "a true lady did not discuss such personal matters." The group was one of Mrs. Mandale's few pleasures, but she feared walking unaccompanied in the city at night and asked that Allen take her each week to "group." She pointed out that she had done much for him, that her very health was involved, and that he should be willing to extend himself for her.

What does the author say?

- Allen's grandmother has diabetes.
- For that reason, her doctor ordered her to lose weight.
- To lose the weight, she participates in a weight-watching group.
- She's not one of the heavier women in the group.
- Even so, she won't reveal her weight, because she thinks true ladies shouldn't discuss such personal issues.
- The weight-watching group is one of Mrs. Mandale's few pleasures.
- The weight-watching group is conducted at night, and Mrs. Mandale does not like to walk in the city by herself at night.
- Mrs. Mandale thinks she's done a lot for Allen so she asks him to take her to her weight-watching group each week.

Half-and-Half
Beware of answer choices that are half good, half bad. They're also deceptive. If an answer is half bad, it's all wrong.

Now evaluate these statements.

	Deceptive Answer	Not a Deceptive Answer
1. Mrs. Mandale is willing to reveal her weight only because she weighs less than others in her weight-watching group.	☑	☒
2. The doctor recommends that Allen's grandmother not walk alone at night.	☑	☐
3. Mrs. Mandale finds her weight reduction group more enjoyable than most of her other activities.	☐	☑
4. Mrs. Mandale thinks that other women in her weight-watching group are not as ladylike as she is.	☑	☐
5. Mrs. Mandale believes she has been a positive force in her grandson's life.	☐	☑

Statements 1, 2, and 4 are deceptive answers. They distort the author's meaning. The key words come straight from the passage, but the statements are distortions. The author does not say

- Mrs. Mandale is willing to reveal her weight
- the doctor advised Mrs. Mandale against walking alone at night
- Mrs. Mandale believes herself to be more of a lady than the other women in the group

Statements 3 and 5 are not deceptive answers. They do not distort. The author does say

- the weight-watching group is one of the few pleasures Mrs. Mandale has
- Mrs. Mandale thinks she has done a lot for her grandson

Read this humanities excerpt.

———————————○———————————

Before the Civil War, Frances Ellen Watkins Harper was the best known of black abolitionist writers. Her greatest true novel, *Iola Leroy,* or *Shadows Uplifted,* appeared in 1892. The work was transitional: It treats both the pre–Civil War and post–Civil War periods. Although it describes the evils of slavery, its principal purpose was considerably different from some of the earlier novels for which Mrs. Harper became famous. In *Iola Leroy,* Mrs. Harper wished to promote justice and interracial tolerance. For that reason, the novel treats some issues with more idealism than realism.

Referring to her own novel, Mrs. Harper wrote: "I have woven a story whose mission will not be in vain if it awakens in the hearts of our countrymen a stronger sense of justice and a more Christlike humanity."

What does the author say?

- Mrs. Harper was a black abolitionist writer—the most famous of her time.
- Her greatest earlier novels dealt primarily with the evils of slavery.
- Her best novel was *Iola Leroy,* which was also called *Shadows Uplifted.*
- Dealing with the periods before and after the Civil War, *Iola Leroy* portrays the evils of slavery; Mrs. Harper primarily intended the novel to promote justice and tolerance among races.
- Because that was her purpose, she sometimes treated issues not in a realistic manner, but in an idealistic manner.

Now evaluate these statements.

	Deceptive Answer	Not a Deceptive Answer
21. *Iola Leroy* depicts situations occurring before and after the Civil War.	☐	☑
22. Frances Ellen Watkins Harper was not well known as an abolitionist until the appearance of her first true novel, *Iola Leroy*.	☑	☐
23. Although best known as abolitionist literature, Mrs. Harper's prewar novels usually concerned justice, not slavery.	☑	☐
24. Mrs. Harper was well known before the Civil War but in the postwar period her fame diminished considerably.	☑	☐
25. Frances Ellen Watkins Harper opposed slavery before the war and attempted to improve relations among blacks and whites after the war.	☐	☑

Statements 22, 23, and 24 are deceptive answers. They distort the author's meaning. The words come right out of the passage, but the meanings have nothing to do with it. The author definitely does not say

- *Iola Leroy* was Mrs. Harper's *first* true novel, or that Mrs. Harper was not well known until that novel appeared
- Mrs. Harper's prewar novels concerned justice and not slavery
- Mrs. Harper lost fame after the Civil War

Statements 21 and 25 are not deceptive answers. They do not distort. The author does indicate that

- *Iola Leroy* concerned both the pre–Civil War and post–Civil War periods
- Mrs. Harper was an abolitionist before the war and that her postwar novel *Iola Leroy* was intended to improve relations among the races

College Lingo

RA: Residence assistant (or residential advisor). Someone, typically an upperclassman or graduate student, who supervises a floor or section of a dorm, usually in return for free room and board.
Source: *Best 366 Colleges,* 2008 Edition

Distracter
2

Distracter 2: Switches

Some ACT distracters take the truth and switch it around. We call this "the switch." Don't let it fool you. For instance, read this.

> 1. Professor Thorne generally explains a technological discovery first in terms of its history and then in terms of the science up on which it was founded.

We've learned that Professor Thorne discusses history *first* and science *second*.

Now look at this statement.

> 2. Professor Thorne generally explains a technological discovery first in terms of the science on which it was founded, and then in terms of its history.

Statement 2 looks like Statement 1, but it's backward. Professor Thorne is doing things in the wrong order: science first and history second. Statement 2 takes the truth and turns it around. That's the essence of "the switch."

But the ACT Test Writers Get Sneaky

When the ACT test writers throw a switch into the answer choices, they don't always write something like Statement 2, which takes the author's statement and literally reverses the order of its words. Sometimes they *change* the wording and at the same time, turn the meaning upside down. Read Statement 1 again, and then look at Statement 3 below.

Use Process of Elimination (POE)
Sometimes it's easier to find the correct answer by eliminating the wrong answer choices. If you can eliminate answer choices with distracters such as deceptive answers, switches, or extremes, as well as answer choices that are too nice, you'll increase your chance of getting the right answer.

> 3. After Professor Thorne describes the scientific aspects of a technological breakthrough, he explains the historical context in which the breakthrough was made.

It's not so easy to see at first, but Statement 3 is a switch. It doesn't use the words *first*, or *then*, and it begins with the word "after." But think about what it says. Professor Thorne discusses history *after* discussing science. That would mean that he discusses science first and history second. That's opposite to what you're told in the passage.

Now read this.

> 4. Irrespective of population, every state elects two members to the United States Senate. The most populous state and the least populous state thus have equal representation in that important legislative body. In contrast, the House of Representatives is population-based and the number of representatives elected by any state depends on the number of citizens residing in that state.

Here's a switch.

> 5. Representation in the United States Senate is dependent on state population.

From Statement 4, we learned

- representation in the Senate is *not* based on population
- representation in the House *is* based on population

Statement 5 is exactly opposite to the original. It's a switch.

Eliminate the Switch

Let's say you're looking at a question. You spot two deceptive answers and eliminate them. That leaves you with two choices, and you aren't sure which is right. One thing you should do is determine whether one of them is a switch. If it is, then the *other* one is right. Here are two passage excerpts—each one followed by two to three questions. For each question, determine which answer choice is the switch.

Read this social sciences excerpt.

The Switch
Look out for
- changes in the wording in the answer choices
- a "flip" in the meaning of the sentence

Twenty or thirty thousand years ago, *Homo Sapiens* were uncommon animals, wandering alone or in small groups in a constant search for food. Primitive humans lived by the hunt, and modern nutritionists like to observe that with meat
5 as a dietary staple, they were seldom iron-deficient as are many farm-based populations today. But the absence of iron deficiency was perhaps the only advantage to the hunting lifestyle of the time. The hunter, it should be remembered, may find himself the hunted, and by anything approaching
10 our own standards today, primitive human life was unstable and incessantly hazardous.

In this regard, however, the advent of agriculture improved the human condition. Between ten and twenty thousand years ago, human beings discovered the use of herding
15 and of growing, which apparently served as inspiration to man's mechanical facilities. Relatively crude weapons of hunt were replaced by more refined farming implements. To be sure, farming is subject to the uncertainties of weather and climate, but it ultimately allows humans a greater degree of
20 control over their food supply and relieves them from the dangers of the hunt.

11. In terms of the tools and implements made by primitive man, the passage suggests that:

   A. farming tools were less sophisticated than hunting weapons.
   B. [Already eliminated]
   C. agriculture is associated with more advanced tool-making skills.
   D. [Already eliminated]

Look at (A). It says farming tools are less sophisticated than hunting weapons. Now look at the passage, lines 16–17. It says that hunting implements were crude and that farming implements were more refined. Choice (A) has it backward—it's a switch. Eliminate it.

12. According to the passage, a life based on agriculture:

   F. [Already eliminated]
   G. provides humans with more iron than is provided by hunting.
   H. [Already eliminated]
   J. offers a greater degree of certainty than does a hunting lifestyle.

Look at (G). It says that agriculture provides more iron than does hunting. The author does discuss iron deficiency, but she says that hunters were *not* iron deficient, and that farmers *are*. Choice (G) is a switch. Eliminate it.

Read this natural science excerpt.

In certain critical respects the magnificence of science lies not in its discovery of what is true but in its identification of that which is not. Pivotal points in scientific learning are those at which some long-held assumption is openly exam-
5 ined and exposed as a falsehood. Copernicus, Kepler, Galileo, and ultimately Newton established that the sun, not the earth, is the fixed center of the solar system and that the earth orbits the sun, thus invalidating the views of Aristotle and Ptolemy, which were largely unquestioned before that time.
10 Toward the turn of the last century, Michelson, Morley, Lorentz, and Einstein successfully challenged a host of assumptions about the absolute quality of space and time. Then, in the 1920s, theories put forward by Heisenberg, Schrodinger, and Dirac together created the science of quantum mechanics and thus
15 destroyed time-honored views about position and velocity. Even Einstein had difficulty accepting Heisenberg's theory, which dealt a lethal blow to the cherished notion, advocated especially by LaPlace, that science could aspire to complete knowledge of the state of the universe and thus predict its future.

20   In 1929, Hubble, versed in the writings of Olbers one hundred years before him, showed that the universe was finite but expanding and more or less did away with the prevailing belief that the universe had to be either finite and static or infinite.

31. According to the passage, Ptolemy differed from Copernicus in that:

    A. Ptolemy envisioned a stationary earth and Copernicus did not.

    B. [Already eliminated]

    C. [Already eliminated]

    D. Ptolemy postulated that the earth followed an orbit about the sun and Copernicus did not.

Look at (D). It says that Ptolemy imagined the earth orbiting the sun and that Copernicus did not imagine the earth orbiting the sun. Now look at lines 5–9 of the passage. They tell us that Copernicus (and others) did *not* believe in a fixed earth. They thought the earth orbited the sun. That view invalidated Ptolemy's view. In other words, Ptolemy thought otherwise. He thought the earth was fixed and that the sun orbited the earth. Choice (D) is a switch. Eliminate it.

32. According to the passage, Heisenberg's theory:

    F. [Already eliminated]

    G. challenged traditional beliefs about position and velocity.

    H. described a universe that could be understood and predicted.

    J. [Already eliminated]

Look at (H). It says that Heisenberg's principle makes the universe seem predictable. Now read the passage, lines 16–19. They say that Heisenberg's theory *dealt a blow* to the idea that science could attain complete knowledge of the universe and predict its future. Heisenberg's principle *destroyed* the belief that science might completely understand the state of the universe. That means (H) is a switch. Eliminate it.

Sometimes the Switch Involves a Sneaky Word Substitution

Sometimes the switch involves the substitution of a wrong word (or name) for a right one. The answer choice looks correct but isn't because one word doesn't belong. Recall the natural science passage and look at the question on the next page.

33. The Aristotelian conception of the solar system was:

    A. inconsistent with Newtonian and Galilean insights.
    B. at odds with Copernican and Ptolemic views.
    C. [Already eliminated]
    D. [Already eliminated]

Look at (B). It indicates that Aristotle's views were different from those of Ptolemy and Copernicus. Now look at lines 5–9 of the passage. They tell us that Copernicus, Kepler, Galileo, and Newton challenged the views of Aristotle and Ptolemy. In other words, Aristotle and Ptolemy believed one thing and the other four, including Copernicus, believed another. "Copernican" belongs in the answer choice, but "Ptolemic" does not. Answer choice (B) is a switch. Eliminate it.

Sometimes the Switch Gives You a Simple Shortcut to the Right Answer

If the answer choices happen to feature two statements that are basically opposites, then one of them is usually right (and the other, of course, is the switch). That means you can focus on these two and ignore the other two answer options unless neither of the first two is correct.

For instance, consider the natural science excerpt we just read, and look at the following answer choices:

34. Blah, blah, blah…

    F. important in that it shows certain propositions to be true.
    G. important in that it shows certain propositions to be false.
    H. less precise than most scientists believe.
    J. extremely misleading to those who fail to question its premises.

Notice that (F) and (G) are opposites. Without even looking at the question, you can conclude that one of them will probably be the right answer. Why? Because the ACT test writers are predictable that way. They tend not to present opposing statements unless one of them is right. In this case, answer choices (H) and (J) are wrong, and you can eliminate them.

Now let's look at the question.

———○———

34. In the first paragraph, the author makes the point that natural science can be:

   F. important in that it shows certain propositions to be true.

   G. important in that it shows certain propositions to be false.

   H. less precise than most scientists believe.

   J. extremely misleading to those who fail to question its premises.

Here's How to Crack It

You know that either (F) or (G) is probably right, so focus on these two. In the first sentence of the paragraph, the author states, "In certain critical respects the magnificence of science lies not in its discovery of what is true but in its identification of that which is not." Answer choice (G) makes the same statement—in camouflage. Answer choice (F) is the switch. Answer choice (G) is correct.

———○———

Distracter 3: Extremes

If an answer choice indicates that something is *always* so, *invariably* so, or *never* so, then it's usually wrong. We call such choices *extremes,* and you should be very suspicious of them.

Words like *completely, perfectly,* and *absolutely* also signal an extreme choice.

Extremes tend to be wrong because they're usually *debatable,* and the ACT test writers know that. Think about these statements:

> *Patients who are chronically depressed never enjoy their lives.*

Never? *Ever?* It's pretty hard to prove the truth of such a statement.

It's one thing to say that depressed patients *have difficulty* enjoying their lives or that they *tend not* to enjoy their lives. But to say they *never* enjoy their lives just can't be correct.

> *A political leader should seek to make peace at all costs.*

All costs? No matter what? That's pretty tough to defend. Such a statement is too one-sided to constitute a right answer on the ACT.

Distracter
3

Extreme Answer Choices

Look out for answer choices that are too extreme to be the correct answer. These are answer choices to eliminate. These answer choices include words such as *always, completely,* and *absolutely.*

In order to lead a productive life, a citizen must devote all of his energy to his work.

All of his energy? Come on. That statement is too easy to dispute, and the ACT test writers know it. They can't call it correct.

Extreme statements are easy to write and they're very useful to standardized test writers. When a standardized test writer has trouble thinking of a wrong answer choice for one of the questions, he or she often constructs an extreme.

Without reading any passage, consider this question and determine which answer choice is an extreme statement.

---

31. The author's claim that "cause is relative only to perspective" introduces his argument that:

    A. mental well-being depends on physical strength.
    B. how something is perceived depends on its nature.
    C. psychological health requires a perfect upbringing.
    D. psychiatric condition depends on numerous factors, environmental and internal.

Here's How to Crack It

Answer choice (C) is extreme. The idea that anything has to be "ideal" or "perfect" or "absolutely precise" or "completely objective" or "totally honest" is usually contrary to ACT philosophy. Eliminate it.

Look at this question and determine which answer choice or choices are extremes.

---

32. The author believes that practicing psychiatrists:

    F. cannot possibly help patients unless they are completely objective.
    G. are hopelessly confused over the genesis of mental illness.
    H. are scientists notwithstanding the uncertainties that surround psychiatry.
    J. should, for the time being, treat mental disease in terms of environment.

Here's How to Crack It

Answer choices (F) and (G) are extremes. The phrases "cannot possibly," "completely objective," and "hopelessly confused" should tip you off.

Read this next question and determine which answer choice or choices are extremes.

---

33. According to information presented in the third paragraph, an individual organism will not survive to reproductive age unless:

    A. all of its compensatory mechanisms are in ideal balance.
    B. it has adequate homeostatic and feedback responses.
    C. it is capable of complete adaptation to every form of stress.
    D. other individuals of the same species fail to reproduce.

Here's How to Crack It

Answer choices (A) and (C) are extremes. "Ideal balance," "complete adaptation," and "every...stress" are the tip-off phrases.

Distracter 4: Choices That Sound Too "Nice"

Some distracters will appeal to you simply because they sound "nice," even though they have little to do with the question or the passage. Such distracters might draw on something you already know, or on the surface they might just seem reasonable and correct. Think, for instance, about statements like the following:

> *Ultimately, the voting public knows its own best interest.*
>
> *Structure is important, but it should not be imposed in such a way as to stifle creativity.*
>
> *The ideal society is one that allows for individual difference, but at the same time creates a people united in interest.*
>
> *All people have a right to live and die with dignity.*

These thoughts are so "nice" and "sensible" as to seem practically beyond challenge. Some students read them and think, "This must be right." Sometimes these kinds of statements do represent the correct answer. But at other times they don't. When you find yourself drawn to such an answer choice, you should check back with the question and ask yourself whether the answer choice is just a sweet and easy sentiment or whether it really *answers* the question you are asked.

For example, look at this prose fiction excerpt and consider the question that follows:

Too Nice
Don't automatically fall for answer choices that sound too "nice." Check to see if the statement was actually made in the passage. If not, eliminate that answer choice.

"And then the men!" said Jonathan, "the men coming aboard drunk, and having to be pounded sober!..." "Well, what can you do?" he went on. "If you don't strike, the men think you're afraid of them...." Jonathan Tinker was plainly part of the horrible tyranny that we all know exists on shipboard; and his listener respected him the more that, though he had heart enough to be ashamed of it, he was too honest not to own it.

1. Jonathan's listener respected him because he believed:

    A. [Already eliminated]
    B. Jonathan did not attempt to conceal his participation in maritime abuse.
    C. Jonathan had a good heart and basically cared for his men.
    D. [Already eliminated]

Here's How to Crack It

Look at (C). What could be more correct than a good heart and an honest concern for other people? Answer choice (C) is tempting, but it isn't right. Nice or not, the author does not state that the listener's respect for Jonathan had anything to do with a good heart or a concern for his men. Read the last two lines of the passage. The listener respected Jonathan because he had the honesty to "own" his acts. He acknowledged his participation in the tyranny.

Read this social studies excerpt.

The thought that older citizens might be denied health care on the basis of cost effectiveness is very troublesome and probably not acceptable to modern American society. Yet there is precedent for such policies in other westernized
5 nations. In Sweden, for example, where the overwhelming majority of health care is funded by the government, patients over the age of 55 are not eligible for long-term life-saving renal dialysis. The nation has made a decision to invest a certain amount of its resources in renal dialysis, and it does
10 not consider it sensible to provide the service to kidney patients over a certain age. Because Sweden is founded largely on egalitarian principles, a citizen over 55 is not permitted access to renal dialysis even if he is willing to pay for it on his own. The society does not believe that wealth should play a
15 role in longevity. Recently, the United States has inaugurated a number of systems aimed at controlling health care costs and avoiding waste. These include requirements that patients obtain a second opinion before undergoing surgery and utilize review systems aimed at shortening hospital stays. To date,
20 however, no agency or insurer in the United States premises its willingness to pay for health care on the age or the youth of the patient.

11. In Sweden, which of the following measures is designed to promote egalitarianism?

    A. [Already eliminated]
    B. The Swedish government denies certain life-saving medical resources to older citizens.
    C. [Already eliminated]
    D. The Swedish government attempts to provide the same health care to all citizens regardless of wealth or age.

Here's How to Crack It

Look at (D). Very, very attractive. What could be nicer than equal health care for all? But look at lines 5–15. In Sweden, we are told, citizens over 55 are denied access to renal dialysis. (D) is wrong, and (B) is right.

Summary

○ ACT test writers love distracting answers. They try to get you to you to pick one of their wrong answers by taking you off track.

○ Be careful of deceptive answers, switches, and extreme answer choices, as well as answers that are too good to be true.

○ Don't forget to always guess your Letter of the Day if there are questions that you can't answer or don't get to in time.

Chapter 18
The Four-Step System

The best way to beat the ACT system is to use a different one. The four-step system outlined in this chapter provides a way to look at the questions and passages methodically to maximize your points. Start by identifying any significant words in the questions. Scan the passage for these words, skim the passage and jot down notes, and then go back to the questions. We call this the loop.

Now that you've learned how to recognize right and wrong answer choices, we're going to teach you a four-step process that systematically leads you to the correct answers. We take time to explain each step slowly, so we can be sure you learn it. Because of that, you might at first think our system is lengthy or cumbersome. It isn't. It's streamlined and efficient. When we're all through, you'll see how speedily it works. (Think about how long it takes to tie a shoe. Now think about how long it would take to tell—not show—someone how to tie a shoe.)

We'll begin by answering the following simple question:

Why Are ACT Passages Hard to Follow?

You know how to read. So why is it so tough to read an ACT passage? It's tough, first of all, because the passage is pulled out of the middle of some larger work; you're reading it out of context. It's also tough to read an ACT passage because you don't know why you're reading it. You don't know what you're looking for or what you're supposed to "understand."

Stop thinking about the ACT for a second and suppose someone offers you a $20 per hour job. She points from her office window to a building sitting on a nearby lot. Then she hands you a key and says, "Check the place out and come back with a report."

That sounds easy enough, except for one thing.

You Don't Know What You're Looking For

What are you supposed to "check out?" The landscaping? The driveway? Are you looking for chipped paint? Leaky pipes? Broken windows?

You have no idea. So you roam around the place. An hour goes by and you roam back to your boss's office. She asks,

"Are there any mice in the basement?"

You tell her you don't know.

"In a whole hour you couldn't look in the basement and see if there were any mice?"

Of course you could have, but you didn't know she wanted you to. You had a simple job, and you blew it. Why? Because you never really knew what the job was. You didn't know what you were supposed to do.

The same sort of thing holds true for ACT reading passages. The passages are usually tough to read because you don't know what you're supposed to look for. They become much easier if you solve that problem. Having said that, we're ready to tell you about the first two steps of our system.

Step 1: Find the Lead Words and Phrases

Step 1 should take you about 30 seconds, and here's what it's all about. Before you read the passage, look at the questions (but not the answer choices) and underline any lead words they contain. Look, for instance, at the following question. (We'll help you ignore the answer choices by turning them all into "blah, blah, blah.")

> **11.** Jeremy Bentham probably would have said that lawyers:
>
> **A.** blah, blah, blah…
> **B.** blah, blah, blah…
> **C.** blah, blah, blah…
> **D.** blah, blah, blah…

The question has some pretty ordinary words like "probably," "would," "have," and "that." We might find those words in a lot of different questions. The lead words special to this question are "Jeremy Bentham" and "lawyers." So when we say "lead words," we mean the words, phrases, or names that stand out and tell you what the question's about. Look at this question and underline the lead words or phrases.

> **12.** The author states that the common law differs from the civil law in that:
>
> **F.** blah, blah, blah…
> **G.** blah, blah, blah…
> **H.** blah, blah, blah…
> **J.** blah, blah, blah…

There are of course some ordinary words like "author," "states," "from," "differs." This question's lead phrases are "common law" and "civil law."

Try three more.

> **21.** According to the passage, Peters differs from Jefferson in that:
>
> **A.** blah, blah, blah…
> **B.** blah, blah, blah…
> **C.** blah, blah, blah…
> **D.** blah, blah, blah…

> **22.** As discussed in the passage, the integrative movement produced:
>
> **F.** blah, blah, blah…
> **G.** blah, blah, blah…
> **H.** blah, blah, blah…
> **J.** blah, blah, blah…

33. According to the passage, edema and hypoproteinemia:

    A. blah, blah, blah…
    B. blah, blah, blah…
    C. blah, blah, blah…
    D. blah, blah, blah…

- In question 21, the lead words are "Peters" and "Jefferson."
- In question 22, the lead phrase is "integrative movement."
- In question 33, the lead words are "edema" and "hypoproteinemia."

By the way, when you find lead words, don't worry about their meaning. You don't have to know who Peters is or what *edema* means. Your job at step 1 is to see that some name, word, or phrase is the focus of a question. Its meaning doesn't matter.

Some Questions Don't Have Lead Words

When you follow step 1, you're going to notice that some questions don't really have any lead words. Look at these three.

1. It can be most reasonably inferred that the author believes that:

    A. blah, blah, blah…
    B. blah, blah, blah…
    C. blah, blah, blah…
    D. blah, blah, blah…

2. Which of the following conclusions is drawn by the passage?

    F. blah, blah, blah…
    G. blah, blah, blah…
    H. blah, blah, blah…
    J. blah, blah, blah…

3. The author's discussion would best support which of the following statements?

    A. blah, blah, blah…
    B. blah, blah, blah…
    C. blah, blah, blah…
    D. blah, blah, blah…

As you can see, none of these three questions offers any critical words. "Writer," "opinion," "support," and "conclusion" are pretty ordinary. We might find them in lots of different questions. What do you do with these questions when you're pursuing step 1? You ignore them. Among the ten questions that follow a passage, usually 8 or 9 will offer you lead words. Those are the questions you're looking for when you follow step 1.

Take a look at the following ten questions (we've deleted the answer choices completely). Figure out which five have lead words and which five do not. We will revisit these questions as we cover the various techniques for the Reading test.

21. Which of the following conclusions is drawn by the passage?

22. As discussed in the passage, Quentin Bell believes that historians and critics:

23. The author expresses the idea that:

24. According to the passage, academicism and mannerism:

25. It can be most reasonably inferred that the author believes that:

26. According to the passage, Renoir differs from Daleur in that:

27. According to the passage, Cezanne's work is characterized by:

28. According to the sixth paragraph, the author implies that:

29. In the author's view, the phrase "modern sculpture" means sculpture that:

30. According to the author, subjectivism affected Rodin in which of the following ways?

Questions 22, 24, 26, 27, 29, and 30 have lead words: "Quentin Bell," "academicism," "mannerism," "Renoir," "Daleur," "Cezanne," "modern art," "subjectivism." On the contrary, questions 21, 23, 25, and 28 are more general. They don't have lead words. If you were to encounter these ten questions while pursuing step 1, you'd focus on 22, 24, 26, 27, 29, and 30. You'd ignore 21, 23, 25, and 28.

Step 2: Scan the Passage for Lead Words

Step 2 of our system should take you about 30 seconds. In step 2, you *scan* the passage very quickly looking for the same lead words you noticed in step 1. You don't read the passage; you scan it. That means you pass your eyes over all of it, trying only to spot the lead words. Every time you see a lead word, underline it.

Here's part of the humanities passage followed by five of the questions we just reviewed with good lead words. We want you to

- First follow step 1: Look at the questions and notice the lead words.
- Then follow step 2: Scan the passage and underline those same lead words wherever you see them.

Refer Back to the Passage for the Lead Words
Now that you have identified the lead words in the question, you can look for them in the passage.

At step 2, you should also underline any words or phrases that seem to be very much like the lead words you find in the questions. For instance, if a question uses the phrase "modern art forms," and the phrase "modern styles of art" appears in the passage, you should underline it.

Rodin was surely a great artist, but he was not an innovator as was Cezanne; prevailing tides of subjectivism came over him. Rodin's mission was to reinvest sculpture with the integrity it lost when Michelangelo died. Rodin succeeded in this mission. His first true work, *The Age of Bronze* (1877), marked the beginning of the end of academicism, mannerism, and decadence that had prevailed since Michelangelo's last sculpture, the *Rondanini Pieta*.

Yet it is largely Cezanne, not Rodin, who was artistic ancestor to Picasso, Gonzalez, Brancusi, Archipenko, Lipchitz, and Laurens, and they are unquestionably the first lights in the "new art" of sculpture. This "new art," of course, is the sculpture we call "modern." It is modern because it breaks with tradition and draws little on that which preceded it.

When I speak of "modern" sculpture, I do not refer to every sculptor nor even to every highly talented sculptor of our age. I do not exclude, necessarily, the sculptors of an earlier time. Modern sculpture, as far as I am concerned, is any that consciously casts tradition aside and seeks forms more suitable to the senses and values of its time. Renoir and Daumier are, in this light, modern sculptors notwithstanding the earlier time at which they worked. Daleur and Carpeaux are not modern, although they belong chronologically to the recent era.

Professor Quentin Bell argues that historians and critics name as "modern" those sculptors in whom they happen to be interested and that the term when abused in that way has no historical or artistic significance. That, I think, is not right. The problem is that Professor Bell thinks "modern" means "now," when in fact it means "new."

22. As discussed in the passage, Quentin Bell believes that historians and critics:

   A. blah, blah, blah…
   B. blah, blah, blah…
   C. blah, blah, blah…
   D. blah, blah, blah…

24. According to the passage, academicism and mannerism:

   F. blah, blah, blah…
   G. blah, blah, blah…
   H. blah, blah, blah…
   J. blah, blah, blah…

26. According to the passage, Renoir differs from Daleur in that:

   A. blah, blah, blah…
   B. blah, blah, blah…
   C. blah, blah, blah…
   D. blah, blah, blah…

27. According to the passage, Cezanne's work is characterized by:

    A. a return to subjectivism.
    B. a pointless search for form.
    C. excessively personal expressions.
    D. rejection of the impressionistic philosophy.

29. In the author's view, the phrase "modern sculpture" means sculpture that:

    F. blah, blah, blah…
    G. blah, blah, blah…
    H. blah, blah, blah…
    J. blah, blah, blah…

30. According to the author, subjectivism affected Rodin in which of the following ways?

    A. blah, blah, blah…
    B. blah, blah, blah…
    C. blah, blah, blah…
    D. blah, blah, blah…

In the first question, you see the name Quentin Bell (whoever he is). In the second, you notice the words "academicism" and "mannerism" (whatever they mean). In question 26, the lead words are "Renoir" and "Daleur." In question 27, "Cezanne" is a great lead word. In question 29, the lead phrase is "modern sculpture." For question 30, you should notice the words "subjectivism" and "Rodin."

So Your Underlined Passage Should Look Something Like This

    Rodin was surely a great artist, but he was not an innovator as was Cezanne; prevailing tides of subjectivism came over him. Rodin's mission was to reinvest sculpture with the
50 integrity it lost when Michelangelo died. Rodin succeeded in this mission. His first true work, *The Age of Bronze* (1877), marked the beginning of the end of academicism, mannerism, and decadence that had prevailed since Michelangelo's last sculpture, the *Rondanini Pieta*.

55   Yet it is largely Cezanne, not Rodin, who was artistic ancestor to Picasso, Gonzalez, Brancusi, Archipenko, Lipchitz, and Laurens, and they are unquestionably the first lights in the "new art" of sculpture. This "new art," of course, is the sculpture we call "modern." It is modern because it breaks with tradition
60 and draws little on that which preceded it.

    When I speak of "modern" sculpture, I do not refer to every sculptor nor even to every highly talented sculptor of our age. I do not exclude, necessarily, the sculptors of an earlier time. Modern sculpture, as far as I am concerned, is
65 any that consciously casts tradition aside and seeks forms more suitable to the senses and values of its time. Renoir and Daumier are, in this light, modern sculptors notwithstanding the earlier time at which they worked. Daleur and Carpeaux are not modern, although they belong chronologically to the
70 recent era.

Professor <u>Quentin Bell</u> argues that historians and critics name as "<u>modern</u>" those sculptors in whom they happen to be interested and that the term when abused in that way has no historical or artistic significance. That, I think, is not right. The problem is that Professor <u>Bell</u> thinks "<u>modern</u>" means "now," when in fact it means "new."

Let's Do It Again

Here's another short passage followed by four questions. Follow steps 1 and 2 just as you did before.

Such relatively reliable insights as we have into the nature of Halley's comet's nucleus derive largely from the work done by the Giotto imaging team. Named for the spacecraft from which six key photographs of the comet were taken at distances ranging from 14,430 to 2,730 kilometers, the team forged a single composite photograph under the directorship of H. Use Keler. As the photograph is normally held, north is up and the sun is at the left.

Discernibility of detail varies at different points in the photograph. The greatest resolution, 100 meters, is found in the upper left portion of the image and the poorest resolution, 400 meters, is found at the lower right. This circumstance and other of the photograph's features largely reflect the "instructions" that were given to the Giotto camera, which had been systematically programmed to track the brightest feature in its visual field. This, for example, explains why the greatest detail in the composite photograph is of the nucleus's uppermost aspect; it was photographed when the comet was closest to Giotto.

The Giotto photographs have allowed investigators to conclude that the surface of the nucleus is rough. This conclusion emanates from the observation that the border area between light and dark portions of the comet is irregular. In addition, the light side reveals a large crater and a hill. The most noticeable of the comet's features relate to the movement of dust away from selected portions of the comet's nucleus toward the sun. The resulting dust jets are brightly colored and likely arise from points and places that lack surface crust, which then would expose the deeper lying ices to the sun.

35. According to the passage, the nuclear surface of Halley's comet is believed to be:

    A. blah, blah, blah…
    B. blah, blah, blah…
    C. blah, blah, blah…
    D. blah, blah, blah…

36. As described in the passage, Giotto's camera was specifically programmed to:

    F. blah, blah, blah…
    G. blah, blah, blah…
    H. blah, blah, blah…
    J. blah, blah, blah…

37. As used in the passage, the word *resolution* (line 11) means:

    A. blah, blah, blah…
    B. blah, blah, blah…
    C. blah, blah, blah…
    D. blah, blah, blah…

38. The passage indicates that H. Use Keler:

    F. blah, blah, blah…
    G. blah, blah, blah…
    H. blah, blah, blah…
    J. blah, blah, blah…

For question 35, the lead phrases are "Halley's comet" and "nuclear surface." For question 36, it's "Giotto's camera." For question 37, it's "resolution." For question 38, it's "H. Use Keler."

Your Underlined Passage Should Look Something Like This

Such relatively reliable insights as we have into the nature of Halley's comet's nucleus derive largely from the work done by the Giotto imaging team. Named for the spacecraft from which six key photographs of the comet were taken at
5 distances ranging from 14,430 to 2,730 kilometers, the team forged a single composite photograph under the directorship of H. Use Keler. As the photograph is normally held, north is up and the sun is at the left.

Discernibility of detail varies at different points in the
10 photograph. The greatest resolution, 100 meters, is found in the upper left portion of the image and the poorest resolution, 400 meters, is found at the lower right. This circumstance and other of the photograph's features largely reflect the "instructions" that were given to the Giotto camera, which
15 had been systematically programmed to track the brightest feature in its visual field. This, for example, explains why the greatest detail in the composite photograph is of the nucleus's uppermost aspect; it was photographed when the comet was closest to Giotto.

20 The Giotto photographs have allowed investigators to conclude that the surface of the nucleus is rough. This conclusion emanates from the observation that the border area between light and dark portions of the comet is irregular. In addition, the light side reveals a large crater and a hill. The
25 most noticeable of the comet's features relate to the movement of dust away from selected portions of the comet's nucleus toward the sun. The resulting dust jets are brightly colored and likely arise from points and places that lack surface crust, which then would expose the deeper lying
30 ices to the sun.

How Steps 1 and 2 Help You

If you were actually to read a passage from beginning to end, you'd never know, as you read, which words or lines you're supposed to understand. Furthermore, when you then went to look at questions about Renoir, H. Use Keler, or the Giotto camera, you'd have to start hunting through the passage to find those words and to figure out what they're all about. By following steps 1 and 2, you help yourself in two important ways.

1. You avoid wasting time trying to read and comprehend the whole passage.
2. You identify those places in the passage likely to provide answers to the questions you're going to be asked. It's *those* portions of the passage that you'll read carefully when the time comes to answer questions.

Here's What We Mean

Below is a small piece of the sculpture passage with our underlining in it. There's also a question you've seen before, except this time it has answer choices. Read the question carefully and look at the answer choices. Then take a look back at the sentence and read *it* very carefully. Think about what it means and figure out which answer choice expresses the same thing—in camouflage. That's the right answer.

> Professor Quentin Bell argues that historians and critics name as "modern" those sculptors in whom they happen to be interested and that the term when abused in that way has no historical or artistic significance.

22. As discussed in the passage, Quentin Bell believes that historians and critics:

    A. should be open-minded to new and innovative art forms.
    B. misuse art and fail to understand its history.
    C. are generally uninterested in modern art.
    D. attach the phrase "modern art" to those sculptors that intrigue them.

The correct answer to this question is (D), and reading the whole passage definitely would *not* help you answer it any more quickly or accurately. The answer is wholly contained in a single sentence. The author says that Professor Quentin Bell (whoever he is) thinks historians and critics give the name "modern" to the sculptors in whom they happen to be interested. Choice (D) expresses that same thought—in camouflage.

You Won't *Always* Find the Answer in a Single Sentence

When you're looking for an answer, you might have to go to the underlined words and "read around" a little. You might have to read the sentences that appear immediately before and after the one that has your mark. Sometimes you'll have to read a whole paragraph.

Here again is the short passage about comets. It's followed by two questions you've already seen, except this time they have answer choices. Follow steps 1 and 2, and then answer the questions.

Such relatively reliable insights as we have into the nature of Halley's comet's nucleus derive largely from the work done by the Giotto imaging team. Named for the spacecraft from which six key photographs of the comet were taken at
5 distances ranging from 14,430 to 2,730 kilometers, the team forged a single composite photograph under the directorship of H. Use Keler. As the photograph is normally held, north is up and the sun is at the left.

Discernibility of detail varies at different points in the
10 photograph. The greatest resolution, 100 meters, is found in the upper left portion of the image and the poorest resolution, 400 meters, is found at the lower right. This circumstance and other of the photograph's features largely reflect the "instructions" that were given to the Giotto camera, which
15 had been systematically programmed to track the brightest feature in its visual field. This, for example, explains why the greatest detail in the composite photograph is of the nucleus's uppermost aspect; it was photographed when the comet was closest to Giotto.

20 The Giotto photographs have allowed investigators to conclude that the surface of the nucleus is rough. This conclusion emanates from the observation that the border area between light and dark portions of the comet is irregular. In addition, the light side reveals a large crater and a hill. The
25 most noticeable of the comet's features relate to the movement of dust away from selected portions of the comet's nucleus toward the sun. The resulting dust jets are brightly colored and likely arise from points and places that lack surface crust, which then would expose the deeper lying ices
30 to the sun.

31. According to the passage, the nuclear surface of Halley's comet is believed to be:

A. smooth, because the interface of light and dark shows high resolution.

B. rough, because a visible border area is irregularly shaped.

C. smooth at some points and rough at others, depending on the relative degrees of light and dark.

D. undetectable, because even the most sophisticated instruments have limitations.

Reminder
Underline key words or phrases that resemble the critical words in the question. If you don't find the answer, read the sentences surrounding the underlined portion of the passage.

32. As described in the passage, the Giotto camera was specifically programmed to:

    F. send "instructions" to Halley's comet regarding detail and resolution.

    G. identify the portions of the comet that had relatively low light intensity.

    H. detect areas of Halley's comet that bordered on light and dark.

    J. photograph those areas of Halley's comet that gave off the most light.

Here's How to Crack It

The first question concerns the "nuclear surface" of "Halley's comet." That precise phrase does not appear in the passage, but the phrase "surface of the nucleus" shows up on line 21. That sentence and the one immediately following it give you the answer to the first question.

> The Giotto photographs have allowed investigators to conclude that the surface of the nucleus is rough. This conclusion emanates from the observation that the border area between light and dark portions of the comet is irregular.

These two sentences are telling you that Halley's comet has light and dark areas and that the border between these areas is irregular. When scientists noticed this they concluded that the surface of the nucleus was rough. You don't have to understand *why* that observation led to that conclusion. You just have to realize that these two sentences are telling you it did. Once you realize that, you know that the correct answer is (B).

The second question refers to "the Giotto camera." So when we first scanned the passage, we underlined the word "Giotto" everywhere it appeared. Look at the sentence that specifically mentions the "Giotto camera." What does it say?

> This circumstance and other of the photograph's features largely reflect the "instructions" that were given to the Giotto camera, which had been systematically programmed to track the brightest feature in its visual field.

The Giotto camera was systematically programmed to track the brightest feature in its visual field. Among the answer options, (J) is best. "Brightest feature" is camouflage for "areas…that gave off the most light."

Step 3: Skim and Scribble

Step 3 should take you about 60 seconds. In step 3, you skim the passage, and in the margin of each paragraph, you scribble a few words that describe its main idea. When we say "skim," we mean you should read fast—so fast that you're uncomfortable and not at all sure you comprehend the passage in detail. (Remember, you're not trying to understand the passage. You're trying to earn a high score on the ACT.) As you speed through each paragraph, you should

- direct a little more attention to the first two sentences than to the remainder
- ask yourself, "What, basically, is this paragraph about?"

Then, in two or three words, scribble an answer in the margin. Here are three paragraphs from a humanities passage. Let's skim and scribble.

artist > period

    If we were to start fresh in the study of sculpture or any art, we might observe that the record is largely filled by works of relatively few great contributors. Next to the influences of these great geniuses, time periods themselves are of little significance. The study of art and art history are properly directed to the achievements of outstanding individual artists, not the particular decades or centuries in which any may have worked.

movements

    Nonetheless, when we study art in historical perspective we select a convenient frame of reference through which diverse styles and talents are to be compared. Hence we write of "movements" and attempt to understand each artist in terms of the one to which he "belongs." Movements have limited use, but we should not talk of realism, impressionism, cubism, or surrealism as though they genuinely had lives of their own to which the artist was answerable. We regard the movement as the governing force and the artist as its servant. Yet it is well to remember that the movements do not necessarily present themselves in orderly chronological series and the individual artist frequently weaves her way into one and out of another over the course of a single career.

artist switch styles

    Great artists are not normally confined by the "movements" that others may name for them. Rather, they transcend the conventional structure working now in one style, then in another, and later in a third. Picasso's work, for example, echoes many of the artistic movements, and other artists, too, moving from one style through another. Indeed, artists are people, and any may decide to alter her style for no more complex a reason than that which makes most people want to "try something new" once in a while.

Skim the Passage
As you read the passage, underline key phrases in the passage or jot down notes next to each paragraph. Don't try to memorize information in the passage, just know the lay of the land.

Paragraph 1

The first paragraph seems to be about the fact that individual artists are more important than the time periods in which they work.

artist > periods

That's enough.

Paragraph 2

The second paragraph has something to do with artistic "movements." What should you scribble?

movements

Paragraph 3

The third paragraph tells us that great artists don't really conform to movements. They vary their styles over time. So for paragraph 3, you scribble

artists switch styles

Enough said, and enough scribbled.

With enough practice, skim and scribble should take you about one minute per passage.

Use Trigger Words

When you're skimming a passage, pay attention to words that signal a change in direction. In line 1 of the second paragraph, for instance, we see the word "nonetheless," which means the author is about to criticize, negate, or "take something away" from thoughts previously expressed. "Nonetheless" is what we call a *trigger word*. Trigger words tell you the author is about to "go somewhere," and you should watch where he's going. Sometimes a trigger word means the author is reaching some sort of conclusion (*therefore, hence*).

Trigger words help you figure out what a paragraph is all about. The "nonetheless" at the beginning of the second paragraph indicates that the author's going to say something that opposes what he said in the first paragraph. He says there's some purpose in thinking of art in terms of "movements," even though he has already said the individual artist is more important than the time periods in which they work.

> ### Look for Trigger Words
> Here are 15 trigger words and/or phrases:
> - *Despite* • *However* • *In spite of*
> - *Nonetheless* • *On the other hand*
> - *On the contrary* • *Yet* • *Notwithstanding* • *But* • *Ironically* • *Rather*
> - *Unfortunately* • *Therefore* • *Hence*
> - *Consequently*

Try Another Skim and Scribble

Here are four paragraphs from the comet passage. Skim and scribble. See if you can do it in one minute.

On the other hand, the Giotto photographs reveal virtually nothing of the interior of the comet's nucleus or its rotational period. For instance, it is not known, even, whether the interior of the nucleus had a density greater than or less than 1 gram per cubic centimeter, which is the density of water. Hans Rickman attempted to estimate the comet's density, hoping, with good reason, that this information would ultimately lead to better understanding of the nuclear interior. Rickman recognized that if he could gain estimates of the comet's mass and volume he would be able to derive an estimate of density from the simple physical formulas relating mass, volume, and density: He would divide the volume into the mass and arrive at an estimate.

The comet's overall dimensions were already known to an approximation, and on this basis Rickman took the volume as 500–550 cubic kilometers. He then employed a rather ingenious method of estimating the nuclear mass. Rickman considered the fact that the comet was losing gas at all times and that the expulsion produced a thrust. He then reasoned, according to simple law, that mass times the thrust due to expelled gas had to equal the product [rate at which mass was lost by expulsion of gas and dust] and the velocity of the expelled substance. Rickman then derived estimates of these values from the comet's motion and from the rate at which the comet visibly produced water. Rickman arrived at a value of 0.1 to 0.3 grams per cubic centimeter for the density of Halley's nucleus.

Using an analogous technique, R. Z. Sagdeev and colleagues arrived at a value of 0.2 to 1.5 grams per cubic centimeter. Stanton J. Peale, however, wrote that he had little confidence in the estimates of mass and volume that had been used in connection with the density calculations. He believed that little could be said about the nuclear density except that it was approximately equal to 1 gram per cubic centimeter.

Zdenek Sekanina and Stephen M. Larson studied the rotational period by first processing images of 1920 photographs in an attempt to improve the image of spiral dust features. They assumed that the spiral dust characteristics were caused by emission from distinct parts of the nuclear surface and that these areas were visible when rotation brought them into sunlight and were invisible in the dark of the cometary night. On these premises, the pair estimated that Halley has a rotation period of 2.2 days, and some spacecraft data have seemed to confirm the figure. However, Robert L. Millis and David G. Schleicher estimated a rotational period of 7.4 days by resorting to filters that allowed them to explore fluorescence of CN, C, and C_2 emissions and the continuum emission from dust particles. Other investigators have reported additional approximations of Halley's rotational period but the issue remains, for the time being, clouded.

Look for Trigger Words

What are trigger words? Trigger words are words that signal a change in a sentence. Some of the most common trigger words are *but*, *although*, *despite*, and *however*.

The first paragraph has something to do with the inside of the comet. Maybe it's about density, too. So we scribble

interior, density

The second paragraph seems to provide details about what someone named Rickman did to calculate the density of the comet's interior.

Rickman, details, density

The third paragraph concerns what other scientists said and did in response to Rickman's work.

other people

The last paragraph has something to do with calculating the comet's rotational period.

rotational period

So that's what we're talking about. It doesn't take long. Steps 1 through 3 together should take maybe one and a half to two minutes.

After Steps 1, 2, and 3

After you've spent about two minutes completing the three steps, go back to the questions.

The entire humanities passage about modern sculpture is on the next page. It's underlined and scribbled, and it includes ten questions. Even though we've already completed steps 1 to 3 for you, you should run through them again yourself so you're familiar with the underlining and scribbling. After you do that, we'll discuss step 4, which is called "practice the loop."

> ### Our Steps So Far
> - **Step 1—Notice Critical Words:** Look quickly at the questions. Notice critical words. Ignore questions that don't have critical words.
>   *Approximate Time*: 30 seconds
> - **Step 2—Scan and Underline:** Scan the passage and underline critical words.
>   *Approximate Time*: 30 seconds
> - **Step 3—Skim and Scribble:** Read the passage at racing speed, giving special attention to the first two or three sentences of each paragraph. For each paragraph, scribble in the margin a few words that describe the main subject.
>   *Approximate Time*: 60 seconds

If we were to start fresh in the study of sculpture or any art we might observe that the record is largely filled by works of relatively few great contributors. Next to the influences of these great geniuses, time periods themselves are of little significance. The study of art and art history are properly directed to the achievements of outstanding individual artists, not the particular decades or centuries in which any may have worked.

Nonetheless, when we study art in historical perspective we select a convenient frame of reference through which diverse styles and talents are to be compared. Hence we write of "movements" and attempt to understand each artist in terms of the one to which he "belongs." Movements have limited use, but we should not talk of realism, impressionism, cubism, or surrealism as though they genuinely had lives of their own to which the artist was answerable. We regard the movement as the governing force and the artist as its servant. Yet it is well to remember that the movements do not necessarily present themselves in orderly chronological series and the individual artist frequently weaves her way into one and out of another over the course of a single career.

Great artists are not normally confined by the "movements" that others may name for them. Rather, they transcend the conventional structure working now in one style, then in another, and later in a third. Picasso's work, for example, echoes many of the artistic movements, and other artists too, moving way from one style through another. Indeed, artists are people, and any may decide to alter her style for no more complex a reason than that which makes most people want to "try something new" once in a while.

In studying modern sculpture one is tempted to begin a history with Auguste Rodin (1840–1917), who was a contemporary of Cezanne. Yet the two artists did not, in artistic terms, belong to the same period. Their strategies and objectives differed. Although Rodin was surely a great artist, he did not do for sculpture what Cezanne did for painting. In fact, although Cezanne was a painter, he had a more lasting effect on sculpture than did Rodin.

Cezanne's work constitutes a reaction against impressionism and the confusion he thought it created. He searched persistently for the "motif." Cezanne strived for clarity of form and was able to convert his personal perceptions into concrete, recognizable substance. He is justly considered to have offered the first glimmer of a new art—a new classicism.

Rodin was surely a great artist, but he was not an innovator as was Cezanne; prevailing tides of subjectivism came over him. Rodin's mission was to reinvest sculpture with the integrity it lost when Michelangelo died. Rodin succeeded in this mission. His first true work, *The Age of Bronze* (1877), marked the beginning of the end of academicism, mannerism, and decadence that had prevailed since Michelangelo's last sculpture, the *Rondanini Pieta*.

artist > period

movements

artists
switch
styles

Rodin
and
Cezanne

Cezanne
vs.
Impressionism

Rodin
not
innovator;
recalled
Michelangelo

Cezanne
influenced
"modern"
sculpture

"modern"
does not
necessarily
mean
"recent"

Bell wrong;
"modern" ≠
now
"modern" =
new

55   Yet it is largely Cezanne, not Rodin, who was artistic ancestor to Picasso, Gonzalez, Brancusi, Archipenko, Lipchitz,
and Laurens, and they are unquestionably the first lights in
the "new art" of sculpture. This "new art," of course, is the
sculpture we call "modern." It is modern because it breaks
60 with tradition and draws little on that which preceded it.

When I speak of "modern" sculpture, I do not refer to
every sculptor nor even to every highly talented sculptor of
our age. I do not exclude, necessarily, the sculptors of an
earlier time. Modern sculpture, as far as I am concerned, is
65 any that consciously casts tradition aside and seeks forms
more suitable to the senses and values of its time. Renoir and
Daumier are, in this light, modern sculptors notwithstanding
the earlier time at which they worked. Daleur and Carpeaux
are not modern, although they belong chronologically to the
70 recent era.

Professor Quentin Bell argues that historians and critics
name as "modern" those sculptors in whom they happen to
be interested and that the term when abused in that way has
no historical or artistic significance. That, I think, is not right.
75 The problem is that Professor Bell thinks "modern" means
"now," when in fact it means "new."

21. Which of the following conclusions is drawn by the passage?

   A. Cezanne had greater influence on modern sculp-
      ture than did Rodin.
   B. Rodin made no significant contribution to modern
      sculpture.
   C. Daumier should not be considered a modern sculp-
      tor.
   D. Carpeaux should be considered a modern sculptor.

22. As discussed in the passage, Quentin Bell believes that
    historians and critics:

   F. have no appreciation for the value of modern art.
   G. abuse art and its history.
   H. should evaluate works of art on the basis of their
      merit without regard to the artist's fame.
   J. attach the phrase "modern art" to those sculptors
      that intrigue them.

23. The author expresses the idea that:

   A. art should never be studied in terms of movements.
   B. true artists are seldom understandable in terms of a
      single movement.
   C. lesser artists do not usually vary their styles.
   D. great artists are always nonconformists.

24. According to the passage, academicism and mannerism:

    F. were readily visible in Rodin's earliest work.

    G. are partially manifest in the *Rondanini Pieta*.

    H. characterized the work of artists who followed Michelangelo.

    J. were primarily part of the Bronze Age.

25. It can be most reasonably inferred that the author believes that:

    A. Rodin was more innovative than Cezanne.

    B. Cezanne was more innovative than Rodin.

    C. Modern art is more important than classical art.

    D. Cezanne tried to emulate impressionism.

26. According to the passage, Renoir differs from Daleur in that:

    F. Daleur had no inspiration and Renoir was tremendously inspired.

    G. Renoir's work was highly innovative and Daleur's was not.

    H. Daleur was a sculptor and Renoir was not.

    J. Renoir revered tradition and Daleur did not.

27. According to the passage, Cezanne's work is characterized by:

    A. a return to subjectivism.

    B. a pointless search for form.

    C. excessively personal expressions.

    D. rejection of the impressionistic philosophy.

28. According to the sixth paragraph, the author implies that:

    F. mannerism reflects a lack of integrity.

    G. Rodin disliked the work of Michelangelo.

    H. Rodin embraced the notion of decadence.

    J. Rodin should have resisted the appeal of subjectivism.

29. In the author's view, the phrase "modern sculpture" means sculpture that:

    A. postdates the *Rondanini Pieta*.

    B. is not significantly tied to work that comes before it.

    C. shows no artistic merit.

    D. genuinely interests contemporary critics.

30. According to the author, subjectivism affected Rodin in which of the following ways?

    F. It ended his affiliation with mannerism.

    G. It caused him to lose his artistic integrity.

    H. It limited his ability to innovate.

    J. It caused him to become decadent.

Questions That Point

With the passage underlined and scribbled, go back to the questions, but don't go necessarily to question 21. Go first to the questions that point you to an answer. Look at questions 21–30 on the last passage. Questions 22, 24, 26, 27, 28, 29, and 30 point to the answer. Questions 22, 24, 26, 27, 29, and 30 have lead words. For those questions, we've already underlined the relevant sections of the passage and we know where to look.

- Question 28 sends us directly to the relevant paragraph.
- Questions 21, 23, and 25 don't point anywhere. We'll save them for last.

Now we're ready to answer questions.

Step 4: Practice the Loop

Step 4 should take you about 40 seconds per question if you're trying to finish all 4 passages.

- Go to the first question that points to an answer. Read it carefully. If it's relatively clear, make sure you remember the question before you go back to the passage. If the question is confusing, reword it so that you know what you're looking for.
- Return to the appropriate portion of the passage (either you've underlined it or the question sends you there).
- Read it carefully. Whenever possible, try to formulate your own answer to the question and jot it down.
- Go back to the question and pick the answer choice that most resembles your answer.

Now suppose something strikes you as correct. Be suspicious. Ask yourself if you're falling for a deceptive answer, a switch, or something too "nice." If you consider those possibilities and still think the answer is right, choose it and go to the next question.

Now suppose you're uncertain about the answer and when you come back to the question, nothing strikes you as right. Fine. Try to eliminate answers that are wrong. Look for a deceptive answer, a switch, an extreme statement, and eliminate it. (In the process, the right answer might strike you, in which case you'll choose it and move on.)

If you don't settle on an answer, take a second pass through the loop.

Practice the Loop
Once you've practiced using these techniques, you can put them together and form "the loop." Read the question, go to the passage, underline the appropriate words or phrases that relate to the question, and then go to the answer choices. As you read each answer choice, watch out for the distracters. If you're stuck, then take another pass through the loop.

- Come back to the question. Sometimes you've missed a clue in the question.
- Go back to the appropriate portion of the passage.
- Read it again. Understand it as best you can.
- Look at the choices that still remain (some were eliminated a few seconds earlier, during your first pass through the loop).

If one of the choices now strikes you as correct, choose it. If nothing strikes you as correct, see if you can eliminate it, and then guess among whatever answer choices remain.

We'll start with question 22 because question 21 doesn't point.

---

22. As discussed in the passage, Quentin Bell believes that historians and critics:

    F. have no appreciation for the value of modern art.
    G. abuse art and its history.
    H. should evaluate works of art on the basis of their merit without regard to the artist's fame.
    J. attach the phrase "modern art" to those sculptors that intrigue them.

Here's How to Crack It

We go to the relevant part of the passage, which we've already underlined.

> Professor <u>Quentin Bell</u> argues that historians and critics name as "<u>modern</u>" those sculptors in whom they happen to be interested and that the term when abused in that way has no historical or artistic significance.

- Read it carefully and try to understand it. Formulate an answer in your own words and write it down.
- Go back to the question and pick the answer choice that best matches what you came up with on your own.

In this case, one might easily answer this question by saying that Professor Bell argued that historians and critics use the word "modern" to describe anything in which they happen to be interested. Hey, that sounds a lot like (J), and thus, (J) is the correct response.

Suppose, however, that you couldn't come up with an answer of your own. Don't panic. Just start eliminating answer choices that are wrong. Answer choice (F) is an extreme statement ("no" appreciation). Eliminate it.

Choice (H) is very "nice" and very irrelevant. Eliminate it.

You're left with (G) and (J), but you're not sure which is right.

So take a second pass through the loop.

- Go back to the relevant part of the passage and read it again.
- Return to the question and try to choose again between choices (G) and (J).

Still not sure? Try to eliminate one of the choices. Answer choice (G) is a deceptive answer. (The author uses the word *abuse* but doesn't say that anyone abuses art or its history.) Eliminate (G). That leaves (J), so that's the answer you choose.

Altogether, you've spent 30 to 50 seconds answering question 22.

***

Use the loop to answer question 24.

***

24. According to the passage, academicism and mannerism:

- **F.** were readily visible in Rodin's first true work.
- **G.** are partially manifest in the *Rondanini Pieta*.
- **H.** characterized the work of artists who followed Michelangelo.
- **J.** were primarily part of the Bronze Age.

Here's How to Crack It

Go to the pertinent part of the passage.

> Rodin was surely a great artist, but he was not an innovator as was Cezanne; prevailing tides of subjectivism came over him. Rodin's mission was to reinvest sculpture with the integrity it lost when Michelangelo died. Rodin succeeded in this mission. His first true work, *The Age of Bronze* (1877), marked the beginning of the end of academicism, mannerism, and decadence that had prevailed since Michelangelo's last sculpture, the *Rondanini Pieta*.

- Read it carefully and try to answer it yourself. Jot down your answer.
- Go back to the question and find the answer choice that best matches what you jotted down.

Maybe you're not sure of the answer, but you realize that (F) and (J) are deceptive answers and eliminate them. You're left with (G) and (H).

Now you take a second pass through the loop.

- Read the question again. Any new insight?
- Go back to the relevant part of the passage and read it again.
- Return to the question.

The last sentence tells us that academicism, mannerism, and decadence were around *since Michelangelo produced his last sculpture*. Answer choice (H) says the same thing—in camouflage. Choose (H) and move on.

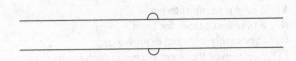

26. According to the passage, Renoir differs from Daleur in that:

   F. Daleur had no inspiration and Renoir was tremendously inspired.
   G. Renoir's work was highly innovative and Daleur's was not.
   H. Daleur was a sculptor and Renoir was not.
   J. Renoir revered tradition and Daleur did not.

Here's How to Crack It
Read the important part of the passage carefully.

> When I speak of "modern" sculpture, I do not refer to every sculptor nor even to every highly talented sculptor of our age. I do not exclude, necessarily, the sculptors of an earlier time. Modern sculpture, as far as I am concerned, is any that consciously casts tradition aside and seeks forms more suitable to the senses and values of its time. Renoir and Daumier are, in this light, modern sculptors notwithstanding the earlier time at which they worked. Daleur and Carpeaux are not modern although they belong chronologically to the recent era.

- First, try to answer the question yourself. This one's fairly easy to answer on your own. The author clearly states that he views Renoir as modern and Daleur as not modern. Thus, (G) is the correct response.
- If you couldn't come up with your own answer, start eliminating bad answer choices.
- Choice (F) is a statement in the extreme. Eliminate it.
- Choice (H) is a switch. (The passage tells you that "Renoir and Daumier are modern sculptors." That means Renoir was a sculptor.) Eliminate it.
- Take a second pass. The author writes that modern sculpture is any that "casts tradition aside…." Then he writes that Renoir is a modern sculptor and Daleur is not. That means Renoir casts tradition aside and Daleur does not. Choice (G) says the same thing in camouflage, so (G) is right. ((J) is a deceptive answer.)

Now use the loop to answer questions 27 to 30. When you're done, you can read on and compare your reasoning with ours.

--------◯--------

27. According to the passage, Cezanne's work is characterized by:

A. a return to subjectivism.
B. a pointless search for form.
C. excessively personal expressions.
D. rejection of the impressionistic philosophy.

Here's How to Crack It

Go to the pertinent part of the passage.

> Cezanne's work constitutes a reaction against impressionism and the confusion he thought it created. He searched persistently for the "motif." Cezanne strived for clarity of form and was able to convert his personal perceptions into concrete, recognizable substance. He is justly considered to have offered the first glimmer of a new art—a new classicism.

- What does the passage tell us? Well, it says that Cezanne rejected impressionism and created a new style called "new classicism." That sounds a lot like (D).
- Not sure? Let's look at the other answer choices and see what we can eliminate.
- Answer choice (B) is extreme (and ridiculous). Eliminate it. With our eye on (A), (C), and (D), we take a second pass. The first sentence tells us that Cezanne reacted against impressionism. Choice (D) says the same thing—in camouflage.

Question 28: (J) is right.

- Choices (F), (G), and (H) are deceptive answers.

Question 29: (B) is right.

- Choices (A) and (D) are deceptive answers. (C) is a statement in the extreme.

Question 30: (H) is right.

- Choices (F), (G), and (J) are deceptive answers.

--------◯--------

What If You *Can't* Settle on an Answer?

Simple. You guess. If you've taken two (or maybe three) passes through the loop and you still can't decide on an answer, look at the choices still remaining, take a guess, and move on. Remember: Having eliminated one or two choices, you've raised the odds that your guess will be right.

Three More Examples

We held questions 21, 23, and 25 for last because they don't point. Now it's time to answer them. For questions that don't point, you

- use the answer choices to tell you what the question is about
- use your scribbles to get you to the right part of the passage

---

Here are the answer choices for question 21.

- **A.** Cezanne had greater influence on modern sculpture than did Rodin.
- **B.** Rodin made no significant contribution to modern sculpture.
- **C.** Daumier should not be considered a modern sculptor.
- **D.** Carpeaux should be considered a modern sculptor.

Apparently, this question has a lot to do with the phrase "modern sculpture."

For Paragraph 8, we scribbled

"modern" does not necessarily mean "recent"

So you go to Paragraph 8. From there on, you follow the loop.

The correct answer is (A).

- Answer choice (B) is extreme.
- Answer choices (C) and (D) are both switches.

Let's look at question 23. Here are the answer choices.

- **A.** art should never be studied in terms of movements.
- **B.** true artists are seldom understandable in terms of a single movement.
- **C.** lesser artists do not usually vary their styles.
- **D.** great artists are always nonconformists.

High School, Sophomore Year

- Stay focused on your studies. If you didn't earn strong grades during your freshman year, start doing so this year.
- Choose one or more extracurricular activities that interest you. But don't overload your schedule with activities...colleges would much rather see you focus on a few worthwhile extracurriculars than divide your time among a bunch of different activities that you're not passionate about.
- Scope out the Advanced Placement course offerings at your school. You'll want to sign up for as many AP courses as you can reasonably take, starting in your junior year.

Source: *Best 368 Colleges*, 2009 Edition

Apparently, the question has something to do with movements and style. It calls our attention to Paragraphs 2 and 3 where we scribbled

(2) *movements*

(3) *artists switch styles*

It turns out that the answer is in Paragraph 3. It's (B).

- Answer choices (A) and (D) are extreme.
- Answer choice (C) is a distortion.

Lastly, look at question 25. Here are the answer choices.

    A. Rodin was more innovative than Cezanne.
    B. Cezanne was more innovative than Rodin.
    C. Modern art is more important than classical art.
    D. Cezanne tried to emulate impressionism.

This question appears to be focusing on the differences between Rodin and Cezanne.

For Paragraph 6, we scribbled

Rodin not innovator

Read Paragraph 6 again. From there on, follow the loop. The best answer is (B).

- (A) is the switch.
- (C) and (D) are deceptive answers.

Steps 1–4
Step 1—Find the Critical Words
Approximate Time: 30 seconds
Step 2—Scan the Passage for Critical Words
Approximate Time: 30 seconds
Step 3—Skim and Scribble
Approximate Time: 60 seconds
Step 4—Practice the Loop
Approximate Time: 40 seconds per question

Special Question Type: State of Mind

When you take the ACT, you'll probably get a few questions that ask you to describe attitudes or states of mind. Often, the answer choices are just one word.

Some Question Types Do Not Require You to Go Through the Loop
Why? The answer is not found in the passage. These question types are: Fact vs. Opinion, State of Mind, Vocab-in-Context, Except/Not/Least, and Roman Numeral

    1. The author's attitude toward…blah, blah, blah…is best described as:

        A. skeptical.
        B. approving.
        C. concerned.
        D. hopeful.

In a literature passage, these questions pertain not to the author, but to some character. Read this final paragraph of a prose fiction passage and look at the question that follows it.

So they parted with a shake of the hand, Jonathan Tinker saying that he believed he should go down to the vessel and sleep aboard, if he could sleep, and murmuring at the last moment the hope of returning the compliment, while the contributor walked homeward, weary to the flesh, but, in spite of his sympathy for Jonathan Tinker, very elated in spirit. The truth is, and however disgraceful to human nature, let the truth be told, he had recurred to his primal satisfaction in the man as calamity capable of being used for such and such literary ends, and, while he pitied him, rejoiced in him as an episode of real life quite as striking and complete as anything in fiction.

1. As final response to his conversation with Jonathan Tinker, the contributor experienced a feeling of

   A. worry.
   B. amusement.
   C. gratification.
   D. disappointment.

Here's How to Crack It

If this kind of item throws you, it's probably because you start thinking about the distracters and lose sight of the question.

- Think about the person and the situation about which you're being asked.
- Turn the item into four true/false questions by saying to yourself:
  TRUE/FALSE "This guy was _____."
  Then fill in the blank with each of the answer choices.
- When you hit a statement that's true, you've got the ACT answer.

Let's try it.

- We think about the contributor as he is described in the last paragraph, and we say to ourselves (very quickly):
  TRUE/FALSE "This guy was <u>worried</u>."
  TRUE/FALSE "This guy was <u>amused</u>."
  TRUE/FALSE "This guy was <u>gratified</u>."
  TRUE/FALSE "This guy was <u>disappointed</u>."

Answer choices (A), (B), and (D) yield statements that sound false. There's nothing in the paragraph to suggest that this guy was worried or disappointed, and he's not particularly amused, either. (He didn't, for example, "chuckle," or "grin.") The paragraph tells us that the contributor experiences "satisfaction" and that he "rejoices." Answer choice (C) yields a statement that seems true.

Many decisions of the United States Supreme Court are inconsistent with the precedents by which they are theoretically balanced. It is true that the court has some freedom to overrule its own precedents, but in such cases it is expected to announce, forthrightly, that it has determined a particular precedent to be erroneous, and that such precedent is renounced.

Contrary to what should be so, however, there are a great many occasions on which the Supreme Court does in fact disavow its own precedents without acknowledging that it has done so. Instead, the Court contrives some implausible distinction between the precedent and the case before it and purports, dishonestly, to abide by a precedent it has in fact determined to repudiate.

11. In this passage, the author's attitude toward the United States Supreme Court is best described as one of:

   A. criticism.
   B. disbelief.
   C. appreciation.
   D. surprise.

Here's How to Crack It

- We consider what the author has said about the Supreme Court's attitude toward precedent. She objects to the dishonesty through which the court sometimes avoids precedent while pretending to honor it.
- We make four true/false questions.
  TRUE/FALSE "This woman is <u>critical</u>."
  TRUE/FALSE "This woman is in a state of <u>disbelief</u>."
  TRUE/FALSE "This woman is <u>appreciative</u>."
  TRUE/FALSE "This woman is <u>surprised</u>."

The correct answer is (A). The author thinks that if the Supreme Court decides not to abide by a precedent, it should do so honestly. Contrary to what should be so, the author explains, the court rejects precedents while pretending to honor them. She's making a criticism.

Special Question Type: Vocab-in-Context

On the ACT, you will encounter a couple of questions that ask you to define words or phrases that are used in the context of specific parts of the passages.

Many artists have spoken of seeing things differently while drawing, and have often mentioned that drawing puts them into a somewhat altered state of awareness. In that different subjective state, artists speak of feeling transported, "at one with their work," able to grasp relations that they ordinarily cannot see.

21. In line 79, the word *transported* is used to mean:

    A. moved from one place to another.
    B. engaged in artistic endeavor.
    C. in an altered state of consciousness.
    D. dreaming.

Here's How to Crack It

Go to the relevant section of the passage and read a couple of lines above and a couple of lines below where you see the word *transported*.

- Draw a line through the word *transported*, and based on your understanding of the lines surrounding it, try to replace it with a word or phrase of your own. In this case, the word *different* or the phrase from the passage, "altered state of awareness," would fit well, so the correct answer is (C).
- Having trouble coming up with your own word? No problem; just go to the answer choices and eliminate those that don't work.
- Answer choice (A) says "moved from one place to another," which is the primary definition of *transported* but has nothing to do with the passage. Eliminate it. Answer choice (B) says "engaged in artistic endeavor." This seems a little suspicious because the whole paragraph is about art. In essence, this is a deceptive answer choice. Eliminate it. Finally, (D) says *dreaming*. It's not a terrible answer choice, but does the passage actually tell us that artists go to sleep while working? No? Well, then, eliminate it.

Special Question Type: Except/Not/Least

If questions contain the words *except*, *not*, or *least*, you should leave them until you have answered all other questions. If you have time to return to them, your job is to identify the answers that are <u>not</u> supported by the passages.

        In Scotland, bees are carried in carts to the Highlands and set free. In France and Poland, bees are carried from pasture to pasture and along rivers in barges so that they can collect the honey from the vegetation that grows along the rivers' banks. In Egypt they are taken up the Nile and floated slowly home again.

13. The passage mentions transportation of bees by river in all of the following countries EXCEPT:

    A. Scotland.
    B. France.
    C. Egypt.
    D. Poland.

Here's How to Crack It

- Skip this question until you have done all the others with the exception of any roman numeral questions. By the time you return to it, you probably will have read most of the passage.
- Look for a lead word in the question. Here, you're interested in the transportation of bees by river, so go back to the passage and see what the passage says on this subject.
- The passage says that bees are transported by river in France, Poland, and Egypt. Because you are looking for the answer choice that is not true, you can eliminate (B), (C), and (D), leaving only the correct answer, which is (A).

Special Question Type: Roman Numeral

A few questions on the ACT will provide you with three statements preceded by roman numerals (and not just in the Reading test). On these questions, your job is to determine which of the statements, according to the passages, are true.

---

16. According to the passage, bees:

    I. are attracted to pastures.
    II. are attracted to cultivated fields.
    III. are attracted to vegetation that grows along river banks.

    F. I only
    G. II only
    H. III only
    J. I and III only

Here's How to Crack It

- You should leave roman numeral questions for last.
- Look at both the question and the roman numeral statements for lead words.
- Take each roman numeral and check, one at a time, to see if the passage makes that statement.
- If you use the last passage and check it for mention of "pastures," you will find that bees do, in fact, like pastures. Because roman numeral I appears to be true, you can quickly eliminate (G) and (H) because they omit roman numeral I.
- Now all you need to do is make a second pass to check and see if the passage states that bees like vegetation that grows along river banks. According to the passage, bees collect honey from these plants, so both roman numerals I and III are true. Thus, (J) is the correct answer.

High School, Senior Year

- Make checklists of what's due when. Deadlines will vary from school to school, and you will have a lot to keep track of.
- If you're not happy with your previous SAT scores, you should take the October SAT.
- If you still need to take any SAT Subject Tests, now's the time.
- If you have found the school of your dreams and you're happy with your grades and test scores, consider filing an Early Decision application.
- Regardless of which route you take, have a backup plan. Make sure you apply to at least one safety school—one that you feel confident you can get into and afford.

Source: *Best 368 Colleges*, 2009 Edition

Summary

- By following a straightforward, four-step system, you can avoid wrong answers and find the right ones more easily.

- The first step is to find the critical words and phrases in the questions.

- The second step is to locate those critical words and phrases in the answer choices.

- Third, skim the passage and scribble a few words that describe the main idea of each paragraph. You aren't reading for comprehension but rather for a general idea.

- Last, practice the loop. Use the techniques to go through the questions as quickly and accurately as possible.

- Be aware of special question types, including Vocabulary-in-Context questions, EXCEPT/NOT/LEAST questions, and roman numeral questions.

- Don't forget to guess your Letter of the Day if there are questions that you can't answer or don't reach in time.

Part V
How to Crack the ACT Science Reasoning Test

Chapter 19
Introduction to the ACT Science Reasoning Test

The ACT Science Reasoning test always comes fourth, after the Reading test and before the optional essay. It really should be called the ACT Science *Reading* test because you aren't required to know any science at all; you just have to read about science and answer questions.

There are three types of passages on the Science test: charts and graphs, experiments, and fighting scientists. To maximize your score on the test, you should do the easiest passages first and the more difficult passages last.

THE SCIENCE REASONING TEST

Remember that tough biology test for which you had to memorize dozens of facts about photosynthesis? When you sat down to take the test, you either knew the answers or you didn't. Well, that's not the case on the science portion of the ACT. Even though the word *science* appears in the title, this test doesn't resemble the science tests you've had in high school. The ACT Science Reasoning test presents you with science-based reading passages and requires that you answer questions about them. Sounds just like the Reading test, doesn't it? That's because it *is* just like the Reading test. Rather than test your knowledge of science, it's supposed to test your ability to "think about science."

Of course, a little science knowledge doesn't hurt. If a passage is about photosynthesis, you'll undoubtedly do better if you know something about photosynthesis. But remember, the information you need to answer each question is contained within the passage itself. So if science has never been your strength, don't worry. In this chapter, we're going to show you techniques that will help you master scientific reasoning, even if you don't know anything about photosynthesis, bacteria, the periodic table, or quantum mechanics.

The ACT Science Reasoning Test Format
You read 7 passages and answer 40 questions in 35 minutes.

What Does the Science Reasoning Test Look Like?

The Science Reasoning test has seven passages, each of which is followed by five to seven questions. The passages cover material drawn from biology, chemistry, physics, and the physical sciences (including geology, astronomy, and meteorology). They vary in organization and difficulty, as well as in the scientific reasoning skills they test.

Sound intimidating? It really isn't—all you need is the ability to answer questions strategically.

You've already developed some of these skills during science lab in school. Others you can borrow from what you learned in the ACT Reading section. (If you had any trouble mastering those skills, this is a good time to review them and make them stick.) The only additional skill you'll need is a basic understanding of math to help you read and interpret charts, figures, and graphs. You are not allowed to use a calculator on the Science Reasoning test. Luckily, you won't need one.

Do You Need to Be a Science Whiz?
Not at all. This test is more like a Reading test whose sole subject matter is science. What you *do* need is an understanding of the scientific method and of how to interpret charts, graphs, and tables. The topics on the test vary widely—no one has taken all these classes in school. If you haven't learned anything about genetics, or if you can't remember what you did learn, don't panic. You are not the only one. Remember that this is an open book test—everything you need to answer the questions is right there in the passage. Just find the information for each passage and you'll do fine.

You'll have 35 minutes to answer 40 questions. That's about five minutes per passage! It's like a car race: You have to move fast but you don't want to crash. In this section, we teach you how to do exactly that.

What Are the Passages Like?

All of the passages fall within three basic categories.

1. Charts and Graphs (aka Data Representation)— 15 questions, 3 passages

These passages provide you with one or more charts, tables, graphs, or illustrations, and are intended to test your ability to understand and interpret the information that's presented. There are three charts and graphs passages per test, and each one has five questions. (Chapter 20 covers charts and graphs.)

2. Experiments (aka Research Summaries)— 18 questions, 3 passages

These passages describe several experiments—and their results—to see whether you can follow the procedures in each experiment (or experiments) and interpret them. There are three experiments passages per test, each with six questions. (Chapter 22 covers experiments.)

Level of Difficulty
Just like on the ACT Reading test, the passages here are not organized in order of difficulty. Prioritize the passages. Before you read a passage, take a good look at the layout. Can you identify the passage type? Do easy passages right away, more difficult passages later.

3. Fighting Scientists (aka Conflicting Viewpoints)— 7 questions, 1 passage

These passages present (usually) two or three conflicting views on a research hypothesis. Typical topics include: "Is There Life on Mars?", "Where Did the Dinosaurs Go?", and "What's Fire?" Frequently, the fight is over something that has already been resolved (such as "What's Fire?"). You will be asked about the conflict and the evidence supporting each view. The ACT test writers may also ask you to figure out what kind of evidence might actually resolve the conflict. There will be only one fighting scientists passage per test, and it will have seven questions. (Chapter 23 covers fighting scientists.)

What Are the Questions Like?

The questions on the ACT Science Reasoning test fall into three general categories.

1. Look It Up (Understanding)

These questions test your ability to paraphrase specific parts of the passage. They're like the questions that you see on the Reading test, and they usually require that you focus on one sentence, paragraph, or chart. You might be asked to think about what happened in the passage and what the underlying assumptions are behind it. You may have to look up a value on a chart.

2. Why? (Analysis)

These questions call for a deeper understanding of the information in the passage, meaning that you may have to consider more than one part of the passage. You'll be required to recognize relationships between different pieces of information in the passage. For instance, you might be asked to put two thoughts together and figure out why something happened, or predict what's *going* to happen.

3. What If? (Generalization)

These questions require that you see things in perspective and look at "the bigger picture." You're asked to understand how events described in the passage may relate to situations not described in the passage. For instance, a passage may describe an experiment and the results. One question might ask you to predict the result if the experiment was performed under different conditions. Or suppose a passage describes an experimental finding. A question might ask you to assess the impact of the finding on the "real world."

Here's Our Step-by-Step Game Plan for Tackling Science Reasoning Passages

We have a step-by-step game plan for reading ACT science passages and answering questions about them. We'll outline the plan first, and then discuss each step in detail.

Step 1. Scan the Passage

Before you read the passage, take a quick look at the format. Your first task is to identify the passage type. Is it a charts and graphs, experiments, or fighting scientists passage? Count the questions. Here's why.

- Charts and graphs passages always have five questions.
- Experiments passages always have six questions.
- Fighting scientists passages always have seven questions.

To Read or Not to Read

Because most of the questions on charts and graphs and experiments passages have nothing to do with the introduction, you don't want to spend any time on it unless you have to. The ACT test writers are trying to waste your time with the introductions—don't let 'em! Just skip those complicated, detailed introductions unless you can't answer a question—then go look at them. From time to time, there is a question that can be answered only by reading the introduction. They're not common though. Fighting scientists passages are different. Often the introductions are critical. So, read the entire passage (quickly!), including any introductions.

If there are tables, illustrations, or graphs, familiarize yourself with their content. This should only take you about 20 seconds. (Remember, time is limited.) If there are experiments, skim the experiments and jot down key words in the margin. For instance, if the first experiment varied the temperature, jot down "temperature change." If the next experiment kept the temperature the same but varied the material used, jot down "material change." Little notes to jog your memory can be very helpful when you get to the questions and can keep you from having to read the entire experiment again.

Step 2. Look at Each Question and Identify Its Type

Once you've scanned the passage, you should move on to the questions. To which category does each question belong? Identify each as either an understanding, analysis, or generalization question. Why? Because knowing the question type will help you eliminate distracters and zero in on the right answer.

Step 3. Guesstimate

Some of the questions will require you to do some pretty simple calculations. Sometimes you can come up with the right answer choice by "guesstimating," which means making a rough estimate. (Remember this from Chapter 14, on geometry?) This technique works particularly well on problems that require you to interpret graphs.

Step 4. Use Process of Elimination (POE)

As on all tests on the ACT, you should use POE to eliminate incorrect answer choices. Once you have eliminated a couple of answer choices, you'll be able to spend a little time on the remaining choices and make a pretty good guess.

Don't Forget to Pace Yourself

To improve your score on the Science Reasoning test, you have to pace yourself. That means you'll have to answer the questions strategically. Remember the "triage" rule? (If not, review Chapter 2.) It applies to the Science Reasoning test as well. At the beginning of the test, take a quick look at all the passages and try to pick the order in which you want to do them based on what looks easiest. As you work on each of the passages, apply the "triage" rule to the questions. Does a question seem difficult or confusing? Then don't waste your time on it. You can always come back to that question later.

Which questions are the easiest? Those that simply require going back to the passage and looking up something tend to be easier. So do questions that ask you to project what will happen based on a trend established in the passage. In contrast, questions about assumptions underlying an experiment or hypothesis tend to be far more difficult.

The "triage" rule, as applied to both the passages and the questions, should allow you to move through the Science Reasoning test much more efficiently. While you want to move through the passages in an efficient manner and at a good pace, you cannot afford to rush yourself. If you have to guess on some questions, that's fine. Your objective is to get as many questions correct as possible, not to spend the same amount of time on each question and each passage.

Use Process of Elimination (POE)
Sometimes it's easier to find the correct answer by eliminating the wrong answer choices. Each time you eliminate a wrong answer choice, you increase your chance of selecting the correct answer.

Time Management
Because you must complete 7 passages in 35 minutes, you need to budget your time accordingly. Don't forget that you're getting the same number of points for correctly answering easy as well as hard questions. Use the "triage" rule. Don't waste time struggling with a hard question when you can move on and answer an easy question. You can always come back to the question if you have time.

Know Your Strengths and Weaknesses

After practicing all three passage types, you may find that you are best at charts and graphs passages. Or perhaps you really like the fighting scientists. Whatever you like best, make sure to do the passages that are easiest *for you* first. Leave the passages that give you the most trouble for last. The ACT Science Reasoning test always comes at the end when you're already tired. By prioritizing the passages, you give yourself the best chance to get the most points that you can.

One More Note

Some questions are fairly long themselves. They're like "mini passages" and usually accompany experiments and fighting scientists passages. These take a lot of time to do, so work these questions only after you've done all of the easy questions. Don't let tough, time-consuming questions delay you from moving on to the next passage, however. Use POE, guess, and move on. Once you have finished all of the questions for a passage, whether by guessing or working on them, don't go back to that passage. You're done with it.

Now that we've outlined our general step-by-step strategy, we'll show you how to apply that strategy to the three passage types that you'll see on the ACT Science Reasoning test.

Summary

o   There are always 7 passages and 40 questions on the ACT Science Reasoning test. There are always three charts and graphs passages, three experiments passages, and one fighting scientists passage. The passages are not in any particular order.

o   Spend the first minute of the test determining which passages will be hardest for you—these are the ones to leave until last. Playing to your strengths early in the test will gain you the most points.

o   You don't need to know any science to do well on the Science Reasoning test. You just need to be able to read passages that are about science topics.

o   Use the Process of Elimination and guesstimation to eliminate incorrect answers.

Chapter 20
Charts and Graphs

There are always three charts and graphs passages on the ACT. Each passage has five questions associated with it. Rather than reading in detail, scan the passages and the charts or graphs and then go straight to the questions. Keep track of variables, units, and trends in the charts. Use POE to eliminate incorrect answers. These passages tend to be shorter and more straightforward.

Step 1: Scan the Passage

You'll notice that the text is pretty skimpy on a charts and graphs passage. (Some passages contain only three sentences.) Because charts, tables, or graphs make up the major part of the passage, you'll need to examine them carefully. This just means using some of the skills you've developed in everyday life.

What do you do when you have to take a bus to a place you've never been? You look at a bus map. To understand the map, you have to figure out how it's designed and what the signs and symbols mean. Well, the same rule applies to the graphs, tables, and charts you'll see on the ACT.

In a charts and graphs passage, the ACT test writers are focusing on your ability to read charts and graphs. No big surprise there, but what that means is that they are not focusing on your ability to read the introduction. On this kind of passage, you want to skip the introduction. If you get into trouble doing the questions, then come back and give the intro a closer look, but otherwise, keep moving. Don't let them waste your time. Time is precious on the Science Reasoning test.

What Is a Variable?
A variable is a quantity ("thing") that has some type of value. There are two types of variables you'll need to know for the ACT: independent variables and dependent variables.

Scanning a Graph: Look at the Variables and Units

When you see a graph, table, or chart, you should ask yourself the following two questions:

1. What are the variables? (sunlight? temperature? number of plants?)
2. How are they measured? (in grams? quarts? meters?) Keep in mind that values can also be represented as percentages.

Let's look at an example.

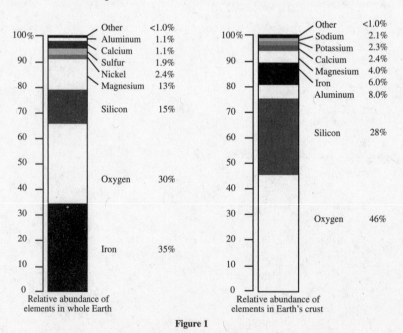

Figure 1

Relative abundance by weight of elements in the whole Earth and in the Earth's crust

We see two bar graphs that describe the composition of the whole earth compared with that of the earth's crust.

1.   What are the variables?
2.   How are they measured?

Do you see the numbers on either side of the bar graphs? They tell you the values are given in percentages (%). The graph on the left describes the percent (by weight) of an element in the whole earth. The one on the right describes the percent (by weight) of an element in the earth's crust.

Now let's see if you can work with a slightly more complicated graph.

Infection Severity Incidence for Four Diseases

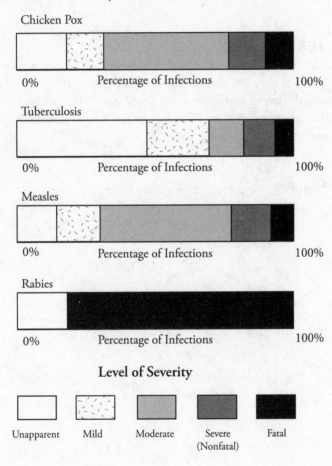

Scan the Bar Graphs

1. What are the variables?
   - There are four diseases: chicken pox, tuberculosis, measles, and rabies.
   - Did you notice the small boxes under the bar graphs? They make up a key that gives you more information about the variables. The graph is about diseases, and the key describes levels of severity.
   - Now how many levels are there?
   - There are five levels: unapparent, mild, moderate, severe (nonfatal), and fatal.

2. How are they measured?
   - The values are in percentages, just as before.

Not Every Graph Is a Bar Graph

The ACT is filled with graphs. There are different types of graphs, so you must learn how to read not only bar graphs, but also graphs in general. We started with bar graphs because they're usually easy to understand. But all graphs illustrate how one variable relates to another. Now let's look at another of the ACT test writers' favorite graphs: the coordinate graph.

Coordinate Graphs

What Are the Four Types of Coordinate Graphs?
- linear graphs
- graphs with curves
- scatter diagrams
- flat lines

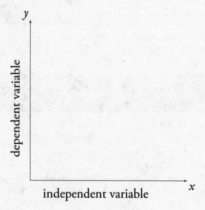

Look at the coordinate graph above. It has a horizontal axis (x-axis) and a vertical axis (y-axis). The x-axis shows the independent variable, the thing that's being manipulated (or changed purposely). The y-axis contains the dependent variable, the thing that is affected when the independent variable is changed.

Now let's look at what happens when we put some points on the graph.

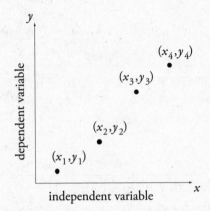

Every point on the graph represents a value for both the independent variable (*x*-variable) and the dependent variable (*y*-variable). In other words, each point represents an (*x,y*) pair. Don't forget that. Whenever you see a point on a graph, you should remember that it has both an *x*-component and a *y*-component.

Now let's look at what happens when we take the same graph and indicate that the graph represents an experiment performed by Dr. Frankenstein.

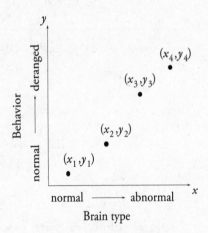

Dr. Frankenstein's Experiment

Take a look at the axes. The variables are brain type and behavior. The brain type is an independent variable and is represented along the *x*-axis. The brain type affects the monster's behavior, which is represented along the *y*-axis.

When building his monster, Dr. Frankenstein can use the brain of either a normal person or a psychopath. In this experiment (x_1, y_1) represents a normal brain (the independent variable) with a normal behavior (dependent variable). The point (x_4, y_4) represents a psychopath's brain and the associated tendency toward deranged behaviors.

Let's look, for example, at point (x_2, y_2) on the graph. When the monster is given this brain type (x_2), what type of behavior does he exhibit? Does he behave normally, or is he deranged?

Point (x_2, y_2) represents a fairly normal brain and, consequently, a reasonably well-behaved individual.

Unfortunately, most graphs on the ACT won't be as interesting as the one about Dr. Frankenstein's experiment. However, we'll show you how interpreting even the most boring graphs can be just as easy.

Know Four Kinds of Coordinate Graphs
On the ACT, you will see four kinds of coordinate graphs. Just remember to look at what the variables are, how they're measured, and how they're related.

Linear Graphs

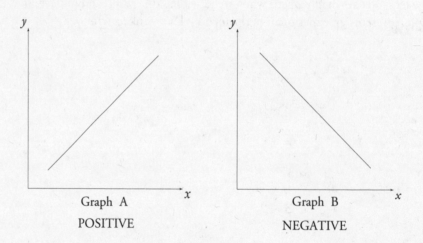

Graph A
POSITIVE

Graph B
NEGATIVE

The graphs above show a linear relationship. *Linear* is a fancy word meaning that the points follow a straight line. A positive linear relationship occurs when an increase in x (as you move to the right along the x-axis) leads to an increase in y (Graph A). A negative, or an inverse, relationship occurs when an increase in x leads to a decrease in y (Graph B).

Let's see if you can recognize the relationship on the next page.

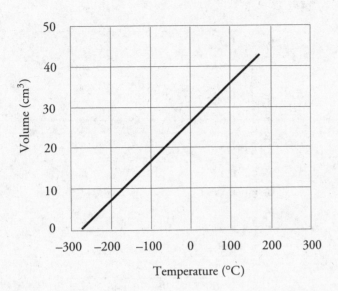

Does the graph show a positive or a negative linear relationship between temperature and volume?

If you answered positive, you're right. If, for some reason, you forget which graph shows a positive relationship, just remember that positive means that the line is pointing upward to the right.

Graphs with Curves

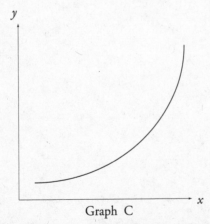

Graph C

Another common graph displays a curve, as shown in Graph C. The curve above means that for every increase in x, the y-values become larger. The changes in y are exponential and become greater the more x increases. If a graph is curved, that means that the amount y changes with each change in x is different at different points on the graph. Let's look at another example.

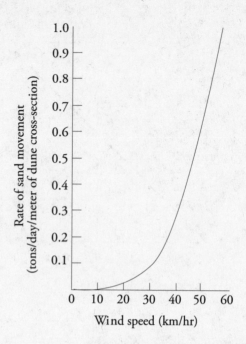

When the wind speed is 40 km/hr, what is the rate of sand movement?

The answer is 0.3. Now let's see what happens when the wind speed is 50 km/hr. The rate of sand movement increases to 0.6. Did you notice that the rate of sand movement doubled? Now what happens when the wind speed is 60 km/hr? The rate of sand movement increases even more. As you pick larger values for wind speed, the rate of sand movement will shoot up in value.

Scatter Diagrams

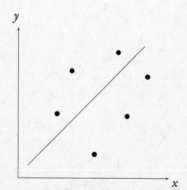

The ACT test writers expect you to understand a scatter diagram. See the line that runs through the center of the graph? It's called a "best-fit" line. It tells you that if you took the average of all the points on the graph and lined them up, they would form the straight line above. Therefore, the graph tells you two things: (1) what the points would look like if they were averaged and lined up (a straight line), and (2) how they *really* look on the graph (scattered).

Flat Lines

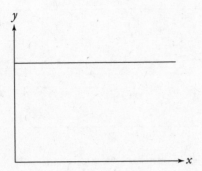

Every so often, the ACT will plot data on a graph in which there is no relationship between the variables. That is to say, the two elements plotted on the graph have no effect on each other. When this occurs, the result is a flat line. A line with no slope accurately graphs data in which there is no change. For example

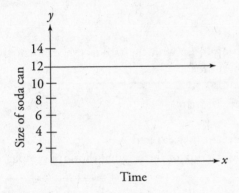

Here, the graph displays the effect of time on the size of a soda can. Does time actually affect the size of the can? Of course not. As a result, we get a line with no slope.

Now that we have tackled scanning graphs, let's see if we can apply the same technique to scanning tables and illustrations.

Scanning a Table: Look at the Variables

Just as you did with graphs, look at the table or chart to figure out what the variables are. You want to know what's being compared with what. As you read the chart, take the time to understand how these variables are related to each other (don't skimp on this part). Let's look at the example on the following page.

Number of half-lives expired for radioactive thorium	Remaining fraction of original thorium sample
0	1
1	$\frac{1}{2}$
2	$\frac{1}{4}$
3	$\frac{1}{8}$
4	$\frac{1}{16}$

This table has something to do with the radioactive element thorium, which has something called a "half-life."

What are the variables? They are

A. the number of half-lives expired
B. the remaining fraction of the original thorium sample

As you can see, the more half-lives that expire, the less we have of the original thorium sample.

Scanning an Illustration: Look at the Variables

Instead of a chart or graph, sometimes the ACT test writers will give you an illustration. Sometimes these illustrations will have text within the picture, but usually they will not have a specific explanation accompanying them. The ACT test writers want to see if you can follow a flow chart or interpret a diagram. Look at the example on the next page.

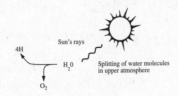

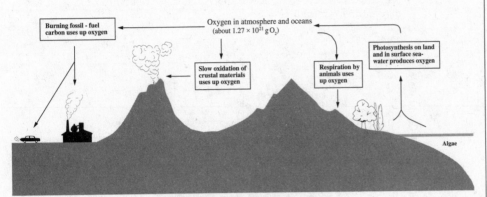

The Cycle of Oxygen Through the Atmosphere

The figure above illustrates the oxygen cycle. Based on this figure, which of the processes releases oxygen into the atmosphere? Look at the arrows associated with each box. The information inside every box is the variable. Which of the boxes has an arrow that shows that oxygen is released into the atmosphere? The box labeled "photosynthesis on land and in surface seawater produces oxygen."

Now what if the ACT test writers ask you what kinds of living organisms produce oxygen? According to this diagram, the answer is algae and plants on land. The direction of the arrow indicates that oxygen is moving from algae and the ground to the atmosphere. All the other arrows are pointing away from the atmosphere.

Step 2: Identify the Question Type

Now that you know how to scan the various charts, graphs, and illustrations, let's go right to the questions. Remember that there are only three basic question types, each addressing a different skill.

Question Type 1: Look It Up

The majority of these questions test your ability to understand the figures. They want you to explain, describe, and identify some of the basic scientific concepts or assumptions that underlie the information provided in the figures. Some questions involve only one figure in the passage, while others require two or more. So for "Look It Up" questions, identify the piece of information needed.

Know the Three Question Types
- Look It Up
- Why?
- What If?

Here's an example.

The term *solubility* refers to the amount of a substance (solute) that will dissolve in a given amount of a liquid substance (solvent). The solubility of solids in water varies with temperature. The graph below displays the water solubility curves for six crystalline solids.

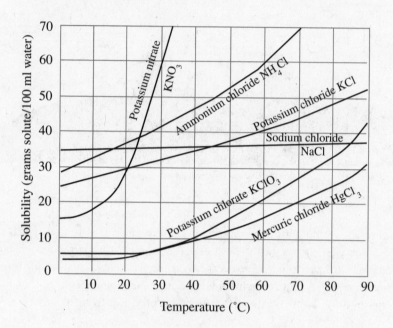

1. Which of the following factors affects the degree to which KCl is soluble in water?

   A. Only the quantity of KCl added to 100 ml of water
   B. The temperature of the solution
   C. Only the amount of solvent present in the solution
   D. The weight of KCl

Here's How to Crack It

This question requires that you understand the variables—what's being compared with what. The variables are

- the solution's temperature; and
- solubility, or the mass of solute that will dissolve in 100 ml of water

The graph shows you that for KCl, the solubility varies with the solution's temperature. That's why the answer is (B).

Translating Tables to Graphs

Sometimes you will be given a question that asks, "Which of the following graphs would best represent the results in the passage?" If you're given a table, you might have to translate the information into a graph.

Luckily, we've just learned a few things about graphs and tables. Now we have to learn how to read a table and translate this information into a graph. To make a graph, draw both axes and label the axes x and y. Remember, the x-axis is the independent variable, and the y-axis is the dependent variable. After you have drawn your axes, you can begin to plot some points on the graph.

Let's see if we can translate the information in the table about radioactive thorium into a graph.

What If You Just Don't Understand the Table, Graph, or Chart?

Sometimes the ACT includes tables, graphs, or charts that seem utterly incomprehensible. Don't get stuck on them. Just see if you can figure out the variables and then go to the questions. Perhaps there's only one question relating to that particular table, graph, or chart. Don't panic. Most of the time you aren't required to understand the entire passage; you just need to search for the information you need to answer each question.

Number of half-lives expired for radioactive thorium	Remaining fraction of original thorium sample
0	1
1	$\frac{1}{2}$
2	$\frac{1}{4}$
3	$\frac{1}{8}$
4	$\frac{1}{16}$

The first thing to do is draw your axes.

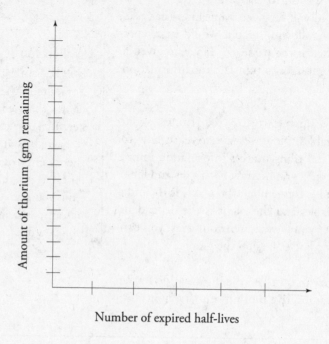

What is the independent variable? It's the number of expired half-lives. Label your x-axis with the numbers 0 through 4. Now, what is the dependent variable? It's the amount of thorium left after each expired half-life. Label the y-axis with the numbers $\frac{1}{16}$ to 1. Now you can plot the values on the graph and connect the dots!

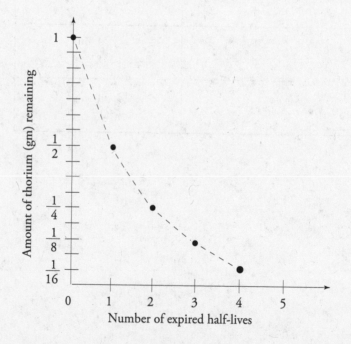

Now let's see if you can translate a table into a graph.

An investigator conducted a study to determine the relationship between temperature and pH of the enzyme chymotrypsin. Her findings are listed in the table below.

What's Chymotrypsin?
Who knows? Who cares? You don't need to understand it to answer the question. You just need to be able to read a chart.

Temp. (C°)	pH level
47	2
42	5
37	7
32	4
27	3

Chymotrypsin acidity: temperature dependence

Use the space in the margin to draw a graph that represents the relationship between temperature and pH in this experiment.

This Is What Your Graph Should Look Like

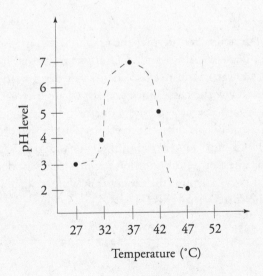

Did you label your axes? Temperature is the independent variable, and pH is the dependent variable. Now here's where it can get a little tricky. You should have labeled your x-axis with the units increasing as you move to the right. If you plotted your numbers differently, you probably got the wrong answer. Are you ever going to have to draw a graph on the ACT? No, but you will have to recognize which of the graphs in the answer choices best represents the information in the chart or passage. These questions are fairly easy if you practice how to read the axes, and look at the points (or lines) on the graphs.

Question Type 2: Why?

For this type of question, you're supposed to have a slightly deeper understanding of the passage. The question will usually require you to look at several pieces of information to get the right answer. Basically, you're being asked to figure out how different pieces of information are related to one another.

Draw on More Than One Piece of Information

Here's an example using the previous passage about solubility. Don't forget to refer to the graph on page 320.

2. How many grams of NH_4Cl can be dissolved in 200 milliliters of water at 70°C ?

    F.   70 grams
    G.   90 grams
    H.   140 grams
    J.   180 grams

Here's How to Crack It

The passage tests your ability to interpret the graph. What are the units? Temperature is measured in degrees Celsius and solubility is measured in grams of solute per 100 milliliters of water. You need to identify which line represents NH_4Cl on the graph. Then follow the curve until you see where it crosses 70°C. You can then look at the y-axis to see how many grams of NH_4Cl can dissolve in water. The answer is 70 grams. But hold it. The question is asking you to determine how many grams of NH_4Cl dissolve in *200* milliliters of water at 70°C. (This is what makes it an analysis question.) This question requires that you double the number of grams of NH_4Cl because you're dissolving the solute in double the amount of water. Therefore, the correct answer is (H).

Question Type 3: Generalization

In this type of question, you need to go beyond the information given. You may be presented with a new situation and be asked to apply the concepts provided in the passage.

Step Back and Look at the Big Picture

Here's an example using the same passage about solubility.

3. Based on the passage, what can you conclude about the relationship between solubility and temperature?

A. The solubility of a substance has little to do with the concentration of the solvent or the temperature.

B. Temperature is a dependent variable in the study.

C. For any given solution, a temperature increase allows for more solute to be dissolved in a solvent.

D. An increase in temperature will always lead to a decrease in solubility.

Here's How to Crack It

This is a What If? question, which means you're supposed to look at the "big picture." The ACT test writers want you to make a generalization not just about the six solids on the graph, but about substances in general. What are some of the trends you notice among all the solutes? As the temperature increases, the number of grams that can be dissolved in water increases (more stuff can be added). This means that higher temperatures allow for more solute to be dissolved in water. Therefore, (C) is the correct answer.

Answer choice (A) is clearly wrong because solubility and temperature are related (just look at the graph). Is temperature an independent variable or a dependent variable? Well, an independent variable is one with which you can play around. Therefore, temperature is the independent variable, so (B) is wrong. Answer choice (D) is incorrect because it is opposite—an increase in temperature leads to an increase rather than a decrease in solubility.

Step 3: Guesstimate

Interpolation

Sometimes the ACT test writers will give you a graph and ask you to predict the position of an unplotted point. This means that you may have to make a guess about where a point will lie on the graph based on the data you already have. The word for this is **interpolation**, and it's a skill you'll need for analyzing graphs. It's not too difficult to develop. The values that they want you to guess are within the range of points on the graph. Let's look at the graph below.

Interpolation
To estimate values on a graph between two known values

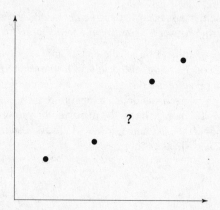

What if the ACT test writers asked you to predict the value of *y* if you were given a value *x* on the graph? Based on the position of the other points (the **trend**), you would predict the point would be located where the question mark is.

Let's try an example.

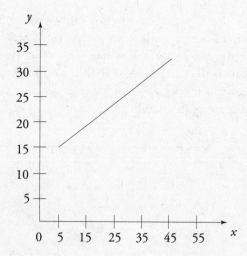

If x is 10, what is the value of y?

We're not sure! The ACT test writers didn't give you a value of 10 on the x-axis. What should you do? First, determine where 10 would lie on the x-axis. This is the first step in guesstimating. Remember, guesstimating will help you approximate an answer. Because 10 falls between 5 and 15, you can guesstimate where x and its corresponding y-value lie on the graph. Can you make a guess as to the value of y on the graph? Move across the x-axis to the approximate position of 10, and then move up from the x-axis until you reach the line. From there, draw a horizontal line to the y-axis. What is the value of y? It's about 17 or 18. Piece of cake, right?

Let's Do It Again

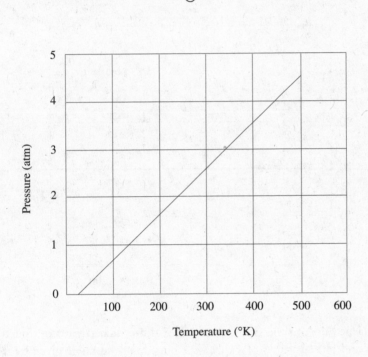

1. Based on the graph above, what is the atmospheric pressure when the temperature is 350°K?

   A. 2.0 atm
   B. 2.5 atm
   C. 3.0 atm
   D. 3.5 atm

Here's How to Crack It

Once again, the ACT test writers didn't give a value of 350°K for *x*. But you do know that 350°K is half way between 300°K and 400°K. So what do you do next? Guesstimate. Move across the *x*-axis until you reach the midpoint between 300°K and 400°K. Then move up until you reach the line and move across to the *y*-axis. What is the approximate value of *y*? The answer is 3.0 atm, (C).

Extrapolation

The ACT test writers want to test another skill. Sometimes they want you to extend the line on a graph.

Extrapolation
To project or expand known data into an area not known

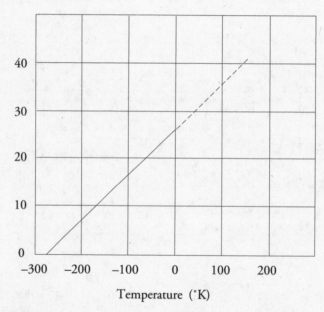

Temperature (°K)

See the dashed line on the graph above? This shows that if you continued the experiment and picked values of *x* that were outside of the range given by the solid line, you would get the dashed line shown above. This is called **extrapolation**. Let's look at an example.

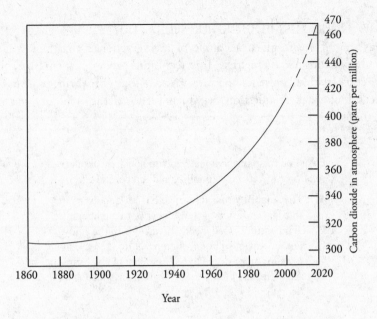

Estimated CO_2 concentration in the atmosphere up to the year 2020

What will be the CO_2 concentration in the atmosphere in the year 2020?

This is a graph of the concentration of CO_2 in the atmosphere since 1860. Notice that the graph gives values of CO_2 concentration all the way up to the year 2020. But we're barely in the twenty-first century! So how did they arrive at these values? They "projected" the CO_2 concentration level based on previous trends in the data. Therefore, the CO_2 concentration will be about 470 parts per million. That's extrapolation. You'll probably need this skill to answer several questions.

Step 4: Use Process of Elimination

Often the ACT test writers will give you several answer choices that look a lot alike. Why's that? They are attempting to disguise the correct answer choice. Test writers usually write the question first, then the correct answer, and finally the incorrect answers. Because they don't want the correct answer to be too obvious, they often surround it with several similar (but wrong) answers.

So How Does This Information Help You?

It means that if you're given a couple of answer choices that look alike, you should always consider them first. This technique works particularly well with answer choices that present opposite trends—one of them is usually correct. Let's look back at question 3, which refers to the solubility passage on page 320.

page 320.

3. Based on the passage, what can you conclude about the relationship between solubility and temperature?

   A. The solubility of a substance has little to do with the concentration of the solvent or the temperature.

   B. Temperature is a dependent variable in the study.

   C. For any given solution, a temperature increase allows for more solute to be dissolved in a solvent.

   D. An increase in temperature will always lead to a decrease in solubility.

Did you notice that (C) and (D) are opposites? So which answer choices should you consider first? Answer choices (C) and (D).

Charts and Graphs Drill 1

The kinetic molecular theory provides new insights into the movement of molecules in liquids. It states that molecules are in constant motion and collide with one another. When the temperature of a liquid increases, there will be an increase in the movement of molecules and in the average kinetic energy. The figure below depicts the distribution of the kinetic energy of two volumetrically identical samples of water at different temperatures (T).

Water has attractive intermolecular forces that keep the molecules together. When enough heat is added to water, it will weaken these forces and allow some molecules to evaporate and escape the liquid as a gas. The activation energy (Ea) is the minimum energy necessary for molecules to escape the liquid and undergo a phase change.

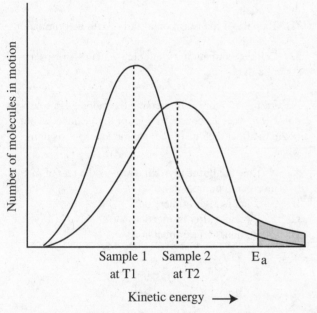

Distribution of Kinetic Energy for Two Samples of Water

Figure 1

1. Which of the following statements best describes the changes observed in the graph?

   A. At T1, Sample 1 has a lower kinetic energy than does Sample 2.
   B. At T2, Sample 1 has a lower kinetic energy than does Sample 2.
   C. An increase in temperature leads to a decrease in kinetic energy.
   D. Water never undergoes a phase change.

2. Assume that water undergoes a phase change to a gas. Which of the following statements would be true?

   F. The attractive intermolecular forces of the escaping molecules are weak.
   G. The average kinetic energy of the water remains the same.
   H. The rate of movement of the gas molecules decreases.
   J. The gas will undergo no further phase changes.

3. Suppose a third sample of water is heated to a higher temperature than Sample 2. It is then found that a greater number of molecules escaped the liquid in Sample 3 than in Sample 2. Would these results be consistent with the results depicted in Figure 1?

   A. Yes, an increase in temperature leads to a decrease in the number of escaping molecules in the liquid.
   B. Yes, as the temperature increases, it leads to more molecules escaping the liquid.
   C. No, the temperature reading of Sample 2 would be five times as high as that of the third sample.
   D. No, the average kinetic energy of the water will decrease.

4. It can be inferred from the passage that when a substance undergoes a phase change from a liquid to a gas it will:

   F. evaporate.
   G. condense.
   H. disintegrate.
   J. remain the same.

5. Given the samples at T1 and T2, and the kinetic energies measured and shown in Figure 1, which temperature produces the highest single kinetic energy measurement?

   A. Both T1 and T2
   B. T2
   C. T1
   D. Neither T1 nor T2

Charts and Graphs Drill 2

Amphibians are unique organisms that undergo drastic physical changes during the transformation from an immature organism into an adult form. This process, called metamorphosis, begins with the determination of cells at the tadpole stage. A study was conducted using tadpoles to determine the influence of thyroxine (a hormone) on metamorphosis.

As shown in the graph below, tadpoles were placed in solutions containing various concentrations of thyroxine. Increased levels of thyroxine correlated with increased rates of tail reabsorption and the appearance of adult characteristics such as lungs and hind legs.

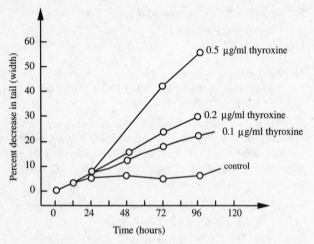

Decrease in tail width in relation to varying levels of thyroxine solutions

Figure 2

1. Suppose that a tadpole was immersed in a 0.3 µg/ml solution for 72 hours. What would be the expected approximate decrease in tail width?

   A. 22%
   B. 30%
   C. 41%
   D. 50%

2. Which of the following generalizations about tadpoles is supported by the results of the study?

   F. They will not undergo metamorphosis if they are not given thyroxine.
   G. Metamorphosis in a normal tadpole takes at least five days.
   H. The most rapid disappearance of the tail is associated with the immersion of tadpoles in the most dilute thyroxine solution.
   J. Temperature plays a major role in metamorphosis.

3. After four days, the tadpoles are checked for development. In all samples other than the control, which of the following concentrations of thyroxine would the tadpoles be likely to show the LEAST development?

   A. 0.5 µg/ml
   B. 0.2 µg/ml
   C. 0.1 µg/ml
   D. All of the tadpoles would show the same development.

4. Based on the information in the passage, which of the following would be a correct order of the stages of tadpole development?

   F. Tadpole → adult → reabsorption of tail → cell determination
   G. Tadpole → cell determination → reabsorption of tail → adult
   H. Tadpole → reabsorption of tail → cell determination → adult
   J. Cell determination → tadpole → adult → reabsorption of tail

5. According to Figure 1, immersing the tadpoles in solutions containing various concentrations of thyroxine does not begin to affect the rate of tadpole metamorphosis until when?

   A. No time at all; the thyroxine affects the rate of metamorphosis immediately.
   B. 0–12 hours after immersion
   C. 12–24 hours after immersion
   D. 24–36 hours after immersion

Charts and Graphs Drill 3

Each element is arranged in the periodic table according to its atomic number, which represents the number of protons in the nucleus. In every neutrally charged atom, the number of electrons equals the number of protons. The table below lists some of the properties of row 2 elements in the periodic table. *Electronegativity* is a measure of the relative strength with which the atoms attract outer electrons. Within a row of the periodic table, the electronegativity tends to increase with increasing atomic number, due to the tighter bonding between protons and electrons. The highest value for electronegativity is 4.0.

Element	Atomic number	Atomic radius	Electro–negativity	Characteristic
Li	3	1.52	1.0	metal
Be	4	1.13	1.5	metal
B	5	0.88	2.0	non-metal
C	6	0.77	2.5	non-metal
N	7	0.70	3.0	non-metal
O	8	0.66	3.5	non-metal
F	9	0.64	4.0	non-metal

Table 1

1. Which of the following graphs best represents the relationship between atomic number and atomic radius for row 2 elements?

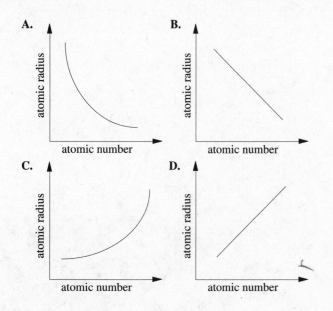

2. What conclusion could be appropriately drawn from the data regarding electronegativity in Table 1 ?

   F. An element with high electronegativity has an even atomic number.
   G. An element with high electronegativity will be a metal.
   H. An element with high electronegativity will have little tendency to attract outer electrons.
   J. An element with high electronegativity will be a non-metal.

3. What generalization can one make concerning the relationship between two properties of elements?

   A. As the atomic radius decreases, the electronegativity decreases.
   B. As the atomic radius decreases, the electronegativity increases.
   C. All metals have higher electronegativity values than non-metals.
   D. The atomic radius of F is larger than that of N.

4. Which of the following is true regarding the comparative electronegativity of fluorine (F) and lithium (Li)?

   F. The electronegativity of F is greater than Li because F has fewer electrons in its outer shell.
   G. The electronegativity of F is greater than Li because F electrons are more tightly bound.
   H. The electronegativity of Li is greater than F because Li has a greater metallic character.
   J. The electronegativity of Li is greater than F because Li has a greater metallic character.

5. Generally speaking, ionization energy follows the same trends as does electronegativity. Elements with a high electronegativity also have a high ionization energy. Which of the following is a correct order of elements with INCREASING ionization energies?

   A. Li, N, F
   B. F, N, Li
   C. B, N, Be
   D. Be, O, Li

Summary

o   There are three charts and graphs passages on the Science Reasoning test. They are identified easily because they do not have summaries of research or experiments. Instead, most of the information is presented in one or more charts or graphs.

o   Look at the variables and units presented in the chart or graph. Scan the charts and graphs and look for trends in the information presented. Then, go directly to the questions.

o   Use Guesstimation and POE to narrow down the answer choices. Often eliminating incorrect answers is easier than only searching for the correct answer.

o   Do the easiest questions first and leave the difficult questions for last. When you've finished all the questions on one passage, go on to another.

o   Don't forget to always guess your Letter of the Day for questions that you have no idea how to do.

Chapter 21
Experiments

There are always three experiments passages on the ACT and each has six questions. Rather than read in detail, scan the experiments, looking for changes in the experiments, and look at any charts; then go straight to the questions. Jot down notes about the overall experimental objective and note what is changing from experiment to experiment; these changes are what the ACT usually asks questions about. Use the Process of Elimination to eliminate incorrect answers.

Experiments passages are easy to spot. They usually contain an introductory paragraph followed by a number of experiments and six questions. Like charts and graphs passages, they may include graphs, tables, illustrations, or charts.

Step 1: Scan the Passage

Identify the Research Objective

Have you ever heard of the *scientific method*? That's a fancy name for the steps an investigator takes in conducting a study. One of the key steps is to state the **objective**. The objective is a statement that tells you the purpose of the study. For every experiment described on the ACT, there will always be an objective.

Example #1
Let's look at an example.

> An investigator was interested in observing whether a chemical reaction occurs when compounds are mixed with water. Chemical reactions are known to produce heat. Three compounds were observed in order to determine whether, based on the release of heat, a reaction took place. A thermometer was placed in each test tube to record any change in temperature.

Test tubes	Temperature Change?	
	Yes	No
1. Powdered bleach + H_2O	x	
2. Salt + H_2O		x
3. Sugar + H_2O		x

Experiments
Look for three things on an experiments passage.

- Identify the objective.
  (*What* were they studying?)
- Identify the method of research.
  (*How* did they study it?)
- Identify the results.
  (*What* did they find?)

How Do You Spot the Objective?
The objective is to determine whether heat was released in any of the reactions listed in the table. Notice that the objective tells you exactly what the investigator wants to know: Did a reaction take place?

Where do you usually find the objective of the study? The objective is usually found in the beginning or at the end of the introductory paragraph. Once you find the objective of the study, underline it. Knowing the objective of the study will keep you focused throughout your reading of the passage.

Your Underlined Passage Should Look Like This

An investigator was interested in observing whether a chemical reaction occurs when compounds are mixed with water. Chemical reactions are known to produce heat. Three compounds were observed in order to determine whether, based on the release of heat, a reaction took place. A thermometer was placed in each test tube to record any change in temperature.

Example #2

A laboratory experiment was conducted to determine whether the lack of sunlight influences photosynthesis (production of glucose). Eight potted *Salvia* flowers were randomly selected and divided into two groups and labeled Group A and Group B. The plants were then subjected to differing light conditions and examined one week later.

Group A

These plants were exposed to sunlight for the duration of the study. At the end of the study, these plants were green in appearance and produced glucose.

Group B

These plants were kept in the dark. At the end of the study, they were yellow in appearance and did not produce glucose.

What Is the Objective of the Study?

The objective of the study is to determine whether the lack of sunlight influences photosynthesis in plants.

A laboratory experiment was conducted to determine whether the lack of sunlight influences photosynthesis (production of glucose). Eight potted *Salvia* flowers were randomly selected and divided into two groups and labeled Group A and Group B. The plants were then subjected to differing light conditions and examined one week later.

So what should you do once you realize you've been given an experimental reasoning passage? Identify the objective and don't answer the questions until you're sure you understand it. Test takers often make careless mistakes when they read the passage too quickly and lose sight of the objective.

Follow the Procedure and Identify the Variables

Write, Write, Write!
Don't forget to take notes on each step within the experiment. You don't have to write a lot—just jot down key changes.

It's a good idea to make some brief notes on each experiment. These notes should highlight the differences between experiments in a passage. (Why else would the ACT test writers include two or more experiments if the experiments weren't different in some way?) Often these notes will refer to the procedure in the experiment. This might seem like a waste of time, but it's not. By noting what each experiment does differently, you will be able to quickly assess which experiment any given question is asking about.

The ACT test writers also want to see whether you can identify the variables in the experiments. Generally, there will be two or more variables that are important in the passage—you're supposed to identify the relationship between them.

So whenever you read an experimental reasoning passage, you should do two things.

1. Follow the procedure used in the experiments.
2. Identify the variables.

Let's take some notes using the experiment about photosynthesis.

> A laboratory experiment was conducted to determine whether the lack of sunlight influences photosynthesis (production of glucose). Eight potted *Salvia* flowers were randomly selected and divided into two groups and labeled Group A and Group B. The plants were then subjected to differing light conditions and examined one week later.

Group A

> These plants were exposed to sunlight for the duration of the study. At the end of the study, these plants were green in appearance and produced glucose.

Group B

> These plants were kept in the dark. At the end of the study, they were yellow in appearance and did not produce glucose.

Look at each of the study groups and follow the procedure.

What happened in Group A? What happened in Group B?

Just refer back to the appropriate sections of the passage. Group A plants, with sun, were green and made glucose. Group B plants, without sun, turned yellow and didn't make glucose (undergo photosynthesis). For experimental reasoning passages on the test, you should scribble a few key words next to each experiment. That way, you'll come away with not only a better understanding of the key points in the paragraph, but you'll also leave out extraneous information.

Here's What the Scribbles Should Look Like

A laboratory experiment was conducted to determine whether the lack of sunlight influences photosynthesis (production of glucose). Eight potted *Salvia* flowers were randomly selected and divided into two groups and labeled Group A and Group B. The plants were then subjected differing light conditions and examined one week later.

Group A

These plants were exposed to sunlight for the duration of the study. At the end of the study, these plants were green in appearance and produced glucose.

sun
green
glucose

Group B

These plants were kept in the dark. At the end of the study, they were yellow in appearance and did not produce glucose.

no sun
yellow
no glucose

Study the Results

The results are the conclusion of the study. When you examine the results, make sure you underline them or scribble some notes in the margin. Once you've completed this step, try to identify any similarities or differences between the results. Do you notice any trends in the data?

Example #3

For example, let's look at a passage about the effects of gibberellins (a plant hormone) on plants.

Dr. Keller examined the influence of gibberellins (a plant hormone) on a crop of dwarf tomato plants for 180 days.

	Amount of gibberellins (ml)	Average height of tomato plants (cm)
Sample 1	0	10.0
Sample 2	2	13.5
Sample 3	4	15.7
Sample 4	6	16.0
Sample 5	8	16.0

What was the trend in the experiment?

The average plant height increased with the addition of the hormone until the plants reached a certain height, at which point they grew no further.

Here's What the Scribbles Should Look Like

Plant height = more with gibb. then leveled off.

What are the variables?

Look at the chart. The variables are the amount of gibberellins and the height of the tomato plants.

Example #4

Let's read a passage about catalysts and apply the same technique.

An investigator was interested in observing whether a chemical reaction occurs when compounds are mixed with water. Chemical reactions are known to produce heat. Three compounds were observed in order to determine whether, based on the release of heat, a reaction took place. A thermometer was placed in each test tube to record any change in temperature.

Test tubes	Temperature Change?	
	Yes	No
1. Powdered bleach + H_2O	x	
2. Salt + H_2O		x
3. Sugar + H_2O		x

What was the procedure in this experiment?

The investigator took a bunch of test tubes and filled them with different mixtures to see if chemical reactions took place.

Here's What the Scribbles Should Look Like

Powdered bleach + H_2O = Reaction

Salt + H_2O ≠ Reaction

Sugar + H_2O ≠ Reaction

What are the variables?

In this case, all you have to do is to look at the chart. The variables are the reactants and the presence or absence of a reaction. Did you need to take a lot of notes for this experiment? Nope. Why not? The key information was already laid out for you in a simple table.

So How Do You Scan Experiments Passages?
1. Look for the objective.
2. Follow the procedure and identify the variables.
3. Study the results.

Step 2: Identify the Question Type
You'll see the same categories of questions as those for data representation.

Question Type 1: Look It Up (Understanding)
The ACT test writers want to know whether you understand the experiment. For instance, do you know the variables? (We now know how to tackle those questions.) If you removed one of the variables in the study, would it change the results? What happened in the experiment?

Let's look at an example using the study about gibberellins on page 339.

1. Which of the following graphs would best represent the effect of gibberellins on dwarf tomato plants in the study?

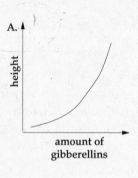

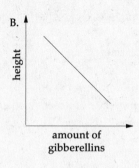

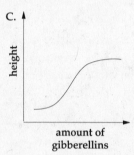

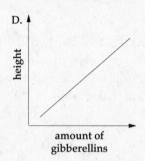

Here's How to Crack It

Remember our technique on how to translate charts into graphs? (If not, review Chapter 20.) Well, we can also use it in this section of the test. Let's go back to the chart.

We can use this information to find the correct graph. The graph that illustrates the same trend as the chart is (C). Look at the numbers in the chart and notice that the height increases up to Sample 5 and then it remains constant, as the amount of gibberellins increases further. You just need to look at the chart to find the answer.

Know How to Identify Controls

The ACT test writers will sometimes ask you to identify the control of the study. A **control** is simply a standard of comparison. What does a control do? It enables the investigator to be certain that the outcome of the study occurs because of changes in the independent variable and nothing else. So a control is something they don't mess with during the experiment. Let's look at an example.

Say the principal of your school thinks that students who eat breakfast do better on standardized tests than those who don't eat breakfast. He takes a group of ten students from your class and gives them free breakfast every day for a year. When the school year is over, he administers the ACT and they all score brilliantly!

Did they do well because they ate breakfast every day? How do you know whether the principal's theory is right? Maybe he just got lucky and picked the best test takers in the class to participate in the study.

The best way to be sure that eating breakfast made a difference in this case is to pick students in the class who *never* eat breakfast and to follow them for a year as well. Have *them* take the ACT and see how they score. What if they do just as well as the group that ate breakfast? Then we'll know that eating breakfast doesn't make a difference.

The group that didn't eat breakfast was the control group. They were not "exposed" to the variable of interest—breakfast.

Let's read the photosynthesis experiment again.

> A laboratory experiment was conducted to determine whether the lack of sunlight influences photosynthesis (production of glucose). Eight potted *Salvia* flowers were randomly selected and divided into two groups and labeled Group A and Group B. The plants were then subjected to differing light conditions and examined one week later.

Group A

> These plants were exposed to sunlight for the duration of the study. At the end of the study, these plants were green in appearance and produced glucose.

Group B

> These plants were kept in the dark. At the end of the study, they were yellow in appearance and did not produce glucose.

Which of the plants served as the control(s) in this study?

The plants in group A served as controls. Why? Because these plants were exposed to sunlight throughout the study. The experimental group was subjected to the factor being investigated—no sunlight. Here's another example using the gibberellin experiment.

Dr. Keller examined the influence of gibberellins (a plant hormone) on a crop of dwarf tomato plants for 180 days.

	Amount of gibberellins (ml)	Average height of tomato plants (cm)
Sample 1	0	10.0
Sample 2	2	13.5
Sample 3	4	15.7
Sample 4	6	16.0
Sample 5	8	16.0

1. Which of the following samples served as the control(s) in the study?

   A. Sample 1
   B. Sample 2
   C. Sample 4
   D. Samples 1 and 2

Here's How to Crack It

Let's find the control in this study. A control in this case is something that is *not* exposed to the hormone. In this case, the control is the first sample. The first measure of the sample was collected *before* the hormone was added to the crop (the chart tells you that the amount of gibberellins found in Sample 1 plants is 0). So the correct answer is (A).

Know How to Identify Assumptions

Another common Look It Up question on the Science Reasoning test asks you to identify the assumption in the argument.

What is an assumption? An **assumption** is a sort of simple logic that everyone takes for granted. Suppose one says

> *Brenda's car is in the driveway; now I can stop by and see her.*

What is the assumption in this statement? The assumption is

> *Brenda is home when her car is in the driveway.*

Yet Brenda could be at a neighbor's house or out of town. For the ACT, an assumption is an unwritten belief that, if false, would make the conclusion of the study invalid.

Here's an assumption question that refers to the passage on photosynthesis.

---

2. Which of the following was NOT assumed in the design of the experiment?

   F. Each plant requires the same amount of water.
   G. The plants are genetically identical.
   H. The plants are naturally green all season.
   J. The plants will be exposed to sunlight.

Here's How to Crack It

Think about it for a moment. What are some of the things you would have to assume about the study for the results to be acceptable? A major assumption is that the plants are genetically identical. If they weren't, then the findings could be invalid. For example, if a bunch of different plants were used, the experimenter couldn't be sure if the differences in the results were because of the lack of sunlight or to the variety of the plants themselves. The researcher also assumed that water was not a factor and that the plants don't turn yellow on their own. The only answer that contains something not assumed is (J).

Question Type 2: Why? (Analysis)

Remember the Why? questions that came with charts and graphs passages? (If not, review Chapter 20.) They required you to integrate two or more pieces of information. Well, that's how it works on experiments questions as well. The only difference is that they may also ask you to compare the results of the data with the ideas presented in the passages. Here are some of the types of questions they may ask.

Can you think of another way to test the same relationship between the independent and dependent variables?

If the experiment were repeated many times and gave different results, what would that mean in terms of the conclusion of the study?

Let's look at an example that refers to the passage on photosynthesis.

———————————○———————————

3. Suppose the Group B plants were placed in the dark for only two days and continued to produce glucose. What would these results mean in terms of the objective of the study?

A. Plants require sunlight to produce glucose.
B. Plants are able to make glucose under any conditions.
C. Photosynthesis occurs in all plants.
D. Photosynthesis is not completely inhibited by the lack of sunlight for two days.

Here's How to Crack It

The ACT test writers want to see if you can relate these new results to the original ones. The Group B plants did not undergo photosynthesis if they were placed in the dark for one week. However, the plants did undergo photosynthesis if they were put in the dark for two days. This must mean that two days wasn't enough time to halt photosynthesis. Therefore, the correct answer is (D).

———————————○———————————

Question Type 3: What If? (Generalization)

Sometimes you'll be asked how the knowledge gained from the experiment might be applied to new situations. As usual, we're supposed to look at the "bigger picture." Here are some sample questions.

> Given the results of the study, can we predict the outcome of some future experiments?

> How do these results influence our understanding of the world?

Let's look at a What If? question that refers to the passage about gibberellins.

---

4. Suppose 20 milliliters of gibberellins was given to a similar crop of tomato plants for 180 days. What would happen to the height of these plants relative to the height of the plants in the initial experiment?

   F. The new plants would be taller than the plants in the experiment.
   G. The new plants would be shorter than the plants in the experiment.
   H. The new plants would die.
   J. The new plants would have the same height as Samples 4 and 5 in the experiment.

Here's How to Crack It

Let's look back at the experiment and review the results. The tomato plants grew when the hormone was added, but eventually leveled off. What would happen if we added even more hormone to the plants? Based on the results of the experiment, their height should remain the same. The correct answer is (J).

Experiments Drill 1

It has been observed that plants exhibit phototropism (bending toward light) when placed in the presence of a light source. The actual part of the plant that bends toward the light source is not the tip of the plant but rather a region farther down the stem. Four flowering plants were exposed to sunlight in order to determine the site of light detection and the response of these plants.

Experiment 1

When light struck Plant 1 from the side, a region a few millimeters down from the tip bent as it grew until the tip pointed directly toward the light source.

Experiment 2

Plant 2 was also placed in the presence of sunlight, but the tip of the plant was covered with a dark cap. The plant failed to bend toward the light source.

Experiment 3

Plant 3 was exposed to the same conditions as was Plant 2, except a clear cap replaced the dark cap. This plant bent toward the light source.

Experiment 4

When a flexible dark collar was placed around the bending region of Plant 4, the plant still bent toward the light source.

1. The results of Experiments 1 and 2 indicate that:

   A. the plant requires both sunlight and nutrition in order to bend.
   B. the tip of the plant detects the light source.
   C. the light-proof cap assists the plant in its bending action.
   D. it is the amount of sunlight that causes the bending of the plant.

What Type of Question Is This? _____

Experiments Drill 1 (cont.)

2. Which of the following plant(s) served as the control(s) in the experiment?

   F. Plant 1 only
   G. Plant 3 only
   H. Plants 1 and 3 only
   J. Plants 2 and 3 only

What Type of Question Is This?_____

3. Based on the results of Experiments 1–4, it can be concluded that:

   A. the strength of the sun's rays correlated with the bending of the plant.
   B. flowering plants are unaffected by sunlight.
   C. the tip of the plant must transmit information about light direction to the lower bending region.
   D. flowering plants respond to light quite differently than do non-flowering plants.

What Type of Question Is This?_____

4. Suppose the tip of the flowering plant is cut off in the presence of a light source, and a new tip does not grow. What will be the response of the plant?

   F. The plant will not bend toward the light.
   G. The plant will exhibit phototropism.
   H. The plant will die.
   J. The plant will produce flowers.

What Type of Question Is This?_____

Experiments Drill 2

Stratification (the horizontal layering of particles) causes settling sediments to form distinct rock formations that contain different types of fossils. Breaks in the sequence of layers may be due to erosion by wind or water. A geologist studied the bedding of different rock formations in an area in order to establish the stratigraphic succession of rock formations and their fossil assemblage.

Study 1

On her expedition, the geologist found rock formations with the order and content shown below.

Rock	Fossil assemblage
1. Limestone	All kinds of marine animal fossils
2. Black shale	Small marine animal fossils only
3. Coal	Plant fossils

Study 2

The geologist examined the rock formation in another location 10 miles away and discovered rock formations with the order and content shown below.

Rock	Fossil assemblage
1. Black shale	Small marine animal fossils
2. Coal	Plant fossils
3. Sandstone	Rare vertebrate bones

Study 3

At a third site 20 miles away, the geologist discovered another rock sequence.

Rock	Fossil assemblage
1. Limestone	All kinds of marine animal fossils
2. Coal	Plant fossils
3. Sandstone	Rare vertebrate bones

The following table gives the types of fossilized organisms normally found in a variety of rock formations.

Rock	Types of fossilized organisms
1. Sandstone	Ancient fish skeletons and shark teeth
2. Coal	Tree stumps, ferns, twigs, and green algae
3. Black shale	Snails, clams, oysters, and periwinkles
4. Limestone	Annelids, sponges, clams, and radiolarians

Experiments Drill 2 (cont.)

1. Which of the following findings would NOT be consistent with the types of fossils normally found in the black shale formation?

   A. Periwinkles
   B. Clams
   C. Oysters
   D. Sponges

   What Type of Question Is This?_____

2. Based on the information presented in the studies, it could be inferred that the remains of ancient pine needles would be found in which of the following types of rocks?

   F. Limestone
   G. Black shale
   H. Coal
   J. Sandstone

   What Type of Question Is This?_____

3. Given the sequence of rock formation in Studies 1 and 2, what might have been the ordered sequence of rock formations in the area at one time?

   A. Limestone, coal, black shale, and sandstone
   B. Limestone, black shale, coal, and sandstone
   C. Coal, sandstone, black shale, and limestone
   D. Black shale, limestone, sandstone, and coal

   What Type of Question Is This?_____

4. The sequence of rock formations in Study 3 is similar but not identical to the sequence of rock formations in Studies 1 and 2. Which of the following factors could be responsible for differences among the three sites?

   F. Weathering
   G. Extreme heat
   H. A mild rainstorm
   J. Cohesion

   What Type of Question Is This?_____

Experiments Drill 3

Consider a massless spring hanging vertically from a stationary wooden block. When a mass is attached to the spring, it causes the spring to vibrate. This is an example of simple harmonic motion in which a force leads to the displacement of the spring.

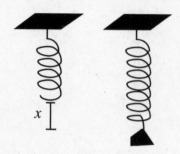

The equation for Hooke's spring law is $F = -kx$. The force (F) is proportional to the displacement (x), where k is called the proportionality constant pertaining to a given spring. The negative sign signifies that the force exerted by the spring is in the opposite direction of the displacement. Several trials were done to observe the relationship between force and the displacement of an object. The results are tabulated in the chart below.

Trial	Mass (gm)	k	x (cm)	F (lb.)
1	2	2.0	4	8
2	3	2.0	6	12
3	4	2.0	8	16
4	5	2.0	10	20

Table 1

1. From the trials above, it can be concluded that the displacement of an object depends on the:

   A. length of the spring.
   B. force according to Hooke's law.
   C. density of air.
   D. height of the wooden block.

What Type of Question Is This?_____

Experiments Drill 3 (cont.)

2. If a downward force of 9 pounds was placed on the mass, the approximate displacement would be:

   F. 2.5 centimeters.
   G. 3.0 centimeters.
   H. 4.5 centimeters.
   J. 18.0 centimeters.

What Type of Question Is This? _____

3. When the weight of the mass attached to the spring is doubled:

   A. the displacement remains the same and the force is doubled.
   B. the displacement is halved and the force is doubled.
   C. the displacement is quadrupled and the force is quadrupled.
   D. the displacement is doubled and the force is doubled.

What Type of Question Is This? _____

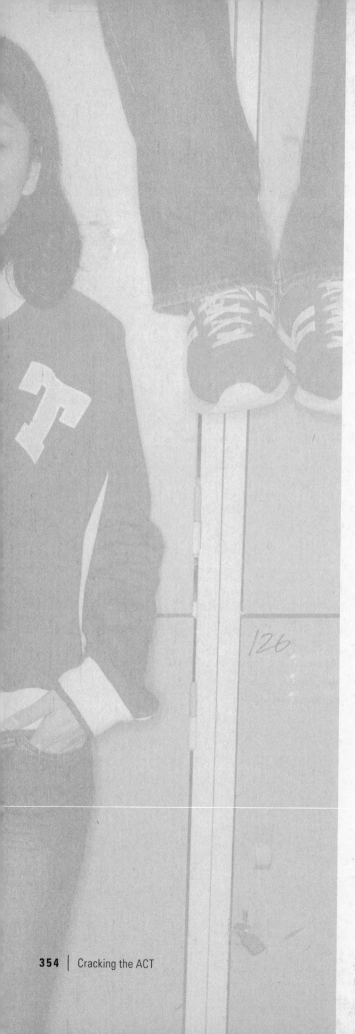

126

Summary

○ There are three experiments passages on the Science Reasoning test. They are identified by the inclusion of two, three, or more experiments. They may also show some information in chart or graph form.

○ First, scan the passage and identify the research objective (what the researcher is trying to test in the experiments). Then, follow the procedures and identify what the researcher is changing from experiment to experiment—this is usually what the questions will relate to.

○ Take notes on each experiment identifying what changed from one to the next.

○ Use Guesstimation and POE to narrow down the answer choices. Often eliminating incorrect answers is easier than finding the correct answer.

○ Do the easiest questions first and leave the difficult questions for last. When you've finished all the questions on one passage, go on to another passage.

○ Don't forget to guess your Letter of the Day on questions that you don't know how to do.

Chapter 22
Fighting Scientists

The third type of passage on the Science Reasoning Test is called "fighting scientists." There will be only 1 of these passages and it will be accompanied by 7 questions. Two, three, or possibly more conflicting views on a scientific phenomenon will be presented. Make a plan of the order in which you will read the scientists, and work one theory at a time before tackling the questions that require comparing and contrasting all the theories.

Think of it as a debate. Each debater proposes a hypothesis and then supports that hypothesis with facts, opinions, and assumptions. The ACT test writers want you to evaluate and compare the arguments made by each debater, but they don't care who wins the debate. We don't care either, but we do want you to answer correctly seven questions about the debate. In order to do that, you must understand each viewpoint and how it agrees and disagrees with the others. Some questions will ask about just one theory, but most of the questions will ask you to compare and contrast two or more. That's a lot to keep track of. Wouldn't it be easier to navigate this passage if you had a plan?

FOLLOW A PLAN

The fighting scientists passage has a lot in common with the Reading test, and you might recognize some of the same strategies we taught you to employ for Reading. Remember when we asked you how you would fare if your boss assigned you the task of checking out an empty building? How well do you do when you don't know what you're looking for? Not very well. How well would you fare if you dived right into a passage on the Reading test if you didn't know what you're looking for? Right. So how can you succeed on the fighting scientists passage if you don't know what you're looking for?

Step 1: Make a Map

Your first task is to map the order in which you will read the scientists. Just as on the Reading test, you should look at the questions first. In the fighting scientists section, the questions help you determine which hypothesis to read and which questions to answer first.

Let's try this with the questions on the next page. Read each question and mark it with a "1" if it asks about Hypothesis 1, a "2" if it asks about Hypothesis 2, and a "B" if it asks about both hypotheses.

1. Hypotheses 1 and 2 agree that the dinosaurs:

2. The basis of Hypothesis 1 is that a meteorite striking Earth was the primary cause of the dinosaurs' demise. Which of the following discoveries would best support this case?

3. Suppose a geologist discovered that the fossilized bones of dinosaurs contained traces of radioactive iridium. How would this evidence influence the two hypotheses?

4. The authors of the two hypotheses would disagree over whether the extinction of the dinosaurs was:

5. If current climatic changes turn out to be as dramatic as those described by the author of Hypothesis 2, which of the following would he say is most likely to occur?

6. Studies have shown that climatic conditions are interdependent. As conditions become less favorable for life in one locale, they improve in another. If fossil evidence were found which showed that this happened at the K-T boundary, how would it affect Hypothesis 2?

7. Both Hypothesis 1 and 2 would be supported by evidence showing that:

You should have a "B" next to questions 1, 3, 4, and 7. Question 2 should have a "1" next to it, and questions 5 and 6 should have a "2" next to them. What does this tell us? We're reading Hypothesis 2 first!

Step 2: One Side at a Time

In order to compare and contrast multiple hypotheses, you need to understand each viewpoint and how it agrees and disagrees with the others. Reading and working the questions for one scientist at a time will give you the firm grasp of each theory you need.

Once the questions have provided a map, read the introduction to identify the disagreement.

> Approximately 65 million years ago (at the boundary between the Cretaceous and Tertiary periods, known as the K-T boundary), the dinosaurs became extinct.
> Here are two of the hypotheses that have been presented to explain their disappearance.

What will the hypotheses debate? They will debate what caused the extinction of the dinosaurs.

Next, read Hypothesis 2. You don't need to comprehend everything in the passage or remember every point of fact or argumentation, and until you read the other hypothesis, you have no basis for comparison. You do need to grasp the argument each is making, so as you read Hypothesis 2, find and underline the scientist's main point.

Hypothesis 2

This event at the K-T boundary was neither sudden nor isolated. It was a consequence of minor shifts in the earth's weather that spanned the K-T boundary. Furthermore, its effect was not as sweeping as some have suggested. While the majority of dinosaurs disappeared, some were able to adapt to the changing world. We see their descendants every day—the birds.

Alterations in the earth's *jet stream* (a steady, powerful wind that blows from west to east, circling the globe) shifted rains away from the great shallow seas that extended across much of what is now North America. As these late-Cretaceous seas began to dry up, a chain reaction of extinctions was set into motion. First affected was plant life. Next, animals that fed on plants began dying off. Ultimately, the lack of prey caused the demise of the dinosaurs. It was the mobility of the winged dinosaurs that saved them, allowing them to move to more favorable locations as conditions in their ancestral homes deteriorated.

What Are They Fighting About?

Some of the scientific theories you'll read about in a fighting scientists passage were settled a long time ago. In reading a passage arguing that Earth is the center of the universe, you may think, "Wait, Earth is NOT the center of the solar system—why in the world are they arguing about this?" For the ACT, the arguments presented are what count. Even though an argument may have been disproved a long time ago, it's still possible to evaluate it scientifically, and that's all you're being asked to do on this test.

What is the main point of Hypothesis 2?

According to Hypothesis 2, the extinction of dinosaurs was caused by a chain reaction prompted by changes in the weather.

Your Underlined Version Should Look Like This

Hypothesis 2

<u>This event at the K-T boundary was neither sudden nor isolated. It was a consequence of minor shifts in the earth's weather that spanned the K-T boundary.</u> Furthermore, its effect was not as sweeping as some have suggested. While the majority of dinosaurs disappeared, some were able to adapt to the changing world. We see their descendants every day—the birds.

Alterations in the earth's *jet stream* (a steady, powerful wind that blows from west to east, circling the globe) shifted rains away from the great shallow seas that extended across much of what is now North America. As these late-Cretaceous seas began to dry up, a chain reaction of extinctions was set into motion. First affected was plant life. Next, animals that fed on plants began dying off. Ultimately, the lack of prey caused the demise of the dinosaurs. It was the mobility of the winged dinosaurs that saved them, allowing them to move to more favorable locations as conditions in their ancestral homes deteriorated.

Did you notice that we didn't underline the details of the theory in the second paragraph? It's not that they are unimportant, but until we dive into the questions, we don't know what to pay attention to other than the main point. As we work the questions for Hypothesis 2, we'll gain a deeper understanding of the details of the theory.

Without further ado, let's go to the questions about Hypothesis 2.

---

5. If current climatic changes turn out to be as dramatic as those described by the author of Hypothesis 2, which of the following would he say is most likely to occur?

   A. A rapid extinction of most of Earth's life, beginning with sea dwellers such as krill (a microscopic crustacean) and progressing through the food chain

   B. A gradual and complete extinction of Earth's life forms that moves through the food chain from the bottom up

   C. An extinction of most life forms on Earth that is gradual and simultaneous, affecting predators as well as prey at roughly the same rates

   D. A progressive extinction that begins with vegetation and eventually reaches to the top of the food chain, affecting most dramatically those life forms least suited to relocation

Here's How to Crack It

The main point of Hypothesis 2 is that changes in the weather prompted a chain reaction of extinctions through the food chain until the dinosaurs were affected. We need to look for an answer that would predict a similar result from today's climactic changes. Use POE as you make your way through the answer choices.

(A) is tempting because it mentions a progression "through the food chain," but the word "rapid" contradicts the first sentence of Hypothesis 2: "The event at the K-T boundary was neither sudden nor isolated." (B) looks good, until we go back to the passage to confirm it and see that some dinosaurs survived, those that evolved into birds. Because of the word "complete," we have to eliminate it. (C) is out because of the word "simultaneous," which we know from evaluating choice (A) is contradicted by the passage. The answer must be (D), and it paraphrases nicely what we underlined as the main point.

6. Studies have shown that climatic conditions are interdependent. As conditions become less favorable for life in one locale, they improve in another. If fossil evidence were found which showed that this happened at the K-T boundary, how would it affect Hypothesis 2?

F. It would strengthen the hypothesis by supporting one of the argument's assumptions.

G. It would weaken the hypothesis, because the area of improving climatic conditions should have provided a means for the survival of the dinosaurs well into the Tertiary period.

H. It would weaken the hypothesis by introducing additional evidence that the author could not have anticipated.

J. It would have no bearing on the hypothesis because the mobility of the winged dinosaurs would render such shifts irrelevant.

Here's How to Crack It

We've learned a lot about Hypothesis 2. We read it and underlined the main point, and then evaluated some of the nuances of the argument to eliminate wrong answers for question number 5. When you consider the import of this new fossil evidence, you should draw upon the deeper understanding you've gained. The correct answer to question 5 reminded us that those *least* suited to relocation are more impacted by the changes in weather. The author stated explicitly that some dinosaurs survived and evolved into birds. Those two facts together allow us to realize this new evidence would make Hypothesis 2 more credible. Eliminate (B), (C), and (D), and select (A) as the correct answer.

Step 3: The Other Side

Now it's time to read Hypothesis 1, but we know more than we did before reading Hypothesis 2 and thus should read more proactively. When you read the second theory, you should look for and underline the following:

- the main idea

- how this hypothesis disagrees from the first

- how this hypothesis agrees with the first

Differentiate Between Theories
Questions on the fighting scientists passages often ask about the areas of agreement as well as disagreement between the scientists' theories. Make sure you know what both the similarities and differences are.

Hypothesis 1

For many years, scientists have speculated about the cause of the extinction of the dinosaurs. Fossil records confirm that dinosaurs as well as other life forms were suddenly wiped out. The natural cause of extinction is the inability of an organism to adapt to environmental changes, yet the extinction of all life forms is unlikely. Chemical analysis of clay found from this era attributes the sweeping extinction of dinosaurs to the collision of a huge meteorite with Earth. These fossil records confirm the presence of a high concentration of iridium, a rare heavy metal that is abundant in meteorites. It is believed that a meteorite hit the earth and created a huge crater, which threw up a dust cloud that blocked the sun for several months. This event led first to the destruction of much plant life and eventually all other life forms that consumed plants and/or herbivores, including the dinosaurs.

Write, Write, Write
Underlining and taking notes in the margins helps you keep track of the differences between the scientists.

What is the main point? Hypothesis 1 believes a meteorite struck Earth and wiped out the dinosaurs.

How do the two hypotheses differ? Hypothesis 2 believes the extinction was gradual; Hypothesis 1 believes it was sudden.

How do they agree? Both hypotheses mention the food chain.

If you didn't come up with those points, look at the underlined portions of the passage below.

Hypothesis 1

For many years, scientists have speculated about the cause of the extinction of the dinosaurs. <u>Fossil records confirm that dinosaurs as well as other life forms were suddenly wiped out.</u> The natural cause of extinction is the inability of an organism to adapt to environmental changes, yet the extinction of all life forms is unlikely.

Fighting Scientists
In a fighting scientists passage, you're given two or more opinions about a scientific phenomenon. Your job is to identify the differences between or among the viewpoints and the information the scientists use to support their points of view.

Chemical analysis of clay found from this era attributes the sweeping extinction of dinosaurs to the collision of a huge meteorite with Earth. These fossil records confirm the presence of a high concentration of iridium, a rare heavy metal that is abundant in meteorites. It is believed that a meteorite hit the earth and created a huge crater, which threw up a dust cloud that blocked the sun for several months. This event led first to the destruction of much plant life and eventually all other life forms that consumed plants and/or herbivores, including the dinosaurs.

Now let's do the one question on Hypothesis 1 before we tackle the questions on both.

2. The basis of Hypothesis 1 is that a meteorite striking Earth was the primary cause of the dinosaurs' demise. Which of the following discoveries would best support this case?

   F. The existence of radioactive substances in the soil
   G. The presence of other rare metals common to meteorites in the clay beds of the ocean from that period
   H. Fossil records of land-dwelling reptiles that roamed Earth for an additional 10 million years
   J. Evidence of dramatic changes in sea levels 65 million years ago

Here's How to Crack It

What type of evidence would support Hypothesis 1? Any evidence that shows that dinosaurs were wiped out as a result of the impact of a meteorite. Would the presence of radioactive substances in the soil support Hypothesis 1? It could support the passage only if the radioactive elements were from meteorites (like iridium). Answer choice (F) did not specify that. Would the fact that some land-dwelling reptiles survived past this period support Hypothesis 1? No, so (H) is out. We can also get rid of (J) because it supports Hypothesis 2. What about (G)? What if other rare metals that are known to be found in meteorites were discovered? Would this support Hypothesis 1? Yes. The correct answer is (G).

Step 4: Compare and Contrast

We are now armed with a clear understanding of each hypothesis's main point, how the two differ, and how they agree.

1. Hypothesis 1 and 2 agree that the dinosaurs

   I. vanished because of a meteorite impact with the earth.
   II. became extinct due to disruptions in their food chain.
   III. became extinct due to some external force other than predation

   A. I only
   B. I and II only
   C. II and III only
   D. III only

Here's How to Crack It

We've already identified the area in which the two agree: the impact on the food chain. We can also eliminate choices that support only one of the theories. Statement 1 supports only Hypothesis 1, so it's out. Eliminate all answer choices with Statement 1 and we're left with (C) and (D) only. Because Statement II is in both answer choices, we know it must be correct. Of course, we'd identified the food chain as a point of agreement. Now let's check Statement III. Do both hypotheses state that dinosaurs became extinct because of some external force? Yes, so the correct answer is (C).

3. Suppose a geologist discovered that the fossilized bones of dinosaurs contained traces of radioactive iridium. How would this evidence influence the two hypotheses?

   A. It would support both hypotheses.
   B. It would support Hypothesis 2 and weaken Hypothesis 1.
   C. It would support Hypothesis 1 and weaken Hypothesis 2.
   D. It would not support Hypothesis 1 or Hypothesis 2.

Here's How to Crack It

Which of the hypotheses would be supported if a geologist found fossil bones that contained traces of radioactive iridium? Hypothesis 1 of course! The passage states that radioactive iridium is abundant in meteorites. If dinosaurs were exposed to the dust of meteorites, their bones would contain this metal. Hypothesis 2 didn't mention anything about iridium, so (C) is the correct answer.

4. The authors of the two hypotheses would disagree over whether the extinction of the dinosaurs was:

    F. a natural process.
    G. rapid.
    H. the result of a disruption on the food chain of the late-Cretaceous period.
    J. preventable.

Here's How to Crack It

The two hypotheses disagreed about the cause of the extinction, but they also disagreed on the pace. Hypothesis 1 believed it was sudden, whereas Hypothesis 2 believed it was gradual. Thus, (G) is the correct answer. Be careful with (H), because that's an issue on which both *agree*.

7. Both Hypothesis 1 and 2 would be supported by evidence showing that:

    A. pterodactyls (winged dinosaurs) survived well into the Tertiary period, adapted to changes in the earth's environment, and eventually evolved into a non-dinosaur life form.
    B. blockage of the sun's rays by particles measurable only on the microscopic scale can still have a significant effect on rates of photosynthesis.
    C. even apparently minor degradation of the plant population in a given ecosystem can have far-reaching effects on the animal population within that ecosystem.
    D. iridium is extremely likely to remain trapped in an ocean's bed when that ocean dries up.

Here's How to Crack It

On what point do the hypotheses agree? Look for an answer choice that provides evidence about the food chain. Eliminate any answer choice that supports only one hypothesis. (A) is out because Hypothesis 1 never mentioned relocation or winged dinosaurs. (B) looks good because it mentions photosynthesis, so keep it. (C) looks much better because it explicitly mentions the effects of plants on animals. (D) is incorrect because Hypothesis 2 never mentioned iridium and Hypothesis 1 never mentioned the ocean drying up. The test writers are trying to distract you with a switch, but you won't fall for it when you take the passages one at a time and learn each thoroughly before working the questions on both. The correct answer is (C).

Fighting Scientists Drill 1

How did the continents take on their current shape? Two differing views are presented below.

Scientist 1

According to a theory based on plate tectonics, the land surface of Earth once comprised a single continent, termed *Pangaea,* which was surrounded by a single vast ocean. Pangaea broke apart because the surfaces of Earth floated on massive plates above the deeper mantle of the ocean's basin. Horizontal movement of the plates began to split up the land about 137 million years ago during the Jurassic period. The continents and the ocean basins moved along convection currents in the mantle, resulting in a continuous degeneration of Earth's physical features. The movement of these rigid plates produced zones of tectonic activity along their margins such as earthquakes, volcanoes, and mountain formations. Fossil records as well as geological evidence show similarities between widely displaced continents. For instance, the coastlines of South America and Africa contain similar rock formations and appear to fit together like a jigsaw puzzle.

Scientist 2

The continents and the ocean basins of Earth are permanent, fixed features of the planet. The hypothesis of plate tectonics is flawed because there is insufficient evidence to support it. The force of gravity is stronger than any known tangential force that can act on Earth's crust. The layers of crust that support the continents and ocean basins are strong enough to preserve Earth's physical features and are too strong to permit horizontal drift. Tectonic activity has always been present, but the hypothesis of plate tectonics explains such activity only in one late period of ancient history. In addition, it is not clear what kind of force could allow the continents, composed largely of granite, to move through areas of dense, iron-rich rock that comprise the ocean basins. Any geological evidence that supports such a theory may be because of the existence of similar conditions on different continents.

1. Which of the following statements is the most inconsistent with the beliefs of Scientist 1?

    A. Continents were once part of a large land mass.
    B. Continents split up and drifted apart.
    C. Ocean basins have not changed for millions of years.
    D. Geological evidence shows similarities between widely displaced continents.

2. Scientist 1 studied the fossils along the coast of South America and Africa and found identical fernlike plants on rocks of the same age. What claim could Scientist 2 make to refute the findings of Scientist 1?

    F. The dating and comparison of plant fossils is an exact science.
    G. The soil and climate conditions along the two coasts must have been very similar at the time the fossils were created.
    H. The ferns were extremely large.
    J. Ferns will only thrive in their original habitat.

3. A new zone of tectonic activity has been discovered in the large land mass of Eurasia. This zone shows geological evidence of having been active for several thousand years. Which scientist is supported by this finding and why?

    A. Scientist 1, because it proves that tectonic activity occurs on the planet.
    B. Scientist 1, because it shows that Pangaea and Eurasia are the same land mass.
    C. Scientist 2, because it proves that tectonic activity occurs in land masses and not solely in the ocean basin and along coastlines.
    D. Scientist 2, because it shows that the continents are made out of granite.

4. Both Scientist 1 and Scientist 2 are experts in plate tectonics. To what discipline of science do these scientists belong?

    F. Physics
    G. Geology
    H. Biology
    J. Chemistry

5. Which of the following claims would be supported by both scientists?

    I. Tectonic activity has always been a factor in the geology of land masses.
    II. The continents and the ocean basins are fixed features of the planet.
    III. Continental drift occurred in the Jurassic period.

    A. I only
    B. II only
    C. I and II only
    D. II and III only

Fighting Scientists Drill 2

How did life on Earth originate? Two differing views are presented.

Hypothesis 1

In 1953, a graduate student attempted to recreate the conditions of primeval Earth in a sealed glass apparatus that he filled with methane, ammonia, hydrogen, and water. Sparks were released into the glass to simulate lightning, and heat was applied to the water. The result was the formation of organic compounds, known as amino acids, which are the building blocks of proteins. Since that time, others have shown how DNA may have been synthesized under various conditions as well. RNA, which is DNA's partner in the translation of genetic information into protein products, has been found to have the ability to reproduce itself under certain conditions. Thus, the origins of life are to be found in the "primordial soup" of the ancient earth that provided conditions for the simplest forms of organic matter to form and develop increasingly sophisticated means of organization. With the ability of compounds to make copies of themselves comes the opportunity for evolution by the mechanisms of heredity and mutation.

Hypothesis 2

Previous assumptions about the makeup of the "primordial soup" are inaccurate. It is not at all clear that methane and ammonia were present on the primeval earth or that conditions were as favorable as in the graduate student's experiment. The ability of RNA to reproduce itself is also limited to particular conditions that the primeval earth is unlikely to have provided. There is a possibility that, given enough time, random events could alone have resulted in the development of entire single-celled organisms, but some have likened that possibility to the chance that a tornado whirling through a junkyard could result in the formation of a 747 jetliner. During much of the time when the "primordial soup" was to have existed, Earth was a regular target of meteors that kept oceans boiling and the atmosphere inhospitable to organic development. Clearly much more research is needed before this theory can be widely accepted.

1. Which of the following statements about the conditions on primeval Earth could be used to support Hypothesis 2?

   A. Atmospheric conditions were too unstable to support the gases essential to the theories of the "primordial soup."
   B. Organic molecules were able to thrive under primeval Earth conditions.
   C. The origin of life began in the "primordial soup."
   D. The atmosphere contained methane, ammonia, hydrogen, and water.

2. To accept Hypothesis 1, one must assume that:

   F. Earth was bombarded by meteors during that time period.
   G. the conditions in the glass were analogous to the conditions on primeval Earth.
   H. proteins are the building blocks of amino acids.
   J. Earth lacked hydrogen in the atmosphere.

3. Which of the following shows how, according to Hypothesis 1, the building blocks of life were formed?

   A. Methane + Ammonia + Hydrogen + Water →Primordial Soup → Amino Acids
   B. Meteors → Primordial Soup → Amino Acids
   C. Amino Acids → Primordial Soup → DNA → Methane + Ammonia + Hydrogen + Water
   D. Primordial Soup → proteins → Amino Acids

Fighting Scientists Drill 3

Will Earth experience another ice age?

Hypothesis 1

Scientists have long speculated whether glaciation will ever take place again. Given that glaciation is an unusual event, it is highly unlikely that such a phenomenon will ever repeat itself. Glaciation usually takes place under periods of extremely cool temperatures. However, it appears that the temperature on Earth has been milder and more stable than at any other period. In fact, it would take a 5°C drop in the average surface temperature in order for glaciation to occur. In addition, there would have to be a significant increase in precipitation.

Hypothesis 2

Although Earth has not experienced glaciation in a long time, the event, no matter how rare, can occur if the right conditions are met. Two factors that are critical to the growth of glaciers are precipitation and temperature. There are a number of areas, specifically land masses in the polar regions, that are currently cold enough to produce glaciers but do not have sufficient snowfall to develop glacier systems. However, if enough events occur simultaneously, they could bring on an ice age. For instance, if there is an increase in the level of snowfall in the winter in these polar regions, this could eventually lead to glaciation. On the other hand, the level of pollution in the atmosphere is also sufficient to gradually cool Earth. Under these conditions, it is quite clear that glaciation is only a matter of the right combination of events at the right time.

1. Which of the following discoveries would most clearly favor Hypothesis 2?

   A. Canada has more snowfall this year than any other year.
   B. When snow falls, it sticks to the ground.
   C. The more pollution in the air, the more the temperature drops.
   D. Earth's bodies of waters are becoming more polluted.

2. Which of the following statements is the strongest argument a supporter of Hypothesis 2 would use to counter Hypothesis 1?

   F. The temperature around polar regions fluctuates.
   G. The precipitation rate has been increasing in the Swiss Alps.
   H. Just because ideal conditions are rare does not mean they will not occur in the future.
   J. The temperature in the North Pole has gone up 2°C.

3. If Hypothesis 2 is correct and glaciation can take place in the future, what regions would be most affected?

   I. Heavily polluted regions
   II. Polar regions
   III. Humid regions

   A. I only
   B. II only
   C. I and II only
   D. II and III only

4. According to Hypothesis 2, what conditions could cause glaciation?

   F. Low levels of pollution leading to high precipitation
   G. High levels of pollution leading to a blanketing effect that blocks out the sun and decreases the temperature dramatically
   H. A lack of snowfall and low temperatures
   J. A 5°C drop in the average surface temperature

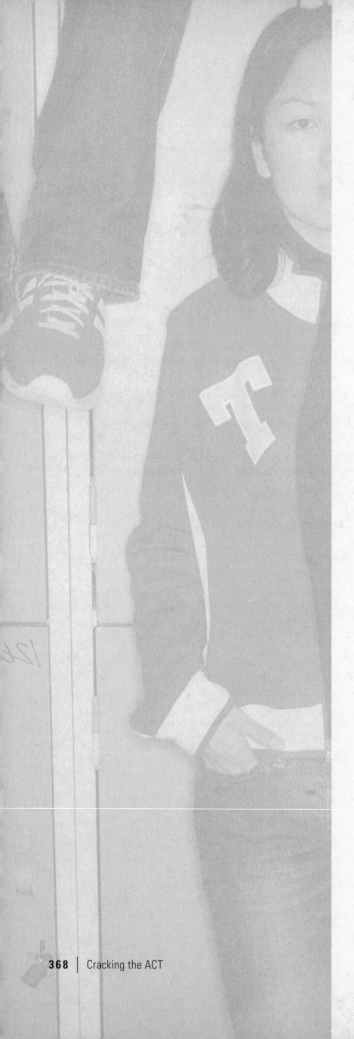

Summary

o   There is one fighting scientists passage on the Science Reasoning test. In this passage, two, three, or more scientists present their differing views on a scientific subject.

o   Don't pick a side. The ACT test writers want you to evaluate and compare the arguments presented, not decide which one is correct. Even if you know something about the topic, answer the questions using only what is presented in the passage.

o   First, use the questions to make a map of the order in which you will read the theories and answer questions on each, one at a time.

o   Leave the questions on more than one theory for last.

o   Don't forget to guess your Letter of the Day if there are questions that you don't know how to do.

Part VI
How to Crack the
ACT Writing Test

Chapter 23
The Essay

The ACT includes an optional Essay section. Some schools are requesting an essay while others are not. We recommend that you take the essay when you take the ACT because you can't take the essay on its own later if you find that you need it; you'd have to take the whole ACT over again. The essay follows a predictable format, so preparation and practice help a lot.

THE KIND-OF OPTIONAL ESSAY

The ACT includes an "optional" essay component, but if you've already started to skip this section, stop for a moment. Although most students would not voluntarily choose to spend an extra half hour on a Saturday morning writing an essay for a standardized test, we **do** recommend that you write the essay. Why? There are two reasons.

- First, some schools require that you take the essay portion. You wouldn't want to have to take the entire test over again if you discover that your dream school wants an essay and you had decided not to write one.
- Second, writing the essay can make your college application look more attractive. Your essay score will appear on every score report you send to colleges, regardless of whether or not the school requires an essay. Every school to which you apply will see that you took the initiative to write the essay, which is a good thing.

Plus, it's not that difficult to get a good score on the essay, especially if you follow the guidelines in this chapter. An impressive score is an impressive score, optional or not.

OK, OK, I'LL WRITE THE ESSAY...
WHAT DO I HAVE TO DO?

The ACT essay will provide you with a prompt "relevant" to high school students—basically it's a topic on which the ACT test writers believe almost any typical high school student will have some opinion. Here's an example of a sample prompt.

> The Children's Internet Protection Act (CIPA) requires all school libraries receiving certain federal funds to install and use blocking software to prevent students from viewing material considered "harmful to minors." However, some studies conclude that blocking software in schools damages educational opportunities for students, both by blocking access to web pages that are directly related to the state-mandated curriculums and by restricting broader inquiries of both students and teachers. In your view, should the schools block access to certain Internet websites?
>
> In your essay, take a position on this question. You may write about either one of the two points of view given, or you may present a different point of view on this question. Use specific reasons and examples to support your position.

Your job is to write an essay in which you take some sort of position on the prompt and develop your position through the use of appropriate supporting examples. You've probably written an essay like this in your high school English class. The only difference is that on the ACT you have a mere 30 minutes to read the prompt, brainstorm some examples, organize the essay, write it, and proofread it. You may be thinking that there's no way that you can write a great essay in such a short amount of time on a topic you've never seen before, and that is indeed true. But that's okay, because the ACT essay graders don't expect a perfect essay; they don't want to penalize you for minor spelling and grammar mistakes. Instead, graders will focus on the major components of your essay.

WHAT THE GRADERS ARE GRADING

If you think you have a tough job writing an essay in only 30 minutes, have some sympathy for the graders. They have to grade each essay in a matter of minutes. Imagine how you would feel if you spent an entire day grading thousands of essays on the same topic. By essay number 50 or so, you probably wouldn't care much if a student used "except" instead of "accept."

ACT graders focus on the big picture. Your essay will be read by two graders, each of whom will assign it a score from 1 to 6 (for a total essay score from 2 to 12) based on how closely it adheres to the standards below. The essays are graded **holistically**, meaning the graders don't keep track of all the good things and bad things in an essay on a checklist or score sheet. Each reader simply reads the entire essay, and based on his or her overall impressions of the essay assigns it a grade.

> ### ACT Graders vs. English Teachers
> The graders who grade for ACT aren't like your English teachers. They don't have the time to focus on the little details of each essay, and frankly, they don't care about your grade the way your English teacher does. So, don't sweat the small stuff. Focus on the big picture for the ACT: good thesis, organization, strong examples, and neatness.

According to the ACT guidelines, essay graders will base your score on your ability to do the following:

1. Take a position on the prompt   To score well on the ACT essay, you need a clear thesis statement. Essay graders will look for one when determining your score.

2. Maintain focus on topic   Once you come up with a thesis, stick to it. Avoid digressions in your essay—or even worse, changing or countering your thesis halfway through the paper.

3. Support your ideas   Good essays support their thesis statements with supporting examples. There is no magic number of examples. However, you do need to show that you understand the issue in the prompt, that you have a position on that issue, that you have a reason for that position, and that you can support that reason with evidence. You have to address the other side of the issue, but you don't want to argue it as strongly as your own side. Address the other issues and then point out why your examples are better.

4. Organize your ideas   This is one of the most important criteria. You must write an organized essay, meaning it needs to contain an introduction, body paragraphs, and a conclusion.

5. Use language clearly and effectively   The graders will look at stylistic issues, but those issues are not as important as the issues above. As a rule of thumb, graders will take issue with your grammar and language only if it detracts from their ability to identify the previous criteria.

HOW TO GET A GOOD SCORE

The way to get a good score on the essay is to make the graders' job easy: Show that you have a thesis, a clear essay structure, and some relevant examples. By following the guidelines presented here, you'll be able to write a clear, effective essay in the limited time available. Let's look at each step in the process. Be sure to practice each step individually, and then try to put all the steps together.

Step 1: Work with the Prompt

Our first task is to read the prompt. Here's the one we saw earlier.

The Children's Internet Protection Act (CIPA) requires all school libraries receiving certain federal funds to install and use blocking software to prevent students from viewing material considered "harmful to minors." However, some studies conclude that blocking software in schools damages educational opportunities for students, both by blocking access to web pages that are directly related to the state-mandated curriculums and by restricting broader inquiries of both students and teachers. In your view, should the schools block access to certain Internet websites?

In your essay, take a position on this question. You may write about either one of the two points of view given, or you may present a different point of view on this question. Use specific reasons and examples to support your position.

After reading the prompt, you must decide what side of the argument you will dfend. Even if you don't have a strong opinion either way, you still must pick a side. Although it is possible to write an essay that examines both sides of the issue at length, it is difficult to do that on the ACT because of the time limit. It's much easier to pick one side and defend it.

Key Words and Phrases

When reading the prompt, underline the key words and phrases. What are some of the key words in the prompt on the previous pages?

_____

_____

Some of the key words we see in the prompt are "school libraries," "blocking software," "prevent students," "harmful to minors," "damages educational opportunities," and "Internet websites." By identifying key words before you start to write, you can focus your essay and find the most pertinent examples.

On your test booklet, jot down something like this:

Pro   Con

Decide which side you wish to defend—there is no right or wrong answer, so just pick the side that you think will be easier to support. Next, brainstorm two or three reasons why you chose the side you did. Fill them in under the appropriate heading.

Pro   **Con**

_____   _____

_____   _____

_____   _____

_____   _____

At this point, you should have something that looks like this

✓ Pro	Con
• Internet contains many offensive/objectionable sites	
• Dangerous spyware and adware can harm computers	
• School computers should be used only for school work	

Of course, your reasons or examples may differ. The actual examples that you come up with do not matter, as long as they are related to the prompt. Now that you have your examples, you're halfway done. But before you move on, you need to think of an example or two for the other side of the argument. To get a top score on the essay, you have to consider both sides of the issue. So let's brainstorm an example or two for the opposing side.

Now you should have something like this

✓ Pro	✓ Con
• Internet contains many offensive/objectionable sites	• Restricting access is a form of censorship
• Dangerous spyware and adware can harm computers	• Students are deprived of opportunities to learn about certain topics
• School computers should be used only for school work	

If you're having trouble coming up with appropriate examples, the prompt usually contains some good ideas.

Step 2: Structure Your Essay

Good ACT essays have a clear, logical structure. Your essay must contain an introductory paragraph, body paragraphs, and a conclusion. Although what you write in each paragraph of any given type will change, the structure of each paragraph should be fairly consistent.

Let's look at an introductory paragraph first.

Introductions

Your introductory paragraph should accomplish two major things.

1. Frame the discussion You must tell the reader exactly what the topic of the essay will be. Introduce the topic by restating or, better yet, paraphrasing the prompt.

2. State your thesis Establish which side of the issue you are on and why. Use the lines below to write your introduction, and then compare it with the sample paragraph that follows.

_____

_____

_____

_____

_____

_____

_____

_____

_____

Here's our sample.

> The Internet has brought many changes to our world. Computers are used in businesses, homes, and of course, schools. However, with increased use of computers comes increased dangers. A new law, the Children's Internet Protection Act, requires schools to use blocking programs to restrict students' Internet access. Although some parents, students, and teachers believe that this law is a bad one, the dangers from the Internet make it clear that schools should block student access to certain Internet sites.

The First Impression
The introduction should be general. Specific examples belong in the body paragraphs and should support the thesis statement that you include in the introduction.

Notice that this introduction accomplishes the two basic goals mentioned previously. It paraphrases the prompt—expanding on it a bit by discussing the impact of the Internet and computers on everyday life—and introduces the question of whether schools should block student access to certain sites. Then the paragraph clearly states the author's position; in this case, the author agrees that schools should block student access.

That is all that is required in an introductory paragraph. Don't try to do too much with the first paragraph. Many writers make the mistake of trying to explain why they chose a particular side, but you should save that for the body paragraphs.

Body Paragraphs, Part I: Supporting Your Position
Body paragraphs are where you will give the reasons or support for your position. A good body paragraph will contain three major things.

1. A good transition/topic sentence   Transition sentences contribute to the flow and organization of the essay. Using transitions will help the grader follow your argument. Topic sentences show the grader that you are focused on your thesis.

2. A relevant example   Each body paragraph should discuss one and only one example. Otherwise, the paragraph becomes muddled and hard to follow. If you are using only one example, however, you'll want to break it up into logical paragraphs.

3. An explanation of how the example supports your position   It's not enough simply to throw a couple of examples into your essay and expect the grader to know what to make of them. Your job as a writer is to show the grader why the examples you chose support your position. Let's try to write a body paragraph. Using the lines below and one of the examples you've chosen (or one of ours) from the Pro/Con list, write a body paragraph. Then, compare it with the sample paragraph that follows.

_____

_____

_____

_____

_____

_____

_____

Here's our sample.

One convincing reason that schools should block access to certain Internet sites is that the Internet contains many offensive or objectionable sites. For example, there are sites on the Internet that contain racist and sexist jokes and content. Other sites might display material that is inappropriate for children. Because there is no censorship, there is no telling what sites a student can visit. This sort of material has no place in a school. If students see violent or offensive sites, they might be influenced. They could insult or hurt other students. For this reason, it is a good idea for schools to block access to certain sites.

Let's examine this body paragraph. The paragraph starts with a good topic sentence. The first sentence repeats the thesis, making it easy for the reader to follow the argument. Next, the author brings in an example—the presence of objectionable sites on the Internet. The following sentences expand on the example, presenting different sites that are inappropriate for a school setting. Finally, and most important, the last sentences tell the grader why the example supports the point—objectionable sites could lead students to insult or harm other students. Also, the last sentence again mentions the thesis. This helps the essay stay focused and makes the argument more forceful.

Practice writing body paragraphs for your remaining examples. For each one, try to start with a transition or topic sentence that restates the thesis. Then, present your example. Finally, state how your example supports your position. Try to end your body paragraph by restating the thesis again.

Writing to Your Grader

We're not talking about writing personal letters here. Rather, we're referring to modifying your writing style to make it fit what the grader wants to see. You do this all the time. When you get a new English teacher, you figure out how that teacher wants you to write your essays, and you tweak your style a little to meet expectations. You should do the same thing for the ACT graders. Figure out what they want to see and write that type of essay. It will help you get a better score.

Body Paragraphs, Part II: Attacking the Other Position

To get a good score on the ACT, you'll also have to write another type of body paragraph—one that discusses the "con," or opposite, side of the argument. This paragraph is similar to the supporting paragraph in structure. The only difference is that you will now attack the example and state why it is not an important consideration. Take a look at our sample paragraph first, and then try to write your own body paragraphs using one of the examples from the other side of the example.

Some people believe that it is wrong for schools to restrict access to certain Internet sites. These people think that restricting access is the same thing as censorship. However, this argument is incorrect. The school is not trying to control what students think or write. It is only trying to control what sorts of things a student can or cannot do at a school computer. This is well within the rights of the school. After all, schools can impose dress codes and dictate what classes students can take. It doesn't make sense to say that a school can determine what books a student reads or what clothes he or she wears, but cannot restrict access to certain Internet sites. Thus, this argument is not convincing.

The purpose of this paragraph is to look at the opposing side of the argument and then show the grader why the opposing side is wrong. The topic sentence clearly states the opposing position, and the next sentence gives a reason that some might consider the opposing side valid. The most important part of this paragraph comes in the third sentence. You must clearly indicate to the grader that you do not agree with this side. If you don't, your essay might seem to support both sides of the issue. Next, attack the opposing side by showing that the reason stated is inadequate, insufficient, or just plain wrong.

If you're having trouble attacking the other position, try one of the three techniques below.

1. The example is true, but... State the example, and then look for ways in which it could still be true but not relevant to the argument.

Example: Although it is true that restricting Internet access is a form of censorship, this is not relevant to the argument. The issue is whether students should be allowed to view the content at school.

2. The example is true, but not as important as...   In this case, acknowledge that the example is relevant, but not as important as some other factor. A good way to attack a position is to compare the con example with the pro example and then state why the pro example is a more important consideration.

Example: It may be true that restricting Internet access is a form of censorship, but there is a more important consideration in this argument. Isn't it more important to keep the students safe than to worry about censorship?

3. The example is flawed because...   Try to attack the actual example.

Example: Some people believe that restricting access to the Internet is a form of censorship. But this is flawed because the school isn't dictating what a student can think or write. It is only stating that students cannot view this material at school.

Now try it on your own. Use the lines on the next page to write a body paragraph attacking one side of the argument.

_____

_____

_____

_____

_____

_____

_____

_____

After you've written your body paragraphs, it's time to wrap things up.

Conclusions

Conclusions have only one purpose. Without looking below, try to guess what that purpose is.

1. A conclusion should restate the thesis

If you said the conclusion should conclude the essay, give yourself a prize. The conclusion should restate the thesis and sum up the essay. Go ahead and use the lines provided to write a conclusion paragraph. Then, compare your conclusion with the sample one.

_____

_____

_____

_____

_____

_____

_____

Here's our sample.

As this essay has shown, it is important and necessary for schools to block student access to certain Internet sites. The Internet has many potential dangers for a student, from objectionable sites to harmful computer viruses and bugs. A school that doesn't restrict access to the Internet puts itself at risk for far more serious issues.

This conclusion gets the job done. The first sentence restates the thesis and the next sentence repeats some of the major arguments of the essay. The final sentence of the conclusion is a good place to get a little sentimental or philosophical. It's the last thing the grader will see, so it's a nice touch.

Putting It All Together

The trick now is to string all of these individual paragraphs into a focused and coherent essay that addresses both sides of the issue, yet still clearly supports only one perspective. At first this seems like a daunting task, but if you practice using the outline below, you'll master it in no time.

Your essay should conform to the following outline:

I. Introduction paragraph
   A. Paraphrase the prompt
   B. State your thesis
II. Con body paragraph
   A. Topic sentence
   B. Con example
III. Pro body paragraph
   A. Topic sentence
   B. Pro example
IV. Pro body paragraph II
   A. Topic sentence
   B. Pro example II
V. Conclusion
   A. Restate thesis

Here's what the essay looks like in its entirety.

The Internet has brought many changes to our world. Computers are used in businesses, homes, and, of course, schools. However, with increased use of computers comes increased dangers. A new law, the Children's Internet Protection Act, requires schools to use blocking programs to restrict students' Internet access. Although some parents, students, and teachers believe that this law is a bad one, the dangers from the Internet make it clear that schools should block student access to certain Internet sites.

Some people believe that it is wrong for schools to restrict access to certain Internet sites. These people think that restricting access is the same thing as censorship. However, this argument is incorrect. The school is not trying to control what students think or write. It is only trying to control what sort of things a student can or cannot do at a school computer. This is well within the rights of the school. After all, schools can impose dress codes and dictate what classes students can take. It doesn't make sense to say that a school can determine what books a student reads or what clothes he or she wears, but cannot restrict access to certain Internet sites. Thus, this argument is not convincing.

One convincing reason that schools should block access to certain Internet sites is that the Internet contains many offensive or objectionable sites. For example, there are sites on the Internet that contain racist and sexist jokes and content. Other sites might display material that is inappropriate for children. Because there is no censorship, there is no telling what sites a student can visit. This sort of material has no place in a school. If students see violent or offensive sites, they might be influenced. They could insult or hurt other students. For this reason, it is a good idea for schools to block access to certain sites.

Another good reason to restrict student access to the Internet is the presence of dangerous computer viruses, spyware, and other harmful computer programs. These programs can infect a computer via the Internet and affect the hardware of the system and all the computers that are attached to it. A student who visits certain restricted sites puts the entire computer network at risk. One infected computer can wipe out or ruin all the other computers in the school. Thus, it would be a very wise move for schools to restrict access to certain dangerous Internet sites.

As this essay has shown, it is important and necessary for schools to block student access to certain Internet sites. Although some people think restricting sites is censorship, the Internet has many potential dangers for a student, from objectionable sites to harmful computer viruses and bugs. A school that doesn't restrict access to the Internet puts itself at risk for far more serious issues.

Now it's your turn. Using the following prompt, write an essay. Don't time yourself; just focus on structuring your essay according to the guidelines.

In recent years, many schools have adopted a "Great Books"–based curriculum. These schools require students to study certain designated classic books of Western civilization, arguing that familiarity with these "Great Books" is essential to education. However, opponents of this curriculum argue that forcing teachers and students to use only the "Great Books," most of which are written by white, European authors, results in a biased view on the world. In your opinion, should schools adopt a "Great Books"–based curriculum?

In an essay, take a position on this question. You may write on either one of the views presented, or on a different point of view relevant to the question. Use examples and reasons to support your position.

Step 3: Proofread

After you finish your essay, spend one or two minutes proofreading your essay if you have time. You don't have to catch every single grammatical and spelling mistake, but try to make sure there are no glaring errors. You can also edit as you go, but a quick review at the very end never hurts.

If you do find an error, erase it completely or cross it out with a single line and then neatly write the correction above it. Although you won't be graded on neatness, it is important. A neatly written essay makes for a happy grader, and a happy grader is a good thing.

OTHER THINGS TO KEEP IN MIND

Here are some other factors to consider when writing your essay. These factors are not nearly as crucial as the ones discussed earlier, but they can help boost your essay grade.

1. Length   ACT graders tend to reward longer essays. Try to write at least five paragraphs spanning one and a half to two pages. If your writing tends to be small, you may want to practice writing larger, especially because it will also make your essay a bit neater and easier to read. If your handwriting is large, make sure you write an extra page to compensate.

2. Sentence structure   Varying your sentence structure helps to improve the rhythm of your essay. If you write a really long sentence with lots of modifiers and dependent clauses, it sometimes helps to follow it with a shorter, more direct sentence. It really works. Don't try to be too fancy, though. The longer the sentence is, the more opportunity there is to confuse the reader or to make a grammatical mistake.

3. Diction   Diction refers to word choice. You certainly want to sprinkle some nice vocabulary words throughout your paper. But make sure to use and spell them correctly. If you're uncertain about the meaning or spelling of a word, it's best just to pick a different word. Using a big word incorrectly makes a worse impression than using a smaller word correctly.

4. Neatness   Make sure you indent each new paragraph. Align your essay using the lines on the paper. Don't go over the lines or write down the side of the page. Avoid messy cross-outs. Although the grader should not take these kinds of things into consideration when determining your grade, a neat, legible essay will be easier to read. Your grader will read hundreds, if not thousands of essays. A neat essay will make the grader happier.

PRACTICE ESSAY PROMPTS

Here are four sample essay prompts on which to practice. After you finish each essay, read it over—or better yet, have someone else read it—and use the Essay Checklist on page 391 to see how well your essay conforms to the ACT's grading standards. When you practice writing essays, it's best to limit your time to 30 minutes to experience how short the alloted time really is.

Practice Prompt #1

New laws are being proposed that would require schools to accommodate students who wish to transfer to a different school if the school falls below a certain level on statewide standardized tests. Supporters of this law believe that it is a student's right to transfer to a new school if his or her current school is not fulfilling its duties. Opponents argue that this law is impractical—what would happen if all the students requested transfers?—and unfairly weights test scores without considering other factors at a school. In your opinion, should students be allowed to transfer if schools score below a certain level on standardized tests?

In an essay, take a position on this question. You may write on either one of the views presented or on a different point of view relevant to the question. Use examples and reasons to support your position.

Practice Prompt #2

Colleges reward professors, who have significant research and teaching experience, with tenure. Once tenured, a professor holds his or her job without review and with little danger of being fired or replaced. Some people believe that high school teachers should be tenured as a reward for dedicated service. These people argue that tenure will attract highly qualified candidates to the profession and also allow teachers to do their jobs without fear of losing them. Opponents of this plan believe that tenure only leads to poor teaching. Without any fear of losing their jobs, teachers will not care as much about their students. In your opinion, should high school teachers receive tenure?

In an essay, take a position on this question. You may write on either one of the views presented, or on a different point of view relevant to the question. Use examples and reasons to support your position.

Practice Prompt #3

Many communities are considering adopting curfews for high school students. Some educators and parents favor curfews because they believe it will encourage students to focus more on their homework and make them more responsible. Others feel curfews are up to families, not the community, and that students today need freedom to work and participate in social activities in order to mature properly. Do you think that communities should impose curfews on high school students?

In an essay, take a position on this question. You may write on either one of the views presented or on a different point of view relevant to the question. Use examples and reasons to support your position.

Practice Prompt #4

In response to articles examining sensitive topics such as dating and partying, many schools are considering censoring their newspapers. Some schools believe that these topics are inappropriate for student-run papers, while others believe that, as long as what is printed is true, student papers should have the same freedoms as regular newspapers do. What is your opinion on this topic?

In an essay, take a position on this question. You may write on either one of the views presented or on a different point of view relevant to the question. Use examples and reasons to support your position.

Summary: An Essay Checklist

Now look at your essays and see if you applied the strategies presented in this chapter.

- o The Introduction
  Did you
  - start with a topic sentence that paraphrases or restates the prompt?
  - clearly state your position on the issue?

- o Body Paragraph 1
  Did you
  - start with a transition/topic sentence that discusses the opposing side of the argument?
  - give an example of a reason that one might agree with the opposing side of the argument?
  - clearly state that the opposing side of the argument is wrong or flawed?
  - show what is wrong with the opposing side's example or position?

- o Body Paragraphs 2 and 3
  Did you
  - start with a transition/topic sentence that discusses your position on the prompt?
  - give one example or reason to support your position?
  - show the grader how your example supports your position?
  - end the paragraph by restating your thesis?

- o Conclusion
  Did you
  - restate your position on the issue?
  - end with a flourish?

- o Overall
  Did you
  - write neatly?
  - avoid multiple spelling and grammar mistakes?
  - try to vary your sentence structure?
  - use a few impressive-sounding words?

Part VII
Drill Answers and Explanations

Chapter 24
Drill Answers and Explanations

Sentence Structure and Punctuation Drill (Chapter 6)

Question	Answer	Explanation
1	B	Did you notice as you were reading that the passage begins with a list of nice things about the town of Roskilde? Lists often mean parallel construction. Because this is a list of things, or nouns, we need to check if everything on the list is presented in the same way. The list is composed of the gingerbread houses of Roskilde with their neatly thatched roofs, the gardens filled with flowers, blooms, and the happy smiles on the fresh-faced inhabitants. Which one of these seems a little out of place? Each of them begins with "the" except for the third item on the list. And come to think of it, the third item is a lot longer. Is "blooms" by itself a nice thing about Roskilde, or does it really belong with the gardens back in the previous item on the list? Let's look at the answer choices. We see several ways to connect the two nouns. Different constructions of the nouns in the answer choices indicate that this could be a parallel construction problem (or possibly a misplaced modifier). Answer choice (A) implies that there are four items on the list, but that these items are not set up the same way. Let's get rid of it. Choice (D) is essentially just the same, but even worse; there is no comma after "blooms." Choice (C) splits the sentence in two. Can the second half of the sentence stand on its own? No way. Answer choice (B) puts the blooms back in the garden, and it clears up all problems of parallel construction. The correct answer is (B).
2	H	The answer choices here provide an immediate clue: One of the choices breaks up the sentence into two pieces, while the others leave it intact. Changes in punctuation may mean a comma splice. They don't always, of course, but we should still check. Can the clauses on both sides of the punctuation stand alone? Yes, they can. Aha! This is definitely a comma splice. We are now probably giving serious thought to (H), which splits the sentence in two. However, because there is more than one way to fix a comma splice, we should check the other answer choices just to see if any of them are better than (H). Choice (G) takes the comma splice and removes the comma, turning it into a run-on sentence. This is no better. Choice (J) merely inserts another pause after "the Vikings," which does not help matters. The correct answer is (H).

Question	Answer	Explanation
3	C	Here the sentence, which is partially underlined, contains a *list* of actions: *The Vikings a) once wandered* and *b) may have travel*. Are the two verbs in the same tense? No. What did we really need here? If you said "traveled," you are absolutely correct. If you missed this as you were reading it the first time, the answer choices provided great clues. Each was just another form of a verb. Anytime you see verb changes in the answer choices, you should immediately think of parallel construction. Each choice is in a different tense. Just read through them until you get a match with "wandered." The correct answer is (C).
4	H	Punctuation again! Three of the choices break up the sentence; one doesn't. Let's see which is better this time. Again, we ask ourselves, can the clauses on both sides of the punctuation stand by themselves? This time, the answer is no. The clause that begins "Where the Viking ships…" is dependent. This is a sentence fragment. We need to combine the two thoughts. Our only option is (H).
5	B	The answer choices here give us a choice of nouns. This could be a parallel construction problem or a misplaced modifier. Because there is no list in this case, let's check for a misplaced modifier. How does the sentence begin? *Until 20 years ago used only by the fishermen who still play their trade in the fiord,…* This is a long modifying phrase. The noun that comes next in the sentence must be what is being modified. Are "tourists" what the fishermen used until 20 years ago? No! This is a misplaced modifier. We can eliminate (A) and (C). In (D), the shore must share itself. Can a shore do something like that? Nope. In choice (B), the construction indicates that the fishermen and the tourists must do the sharing. The correct answer is (B).
6	F	We can spot the *type* of error ACT is looking for this time by going straight to the answer choices. This is one of those construction shift questions. Let's move "in the traditional manner" around in the sentence and find the best fit. You say it was just fine where it was? You're right. The answer is (F).
7	B	More punctuation! Again, our choices either put the sentence together or break it apart. Can the two phrases on either side of the punctuation stand on their own? The answer this time is yes. We have another run-on sentence. There is only one choice that breaks up the two clauses: The correct answer is (B).
8	J	More of the same. Can "who one hopes was only a boy at the time," stand on its own? No. We are down to (H) and (J). The correct answer is (J). How do you decide between "who" and "whom"? To find out, make sure you check out the Grammar and Usage chapter.

Question	Answer	Explanation
9	C	In the underlined portion, the semicolon breaks up two independent clauses. Of course, that is acceptable behavior for a semicolon, but only if there is no conjunction between them. Thus, we can get rid of (A). Looking at the answer choices, none of the alternatives gets rid of the conjunction. Therefore, we cannot break the two clauses into two separate sentences. This allows us to eliminate (D). When you have two independent clauses linked by a conjunction, what kind of punctuation is required? If you said a comma, you were absolutely right. The correct answer is (C).
10	F	Notice that the underlined portion contains two commas. When do we need two commas in a sentence? When we want to set off a clause or phrase that describes a noun in more detail but is not vital to the meaning of the sentence (a nonrestrictive element). Let's remove the phrase "a true adventurer" from the sentence. Do we lose any vital information? No. Therefore, the correct answer is (F). If you weren't sure how to correct the underlined portion, you could have looked at your answer choices. Answer choice (G) has three commas. Do they make the sentence any clearer? No. The comma after the word "true" is unnecessary. Answer choice (H) is incorrect because a colon should come after a complete thought and precede a list of related details. Answer choice (J) supplies only *one* comma. Remember, nonrestrictive elements need a *pair* of commas.
11	B	Because the wording is exactly the same in each of the answer choices, it is easy to see that this question can only concern punctuation. Choice (D) creates an incomplete sentence: "My romantic picture of the West;". Because this cannot stand alone, we can cross off (D). The phrase "complete with cowboys and Indians" is supposed to be a parenthetical description of the author's vision of what the West would be like. As the underlined sentence stands, it is unclear where the main clause ends and the parenthetical thought begins, so cross off (A). If there had been a pair of parentheses in one of the answer choices, that could well have been the correct answer, but there were no parentheses in any of the choices. What is another way to surround a parenthetical thought? If you suggested dashes, you were correct. Now, look at the difference between (B) and (C). In choice (B), there are *two* dashes surrounding the parenthetical thought. In (C), there is only *one* at the beginning of the phrase. The correct answer is (B).
12	H	Again, we can be pretty sure that this is a question about punctuation. Let's look at the entire sentence. It begins with a long introductory phrase, followed by an independent clause. Do we need any punctuation between a long phrase and a clause? Sure. We need a comma. The only answer choice that correctly positions the comma between the phrase and the clause is (H).

Question	Answer	Explanation
13	D	If you look at the answer choices, you'll realize that this question is concerned with proper use of the apostrophe. Whose back is it? It is the mule's back. We need the possessive form here. Thus, (A) is immediately gone. Choice (C) uses the pronoun "our." Does this agree with the first part of the sentence? It could, but look at "back." Do "mules" have only one "back?" Nope. So (C) is out. In (B), "mules" gives the impression that she is riding more than one mule at the same time. The correct answer is (D).
14	J	This sentence contains an independent clause followed by a list of related details, so the best punctuation mark to connect the two is the colon. A period or semicolon would be inappropriate because the sentence does not contain two independent clauses. So (F) and (G) are eliminated. A comma would not be sufficient: The related details should be set off in order to separate the hue from its description. So (H) is eliminated. The best answer to this question is (J).
15	C	Here we have a series of items that need commas. Eliminate (D) because it doesn't have any commas. The original sentence, (A), is missing a comma after the word "shale." In (B), the adjective "freshwater" is split from the noun "shale." Commas should be placed after "limestone" and "shale." Therefore, the correct answer is (C).
16	G	Does the sentence require the word "its" or "it's"? If you use the word "it's," the sentence would be the same as: *It is* imposing peaks. This is clearly wrong. "Its" refers to the Grand Canyon. Thus, (F) is wrong. A comma is unnecessary after the word "its" in (J) because it would break up the thought of the sentence. Two down and two to go. Is an apostrophe needed after the word "its"? Definitely not. There is no such word as "its'." Therefore, the correct answer is (G).

Grammar Drill (Chapter 7)

Question	Answer	Explanation
1	B	Looking at the answer choices, you might notice that there are two potential errors to check: pronoun agreement and tense. Why? Because the answers contained two different pronouns and two different verb tenses. Let's check pronouns first. In the original underlined portion of the sentence, "one" is a pronoun. Does it agree with the other pronouns in the same sentence? Not really. The author begins the passage by addressing "you." It is confusing and incorrect to change to "one" in the same sentence. Which answer choice uses "you" correctly? The correct answer is (B).

Question	Answer	Explanation
2	H	Checking the answer choices, we see that the question seems to revolve around verb tense. The sentence is describing something that happened yesterday, so we can expect that the sentence should be in some form of the past tense. Two events take place in this sentence. The author woke up, and the alarm clock failed to go off. Which of these two events happened first, thus causing the other? If you said that the failure of the alarm clock took place before the author woke up, you were absolutely correct. When two events occur in the past, but one occurs before the other, the sentence requires the past perfect. The correct answer is (H).
3	D	The answer choices here offer us the choice of the adverb "previously" or the adjective "previous." To decide which is correct, we need to know to what "previously" (or "previous") is referring. The word being modified here is "evening," which we all know is a noun. The correct modifier of a noun is an adjective. This eliminates (A) and (B). Now, does an adjective normally precede or follow the noun it modifies? The correct answer is (D).
4	G	The answer choices here indicate that we have to consider either of two errors: tense or subject-verb agreement. Let's check subject-verb agreement first. Find the subject of the sentence. If you said the subject was "each," you were absolutely correct. "Of the first three taxis I saw" is modifying "each." Now check the verb. "Each…were." In our review, we said that the word *each* is always singular—but the verb in this case is plainly plural. Aha! We have found the error. Check the answer choices to see which ones are singular. Our only remaining choices are (G), "was," and (J), "is." In what general tense is this passage written? Check the tense of the verbs in surrounding sentences. The correct answer is (G).
5	A	Clearly this question is testing our understanding of the "who/whom" issue. Remember that the difference between the pronouns "who," and "whom" lies in whether they are being used as subjects or objects in the clause or phrase that contains them. "Who finally picked me up" is a clause modifying the taxi driver. What is the subject of the clause? If you said "who" you are absolutely correct. Thus, "who" is fine just the way it is. We can eliminate (B) and (C), both of which contain "whom." Now let's see what the difference is between (A) and (D). Again, it comes down to tense. Is this passage being told in the present tense? No. The correct answer is (A).

Question	Answer	Explanation
6	J	The answer choices are offering you a variety of options having to do with "and" or "but." This is an idiom question. Try making up your own sentence using the idiomatic expression in question: *My sister Jane is not only stupid….* How would you finish this sentence? Or put it this way: What would be *the next word* in the sentence after "stupid"? *My sister Jane is not only stupid,* but *she is also a pain.* Choices (F) and (G) bite the dust. The answer is either (H) or (J). In the sentence you just made up, did you use "she" or "her" after the "but"? Chances are you used "she." "But she is also a pain" is a clause. Because "she" is the subject of the clause, we have to use the subject form, "she," instead of the object form, "her." The same is true for the sentence in the passage. The correct answer is (J).
7	C	This question is about the proper use of the superlative. The answer choices (including "worser" and "worst") give you a pretty good indication that this is the case. If you are discussing two bad options, you would have to decide which of them was *worse.* If you are discussing three or more bad options, you would have to decide which of them was *the worst.* The correct answer is (C).

Rhetorical Skills Drill (Chapter 8)

Question	Answer	Explanation
1	C	The underlined portion and the answer choices all contain sentence connectors. This is a transition question. Do we need an *also,* a *but,* or a *thus*? It seems pretty clear we need a *but.* The answer is (C).
2	F	Several of the answer choices here seem to use similar words. We should consider redundancy immediately. Choices (G) and (H) are clearly redundant. Answer choice (J) ("famousness") is not a word. Thus, the best answer is (F).
3	D	The underlined portion and the answer choices all seem to contain similar words, so again we should consider redundancy. There is no need to say both "initially" and "for the first time" in the same sentence. Choices (B) and (D) are the only choices that avoid redundancies. Choice (B) is awkward and incorrectly phrased, so (D) is correct.
4	J	At first this might strike you as an idiom question. In fact, style questions often resemble idiom questions. The metaphor of an actor sharpening his or her skills is effective, but how far do we want to take it? Is it necessary to say "to a knife edge" to get the point across? The answer is (J): OMIT the underlined portion.

Question	Answer	Explanation
5	C	As with all organization questions, we should try to spot either the beginning sentence or any pair of sentences we can link together. There is a certain cause and effect visible between Sentence 1 and Sentence 4. Which of the answer choices puts them next to each other in that order? Two of them do. The answer would seem to have to be (C) or (D). Because both choices put Sentence 2 first, the question becomes "where does Sentence 3 belong?" Well, the paragraph begins by saying *Playhouse 90* was a training ground. It is most logical to put the list of future stars after the introductory sentence, so (D) is the best answer.
6	G	We see more sentence connectors, so we are again prepared for transition. "(Blank) the frantic pace, accidents happened frequently." Let's try out the words in the answer choices. Could "despite" fill in the blank? No. We want a causal word. Answer choice (G), "Due to," is the correct answer.
7	C	How do we change the tone of Paragraph 3 with one word? Well, "accidents" sounds a little drastic. Which choice minimizes the sound of that word? If you said (C), "mishaps," you are absolutely correct.
8	G	Summary questions always take a while. Answer choice (F) merely repeats the first half of the first sentence of the passage, entirely missing *Playhouse 90*. Answer choice (G) seems really good. Answer choice (H) concentrates on the third paragraph only. Answer choice (J) concentrates solely on the three actors and writers mentioned. Are they the primary focus of the passage? Not really. The answer is (G).
9	A	Organization of paragraphs requires an overview of the entire passage. As always, try to find one paragraph you feel you can label as first or last, and proceed from there. Because the first paragraph is the best introduction to the passage as a whole, the correct answer is (A).

Basics Drill (Chapter 10)

Question	Answer	Explanation
1	D	Answer choice (C) does not equal 54, so we can eliminate it right away. Answers (A), (B), and (E) all equal 54, but each of these choices includes a factor that is not prime. The correct answer is (D).
2	H	First, ballpark the answer choices. There are 2 negative signs in the question (not including the one inside the absolute value symbols), which means your answer must be positive. Eliminate (F) and (G). Next, you can find that the absolute value of −6 is 6. From here, use your calculator to do the heavy lifting. Just be sure you enter the data correctly; your equation should be (−)5 × 4 × 6/−3, which comes out to 40.

Question	Answer	Explanation
3	D	Work smarter here, not harder. If you're given a list of possible factors/divisors, simply use your calculator to test each answer choice. (D) is the only choice that does not come out to an integer.
4	F	Again, put your calculator to work. You should have entered $(-2)^3 + 3^{(-2)} + (8 \neq 9)$, which yields -7.
5	C	Use the "carat" function, with carefully placed parentheses, to apply a fractional exponent: Enter $27^{(2/3)}$ to get 9.
6	F	$(xy)^3$ equals x^3y^3. Anything to the zero power equals 1, so z disappears from the numerator. The correct answer is (F).
7	C	To make this expression an integer, we need an even numerator. Why? Because it is going to be divided by 2. How can we ensure that the numerator of this fraction is even? The value a must be odd. The correct answer is (C). Another, perhaps simpler, way to approach this question is to plug in numbers and see what happens. Use the answer choices to help you decide what numbers to try. First, let's try 2, which is positive and even. If we put 2 in for a, we get $\frac{9}{2}$, which isn't an integer, so we can cross out (E) and (B). Try 0 next, because that's an easy number to work with. $\frac{11}{2}$ isn't an integer; 0 doesn't work, so (D) is out too. We're down to (A), negative, and (C), odd. Let's try 3 for a. That gives $\frac{8}{2}$, which is 4, which is an integer. So a doesn't have to be negative, but it does have to be odd. (C) is the answer.
8	G	Just count on your fingers. Is 0 even? Yes. The correct answer is (G). Note: If you chose J, it's because you read "between -4 and 4" as "between -4 and 4, inclusive"— that is, including -4 and 4 themselves. Sometimes a math test is actually a vocabulary test.
9	C	As in question 3, we can use our calculator to test the answer choices. For $4,7W6$ to be divisible by 6, the quotient must be an integer. Plug each answer choice in for W and see which answer choice makes this happen. Using (C), you'll find that $\frac{4,746}{6} = 791$.
10	J	Ignore your instinct to start doing the math and pick up your calculator. You're given an equation and a series of possible answers; just test each choice until you get $\frac{1}{3}$. Using (J), type $9^{(-1/2)}$ into your calculator. It should come out to .333, which is the same as $\frac{1}{3}$. You can always hit [MATH] [1:Frac] [ENTER] to make sure you have the right fraction

Arithmetic Drill (Chapter 11)

Question	Answer	Explanation
1	C	A ratio is a $\frac{\text{part}}{\text{part}}$. Because the only actual number of students that we have is a whole, we will need to convert the ratio into a fraction. If the ratio is $\frac{4}{5}$, then the whole is 9. The equation we need is $\frac{4}{9} = \frac{x}{27}$. $x = 12$, and the answer is (C).
2	J	First, let's do some quick elimination. The average of the first 5 tests is 88. Because the sixth test is less than 88, the final average must also be less than 88. Scratch (K). Now let's get to work. Let's use the average pie to think about what information we are given. The first bite-size piece tells us that Linda had 5 scores with an average of 88. It sounds like we are missing the total, so multiply 5×88 to get 440. What does the next piece say? Linda forgot the test on which she scored an 82, so we'll have to tack that onto the total. $440 + 82 = 522$. What is the question asking us to find? We need an average, which means we must have the total and the number of things. Our new total is 522, and because we added on the test Linda forgot, our number of tests is now 6. Divide 522 by 6 to arrive at 87.
3	E	Percent translation should do the trick. Because we are taking percentages, let's start with the original amount. What happens with the 490 tons of grain? We lost both 3 percent and 5 percent of the original; because we aren't asked to take a percent of the remaining grain, we can combine the percentages and do one calculation: What is 8% of 490? Punch (8/100) x 490 into your calculator to get 39.2. Subtract that from 490, circle (E), and move on.
4	F	First, let's convert these numbers into improper fractions. $5\frac{1}{3}$ equals $\frac{16}{3}$. $6\frac{1}{4}$ equals $\frac{25}{4}$. Clearly, when we subtract the second number from the first, the result will be negative. Cross off (J) and (K) because they are both positive. Your calculator can easily subtract mixed numbers—as long as you enter them correctly. In order to do so, add each integer to the attached fraction prior to subtracting by using parentheses. Your equation should look like this: $(5 + (\frac{1}{3})) - (6 + (\frac{1}{4}))$. After hitting enter, you should get $-.91667$. Can you eliminate anything? Definitely (J) and (K); if you know your common fractions, you can strike (G) as well. Ballpark the remaining two answers by figuring out which fraction is closer to -1. (F) it is.

Question	Answer	Explanation
5	D	This is straight calculator work! Just be sure you enter 1,245/.05 and NOT 1,245/.5, or your answer will be off by a significant amount.

Algebra Drill (Chapter 12)

Question	Answer	Explanation
1	A	If $x = -3$, then the first term of the numerator $(x + 3)$ equals 0. 0 times any number equals 0, so the correct answer is (A).
2	H	If we factor the equation, we get $(x - 3)(x - 1) = 0$. x could be either 3 or 1. Because we are being asked for the larger value, the correct answer is (H). Note that you could have worked backward on this question, starting with (K), because the question wants you to find the "largest value."
3	D	Because this question contains two equations with two different variables, this is a simultaneous equations question. Let's get rid of the fraction in the second equation. Multiply the entire equation by 2. We get $$x + 2y = 8$$ $$x - 2y = 20$$ If we add the two equations together, we get $2x = 28$, or $x = 14$. The correct answer is (D).
4	G	If we factor, we get $\dfrac{(x+9)(x-3)}{(x+9)}$ The $(x + 9)$s cancel out, so the correct answer is (G). Note that you could have plugged in on this question. Also, you could have used the denominator to help you factor the numerator.
5	A	The correct translation of the equation is $3x - 2 = 5(3) + 4$. Thus, the correct answer is (A).

Question	Answer	Explanation
6	G	"A certain number" sounds pretty cosmic to us. This is a Plugging In question. Let's pick a number of books. Because we will be dividing by 5 and by 3, a good number might be 15. $\frac{2}{5}$ of 15 = 6. If 6 are gone, then 9 remain to be given out. In the afternoon, $\frac{1}{3}$ of 9 are given out: This equals 3. If 3 are given out in the afternoon, that leaves 6. The question asks for the fraction of books that remains. Every fraction is a part over a whole. The part is 6; the whole is 15. $\frac{6}{15}$ reduces to $\frac{2}{5}$. The correct answer is (G).

Geometry Drill (Chapter 13)

Question	Answer	Explanation
1	B	Let's say $\angle A$ equals $x°$. $\angle B$ also equals $x°$. $\angle C$ is therefore $2x°$. We have a total of $4x°$. Because there are 180° in a triangle, $4x = 180$. x equals 45, and therefore, the correct answer is (B). Note that you could have worked backward on this problem.
2	F	When two parallel lines are cut by a third line, there are really only two angles formed—a big one and a little one. We need to find an answer choice with two big angles or two little angles. Remember, any answer choice with $\angle D$ in it must be wrong because this angle is not formed by two parallel lines being cut by a third. The correct answer is (F).
3	D	You could use the Pythagorean theorem to solve this question, but you will be done much faster if you know the triples that ACT likes to use. The triangle on the left is a multiple of a 3-4-5 triangle: 15-20-25. The triangle on the right is a 7-24-25 triangle. The correct answer is (D).
4	G	The radius of circle A is 4. If circle B has a radius that is half of circle A, its radius is 2. Therefore, the circumference is 4π. The correct answer is (G).
5	A	This time we have to use the Pythagorean theorem because all we know about $\triangle LMO$ is that it is a right triangle. Using the Pythagorean theorem, we find that $\overline{MO}$ is equal to $\sqrt{20}$ or $2\sqrt{5}$. $\triangle MON$ is an isosceles right triangle, so the hypotenuse is equal to the side times $\sqrt{2}$. The correct answer is (A).

Graphing and Coordinate Geometry Drill (Chapter 14)

Question	Answer	Explanation
1	E	We can immediately cross off (B) and (D) because the equation does not contain a greater-than-or-equal-to sign. If you chose (C), you forgot that the sign flips when you multiply or divide an inequality by a negative number. The correct answer is (E).
2	G	If you don't remember the formula for finding a midpoint, just make a rough graph. Which quadrant should the answer be in? If you said the second, you are correct. The x-coordinate should be negative, the y-coordinate should be positive. Which answer choices are possible? There's only one. The correct answer is (G).
3	B	We need to put this into the standard $y = mx + b$ form. In this case, the equation becomes $y = 12x - 6$. The slope is 12, and the answer is (B).
4	H	Forget the distance formula. Instead, try sketching out a graph. Make the line between the two points the hypotenuse of a right triangle. It turns out to be a 3-4-5 triangle. The correct answer is (H).
5	C	Just use the slope formula—the difference in y over the difference in x. The correct answer is (C).

Trigonometry Drill: Answers and Explanations (Chapter 15)

Question	Answer	Explanation
1	D	This is a 5-12-13 triangle. The tangent of an angle is opposite over adjacent. The correct answer is (D).
2	H	The cotangent of an angle is the reciprocal of the tangent. If the tangent is 1, then so is the cotangent. The correct answer is (H).
3	C	$\sin^2\theta + \cos^2\theta$ always equals 1. Therefore, x must equal 3. The correct answer is (C).

Charts and Graphs Drill 1 (Chapter 20)

Question	Answer	Explanation
1	B	This is a Look It Up question on which you can use POE. As you were reading the question, did you notice that (A) and (B) were the same except that the words "T1" and "T2" were switched? The answer choices are opposites, and one of them will probably be correct. Let's try (A) and (B) first. At T1, Sample 1 has a greater number of molecules in motion. The introduction clarifies that this corresponds to an increase in kinetic energy. The graph contradicts (A), so the answer appears to be (B). Now let's check the other two choices. Does an increase in temperature lead to a decrease in kinetic energy? No. The passage states that an increase in temperature leads to an increase in kinetic energy. So we can eliminate (C). Now let's look at (D). Is it true that water never undergoes a phase change? No; in fact, the text accompanying the graph says just the opposite. So we can eliminate (D). Also, remember to be cautious of extreme language such as "never." The correct answer is (B).
2	F	This is a Why? question because it requires a greater understanding of the passage than does question 1. The question refers to the second paragraph, which mentions phase changes. What happens during a phase change? Two things happen: (1) Increased kinetic energy weakens the attractive intermolecular forces in the water, and (2) Some molecules escape the liquid as a gas. Now that we have reviewed this information, it's pretty easy to eliminate (G) and (H). Now let's look at (J). Did we read anything in the passage that told us about other phase changes? No. This answer is beyond the realm of the passage and can be eliminated. So the correct choice is (F), and again we've reached it by using POE.

Question	Answer	Explanation
3	B	This is a What If? question. The ACT test writers want to see if you can predict what will happen if you raise the temperature of water higher than that of Sample 2. What answer choices should you eliminate? Decide whether the correct answer should begin with a yes or a no. How do we do that? Just check the graph with the results for Samples 1 and 2. When you increase the temperature, will the sample have more or less kinetic energy? It will have more. That means we can rule out (D). We can eliminate (C) because the temperature reading of Sample 2 is lower than the third sample. Now compare (A) with (B) to see which one is correct. Does an increase in temperature lead to greater or fewer numbers of molecules escaping the liquid? Greater. Thus, the correct answer is (B).
4	F	This is a Why? question. The passage states that when a substance goes from the liquid to the gas phase, it will evaporate. When a substance has reached the temperature at which it undergoes the phase change, it will evaporate. That's how molecules will escape. Therefore, the answer is (F).
5	C	This is a Look It Up question. When you look at the figure, which line goes the highest? Which has the highest kinetic energy at any one point? Well, the curve for T1 goes higher than the curve for T2. T2 has the highest average kinetic energy, but that's not what this question asks us to find. Therefore, (A) and (B) can be eliminated. (D) is a nonsensical answer choice. (C) is the best answer.

Charts and Graphs Drill 2 (Chapter 20)

Question	Answer	Explanation
1	B	This is a Why? question. Do we see a solution of thyroxine that is 0.3 μg/ml? No. The ACT test writers want you to "guesstimate" where 0.3 μg/ml would fall on the table. This value would have to lie somewhere between 0.2 μg/ml and 0.5 μg/ml. The question requires that you make a guess within the values given. What do we call this skill? Interpolation! Now if we move across the x-axis to the value of 72 hours, and we move up to the range of values between 0.2 μg/ml and 0.5 μg/ml, we see that the y-values range from about 23 percent to 37 percent. The only one that falls in that range is (B)—30 percent.

Question	Answer	Explanation
2	G	This is a What If? question. Notice that they want to know what is true for tadpoles in general. Let's start with (F). This is a ridiculous answer choice. We know that all normal tadpoles undergo metamorphosis. If you're not sure, take a look at the graph. The control group in the graph represents normal tadpoles. They do have some decrease in tail width, although not a lot, in 120 hours or 5 days. (Notice that you needed to know that 5 days is the same as 120 hours.) Thus, (F) is incorrect. You can also rule out (H) because the figure clearly shows that high concentrations of thyroxine solutions lead to the greatest decrease in tail width. The passage doesn't mention anything about temperature, thus (J) is out. The correct answer is (G). We see that the control sample shows some reduction in tail size in 120 hours, so it must take longer for the process to be complete.
3	C	This is a Look It Up question. You must realize that as the tadpole develops, the tail is reabsorbed—or it shrinks. The graph compares percent decrease in tail width to hours. At 96 hours (4 days), the tadpoles showing the lowest percent decrease in tail width would be the least developed. Therefore, the answer must be (C), the tadpoles in 0.1 µg/ml.
4	G	This is also a Look It Up question. Thyroxine affects the metamorphosis of the tadpole by influencing the process of cell determination from tadpole cells into mature adult cells. You don't have to understand this process—just realize that it occurs between tadpole and adult stages. Begin with (F), (G), and (H), because you need a tadpole to start the process. Using POE, the correct answer can be only (G).
5	C	Take a look at the figure provided. When do the lines start to differentiate from one another (showing different rates of tail reabsorption)? We can see that by 24 hours, the tadpoles placed in the various thyroxine solutions have each had a larger percent of their tails reabsorbed than the tadpoles in the control group. (D) can be eliminated. Now look between 0 and 24 hours. At 0 hours and at 12 hours, the percent decrease in tail width is the same for all the tadpoles. Therefore, the change in metamorphosis rate must occur between 12 and 24 hours, so (C) is correct.

Charts and Graphs Drill 3 (Chapter 20)

Question	Answer	Explanation
1	A	Finally, a question about drawing a graph! This question was easy because you only needed to look at the *x*- and *y*-axes (a typical Look It Up question). The atomic number of the elements was the independent variable, and the atomic radius was the dependent variable. What happens to the atomic radius as you increase the atomic number? It gets smaller. That means we can eliminate (C) and (D). Now we have to decide if it's a linear relationship or an exponential one. Just check the numbers. Notice that the numbers decrease by a smaller amount each time—so it's a curve, not a straight line. Thus, the correct answer is (A).
2	J	This question requires that you integrate information from two parts of the table, so it's a Why? question. You should look at relationships between electronegativity and one of the other properties of elements. Let's start with (G) and (J). Why? They are opposites (the switch again), so they can't both be true. If an element has a high electronegativity, is it a metal or a non-metal? It's a non-metal, so eliminate (G). Now we can check the other answer choices. Must an element with a high electronegativity have an even or an odd atomic number? Let's check. If you look at the two highest electronegative elements, O and F, one is even and one is odd. So (F) is not true. As for (H), we know that elements with high electronegativity pull their outer electrons (the passage defines electronegativity as a measure of that strength). Therefore, we can eliminate (H). The correct answer is (J).
3	B	This question asks you to make a generalization about trends in the chart, with regard to the bigger picture. Let's take a moment to think about the answer choices. If we want to make generalizations about elements, would an answer that refers to specific elements be the correct one? Probably not. So we can probably eliminate (D). But let's look at (D) more closely to be sure. Is the atomic radius of F larger than that of N? No. Do all metals have high electronegativity values? No. Now notice that (A) and (B) state opposite trends. Use the chart to determine which is correct. As the atomic radius decreases, electronegativity increases. Thus, the correct is (B).

Question	Answer	Explanation
4	G	This is a Why? question because you have to integrate the information on the chart and information in the passage. The first part is easy. Look at the chart to tell you which has a greater electronegativity, Li or F. F, of course! So we can get rid of (J). Now why is the electronegativity of F greater than that of Li? We have to choose between (F) and (G). Can you determine which one of these is correct by using the information in the chart? NO. Go back to the introduction and skim for information about electronegativity. The passage says specifically that within a row of the periodic table, the electronegativity tends to increase with increasing atomic number, due to the tighter bonding between protons and electrons. Its not the number that's important, but rather how tightly bound they are. F has a higher atomic number than Li and more electrons than Li, so, F's electrons are more tightly bound than Li's. Therefore, the best answer is (G).
5	A	This is a Why? question. You must take new information given in the question and apply it to the chart given in the passage. Fortunately, this is very easy. Be careful; the question asks for increasing order of ionization energies. Because it follows the same trend as electronegativity, just find the answer that lists elements with increasing electronegativities. The answer can only be (A).

Experiments Drill 1 (Chapter 21)

Question	Answer	Explanation
1	B	This is a Look It Up question, and it directs your attention to Experiments 1 and 2. In Experiment 1, the plant bends when exposed to sunlight. In Experiment 2, the light-proof cap inhibits the influence of sunlight in such a way that prevents the bending of the plant. Clearly, the cap prevented sunlight from having any effect. So we can eliminate (C). The passage doesn't give any information on the amount of sunlight (D) or the influence of nutrition (A). The only answer that correctly addresses the effect of the cap on the plant tip is (B). It was the tip of the plant that was covered by the cap; therefore, the tip of the plant must somehow perceive sunlight.
2	F	Here is a Look It Up question about the control of the study. The control sample is Plant 1. Nothing was done to this plant. Plants 2, 3, and 4 were all manipulated to some degree to determine the influence of sunlight on phototropism. Plant 1 is left as is in the sunlight. Therefore, the answer is (F).

Question	Answer	Explanation
3	C	This is a Why? question that requires more than one piece of information, so you need to look at the results of all of the experiments. Did you notice that when the tip was covered, the plant didn't bend? Actually, it's not the tip that bends but a region farther down from the tip. That means there must be some sort of communication between the tip of the plant and that region for this response to take place. Therefore the answer is (C). (B) is incorrect because plants *do* respond to sunlight—they bend. The passage does not give any information about differences between flowering plants and non-flowering plants, (D) or the strength of the sun's rays, (A).
4	F	This is a What If? question. Did you notice that the question begins with the word *suppose*? That's a hint that you're supposed to predict the outcome of a similar study. You already know that the initial communication for phototropism occurs in the tip of the plant. If the tip is cut off, the most likely reaction would be that the plant will no longer be able to send information to the lower bending region, and, therefore, the plant will not bend. If you followed all the results of the study, then this should have been a logical follow-up based on the results. The answer to this question is (F).

Experiments Drill 2 (Chapter 21)

Question	Answer	Explanation
1	D	This is a Look It Up question. You need to find the types of fossilized organisms that are found in the black shale layer. You should therefore look at the table. What types of fossilized organisms are found in the black shale layer? There are snails, clams, oysters, and periwinkles. You can eliminate any of these answer choices because you're looking for the wrong answer choice. The only one that is not found in this layer is sponges. So the answer is (D).
2	H	This is a Why? question. Pine needles are not mentioned in any of the studies, but if you look at the data in each study, you will notice that plant fossils occur in only one kind of rock: coal. Thus the correct answer is (H).
3	B	This is a Why? question. You're supposed to observe the results of Studies 1 and 2 and figure out the correct sequence of the rock formations. Did you notice that the layers of Studies 1 and 2 overlap? The ordering of the layers must have been limestone, black shale, coal, and sandstone. The only one with the correct sequence is (B).

Question	Answer	Explanation
4	F	This is a Look It Up question. The ACT test writers want you to read the part of the passage that mentions that the rock formations can be altered by various types of erosions. Which of the answer choices is an example of erosion? The correct answer is the term "weathering," which refers to the break-up of rock formations by physical or chemical means. Answer choice (J) is ridiculous because it has nothing to do with the passage. In addition, a mild rainstorm or extreme heat would not be sufficient to wear away rock formations. So the correct answer is (F).

Experiments Drill 3 (Chapter 21)

Question	Answer	Explanation
1	B	This is a Why? question. You can use the table to help you answer this question. Displacement changes according to what other variable? Force. As force changes, the displacement also changes. You could have looked at the formula $F = -kx$, which shows that force is related to displacement (x). None of the other factors listed will affect the displacement. So the answer to this question is (B).
2	H	This is a Why? question that requires you to predict the displacement that would result from a hypothesized value of force. This is an example of interpolation. We're looking for a value that is going to fall within the range of values provided. What do we do? Guesstimate using the chart. The displacement from a force of 8 pounds is 4 pounds and from 10 pounds would be 5. The only answer choice in that range is (H), 4.5; (H) is the correct answer.
3	D	This is a Why? question. Where in the chart do we look to see what happens when the weight of the mass is doubled? Only trials 1 and 3 do this. Between Trials 1 and 3, the displacement and the force are both doubled, so (D) is correct.

Fighting Scientists Drill 1 (Chapter 22)

Question	Answer	Explanation
1	C	This is a Look It Up question. What are the beliefs of Scientist 1? His main point is that Pangaea (one continent) existed 137 million years ago. Now let's start by looking at each of the answer choices. Were the continents once part of one large land mass? Yes. We read that in the passage. What about (B)? Did the continents break up and drift apart? Definitely. Does the statement that the ocean basins remained fixed agree with the theory? No. If so, how would the continents drift apart? So (C) is inconsistent. (D) is not inconsistent with the theory of Scientist 1. So the correct answer choice is (C).

Question	Answer	Explanation
2	G	This is a Why? question. Scientist 2 needs to show how what Scientist 1 said fits with Scientist 2's hypothesis. It will also probably be something which disagrees with Scientist 1's argument. Answer choice (F) states that the techniques used to date and compare fossils are accurate. This is an argument Scientist 1 makes but that Scientist 2 doesn't mention. Cross it out. Answer choice (G) says that the soil and climate conditions were once the same—a nice paraphrase of what Scientist 2 says at the end of the argument. Keep (G) for now. Answer choice (H) supports Scientist 1 because extremely large ferns would have a hard time floating thousands of miles across the ocean. You can eliminate (J) because it doesn't support either scientist. Scientist 2 would infer that these ferns grew well in both places; (G) has to be right.
3	C	This is a Why? question, and it's kind of tricky. Either scientist could use this information to support his theory if he could come up with a valid reason. Answer choice (A) says that Scientist 1 is supported because the finding shows tectonic activity. But we already knew about that and besides, that's a point on which the scientists agree. So eliminate (A). Answer choice (D) also gives us information that was already stated in Scientist 2's statement, so this choice is weak. Choice (B) is ridiculous because neither scientist believes that Pangaea exists today, so cross it out. At this point, (C) is looking pretty good. Scientist 2 could soundly reason that tectonic activity in a solid land mass demonstrates that this geological phenomenon does not lead to continental drift. The best answer is (C).
4	G	This is a Look It Up question. The passage tells us about the formation of land masses, tectonic plates, and other geological evidence—namely fossils. You must be able to add this together and determine that the scientists know something about geology. So only (G) can be correct.
5	A	This is a Look It Up question. You must know what each scientist supports. Let's go through the choices one by one. Statement I is supported by both scientists because both believe that tectonic activity exists and changes geological formations. (Scientist 1 thinks it's more important than does Scientist 2, but that doesn't matter here.) So Statement I is correct and we're down to (A) and (C). Let's keep checking. Only Scientist 2 supports Statement II and only Scientist 1 supports Statement III. Therefore, (A) must be the correct answer.

Fighting Scientists Drill 2 (Chapter 22)

Question	Answer	Explanation
1	A	This is a Why? question because we're asked to find an answer that supports the argument. To do this, we must understand the argument. What's the main point of Hypothesis 2? The debater believes that the chance of RNA reproducing as the graduate student described is extremely small. Look for an answer choice that supports this argument. Answer choice (A) states that conditions in the atmosphere were too unstable to support the necessary gases. Does this statement support Hypothesis 2? Yes. How? Because it weakens Hypothesis 1. So (A) is correct. Answer choices (B), (C), and (D) are wrong because they support Hypothesis 1.
2	G	This is a Look It Up question, and we're looking for an assumption in the argument. What does Scientist 1 believe? That the experiment shows how the first organic compounds were made. Is (F) an assumption in this argument? No. It refers to Hypothesis 2. What about (G)? Yes. The scientist assumed that the experiment mimicked the conditions of primeval Earth. So (G) is correct. Answer choice (H) states that proteins are the building blocks of amino acids. That's wrong; as stated in Hypothesis 1, amino acids are the building blocks of proteins. So get rid of (H). Answer choice (J) is incorrect because Earth had to have hydrogen in order to form organic compounds.
3	A	This is a Look It Up question. What does Hypothesis 1 say about amino acids? The passage tells us that amino acids are the building blocks of life, so let's start with the answer choices that list amino acids last. We can quickly eliminate (C). We can also eliminate (B) because the meteor theory was part of Hypothesis 2, not Hypothesis 1. And we're down to (A) and (D). We can also find in the passage that amino acids are the building blocks of proteins, so amino acids should be before proteins in the list. So by POE and understanding the passage, we arrive at the correct answer, (A).

Fighting Scientists Drill 3 (Chapter 23)

Question	Answer	Explanation
1	C	This is a Why? question. We are looking for an answer that supports Hypothesis 2. Hypothesis 2 states that an increase in precipitation or an increase in pollution would lead to a significant drop in temperature. Answer choice (A) states that there is more snow in Canada this year, but we don't know if that's enough snow for glaciation. So we can eliminate it. Let's look at (B). If snow didn't stick to the ground, would there be an ice age? Answer choice (B) is silly; eliminate it. What about (C)? If there is a drop in temperature for every increase in the pollution rate, could that lead to glaciation? Yes. Let's look at (D). If the water became more polluted, would that necessarily lead to the next ice age? We're not sure. The passage states that pollution in the air, not necessarily in the water, leads to a decrease in temperature. So the correct answer is (C).
2	H	This is a Why? question. For this question we're looking for an answer that could disprove Hypothesis 1. What is the main point of Hypothesis 1? The debater says that it is highly unlikely that Earth will experience another ice age. Why? Because he believes that the necessary conditions will not be met in the future. What is the best way to disprove this point? Just indicate that the conditions could change in the future and then the chance for glaciation could increase. Which choice states that? Answer choice (H). Now let's look at (F). A fluctuation in temperature would not necessarily mean that the temperature was low enough for glaciation to occur. We therefore can eliminate this choice. Even if there was more snowfall in the Swiss Alps, we are not given an indication of how long it lasted. So you can get rid of (G). Now, if the temperature went up 5°C in the North Pole, it would be warmer, not colder, so (J) is out. So the correct answer choice is (H).
3	C	This is a Look It Up question because you are being asked to identify the regions in which glaciation would take place. Let's start with Statement II, because it appears in the most answer choices. Based on the passage, would glaciation take place in polar regions? The passage tells us that polar regions would be one of the first locations in which glaciation would take place. Now that you can eliminate answer choices that don't include Statement II, you can eliminate (A). What about heavily polluted regions? Yes. The passage refers to the other possible cause of a temperature drop—pollution. We can eliminate (B) and (D) because they don't include Statement II. Therefore, (C) must be correct.

Question	Answer	Explanation
4	G	This is also a Look It Up question. According to Hypothesis 2, there are two conditions that are critical to glaciation: temperature and precipitation. Answer choice (F) is incorrect because pollution doesn't cause precipitation. Answer choice (G) sounds good because it states that pollution leads to a major drop in temperature (it has one of the conditions). What about (H)? You can eliminate (H) because glaciation needs both low temperatures and high precipitation. (J) supports Hypothesis 1, not Hypothesis 2, so we can eliminate it. The best answer is (G).

Part VIII

The Princeton Review
ACT Practice Exam 1
and Answers and Explanations

Chapter 26
Practice Exam 1

ENGLISH TEST
45 Minutes—75 Questions

DIRECTIONS: In the five passages that follow, certain words and phrases are underlined and numbered. In the right-hand column, you will find alternatives for each underlined part. You are to choose the one that best expresses the idea, makes the statement appropriate for standard written English, or is worded most consistently with the style and tone of the passage as a whole. If you think the original version is best, choose "NO CHANGE."

You will also find questions about a section of the passage or the passage as a whole. These questions do not refer to

an underlined portion of the passage but rather are identified by a number or numbers in a box.

For each question, choose the alternative you consider best and blacken the corresponding oval on your answer sheet. Read each passage through once before you begin to answer the questions that accompany it. You cannot determine most answers without first reading several sentences beyond the question. Be sure that you have read far enough ahead each time you choose an alternative.

PASSAGE I

Animal Migration

It seems inconceivable to us <u>when</u> some animals
₁

1. A. NO CHANGE
   B. whereby
   C. that
   D. if

travel thousands of miles during their life cycles. <u>Yet,</u> an
₂
amazingly wide variety of creatures annually make long
and even arduous journeys.

2. F. NO CHANGE
   G. So,
   H. Happily,
   J. For,

<u>For understanding</u> why they do it, we need only look
₃
at the changing seasons in the North. As summer fades
into fall, which in turn fades into winter, we turn on our
furnaces and take our warm coats out of storage
<u>because it is cold.</u> We eat less fresh food. If our winter
₄

3. A. NO CHANGE
   B. To understand
   C. As understanding
   D. If we understand

4. F. NO CHANGE
   G. as if it was cold
   H. because it was cold
   J. OMIT the underlined portion.

food is <u>fresh, it has</u> probably been shipped from a warmer
₅
climate.

5. A. NO CHANGE
   B. fresh. They have
   C. fresh; it has
   D. fresh. It has

Wild animals, <u>nevertheless,</u> have not developed the
₆
sophisticated technologies necessary for the

6. F. NO CHANGE
   G. however
   H. although
   J. in addition

GO ON TO THE NEXT PAGE.

adaptations and adjustments that we employ and utilize.
⁷
They are at the mercy of the environment in terms of

climatological change and the subsequent availability

of food. Some animals have developed it's own ways of
⁸
surviving seasonal changes. In order to endure the harsher

seasons, some change their coats as we do. Even the

family dog or cat, long removed from the wild, follows

this adaptive pattern.

Others, though, are not able to adapt to the

fluctuating temperatures. They follow the warm weather

south (or north, if they live south of the equator). These

migratory creatures, a group that encompasses birds,
⁹
whales, fish, insects, and quadrupedal mammals, have

bodies adapted to the demands of long seasonal journeys.

[1] Why do they travel so very far? [2] During its

migration from equatorial Africa to northern Europe,

the white stork crossed the Sahara Desert and the
¹⁰
Mediterranean Sea. [3] This is something of a mystery,

especially because some creatures must traverse

inhospitable areas during the trip to their seasonal homes.

[4] For example, certain sea birds must cross oceans to

get to their winter nesting grounds.[11]

Although the exact cause for such journeys is

impossible to determine. Scientists speculate that
¹²

7. A. NO CHANGE
   B. adaptations and adjustments that we employed and utilized.
   C. adaptations and adjustments that we are employing.
   D. adaptations we employ.

8. F. NO CHANGE
   G. each's
   H. theirs
   J. their

9. A. NO CHANGE
   B. encompasses: birds
   C. encompasses, birds
   D. encompass birds

10. F. NO CHANGE
   G. having crossed
   H. crosses
   I. had crossed

11. Which of the following best sequences of sentences makes this paragraph most logical?

   A. NO CHANGE
   B. 1, 3, 2, 4
   C. 4, 2, 1, 3
   D. 3, 2, 1, 4

12. F. NO CHANGE
   G. determine—scientists
   H. determine; scientists
   J. determine, scientists

GO ON TO THE NEXT PAGE.

continental drift has pulled traditional

seasonal homes far apart and that instinct
        ———————
         13

having precluded a change in territorial preference.
————————
   14

Perhaps more study into the past may shed light on the

causes of migration. Evidence also suggests that some

species of dinosaurs migrated. The Elmisaurus has been

found in both Mongolia and North America, indicating

that this dinosaur migrated.

13. **A.** NO CHANGE
    B. apart and,
    C. apart: and
    D. apart; and

14. **F.** NO CHANGE
    G. had precluded
    H. was precluding
    J. has precluded

Item 15 poses a question about Passage I as a whole.

---

15. Which of the following best describes the tone and purpose of this essay?

    A. The tone is ironic; the purpose is to point out the similarities between people and animals.
    B. The tone is objective; the purpose is to discuss some possible reasons for migration in animals.
    C. The tone is critical; the purpose is to condemn animals for being unable to adapt to the seasons.
    D. The tone is humorous; the purpose is to present an amusing anecdote.

PASSAGE II

The Dada Movement

[1]

Max Ernst, in the Dada movement, was a German
———————————————————————————
                         16

artist and a leading figure.
——————————————
        16

However, Ernst cut up photographs, engravings, and
————————
   17

illustrations, and recombined the images in collage form.

The featured objects thereby assumed new, sometimes

multiple, identities.

16. **F.** NO CHANGE
    G. In the Dada movement, a leading figure and a German artist, was Max Ernst.
    H. Max Ernst was a German artist and a leading figure in the Dada movement.
    J. A German artist and a leading figure in the Dada movement was Max Ernst.

17. **A.** NO CHANGE
    B. As a consequence,
    C. Despite the fact,
    D. OMIT the underlined portion.

GO ON TO THE NEXT PAGE.

[2]

Horrified by trench warfare, a lasting imprint was
<u>left</u> on the generation of European intellectuals who
18

came of age during World War I. Painters, sculptors, and

<u>people who wrote</u> turned their expressions of protest into
19

works of art and gave their movement the <u>nonsensical and</u>
20

<u>meaningless</u> name Dada. Dada condemned the existing
20

cultural institutions and advocated the liberation of

artistic form.

[3]

The loosely knit group found refuge in Zurich,

Switzerland, a <u>neutrally</u> country. From this safe haven,
21

the Dadaists <u>hurled</u> ridicule and abuse at nationalism,
22

rationalism, materialism, and any other modern "ism"

that they believed had contributed to the breakdown

of society and allowed the war. Some analysts have

portrayed the Dada movement as the <u>forerunners</u> of what
23

has become known as "Shock Art."

<u>Marcel Duchamp was an example of a leading French</u>
24

<u>artist in the group and he</u> painted a mustache on a copy
24

of the *Mona Lisa* and put a coded obscenity beneath the

portrait.

[4]

<u>Max Ernst is best known for contributing</u> to this
25

movement was the development of the frottage technique.

18. **F.** NO CHANGE
   G. Horrified, trench warfare left a lasting imprint
   H. The horror of trench warfare left a lasting imprint
   J. A lasting imprint left by trench warfare

19. **A.** NO CHANGE
   B. writers
   C. writing people
   D. OMIT the underlined portion.

20. **F.** NO CHANGE
   G. nonsensical, and meaningless
   H. nonsensical and absurd
   J. nonsensical

21. **A.** NO CHANGE
   B. neutral
   C. neutralist
   D. notorious

22. **F.** NO CHANGE
   G. would hurl
   H. hurl
   J. were hurling

23. **A.** NO CHANGE
   B. foreshadowing
   C. forerunner
   D. champions

24. **F.** NO CHANGE
   G. An example of a leading French Dada artist, Marcel Duchamp,
   H. For example, the Frenchman Marcel Duchamp,
   J. For example, Marcel Duchamp, a leading French artist in the group,

25. **A.** NO CHANGE
   B. Max Ernst's best-known contribution
   C. Max Ernsts' best-known contribution
   D. Max Ernst is best known for his contribution

GO ON TO THE NEXT PAGE.

Ernst lay down paper over raised surfaces, rubbed a
pencil over the paper, and then isolated images in the
haphazard design that resulted. These images were then
to be translated into paintings. The desolate landscapes
portrayed in many of Ernsts' later works suggest the
destruction of a depraved society.

[5]

The Dada movement had lost much of their impetus
by the early 1920s. At that time, Ernst moved to Paris
where another artistic movement, surrealism, was in
its formative stages. Surrealists sought to capture the
images produced by free association of the unconscious
mind. They combined these images in incongruous ways,
creating effects that were sometimes humorous, but
sometimes frightening.

26. F. NO CHANGE
    G. placed down
    H. placed
    J. placed and lay

27. A. NO CHANGE
    B. Ernsts' later work
    C. the later work of Ernst's
    D. Ernst's later works

28. F. NO CHANGE
    G. its
    H. the movement's
    I. the movements'

Items 29 and 30 pose a question about Passage II as a whole.

29. Which of the following best describes the writer's tone in the passage?

    A. Annoyed
    B. Informative
    C. Caustic
    D. Upbeat

30. Which of the following sequences of paragraphs will make the essay most logical?

    F. NO CHANGE
    G. 4, 2, 1, 3, 5
    H. 2, 3, 1, 4, 5
    J. 2, 3, 4, 5, 1

GO ON TO THE NEXT PAGE.

PASSAGE III

Ella Fitzgerald

Jazz singer, Ella Fitzgerald, was born in 1918 in
Newport News, Virginia. She took part in a performance
on amateur night at the Apollo Theater in New York when
she caught the eye and ear of bandleader Chick Webb,
who hired her immediately. Fitzgerald performed with
Webb's band until his death in 1935, at which time she
took over the group. Two years later, she left
to pursue a career as a soloist.

As a black female performer in nightclubs, Fitzgerald
contended with racism as well as sexism. This, combined
with a poverty-stricken background, a father who
abandoned her, and a runaway as a teen, could have

pushed she over the edge into drug addiction, as it did her
friend and fellow jazz star, Billie Holiday. But Fitzgerald
remained so strongly, and her songbook albums led to the
growth of her popularity and her legend.

[1] She flawlessly interpreted the works of such
musical legends as Jerome Kern, Cole Porter, and George
Gershwin, who are very famous. [2] She sang songs from

31. A. NO CHANGE
    B. singer: Ella Fitzgerald,
    C. singer Ella Fitzgerald
    D. singer Ella Fitzgerald,

32. F. NO CHANGE
    G. was performing
    H. has been performing
    J. is performing

33. A. NO CHANGE
    B. having pursued
    C. only to pursue
    D. and pursuing

34. F. NO CHANGE
    G. black, female, performer
    H. female, black performer
    J. performer who happened to be black and female

35. A. NO CHANGE
    B. a running away to the city when she was a teenager
    C. a life on the streets as a teen
    D. as a teen runaway to live on the streets

36. F. NO CHANGE
    G. herself
    H. them
    J. her

37. A. NO CHANGE
    B. strong
    C. the stronger of the two
    D. strongest

38. F. NO CHANGE
    G. all of who are famous
    H. all famous
    J. OMIT the underlined portion and end the sentence with a period.

GO ON TO THE NEXT PAGE.

a broad spectrum of music, ranging from slow and sultry to upbeat and swinging. [3] Nicknamed "the First Lady of Song," Fitzgerald had a long and illustrious career. [4] Her contribution to the world of

39

music, and indeed to society as a whole, was great. 40

Fitzgerald helped pave the way for other black

41

singers and brought jazz to a larger audience. Her singing

42

facilitated the integration of blacks and whites, at least within the confines of the music hall. Either blacks

43

or whites flocked to hear her sing,

43

united under a brief time by the magic of her sound.

44

39. A. NO CHANGE
    B. contributions
    C. contributing
    D. having contributed

40. For the sake of unity and coherence, Sentence 3 should be:
    F. left where it is now.
    G. placed after Sentence 1.
    H. placed before Sentence 1.
    J. OMITTED.

41. A. NO CHANGE
    B. the paving of
    C. paving
    D. OMIT the underlined portion.

42. F. NO CHANGE
    G. Since her singing
    H. Since Fitzgerald's singing
    J. That her singing

43. A. NO CHANGE
    B. All blacks and whites
    C. Both blacks and whites
    D. Because blacks and whites

44. F. NO CHANGE
    G. united for a brief time
    H. united—for a brief time
    J. united, for a brief time

Item 45 poses a question about Passage III as a whole.

45. Suppose that a newspaper editor had assigned the writer to describe an instance of racial unity in the arts. Does the essay successfully fulfill the assignment?

    A. No, because its main focus is on the career of Fitzgerald.
    B. Yes, because Fitzgerald sang works by white composers.
    C. Yes, because blacks and whites alike went to see Fitzgerald sing.
    D. No, because very few people listen to jazz.

GO ON TO THE NEXT PAGE.

PASSAGE IV

The Change to Agriculture

Approximately ten thousand years ago, a radical change took place in the way people lived, significantly altering their lives. Ancient peoples abandoned the traditional methods of hunting and gathering their food, which required an arduous seasonal migration. Instead, they domesticated the plants and animals they needed for surviving.

The shift to domestication and a sedentary lifestyle wrought great change. Lost to us is the knowledge of whether or not the lifestyle change itself gave rise to new technologies (or at least improvements and adaptations of the way things had been done) or whether the development of new technologies made the lifestyle shift possible.

What is known is that after the initial adaptations, the two have seemed to move in tandem ever since. For example, a given area of land could now support more people than were ever before possible. More people in a given area made finding a mate easier, and more children had been born and lived longer. Thus, the ability of the land to support more people ineluctably led to more people in the area.

46. **F.** NO CHANGE
G. to alter their lives
H. which significantly altered their lives
J. OMIT the underlined portion and end the sentence with a period.

47. **A.** NO CHANGE
B. Nevertheless,
C. However,
D. Even so,

48. **F.** NO CHANGE
G. surviving.
H. to survive.
J. to have survived.

49. **A.** NO CHANGE
B. from
C. of
D. for

50. **F.** NO CHANGE
G. whether
H. regardless
J. how or even whether

51. **A.** NO CHANGE
B. What is known, is
C. We know
D. Our wisdom tells us

52. **F.** NO CHANGE
G. than was
H. than they were
J. than it were

53. **A.** NO CHANGE
B. were being borned to live longer
C. were being born and living longer
D. were born and lived longer

GO ON TO THE NEXT PAGE.

Agriculture necessitated the storage of seed stock, the division of labor, and <u>allocating</u> land. The increased
₅₄
populace could now be put into productive

<u>service working</u> additional land, producing additional
₅₅
food, and providing more varied services. Economies of scale led to an increased specialization of crops, which in turn led to an increased need for other specialized products.

As each region became more specialized in what <u>they produced, the need</u> for greater trade and
₅₆
communication intensified. The population in each area became situated around natural, centrally located <u>points, which</u> developed into the first cities. It became
₅₇

necessary to organize the increasingly <u>complex and</u>
₅₈
<u>complicated</u> economic relationships and to develop a
₅₈
structure capable <u>to deal</u> with the many societal changes.
₅₉

Thus, a <u>centrally located</u> authority developed, giving rise
₆₀
to some of the first real governments.

54. **F.** NO CHANGE
    G. to allocate
    H. allocated
    J. the allocation of

55. **A.** NO CHANGE
    B. service: working
    C. service. Working
    D. servitude and working

56. **F.** NO CHANGE
    G. it produced. The need
    H. they produced. The need
    J. it produced, the need

57. **A.** NO CHANGE
    B. points: which
    C. points: which,
    D. points; which

58. **F.** NO CHANGE
    G. complex, and complicated
    H. complex but complicated
    J. complex

59. **A.** NO CHANGE
    B. of dealing
    C. to have dealt
    D. OMIT the underlined portion.

60. **F.** NO CHANGE
    G. central location
    H. central located
    J. centrally location

GO ON TO THE NEXT PAGE.

PASSAGE V

Who Was Dracula?

[1] Many legends, such as those of Bluebeard and King Arthur, are based on real people and events. [2] One of the most striking examples of a legendary character who is based on real people is Count Dracula. [3] Many people believe that Dracula is a fictional character invented by Bram Stoker, the nineteenth-century writer, and that tales of vampires in turn derive from Stoker's popular story. [4] In actuality, though, Stoker based his character on Prince Vlad IV, a Transylvanian resistance fighter also known as "Vlad the Impaler." [5] The history and derivations of Vlad's several names is itself an interesting story. [6] The name "Dracula" may come from the Romanian word *drac*, meaning both "dragon" and "devil," and thus referring to Vlad's bloody activities. [7] On the other hand, the father of Prince Vlad IV was named Vlad Dracul, an honor and title bestowed by the Order of the Dragon that was probably hereditary, at least in part. [8] Thus, Vlad IV could, and did, refer to himself as "Dracula" and even signed official documents with that sobriquet. [9] Even such historical evidence, notwithstanding, is not sufficient to outweigh the political and cultural distaste present-day Romanians have for referring to their prince as "Dracula." [10] To many, Prince Vlad was a national hero and call him Dracula reduces him to Stoker's fictional monster. [11] Despite its suggestions of brutality, "Vlad Tepes," or Vlad the Impaler, is the name preferred by these patriots.

61. **A.** NO CHANGE
    B. on real people was
    C. on a real person was
    D. on a real person is

62. **F.** NO CHANGE
    G. were deriving
    H. are deriving from
    J. being derived from

63. **A.** NO CHANGE
    B. history
    C. derivations
    D. beginning

64. **F.** NO CHANGE
    G. refers
    H. has referred
    J. could have referred

65. **A.** NO CHANGE
    B. could, and did refer
    C. could and did, refer
    D. calls and refers

66. **F.** NO CHANGE
    G. yet
    H. nevertheless
    J. however

67. **A.** NO CHANGE
    B. to call
    C. having called
    D. by calling

GO ON TO THE NEXT PAGE.

[12] Vlad had been living in the fifteenth century, when
68
Transylvania was under constant attack. [13] He united

armies to fight the invaders, who were notorious for their

cruelty and barbarity, for which they were famous.
69
[14] Vlad earned his nickname by outdoing his enemies

at their own game; when he captured them alive, he

would impale them on stakes and watch them die slow,

excruciating deaths. [15] The prince's cruelty was not

limited to foes, however. [16] When soldiers deserted his

army or failed to meet his military standards received the
70
same treatment. [17] Hundreds of thousands of people
70
died while Vlad calmly went about his everyday business.

71

68. F. NO CHANGE
G. Vlad, living
H. Vlad lived
J. Vlad, who lived

69. A. NO CHANGE
B. and which made them famous
C. which they were famous for
D. OMIT the underlined portion.

70. F. NO CHANGE
G. standards receiving the same treatment.
H. standards, they received the same treatment.
J. standards, received the same treatment.

71. The writer has been told that the first paragraph needs to be broken into two. Where would be the best place to split the paragraph?

A. between Sentences 3 and 4
B. between Sentences 4 and 5
C. between Sentences 12 and 13
D. between Sentences 15 and 16

GO ON TO THE NEXT PAGE.

[1] For example, the stakes upon which Vlad impaled his victims became, in popular legend, the only weapon that could kill a vampire. [2] The enduring legend of Dracula is one of countless examples of the merging of fact and fiction. [3] It is not surprising that Vlad's legend lived on long after his death, nor is it surprising that in the retelling, several details were changed and exaggerated. [4] Similarly, Vlad's bloodthirsty nature was <u>also likewise</u> transformed into a central feature of vampire <u>lore—by the</u> vampire's grisly habit of sucking his victim's blood. 74

72. **F.** NO CHANGE
    G. also
    H. likewise
    J. OMIT the underlined portion.

73. **A.** NO CHANGE
    B. lore: the vampire's
    C. lore as evidenced by the vampire's
    D. lore: as evidenced by the vampire'

74. Which of the following sequences of sentences makes this paragraph most logical?

    F. NO CHANGE
    G. 4, 2, 1, 3
    H. 3, 2, 1, 4
    J. 3, 1, 4, 2

Item 75 poses a question about Passage V as a whole.

---

75. Which of the following sentences most effectively summarizes the conclusion drawn by the essay as a whole?

    A. Vlad the Impaler was very famous.
    B. Dracula is an example of a fictional character who is based on an actual historical figure.
    C. Vlad the Impaler was also known as Count Dracula.
    D. History often repeats itself.

END OF TEST 1
STOP! DO NOT TURN THE PAGE UNTIL TOLD TO DO SO.

MATHEMATICS TEST

60 Minutes—60 Questions

DIRECTIONS: Solve each problem, choose the correct answer, and then darken the corresponding oval on your answer sheet.

Do not linger over problems that take too much time. Solve as many as you can; then return to the others in the time you have left for this test.

You are permitted to use a calculator on this test. You may use your calculator for any problems you choose, but some of the problems may best be done without using a calculator.

Note: Unless otherwise stated, all of the following should be assumed:

1. Illustrative figures are NOT necessarily drawn to scale.
2. Geometric figures lie in a plane.
3. The word *line* indicates a straight line.
4. The word *average* indicates arithmetic mean.

---

1. In the figure below, the measure of ∠A is 80°. If the measure of ∠B is half the measure of ∠A, what is the measure of ∠C ?

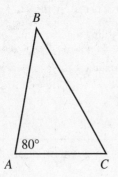

A. 40°
B. 60°
C. 80°
D. 100°
E. 120°

2. Property tax is 8% of the assessed value of a house. How much would the property tax be on a house with an assessed value of $80,000 ?

F. $100
G. $640
H. $1,000
J. $6,400
K. $10,000

DO YOUR FIGURING HERE.

GO ON TO THE NEXT PAGE.

3. If $4p - 2 = -3(p - 4)$, then $p = $?

   A. -2

   B. $\dfrac{1}{2}$

   C. 2

   D. 10

   E. 12

4. A plumber charges \$75 for the first 30 minutes of each house call plus \$2 for each additional minute that she works. The plumber charges Adam \$113 for her time. For what amount of time, in minutes, did the plumber work?

   F. 19
   G. 38
   H. 49
   J. 59
   K. 64

5. In a group of 48 pianos, 18 are out of tune. What percentage of the pianos is out of tune?

   A. 18%

   B. 30%

   C. $37\dfrac{1}{2}\%$

   D. $62\dfrac{1}{2}\%$

   E. $66\dfrac{2}{3}\%$

6. A group of musicians includes 3 drummers, 4 trumpet players, and 5 pianists. How many different jazz trios, each consisting of a drummer, a trumpet player, and a pianist, can be formed from this group of musicians?

   F. 3
   G. 5
   H. 12
   J. 17
   K. 60

GO ON TO THE NEXT PAGE.

7. If $x = -2$, then $3x^2 - 5x - 6 = $?

   A. -30
   B. -8
   C. -4
   D. 10
   E. 16

DO YOUR FIGURING HERE.

8. Which of the following algebraic inequalities is represented by the graph below?

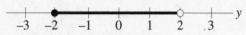

   F. $-2 \geq y < 2$
   G. $-2 < y > 2$
   H. $-2 < y < 2$
   J. $-2 \leq y < 2$
   K. $-2 < y \leq 2$

9. The formula for calculating sales tax is $S = Ar$, where S is the sales tax, A is the cost of the product, and r is the local sales-tax rate. If the cost of a television was $400 and the sales tax was $24, what was the local sales-tax rate?

   A. $.60\%$
   B. 1.67%
   C. 6.00%
   D. 16.67%
   E. 60.00%

10. In the figure below, D, B, and E are collinear. What is the measure of $\angle ABC$?

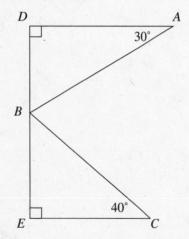

   F. $20°$
   G. $35°$
   H. $50°$
   J. $60°$
   K. $70°$

GO ON TO THE NEXT PAGE.

11. If a circle's area is 16π square centimeters, what is the length, in centimeters, of its diameter?

   A. 2
   B. 4
   C. 8
   D. 16
   E. 32

12. If $g(x) = (x^2 + 3x - 5)(2x + 4)$, what is the value of $g(-3)$?

   F. -50
   G. -46
   H. -10
   J. 10
   K. 46

13. After N chocolate bars are divided equally among 6 children, 3 bars remain. How many would remain if $(N + 4)$ chocolate bars were divided equally among the 6 children?

   A. 0
   B. 1
   C. 2
   D. 3
   E. 4

14. Of the 40 dogs at the animal shelter, 12 are purebred. If 1 of the 40 dogs is selected at random, what is the probability that it is purebred?

   F. .12
   G. .30
   H. .40
   J. .70
   K. .78

15. For all x, $(10x^4 - x^2 + 2x - 8) - (3x^4 + 3x^3 + 2x + 8) = ?$

   A. $7x^4 - 3x^3 - x^2 - 16$
   B. $7x^4 - 4x^2 - 16$
   C. $7x^4 + 3x^3 - x^2 + 4x$
   D. $7x^4 + 2x^2 + 4x$
   E. $13x^4 - 3x^3 - x^2 + 4x$

DO YOUR FIGURING HERE.

GO ON TO THE NEXT PAGE.

16. What is the y-coordinate at which the line determined by the equation $5x + 2 = 7y - 3$ intercepts the y-axis?

    F. -1

    G. $-\dfrac{1}{7}$

    H. $\dfrac{1}{7}$

    J. $\dfrac{5}{7}$

    K. 5

17. A rectangular garden is surrounded by a 60-foot-long fence. One side of the garden is 6 feet longer than the other. Which of the following equations could be used to find s, the shorter side, of the garden?

    A. $8s + s = 60$
    B. $4s = 60 + 12$
    C. $s(s + 6) = 60$
    D. $2(s - 6) + 2s = 60$
    E. $2(s + 6) + 2s = 60$

18. Which of the following is the sum of both solutions to the equation $x^2 - 2x - 8 = 0$?

    F. -6
    G. -4
    H. -2
    J. 2
    K. 6

19. If the legs of a right triangle measure 10 inches and 24 inches, what is the length, in inches, of the hypotenuse?

    A. $\sqrt{34}$
    B. $2\sqrt{17}$
    C. 14
    D. 26
    E. 34

20. $\sqrt{64 + 36} = ?$

    F. 10
    G. 14
    H. 28
    J. 48
    K. 100

GO ON TO THE NEXT PAGE.

DO YOUR FIGURING HERE.

21. For all $y \neq 3$, $\dfrac{y^2 - 9}{3y - 9} = ?$

   A. y

   B. $\dfrac{y+1}{8}$

   C. $y + 1$

   D. $\dfrac{y}{3}$

   E. $\dfrac{y+3}{3}$

22. $\left(\dfrac{1}{2} \times 0.25\right)^3 = ?$

   F. 1.95×10^{-1}
   G. 1.95×10^{-2}
   H. 1.95×10^{-3}
   J. 1.95×10^{-4}

23. In the figure below, $\angle A$ is a right angle. $\overline{AB}$ is 3 units long and $\overline{BC}$ is 5 units long. If the measure of $\angle C$ is θ, what is the value of $\cos \theta$?

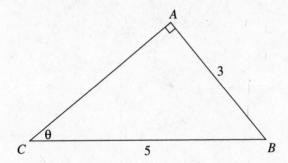

   A. $\dfrac{3}{5}$

   B. $\dfrac{3}{4}$

   C. $\dfrac{4}{5}$

   D. $\dfrac{5}{4}$

   E. $\dfrac{5}{3}$

GO ON TO THE NEXT PAGE.

24. Liam's lawnmower uses $\frac{3}{5}$ of a gallon of gasoline every time he mows his lawn. How many times can Liam mow his lawn if he has only 3 gallons of gasoline?

DO YOUR FIGURING HERE.

    F. 5

    G. 6

    H. 10

    J. $1\frac{4}{5}$

    K. $\frac{5}{3}$

25. $\sqrt[3]{64x^6y^3} = ?$

    A. $4x^2y$
    B. $8xy$
    C. $8x^2y$
    D. $4xy$
    E. $16x^2y$

26. If $x = 2$ and $x = 8$ are the solutions to the quadratic equation $x^2 + Bx + 16 = 0$, what is the value of the constant B ?

    F. −10
    G. −8
    H. −6
    J.   6
    K. 10

27. Triangle A has sides of lengths 8 centimeters, 12 centimeters, and 20 centimeters. Triangle B is similar to triangle A and has a perimeter of 10 centimeters. What is the length, in centimeters, of the shortest side of triangle B ?

    A.   2
    B.   3
    C.   5
    D. 40
    E. 160

GO ON TO THE NEXT PAGE.

28. If $20 - 2(4 - y) = y + 9$, then $y = ?$

DO YOUR FIGURING HERE.

    F. −6
    G. −3
    H. −1
    J.   1
    K. 3

29. What is the slope of the line that passes through the points (4,−1) and (−2,8) ?

    A. $\dfrac{3}{2}$

    B. $\dfrac{1}{4}$

    C. $-\dfrac{1}{4}$

    D. $-\dfrac{3}{2}$

    E. −4

30. If $\sqrt[N]{48} = 2\sqrt[N]{3}$, then $N = ?$

    F. 1
    G. 2
    H. 3
    J. 4
    K. 5

31. Grace tried to compute the average of her 5 test scores. She mistakenly divided the correct total (T) of her scores by 6, and her result was 14 less than what it should have been. Which of the following equations would determine the value of T ?

    A. $5T + 14 = 6T$

    B. $\dfrac{T}{6} = \dfrac{(T - 14)}{5}$

    C. $\dfrac{T}{6} - 14 = \dfrac{T}{5}$

    D. $\dfrac{(T - 14)}{6} = \dfrac{T}{5}$

    E. $\dfrac{T}{6} + 14 = \dfrac{T}{5}$

GO ON TO THE NEXT PAGE.

32. The line $y = \dfrac{4}{5}x - 2$ passes through which one of the following points?

   F. (–5, 4)
   G. (–4, –7)
   H. (4, 3)
   J. (5, 2)
   K. (6, 10)

33. If $x = yz - 2$, which of the following provides the value of z in terms of x and y ?

   A. $\dfrac{x}{y} + 2$

   B. $\dfrac{x}{y} - 2$

   C. $\dfrac{x - 2}{y}$

   D. $\dfrac{2 - x}{y}$

   E. $\dfrac{x + 2}{y}$

34. In the figure below, ABC is an equilateral triangle, and $\overline{BC}$ is 7 units long. If $\angle DCA$ is a right angle and $\angle D$ measures 45°, what is the length of $\overline{AD}$, in units?

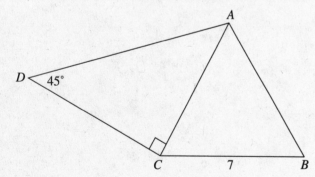

   F. 7
   G. $7\sqrt{2}$
   H. 14
   J. $14\sqrt{2}$
   K. It cannot be determined from the information given.

GO ON TO THE NEXT PAGE.

35. In the figure below, A and ADC are right angles, the length of $\overline{AD}$ is 7 units, the length of $\overline{AB}$ is 10 units, and the length of $\overline{DC}$ is 6 units. What is the area, in square units, of $\triangle DCB$?

DO YOUR FIGURING HERE.

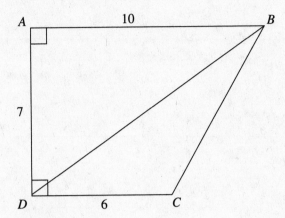

A.   21
B.   24
C. $3\sqrt{149}$
D.   42
E.   210

36. An ellipse can be defined as the set of points the sum of whose distances from two focus points is constant. What is the distance between the focus B and the point C as shown in the standard (x,y) coordinate plane below?

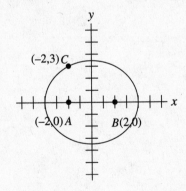

F.   3
G.   4
H.   5
J. $4\sqrt{3}$
K.   8

GO ON TO THE NEXT PAGE.

37. If $(x-2)(x-3) = 3x - 10$, how many possible values for x exist?

   A. 0
   B. 1
   C. 2
   D. 4
   E. Infinitely many

38. Which of the following represents the solution to the inequality $x^2 - 9x + 8 < 0$?

   F. $-8 < x < -1$

   G. $-\dfrac{1}{8} < x < 1$

   H. $1 < x < 8$

   J. $x < 8 \text{ or } x > 1$

   K. $x < -1 \text{ or } x > 8$

39. A line in the standard (x,y) coordinate plane has the same slope as the line $12 = 3y - 7x$. If the line passes through the point $(3,6)$, what is its y-intercept?

   A. $(0, -3)$

   B. $(0, -\dfrac{7}{3})$

   C. $(0, -1)$

   D. $(0, 1)$

   E. $(0, \dfrac{7}{3})$

40. What graph would be created if the equation $x^2 + y^2 = 12$ were graphed in the standard (x,y) coordinate plane?

   F. Circle
   G. Ellipse
   H. Parabola
   J. Straight line
   K. Two rays forming a "V"

DO YOUR FIGURING HERE.

GO ON TO THE NEXT PAGE.

DO YOUR FIGURING HERE.

41. If $AC = 4$ and $CD = 4\sqrt{3}$ in the figure below, what is $\cos x$?

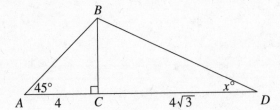

A. $\dfrac{1}{2}$

B. $\dfrac{\sqrt{3}}{3}$

C. $\dfrac{\sqrt{2}}{2}$

D. $\dfrac{\sqrt{3}}{2}$

E. 1

42. Point Y lies on line segment XZ, between X and Z. The (x,y) coordinates for X and Z are $(7,2)$ and $(-3,-3)$, respectively. If the ratio of $\overline{XY}$ to $\overline{YZ}$ is 2 to 3, what are the (x,y) coordinates of Y?

F. $(10, 5)$

G. $(4, -1)$

H. $(3, 2)$

J. $(3, 0)$

K. $(2, 3)$

43. The radius of the circle with center O, as shown below, is 6 inches. What is the area, in square inches, of the shaded region?

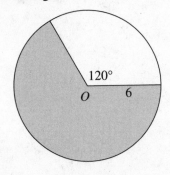

A. 12π

B. 18π

C. 24π

D. 30π

E. 36π

GO ON TO THE NEXT PAGE.

DO YOUR FIGURING HERE.

44. What is the slope of a line that is perpendicular to the line formed by the equation $4x + 12y = 12$?

    F. -3

    G. 3

    H. $-\dfrac{1}{3}$

    J. $\dfrac{1}{3}$

    K. 1

45. In the figure below, $ABCD$ is a square inscribed in the circle centered at O. If $\overline{OB}$ is 6 units long, how many units long is minor arc BC ?

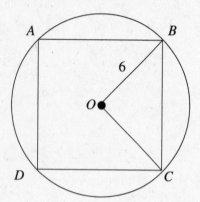

    A. $\dfrac{3}{2}\pi$

    B. 3π

    C. 6π

    D. 12π

    E. 36π

GO ON TO THE NEXT PAGE.

46. Which of the following is a polynomial factor of
$6n^2 - 7n - 10$?

  F. $n + 2$
  G. $2n - 5$
  H. $2n + 1$
  J. $3n - 10$
  K. $6n + 5$

47. For which of the following equations are both $-\dfrac{2}{3}$
and 0 possible solutions for x ?

  A. $3x^2 + 2x = 0$

  B. $3x^2 - 2x = 0$

  C. $2x^2 + 3x = 0$

  D. $2x^2 - 3x = 0$

  E. $x^2 - \dfrac{2}{3} = 0$

48. If y is a positive integer, for how many values of y is
$\dfrac{3}{2y}$ greater than $\dfrac{1}{4}$ and less than $\dfrac{1}{2}$?

  F. 0
  G. 1
  H. 2
  J. 3
  K. 4

49. Which of the following expresses all possible solutions for the inequality $3n - 7(n - 2) \geq 2 + 4(3 - n)$?

  A. All real numbers
  B. $n \geq 0$
  C. $n \leq 0$
  D. $n \geq 2$
  E. No real numbers

DO YOUR FIGURING HERE.

GO ON TO THE NEXT PAGE.

50. In the figure below, *ABCD* is a square. What is the area, in square units, of the shaded region?

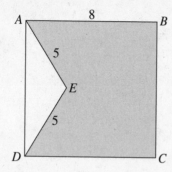

    F. 64
    G. 52
    H. 48
    J. 44
    K. 24

51. At what point (x,y) do the two lines with equations $y = 2x - 2$ and $7x - 3y = 11$ intersect?

    A. (5,8)

    B. (8,5)

    C. $\left(\dfrac{5}{8}, -1\right)$

    D. $\left(\dfrac{5}{8}, 1\right)$

    E. $\left(\dfrac{25}{16}, \dfrac{9}{8}\right)$

52. If $\dfrac{61}{37}$ is written as a decimal, what is the 19th digit to the right of the decimal place?

    F. 1
    G. 4
    H. 6
    J. 8
    K. 9

GO ON TO THE NEXT PAGE.

53. Two vertical poles, one 3 meters tall and the other 5 meters tall, stand a certain distance apart, as shown below. A line from the top of the shorter pole to the top of the taller pole makes a 15° angle with a horizontal line. Which of the following expresses the horizontal distance, in meters, between the bases of the two poles?

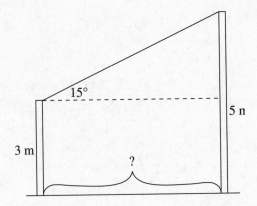

3 m

15°

5 n

?

A. 2 tan 15°

B. 2 tan 105°

C. 5 tan 15°

D. $\dfrac{\tan 15°}{2}$

E. $\dfrac{2}{\tan 15°}$

54. The hypotenuse of an isosceles right triangle has a length of 20 units. What is the length, in units, of one of the legs of the triangle?

F. 10
G. $10\sqrt{2}$
H. $10\sqrt{3}$
J. 20
K. $20\sqrt{2}$

GO ON TO THE NEXT PAGE.

DO YOUR FIGURING HERE.

55. If $(\sin \theta + \cos \theta)^2 = \dfrac{5}{2}$, then $\sin \theta \cos \theta = ?$

   A. 1

   B. $\dfrac{1}{2}$

   C. $\dfrac{1}{4}$

   D. $\dfrac{3}{2}$

   E. $\dfrac{3}{4}$

56. For what values of x is the expression $\dfrac{x^2 - x - 30}{x^2 - 25}$ undefined?

   F. All real numbers
   G. −5 and 6
   H. −5 and 5
   J. 5 only
   K. No real numbers

57. In comparison to $y = \sin \theta$, which of the following has twice the amplitude and half the period?

   A. $y = \dfrac{1}{2} \sin\left(\dfrac{\theta}{2}\right)$

   B. $y = \dfrac{1}{2} \sin (2\theta)$

   C. $y = 2 \sin\left(\dfrac{\theta}{2}\right)$

   D. $y = 2 \sin \theta$

   E. $y = 2 \sin (2\theta)$

GO ON TO THE NEXT PAGE.

58. Ali and Bo were paid a total of $40 to wash 5 cars. Ali washed 3 of the cars, and Bo washed 2 of the cars. If A represents Ali's share of the money and B represents Bo's share, which of the following systems of equations divides the money so that each person receives an equal amount for each car washed?

F. $3A + 2B = 40$
     $3A - 2B = 0$

G. $3A = 40 - 2B$
     $A - B = 1$

H. $A - B = 40$
     $2A = 3B$

J. $A + B = 40$
     $2A - 3B = 0$

K. $A = 40 - B$
     $3A = 2B$

59. Which of the following expressions is equal to $|x - y|$ for all real numbers x and y ?

I. $|x| - |y|$
II. $|y - x|$
III. $|y| - |x|$

A.   None
B.   I only
C.   II only
D.   II and III only
E.   I, II, and III

60. Right circular cylinder A has a height of 4 inches and a radius of 10 inches. Right circular cylinder B has a height of 8 inches and a radius of 5 inches. What is the ratio of the volume of A to the volume of B ?

F. $\dfrac{1}{4}$

G. $\dfrac{1}{2}$

H.   1

J.   2

K.   4

END OF TEST 2

STOP! DO NOT TURN THE PAGE UNTIL TOLD TO DO SO.
DO NOT RETURN TO THE PREVIOUS TEST.

READING TEST

35 Minutes—40 Questions

DIRECTIONS: There are four passages in this test. Each passage is followed by several questions. After reading each passage, choose the best answer to each question and blacken the corresponding oval on your answer sheet. You may refer to the passages as often as necessary.

Passage I

PROSE FICTION: The following passage is excerpted from the coming-of-age novel *The Year of the Unicorn* by Krista Prouty.

It was always the same, every Christmas. My sister and I would wake up early, my parents would send us back to bed, and we would instead huddle in my room, discussing which gifts might be waiting for
5   us downstairs. One year it was a bicycle that I wanted, and I can still remember telling my sister exactly what it would look like: pink, with silver streamers and a sparkly silver seat. Eventually we would hear our parents moving around downstairs and we would know that it
10 was almost time. Once the scent of coffee made it to our rooms, we would hurl ourselves downstairs since that signified that our parents were not only awake but caffeinated and ready for gift-giving.

The year that I was nine, and Lily was six, the gift
15 that I had been craving was the Barbie Dream House. Another girl from my school had one and I had been lucky enough to be allowed a glimpse of it after school one day. She was like a princess bestowing largesse; allowing one or two people over after school most days,
20 demonstrating the various clever mechanisms, then sitting quietly, contentedly, while we gazed in wonder for a few minutes. Then, she sent us on our way. I knew that if I could only have a Dream House of my own, my life would be complete. It was a bigger gift than I usually
25 requested but, logically, I felt, that meant I was all the more likely to have my wish granted.

One night I overheard my parents, after they thought Lily and I had gone to bed.

"Bill, what are we going to do about Christmas
30 this year?" My mother's voice, quiet and unsettlingly uncertain, came from the kitchen.

"I don't know yet, Mel, but we'll figure something out. We always do, honey."

"I know. I just can't help but worry." Whatever my
35 mother said next was drowned out by the running water- she must have been washing up after dinner. I crept back to my bedroom, a little bit troubled by what I had heard but, as is the way of children, soon forgot and went back to Barbie Dream House dreaming.

40   On the Christmas morning in question, Lily and I huddled in my room, waiting for the signal to appear. She wanted a new bike and kept asking me if Santa would get it for her, but all I could think about was my Dream House. Somehow, I had convinced myself that
45 I was certain to get it, that life and the fates could not possibly be cruel enough to deny me this. I could see the wallpaper that was printed on the plastic walls, the darling matching furniture, and the ingenious hand-operated elevator. It would smell like new plastic. I
50 inhaled deeply, imagining myself showing my gift off to friends and foes alike. Instead of new plastic, however, my nostrils quivered to the odor of freshly brewed coffee. It was time.

My eyes still full of the glories I expected, I bar-
55 reled down the stairs, almost knocking Lily down in my haste. Both of my parents were standing in the kitchen, sipping coffee. I tore past them, even though I knew that they would expect me to stop and wait for them to walk into the living room with me. My longing was
60 simply too exquisite to wait any longer. I burst through the double doors into our living room, words of joy and gratitude ready on my lips, only to find- there was no dream house. Frantically, I began to paw through the boxes under the tree, certain that it had to be there,
65 somewhere, blind to the movement of my parents and sister entering the room behind me, nervous smiles on both my parents' faces. Eventually I was forced to concede that the tree was not somehow harboring a dream house under its limbs. I looked up at my parents, grief
70 and confusion painted large on my features.

"Hold up a minute, honey. Santa brought you one more gift that wouldn't quite fit under the tree. Bill, go ahead- show her."

As I watched my father head towards a corner
75 where a large blanket was draped over some bulky object, hope flickered back to life a bit. But the size was all wrong, as was the shape. Still smiling anxiously,

GO ON TO THE NEXT PAGE.

my father pulled the blanket away from what appeared
to be a huge dollhouse. If Barbie's Dream House was
80　sleek and modern, this was awkward and old-fashioned.
It had a peaked roof and a patio, with what looked like
handmade furniture and wallpaper that looked suspi-
ciously like the paper my parents had hung in Lily's
room last fall. Slowly, realization dawned- my father
85　had made it for me.

Looking back, I can only recall the rest of that day
hazily, even though the events up until that moment are
as clear today as they were at the time. I remember the
feeling of devastation that I felt, as I realized that the
90　other girls from school would not, in fact, be blown
away by my Christmas gift. I tried to be as grateful as
I could, understanding even then that my father had
probably spent countless hours working on the house,
but my disappointment was only too evident. I just
95　couldn't understand why they had given me this crude
approximation instead of my heart's desire. As an adult,
I wish I could go back in time, whisper the reason to
my younger self, try to be more appreciative of my
father's efforts, but that is not the way of the world. I
100　still have the house, though, and when I have children
of my own, I will tell them the whole story, and I hope
they will understand better than I did.

1. Which of the following statements does NOT describe one of the narrator's reactions to her Christmas
gift?

   A. She is devastated by the realization that the other
   children at school will not be impressed by this
   gift.
   B. She wishes that her parents had bought her a real
   Barbie Dream House instead of a handmade one.
   C. She despises the house for its old-fashioned appearance and lack of modern conveniences, such
   as an elevator.
   D. She appreciates all the effort her father went to
   in order to give her this gift and tries to convey a
   sense of gratitude.

2. According to the passage, when the narrator smells
coffee on Christmas morning, it means that

   F. her parents are ready to proceed with the Christ-
   mas festivities
   G. she and her sister should hurry to the kitchen for
   breakfast
   H. her father has finally finished preparing her
   Christmas gift
   J. it is time to burst into the living room in front of
   her parents

3. The narrator would most likely agree with which
of the following statements about owning a Barbie
Dream House?

   A. She would become a princess able to bestow
   largesse on other children.
   B. She would, at least for the moment, be content
   with her life.
   C. It would allow her to appreciate her parents' hard
   work and sacrifices.
   D. She would then be able to pass it on to her own
   children someday.

4. What is the main point of the first paragraph?

   F. The smell of coffee still reminds the narrator of
   the Christmases of her childhood.
   G. The narrator's family had a specific ritual that
   was followed every Christmas morning.
   H. Most years, the narrator and her sister would
   hurl themselves into their gifts without warning.
   J. The narrator had once desperately wanted a pink
   and silver bicycle.

5. Which of the following statements most accurately
expresses the narrator's feelings when she first sees
the gift that her father made for her?

   A. She is disappointed that it is not the exact gift
   that she had hoped to receive.
   B. She gratefully acknowledges the long hours her
   father must have put into the gift.
   C. She admires the traditional architecture of the
   house and its attractive wallpaper.
   D. She looks forward to showing her new house off
   to all of the other girls at school.

6. The narrator's father can most accurately be characterized as

   F. ignorant and cruel
   G. thoughtful but lazy
   H. concerned and hard-working
   J. caring but inaccessible

GO ON TO THE NEXT PAGE.

7. It can logically be inferred from the passage that the reason the narrator was not given the official Barbie Dream House for Christmas is because

   A. it is too costly a gift for her parents to buy that year
   B. she had already been given the pink and silver bicycle that she wanted
   C. her father had always wanted to make his daughter a dollhouse
   D. her parents do not wish for their daughter to be happy

8. According to the passage, the reason why the narrator hopes to someday give her dollhouse to her children is that she

   F. wants them to be able to impress the other children at school as she once did
   G. knows that, by that time, it is likely to be worth a great deal of money
   H. remembers how much she appreciated the gift when it was given to her
   J. hopes that they will be better able to understand the meaning behind the gift than she was

9. A reasonable conclusion that the narrator draws regarding her dollhouse is that

   A. it is far more beautiful than was the plastic Barbie Dream House that she had initially desired
   B. without an elevator, it is less valuable than it would otherwise have been
   C. it was given to her with the intention that she keep it to pass on to her own children someday
   D. constructing it must have been time-consuming and labor-intensive

10. The main point of the last paragraph is that:

   F. the narrator would have been much happier if she had been given a Barbie Dream House
   G. it is not fair to give one child a long-desired gift and not give the same to another child
   H. the disappointments suffered in childhood affect people well into adulthood
   J. the passage of time can alter the way events from the past are viewed

GO ON TO THE NEXT PAGE.

Passage II

SOCIAL SCIENCE: This passage discusses the development of the steamboat business in and around New York City in the early 1800s.

Every school child is taught that Robert Fulton was the first American to build and operate a steamboat on New York waters. When his *Clermont* sauntered four miles per hour upstream on the Hudson River in 1807,
5 Fulton opened up new possibilities in transportation, marketing, and city building. What is not often taught about Fulton is that he had a monopoly enforced by the state. The New York legislature gave Fulton the privilege to carry all steamboat traffic in New York for
10 30 years. It was this monopoly that Thomas Gibbons, a New Jersey steamboat man, tried to crack when he hired young Cornelius Vanderbilt in 1817 to run steamboats in New York by charging less than the monopoly rates.

15 Vanderbilt was a classic market entrepreneur, and he was intrigued by the challenge of breaking the Fulton monopoly. On the mast of Gibbons's ship, Vanderbilt hoisted a flag that read "New Jersey must be free." For 60 days in 1817, Vanderbilt defied capture as he raced
20 passengers cheaply from Elizabeth, New Jersey, to New York City. He became a popular figure on the Atlantic as he lowered the fares and eluded the law. Finally, in 1824, in the landmark case *Gibbons v. Ogden*, the Supreme Court struck down the Fulton monopoly. Chief Justice
25 John Marshall ruled that only the federal government, not the states, could regulate interstate commerce. This extremely popular decision opened the waters of America to complete competition. A jubilant Vanderbilt was greeted in New Brunswick, New Jersey, by can-
30 non salutes fired by "citizens desirous of testifying in a public manner their goodwill." Ecstatic New Yorkers immediately launched two steamboats named for John Marshall. On the Ohio River, steamboat traffic doubled in the first year after *Gibbons v. Ogden* and quadrupled
35 after the second year.

The triumph of market entrepreneurs in steamboating led to improvements in technology. As one man observed, "The boat builders, freed from the domination of the Fulton-Livingston interests, were quick to
40 develop new ideas that before had no encouragement from capital." These new ideas included tubular boilers to replace the heavy and expensive copper boilers Fulton used. Cordwood for fuel was also a major cost for Fulton, but innovators soon found that anthracite
45 coal worked well under the new tubular boilers, so "the expense of fuel was down one-half."

The real value of removing the Fulton monopoly was that the costs of steamboating dropped. The price for passenger traffic, for example, from New York City
50 to Albany immediately dropped from seven to three dollars per person after *Gibbons v. Ogden*. Fulton's group couldn't meet the new rates and soon went bankrupt. Gibbons and Vanderbilt, meanwhile, adopted the new technology, cut their costs, and earned $40,000
55 profit each year during the late 1820s.

With such an open environment for market entrepreneurs, Vanderbilt decided to quit his pleasant association with Gibbons, buy the two steamboats, and go into business for himself. During the 1830s,
60 Vanderbilt would establish trade routes all over the Northeast. He offered fast and reliable service at low rates. He first tried the New York to Philadelphia route and forced the "standard" three-dollar fare down to one dollar. On the New Brunswick to New York City
65 run, Vanderbilt charged six cents per trip and provided free meals. As *Niles' Register* said, the "times must be hard indeed when a traveler who wishes to save money cannot afford to walk."

11. According to the passage, Vanderbilt was a "market entrepreneur" (line 15) because he:

   A. broke from the Fulton family.
   B. ran a successful steamboat company.
   C. operated the cheapest steamboat line on the Hudson.
   D. believed in the free market as opposed to a state-enforced monopoly.

12. The phrase "New Jersey must be free" (line 18) meant that:

   F. there should be no fares on the Hudson line.
   G. the New Jersey market should be open to competition.
   H. Fulton's line should be dismantled.
   J. the government should regulate the steamboat industry.

13. According to the passage, Vanderbilt was able to expand all over the Northeast because:

   A. demand was very high there for steamboat transportation.
   B. Gibbons's monopoly was broken.
   C. there were very few rival steamboat lines.
   D. he offered cheap and efficient service.

GO ON TO THE NEXT PAGE.

14. Based on the information presented, Gibbons and Vanderbilt were:

    F. competitors.
    G. employer and employee.
    H. equal partners.
    J. legal experts.

15. After *Gibbons v. Ogden*, steamboat travel most probably increased because of:

    A. larger steamboats.
    B. more efficient technology.
    C. reduced fares.
    D. a population explosion.

16. It can be inferred that Fulton's business faltered while Gibbons's and Vanderbilt's business flourished because:

    F. Fulton didn't adopt the new technology.
    G. Gibbons and Vanderbilt took over Fulton's state-enforced monopoly.
    H. Fulton was less popular than Vanderbilt.
    J. steamboat travel on the Hudson, Fulton's primary route, decreased.

17. It can be inferred from the passage that:

    A. Fulton was essentially dishonest.
    B. everything that children are usually taught about Fulton is wrong.
    C. schoolchildren learn only part of Fulton's story.
    D. Fulton does not deserve to be honored.

18. The author's tone toward Vanderbilt is one of:

    F. admiration.
    G. glorification.
    H. understanding.
    J. empathy.

19. The Supreme Court's decision in *Gibbons v. Ogden* had all of the following effects EXCEPT:

    A. it struck down the Fulton monopoly.
    B. it led to cheaper fares.
    C. it enabled Fulton to expand.
    D. it opened America's waterways to competition.

20. The quote from *Niles' Register* implies that:

    F. toll bridges for pedestrians had become too expensive.
    G. the expansion of steamboat companies had hurt the economy.
    H. the increase in the price of steamboat passenger tickets was finally slowing.
    J. steamboat travel had become an incredible bargain.

GO ON TO THE NEXT PAGE.

Passage III

HUMANITIES: This passage is adapted from Roald Williken's *A History of Art and Its Movements* (© 1973 by Roald Williken).

We know today that tribal art is more complex and less "primitive" than its discoverers believed; we have even seen that the imitation of nature is by no means excluded from its aims. In fact, the style of
5 these ritualistic objects could still serve as a common focus for that search for expressiveness, structure, and simplicity that the new movements had inherited from the experiments of the three lonely rebels: van Gogh, Cezanne, and Gauguin.

10 The experiments of Expressionism are, perhaps, the easiest to explain in words. The term itself may not be happily chosen, for we know that we are all expressing ourselves in everything we do or leave undone, but the word became a convenient label because of its
15 easily remembered contrast to Impressionism, and, as a label, it is quite useful. In one of his letters, van Gogh had explained how he set about painting the portrait of a friend who was very dear to him. The conventional likeness was only the first stage. Having painted a
20 "correct" portrait, he proceeded to change the colors and the setting: "I exaggerate the fair color of the hair, I take orange, chrome, lemon color, and behind the head I do not paint the trivial wall of the room; instead, I paint the Infinite. I make a simple background out
25 of the most intense and richest blue the palette will yield. The blond luminous head stands out against this strong blue background mysteriously, like a star in the azure. Alas, my dear friend, the public will see nothing but caricature in this exaggeration, but what does that
30 matter to us?"

Van Gogh was right in saying that the method he had chosen could be compared to that of the caricaturist. Caricature had always been "expressionist," for the caricaturist plays with the likeness of his victim, and
35 distorts it to express just what he feels about his fellow man. As long as these distortions of nature sailed under the flag of humor nobody seemed to find them difficult to understand. Humorous art was a field in which everything was permitted, because people did not approach it
40 with the prejudices they reserved for "Art with a capital A." The idea of a serious caricature, however, of an art that deliberately changed the appearance of things not to express a sense of superiority, but maybe love, or admiration, or fear, proved indeed a stumbling block,
45 as van Gogh had predicted. Nevertheless, there is nothing inconsistent about it. It is the sober truth that our feelings about things do color the way in which we see them and, even more, the forms that we remember. Everyone must have experienced how different the
50 same place looks when one is happy compared to when one is sad.

What upset the public about the Expressionist art was, perhaps, not so much the fact that nature had been distorted as that the result led away from beauty. That
55 the caricaturist may show up the ugliness of man was granted—it was his job. Nevertheless, the fact that men who claimed to be serious artists should forget that if they must change the appearance of things, they should idealize them, rather than make them ugly, was strongly
60 resented. An Expressionist, however, would probably have retorted that a shout of anguish is not beautiful and that it would be insincere to look only at the pleasing side of life. The Expressionists felt so strongly about human suffering, poverty, violence, and passion that
65 they were inclined to think that the insistence on harmony and beauty were only born out of a refusal to be honest. The art of the classical masters, of a Raphael or Correggio, seemed to them insincere and hypocritical. The Expressionists wanted to face the stark facts
70 of our existence and to communicate their compassion for the disinherited and the ugly. It became almost a point of honor with them to avoid anything that smelt of prettiness and polish; instead, they were determined to create art that would, among other things, shock the
75 "bourgeois" out of his real or imagined complacency.

21. The term "correct" in line 20 means:

   A. critically acclaimed.
   B. traditionally accepted.
   C. objectively beautiful.
   D. simple and trivial.

22. Van Gogh, Cezanne, and Gauguin all:

   F. used the same methods of distortion.
   G. began their careers as caricaturists.
   H. experimented with new styles of expression.
   J. were concerned with educating people about the "new" art.

23. It can be inferred from the passage that people found it easier to accept distortions in humorous art for all of the following reasons EXCEPT:

   A. people had fewer preconceptions toward it.
   B. people didn't take it seriously.
   C. they thought of the distortions as deliberate attempts at humor.
   D. they accepted the distortions as expressions of love, admiration, and fear.

GO ON TO THE NEXT PAGE.

24. According to the passage, what was the Expressionist position regarding beauty in art?

   F. There was essentially no such thing as true beauty.

   G. It resulted from conformity and fear of change.

   H. It was totally unnecessary.

   J. It stemmed from dishonesty.

25. According to the passage, the Expressionists believed that an insistence on harmony and beauty was:

   A. necessary to great art.

   B. similar to a shout of anguish.

   C. important to shock people.

   D. insincere and hypocritical.

26. The author quotes van Gogh's description of his painting (lines 21–30) in order to:

   F. show how the Expressionist style differed from conventional painting.

   G. show that van Gogh was essentially a caricaturist.

   H. give the reader a feel for a typical Expressionist work.

   J. demonstrate van Gogh's importance to the new movement.

27. The author implies that the art of Raphael and Correggio:

   A. was similar to that of the Expressionists.

   B. used caricature to show the darker side of the human condition.

   C. was characterized by an insistence on harmony and beauty.

   D. expressed compassion for the disinherited and the ugly.

28. Based on the passage, it can be inferred that the Expressionists:

   F. were lonely people.

   G. were motivated by a desire to change for the sake of changing.

   H. were not immediately accepted by the public.

   J. were appreciative of the influence of caricatures on their work.

29. The author believes that:

   A. Expressionism is a more advanced style of art than conventional painting.

   B. caricatures are not serious art.

   C. Expressionism was responsible for an eventual decrease in the importance of beauty in twentieth-century art.

   D. Expressionism shares characteristics with the art of caricature.

30. According to the author, which of the following factors entered into van Gogh's decision to employ methods similar to those of a caricaturist?

   I.   A desire to upset the public

   II.   A desire to express a sense of superiority

   III.   A desire to express what he felt about his fellow man

   F. III only

   G. II and III only

   H. I and II only

   J. I only

GO ON TO THE NEXT PAGE.

Passage IV

NATURAL SCIENCE: This passage discusses the discoveries of certain elements.

In the 1740s, gold was discovered in what was then eastern Hungary and is now northwestern Romania. The usual avid search uncovered more veins of gold elsewhere in Hungary, but sometimes the quantity of
5　gold obtained from such veins was disappointingly small. Hungarian mineralogists naturally got to work in order to find out what was wrong.

One of them, Anton von Rupprecht, analyzed ore from a gold mine in 1782 and found that a non-gold
10　impurity accounted for the gold that was not obtained. Studying this impurity, Rupprecht found that it had some properties that resembled those of antimony, an element well known to the chemists of the day. Judging from its appearance, therefore, he concluded that the
15　impurity was antimony.

In 1784, another Hungarian mineralogist, Franz Joseph Muller, studied Rupprecht's ore and decided that the metal impurity was not antimony because it did not have some of that metal's properties. He began
20　to wonder whether he had a completely new element, but didn't dare commit himself to that. In 1796, he sent samples to the German chemist Martin Heinrich Klaproth, a leading authority, telling him of his suspicions that he had a new element and asking him to
25　check into the matter.

Klaproth gave it all the necessary tests and, by 1798, was able to report it as a new element. He carefully, as was proper, gave Muller credit for the discovery, and supplied it with a name. He called it "tellurium,"
30　from the Latin word for "earth."

Tellurium is a very rare element, less than half as common in the earth's crust as gold is. However, it is commonly associated with gold in ores, and since few things are as assiduously searched for as gold, tellurium
35　is found more often than one would expect considering its rareness.

Tellurium is (as was eventually understood) one of the sulfur family of elements, and the Swedish chemist Jons Jakob Berzelius was not surprised, therefore,
40　when, in 1817, he found tellurium in the sulfuric acid being prepared in a certain factory. At least, he found an impurity that looked like tellurium, so he took it for granted that it was.

Working with the supposed tellurium, he found
45　that some of its properties were not like those of tellurium. By February 1818, he realized that he had still another new element on his hands, one that strongly resembled tellurium…he called it "selenium."

In the periodic table, selenium falls between sulfur
50　and tellurium. Selenium is not exactly a common element, but it is more common than either tellurium or gold. Selenium is, in fact, nearly as common as silver.

Selenium and tellurium were not particularly important elements for nearly a century after their
55　discovery. Then, in 1873, there came a peculiar and completely unexpected finding. Willoughby Smith found that selenium conducts an electric current with much greater ease when it is exposed to light than when it is in the dark. This was the first discovery ever made of something that was eventually called "the
60　photoelectric effect"; that is, the effect of light upon electrical phenomena.

31. Which of the following best states the main idea of the passage?

   A. Tellurium and selenium are elements that are not particularly important to science.
   B. New elements can be discovered when scientists are looking for other things.
   C. Tellurium is a common element, much like silver.
   D. Anton von Rupprecht made many important discoveries.

32. According to the passage, the credited discoverer of tellurium is:

   F. Klaproth.
   G. Rupprecht.
   H. Berzelius.
   J. Muller.

33. Based on the information in the passage, the periodic table (line 49) is most likely:

   A. a list of new elements.
   B. a listing of all elements.
   C. a description of selenium, sulfur, and tellurium.
   D. a list of the properties of common elements.

GO ON TO THE NEXT PAGE.

34. The passage asserts that selenium and tellurium:

    F. have no important applications.
    G. were ignored until 1873.
    H. were not utilized practically until well after their discovery.
    J. are equally important in terms of practical applications.

35. According to the passage, which event most contributed to the discovery of selenium?

    A. The discovery of tellurium in gold ore
    B. The analysis of sulfuric acid
    C. The discovery of the photoelectric effect
    D. The discovery that tellurium is similar to sulfur

36. Given the information on the photoelectric effect (lines 56–63), which of the following can be inferred?

    F. Electricity and light are the same thing.
    G. Electricity is usually the result of light.
    H. Electricity and light are related phenomena.
    J. Electricity has little effect on light.

37. It can be inferred from the passage that silver is:

    A. slightly more common than selenium.
    B. slightly less common than gold.
    C. as common as sulfur.
    D. as common as tellurium.

38. It can be inferred from the passage that all of the following are elements EXCEPT:

    F. sulfuric acid.
    G. antimony.
    H. selenium.
    J. gold.

39. According to the passage, Rupprecht found that:

    A. gold is impure.
    B. a non-gold impurity accounted for the little gold obtained.
    C. antimony is an element just like gold.
    D. the impurity was not antimony.

40. Based on the information in the passage, the frequency with which tellurium is discovered in the earth is due to:

    F. the mistaken assumption that it is antimony.
    G. its relative abundance in the earth's crust.
    H. its name being derived from the Latin word for "earth."
    J. its tendency to be found with gold.

END OF TEST 3

**STOP! DO NOT TURN THE PAGE UNTIL TOLD TO DO SO.
DO NOT RETURN TO THE PREVIOUS TEST.**

NO TEST MATERIAL ON THIS PAGE.

SCIENCE REASONING TEST

35 Minutes—40 Questions

DIRECTIONS: There are seven passages in the following section. Each passage is followed by several questions. After reading a passage, choose the best answer to each question and blacken the corresponding oval on your answer sheet. You may refer to the passages as often as necessary.

You are NOT permitted to use a calculator on this test.

Passage I

Astronauts exposed to weightlessness over a long period of time experience a variety of adverse effects. This has been studied extensively in a weightless environment, but not in an environment with partial gravity, such as that found on the Moon. To study the effects of prolonged reduced gravity environments on the body, 12 pigs (6 male and 6 female) were sent to the International Space Station and then subjected to various levels of exercise and partial gravity to examine any deleterious effects of prolonged exposure to this environment.

Experiment 1

While on the International Space Station, pigs were placed on different exercise regimes. The station created reduced artificial gravity to one-sixth of that of the Earth by spinning the sections of the space station that housed the pigs' living quarters and exercise spaces. Different pigs exercised for different amounts of time during the day over the course of 1 month. Measurements were taken of the pigs' starting mass, the length of time that the pigs exercised per day, the percentage of bone loss per pig, and the pigs' final mass. In addition, any unusual symptoms were recorded during this period. The results are shown in Table 1.

Table 1

Name/Gender	Starting mass (kg)	Amount of Exercise (hrs/day)	Percentage of bone loss (%)	Week 1 mass (kg)	Week 2 mass (kg)	Week 3 mass (kg)	Week 4 mass (kg)	Symptoms
Ari/Male	75 kg	0 hrs/day	30%	65 kg	55 kg	45 kg	35 kg	Nausea, dizziness, irritability
Betty/Female	75 kg	0 hrs/day	50%	60 kg	45 kg	30 kg	15 kg	Nausea, dizziness, irritability
Chip/Male	75 kg	1 hr/day	20%	68 kg	61 kg	52 kg	45 kg	Nausea, dizziness, irritability
Dale/Female	75 kg	1 hr/day	45%	64 kg	53 kg	42 kg	31 kg	Nausea, dizziness, irritability
Earnie/Male	75 kg	2 hr/day	15%	70 kg	65 kg	60 kg	55 kg	Nausea, dizziness
Fifi/Female	75 kg	2 hr/day	30%	65 kg	55 kg	45 kg	35 kg	Nausea, dizziness, irritability
Greg/Male	75 kg	3 hr/day	8%	70 kg	65 kg	62 kg	62 kg	Dizziness
Hana/Female	75 kg	3 hr/day	10%	70 kg	65 kg	62 kg	62 kg	None
Irwin/Male	75 kg	4 hr/day	5%	71 kg	70 kg	71 kg	72 kg	None
Jess/Female	75 kg	4 hr/day	3%	73 kg	70 kg	70 kg	75 kg	None
Ken/Male	75 kg	5 hr/day	2%	73 kg	75 kg	76 kg	78 kg	None
Laura/Female	75 kg	5 hr/day	2%	72 kg	74 kg	80 kg	85 kg	None

GO ON TO THE NEXT PAGE.

Experiment 2

After the 12 pigs were rehabilitated and brought back to their original mass, a second experiment was conducted to examine the effect of lower gravity on sleep. The pigs were divided by gender and placed in the space station. The space station was spun again to produce one-sixth the gravity of Earth. Half of each group did not exercise and the other half of each group exercised for four hours per day. After one week an average amount of sleep per night was calculated for each group. The results are shown in Table 2.

Table 2

Pig group	Amount of Exercise (hrs/day)	Amount of Sleep (hrs/night)
Male	0 hrs/day	4 hrs/night
	4 hr/day	6 hrs/night
Female	0 hrs/day	3 hrs/night
	4 hr/day	7 hrs/night

Experiment 3

In order to determine what effect lower gravity has on mental ability, the pigs were each given four hours of exercise per day for a week and then placed in a maze in the space station. Maze completion time was recorded for the individual pigs and then averaged for each gender of pig. The pigs were then tested at the end of each week for a total of four weeks. The results are shown in Table 3.

Table 3

Pig group	Time to complete maze (mins.)			
	Week 1	Week 2	Week 3	Week 4
Male	20 mins.	25 mins.	40 mins.	60 mins.
Female	16 mins.	32 mins.	20 mins.	16 mins.

1. Based on the information in Experiment 1, the mass of the female pig that exercised five hours per day

A. increased
B. decreased
C. decreased then increased
D. remained constant

2. Pigs, regardless of gender, normally sleep 6 hours per night, according to Table 2, which pigs are least affected by the change of gravity?

F. Male pigs that exercise zero hours per day
G. Male pigs that exercise four hours per day
H. Female pigs that exercise zero hours per day
J. Female pigs that exercise four hours per day

3. According to Table 1, which of the following statements could be made about the relationship between the amount of exercise and the gender of the individual pig?

A. Male pigs lose less weight than female pigs when the pigs exercise at low levels.
B. Male pigs gain less weight than female pigs when the pigs exercise at low levels.
C. Female pigs lose less weight than male pigs when the pigs exercise at low levels.
D. There is no relationship between the amount of exercise and gender.

4. Based upon the information in Experiment 3, which pigs are most likely to get lost in the maze?

F. Female pigs after 1 week
G. Male pigs after 1 week
H. Female pigs after 4 weeks
J. Male pigs after 4 weeks

5. According to the data on Table 1, which two pigs had the most similar reactions to their exercise regimens?

A. Ari and Fifi
B. Dale and Ernie
C. Greg and Hana
D. Irwin and Jess

6. In Experiment 1, Ken and Laura experienced a gain in mass, yet still had a net percentage bone loss. What best explains this?

F. The loss of bone was countered by an increase in other tissues such as muscle.
G. The loss of bone was not accounted for in the measure of pig mass.
H. The loss of bone was made up for by an increase in the amount of exercise.
J. The loss of bone was not effected by the reduced weight environment.

GO ON TO THE NEXT PAGE.

Passage II

In the full electromagnetic spectrum, waves vary greatly in length and frequency. Radio waves, which can measure up to many miles, are approximately 10 million times longer than visible light rays, which are 10 million times longer than gamma rays. How we use waves is indicative of these characteristics. For instance, television, AM/FM broadcasts, and short-wave signals are types of radio waves that can travel long distances.

Visible light rays are composed of several waves at different wavelengths. White light can be refracted through a prism to display the different color components of the light. Each color band represents a distinct wavelength. Figure 1 below depicts the wavelengths (cm) and frequencies (cycles/second) of some common waves.

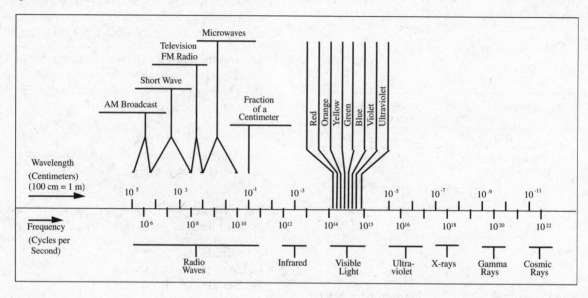

Figure 1

7. Vitamin D can be collected from rays with a wavelength of 1×10^{-6} cm. These rays could be:

   A. radio waves.
   B. visible light rays.
   C. ultraviolet rays.
   D. gamma rays.

8. A short-wave radio emits waves of a wavelength 5×10^4 cm. Express this term in meters.

   F.   400 m
   G.   500 m
   H. 40,000 m
   J. 50,000 m

9. Which of the following is a correct sequence of waves in order of increasing frequency?

   A. Cosmic rays, gamma rays, infrared
   B. Infrared, ultraviolet, visible light
   C. Yellow, orange, and red light
   D. Radio waves, visible light, X-rays

10. Wavelength, frequency, and velocity are interrelated characteristics of an electromagnetic wave. According to Figure 1, as wavelength increases at a constant velocity, the frequency of a wave would:

   F. decrease.
   G. increase.
   H. increase by a factor of 2.
   J. be unchanged.

11. When a prism refracts white light, the longest component rays are refracted the least, while the rays with the shortest wavelengths are refracted the most. In the visible light spectrum, which color is refracted the LEAST?

   A. Ultraviolet
   B. Blue
   C. Red
   D. White

GO ON TO THE NEXT PAGE.

Passage III

The complex behavior of the poor-sighted, three-spined male stickleback fish has been studied extensively as a model of species behavior in courtship and mating. After a male has migrated to a suitable spot, he builds a spawning nest of sand and sediment. When in courting, he performs a special "zigzag" dance. The female then follows the male to the nest where she spawns and he fertilizes the spawned eggs. Also, male sticklebacks have been shown to exhibit territorial behaviors, such as defending nesting or feeding sites from other fish. A biologist performed three experiments to learn more about the behavior of the stickleback.

Experiment 1

Tank 1 and Tank 2 are set up with identical conditions and one male stickleback is placed in each tank. Both fish build nests in their respective tanks. The male from Tank 1 is removed from his tank and is replaced with an egg-laden female; the male from Tank 2 is removed from his tank and is introduced into Tank 1. In Tank 1, the male does not perform the zigzag dance and no spawning occurs. The male retreats to a corner of the tank.

Experiment 2

A male stickleback in an aquarium builds his nest. A fat, round male is introduced into the environment. The original male performs the zigzag dance and attempts to lead the round male to the nest. The round male refuses and begins to flap his fins and swim in circles. The first male then begins to flap his fins, circle his nest, and occasionally prod the other fish to a far corner of the tank.

Experiment 3

A small, flat-shaped female is introduced into a tank where a male has built a nest. The male circles the female a few times and then retreats to a corner of the tank.

12. The experimental data would support the hypothesis that the purpose of the male stickleback's mating dance is to:

F. keep away other male sticklebacks.
G. lure and entice the female to the nest.
H. fertilize the eggs.
J. establish territorial rights.

13. Based on observations from experiments 1–3, which factor initially stimulates the male to do the zigzag dance?

A. The physical environment
B. The number of fish in the tank
C. The sex of the fish
D. The shape of the fish

14. Which experiment supports the hypothesis that the male exhibits territorial behavior?

F. Experiment 2 only
G. Experiment 3 only
H. Experiments 2 and 3 only
J. Experiments 1, 2, and 3

15. To further investigate the territorial behavior of the stickleback, the biologist should vary which of the following factors in Experiment 2?

A. The temperature of the water
B. The sediment and sand in the tank
C. The fatness of the male fish
D. The size of the tank

16. To clarify the results of Experiment 1, the biologist should set up which of the following test situations?

F. Return the original male stickleback to Tank 1 and observe its behavior with the female fish.
G. Maintain the positions of the male sticklebacks and add another egg-laden female to Tank 1.
H. Place both male sticklebacks in Tank 2.
J. Repeat the experiment using a different species of fish.

17. A male stickleback has been established in an aquarium and has built a nest. If one egg-laden female and several flat-shaped male sticklebacks are placed in the tank, one would most likely observe:

A. all the males performing the zigzag dance.
B. only the male that was originally in the tank performing the zigzag dance.
C. all the males circling the female.
D. the female retreating to a corner.

GO ON TO THE NEXT PAGE.

Passage IV

Photosynthesis is a biological process in which light energy is converted to chemical bond energy. This essential process takes place on the primary level of the food chain and provides most of the food energy available to living organisms. Also, photosynthesis is the source for most of the oxygen in Earth's atmosphere. Photosynthesis takes place in two distinctive stages called the "light" reactions and the "dark" reactions.

Light reactions:

These reactions are also known as the photochemical reactions. Plants and some types of microorganisms contain specialized organelles called chloroplasts. In the chloroplasts, light energy is absorbed by the pigment chlorophyll. Some of this energy is used to convert water molecules into hydrogen ions and oxygen gas. The oxygen gas is released into the atmosphere through specialized openings on the plant's leaves. Some of the light energy is used to produce molecules of ATP.

Dark reactions:

These reactions, also called "carbon-fixing" reactions, are not dependent on light. During the dark reactions, the hydrogen ions produced in the light reactions and carbon dioxide from the atmosphere pass through a series of chemical changes to form the simple sugar glucose and other compounds, including water. This glucose can be either consumed immediately or stored for later use. To test the effect of various environmental factors on the process of photosynthesis, a student observed the growth of plants over a period of time. The conditions and the results are described in Table 1. All plants were watered on a regular basis.

Table 1

Plant	Conditions	Results
1	Sunlight	Normal growth Green
2	Darkness	Plant sickly Yellow
3	Sunlight Cut off all the leaves, but left the flowers intact	Plant dead Brown
4	Sunlight Cut off all the flowers, but left the leaves intact	Normal growth Green
5	Sunlight Entire plant covered with plastic wrap	Normal growth Green Condensed water on the plastic wrap

18. Which word equation represents the process of photosynthesis?

   F. Sunlight + Carbon Dioxide + Water → Glucose + Oxygen + Water
   G. Glucose + Sunlight → Alcohol + Carbon Dioxide
   H. Oxygen + Sunlight + Water → Glucose + Carbon Dioxide + Water
   J. Glucose + Sunlight + Oxygen → Carbon Dioxide + Water

19. According to the passage, oxygen gas is produced in which of the following processes?

   A. Carbon-fixing reactions only
   B. Photochemical reactions only
   C. Chlorophyll-fixing reactions
   D. Both the photochemical and carbon-fixing reactions

GO ON TO THE NEXT PAGE.

20. Which of the following substances undergoes a transformation during the dark reactions of photosynthesis?

  I.   Chlorophyll
  II. Hydrogen ions
  III. Carbon dioxide

F. I only
G. III only
H. I and III only
J. II and III only

21. Which of the plants represents the control for the experiments?

A. Plant 1 only
B. Plants 1 and 2 only
C. All of the plants
D. None of the plants

22. Which of the following hypotheses is supported by the comparison of changes in Plant 3 and Plant 4 ?

F. Chloroplasts are found in leaves but not in flowers.
G. Chloroplasts are found in flowers but not in leaves.
H. Oxygen is an essential requirement for photosynthesis.
J. No chemical reactions occur in the stems.

GO ON TO THE NEXT PAGE.

Passage V

Social insects live in colonies. The survival of the colony is dependent on all of its members working together to obtain food, to secure safe home sites, and to continue the reproductive cycle of the species. All species of termites exhibit this social behavior. Biologists have observed that certain members of a termite colony, called soldiers, patrol the area surrounding a colony and, if alarmed, alert other soldier termites to the danger. At this time, the soldier termite exhibits synchronous, convulsive movements, and it may strike its head against wood or other nest materials. Two divergent theories exist concerning what kind of information is exchanged by these motions.

Hypothesis 1

Termites have highly specialized appendages that enable them to receive vibrations sent through the air. Soldier termites are the colony's first line of defense. The convulsive movements of an alarmed soldier termite create "sound waves," which can be perceived by other termites but not by humans. This method is used to communicate with nearby termites. When a soldier termite strikes its head against wood, it creates a louder sound message, which provides a warning to distant termites. The rate of these movements indicates how near the danger is to the colony—the closer the source, the more convulsions or head-strikes occur within a certain time period.

Hypothesis 2

Termites are known to have highly developed sensory organs for smell. The convulsive motions of a soldier termite do not emit sound messages, but instead accompany the release of pheromones, or scent. Every termite colony has its own distinctive pheromone. The characteristic scent of the soldier termite is received quickly throughout the colony and serves as a warning to members of the colony. Head-striking is a ritual that does not, by itself, carry any information about the danger or its distance from the colony. Rather, it is the convulsions involved with the striking that cause the warning pheromone to be released.

23. Hypothesis 2 differs from Hypothesis 1 in that only in Hypothesis 1 is it believed that soldier termites warn the colony by:

A. creating sound waves through convulsive movements that are perceived by termites nearby.
B. releasing pheromones through convulsive movements that are perceived by the other termites.
C. patrolling the area surrounding the colony.
D. receiving vibrations through the air from other soldier termites.

24. Scientists observing a termite colony disturbed the colony and noticed that the soldier termites only exhibited the convulsive movements discussed in the passage and did not strike their heads against wood or nest materials. The entire nest received the warning, as evidenced by the behavior of the termites after the convulsive movements. Which of the two hypotheses would this data best support, and why?

F. Hypothesis 1, because the convulsive movements would be enough to warn all the termites, both nearby and far away.
G. Hypothesis 2, because the pheromones released with the convulsions would warn the entire colony.
H. Hypothesis 1, because the pheromones released with the convulsions would warn the entire colony.
J. Hypothesis 2, because head-striking by termites is only a ritual movement and does not convey any warning.

GO ON TO THE NEXT PAGE.

25. In order to support Hypothesis 2, what must be assumed?

   A. Termites do not have well-developed sensory organs for sight.

   B. All termites can release different types of scents in order to send the colony different messages.

   C. Termites cannot perceive sources of danger that are more than 500 feet from the colony.

   D. The soldier termite scent is sufficient to alert the colony that a danger is present.

26. These hypotheses are similar because they both suggest that termites:

   I. use a symbolic language to communicate information to the other members of the colony.

   II. require exact information about a danger source in order to respond to a warning.

   III. are social insects that work together within a colony.

   F. I only

   G. II only

   H. III only

   J. II and III only

27. Which of the following observations would support Hypothesis 2?

   A. Soldier termites strike their heads against wood or other nest materials in response to various stimuli, including food.

   B. All types of termites, not just soldier termites, convulse and strike their heads when a danger source is present.

   C. Termites respond more quickly to danger signals when no wind is present.

   D. Termites respond more quickly to danger signals during the daylight hours.

28. Using a device that emits a high-pitched sound, a biologist determined the frequency of sound that triggers the soldier termites' danger mechanisms. These devices were placed at different distances from the colony. Data were collected to compare the rate of a soldier termite's convulsions to the distance the danger was from the colony. All experiments were performed on calm days and the sound devices were placed on flat land in a straight line from the colony. A significant variation in convulsion rates was reported in different soldiers reacting to a sound source at an equal distance. Furthermore, each soldier seemed to exhibit a uniform number of convulsions, regardless of the distance the sound source was placed from the colony. Which of the following explanations for this behavior was NOT investigated in this study?

   I. Wind may affect a soldier termite's perception of the distance of a danger source.

   II. The convulsion rate does not convey information about the distance of a danger source.

   III. Experienced soldiers can more accurately determine the distance of a danger source than can a novice soldier.

   F. I only

   G. II only

   H. I and II only

   J. I and III only

29. Which of these discoveries would weaken Hypothesis 1?

   A. When a soldier termite's scent has been re- moved, it can still effectively warn a colony of danger.

   B. Termites have a range of hearing that is exactly the same as humans.

   C. If a termite loses its specialized appendages, it is forced out of the soldier position by other members of the colony.

   D. On a windy day, a soldier termite cannot as accurately warn the colony of danger as it can on a calm day.

GO ON TO THE NEXT PAGE.

Passage VI

Ionization energy is the amount of energy needed to take one electron from the outer shell of an elemental atom. Ionization energies are measured by removing successive electrons from the shells of an atom. The energy needed to withdraw the first electron is termed the first ionization energy, and each successive stage of electron withdrawal—named the second or third ionization energy, accordingly—requires more energy than the stage preceding it. Yet, an atom just beginning a new shell or subshell will have a smaller first ionization energy than the atom preceding it.

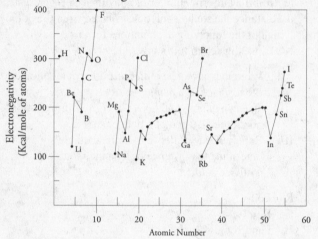

Figure 1

Figure 1 shows the first ionization energies (Kcal/mole of atoms) of the first 53 elements on the periodic table. Each of the first five periods is represented by a line connecting the elements of that period. The first period, containing only hydrogen, is represented by a dot. The noble gases are excluded.

If an element has a low first ionization energy, the atom is likely to form a positive cation, while an element with a high first ionization energy is less likely to lose an electron and more likely to form a negative anion. Also, metals tend to have lower first ionization energies and tend to give away electrons, forming positive cations. Figure 2 shows an expanded graph of Group IA to give a clearer representation of the trend down a group on the periodic table.

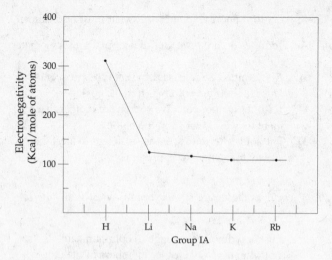

Figure 2

30. Some cations and anions will form ionic bonds with each other. Which of the following pairs of atoms could form a cation and an anion pair, respectively?
    F. Na and Mg
    G. Na and K
    H. Br and I
    J. Li and F

GO ON TO THE NEXT PAGE.

31. As a general trend, the lower the first ionization energy, the more metallic character the element exhibits. According to Figure 1, which three elements are the MOST metallic?

A. Na, K, Rb
B. Li, Na, Al
C. In, Ga, Sr
D. F, Cl, O

32. Comparing the first ionization energies of Mg and Al, what is a possible explanation for their different values?

F. Mg > Al because Mg contains more electrons than Al.
G. Mg > Al because Mg is more metallic and more energy is required to remove its outermost electron.
H. Mg > Al because Al represents a new subshell and less energy is required to remove its outermost electron.
J. Al > Mg because each successive ionization stage requires more energy.

33. Using Figure 2, predict the approximate first ionization energy for Cesium (Cs), element #55 (Group IA, Period 6).

A. 55
B. 90
C. 160
D. 280

34. Hydrogen (H), element #1, has a high first ionization energy compared to Lithium (Li), element #3, although they both have only one electron in their outermost shell. What is a possible explanation for this phenomenon?

F. Hydrogen is heavier than lithium.
G. Hydrogen has fewer shells than lithium, and its nucleus exerts a greater comparative force on its one electron.
H. In a vacuum, hydrogen and lithium would have the same first ionization energy.
J. Hydrogen is an anomaly, and it is usually not included in first ionization energy charts.

GO ON TO THE NEXT PAGE.

Passage VII

Capacitors are used to store energy. Unlike batteries, capacitors discharge this energy very rapidly. There are a variety of applications for capacitors. Commonly they are used in devices that must deliver a large sudden burst of electricity. For instance, they are commonly found in flashbulbs for cameras and in defibrillators in hospitals. In addition, capacitors can be used to change the direction of the charged particles that pass through them. This application is often used in printers and television sets.

A standard capacitor is made up of two parallel plates separated by a small distance. To charge the capacitor, one plate is connected to the positive terminal of a battery and the other plate is connected to the negative terminal of the same battery.

Experiment 1

A student placed several capacitors of different sizes and shapes and attached them to 12 V batteries to determine the factors that might affect capacitance, charge, and energy within a capacitor. Each capacitor varied in the distance between the plates (measured in millimeters) and the size of the plates themselves (measured in cm²). The amount of capacitance and charge was measured for each capacitor. The results are shown in Table 1.

Capacitor	Distance between plates (mm)	Area of plates (cm²)	Capacitance (pF)	Charge (nC)
1	0.5 mm	10 cm²	177 pF	2.12 nC
2	0.5 mm	20 cm²	708 pF	8.49 nC
3	1.0 mm	10 cm²	88.5 pF	1.06 nC
4	1.0 mm	20 cm²	354 pF	4.24 nC
5	1.5 mm	10 cm²	59 pF	0.71 nC
6	1.5 mm	20 cm²	236 pF	2.83 nC

Table 1

Experiment 2

The student used capacitor 3 from Experiment 1 to test the effect of different dielectrics within the capacitor. A dielectric is any material that is placed between the plates of the capacitor that acts to multiply the capacitance. A stronger the dielectric equates to a greater increase in capacitance. The amount of capacitance and charge was measured for each of the materials. The results are shown in Table 2.

Dielectric	Capacitance (pF)	Charge (nC)
Air/None	88.5 pF	1.06 nC
Glass	685.9 pF	8.22 nC
Paper	265.5 pF	3.18 nC
Polystyrene	230.1 pF	2.76 nC
Quartz	336.3 pF	4.03 nC
Teflon	185.9 pF	2.23 nC

Table 2

35. Based on the information in Experiment 1, what shape of capacitor would have the most capacitance?

A. Small distance and small area
B. Small distance and large area
C. Large distance and small area
D. Large distance and large area

36. If the student were test a seventh capacitor with twice the distance between the plates and twice the area of Capacitor 6 what would the charge on the capacitor be closest to:

F. 0.71 nC
G. 2.83 nC
H. 5.66 nC
J. 11.32 nC

37. According to Table 2, which of the following is a correct sequence of dielectrics in order of decreasing strength?

A. Glass, Quartz, Paper, Teflon
B. Glass, Paper, Quartz, Teflon
C. Teflon, Quartz, Paper, Glass
D. Teflon, Paper, Quartz, Glass

38. If an additional capacitor were tested with an plates of 10 cm² and a distance between the places of 1.25 mm, which of the following would be the closest to the resulting amount of capacitance?

F. 29 pF
G. 59 pF
H. 74 pF
J. 88.9 pF

GO ON TO THE NEXT PAGE.

4 **4**

39. According to both experiments, which of the following combinations would have the lowest charge?

    A. Capacitor 1 with a Paper Dielectric
    B. Capacitor 2 with a Glass Dielectric
    C. Capacitor 3 with a Teflon Dielectric
    D. Capacitor 4 with a Quartz Dielectric

40. If the student were to modify one of the capacitors by doubling the area of the plates and reducing the distance between the plates to one third of the original amount, how would the capacitance be affected?

    F. Decreased by a factor of 3
    G. Decreased by a factor of 12
    H. Increased by a factor of 3
    J. Increased by a factor of 12

END OF TEST 4

**STOP! DO NOT TURN THE PAGE UNTIL TOLD TO DO SO.
DO NOT RETURN TO THE PREVIOUS TEST.**

DIRECTIONS

This is a test of your writing skills. You will have thirty (30) minutes to write an essay. Before you begin planning and writing your essay, read the writing prompt carefully to understand exactly what you are being asked to do. Your essay will be evaluated on the evidence it provides of your ability to express judgments by taking a position on the issue in the writing prompt; to maintain a focus on the topic throughout your essay; to develop a position by using logical reasoning and by supporting your ideas; to organize ideas in a logical way; and to use language clearly and effectively according to the conventions of standard written English.

You may use the unlined pages in this test booklet to plan your essay. These pages will not be scored. *You must write your essay on the lined pages in the answer folder.* Your writing on those lined pages will be scored. You may not need all the lined pages, but to ensure you have enough room to finish, do NOT skip lines. You may write corrections or additions neatly between the lines of your essay, but do NOT write in the margins of the lined pages. *Illegible essays cannot be scored, so you must write (or print) clearly.*

If you finish before time is called, you may review your work. Lay your pencil down immediately when time is called.

DO NOT OPEN THIS BOOK UNTIL YOU ARE TOLD TO DO SO.

ACT Assessment Writing Test Prompt

Schools in some states have changed their school calendars so that they are now year-round schools. Advocates of year-round schooling argue that the traditional summer break is a waste of students' time that could otherwise be spent learning. Opponents charge that today's students are already overburdened with the stresses of school and need the summer to get a much-needed break. In your view, should the traditional three-month summer vacation from school be maintained?

In your essay, take a position on this question. You may write about either one of the two points of view given, or you may present a different point of view on this question. Use specific reasons and examples to support your position.

ACT Diagnostic Test Form

Use a No. 2 pencil only. Be sure each mark is dark and completely fills the intended oval. Completely erase any errors or stray marks.

1. **YOUR NAME:** _____
(Print)　　　　　　Last　　　　　　　　First　　　　　　　　M.I.

SIGNATURE: _____　**DATE:** _____ / _____ / _____

HOME ADDRESS: _____
(Print)　　　　　　　　Number and Street

_____
City　　　　　　　　　State　　　　　　Zip

E-MAIL: _____

PHONE NO.: _____
(Print)

SCHOOL: _____

CLASS OF: _____

IMPORTANT: Please fill in these boxes exactly as shown on the back cover of your tests book.

2. TEST FORM

_____

3. TEST CODE

⓪	⓪	⓪	⓪
①	①	①	①
②	②	②	②
③	③	③	③
④	④	④	④
⑤	⑤	⑤	⑤
⑥	⑥	⑥	⑥
⑦	⑦	⑦	⑦
⑧	⑧	⑧	⑧
⑨	⑨	⑨	⑨

4. PHONE NUMBER

⓪	⓪	⓪	⓪	⓪	⓪	⓪	⓪
①	①	①	①	①	①	①	①
②	②	②	②	②	②	②	②
③	③	③	③	③	③	③	③
④	④	④	④	④	④	④	④
⑤	⑤	⑤	⑤	⑤	⑤	⑤	⑤
⑥	⑥	⑥	⑥	⑥	⑥	⑥	⑥
⑦	⑦	⑦	⑦	⑦	⑦	⑦	⑦
⑧	⑧	⑧	⑧	⑧	⑧	⑧	⑧
⑨	⑨	⑨	⑨	⑨	⑨	⑨	⑨

5. YOUR NAME

First 4 letters of last name				FIRST INIT	MID INIT
Ⓐ	Ⓐ	Ⓐ	Ⓐ	Ⓐ	Ⓐ
Ⓑ	Ⓑ	Ⓑ	Ⓑ	Ⓑ	Ⓑ
Ⓒ	Ⓒ	Ⓒ	Ⓒ	Ⓒ	Ⓒ
Ⓓ	Ⓓ	Ⓓ	Ⓓ	Ⓓ	Ⓓ
Ⓔ	Ⓔ	Ⓔ	Ⓔ	Ⓔ	Ⓔ
Ⓕ	Ⓕ	Ⓕ	Ⓕ	Ⓕ	Ⓕ
Ⓖ	Ⓖ	Ⓖ	Ⓖ	Ⓖ	Ⓖ
Ⓗ	Ⓗ	Ⓗ	Ⓗ	Ⓗ	Ⓗ
Ⓘ	Ⓘ	Ⓘ	Ⓘ	Ⓘ	Ⓘ
Ⓙ	Ⓙ	Ⓙ	Ⓙ	Ⓙ	Ⓙ
Ⓚ	Ⓚ	Ⓚ	Ⓚ	Ⓚ	Ⓚ
Ⓛ	Ⓛ	Ⓛ	Ⓛ	Ⓛ	Ⓛ
Ⓜ	Ⓜ	Ⓜ	Ⓜ	Ⓜ	Ⓜ
Ⓝ	Ⓝ	Ⓝ	Ⓝ	Ⓝ	Ⓝ
Ⓞ	Ⓞ	Ⓞ	Ⓞ	Ⓞ	Ⓞ
Ⓟ	Ⓟ	Ⓟ	Ⓟ	Ⓟ	Ⓟ
Ⓠ	Ⓠ	Ⓠ	Ⓠ	Ⓠ	Ⓠ
Ⓡ	Ⓡ	Ⓡ	Ⓡ	Ⓡ	Ⓡ
Ⓢ	Ⓢ	Ⓢ	Ⓢ	Ⓢ	Ⓢ
Ⓣ	Ⓣ	Ⓣ	Ⓣ	Ⓣ	Ⓣ
Ⓤ	Ⓤ	Ⓤ	Ⓤ	Ⓤ	Ⓤ
Ⓥ	Ⓥ	Ⓥ	Ⓥ	Ⓥ	Ⓥ
Ⓦ	Ⓦ	Ⓦ	Ⓦ	Ⓦ	Ⓦ
Ⓧ	Ⓧ	Ⓧ	Ⓧ	Ⓧ	Ⓧ
Ⓨ	Ⓨ	Ⓨ	Ⓨ	Ⓨ	Ⓨ
Ⓩ	Ⓩ	Ⓩ	Ⓩ	Ⓩ	Ⓩ

6. DATE OF BIRTH

MONTH	DAY		YEAR	
◯ JAN				
◯ FEB				
◯ MAR	⓪	⓪	⓪	⓪
◯ APR	①	①	①	①
◯ MAY	②	②	②	②
◯ JUN	③	③	③	③
◯ JUL		④	④	④
◯ AUG		⑤	⑤	⑤
◯ SEP		⑥	⑥	⑥
◯ OCT		⑦	⑦	⑦
◯ NOV		⑧	⑧	⑧
◯ DEC		⑨	⑨	⑨

7. SEX

◯ MALE
◯ FEMALE

8. OTHER

1　Ⓐ Ⓑ Ⓒ Ⓓ Ⓔ
2　Ⓐ Ⓑ Ⓒ Ⓓ Ⓔ
3　Ⓐ Ⓑ Ⓒ Ⓓ Ⓔ

OpScan *i*NSIGHT™ forms by Pearson NCS EM-255315-1:654321　　Printed in U.S.A.

THIS PAGE INTENTIONALLY LEFT BLANK

The Princeton Review
Diagnostic ACT Form

ENGLISH

1 Ⓐ Ⓑ Ⓒ Ⓓ	21 Ⓐ Ⓑ Ⓒ Ⓓ	41 Ⓐ Ⓑ Ⓒ Ⓓ	61 Ⓐ Ⓑ Ⓒ Ⓓ
2 Ⓕ Ⓖ Ⓗ Ⓙ	22 Ⓕ Ⓖ Ⓗ Ⓙ	42 Ⓕ Ⓖ Ⓗ Ⓙ	62 Ⓕ Ⓖ Ⓗ Ⓙ
3 Ⓐ Ⓑ Ⓒ Ⓓ	23 Ⓐ Ⓑ Ⓒ Ⓓ	43 Ⓐ Ⓑ Ⓒ Ⓓ	63 Ⓐ Ⓑ Ⓒ Ⓓ
4 Ⓕ Ⓖ Ⓗ Ⓙ	24 Ⓕ Ⓖ Ⓗ Ⓙ	44 Ⓕ Ⓖ Ⓗ Ⓙ	64 Ⓕ Ⓖ Ⓗ Ⓙ
5 Ⓐ Ⓑ Ⓒ Ⓓ	25 Ⓐ Ⓑ Ⓒ Ⓓ	45 Ⓐ Ⓑ Ⓒ Ⓓ	65 Ⓐ Ⓑ Ⓒ Ⓓ
6 Ⓕ Ⓖ Ⓗ Ⓙ	26 Ⓕ Ⓖ Ⓗ Ⓙ	46 Ⓕ Ⓖ Ⓗ Ⓙ	66 Ⓕ Ⓖ Ⓗ Ⓙ
7 Ⓐ Ⓑ Ⓒ Ⓓ	27 Ⓐ Ⓑ Ⓒ Ⓓ	47 Ⓐ Ⓑ Ⓒ Ⓓ	67 Ⓐ Ⓑ Ⓒ Ⓓ
8 Ⓕ Ⓖ Ⓗ Ⓙ	28 Ⓕ Ⓖ Ⓗ Ⓙ	48 Ⓕ Ⓖ Ⓗ Ⓙ	68 Ⓕ Ⓖ Ⓗ Ⓙ
9 Ⓐ Ⓑ Ⓒ Ⓓ	29 Ⓐ Ⓑ Ⓒ Ⓓ	49 Ⓐ Ⓑ Ⓒ Ⓓ	69 Ⓐ Ⓑ Ⓒ Ⓓ
10 Ⓕ Ⓖ Ⓗ Ⓙ	30 Ⓕ Ⓖ Ⓗ Ⓙ	50 Ⓕ Ⓖ Ⓗ Ⓙ	70 Ⓕ Ⓖ Ⓗ Ⓙ
11 Ⓐ Ⓑ Ⓒ Ⓓ	31 Ⓐ Ⓑ Ⓒ Ⓓ	51 Ⓐ Ⓑ Ⓒ Ⓓ	71 Ⓐ Ⓑ Ⓒ Ⓓ
12 Ⓕ Ⓖ Ⓗ Ⓙ	32 Ⓕ Ⓖ Ⓗ Ⓙ	52 Ⓕ Ⓖ Ⓗ Ⓙ	72 Ⓕ Ⓖ Ⓗ Ⓙ
13 Ⓐ Ⓑ Ⓒ Ⓓ	33 Ⓐ Ⓑ Ⓒ Ⓓ	53 Ⓐ Ⓑ Ⓒ Ⓓ	73 Ⓐ Ⓑ Ⓒ Ⓓ
14 Ⓕ Ⓖ Ⓗ Ⓙ	34 Ⓕ Ⓖ Ⓗ Ⓙ	54 Ⓕ Ⓖ Ⓗ Ⓙ	74 Ⓕ Ⓖ Ⓗ Ⓙ
15 Ⓐ Ⓑ Ⓒ Ⓓ	35 Ⓐ Ⓑ Ⓒ Ⓓ	55 Ⓐ Ⓑ Ⓒ Ⓓ	75 Ⓐ Ⓑ Ⓒ Ⓓ
16 Ⓕ Ⓖ Ⓗ Ⓙ	36 Ⓕ Ⓖ Ⓗ Ⓙ	56 Ⓕ Ⓖ Ⓗ Ⓙ	
17 Ⓐ Ⓑ Ⓒ Ⓓ	37 Ⓐ Ⓑ Ⓒ Ⓓ	57 Ⓐ Ⓑ Ⓒ Ⓓ	
18 Ⓕ Ⓖ Ⓗ Ⓙ	38 Ⓕ Ⓖ Ⓗ Ⓙ	58 Ⓕ Ⓖ Ⓗ Ⓙ	
19 Ⓐ Ⓑ Ⓒ Ⓓ	39 Ⓐ Ⓑ Ⓒ Ⓓ	59 Ⓐ Ⓑ Ⓒ Ⓓ	
20 Ⓕ Ⓖ Ⓗ Ⓙ	40 Ⓕ Ⓖ Ⓗ Ⓙ	60 Ⓕ Ⓖ Ⓗ Ⓙ	

MATHEMATICS

1 Ⓐ Ⓑ Ⓒ Ⓓ Ⓔ	16 Ⓕ Ⓖ Ⓗ Ⓙ Ⓚ	31 Ⓐ Ⓑ Ⓒ Ⓓ Ⓔ	46 Ⓕ Ⓖ Ⓗ Ⓙ Ⓚ
2 Ⓕ Ⓖ Ⓗ Ⓙ Ⓚ	17 Ⓐ Ⓑ Ⓒ Ⓓ Ⓔ	32 Ⓕ Ⓖ Ⓗ Ⓙ Ⓚ	47 Ⓐ Ⓑ Ⓒ Ⓓ Ⓔ
3 Ⓐ Ⓑ Ⓒ Ⓓ Ⓔ	18 Ⓕ Ⓖ Ⓗ Ⓙ Ⓚ	33 Ⓐ Ⓑ Ⓒ Ⓓ Ⓔ	48 Ⓕ Ⓖ Ⓗ Ⓙ Ⓚ
4 Ⓕ Ⓖ Ⓗ Ⓙ Ⓚ	19 Ⓐ Ⓑ Ⓒ Ⓓ Ⓔ	34 Ⓕ Ⓖ Ⓗ Ⓙ Ⓚ	49 Ⓐ Ⓑ Ⓒ Ⓓ Ⓔ
5 Ⓐ Ⓑ Ⓒ Ⓓ Ⓔ	20 Ⓕ Ⓖ Ⓗ Ⓙ Ⓚ	35 Ⓐ Ⓑ Ⓒ Ⓓ Ⓔ	50 Ⓕ Ⓖ Ⓗ Ⓙ Ⓚ
6 Ⓕ Ⓖ Ⓗ Ⓙ Ⓚ	21 Ⓐ Ⓑ Ⓒ Ⓓ Ⓔ	36 Ⓕ Ⓖ Ⓗ Ⓙ Ⓚ	51 Ⓐ Ⓑ Ⓒ Ⓓ Ⓔ
7 Ⓐ Ⓑ Ⓒ Ⓓ Ⓔ	22 Ⓕ Ⓖ Ⓗ Ⓙ Ⓚ	37 Ⓐ Ⓑ Ⓒ Ⓓ Ⓔ	52 Ⓕ Ⓖ Ⓗ Ⓙ Ⓚ
8 Ⓕ Ⓖ Ⓗ Ⓙ Ⓚ	23 Ⓐ Ⓑ Ⓒ Ⓓ Ⓔ	38 Ⓕ Ⓖ Ⓗ Ⓙ Ⓚ	53 Ⓐ Ⓑ Ⓒ Ⓓ Ⓔ
9 Ⓐ Ⓑ Ⓒ Ⓓ Ⓔ	24 Ⓕ Ⓖ Ⓗ Ⓙ Ⓚ	39 Ⓐ Ⓑ Ⓒ Ⓓ Ⓔ	54 Ⓕ Ⓖ Ⓗ Ⓙ Ⓚ
10 Ⓕ Ⓖ Ⓗ Ⓙ Ⓚ	25 Ⓐ Ⓑ Ⓒ Ⓓ Ⓔ	40 Ⓕ Ⓖ Ⓗ Ⓙ Ⓚ	55 Ⓐ Ⓑ Ⓒ Ⓓ Ⓔ
11 Ⓐ Ⓑ Ⓒ Ⓓ Ⓔ	26 Ⓕ Ⓖ Ⓗ Ⓙ Ⓚ	41 Ⓐ Ⓑ Ⓒ Ⓓ Ⓔ	56 Ⓕ Ⓖ Ⓗ Ⓙ Ⓚ
12 Ⓕ Ⓖ Ⓗ Ⓙ Ⓚ	27 Ⓐ Ⓑ Ⓒ Ⓓ Ⓔ	42 Ⓕ Ⓖ Ⓗ Ⓙ Ⓚ	57 Ⓐ Ⓑ Ⓒ Ⓓ Ⓔ
13 Ⓐ Ⓑ Ⓒ Ⓓ Ⓔ	28 Ⓕ Ⓖ Ⓗ Ⓙ Ⓚ	43 Ⓐ Ⓑ Ⓒ Ⓓ Ⓔ	58 Ⓕ Ⓖ Ⓗ Ⓙ Ⓚ
14 Ⓕ Ⓖ Ⓗ Ⓙ Ⓚ	29 Ⓐ Ⓑ Ⓒ Ⓓ Ⓔ	44 Ⓕ Ⓖ Ⓗ Ⓙ Ⓚ	59 Ⓐ Ⓑ Ⓒ Ⓓ Ⓔ
15 Ⓐ Ⓑ Ⓒ Ⓓ Ⓔ	30 Ⓕ Ⓖ Ⓗ Ⓙ Ⓚ	45 Ⓐ Ⓑ Ⓒ Ⓓ Ⓔ	60 Ⓕ Ⓖ Ⓗ Ⓙ Ⓚ

The Princeton Review
Diagnostic ACT Form

Completely darken bubbles with a No. 2 pencil. If you make a mistake, be sure to erase mark completely. Erase all stray marks.

READING

1 Ⓐ	Ⓑ	Ⓒ	Ⓓ	11 Ⓐ	Ⓑ	Ⓒ	Ⓓ	21 Ⓐ	Ⓑ	Ⓒ	Ⓓ	31 Ⓐ	Ⓑ	Ⓒ	Ⓓ
2 Ⓕ	Ⓖ	Ⓗ	Ⓙ	12 Ⓕ	Ⓖ	Ⓗ	Ⓙ	22 Ⓕ	Ⓖ	Ⓗ	Ⓙ	32 Ⓕ	Ⓖ	Ⓗ	Ⓙ
3 Ⓐ	Ⓑ	Ⓒ	Ⓓ	13 Ⓐ	Ⓑ	Ⓒ	Ⓓ	23 Ⓐ	Ⓑ	Ⓒ	Ⓓ	33 Ⓐ	Ⓑ	Ⓒ	Ⓓ
4 Ⓕ	Ⓖ	Ⓗ	Ⓙ	14 Ⓕ	Ⓖ	Ⓗ	Ⓙ	24 Ⓕ	Ⓖ	Ⓗ	Ⓙ	34 Ⓕ	Ⓖ	Ⓗ	Ⓙ
5 Ⓐ	Ⓑ	Ⓒ	Ⓓ	15 Ⓐ	Ⓑ	Ⓒ	Ⓓ	25 Ⓐ	Ⓑ	Ⓒ	Ⓓ	35 Ⓐ	Ⓑ	Ⓒ	Ⓓ
6 Ⓕ	Ⓖ	Ⓗ	Ⓙ	16 Ⓕ	Ⓖ	Ⓗ	Ⓙ	26 Ⓕ	Ⓖ	Ⓗ	Ⓙ	36 Ⓕ	Ⓖ	Ⓗ	Ⓙ
7 Ⓐ	Ⓑ	Ⓒ	Ⓓ	17 Ⓐ	Ⓑ	Ⓒ	Ⓓ	27 Ⓐ	Ⓑ	Ⓒ	Ⓓ	37 Ⓐ	Ⓑ	Ⓒ	Ⓓ
8 Ⓕ	Ⓖ	Ⓗ	Ⓙ	18 Ⓕ	Ⓖ	Ⓗ	Ⓙ	28 Ⓕ	Ⓖ	Ⓗ	Ⓙ	38 Ⓕ	Ⓖ	Ⓗ	Ⓙ
9 Ⓐ	Ⓑ	Ⓒ	Ⓓ	19 Ⓐ	Ⓑ	Ⓒ	Ⓓ	29 Ⓐ	Ⓑ	Ⓒ	Ⓓ	39 Ⓐ	Ⓑ	Ⓒ	Ⓓ
10 Ⓕ	Ⓖ	Ⓗ	Ⓙ	20 Ⓕ	Ⓖ	Ⓗ	Ⓙ	30 Ⓕ	Ⓖ	Ⓗ	Ⓙ	40 Ⓕ	Ⓖ	Ⓗ	Ⓙ

SCIENCE REASONING

1 Ⓐ	Ⓑ	Ⓒ	Ⓓ	11 Ⓐ	Ⓑ	Ⓒ	Ⓓ	21 Ⓐ	Ⓑ	Ⓒ	Ⓓ	31 Ⓐ	Ⓑ	Ⓒ	Ⓓ
2 Ⓕ	Ⓖ	Ⓗ	Ⓙ	12 Ⓕ	Ⓖ	Ⓗ	Ⓙ	22 Ⓕ	Ⓖ	Ⓗ	Ⓙ	32 Ⓕ	Ⓖ	Ⓗ	Ⓙ
3 Ⓐ	Ⓑ	Ⓒ	Ⓓ	13 Ⓐ	Ⓑ	Ⓒ	Ⓓ	23 Ⓐ	Ⓑ	Ⓒ	Ⓓ	33 Ⓐ	Ⓑ	Ⓒ	Ⓓ
4 Ⓕ	Ⓖ	Ⓗ	Ⓙ	14 Ⓕ	Ⓖ	Ⓗ	Ⓙ	24 Ⓕ	Ⓖ	Ⓗ	Ⓙ	34 Ⓕ	Ⓖ	Ⓗ	Ⓙ
5 Ⓐ	Ⓑ	Ⓒ	Ⓓ	15 Ⓐ	Ⓑ	Ⓒ	Ⓓ	25 Ⓐ	Ⓑ	Ⓒ	Ⓓ	35 Ⓐ	Ⓑ	Ⓒ	Ⓓ
6 Ⓕ	Ⓖ	Ⓗ	Ⓙ	16 Ⓕ	Ⓖ	Ⓗ	Ⓙ	26 Ⓕ	Ⓖ	Ⓗ	Ⓙ	36 Ⓕ	Ⓖ	Ⓗ	Ⓙ
7 Ⓐ	Ⓑ	Ⓒ	Ⓓ	17 Ⓐ	Ⓑ	Ⓒ	Ⓓ	27 Ⓐ	Ⓑ	Ⓒ	Ⓓ	37 Ⓐ	Ⓑ	Ⓒ	Ⓓ
8 Ⓕ	Ⓖ	Ⓗ	Ⓙ	18 Ⓕ	Ⓖ	Ⓗ	Ⓙ	28 Ⓕ	Ⓖ	Ⓗ	Ⓙ	38 Ⓕ	Ⓖ	Ⓗ	Ⓙ
9 Ⓐ	Ⓑ	Ⓒ	Ⓓ	19 Ⓐ	Ⓑ	Ⓒ	Ⓓ	29 Ⓐ	Ⓑ	Ⓒ	Ⓓ	39 Ⓐ	Ⓑ	Ⓒ	Ⓓ
10 Ⓕ	Ⓖ	Ⓗ	Ⓙ	20 Ⓕ	Ⓖ	Ⓗ	Ⓙ	30 Ⓕ	Ⓖ	Ⓗ	Ⓙ	40 Ⓕ	Ⓖ	Ⓗ	Ⓙ

I hereby certify that I have truthfully identified myself on this form. I accept the consequences of falsifying my identity.

Your signature

Today's date

**The Princeton Review
Diagnostic ACT Form**

ESSAY

Begin your essay on this side. If necessary, continue on the opposite side.

Continue on the opposite side if necessary.

The Princeton Review
Diagnostic ACT Form

Continued from previous page.

_____

_____

_____

_____

_____

_____

_____

_____

_____

_____

_____

_____

_____

_____

_____

_____

_____

_____

_____

_____

_____

_____

**PLEASE PRINT
YOUR INITIALS**

First	Middle	Last

The Princeton Review
Diagnostic ACT Form

Continued from previous page.

PLEASE PRINT
YOUR INITIALS

First	Middle	Last

The Princeton Review
Diagnostic ACT Form

Continued from previous page.

_____

_____

_____

_____

_____

_____

_____

_____

_____

_____

_____

_____

_____

_____

_____

_____

_____

_____

_____

_____

_____

_____

PLEASE PRINT
YOUR INITIALS

First	Middle	Last

Chapter 26
Practice Exam 1:
Answers and Explanations

EXAM 1 ANSWER KEY

English Test		Mathematics Test		Reading Test		Science Reasoning Test	
1. C	41. A	1. B	37. B	1. C	37. A	1. C	37. A
2. F	42. F	2. J	38. H	2. F	38. F	2. F	38. H
3. B	43. C	3. C	39. C	3. B	39. B	3. B	39. B
4. J	44. G	4. H	40. F	4. G	40. J	4. J	40. J
5. A	45. A	5. C	41. D	5. A		5. A	
6. G	46. J	6. K	42. J	6. H		6. F	
7. D	47. A	7. E	43. C	7. A		7. C	
8. J	48. H	8. J	44. G	8. J		8. G	
9. A	49. A	9. C	45. B	9. D		9. D	
10. H	50. G	10. K	46. K	10. J		10. F	
11. B	51. C	11. C	47. A	11. D		11. C	
12. J	52. G	12. J	48. H	12. G		12. G	
13. A	53. D	13. B	49. A	13. D		13. D	
14. J	54. J	14. G	50. G	14. G		14. F	
15. B	55. B	15. A	51. A	15. C		15. C	
16. H	56. J	16. J	52. H	16. F		16. F	
17. D	57. A	17. E	53. E	17. C		17. B	
18. H	58. J	18. J	54. G	18. F		18. F	
19. B	59. B	19. D	55. E	19. C		19. B	
20. J	60. F	20. F	56. H	20. J		20. J	
21. B	61. D	21. E	57. E	21. B		21. A	
22. F	62. F	22. H	58. J	22. H		22. F	
23. C	63. B	23. C	59. C	23. D		23. A	
24. J	64. F	24. F	60. J	24. J		24. G	
25. B	65. A	25. A		25. D		25. D	
26. H	66. J	26. F		26. F		26. H	
27. D	67. B	27. A		27. C		27. A	
28. G	68. H	28. G		28. H		28. J	
29. B	69. D	29. D		29. D		29. B	
30. H	70. H	30. J		30. F		30. J	
31. C	71. B	31. E		31. B		31. A	
32. G	72. J	32. J		32. J		32. H	
33. A	73. B	33. E		33. B		33. B	
34. F	74. J	34. G		34. H		34. G	
35. C	75. B	35. A		35. B		35. B	
36. J		36. H		36. H		36. H	
37. B							
38. J							
39. A							
40. H							

ENGLISH TEST

Answers and Explanations

Question	Answer	Explanation
1	C	"When" is only used to refer to time, so even though it sounds right, it's wrong here. The only choice that makes sense is (C).
2	F	The first sentence indicates that long migrations are "inconceivable," but the second sentence indicates that animals do so anyway, so you need to change the direction here. (G), (H), and (J) all indicate the same direction; only (F) changes the direction as required, so (F) it is.
3	B	This is a parallelism question, and only (B) and (D) are parallel with "look." (J) would be grammatically correct but would change the meaning, and the right answer never changes the meaning.
4	J	OMIT is right more than half the time it shows up, so always pay it special attention. The test writers love brevity. Telling us winter is "cold" is redundant, so (J) is the best answer.
5	A	The answer choices give you a clue: This is a punctuation question. The part before the comma is a dependent clause and can't stand alone, so you can't have a period or semicolon there.
6	G	You can cross out (H) because it doesn't fit grammatically. (F) and (J) both require the author to have just been discussing something to do with "wild animals," but he wasn't. So that leaves (G).
7	D	Try the shortest first. All the answer choices have redundancies besides (D).
8	J	The subject is plural, so get rid of singular pronouns right away: (F) and (G) both go. You want the possessive here, which is (J). (H) is the form of the plural possessive that would be placed after the verb, as in "The book is theirs."
9	A	There's a list, and you need to keep everything parallel. The list uses commas after each item, so (A) is the best answer because it's the only choice with a comma in the right place.
10	H	This is testing parallelism. Only (H) has the same tense as the rest of the passage. Be sure to pay attention to the non-underlined parts.
11	B	Remember to look for sentences that seem to belong together. In this paragraph, Sentence 4 discusses bird migrations. Logically, Sentence 2, which gives a specific example, should go after it. Also, Sentence 3 leads into Sentence 4. The only answer choice that puts 3, 2, and 4 in order is (B).
12	J	The answer choices give you a clue that this is testing punctuation. The stuff before the punctuation is a dependent clause, so only (J) will work. (G) is no good because there isn't another dash somewhere else in the sentence with which to pair it.
13	A	The answer choices give you a clue that this is testing punctuation. The stuff after the punctuation is a dependent clause, so (C) and (D) are out. B has the comma in the wrong place, so it goes, too.

ENGLISH TEST

Question	Answer	Explanation
14	J	This is testing parallelism. They have "has pulled" earlier in the sentence, so you want "has precluded" here to match.
15	B	The best way to do these is to get rid of the wrong answers using POE. The passage doesn't point out similarities, so (A) is out. It doesn't "condemn" animals, so (C) is out. It doesn't have a funny tone, so (D) is out. That leaves (B).
16	H	Go for the simplest sentence structure available, and one that puts your subject, Max Ernst, at the beginning. That's (H).
17	D	OMIT is right more than half the time it shows up, so always pay special attention to it. This sentence just continues telling us about Ernst, so no transition is needed.
18	H	This is a misplaced modifier: The "imprint" is "horrified," and that can't be right. (H) and (J) both fix that problem, but (J) creates a sentence fragment, so (H) is the best answer.
19	B	If you OMIT here, you're left with a very confusing sentence. OMIT is not right *all* the time. This is testing parallelism. Only "writers" fits into the list.
20	J	Remember that the ACT test writers don't like redundancies. The first three answers all contain pairs of words with pretty much the same meaning. Always give the shortest answer choice a close look.
21	B	The underlined word modifies a noun, so an adjective is needed. (A) is an adverb, (C) is not a word, and (D) has the wrong meaning.
22	F	This question is testing parallelism. The non-underlined verb in the sentence is "believed," and more generally, the passage is written in the simple past. Only (F) is parallel.
23	C	The underlined word is a noun that refers back to the "movement," so this is a noun agreement question. The noun needs to be singular, which (C) is. (A) and (D) are plural, and, therefore, wrong. (B) changes the meaning of the sentence, and the right answer never does that.
24	J	Try to make things as brief as possible without losing the meaning. (F) creates a sentence fragment, (G) is an awkward construction, and (H) loses information. Thus, only (J) could be correct.
25	B	(C) makes Ernst plural, so eliminate it; we want the possessive here. (A) and (D) are too wordy, so eliminate them and pick (B).
26	H	This is testing parallelism. The non-underlined parts of the passage are always right and should guide you. Here, only "placed" is parallel with "rubbed" and "isolated."
27	D	Another good POE question. (C) is too wordy, so eliminate it. (A) and (B) make Ernst plural and we want the possessive as in (D), so pick (D).

ENGLISH TEST

Question	Answer	Explanation
28	G	The subject is singular here, so "their" isn't parallel. Both (H) and (J) would be redundant, and (J) has the wrong possessive. The ACT test writers prefer brevity, so (G) is correct.
29	B	The writer is not annoyed, caustic, or upbeat. The writer is simply providing information, so (B) is correct.
30	H	When ordering paragraphs, try to find one paragraph that is clearly the beginning or end of the story and use POE from there. Paragraph 2 introduces everything, so it should go first; that eliminates (F) and (G). The paragraph at the end right now tells about the end of the movement, so it should stay where it is; that eliminates (J).
31	C	"Jazz singer Ella Fitzgerald" is the subject, so you don't need any punctuation around it at all here. (D) is no good because if you took out the stuff between the pair of commas, the sentence wouldn't make any sense.
32	G	Remember that the non-underlined parts of the passage are correct and should guide you. She was hired "immediately" so she must have been doing something at the time. Because this is all in the past, only (G) has the right tense.
33	A	This is testing idioms. You leave "to do" something, so (A) is right.
34	F	The underlined words create a compound noun and, therefore, do not need to be separated by commas. (G) and (H) introduce unnecessary commas. You should have crossed out (J) for being far too wordy for the ACT.
35	C	This is a parallelism question. The sentence has "a background" and "a father," so the third piece in the series needs to be parallel to those. (A) refers to Ella herself, not a condition, and, therefore is not correct. (B) is an extremely awkward construction, and (D) creates a sentence fragment.
36	J	The sentence requires an objective case pronoun; that's (J). This choice is also parallel with the "her" later in the sentence.
37	B	As it is written, "so" would need to be followed by "that," and it's not, so (A) is out. You can eliminate (D) because you're not comparing three or more things, and (C) simply doesn't make sense.
38	J	OMIT is right more than half the time it shows up, so always pay special attention to it. The test writers love brevity. They already said these guys are "legends," so calling them "famous" would be redundant.
39	A	This is testing subject-verb agreement. The verb is "was," which is singular, so only (A) works for the subject.
40	H	Sentence 3 sounds like an introductory sentence. It fits before Sentence 1, so (H) is right. If it were omitted, the whole paragraph would refer to "she" and "her" without telling us who that person is.

ENGLISH TEST

Question	Answer	Explanation
41	A	If you OMIT this, you'll have a very weird sentence. This is testing parallelism. The only choice that matches up with "brought" is "pave."
42	F	The underlined portion here has to be the subject of the sentence, so only (F) works. All the others create dependent clauses.
43	C	(D) would make a sentence fragment, so it's out. Of the others, only (C) makes sense logically. It's not possible for "all" blacks and whites to have gone to hear her sing.
44	G	This is testing both idioms and punctuation. (F) is out because you're not united "under" a time, you're united "for" a time. All the others have the idiom right, but (H) and (J) add unnecessary punctuation that creates sentence fragments.
45	A	First, answer the question "yes" or "no," and then look at the reasons given. This essay was about Fitzgerald, not racial unity, so cross off (B) and (C). Now look at the reasons given. (D) just doesn't make sense: The passage said people "flocked to hear her sing." So (A) is correct.
46	J	OMIT is right more than half the time it shows up, so always pay it special attention to it. The ACT test writers love brevity. They already said that there was a "radical change," so (F), (G), and (H) all are redundant.
47	A	The transition here is one of substituting one thing (domestication) for another (hunting and gathering), so only (A) makes sense.
48	H	This is testing verb tenses. You need something in order "to do" something, so only (H) works.
49	A	A "shift" goes "from" somewhere "to" somewhere. They began with hunting and gathering and ended at domestication, so "to" is right.
50	G	The ACT test writers love brevity, and there's a shorter choice that's better than the underlined words. (G) has the same meaning and is grammatically correct, so it's right. (H) would have changed the meaning of the sentence.
51	C	This question is testing parallelism. The underlined part is grammatically correct but not parallel with the rest of the passage. The previous sentence refers to "us" so you want (C) or (D). You want to avoid colorful language when given a choice; get rid of (D).
52	G	The subject here is "area of land," and it's singular, so that eliminates (F), (H), and (J).
53	D	This question is testing parallelism. The only choice that matches the verbs in the rest of the passage is (D).
54	J	This is testing parallelism. The non-underlined part should guide you. The passage has "the storage of" and "the division of," so only (J) matches.

ENGLISH TEST

Question	Answer	Explanation
55	B	Punctuation is needed between "service" and "working." A colon can be used to introduce a list, and that's what it is doing here. (C) might sound OK at first, but it turns the second half into a fragment. (D) is grammatically correct but changes the meaning, so it's out.
56	J	The subject here is "each region," and it's singular, so you can eliminate (F) and (H). (G) would turn the first part into a sentence fragment, so (J) is right.
57	A	The answer choices give you a clue that this is testing punctuation. The part after the punctuation is a dependent clause, so you have to use a comma.
58	J	Watch out for redundancies! The adjectives "complex" and "complicated" mean pretty much the same thing, so you don't need both of them.
59	B	If you OMIT here, you'll be missing a verb, so (D) is out. This is testing idioms. "Capable" goes with "of doing" something, so (B) is right even though (A) sounds right.
60	F	The word "centrally" is an adverb modifying "located," an adjective, and that's exactly how things should be. The other answer choices do not provide this correct combination of parts of speech.
61	D	Later in the passage they tell you Dracula was based on Prince Vlad IV, not a bunch of "people," so (A) and (B) are out. The next sentence is in the present tense, so make this one parallel with it by picking (D).
62	F	This is testing parallelism. The non-underlined part is in the present tense, so this should be, too.
63	B	You want to avoid redundancies whenever you can, so get rid of (A). Only (B) makes sense with the passage, which is telling the history of Dracula.
64	F	You want to keep everything parallel. Even though -ing words are often wrong, here you need to stay parallel with "meaning" in the non-underlined part of the passage, and only (F) works.
65	A	If you look at (C) and (D), you'll see that they change the meaning or create sentence fragments, so you can eliminate them. This question is testing commas. You could pull out the stuff between the commas and the sentence would still be correct, so you need the pair in (A), not the single comma in (B).
66	J	All of these transitions do similar things, but only (J) works grammatically because of the structure of the non-underlined part of the sentence.
67	B	The underlined part here is part of the *subject* of what comes after the "and." The only form of "call" that can be used in that way is (B).
68	H	This sentence needs to be parallel to "he united" in the next sentence, so (F) is out. (G) and (J) create sentence fragments, which leaves (H).

ENGLISH TEST

Question	Answer	Explanation
69	D	OMIT is right more than half the time it shows up, so always pay special attention to it. The test writers love brevity. They already told you that the invaders were "notorious," so "famous" is redundant.
70	H	As written, this is a misplaced modifier. The "standards" are receiving "treatment" instead of the "soldiers." Only (H) fixes the problem by adding a pronoun.
71	B	The ACT test writers like paragraphs to be about one idea each. The beginning of this paragraph is talking about legends. Then it goes into specifics about Vlad. The best place to break it is between those two ideas.
72	J	OMIT is right more than half the time it shows up, so always pay special attention to it. The ACT test writers love brevity. They already used "similarly" in the sentence, so "also" and "likewise" are redundant.
73	B	The answer choices give you a clue that they are testing punctuation here. The second part of the sentence is an example of what the first part is describing, so a colon makes sense. Then, go with the shortest answer choice that is grammatically correct: (B).
74	J	The most logical opening sentence for the paragraph is the third sentence and the most logical closing sentence is the second sentence. Only (J) combines both of these sentences in these locations.
75	B	Always look back to the introductory paragraph when they ask you about the meaning of the whole passage. Then put the answer in your own words before going to the answer choices. The right answer will tie all the big ideas together, which (B) does here.

MATHEMATICS TEST

Question	Answer	Explanation
1	B	You know that there are 180° in a triangle, so the other two angles here have to add up to 100°. You can cross off (D) and (E) right away. They tell you that angle B is half of angle A, so take half of 80° and you'll get 40°. So write that in for angle B. Subtract 40° from 100° and you get 60°—(B).
2	J	If you got (G), you forgot that 8% is 0.08, not 0.008. Because 10% of $80,000 is $8,000 and we want just a little less than that, cross off (F), (G), and (K) right away. To find percentages, just translate: 8% of $80,000 becomes $\frac{8}{100} \times 80,000 = 6,400$.
3	C	The easiest way to approach this is to just solve the equation. First, multiply the –3 through to get this: $4p - 2 = -3p + 12$. Note that the 12 is positive, because the two negative signs cancel out each other. Next, add $3p$ to each side: $7p - 2 = 12$. Then, add 2 to each side: $7p = 14$. Finally, divide both sides by 7 to get $p = 2$. Alternatively, you can work backward; substitute each answer for p until you find the one that works, remembering to start in the middle. With (C), you get $4(2) - 2 = -3(2 - 4)$, which becomes $6 = -3(-2)$.
4	H	This is a great Working Backward question. Start with the answer choice in the middle, and see what happens. If she works 49 minutes, the first 30 minutes will cost $75 and the rest (19 minutes) will cost $2 per minute. The total will be 75 + (2×19), which works out to 75 + 38 = 113. Exactly right!
5	C	Because less than half of the pianos are out of tune, you should have eliminated (D) and (E) by ballparking. Always think about the question before you begin solving it. Then translate the question to get $\frac{x}{100} \times 48 = 18$. When you solve that, you get $x = \frac{18}{48} \times 100 = \frac{3}{8} \times 100 = 37.5$. That's (C).
6	K	Be sure to ballpark when you can. Both (F) and (G) are way too small to be right. To find the number of different possible groups, multiply the number of choices for each position: 3 drummers × 4 trumpet players × 5 pianists = 60 different trios.
7	E	Whenever you have this many negative numbers and minus signs in a question, be sure to work it through twice. Just plug x into the equation and solve: $3(-2)^2 - 5(-2) - 6 = 16$.

MATHEMATICS TEST

Question	Answer	Explanation
8	J	The only things really changing here are the inequality signs in the answer choices. If you remember the difference between open and closed circles, you can eliminate some of the answers. The closed circle on the left means that y can equal –2. Eliminate (G), (H), and (K). Now, you just need to figure out which direction the inequality sign should be facing. Could y be less than –2? Not according to the picture. Eliminate (F) and pick (J).
9	C	Use the values provided in the question; if a \$400 purchase had a \$24 sales tax, you should simply be able to divide the two to find the percentage. Because $\frac{24}{600} = 0.06$, you can at least eliminate (B) and (D). To get the actual percentage, just multiply by 100.
10	K	There are 180° in a line, right? So if you figure out the angles *next to* $\angle ABC$, you can subtract from 180 and find $\angle ABC$. $\angle ADB$ and $\angle BEC$ are both 90°, so you can solve for the missing angle in each triangle by subtracting the given angles from 180°. The missing angle in the top triangle is $180° - 90° - 30° = 60°$, and the missing angle in the bottom triangle is $180° - 90° - 40° = 50°$. Now solve for $\angle ABC$: $180° - 60° - 50° = 70°$.
11	C	Remember, there are only four things you need to know about circles on the ACT: area, circumference, radius, and diameter. In this question, we are given the area and asked to find the diameter. What other part of the circle could bridge the gap between those two pieces of information? The radius! If the area is 16π, the radius is the square root of 16, or 4. Because the diameter is twice the length of the radius, you know your answer must be 8.
12	J	Plug in –3 for x in the formula and then solve it: $[(-3)^2 + 3(-3) - 5][2(-3) + 4] = (9 - 3 - 5)(-6 + 4) = (-5)(-2) = 10$. That's (J)! If you got something else, you probably need to be more careful with your negative signs or with your calculator.
13	B	Plug in! There are 3 bars left when they are split among 6 kids, so how about making $N = 9$? That would be 1 bar per kid and 3 left over. Now do the rest of the question with $N = 9$: $9 + 4 = 13$; that means each kid will get 2, and there will be 1 left over.
14	G	Because fewer than half of the dogs are purebred, you can eliminate (J) and (K) by ballparking. To find a probability, set up a fraction with the number of desired things in the top and the total number of things in the bottom. You want a purebred dog, so put 12 in the top and 40 in the bottom: $\frac{12}{40} = 0.3$.
15	A	If you have a great calculator and really quick fingers, you might be able to do this one by Plugging In, but there's an easier way. Subtract the terms, being very careful with the minus signs, using POE as you go. First, $10x^4 - 3x^4 = 7x^4$; cross off (E). Next, $-(3x^3) = -3x^3$; cross off (B), (C), and (D). Done!

MATHEMATICS TEST

Question	Answer	Explanation
16	J	To find the y-intercept you have to put the equation into the $y = mx + b$ form, and b will be the y-intercept. First, rewrite the equation with the y-term on the left, and move the 3 over: $7y = 5x + 5$. Then divide by 7 to isolate y on the left: $y = \frac{5}{7}x + \frac{5}{7}$.
17	E	This might look like a Plugging In question, but what they really want you to do here is *translate*. You can tell because the answer choices are all complete equations; you could plug in all day before figuring out which one is right. They tell you that the long sides of the rectangle are 6 more than the short sides: s and $s + 6$. Because rectangles have two pairs of equal sides, you'll have to double each of them: $2s + 2(s + 6) = 60$.
18	J	Because you have a minus sign at the end of the equation, you will have a plus and minus when you factor because that's the only way multiplication comes out negative. What factors of 8 have a difference of 2? 4 and 2. So this will have to factor into $(x - 4)(x + 2) = 0$, which means that the solutions to the equation are 4 and -2. The question asks for the sum of the solutions, so $-2 + 4 = 2$.
19	D	Use the Pythagorean theorem: $a^2 + b^2 = c^2$. Plug in 10 and 24 for the legs to get $10^2 + 24^2 = c^2$, so $c^2 = 676$. That means $c = \sqrt{676} = 26$. You could also recognize that the legs fit the 5-12-13 right triangle pattern and solve it that way.
20	F	Just take this one step at a time. First add the numbers under the square root sign, and then take the square root. $64 + 36 = 100$. $\sqrt{100} = 10$.
21	E	Plug in! Let $y = 4$, and you'll get $\frac{4^2 - 9}{3 \times 4 - 9} = \frac{16 - 9}{12 - 9} = \frac{7}{3}$. Then check the answer choices, still using 4 for y. Alternatively, you could use FOIL to crack this problem. If you factor a 3 out of the denominator and FOIL the numerator, you're left with $\frac{(y + 3)(y - 3)}{3(y - 3)}$. Cancel out like terms and you're done!
22	H	This question is a fun blend of fractions and decimals. First, let's make everything look the same. Because 0.25 is the same as $\frac{1}{4}$, you can multiply it by $\frac{1}{2}$ to get $\frac{1}{8}$. Now, enter $\left(\frac{1}{8}\right)^3$ into your calculator. You should get 0.001953125. Of course, nothing in the answer choices is a direct match, so you'll have to translate the decimal into scientific notation. How many decimal places to the right would you need to travel to make .00195 into 1.95? If you counted 3, you should be able to eliminate everything but (H).

MATHEMATICS TEST

Question	Answer	Explanation
23	C	Use SOHCAHTOA. Cosine is $\dfrac{\text{adjacent}}{\text{hypotenuse}}$. Either use the Pythagorean theorem to solve for $\overline{AC}$, or recognize that this is a 3-4-5 right triangle, and you'll get $\cos\theta = \dfrac{4}{5}$.
24	F	Use the rate formula: rate × time = amount. Plug in $\dfrac{3}{5}$ for the rate and 3 for the amount: $\dfrac{3}{5} \times t = 3$. Solving the equation gives you $t = 5$ times.
25	A	For starters, do a little ballparking. Do you know the cube root of 64? If not, your calculator does; it's 4. This allows you to eliminate (B), (C), and (E). What's the only difference between the remaining answers? The exponent on your x-variable! If you look at the answers, you'll notice that y^3 became y when the root was taken. Even if you aren't good at exponents, you can choose the answer that reflects the same trend; x^6 should become x^2.
26	F	The solutions of an equation are the values that work in the equation. So plug in either 2 or 8 for x. With $x = 2$, you get $2^2 + B(2) + 16 = 0$, or $2B + 20 = 0$. Solving the equation, you get $B = -10$. You could also use the FOIL method; if the solutions are 2 and 8, then the factors would be $(x - 2)$ and $(x - 8)$. Multiply these out and you will find B.
27	A	You can eliminate (D) and (E) by ballparking, because the perimeter of B is only 10, so the shortest side can't be more than that. The sides of similar triangles are proportional, as are their perimeters. The perimeter of A is $8 + 12 + 20 = 40$, and the perimeter of B is 10. Set up a proportion using the perimeters of each triangle and the shortest side of A, which is 8, to find the shortest side of B: $\dfrac{8}{40} = \dfrac{x}{10}$. Thus, $x = 2$.
28	G	To solve the equation, start by multiplying the -2 through the parentheses: $20 - 8 + 2y = y + 9$. Notice that the 2 is positive, because the two negative signs cancel. Next, subtract 8 from 20 to get $12 + 2y = y + 9$. Subtract y from each side: $12 + y = 9$. Finally, subtract 12 from each side: $y = -3$. Or you can work backward and see which answer works. Remember to start in the middle. (H) doesn't work, but with (G), you get $20 - 2(4 - (-3)) = -3 + 9$ or $20 - 2(7) = 6$, which is right.
29	D	Plug the numbers into the formula for slope, $m = \dfrac{\text{rise}}{\text{run}} = \dfrac{y_2 - y_1}{x_2 - x_1} = \dfrac{8 - (-1)}{-2 - 4} = \dfrac{9}{-6} = -\dfrac{3}{2}$. That's (D).
30	J	If you're good at doing roots on your calculator, you should work backward on this one. If not, you're going to have to factor. The right side of the equation gives you a hint: Only a 3 will be left under the radical sign, so factor 48 into $2^4 \times 3$. Because 2 is to the 4th power, that tells you that $N = 4$.

MATHEMATICS TEST

Question	Answer	Explanation
31	E	It's time to translate. Put what she did on the left and what she should have done on the right. She divided her total by 6, so start by writing $\frac{T}{6}$. That was 14 too low, so add 14: $\frac{T}{6}+14$. She should have been dividing by 5 so $\frac{T}{5}$ goes on the right: $\frac{T}{6}+14=\frac{T}{5}$.
32	J	If you don't know how to do this on your calculator, the best way is to work backward with the answer choices. Try the coordinates for each answer choice to see which one works. With (H), you have 4 for x and 3 for y: $3=\frac{4}{5}(4)-2$. That doesn't work, so eliminate it. With (J), you get $2=\frac{4}{5}(5)-2$, or $2=4-2$. That works.
33	E	Plug in. If $y=3$ and $z=4$, then $x=(3)(4)-2=10$. Your target is 4, because that's the value of z. Plug $x=10$ and $y=3$ into the answers to see which one equals 4. With (E), you get $\frac{x+2}{y}=\frac{10+2}{3}=\frac{12}{3}=4$. That matches your target.
34	G	Write everything you know on the figure while you're working. Because you have an equilateral and an isosceles triangle, and they share a side, right away you know that *all* the sides other than $\overline{AD}$ are 7. Isosceles right triangles have sides in a $s:s:s\sqrt{2}$ ratio, so $\overline{AD}$ is $7\sqrt{2}$. (Remember that "It cannot be determined from the information given" is frequently a trap.)
35	A	The area of a triangle is $A=\frac{1}{2}bh$. For triangle DCB, the base is 6. The height is trickier; extend line segment $\overline{DC}$ to the right, then drop a line straight down from point B. That line segment, the height, is equal to $\overline{AD}$, because a rectangle is created. So the base is 6 and the height is 7, and the area is $A=\frac{1}{2}(6)(7)=21$. Choose (A).
36	H	Even though this problem talks about an ellipse, it's really asking about the distance between two points, which you can find by drawing a right triangle and using the Pythagorean theorem or the distance formula. On the diagram, connect the three points. $\overline{AC}$ has a length of 3, and $\overline{AB}$ has a length of 4. With the Pythagorean theorem, $3^2+4^2=c^2$, so $c=5$. Alternatively, you could recognize that the triangle fits the 3-4-5 pattern for right triangles. Either way, you end up with (H).
37	B	To solve this equation for the possible values of x, you need to get one side equal to 0. First, use FOIL on the left side of the equation: $x^2-5x+6=3x-10$. Next, subtract $3x$ and add 10 to both sides: $x^2-8x+16=0$. Now factor (or un-FOIL) the left side: $(x-4)(x-4)=0$. The only way the left side equals 0 is when $x-4=0$, so the only possible solution is $x=4$. There is only 1 solution, so choose (B).

MATHEMATICS TEST

Question	Answer	Explanation
38	H	You can solve this on your graphing calculator or use Working Backward. Make things easy on yourself and try $x = 0$ first. That gives you $8 < 0$, which isn't true, so you can eliminate (F), (G), and (J). Now try $x = 2$. That gives you $-6 < 0$, which is true, so eliminate (K). The answer is (H).
39	C	Do this one in two steps, using the $y = mx + b$ equation for a line both times. Remember that m is the slope and b is the y-intercept. First, find the slope of the line they give you by rearranging it into $y = mx + b$ form: $y = \frac{7}{3}x + 4$. Now put the slope and the point they give you into the $y = mx + b$ equation and solve for the y-intercept: $6 = \frac{7}{3} \times 3 + b$. So $b = -1$.
40	F	If you have a graphing calculator, this is the time to use it. If you don't, you're going to have to do some clever POE work. You know that equations for lines don't have any squared terms, so eliminate (J) and (K). If you remember that parabolas have only one term squared, cross off (H). Last, if you remember your equations, you know that (F) is your answer.
41	D	Because ABC is an isosceles right triangle (45-45-90 triangle), $\overline{BC}$ and $\overline{AC}$ must be equal, so $\overline{BC}$ is 4. Now use the Pythagorean theorem to find the length of $\overline{BD}$ in the triangle on the right. Plugging in the lengths, you get $4^2 + \left(4\sqrt{3}\right)^2 = c^2$, or $c^2 = 64$, so $c = 8$. That's $\overline{BD}$. Now use SOHCAHTOA. Cosine is adjacent over hypotenuse, so $\cos = \frac{\text{adjacent}}{\text{hypotenuse}}$, and $\cos x = \frac{4\sqrt{3}}{8} = \frac{\sqrt{3}}{2}$.
42	J	If they don't give you a diagram, draw one. Because Y is on the line between X and Z, you can eliminate some answers by ballparking. Get rid of (F), (H), and (K), because point Y must be lower than X, so the y-coordinate is less than 2 Then plug in answers. The distance between X and Y should have a ratio of 2 to 3, with the distance between Y and Z. If you plug in (G), using the distance formula, the distance between X and Y is $3\sqrt{2}$, and the distance between Y and Z would be $\sqrt{52}$. That ratio is not 2:3, so eliminate it and pick (J).
43	C	Start by finding the area of the whole circle. $A = \pi r^2 = 36\pi$. Because the shaded region is more than half (but less than the whole thing), you can eliminate (A), (B), and (E). The shaded part of the circle has an angle of 240°, so it constitutes $\frac{240}{360} = \frac{2}{3}$ of the circle. Thus, its area is $\frac{2}{3}$ of the total area, or $\frac{2}{3} \times 36\pi = 24\pi$.

MATHEMATICS TEST

Question	Answer	Explanation
44	G	First, put the line in slope-intercept form. You should end up with $y = -\dfrac{1}{3}x + 1$. Because the slope of a perpendicular line is the negative reciprocal of the original slope, you should "flip and negate" $-\dfrac{1}{3}$, which gives you a slope of 3.
45	B	If you've forgotten the formulas for circles, try measuring the figure and ballparking. To solve it, though, first you need to find the circumference of the circle. They tell you that the radius is 6. $C = 2\pi r$, so $C = 12\pi$. You should be able to eliminate (C), (D), and (E) because they are all too big. The length of an arc is going to be a fraction of the whole circumference. If you finish drawing the diagonals of the square, you should see that minor arc BC is a quarter of the whole circle, so divide the circumference by 4: $\dfrac{12\pi}{4} = 3\pi$.
46	K	Because there are variables in the answer choices, try Plugging In. If $n = 4$, then $6n^2 - 7n - 10 = 6(16) - 28 - 10 = 58$. So you want the answer that is a factor of 58 when you plug in $n = 4$, (F) is 6, (G) is 3, (H) is 9, (J) is 2, and (K) is 29. Because (J) and (K) both work (i.e., 2 and 29 are factors of 58), eliminate the other answers and try another number. If $n = 7$, then $6n^2 - 7n - 10 = 6(49) - 49 - 10 = 235$. So you want the answer that is a factor of 235 when you plug in $n = 7$. (J) is 11 and K is 47. (K) works, but (J) doesn't.
47	A	Plug in both $-\dfrac{2}{3}$ and 0 for x in the answer choices and see which one works for both values. When $x = 0$, all of the answers except (E) work. Eliminate (E) and try $x = -\dfrac{2}{3}$. Now only (A) works; $3\left(-\dfrac{2}{3}\right)^2 + 2\left(-\dfrac{2}{3}\right) = 3\left(\dfrac{4}{9}\right) - \dfrac{4}{3} = \dfrac{4}{3} - \dfrac{4}{3} = 0$.
48	H	First, translate the inequality. The question is telling you that $\dfrac{1}{4} > \dfrac{3}{2y} > \dfrac{1}{2}$. How many values of y could fit within that range? If you plug in the basic digits starting with 1, you'll find that only 4 and 5 make the inequality true.
49	A	Try plugging in various numbers for n to see which answers you can eliminate. For example, if $n = 0$, the inequality becomes $0 - 7(-2) \geq 2 + 4(3)$, or $14 \geq 2 + 12$. That's true, so the right answer must include 0; eliminate (D) and (E). If $n = 1$, the inequality becomes $3 - 7(1 - 2) \geq 2 + 4(3 - 1)$, or $3 + 7 \geq 2 + 8$. That's true, so the right answer must include 1; eliminate (C). If $n = -1$, the inequality becomes $-3 - 7(-1 - 2) \geq 2 + 4(3 + 1)$, or $-3 + 21 \geq 2 + 16$. That's true, so the right answer must include -1; eliminate (B). Only (A) is left.

MATHEMATICS TEST

Question	Answer	Explanation
50	G	Draw a line from point E to the midpoint of $\overline{AD}$, creating 2 small right triangles. Each half of $\overline{AD}$ is 4 units long. By the Pythagorean theorem (or the 3-4-5 pattern), the third side of the right triangle is 3. So each little triangle has an area of $\frac{1}{2} \times 3 \times 4 = 6$, or 12 combined. The shaded region is the area of the square minus the combined area of the unshaded triangles, or $8^2 - 12 = 64 - 12 = 52$. Choose (G).
51	A	You can either put these equations into your graphing calculator or solve the equations by substitution (Working Backward would take a really long time with those fractions). If you substitute, you should get this $7x - 3(2x - 2) = 11$, so $x = 5$. Only (A) has a 5 for x, so you're done.
52	H	Use your calculator to find $\frac{61}{37} = 1.6\overline{48648}$. Because the answer is a repeating decimal, you need to use the pattern to determine the 19th digit. The decimal repeats every 3 digits, so the 19th digit is the same as the 1st digit after the decimal point, 6.
53	E	The top part of the diagram makes a right triangle with a 15° angle and a height of 2 meters. You can use trigonometry to find the horizontal length (the answer choices should have clued you in on that one). In relation to the 15° angle, the known side, 2 meters, is the opposite side, and the question asks for the horizontal side, adjacent to the angle. Remember SOHCAHTOA? The trig function that uses the opposite and adjacent sides is the tangent. Set up the $\tan = \frac{\text{opposite}}{\text{adjacent}}$, or $\tan 15° = \frac{2}{x}$. To find x, the horizontal length, multiply both sides by x and divide by $\tan 15°$: $x = \frac{2}{\tan 15°}$.
54	G	If they don't give you a figure, sketch one. Isosceles right triangles have sides in a $s : s : s\sqrt{2}$ ratio, and they've given you the hypotenuse here. So divide 20 by $\sqrt{2}$ to get (G).
55	E	First, you need to use FOIL to expand the polynomial. You should end up with $\sin^2 \theta + 2 \cos \theta \sin \theta + \cos^2 \theta = \frac{5}{2}$. If you recall your trig identities, you know that $\sin^2 \theta + \cos^2 \theta = 1$. You can then subtract 1 from the right side of the equation to end up with $2 \cos \theta \sin \theta = \frac{3}{2}$. Finally, divide the equation by 2 to arrive at $\frac{3}{4}$.

MATHEMATICS TEST

Question	Answer	Explanation
56	H	"Undefined" means the bottom of the fraction is zero. Try plugging in the answers by seeing whether –5, 5, or 6 make the bottom zero. When $x = 5$ or –5, the fraction has a 0 in the bottom. When $x = 6$, however, you get $\frac{36 - 6 - 30}{36 - 25} = \frac{0}{11}$. A zero in the numerator is okay. So 5 and –5 are trouble, but 6 is not, so you want (H).
57	E	A multiplier in front of the sine function affects the amplitude. You want twice the amplitude, so eliminate (A) and (B). A multiplier on the θ affects the period, but inversely; a higher multiplier leads to a shorter period. To get half the period, you need to multiply θ by 2. Eliminate (C) and (D), and pick (E).
58	J	They got \$40 for 5 cars, so each car was worth $\frac{40}{5} = \$8$. So Ali should receive $3 \times 8 = \$24$, and Bo should receive $2 \times 8 = \$16$. Plug those numbers into the equations in the answers to see which pair works. With (J), you get $24 + 16 = 40$ and $2(24) - 3(16) = 0$. Bingo.
59	C	You're going to have to use trial and error here to work through the possibilities, so plug in. If $x = 3$ and $y = 2$, then $|x - y| = |3 - 2| = |1| = 1$, so your target is 1. Checking the answers, you get $|3| - |2| = 1$ for I; you get $|2 - 3| = 1$ for II; and you get $|2| - |3| = -1$ for III. Because III doesn't match the target, eliminate (D) and (E) and then try another set of numbers. If $x = 3$ and $y = 4$, then $|x - y| = |3 - 4| = |-1| = 1$, so 1 is your target. Checking the answers, you get $|3| - |4| = -1$ for I, and you get $|4 - 3| = 1$ for II. Because I doesn't work, eliminate (B). You can try some other sets of numbers to confirm that II always works and then pick (C).
60	J	The volume of a cylinder is $V = \pi r^2 h$. If you didn't remember that, all you could do was guess. The volume of A is $10^2 \times 4 \times \pi = 400\pi$. The volume of B is $5^2 \times 8 \times \pi = 200\pi$. The ratio of A's volume to B's volume is $\frac{400\pi}{200\pi} = \frac{2}{1}$ or 2 Choose (J).

READING TEST

Question	Answer	Explanation
1	C	When the narrator first sees her gift, her first response is confusion, followed by devastation that she won't be able to show her gift off to the other girls at school. Eliminate choice (A). She then recognizes that her father put a lot of effort into her gift and tries to be grateful. Eliminate choice (D). She then returns to being confused as to why they made her this house instead of buying her the real Barbie Dream House. Eliminate choice (B). That leaves choice (C), the correct answer. Disappointed and upset as the narrator is, the passage does not state that she hates the house.
2	F	The narrator of the story explains that only when she and her sister could smell coffee were they allowed to go downstairs to start Christmas. Therefore, choice (F) is the best answer. Choice (G) incorrectly refers to breakfast, which is not mentioned in the passage. Choice (H) incorrectly refers to the narrator's father preparation of a gift instead of general morning readiness. Choice (J) is incorrect because the passage explicitly states that the narrator was expected to wait in the kitchen for her parents; she just burst in ahead of them one year because she was too excited to wait.
3	B	The narrator talks about her dream of owning the Dream House in the second paragraph, where she says "I knew that if I could only have a Dream House of my own, my life would be complete." Therefore, choice (B) is the best answer, as it is a good paraphrase of that statement. Choice (A) incorrectly refers to the other girl that owns the house and is not meant to be taken literally. Choice (C) confuses the actual result, based on her parents' hard work, with the narrator's dream, based on buying a particular toy. Choice (D) refers to the narrator's eventual comment that she will pass her gift on to her children someday, but that refers not to the Dream House but to her father's actual gift.
4	G	The first paragraph describes the family's tradition of waiting until the parents have had a chance to wake up and make coffee before beginning to open the presents. Choice (G) is the best paraphrase of that summary and is the best answer. Choice (F) might be true but it not mentioned in the passage and is not the best summary of the entire paragraph. Choice (H) states the opposite of what the passage says. Choice (J) is true, but is not the main point of the paragraph.

READING TEST

Question	Answer	Explanation
5	A	When the narrator first sees her handmade doll house, she is confused and upset as she compares her house to her idealized Barbie Dream House. Choice (A) is the best paraphrase of her reaction. Choice (B) is incorrect because although the narrator does eventually try to be grateful, that is not her first response and she is not immediately successful in her attempt. Choice (C) goes against the passage- she compares the old-fashioned style of her house with the modern Barbie house and finds her house lacking. Choice (D) is incorrect because that was her goal before she saw her house, when she believed she would receive the official Barbie Dream House.
6	H	The narrator's father is described in a few different places in the passage. First, he is overheard reassuring Mel, the mother, regarding Christmas. Then, when he is preparing to present his daughter with her gift, he is described as smiling anxiously. Finally, the narrator eventually realizes that her father had "spent countless hours working on the house." Therefore, choice (H) is the best characterization of the father in the story. Choice (F) is incorrect because nowhere is the father described as cruel. Choice (G) correctly identifies him as thoughtful but then adds lazy, which is the opposite of how he is described. Choice (J) correctly includes caring but then incorrectly adds inaccessible, which is not supported by the passage.
7	A	In lines 29–34, the narrator overhears her parents discussing Christmas, wondering what they will do. This implies that there is some kind of problem. Her father then proceeds to make a homemade version of the Dream House that his daughter wants, implying that for some reason, he cannot give her the gift she wants but is willing to work very hard to give her something similar. Therefore, choice (A) is the best answer, because it explains what problem might cause him to act in such a manner. Choice (B) is incorrect because it refers to an early comment regarding a previous Christmas, not the one being described. Choice (C) is incorrect because there is no evidence that the father made the dollhouse because he had always wanted to do so. Choice (D) is incorrect because the fact that the father put so much time and effort into making the dollhouse implies that they do in fact want their daughter to be happy.
8	J	At the end of the passage, the narrator comments that she still has the dollhouse and that she hopes to someday give it to her own children along with the story of how she got it. Therefore, choice (J) is the best answer, since it refers only to her hopes of passing on the story. Choice (F) incorrectly refers to the narrator's initial hopes of impressing other children with an official Barbie Dream House. Choice (G) focuses on the possible value of the house, which is not discussed in the passage. Choice (H) is incorrect because the narrator did not in fact appreciate the gift initially.

READING TEST

Question	Answer	Explanation
9	D	The narrator concludes, at the time of the gifting, that although she does not like her dollhouse as much as she would have liked a Barbie Dream House, it must have taken her father a lot of time and effort to build. Therefore, choice (D) is the best answer. Choice (A) is incorrect because she refers to the dollhouse as a crude approximation of what she wanted. Choice (B) is incorrect because the absence of an elevator is not mentioned in the passage. Choice (C) is incorrect because there is no evidence that her eventual decision to pass the house on to her children was anticipated by her or her parents at the time when it was given to her.
10	J	The last paragraph is told as if the narrator is looking back on her childhood and having trouble remembering the events that followed the previous part of the passage. She reflects that she now more fully understands her parents' actions and wishes she could go back in time and explain things to her younger self. Therefore, the best answer is choice (J). Choice (F) might be true, but the focus of the last paragraph is on the narrator as an adult, not as a child. Choice (G) is incorrect because the passage does not discuss the narrator's sister's gift. Choice (H) is too negative- the narrator is looking back on the events with greater wisdom and understanding, not bitterness.
11	D	Vanderbilt was hired to break the Fulton monopoly, which was enforced by the state. (A) is not stated. (B) is true, but it is not the reason he is described as a "market entrepreneur." (C) is mentioned, but later in the passage.
12	G	Vanderbilt was trying to break Fulton's monopoly, so his flag referred to breaking free of that monopoly so that others, like Gibbons, could have steamboats running alongside Fulton's. (G) best expresses this idea. (F) is incorrect; Vanderbilt "raced passengers cheaply," not free. (H) is too extreme. (J) is the opposite of what was meant.
13	D	In the last paragraph, it says that Vanderbilt "offered fast and reliable service at low rates." (D) is the best paraphrase of this idea. (A) and (C) are not stated. (B) is wrong; Gibbons was the one fighting the monopoly.
14	G	Lines 10–12 describe how Gibbons hired Vanderbilt to run his steamboats; therefore, (G) is correct. (H) and (J) are not stated. (F) is wrong, because in lines 57–59 it states that Vanderbilt bought the two steamboats from Gibbons, leaving Gibbons with none.
15	C	Lines 47–48 indicate that lower costs resulted from the end of the monopoly and that Vanderbilt's business grew quickly as a result. Also, in the first paragraph it mentions that the whole point of breaking the monopoly was to allow other companies to charge less. (A) and (D) are not mentioned. (B) is incorrect because newer technology helped reduce prices and only indirectly affected the growth of steamboat travel.

READING TEST

Question	Answer	Explanation
16	F	The third paragraph describes how the adoption of newer technologies allowed Vanderbilt and Gibbons to cut costs and charge less. From the result, it can be inferred that Fulton did not do so as well. (G) is wrong because the monopoly was over altogether, not taken over by anyone. (H) and (J) are not stated in the passage.
17	C	Lines 6–7 note that there is something that "is often not taught about Fulton," a good match for (C). (A) is not stated and is too extreme. (B) and (D) are also too extreme.
18	F	The passage as a whole describes Vanderbilt in positive terms. (G) is too strong. (H) and (J) aren't indicated.
19	C	(C) is correct because Fulton didn't expand; he went bankrupt (lines 51–53). (A) is indicated in lines 23–24, (B) is in lines 47–51, and (D) is in lines 27–28.
20	J	The quote from the paper implies that taking the steamboat was even cheaper than walking; (J) is the best answer. (F) and (G) are not mentioned. (H) is incorrect because the ticket prices had been decreasing, not increasing.
21	B	The sentence immediately preceding the one in line 20 notes that he began with a "conventional likeness," meaning a traditional portrait, which he then altered. (B) best expresses this meaning. None of the other choices is indicated in the passage.
22	H	The first paragraph describes these three artists as "lonely rebels" whose experimental work influenced others. (H) best expresses this idea. (F) and (J) are not indicated in the passage. (G) is intended to mislead; van Gogh admitted that his method could be compared to that of the caricature, not that it actually was caricature.
23	D	(A) is mentioned in lines 38–41, as is (B). Lines 41–46 indicate that (C) is true, but that (D) is not true. Therefore, (D) is the correct answer.
24	J	Lines 63–67 indicate that the Expressionists felt that "the insistence on harmony and beauty were only born out of a refusal to be honest." (J) best expresses this idea.
25	D	Three of the answers take information out of the passage and twist it so that it is incorrect. (A) is the opposite answer. The expressionists did not believe that harmony and beauty were necessary to great art. (B) is a deceptive answer because the expressionists saw a shout of anguish as not beautiful (line 61). In (C), the language is deceptive as well; the expressionists felt it necessary to shock people, but not by using beauty and harmony in their art. (D) is the best answer.
26	F	The quote shows how van Gogh understands his own creative motivations and techniques as contrasted with how a conventional portrait is painted. (F) best expresses this idea. (G) is incorrect, because van Gogh is never labeled a caricaturist by the author. (H) is not the author's intent, because lines 11–16 show that the intent was to contrast Expressionism with Impressionism. (J) is not stated anywhere in the passage.

READING TEST

Question	Answer	Explanation
27	C	Raphael and Corregio were mentioned as the kind of artists whom the Expressionists would consider "insincere" because of their insistence on beauty and harmony in their work. (C) best expresses this idea. (A) is wrong; these artists embodied the opposite of what the Expressionists believed in. (B) is wrong; caricature was mentioned in relation to Expressionism, not classical art. (D) is also the opposite of what is stated in the passage.
28	H	In the fourth paragraph, the public is described as "upset" by Expressionist art. (H) best expresses this idea. None of the other answers is stated in the passage. (F) may be tempting, but the author describes only three artists as "lonely," not all Expressionist artists.
29	D	Lines 31–33 indicate that the author agreed with van Gogh regarding the similarity between caricature and Expressionism. (A) is not stated. (B) is what the public feels about caricatures, not how the author feels. (C) goes too far; we don't know this from the passage.
30	F	III is supported in lines 32–36, so eliminate (H) and (J). Now just see if II is correct, because the two answers left both contain III. II is wrong; the passage explicitly states that the purpose of van Gogh's methods was "*not* to express a sense of superiority" (line 43). Therefore, eliminate (G) and pick (F).
31	B	The blurb sums up the main idea: It is about the discovery of new elements. (B) best expresses this. (A) is true (at least until 1873), but too specific to be the main idea. (C) is not true (line 31). (D) is too specific and is not stated in the passage.
32	J	Lines 26–30 indicate that it was Muller who was credited with the discovery.
33	B	(A) is not true, because sulfur wasn't a new element. (C) is incorrect because there is no description mentioned. (D) is wrong because tellurium and selenium are not common. Therefore, (B) is the best answer.
34	H	Lines 57–59 indicate that these two elements weren't important until 100 years after they were discovered. (H) best expresses this idea. (F) is too extreme. (G) is untrue; they weren't completely ignored, just not seen as important. (J) is not mentioned in the passage.
35	B	Lines 37–43 describe how Berzelius, in working with sulfuric acid, found something that was later labeled as "selenium," so (B) is the best answer. (A) happened earlier in the passage, but was not connected to selenium's discovery. (C) is also mentioned, but happened a century after selenium was discovered. (D) by itself didn't lead to the discovery of selenium.
36	H	Lines 52–62 show that light can affect electricity, so (H) is the correct answer. (F) is not true. The "usually" in (G) is not supported by the passage. (J) is the opposite of what is stated in the passage.

READING TEST

Question	Answer	Explanation
37	A	Lines 49–52 say that "selenium is…nearly as common as silver," which means that silver is just a bit more common than selenium, (A). (B) is the opposite of what is stated in the passage. (C) is not mentioned. (D) is wrong according to the passage.
38	F	Antimony (line 15), selenium (line 48), and gold (line 1) are all elements. Sulfuric acid is described as "being prepared" (line 41), which means it is not an element.
39	B	Lines 9–13 describe Rupprecht's discovery of the impurity, (B). (A) goes too far; it doesn't say that all gold is impure. (C) is wrong; antimony is not described as just like gold. (D) is incorrect because Klaproth, not Rupprecht, found this.
40	J	Lines 31–36 indicate that tellurium, despite its rarity, is found more often than one would expect because it is found with gold, (J). (F) and (H) are irrelevant. (G) is the opposite of what is stated in the passage (line 31).

SCIENCE REASONING

Question	Answer	Explanation
1	C	According to Table 1, the female pig that exercised 5 hours per day, Laura, started at 75 kg, dropped to 72 kg, and then increased to 85 kg. She decreased, which eliminates answers (A) and (D) and then she increased which eliminates (B), leaving answer (C).
2	G	Since pigs normally sleep 6 hours per night, the correct answer should be closest to 6. Answer choice (G) male pigs that exercise 4 hours a day sleep 6 hours a night. Since no other experimental pig does this, the answer must be (G).
3	A	According to Table 1, at low levels male pigs lost less weight than did their female counterparts when the pigs exercised between 0-2 hours a day. This eliminates (B) and (C) that both say the opposite, as well as (D) because there is in fact a relationship between levels of exercise, gender, and weight loss. This leaves (A), which states, "Male pigs lose less weight than female pigs when the pigs exercise at low levels."
4	J	According to Table 3, female pigs's speed through the maze decreases then increases back to the original speed over the four weeks. Male pigs, however, go increasingly slower over time. Therefore, male pigs after 4 weeks are the most likely, out of the options, to get lost in the maze, answer (J).
5	A	According to Table 1, Ari and Fifi (A) both lost the same amount of bone mass, the same amount of weight each week, and had the same symptoms. Dale and Ernie (B) had different percentages of bone loss, different rates of total weight loss, and different symptoms. Greg and Hanna had different percentages of bone loss, the same weight loss rates, and different symptoms. Irwin and Jess (D) had different percentages of bone loss, different weight loss rates, but the same symptoms. Therefore, overall the best answer is (A).
6	F	Answer choice (F) seems logical, so we should keep it. Answer choice (G) does not make sense since bone is part of the mass of an animal. Eliminate it. Answer choice (H) bone mass and exercise are not related, eliminate it. Answer choice (J) is not accurate since ALL of he pigs experienced weight loss in the environment. This leaves us with answer choice (F) as the best answer.
7	C	Find wavelength on the left and then go across until you find the value listed in the problem. This is a straight Look It Up question, and if you didn't get it, you need to slow down.
8	G	First, write this out without the exponent: 50,000. Then, convert centimeters into meters by moving the decimal to the left two places.
9	D	Frequency and wavelength go in opposite directions on this graph, so be sure you've got the right units. If you picked (C) or (A), you were on the wrong side of the graph.
10	F	Find wavelength on the graph. It increases from left to right. What is frequency doing at the same time? It's decreasing.

SCIENCE REASONING

Question	Answer	Explanation
11	C	Wavelength is on the top, and the bigger wavelengths are to the left (look at the exponents). Red is the color most to the left, so it's the right answer.
12	G	In the introduction they tell you why the stickleback dances: for courtship.
13	D	Only in Experiment 2 did the stickleback dance, and they told you that the other fish was fat and round. In Experiment 3, the stickleback didn't dance, even though the other stickleback was a female. So it's not (C).
14	F	The passage describes territorial behavior as "defending nesting or feeding sites from other fish." This behavior is seen only in Experiment 2, so (F) is correct.
15	C	The stickleback is territorial toward other sticklebacks, so to experiment on territorial behavior, some change should be made in the fish. Only (C) suggests that.
16	F	Because the biologist is studying sticklebacks, (J) just doesn't make sense. To find out if the stickleback who made the nest will dance for the female, the original male should be returned to Tank 1.
17	B	The only time a stickleback danced or circled a female was when the male was near its own nest, so you can eliminate (A) and (C) because only one of the males has a nest here. Only males retreated to corners in the experiments, so you can eliminate (D).
18	F	The two "reactions" passages together tell you all the stages of photosynthesis, so you'll need to look at both. The second passage tells you that glucose is a product of the reaction, so you can cross out (G) and (J), because they have it on the wrong side of the arrow. You can cross out (H) because it doesn't produce oxygen.
19	B	Oxygen is mentioned only in the first "light reactions" passage, so only (B) works.
20	J	Tackle roman numeral questions one step at a time, using POE as you go. Chlorophyll isn't mentioned in the "dark reactions" passage, so cross out (F) and (H). Because III is listed on both the remaining answers, check for hydrogen ions (II) next. It is mentioned, so (J) is right.
21	A	The control is the one that had nothing special done to it. That's the plant they left in sunlight.
22	F	Whenever you have answers that are opposites, start with them. The "light reactions" passage tells you that chloroplasts are needed for the plant to survive, so because Plant 4 survived without its flowers, (F) is right.
23	A	Hypothesis 1 is the one dealing with waves and noise. Neither hypothesis mentions the patrolling of the termites, so (C) can be eliminated. (B) supports Hypothesis 2, not 1. Of (A) and (D), which is better? Well, the question asks how the soldier termites "warn" the colony. What is described in (D) is how the soldier termites "receive the warning," not how they provide it. (A) is the best answer.

SCIENCE REASONING

Question	Answer	Explanation
24	G	In this question, the scientists noticed that the action of the termites was sufficient to warn the entire colony. Hypothesis 1 says that the convulsions on their own are sufficient to warn "nearby termites" but presumably not enough to warn the whole colony, which is why soldier termites strike their heads on wood as well. Hypothesis 2 says that the pheromone released is enough to warn the entire colony. Therefore, (G) is the best answer.
25	D	An assumption is something that has to be true for the hypothesis to work, so it will be directly related to the hypothesis. That eliminates (A) and (C). (D) is better than (B) because the hypothesis mentions only soldier termites producing warning scents, not "all" termites.
26	H	Tackle roman numeral questions one step at a time, using POE as you go. Symbolic language isn't really mentioned in either hypothesis, so eliminate (F). The first hypothesis does talk about pretty specific information being communicated, but the second only talks about a general warning being communicated, so II isn't a similarity. Cross off (G) and (J), and you're done!
27	A	Hypothesis 2 says that head-striking has no relationship to danger, which is a nice paraphrase of (A).
28	J	Tackle roman numeral questions one step at a time, using POE as you go. You're looking for what they didn't investigate, so you want to keep things that weren't varied during the experiment. They didn't alter the wind, so I is true and you can cross off (G). They DID alter the distance, so II is false and you can cross off (H). They didn't use termites of different experience levels, so III is true and you can cross off (F).
29	B	Hypothesis 1 says termites make sounds that humans cannot hear. Hypothesis 2 talks about scent. Cross off (A) and (D) right away. Only (B) talks about sound, and if termites heard only what humans did, then they couldn't hear their own warnings! So (B) is right.
30	J	The passage tells you that cations are at the bottom and anions are at the top of the graph. Li and F are the pair with the biggest split, so (J) is right.
31	A	Low ionization energies are at the bottom of the graph. The only group with all three members near the bottom is (A).
32	H	The graph shows you that Mg is higher than Al, so cross out (J) right away. The passage told you that metals are toward the bottom, so cross out (G). Finally, the intro told you that subshells have smaller ionization energies, so that means (H) is right.
33	B	Continue the trend in Figure 2. They tell you that they've given you the first 53 elements, and Cesium is number 55, so it will have to be just a little lower than Rb. Only (B) fits because (A) is way too low and (C) and (D) are both higher than Rb.

SCIENCE REASONING

Question	Answer	Explanation
34	G	This one's tough, but if you keep in mind what the passage was about, you can cross off the three wrong answers. All the passage discussed was the relationship between the shells and the energy, and only (G) talks about that. (J) just doesn't make sense; how could an element be left out of the charts?
35	B	According to Table 1, if you compare capacitor 1 to capacitor 3, the area of the plates remains the same, but the distance between the plates is different. Capacitor 1 has a smaller distance between its plates than does Capacitor 3 with a resulting larger capacitance. If you compare capacitor 2 to capacitor 1, the distance between the plates remains the same, but the area of the plates is different. Capacitor 2 has a larger area than capacitor 1 with a resulting large capacitance. Therefore, you want a smaller distance between the plates and plates with a larger area to increase capacitance. Answer choice B says this.
36	H	In Experiment 1, the student manipulates both the area of the plates and the distance between the plates of the capacitor. The question asks to determine what happens when capacitor 6's area and distance are both doubled. Capacitance 1 and 4 on Table 1 show this same relationship: the area is doubled from 0.5 mm to 1.0 mm and the area is doubled from 10 cm^2 to 20 cm^2. When this occurs the charges increases from 2.12 nC to 4.24 nC or doubling. Answer choice H's charge of 5.66 nC is double the original charge of 2.83 nC. So the Answer is H.
37	A	The question asks for decreasing strength so we must start with the strongest dielectric. The first and last dielectric in each answer choice is either Glass or Teflon. According to Table 2, Glass is a stronger dielectric than Teflon so we can eliminate answer choices C and D. A and B both have Paper and Quartz as their middle two dialectic. According to Table 2 Quartz is a stronger dielectric than Paper so we can eliminate B and we are left with Answer choice A.
38	H	According to Table 1, capacitors 3 and 5 both have the same area for their plates. Capacitor 3 has a distance of 1.0 mm between its plates and a capacitance of 88.5 pF. Capacitor 5 has a distance of 1.5 mm between its plates and a capacitance of 59 pF. Therefore a third plate with the same area as the capacitors 3 and 5, but a distance between 1.0 mm and 1.5 mm should have a capacitance between 88.5 pF and 59 pF. Answer choice H is the only answer between these two numbers.

SCIENCE REASONING

Question	Answer	Explanation
39	B	According to Table 2, the charge of the capacitor without a dielectric is 1.06 nC. A Teflon dielectric increases this to 2.23 nC or twice as large; a Paper dielectric increases this to 3.18 nC or three times greater; a Quartz dielectric increases this to 4.03 or four times greater; a Glass dielectric increases this to 8.22 nC or eight times greater. Capacitor 1 has a charge of 2.2 nC; capacitor 2 has a charge of 8.49 nC; capacitor 3 has a charge of 1.06 nC; capacitor 4 has a charge of 4.24 nC. Consequently, answer (A) has a charge of 2.2 nC X 2 = 4.4 nC. Answer (B) has a charge of 8.59 X 8 = 68.72, which is larger than (A) so you should eliminate (B). Answer (C) has a charge of 1.06 X 2 = 2.23 nC, which is smaller than (A) so you should eliminate (A). Answer (D) has a charge of 4.24 X 4 = 16.96 nC, so you should eliminate (D) and you are left with (C).
40	J	Comparing capacitors 1 and 2 in Table 1, we see that when the area is doubled from 10 cm^2 to 20 cm^2, the capacitance increases from 177pF to 708 pF or 4 times. Comparing capacitors 5 and 1 we see that when the distance is decreased from 1.5 mm in capacitor 5 to 0.5 mm in capacitor 1 the capacitance increases from 59 pF to 177 pF or three times. Consequently, an increase of 3 times multiplied by and increase of 4 times yields an overall increase of 12 times of (J).

WRITING TEST

To grade your essay, see the Essay Checklist on the following page. The following is an example of a top-scoring essay for the prompt given in this test. Note that it's not perfect, but it still follows an organized outline and has a strong introductory paragraph, a concluding paragraph, and transitions throughout.

The traditional academic calendar of school in the fall, winter, and spring, with summers off, was developed to accommodate the needs of an agrarian society. Simply put, children were needed to work in the fields during the summer. There is an argument that spring break existed to allow for help with planting, and fall break to help with the harvests. Although the shape of our nation has changed dramatically since the academic calendar was created, there are still powerful reasons for keeping it in place: School has become much more stressful, and students need the break during summer; colleges have become much more expensive, and students need the chance to earn money in the summer; childhood is something special, and the things which make it special should not be casually stripped from the young simply because we're no longer a nation of farmers.

Contrary to high school in years past, high school is no longer a gentle nine-month trek through classes. High school today is a very difficult academic exercise designed to prepare students for college, not just for getting a job when they graduate. Consequently, the classes have become harder, and the amount of homework and other preparation has increased. Every student has heard his or her parents comment that they never worked so hard when they were in school. The fact is, this is the truth. Students today have to take AP classes (which are really college-level classes in high school) if they are serious about getting into a top college. These classes run all year and end with a very difficult exam in May. The amount of work being demanded from students is so high that during the year many students need help coping with the stress. If summer vacation did not exist and students had to go at this pace all the time, it would be disasterous.

Furthermore, summer is also for more than just recovering from the school year. Most students today have jobs in the summer, which are critically important to their ability to pay for college. Because college has become more expensive, and because financial aid is so hard to get, many high school students work during the summers. The money they earn is usually for their college savings, although some of them even give this money to their families to help support them. If this flow of money were cut off, perhaps some students would not be able to afford college, or their families would suffer.

Also, we should be cautious about altering the academic calendar in high school because summer vacation is one of those things that make being a child special. Every parent has fond memories of their summers playing, and tells those stories to his or her children. Teachers talk about this in classes as well. The truth is, there is a difference between children and adults, and we should not act rashly to take away those things which mark that difference. We should be cautious when considering decisions that will make childhood less like childhood and more like the "real world" inhabited by adults. Although it is hard to explain in a concrete way exactly how this is a damaging thing to do, that difficulty makes it no less damaging. The simple pleasures mean a lot and should be protected, not eliminated in the name of efficiency.

For a wide variety of reasons, from the very concrete to the somewhat abstract, it would be a bad idea to force students to go to school year-round. Although there may be problems like overcrowding, which cause administrators to consider abolishing the academic calendar and going to a year-round calendar, the proper solution is not changing the calendar, the proper solution is spending more money on education. Because students need a break from the rigors of the classroom, a chance to earn much needed money, and a childhood full of memories to pass on to their own kids, the academic calendar should remain the way it is.

WRITING TEST

Essay Checklist

1. The Introduction
   Did you
   - start with a topic sentence that paraphrases or restates the prompt?
   - clearly state your position on the issue?

2. Body Paragraph 1
   Did you
   - start with a transition/topic sentence that discusses the opposing side of the argument?
   - give an example of a reason that one might agree with the opposing side of the argument?
   - clearly state that the opposing side of the argument is wrong or flawed?
   - show what is wrong with the opposing side's example or position?

3. Body Paragraphs 2 and 3
   Did you
   - start with a transition/topic sentence that discusses your position on the prompt?
   - give one example or reason to support your position?
   - show the grader how your example supports your position?
   - end the paragraph by restating your thesis?

4. Conclusion
   Did you
   - restate your position on the issue?
   - end with a flourish?

5. Overall
   Did you
   - write neatly?
   - avoid multiple spelling and grammar mistakes?
   - try to vary your sentence structure?
   - use a few impressive-sounding words?

SCORING YOUR PRACTICE EXAM

Step A

Count the number of correct answers for each section and record the number in the space provided for your raw score on the Score Conversion Worksheet below.

Step B

Using the Score Conversion Chart on the next page, convert your raw scores on each section to scaled scores. Then compute your composite ACT score by averaging the four subject scores. Add them up and divide by four. Don't worry about the essay score; it is not included in your composite score.

Score Conversion Worksheet		
Section	Raw Score	Scaled Score
1	_____/75	_____
2	_____/60	_____
3	_____/40	_____
4	_____/40	_____

SCORE CONVERSION CHART

Scaled Score	Raw Score			
	English	Mathematics	Reading	Science Reasoning
36	75	60	39–40	40
35	74	59	38	39
34	72–73	58	37	38
33	71	57	36	—
32	70	55–56	35	37
31	69	53–54	34	36
30	67–68	52	33	—
29	65–66	50–51	32	35
28	62–64	46–49	30–31	33–34
27	59–61	43–45	28–29	31–32
26	57–58	41–42	27	30
25	55–56	39–40	26	29
24	52–54	37–38	25	28
23	50–51	35–36	24	27–26
22	49	33–34	23	25
21	48	31–32	21–22	24
20	45–47	29–30	20	23
19	43–44	27–28	19	22
18	40–42	24–26	18	20–21
17	38–39	21–23	17	18–19
16	35–37	18–20	16	16–17
15	32–34	16–17	15	15
14	29–31	13–15	14	13–14
13	27–28	11–12	12–13	12
12	24–26	9–10	11	11
11	21–23	7–8	9–10	10
10	18–20	6	8	9
9	15–17	5	7	7–8
8	13–14	4	—	6
7	11–12	—	6	5
6	9–10	3	5	—
5	7–8	2	4	4
4	5–6	—	3	3
3	3–4	1	2	2
2	2	—	1	1
1	0	0	0	0

Part IX

The Princeton Review
ACT Practice Exam 2
and Answers and Explanations

Chapter 27
Practice Exam 2

ENGLISH TEST
45 Minutes—75 Questions

DIRECTIONS: In the five passages that follow, certain words and phrases are underlined and numbered. In the right-hand column, you will find alternatives for each underlined part. You are to choose the one that best expresses the idea, makes the statement appropriate for standard written English, or is worded most consistently with the style and tone of the passage as a whole. If you think the original version is best, choose "NO CHANGE."

You will also find questions about a section of the passage or the passage as a whole. These questions do not refer to

an underlined portion of the passage but rather are identified by a number or numbers in a box.

For each question, choose the alternative you consider best and blacken the corresponding oval on your answer sheet. Read each passage through once before you begin to answer the questions that accompany it. You cannot determine most answers without first reading several sentences beyond the question. Be sure that you have read far enough ahead each time you choose an alternative.

PASSAGE I

Lindbergh's Journey

[1]

On May 20, 1927, Charles Lindbergh, a 25 year old from the Midwest, embarked on a journey. Destined to become the first
₁
successful solo, nonstop flight from New York to Paris. Flying in

his single-engine plane, it was *The Spirit of St. Louis*, Lindbergh
₂
took off from Roosevelt Field in Long Island at 7:24 A.M. and

did not touch down in France until 33.5 hours later.

[2]

Lindbergh's flight was unique in several respects that it was
₃
unlike any previous flights. First, Lindbergh flew without a co-
₃

pilot, an extremely risky undertaking despite the duration of the
₄

flight and the exhaustion that would be an inevitable threat to a
₅
solo pilot. Second, Lindbergh's flight was four hundred miles

longer than any that had come before it. A French attempt to fly

the same route shortly before had ended in the death of the two

pilots when their plane crashed before reaching its destination.

1. A. NO CHANGE
   B. embarked, on a journey destined
   C. embarked on a journey destined
   D. embarked. On a journey destined

2. F. NO CHANGE
   G. plane,
   H. plane, being
   J. plane. This was

3. A. NO CHANGE
   B. respects, and unlike flights previous to it.
   C. differences from flights that came before.
   D. respects.

4. F. NO CHANGE
   G. except for
   H. given
   J. regardless of

5. A. NO CHANGE
   B. that would inevitably threaten
   C. in an inevitably threatening regard to
   D. however inevitable the threat of

GO ON TO THE NEXT PAGE.

[3]

It was, therefore, not surprising that Lindbergh's success was met with such a trickle of joy and admiration. When Lindbergh landed in Paris, nearly 34 hours after leaving New York, the crowd descended on him, carrying the exhausted pilot on their shoulders for half an hour. Finally, he was whisked off to the American Embassy, where he can get some well-deserved sleep.

[4]

When he got back to the United States, the uproar only has grown. Thousands of songs and poems were written for him, and throngs made up of American admirers followed him everywhere he went. Every day brought more fan letters, even though proposals of marriage from female devotees. Lindbergh became, and to some extent still becoming, the quintessential American hero. Indeed, who could typify the American ideal better than one who beat the odds, challenged the laws of nature, and showed the world the optimism, dynamism, and capability of the American people?

6. F. NO CHANGE
   G. an outpouring
   H. an undercurrent
   J. a murmur

7. A. NO CHANGE
   B. him: to carry
   C. him; carrying
   D. him. And carried

8. F. NO CHANGE
   G. will
   H. might
   J. was able to

9. A. NO CHANGE
   B. growed.
   C. grew.
   D. had been growing.

10. F. NO CHANGE
    G. consisting of admirers from the United States
    H. of admiring, Americans
    J. of admirers

11. A. NO CHANGE
    B. letters—even
    C. letters, despite
    D. OMIT the underlined portion.

12. F. NO CHANGE
    G. has already become,
    H. remains,
    J. remain,

13. A. NO CHANGE
    B. challenged the natural odds as well as the laws
    C. beat the odds, and challenged the laws of nature
    D. beat upon the most challenging laws of nature,

14. Which of the following would best convey the idea that Lindbergh is emblematic of the hope and pride of America?

    F. NO CHANGE
    G. a plane could indeed be aerodynamically sound?
    H. America was a land of great economic power?
    J. Charles Lindbergh was a truly extraordinary pilot?

Question 15 asks about the preceding passage as a whole.

15. Suppose the author wanted to include the following sentence in the passage: "All Lindbergh wanted to do was get some sleep." This sentence would best be incorporated into Paragraph:

    A. 1
    B. 2
    C. 3
    D. 4

GO ON TO THE NEXT PAGE.

PASSAGE II

The War of the Worlds

In 1938, CBS Radio hired the young Orson Welles to

direct a sophisticated but deft weekly drama series to go
16

opposite *Chase and Sanborn Radio Hour*, a particularly

popular show on the rival station, NBC. [17] CBS hoped

to draw on highbrow viewers who were more interested

in serious literary material, than in the songs and jokes
18

that dominated *Chase and Sanborn.* Welles was so rising
19

a promising stage director that he seemed like the perfect
19

person for the job.

The first episode of the series was to be an adaptation of

H.G. Wells' *The War of the Worlds*, the story of a Martian

invading of Earth. Rather than tell the story in traditional radio
20

play format, however, he decided to present it as an unfolding
21

news story, complete with actors playing radio

---

16. The author would like to convey the idea that CBS wanted Orson Welles's series to appeal to a wide range of listeners. Which of the following would best accomplish this?

   F. NO CHANGE
   G. accessible
   H. smart
   J. wordy

17. The author would like to insert a sentence to give a sense of the popularity of *Chase and Sanborn Radio Hour*. If all of the following are true, which would best accomplish this?

   A. *Chase and Sanborn* starred the well-known ventriloquist Edgar Bergan and his hilariously insolent dummy, Charlie McCarthy.
   B. *Chase and Sanborn*, like many radio shows of its era, was a variety show, and may be seen as the prototype for the many television variety shows of the 1970s.
   C. Although *Chase and Sanborn* was enjoyed by many, others felt that its vapid subject matter did little to enrich the minds of its listeners.
   D. *Chase and Sanborn* had such a large and devoted audience that most sponsors refused to advertise on any show that broadcast at the same time.

18. F. NO CHANGE
   G. serious, literary material, than
   H. serious literary, material than
   J. serious literary material than

19. A. NO CHANGE
   B. Welles was a rising, promising stage director,
   C. Welles, a rising stage director of great promise,
   D. On the promising rise as a stage director, Welles

20. F. NO CHANGE
   G. invasion
   H. invades
   J. invaded

21. A. NO CHANGE
   B. they
   C. he then
   D. Orson Welles

GO ON TO THE NEXT PAGE.

reporters "stunned" by the horrific events unfolding before their eyes. The director, realizing that some might mistake the program for a real newscast, made sure that the program started with a disclaimer; he assured listeners that the program to come
₂₂
was a work of fiction.

It did not occur to him, however, that a great number of people would tune in after the broadcast had started. Many of
₂₃
them, assuming that what they were hearing was genuine on-the-scene coverage, panicked; they were very frightened. The
₂₄
broadcast lasted only an hour, but by the time it ended, much
₂₅
of the country was convinced that the United States had been largely overtaken by Martians (this simultaneous fear of and
₂₆
fascination with extraterrestrials is present in many cultures).
₂₆

In retrospect, it seems strange that so many could have been fooled by what surely could not have been all that
₂₇
convincing a radio play. One cannot help but wonder why people did not question why all of the other radio stations

22. F. NO CHANGE
G. disclaimer he
H. disclaimer, he
J. disclaimer of which

23. A. NO CHANGE
B. been started.
C. start.
D. starting.

24. If all of the choices below are true, which of them best uses specific detail to convey the panic that the broadcast of *The War of the Worlds* caused?

F. NO CHANGE
G. the highways were clogged with cars full of people seeking escape, and train stations were crowded with mobs willing to buy tickets to anywhere far away.
H. many felt that they had never encountered anything as terrifying in their lives and fully believed that what they were hearing was the absolute truth.
J. they did not stop to think that what they were hearing might be fiction; instead they leaped to the unlikely conclusion that an interplanetary invasion was indeed occurring.

25. A. NO CHANGE
B. hour, by
C. hour by
D. hour but, by

26. F. NO CHANGE
G. Martians. This simultaneous fear of and fascination with Martians exists in many cultures.
H. Martians, who continue to frighten and fascinate people of various cultures.
J. Martians.

27. A. NO CHANGE
B. fooled at
C. foolish by
D. foolhardy in

GO ON TO THE NEXT PAGE.

continued to play their normal programs; while a disaster of
<u>   </u>
                                  28

global proportions <u>was underway.</u> [30]
                        29

28. F. NO CHANGE
   G. programs while
   H. program's while
   J. programs' while

29. A. NO CHANGE
   B. is
   C. will be
   D. had become

30. The author would like to end the passage with a sentence that places the response to *The War of the Worlds* in a larger context of other stories of alien invasion. Assuming all are true, which of the following, if inserted at this point, would best accomplish this?

   F. During that period, people relied on radio to tell them about news stories as they were occurring; newspapers did not report on such events until hours after the fact.
   G. Perhaps they assumed that the invasion had happened so suddenly that none of the other stations were even aware of it and were learning about it along with the listeners.
   H. However, humans have always been inclined to believe in unearthly forces; the response to *The War of the Worlds* is no more absurd than the responses to many equally unlikely rumors in the past and, doubtless, in the future.
   J. Certainly there were those who immediately recognized it for what it was, and turned the dial back to the *Chase and Sanborn Radio Hour*, aware that *The War of the Worlds* was entirely fictional.

GO ON TO THE NEXT PAGE.

PASSAGE III

Our Family Has Chemistry

[1]

There was always one big difference between my twin

brother and I. He was good at subjects such as English and his-
___
31

tory, while I was better at math and science. We were always
___
32

thoughtful; he would be a professor and I would be a doctor.
___
32

Because of this, I never felt particularly competitive with him and

was unconcerned when we accepted offers from the same college.

However, once we started, we would find that things did not
___
33

work out quite as I would expect. Continuing to pursue his high
___
34

school passions, he immediately joined the editorial board of the

school's literary magazine and convinced a professor to let him

into a graduate-level poetry seminar. [35]

[2]

I would never believe it if he hadn't told me himself, but all
___
36

of a sudden, my brother wanted to be a doctor, too. I can't say

---

31. A. NO CHANGE
   B. and me.
   C. and me were.
   D. and I had.

32. F. NO CHANGE
   G. Thoughtful as we were,
   H. I always thought that
   J. Although we were thoughtful,

33. A. NO CHANGE
   B. he found
   C. one had found
   D. I found

34. F. NO CHANGE
   G. had expected.
   H. was expecting.
   J. expect.

35. Which of the following sentences, if added here, would best link this paragraph to the one that follows?

   A. My brother had been editor of our high school's literary magazine and also a frequent contributor, so he was well qualified for both of these things.
   B. This was, however, the least of my problems.
   C. However, he also signed up for biology and chemistry, the very same premed classes that I was taking.
   D. I flipped right by the English courses in the catalogue, opting instead for biology and chemistry.

36. F. NO CHANGE
   G. of believed
   H. believed
   J. have believed

GO ON TO THE NEXT PAGE.

that I was too happy about the situation, and I told him so. It was

fine if he wanted to "make a difference" and "help humanity," but

as far as I was concerned, he could find his own way to do it. 37

Not surprisingly, he didn't see things that way; the next day, he

was sitting beside me in the front row of the lecture hall, waiting

for biology class to begin.

[3]

I wasn't too worried; I thought that a few days of lectures
                   38

on stoichiometry and the Krebs cycle would be enough to send

him running back to the English department for good. However,

as the weeks passed, this did not happen. I found that while

we were struggling to maintain a B+ average, my brother was
    39

getting straight A's. To make matters worse, he seemed to be

enjoying himself.

[4]

[1] Determined to outdo him, I was thrown into my work.
                              40

[2] I went to the library every night, smuggling in big cups of

coffee, to keep me awake, and stayed until closing time.
    41

[3] Including my brother, I soon had a grade-point average as
                        42

high as any premed. [4] I didn't stop there.
    42

37. The two sets of quotation marks in this sentence serve to:
   I.   show that the writer's brother was justified in his decision to become a doctor.
   II. present some of the phrases used during the writer's discussion with his brother.
   III. suggest that the writer was slightly skeptical of his brother's reasoning.

   A. II only
   B. I and II only
   C. II and III only
   D. I, II, and III

38. F. NO CHANGE
    G. worried, but
    H. worried,
    J. worried however much

39. A. NO CHANGE
    B. he was
    C. I was
    D. they were

40. F. NO CHANGE
    G. threw it
    H. threw myself
    J. was throwing everything

41. A. NO CHANGE
    B. coffee, to keep me awake
    C. coffee to keep me awake,
    D. coffee to keep me awake

42. F. NO CHANGE
    G. None of the grade-point averages of my brother and all of the other premeds were soon higher than mine.
    H. My grade-point average was soon at least as high as my brother's grade-point average, and also the grade-point averages of the other premeds.
    J. Soon no other premed, including my brother, had a grade-point average higher than mine.

GO ON TO THE NEXT PAGE.

[5] I took a summer job working in a professor's chemistry lab, set on getting a letter of recommendation more impressive than any that my brother could get. [6] At first, I thought only of impressing the professor; but soon I realized that I not only en-
43
joyed the work, but also had a real feel for it. [7] By the end of the summer, I decided to apply to graduate school in chemistry instead of medical school. 44

43. A. NO CHANGE
   B. professor but soon I
   C. professor. However, I soon
   D. professor: however I soon

44. The writer would like to divide the final paragraph into two shorter paragraphs. The most logical way to accomplish this would be to start a new paragraph beginning with:

   F. Sentence 3.
   G. Sentence 4.
   H. Sentence 6.
   J. Sentence 7.

> Question 45 asks about the preceding passage as a whole.

45. The writer wishes to add a sentence at the end of the essay that will demonstrate a sense of perspective gained by the experience described in the essay. Which of the following would accomplish this most effectively?

   A. We are both very happy in our chosen fields and have become much closer than we were in college.
   B. Although at the time there seemed to be nothing positive about my brother becoming a premed, it ultimately led me into a career that was perfect for me.
   C. Had I become a doctor, I probably would have chosen to become a surgeon; however, my brother hopes to become a pediatrician.
   D. I often wonder what would have happened had I gotten a job at a biology lab rather than a chemistry lab that summer.

GO ON TO THE NEXT PAGE.

PASSAGE IV

A Year in Ireland

[1]

We had just touched down in Shannon airport in Dub-
lin, Ireland. Left our native Chicago many hours before, and
46
although we were exhausted, we were all charged with the

excitement, that comes from embarking on a great adventure.
47

Being as everyone had a thick accent, we could barely under-
48
stand them as they tried to direct us where we should claim our
48
baggage.
48

[2]

I was six years old, and my parents, my sister, and I were
49

spending a year in Ireland. It all started, nonetheless, when my
50
parents received a grant to work at Trinity College. The next

thing I knew, we were subletting our apartment, packing all of

our clothes into big duffel bags, and convincing my grandfather

to take care of our cat. Finally, we piled everything into the car
51

and drove off. Watching our house and then our neighborhood
52
disappear in the distance, my apprehension grew.
52

46. F. NO CHANGE
    G. Having left
    H. We had left
    J. We left

47. A. NO CHANGE
    B. excitement that comes from embarking,
    C. excitement, that comes from embarking,
    D. excitement that comes from embarking

48. F. NO CHANGE
    G. Having thick accents, those who tried to help us claim
       our baggage were hard for us to understand.
    H. Everyone had such thick accents that we could barely
       understand their directions to the baggage claim area.
    J. Directions to the baggage claim area were barely
       understandable because of everyone's thick accents.

49. A. NO CHANGE
    B. old. And
    C. old
    D. old,

50. F. NO CHANGE
    G. started, in addition,
    H. started, despite this,
    J. started

51. Which of the following alternatives to the underlined portion
    would NOT be acceptable here?

    A. On our last day,
    B. In the end,
    C. Last,
    D. Yet,

52. F. NO CHANGE
    G. In the distance, my apprehension grew as I watched our
       house and then our neighborhood disappear.
    H. Our house and then our neighborhood disappeared as I
       watched apprehensively in the distance.
    J. My apprehension grew as I watched our house and then
       our neighborhood disappear in the distance.

GO ON TO THE NEXT PAGE.

[3]

Even after we arrived and got settled in, I remained uneasy. Everything was different, from the shape of the milk cartons to the characters in the comic books.

[4]

These may seem like trivial things, but to a first grader,
53
they were very important. A week after we arrived, I told my mother that it was time for us to go home. We could buy our plane tickets that night and the next day could be the one when
54
we would leave.
54

55 My mother smiled sympathetically and promised me that I would get used to it.

[5]

This, in fact, turned out to be true. A few days later, I started school and immediately achieved celebrity status. There were no other Americans in class P–1 as the first grade, was called, and
56
only three other foreigners in the whole school. During recess, I would hold court on the playground, teaching everyone my own version of American history and culture.

[6]

57 As I walked with my family through O'Hare airport

53. **A.** NO CHANGE
B. (Do NOT combine paragraphs 3 and 4) Seeming
C. (Combine paragraphs 3 and 4) Seeming
D. (Combine paragraphs 3 and 4) These may seem

54. **F.** NO CHANGE
G. a departure tomorrow.
H. leave the next day.
J. the following day would be the day of our departure.

55. The writer wants to include a detail to show that she was serious about her suggestion to her mother. Assuming all are true, which of the following sentences, if inserted at this point, would best accomplish this?

A. I showed her my little red suitcase, which I had already neatly packed with all of my dolls, books, and stuffed animals.
B. I then reminded her that Father would be home very soon and that she should start his supper right away.
C. My sister didn't mind it there, but because she was only two years old, she didn't know any better.
D. I didn't know whether it would be possible to get plane tickets on such short notice; our tickets to Ireland came in the mail only two weeks before we left.

56. **F.** NO CHANGE
G. P–1, as the first grade was called,
H. P–1, as the first grade was called
J. P–1 as the first grade was called,

57. The author wishes to add a sentence at the beginning of Paragraph 6 in order to provide a graceful transition and convey the passage of time. Which of the following sentences best accomplishes this?

A. The flight back was a little bumpy, but the plane landed safely.
B. The year flew by, and it was soon time to return home.
C. Air travel can be exhausting, especially for a family with children.
D. I ended up having a wonderful time in Ireland.

GO ON TO THE NEXT PAGE.

in Chicago, I was glad to be home, <u>but one at a time,</u> a little
58
sad to go back to being just like everyone else. Soon, however,

something happened that made me smile. A little boy overheard

me talking to my father in the Irish lilt that I had unknowingly

picked up over the course of the year. He immediately turned to

his mother and said, "Wow, look at that! There's a kid over there

from Ireland."

58. F. NO CHANGE
G. from time to time,
H. at the same time,
J. all in good time,

Questions 59 and 60 ask about the preceding passage as a whole.

59. This essay was written in response to an assignment to describe the personal relationships among the writer's family. Does it successfully do so?

A. Yes, because it describes how the writer's family responded to a difficult year.
B. Yes, because it mentions a conversation between the writer and her mother.
C. No, because it focuses mostly on the writer's response to a series of events.
D. No, because it does not explain how the writer's parents met.

60. The writer is deciding where to include the following sentence in the essay, in order to emphasize her eventual adjustment to life in Ireland.

> Soon, Dublin was like a second home to me.

The best place to insert this sentence would be:
F. at the beginning of Paragraph 4.
G. at the beginning of Paragraph 5.
H. at the end of Paragraph 5.
J. at the end of Paragraph 6.

GO ON TO THE NEXT PAGE.

PASSAGE V

Wait Just a Minute . . .

I <u>crept</u> in for my first shift as a waiter without a
61
care in the world. Everyone told me that waiting tables

was much harder than it looked, <u>and</u> I knew that they
62
were just exaggerating. After all, if you're a college

graduate and you've already spent two nights training,

how much trouble <u>must I</u> have working at a place called
63

Harry's Burritos? Besides, <u>I reasoned,</u> it was a Tuesday
64
night, which was sure to be slow.

I changed into my uniform and immediately got my

<u>first customers, a father,</u> with two little boys. I brought
65
over some chips and salsa, and before I could even take the

family's order, the older boy started to pelt his little brother

with tortilla chips. The younger <u>boy, who was probably</u>
66
<u>about the same age as my little sister,</u> got so upset that he
66
spilled his water all over the table. The boys' father apolo-

gized for <u>there</u> behavior, but I assured him that it was all
67
right. I cleaned up the mess, and within ten minutes, they

were all happily digging into their burritos. I silently con-

gratulated myself, thinking that I was obviously a natural.

61. Which of the following best conveys the way the writer entered the restaurant?

  A. NO CHANGE
  B. trudged
  C. skipped
  D. staggered

62. F. NO CHANGE
  G. but
  H. while
  J. so

63. A. NO CHANGE
  B. could I
  C. could you
  D. can one

64. F. NO CHANGE
  G. for many reasons,
  H. within reason,
  J. being reasonable,

65. A. NO CHANGE
  B. customers: a father
  C. customers; a father
  D. customers. A father,

66. F. NO CHANGE
  G. boy was about the same age as my little sister. He
  H. boy (about the same age as my younger sister)
  J. boy

67. A. NO CHANGE
  B. they're
  C. their
  D. his

GO ON TO THE NEXT PAGE.

Then came the seven o'clock rush. All of a sudden, five

of my six tables were full. I was running around like a crazy

man, barely able to remember whose order I had taken.
68

The manager seated a couple at my last empty table and

whispered that they were friends of the owner. I nodded, but

with one group needing its check, another demanding
69

about its nachos, and a third complaining that the vegetarian
70

tacos had beef in them, so I didn't have time to lavish attention
71

on anyone.

[1] Before I knew it, half an hour had passed, and I

hadn't even brought the owner's friends their margaritas.

[2] I grabbed the drinks and ran toward their table, but the

manager stopped me in my path. [3] She wanted to know

what was going on. [4] I admitted that I had not been com-

pletely truthful. [5] She asked me whether I really had three

years of experience waiting tables, as I had indicated on my
72

application. [6] However, I had no choice. [7] Since no one

would hire an inexperienced waiter, no waiter could get a

first job without lying. [8] She found my argument less than

compelling, and by eight-fifteen, I was unemployed. [73]

68. **F.** NO CHANGE
    G. man so
    H. man, then
    J. man, but

69. **A.** NO CHANGE
    B. one group needed their check,
    C. the check was what one group was needing,
    D. checking one group,

70. **F.** NO CHANGE
    G. of
    H. for
    J. OMIT the underlined portion.

71. **A.** NO CHANGE
    B. them, I
    C. them, and I
    D. them. I

72. **F.** NO CHANGE
    G. years, of experience,
    H. years of experience,
    J. years, of experience

73. In order to make the final paragraph easier to understand, the writer should reverse the order of which two sentences?

    A. Sentence 1 and Sentence 2
    B. Sentence 3 and Sentence 4
    C. Sentence 4 and Sentence 5
    D. Sentence 7 and Sentence 8

GO ON TO THE NEXT PAGE.

> Questions 74 and 75 ask about the preceding passage as a whole.

74. Assuming each is true, which of the following sentences, if added at the end of the final paragraph, would be most consistent with the writer's tone in the rest of the essay?

    F. She was wholly justified in her actions; except in cases when a life is at stake, dishonesty is never justifiable.
    G. I had never been treated with so little care or respect, and I told her so.
    H. My brilliant career as a waiter was officially over, only three hours after it had begun.
    J. I had to fight back the tears as I walked to the bus stop, but I soon started to put things in perspective.

75. The writer has written the following sentence and is considering adding it to the essay.

    Harry's Burritos is a moderately priced Mexican restaurant on Manhattan's Upper West Side.

    Should this sentence be included in the essay, and if so, where?
    A. Yes, at the beginning of the first paragraph, because it helps the reader to envision the setting in which the events described take place.
    B. Yes, at the end of the first paragraph, because it explains why the writer is not nervous before his first shift.
    C. No, because the readers should be expected to be familiar with Harry's Burritos.
    D. No, because the location and cost of the restaurant are not central to the events that the writer describes.

END OF TEST 1

STOP! DO NOT TURN THE PAGE UNTIL TOLD TO DO SO.

MATHEMATICS TEST
60 Minutes—60 Questions

DIRECTIONS: Solve each problem, choose the correct answer, and then darken the corresponding oval on your answer sheet.

Do not linger over problems that take too much time. Solve as many as you can; then return to the others in the time you have left for this test.

You are permitted to use a calculator on this test. You may use your calculator for any problems you choose, but some of the problems may best be done without using a calculator.

Note: Unless otherwise stated, all of the following should be assumed:

1. Illustrative figures are NOT necessarily drawn to scale.
2. Geometric figures lie in a plane.
3. The word *line* indicates a straight line.
4. The word *average* indicates arithmetic mean.

---

1. If $4x + 2 = 20$, then $x = ?$

   A. 4.5
   B. 6.0
   C. 9.0
   D. 12.5
   E. 18.0

2. On a real number line, what is the distance, in coordinate units, between points M and N if point M has coordinate 9 and point N has coordinate –5 ?

   F. 2
   G. 4
   H. 7
   J. 12
   K. 14

3. Each week, a store sells x hats and y shirts. If the store earns $5 for each hat and $10 for each shirt, which of the following expressions shows the total amount of money, in dollars, that the store earns each week?

   A. $10x + 5y$
   B. $5x + 10y$
   C. $15(x + y)$
   D. $50(x + y)$
   E. $15xy$

4. Of the following numbers, which is the greatest in value?

   F. 2.1×10^{-5}
   G. 21×10^5
   H. $.0021 \times 10^{10}$
   J. 210,000
   K. $.21 \times 10^9$

DO YOUR FIGURING HERE.

GO ON TO THE NEXT PAGE.

5. On Monday, Alice bought a bag of marbles. On Tuesday, she gave $\frac{2}{3}$ of her marbles to a friend. On Wednesday, she gave away $\frac{1}{3}$ of her remaining marbles. If she then had 8 marbles left, how many marbles did she buy originally?

A. 36
B. 30
C. 24
D. 18
E. 12

6. If $a = 4y + 2z$ and $b = z - y$, then what is the value of $a + b$?

F. $5y + 3z$
G. $5y - 3z$
H. $3y + 3z$
J. $3y - 3z$
K. $3y + z$

7. Susan recorded the number of customers visiting her book-store each day for five days, as shown in the table below. What was the average number of customers for these five days?

Day	Number of Customers
Monday	56
Tuesday	47
Wednesday	43
Thursday	55
Friday	64

A. 48
B. 50
C. 53
D. 55
E. 56

8. If $x = -2$, then $x^2 + 3x + 15 = ?$

F. 19
G. 13
H. 11
J. 7
K. 5

9. By the end of the year, the population of Greenville is expected to increase 8% from its current population of 45,000. If this prediction is accurate, what would be its new population at the end of the year?

A. 48,600
B. 48,000
C. 46,400
D. 45,800
E. 41,400

DO YOUR FIGURING HERE.

GO ON TO THE NEXT PAGE.

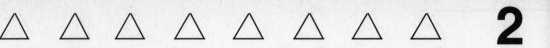

DO YOUR FIGURING HERE.

...ion shows the slope-intercept form of
... $= 1$?

F. $y = \dfrac{2}{5}x - \dfrac{9}{2}$

G. $y = -\dfrac{2}{5}x + \dfrac{9}{2}$

H. $y = -\dfrac{5}{2}x + \dfrac{9}{2}$

J. $y = \dfrac{5}{2}x + \dfrac{9}{2}$

K. $y = \dfrac{5}{2}x - \dfrac{9}{2}$

11. For all real values of x, y, and z, the expression $(x + y)(x + z) = ?$

A. $2x + x(y + z) + yz$
B. $x^2 + x(y + z) + yz$
C. $x^2 + yz + xz$
D. $x(x + y + z)$
E. $x(yz + xz)$

12. The lengths of the sides of a triangle are 4, 7, and 10 inches. How many inches long is the longest side of a similar triangle that has a perimeter of 42 inches?

F. 16
G. 20
H. 24
J. 36
K. 30

13. $|2 - 4| \times |-2| = ?$

A. −4
B. −2
C. 2
D. 4
E. 8

14. John needs to pick his clothes for the day. He can choose from 6 different shirts, 4 different pairs of pants, and 8 different pairs of socks. If an outfit consists of 1 shirt, 1 pair of pants, and 1 pair of socks, how many different outfits could he choose?

F. 18
G. 48
H. 64
J. 96
K. 192

GO ON TO THE NEXT PAGE.

15. A formula for the volume of a cylinder with radius r and height h is $V = \pi r^2 h$. What is the volume, to the nearest cubic inch, of a cylindrical can with a radius of 3 inches and a height of 5 inches?

    A. 707
    B. 444
    C. 236
    D. 188
    E. 141

16. Which of the following functions will have the greatest value if $x = -10$?

    F. $f(x) = x^2 - 2x$
    G. $g(x) = x^2 + 2x$
    H. $h(x) = -x^2$
    J. $j(x) = x^3 - x^2$
    K. $k(x) = x^0$

17. If 50 is 20 percent of x, then $x = ?$

    A. 10
    B. 100
    C. 250
    D. 1,000
    E. 2,500

18. The cost of a long-distance phone call is 15 cents for the first minute, and then 3 cents for every additional minute. How many cents would a 24-minute phone call cost?

    F. 42
    G. 45
    H. 72
    J. 84
    K. 87

19. What is the slope of the line that passes through the points $(-1,3)$ and $(1,2)$?

    A. $-\dfrac{1}{3}$

    B. $-\dfrac{1}{2}$

    C. $\dfrac{1}{2}$

    D. 1

    E. 2

20. If $8 - 3(x - 2) = 5$, then $x =$

    F. -3

    G. -1

    H. $-\dfrac{1}{3}$

    J. 1

    K. 3

GO ON TO THE NEXT PAGE.

21. Which of the following is a simplified equivalent of $\dfrac{3x + 9y}{6z}$?

A. $\dfrac{12xy}{z}$

B. $\dfrac{6xy}{z}$

C. $\dfrac{3x + 3y}{2z}$

D. $\dfrac{2x + 3y}{z}$

E. $\dfrac{x + 3y}{2z}$

22. Three vertices of a square lie at the points $(-2,2)$, $(2,3)$, and $(3,-1)$ in the standard (x,y) coordinate plane. What are the coordinates of the fourth vertex of the square?

F. $(-1,-2)$
G. $(-2,-1)$
H. $(1,2)$
J. $(2,-1)$
K. $(2,1)$

23. What is the slope of a line that is perpendicular to the line with equation $2y = 10 - 3x$?

A. $-\dfrac{2}{3}$

B. $\dfrac{2}{3}$

C. $\dfrac{3}{2}$

D. 2

E. 3

24. If $x^2 + 4x = 12$, what are all possible values of x ?

F. -6 and 2 only
G. -2 and 6 only
H. 3 and 4 only
J. 4 only
K. 6 only

DO YOUR FIGURING HERE.

GO ON TO THE NEXT PAGE.

DO YOUR FIGURING HERE.

25. A certain lemonade mix requires $3\frac{1}{2}$ cups of lemon juice to make 4 quarts of lemonade. How many cups of lemon juice would be required to make 10 quarts of lemonade?

    A. $4\frac{1}{2}$

    B. $6\frac{2}{3}$

    C. 8

    D. $8\frac{3}{4}$

    E. $9\frac{1}{2}$

26. What is the length, in inches, of the hypotenuse of a right triangle with legs measuring 12 inches and 16 inches?

    F. 18

    G. 20

    H. 28

    J. $\sqrt{28}$

    K. $\sqrt{90}$

27. Which of the following is a polynomial factor of $8x^2 + 22x - 6$?

    A. $(4x - 3)$
    B. $(4x + 3)$
    C. $(8x - 2)$
    D. $(8x + 3)$
    E. $(8x + 6)$

28. Which of the following is the graph of the solution set for $2(3x + 4) < 20$?

GO ON TO THE NEXT PAGE.

29. If, for all x, $(x^{a+1})^3 = x^9$, then $a = ?$

    A. 2
    B. 3
    C. 4
    D. 5
    E. 6

DO YOUR FIGURING HERE.

30. What is the cosine of $\angle C$ in $\triangle ABC$ below?

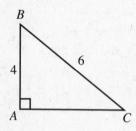

    F. $\dfrac{2}{3}$

    G. $\dfrac{3}{2}$

    H. $\dfrac{\sqrt{13}}{3}$

    J. $\dfrac{\sqrt{5}}{3}$

    K. $\dfrac{\sqrt{5}}{2}$

31. What is the area of the shaded triangle below?

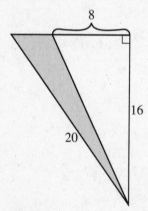

    A. 16
    B. 32
    C. 64
    D. 128
    E. 192

GO ON TO THE NEXT PAGE.

32. In the complex numbers, where $i^2 = -1$, what is the value of $3i^2 + i^4$?

    F. −2
    G. −1
    H. 0
    J. 1
    K. 2

33. In the figure below, $\overline{BD}$ is the altitude of equilateral triangle ABC. If $\overline{BD}$ is 8 units long, what is the perimeter of $\triangle ABC$?

(Note: An altitude of a triangle is perpendicular to the opposite side.)

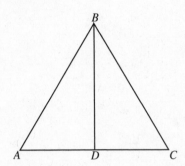

    A. 12

    B. $8\sqrt{3}$

    C. 16

    D. 24

    E. $16\sqrt{3}$

34. A triangle has sides of length 4 inches and 7.5 inches. Which of the following CANNOT be the length of the third side?

    F. 3.5 inches
    G. 4.0 inches
    H. 5.0 inches
    J. 5.5 inches
    K. 9.5 inches

35. What is the x-intercept of the line formed by the equation $y = 4x + 5$?

    A. (5,−4)

    B. $(4, \frac{5}{4})$

    C. $(-\frac{5}{4}, 0)$

    D. $(\frac{4}{5}, 0)$

    E. $(0, \frac{5}{4})$

DO YOUR FIGURING HERE.

GO ON TO THE NEXT PAGE.

36. The line $y = \frac{1}{2}x - 2$ passes through which one of the following points?

    F. (0,2)
    G. (1,3)
    H. (2,4)
    J. (2,–1)
    K. (1,–3)

DO YOUR FIGURING HERE.

37. In the figure below, $\overleftrightarrow{BD}$ and $\overleftrightarrow{AE}$ are parallel and crossed by two transversals. The points of intersection and some lengths are shown. What is the length of $\overline{AE}$?

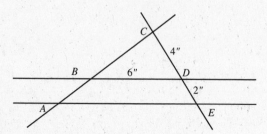

    A. 8
    B. 9
    C. 9.5
    D. 10
    E. 12

38. In the right triangle below, how long is side $\overline{AC}$?

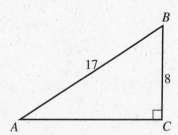

    F. $17 - 8$
    G. $17^2 - 8^2$
    H. $17^2 + 8^2$
    J. $\sqrt{17 - 8}$
    K. $\sqrt{17^2 - 8^2}$

GO ON TO THE NEXT PAGE.

39. At which of the following points does the graph for $2x^2 + x - 10 = y$ cross the x-axis?

   A. $(2,-5)$
   B. $(0,-2)$
   C. $(3,0)$
   D. $(2,0)$
   E. $(0,0)$

40. If $\tan\theta = \dfrac{9}{40}$ and $\sin\theta = \dfrac{9}{41}$ then $\cos\theta = ?$

   F. $\dfrac{41}{9}$

   G. $\dfrac{41}{40}$

   H. $\dfrac{40}{41}$

   J. $\dfrac{9}{39}$

   K. $\dfrac{1}{9}$

41. At how many points do the graphs of $x^2 + y^2 = 16$ and $x^2 + y^2 = 9$ intersect?

   A. 0
   B. 1
   C. 2
   D. 3
   E. infinitely many

42. For what value of b would the graph of the following system of equations be a single line in the standard (x,y) coordinate plane?

$$3x + 4y = 15$$
$$9x + 12y = 5b$$

   F. 3
   G. 5
   H. 7
   J. 9
   K. 11

DO YOUR FIGURING HERE.

GO ON TO THE NEXT PAGE.

43. In the figure below, *ABC* and *ACD* are right triangles. If triangle *ABC* is isosceles, and if $\overline{CD}$ is 6 inches long, how many inches long is $\overline{BC}$?

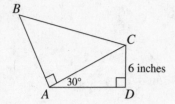

DO YOUR FIGURING HERE.

A. 6

B. $6\sqrt{3}$

C. 12

D. $12\sqrt{2}$

E. 24

44. A certain rectangle has a length that is 2 feet less than 4 times its width. If the area of the rectangle is 240 square feet, how many feet wide is the rectangle?

F. 2

G. 5

H. 6

J. 7

K. 8

45. The (x,y) coordinates of the center of a circle are $(-1,2)$. If the (x,y) coordinates of one endpoint of a certain diameter of the circle are $(-6,5)$, what are the (x,y) coordinates of the other endpoint of the diameter?

A. $(-11,8)$

B. $(-7,7)$

C. $(0,-2)$

D. $(3,0)$

E. $(4,-1)$

46. If $x - y = -4$ and $x + y = -3$, then $x^2 - y^2 = ?$

F. -7

G. -3

H. 7

J. 9

K. 12

GO ON TO THE NEXT PAGE.

47. A circle is inscribed in a square, as shown in the figure below. If the square measures 10 feet on a side, which of the following expressions gives the area of the shaded region in square feet?

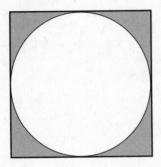

A. $10^2 - 10\pi$
B. $10^2 - 5^2\pi$
C. $10 - 5\pi$
D. $5^2 - 5^2\pi$
E. $5^2 - 10\pi$

48. The figure below shows an isosceles trapezoid. What is its area in square centimeters (cm)?

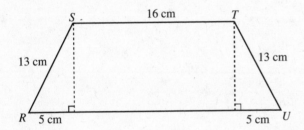

F. 338
G. 312
H. 273
J. 252
K. 192

49. Miko is walking to a bus stop on the other side of a rectangular pool. She walks 20 feet west, then turns and walks 70 feet north, then turns and walks 60 feet west, and then turns and walks 10 feet south to the bus stop. If she had been able to walk in a straight line from her starting point to the bus stop, approximately how many feet shorter would her path have been?

A. 20
B. 47
C. 60
D. 71
E. 88

GO ON TO THE NEXT PAGE.

50. If $\log_x 64 = 2$, then $x = ?$

    F.   2
    G.   4
    H.   8
    J.   16
    K. 64^2

51. If x is a real number, and the value of $\dfrac{x}{x^2 - 7}$ is undefined, then what is the value of $x^3 - 7x$?

    A.   0
    B.   1
    C.   −1
    D.   Undefined
    E.   It cannot be determined from the given information.

52. Bob can drive 3 miles in n minutes. At this rate, how many minutes will it take him to drive 14 miles?

    F. $42n$

    G. $\dfrac{3n}{14}$

    H. $\dfrac{14n}{3}$

    J. $\dfrac{3}{14n}$

    K. $\dfrac{14}{3n}$

53. For real numbers x and y such that $-1 < x < 0 < 1 < y$, which of the following represents the set of all possible values of xy ?

    A.

    B.

    C.

    D.

    E.

GO ON TO THE NEXT PAGE.

54. Which of the following calculations will yield an odd integer for any integer x ?

F. x^2
G. $3x^2$
H. $2x^2 + 1$
J. $3x^2 + 1$
K. $5x^2$

55. If the equation $x^2 - 12x + k = 0$ has only one solution for x, what is the value of k ?

A. 1
B. 6
C. 12
D. 36
E. 48

56. In the figure below, $AE = \dfrac{1}{2} BE$. What is the area of parallelogram $ABCD$?

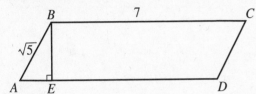

F. 7

G. 14

H. $7\sqrt{5}$

J. 28

K. $14\sqrt{5}$

57. From point A, the top of a pole can be seen at a 29° angle of ascent. If the distance from point A to the base of the pole is 40 feet, which of the following expresses the height of the pole in feet?

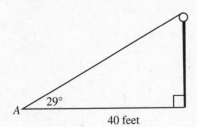

A. $40 \tan 29°$

B. $40 \sin 29°$

C. $\dfrac{40}{\tan 29°}$

D. $\dfrac{40}{\sin 29°}$

E. $\dfrac{40}{\cos 29°}$

58. What is the maximum value of $y = -1 + 4(\sin 2x)$?

DO YOUR FIGURING HERE.

F. 3
G. 4
H. 5
J. 6
K. 7

59. The average of a set of 6 integers is 65. If a seventh number is added to the set, the average of the set increases to 66. What is the seventh number?

A. 66
B. 67
C. 70
D. 72
E. 78

60. Jamie's sock drawer contains 10 black socks, 8 red socks, 8 white socks, and 2 yellow socks. She pulls out a black sock and does not put it back. If she reaches back in the drawer to pull out another sock at random, what is the probability that she will pull out another black sock?

F. $\dfrac{1}{9}$

G. $\dfrac{9}{28}$

H. $\dfrac{1}{3}$

J. $\dfrac{5}{14}$

K. $\dfrac{10}{27}$

END OF TEST 2

STOP! DO NOT TURN THE PAGE UNTIL TOLD TO DO SO.
DO NOT RETURN TO THE PREVIOUS TEST.

NO TEST MATERIAL ON THIS PAGE.

READING TEST
35 Minutes—40 Questions

DIRECTIONS: There are four passages in this test. Each passage is followed by several questions. After reading each passage, choose the best answer to each question and blacken the corresponding oval on your answer sheet. You may refer to the passages as often as necessary.

Passage I

PROSE FICTION: This passage is taken from *The Heart Is a Lonely Hunter,* by Carson McCullers (© 1940 and 1967 by Carson McCullers).

The sun woke Mick early, although she had stayed out mighty late the night before. It was too hot even to drink coffee for breakfast, so she had ice water with syrup in it and cold biscuits. She messed around the kitchen for a while and then
5 went out on the front porch to read the funnies. She had thought maybe Mister Singer would be reading the paper on the porch like he did most Sunday mornings. But Mister Singer was not there, and later on her dad said he came in very late the night before and had company in his room. She waited for Mister
10 Singer a long time. All the other boarders came down except him. Finally she went back in the kitchen and took Ralph out of his high chair and put a clean dress on him and wiped off his face. Then when Bubber got home from Sunday School she was ready to take the kids out. She let Bubber ride in the wagon with
15 Ralph because he was barefooted and the hot sidewalk burned his feet. She pulled the wagon for about eight blocks until they came to the big, new house that was being built. The ladder was still propped against the edge of the roof, and she screwed up nerve and began to climb.

20 "You mind Ralph," she called back to Bubber. "Mind the gnats don't sit on his eyelids."

Five minutes later Mick stood up and held herself very straight. She spread out her arms like wings. This was the place where everybody wanted to stand. The very top. But if you lost
25 your grip and rolled off the edge it would kill you. All around were the roofs of other houses and the green tops of trees. On the other side of town were the church steeples and the smokestacks from the mills. The sky was bright blue and hot as fire. The sun made everything on the ground either dizzy white or black.

30 She wanted to sing. All the songs she knew pushed up toward her throat, but there was no sound. One big boy who had got to the highest part of the roof last week let out a yell and then started hollering out a speech he had learned at High School—"Friends, Romans, Countrymen, Lend me your ears!" There was something
35 about getting to the very top that gave you a wild feeling and made you want to yell or sing or raise up your arms and fly.

She felt the soles of her tennis shoes slipping, and eased herself down so that she straddled the peak of the roof. The house was almost finished. It would be one of the largest buildings in
40 the neighborhood—two stories, with very high ceilings and the steepest roof of any house she had ever seen. But soon the work would all be finished. The carpenters would leave and the kids would have to find another place to play.

She was by herself. No one was around and it was quiet
45 and she could think for a while. She took from the pocket of her shorts the package of cigarettes she had bought the night before. She breathed in the smoke slowly. The cigarette gave her a drunk feeling so that her head seemed heavy and loose on her shoulders, but she had to finish it.

50 M.K.—That was what she would have written on everything when she was seventeen years old and very famous. She would ride back home in a red-and-white Packard automobile with her initials on the doors. She would have M.K. written in red on her handkerchiefs and underclothes. Maybe she would
55 be a great inventor. She would invent tiny little radios the size of a green pea that people could carry around and stick in their ears. Also flying machines people could fasten on their backs like knapsacks and go zipping all over the world. After that she would be the first one to make a large tunnel through the world
60 to China, and people could go down in big balloons. Those were the first things she would invent. They were already planned.

When Mick had finished half of the cigarette she smashed it dead and flipped the butt down the slant of the roof. Then she leaned forward so that her head rested on her arms and began
65 to hum to herself.

1. As it is used in line 18, the phrase *screwed up* most nearly means:

   A. lost.
   B. made a mistake.
   C. examined.
   D. gathered.

GO ON TO THE NEXT PAGE.

2. If the passage describes a typical Sunday, Mick then spends part of her Sundays:

   F. learning grammar from Mister Singer.
   G. cooking breakfast for her family.
   H. going to Sunday School.
   J. caring for her younger brothers.

3. Mick believes that the other children in the neighborhood:

   A. did not want to play with her.
   B. also liked to climb on the roof.
   C. thought that Mick was crazy for climbing on rooftops.
   D. had more housework to do than she did.

4. The name of Mick's father is:

   F. Ralph.
   G. Bubber.
   H. Mister Singer.
   J. not mentioned in the passage.

5. It can be reasonably inferred that one of the reasons that Mick enjoyed being on the roof was that:

   A. she could enjoy some time alone.
   B. her friends did not believe that she could do it and she liked proving them wrong.
   C. she felt very athletic while climbing.
   D. she knew that she was the only one who could climb that high.

6. It is suggested that no sound came out of Mick's throat (line 31) because she:

   F. did not think she had a good singing voice.
   G. could not express all of what she was feeling.
   H. was afraid of heights.
   J. did not want to scare her brothers by yelling too loudly.

7. It can be inferred from the passage that Mister Singer is:

   A. Mick's father.
   B. a boarder at Mick's house.
   C. a schoolteacher.
   D. a journalist.

8. All of the following are included in the list of things Mick would like to invent EXCEPT:

   F. a miniature radio.
   G. a small flying machine.
   H. a big balloon.
   J. a tunnel through the earth.

9. The house that Mick climbs onto is:

   A. three stories tall.
   B. on a hill.
   C. unfinished.
   D. owned by a celebrity.

10. According to the passage, it can reasonably be inferred that Mick spent a great deal of time wishing:

   F. to be famous.
   G. to have children.
   H. to get good grades in school.
   J. to spend more time with her mother.

GO ON TO THE NEXT PAGE.

Passage II

SOCIAL SCIENCE: This passage, which discusses how news is reported in the age of television, is taken from a book by Neil Postman.

"Now…this" is commonly used on radio and television newscasts to indicate that what one has just heard or seen has no relevance to what one is about to hear or see, or possibly to anything one is ever likely to hear or see. The phrase is a means
5 of acknowledging the fact that the world as mapped by the speeded-up electronic media has no order or meaning and is not to be taken seriously. There is no murder so brutal, no earthquake so devastating, no political blunder so costly—for that matter, no ball score so tantalizing or weather report so threatening—that
10 it cannot be erased from our minds by a newscaster saying, "Now…this." The newscaster means that you have thought long enough on the previous matter (approximately 45 seconds), that you must not be morbidly preoccupied with it (let us say, for 90 seconds), and that you must now give your attention to another
15 fragment of news or a commercial.

Television did not invent the "Now…this" worldview. As I have tried to show, it is the offspring of the intercourse between telegraphy and photography. But it is through television that it has been nurtured and brought to a perverse maturity. For on
20 television, nearly every half hour is a discrete event, separated in content, context, and emotional texture from what precedes and follows it. In part because television sells its time in seconds and minutes, in part because television must use images rather than words, in part because its audience can move freely to and
25 from the television set, programs are structured so that almost each eight-minute segment may stand as a complete event in itself. Viewers are rarely required to carry over any thought or feeling from one parcel of time to another.

Of course, in television's presentation of the "news of the
30 day," we may see the "Now…this" mode of discourse in its boldest and most embarrassing form. For there, we are presented not only with fragmented news but news without context, without consequences, without value, and therefore without essential seriousness; that is to say, news as pure entertainment.

35 Consider, for example, how you would proceed if you were given the opportunity to produce a television news show for any station concerned to attract the largest possible audience. You would, first, choose a cast of players, each of whom has a face that is both "likable" and "credible." Those who apply would,
40 in fact, submit to you their eight-by-ten glossies, from which you would eliminate those whose countenances are not suitable for nightly display. This means that you will exclude women who are not beautiful or who are over the age of 50, men who are bald, all people who are overweight or whose noses are too
45 long or whose eyes are too close together. You will try, in other words, to assemble a cast of talking hairdos. At the very least, you will want those whose faces would not be unwelcome on a magazine cover.

Christine Craft has just such a face, and so she applied for a
50 co-anchor position on KMBC-TV in Kansas City. According to a lawyer who represented her in a sexism suit she later brought against the station, the management of KMBC-TV "loved Christine's look." She was accordingly hired in January 1981. She was fired in August 1981 because research indicated that her
55 appearance "hampered viewer acceptance." What exactly does "hampered viewer acceptance" mean? And what does it have to do with the news? Hampered viewer acceptance means the same thing for television news as it does for any television show: Viewers do not like looking at the performer. It also means that
60 viewers do not believe the performer, that she lacks credibility. In the case of a theatrical performance, we have a sense of what that implies: The actor does not persuade the audience that he or she is the character being portrayed. But what does lack of credibility imply in the case of a news show? What character
65 is a co-anchor playing? And how do we decide that the performance lacks verisimilitude? Does the audience believe that the newscaster is lying, that what is reported did not in fact happen, that something important is being concealed?

It is frightening to think that this may be so, that the per-
70 ception of the truth of a report rests heavily on the acceptability of the newscaster. In the ancient world, there was a tradition of banishing or killing the bearer of bad tidings. Does the television news show restore, in a curious form, this tradition?

11. The author of this passage can most reasonably be described as:

A. a detective who tries to find evidence proving that a television network is not guilty of misleading the public.
B. a television executive who discusses important factors for a successful news program.
C. a critic who warns his readers about the effects that television has had on the reporting of news.
D. a journalism teacher who wishes to show his students how to write interesting television news stories.

12. As it is used in line 5, the word *mapped* most nearly means:

F. obscured.
G. explored.
H. destroyed.
J. defined.

GO ON TO THE NEXT PAGE.

13. It can reasonably be inferred that the author would most likely agree with which of the following statements?

    A. News stories are more interesting when they are presented on live television than when they are recorded.

    B. The short amount of time given to news stories on television reduces the value of the facts reported.

    C. Television has done a good job of bringing families together by creating programs that the entire family can watch.

    D. Television news reporters should also write news stories for magazines and newspapers.

14. In the fifth paragraph (lines 49–68) the author offers details about Christine Craft in order to:

    F. illustrate the importance of the appearance of the newscaster on television.

    G. show that television gets its nature from both telegraphy and photography.

    H. support a claim about sexism in America.

    J. present the story of a friend and her experiences in television journalism.

15. It can most reasonably be inferred that the author believes that:

    A. well-trained actors are better than newscasters at delivering news on television.

    B. television is not well suited to a serious presentation of the news.

    C. newspapers will likely disappear in a few years if people continue to get their news from television.

    D. the presentation of the news has not fundamentally changed since ancient times.

16. According to the passage, television has become a medium whose main goal is:

    F. to report the facts in an unbiased manner.

    G. to help television reporters become famous.

    H. to inform the public of important new products.

    J. to entertain viewers.

17. The author's reference to "talking hairdos" (line 46) is a reference to:

    A. people whose faces are pleasing to viewers.

    B. the advertising of hair-care products on television.

    C. animated cartoon characters.

    D. the amount of money spent to make television personalities look good.

18. According to the author, the phrase "Now…this" indicates that the next topic:

    F. will be more important than the previous topic.

    G. will receive less time than the previous topic.

    H. will have no connection to the previous topic.

    J. will begin a new eight-minute segment of news.

19. According to the passage, television viewers' perceptions of whether a story is true or false depends largely on the:

    A. appearance of the person reporting the news.

    B. reputation of the television network.

    C. references cited during the news story.

    D. commentary provided by those being interviewed.

20. Which of the following is NOT cited as having an impact on the presentation of television news?

    F. Airtime is a very valuable commodity for television stations.

    G. People are not expected to remain attentive to the television for more than a short period of time.

    H. Television relies more on images than on words to transmit its message.

    J. Television sets are relatively expensive, and not everyone can afford them.

GO ON TO THE NEXT PAGE.

Passage III

HUMANITIES: This passage is taken from *The Century* by Peter Jennings (© 1998 by ABC Television Network Group).

The show was grandly titled "The International Exhibition of Modern Art," but the dynamite, as *The New Yorker* later commented, was in the word "modern." And while the new painting and sculpture declared itself with the confidence that comes
5　with a revolution, there were many in the New York crowd and in even larger gatherings who greeted the show when it moved on to Boston and Chicago (where art students burned Matisse and Brancusi in effigy) who would have nothing of it. One of America's more distinguished artists, Kenyon Cox, a longtime
10　holdout against the trends that seemed to be undermining the traditional image, saw in the show nothing less than the "total destruction of the art of painting," and on this he could find only one bit of good news: that the Americans represented here seemed to him to have resisted the "depth of badness [attained]
15　by the French and the Germans." Indeed, many of those attending the show looked upon the works before them as the perverse fantasies of the foreigner; Ellis Island art they called it. And no less a chauvinist than Teddy Roosevelt himself, fresh from his unsuccessful 1912 attempt to re-enter the White House
20　with the backing of a third party (Roosevelt and his handpicked Republican successor, William Howard Taft, had had a falling-out), was said to have stomped about the opening, waving his arms and declaring in a loud voice his disapproval of all but the American entries, even as he gave praise to the show's general
25　spirit, in particular in the way that it tolerated no "simpering, self-satisfied conventionality."

The star image of the exhibition was most certainly Duchamp's *Nude Descending a Staircase* (or, as Roosevelt called it, "a naked man going downstairs"), a painting so ab-
30　stract it defied its own title, which, of course, was the point. As critic Robert Hughes has pointed out, the nude had a long and distinguished history with painting, where she (and, more rarely, he) was usually portrayed in a blissful state of recline; by contrast, Duchamp's nude, to the degree that it looked at all like
35　what it was supposed to be, was a nude on the move (indeed, the painting had the quality of a photographic motion study), a metaphor for the change that it heralded. Still, most people saw something else entirely—"an explosion in a shingle factory," "an earthquake on the subway," "a staircase descending a
40　nude"—jokes all, uttered even as the jokesters themselves stood in long lines, necks craning, to see the object of their ridicule. The modern era might be abhorrent, absurd, unnatural, but oh to get a glimpse of it!

Roosevelt said Duchamp's *Nude* reminded him of a Navaho
45　rug he stood upon while shaving each morning in his bathroom. And indeed, to the degree that Roosevelt, Cox, and others saw any merit to modern abstractions like Duchamp's, it was as decoration, fancy wallpaper. But the fact that these artists attached meaning to their creations, that they saw themselves as
50　articulating an ideology, an "ism" of the new, and one that quite blatantly intended to disassemble the world as men and women had known it, was simply too bold and raw for mainstream temperaments. This modern art was, as its name suggested, something different—art as cause—and the condemnation brought
55　upon it by Roosevelt and others was a denunciation of the new work's politics. After all, when before had reasonable men discovered in painting, as they did here, "the chatter of anarchistic monkeys" or "the harbinger of universal anarchy"?

Anticipating a reluctant audience, the organizers of the
60　Armory Show had included an editorial in the exhibition catalog urging viewers to greet the new art with an open mind. "Art," it read, "is a sign of life. There can be no life without change, as there can be no development without change. To be afraid of what is different is to be afraid of life…" Then, perhaps with
65　Roosevelt's legendary machismo in mind, they added a challenge to contemporary pretensions to the rugged life, concluding with the statement that their exhibition was a proclamation "against cowardice."

21. The author mentions a "photographic motion study" (line 36) in order to emphasize what quality of Duchamp's *Nude*?

    A. The different interpretations of the painting
    B. The painting's photographic realism
    C. The painting's inappropriate subject matter
    D. The movement implied in the painting

22. According to the passage, which of the following persons was an artist?

    I. Brancusi
    II. Cox
    III. Hughes

    F. I only
    G. I and II only
    H. II and III only
    J. I, II, and III

GO ON TO THE NEXT PAGE.

23. The first paragraph states that certain early critics of modern art:

    A. viewed modern art as completely unimportant and ignored it entirely.
    B. believed that modern artists were harming the art of painting.
    C. thought that modern art was interesting, but not very beautiful.
    D. preferred the work of European modernists to those of the Americans.

24. It can be inferred from the author's reference to "an explosion" and "an earthquake" (lines 38–40) that Duchamp's *Nude*:

    F. did not look like an ordinary painting of a nude person.
    G. depicted many different natural disasters.
    H. was painted during a time of great social upheaval and unrest.
    J. was so disturbing to viewers that people did not want to look at it.

25. As it is used in line 42, the word *abhorrent* most nearly means:

    A. colorful.
    B. flimsy.
    C. awful.
    D. tiresome.

26. It can be reasonably concluded from the passage that the most important characteristic of "modern" art was that it was:

    F. beautiful.
    G. expensive.
    H. political.
    J. recent.

27. Which of the following best describes Roosevelt's reaction to modern art?

    A. He wholeheartedly approved of it.
    B. He largely approved of it, except for the pieces that he thought were too disorganized.
    C. He largely disapproved of it, although he thought that certain pieces had some merit.
    D. He disapproved of all of it.

28. It can reasonably be inferred that the use of the words "Ellis Island" (line 17) indicated that:

    F. many of the modern artists were from countries outside the United States.
    G. the exhibition took place on Ellis Island.
    H. the exhibition showed many paintings of Ellis Island.
    J. many of the pieces were dedicated to the idea of freedom in the United States.

29. It can be inferred from the last paragraph that the organizers of the Armory Show:

    A. needed a great deal of financial support to put on the exhibition.
    B. tried hard to please the American public.
    C. were immigrants from Europe.
    D. expected that the exhibition would be controversial.

30. According to the passage, some of the supporters of modern art believed that modern art represented:

    F. a return to the themes of classical painting.
    G. the expansion of traditional American tastes into the rest of the world.
    H. a force for change and progress in the world of art.
    J. an attempt to depict the world as precisely as in a photograph.

GO ON TO THE NEXT PAGE.

Passage IV

NATURAL SCIENCE: This passage is adapted from a text on the history of science.

Small beginnings can have great endings—sometimes. As a case in point, note what came of the small, original effort of a self-trained, back-country Quaker youth named John Dalton. Toward the close of the eighteenth century, he became interested
5   in the weather, which led him to construct a crude water gauge to test the amount of rainfall. But this was only a beginning. The simple rain gauge pointed the way to the most important generalization of the nineteenth century in a field of science with which, to the casual observer, it might seem to have no alliance
10 whatever. The wonderful theory of atoms, on which the whole gigantic structure of modern chemistry is founded, was the logical outgrowth of those early studies in meteorology.

The way it happened was this: From studying rainfall, Dalton turned naturally to the complementary process of evapora-
15 tion. He soon came to believe that vapor exists in the atmosphere as an independent gas. But since two bodies cannot occupy the same space at the same time, this implies that the various atmospheric gases are really composed of discrete particles. These ultimate particles are so small that we cannot see them—cannot,
20 indeed, more than vaguely imagine them—yet each particle of vapor, for example, is just as much a portion of water as if it were a drop out of the ocean. But water is a compound substance, for it may be separated, as Cavendish has shown, into the two elementary substances hydrogen and oxygen. Hence the atom
25 of water must be composed of two lesser atoms joined together. Imagine an atom of hydrogen and one of oxygen. Unite them, and we have an atom of water; sever them, and the water no longer exists; whether united or separate, the atoms of hydrogen and of oxygen remain hydrogen and oxygen and nothing else.
30 Differently mixed together or united, atoms produce different gross substances, but the elementary atoms never change their chemical nature—their distinct personality.

Around 1803, Dalton first gained a full grasp of the conception of the chemical atom. At once he saw that the hypothesis,
35 if true, furnished a marvelous key to secrets of matter hitherto insoluble—questions relating to the relative proportions of the atoms themselves. It is known, for example, that a certain bulk of hydrogen gas unites with a certain bulk of oxygen gas to form water. If it is true that this combination consists essentially of the
40 union of atoms one with another (each single atom of hydrogen united to a single atom of oxygen), then the relative weights of the original masses of hydrogen and of oxygen must be also the relative weights of each of their respective atoms. If one pound of hydrogen unites with five and one-half pounds of oxygen
45 (as, according to Dalton's experiments, it did), then the weight of the oxygen atom must be five and one-half times that of the hydrogen atom. Other compounds may be plainly tested in the same way. Dalton made numerous tests before he published his theory. He found that hydrogen enters into compounds in smaller
50 proportions than does any other element known to him, and so, for convenience, determined to take the weight of the hydrogen atom as unity. The atomic weight of oxygen then becomes (as given in Dalton's first table of 1803) 5.5; that of water (hydro-

gen plus oxygen) being of course 6.5. The atomic weights of
55 about a score of substances are given in Dalton's first paper, which was read before the Literary and Philosophical Society of Manchester, October 21, 1803.

During these same years, the rising authority of the French chemical world, Joseph Louis Gay-Lussac, was conducting
60 experiments with gases. In 1809, the next year after the publication of the first volume of Dalton's New System of Chemical Philosophy, Gay-Lussac published the results of his observations, and among other things brought out the remarkable fact that gases, under the same conditions as to temperature and
65 pressure, combine always in definite numerical proportions as to volume. Exactly two volumes of hydrogen, for example, combine with one volume of oxygen to form water.

The true explanation of Gay-Lussac's law of combination by volumes was thought out almost immediately by an
70 Italian savant, Amadeo Avogadro, and expressed in terms of the atomic theory. The fact must be, said Avogadro, that under similar physical conditions every form of gas contains exactly the same number of ultimate particles in a given volume. Each of these ultimate physical particles may be composed of two or
75 more atoms (as in the case of water vapor), but such a compound atom conducts itself as if it were a simple and indivisible atom, as regards the amount of space that separates it from its fellows under given conditions of pressure and temperature. The compound atom, composed of two or more elementary atoms,
80 Avogadro proposed to distinguish, for purposes of convenience, by the name *molecule*.

The other and even more noted advocate of the atomic theory was Johan Jakob Berzelius. This great Swedish chemist at once set to work to put the atomic theory to such tests as might
85 be applied in the laboratory. He was an analyst of the utmost skill, and for years he devoted himself to the determination of the combining weights, "equivalents" or "proportions," of the different elements. These determinations, in so far as they were accurately made, were simple expressions of empirical facts, independent
90 of any theory; but gradually it became more and more plain that these facts all harmonized with the atomic theory of Dalton. So by common consent the proportionate combining weights of the elements came to be known as atomic weights—the name Dalton had given them from the first. Berzelius proposed to
95 improve upon Dalton's method of notation by using the initial of the Latin name of the element represented—O for oxygen, H for hydrogen, and so on—a numerical coefficient to follow the letter as an indication of the number of atoms present in any given compound. This simple system soon gained general
100 acceptance, and with slight modifications it is still universally employed. Every student now is aware that H2O is the chemical way of expressing the union of two atoms of hydrogen with one of oxygen to form a molecule of water.

GO ON TO THE NEXT PAGE.

31. In the first paragraph, the author discusses Dalton's instrument for measuring rainfall in order to show that:

  A. meteorology is more important than chemistry.
  B. water is an important chemical compound found in many more complex substances.
  C. some scientific discoveries arise unexpectedly from simple observations.
  D. many scientists in the eighteenth century had little or no formal training in the scientific method.

32. The scientist who is credited with the modern chemical notation in which water is expressed as H_2O is:

  F. Berzelius.
  G. Dalton.
  H. Avogadro.
  J. Gay-Lussac.

33. The author's attitude toward the work of Dalton is best characterized as one of:

  A. scholarly detachment.
  B. restrained criticism.
  C. admiring interest.
  D. scientific indifference.

34. The passage states that Gay-Lussac was:

  F. English.
  G. French.
  H. Swedish.
  J. Italian.

35. The author credits Avogadro with:

  A. discovering the law that explains the observations of Gay-Lussac.
  B. measuring the atomic weight of oxygen.
  C. showing that some substances were combinations of more basic elements.
  D. realizing that hydrogen was the lightest atom.

36. In the final paragraph, the author states that Berzelius:

  F. disproved Dalton's version of atomic theory and replaced it with his own.
  G. was an important influence on the work of Avogadro and Gay-Lussac.
  H. found more evidence that supported Dalton's work.
  J. was the first to show that water can be divided into oxygen and hydrogen.

37. The passage states that Dalton believed that the weight of an atom of oxygen is:

  A. about twice the weight of an atom of hydrogen.
  B. between five and six times the weight of an atom of hydrogen.
  C. between six and seven times the weight of an atom of hydrogen.
  D. slightly more than the weight of a molecule of water.

38. As described in the passage, the works of Gay-Lussac concerned the:

  F. weight of gases.
  G. volume of gases.
  H. transformation of liquids into gases.
  J. number of electrons in an atom.

39. Which of the following assumptions made by Dalton led to a flaw in his atomic theory?

  A. All atoms have the same volume.
  B. All atoms have the same weight.
  C. Two atoms can occupy the same space at the same time.
  D. Atoms combine only in pairs.

40. The passage associates the origin of the word *molecule* with:

  F. Dalton.
  G. Avogadro.
  H. Cavendish.
  J. Gay-Lussac.

END OF TEST 3

**STOP! DO NOT TURN THE PAGE UNTIL TOLD TO DO SO.
DO NOT RETURN TO THE PREVIOUS TEST.**

SCIENCE REASONING TEST
35 Minutes—40 Questions

DIRECTIONS: There are seven passages in the following section. Each passage is followed by several questions. After reading a passage, choose the best answer to each question and blacken the corresponding oval on your answer sheet. You may refer to the passages as often as necessary.

You are NOT permitted to use a calculator on this test.

Passage I

An enzyme is a biological catalyst that uses a substrate to make a product. The enzyme converts the substrate to the product at a certain rate, V, measured in reactions per second. The rate of the reaction is a measure of the efficiency of the enzyme. The maximum rate of the reaction, V_{max}, is independent of the amount of substrate. The substrate concentration at which $V = \frac{1}{2} V_{max}$ is known as the K_m. A typical reaction rate graph is shown in Figure 1.

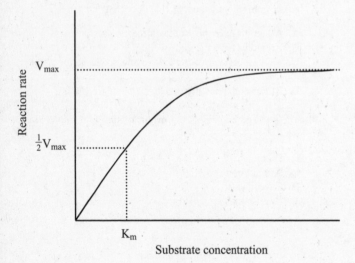

Figure 1

Monoamine oxidase inhibitors (MAOI) are a class of drugs designed for use as antidepressants. Because a similar enzyme is present in the heart, patients taking these drugs may experience potentially fatal drug and food interactions. Scientists are interested in designing a drug that will effectively inhibit the enzyme found in the brain (bMAO) while minimizing the drug's action on the heart enzyme (hMAO).

Experiment 1

Brain tissue from an experimental animal was homogenized, and the protein fraction was obtained and purified. Drug X was added in increasing concentrations to bMAO and the reaction rate was measured. The trials were performed using 10 μg/mL of the enzyme. The results are shown in Figure 2.

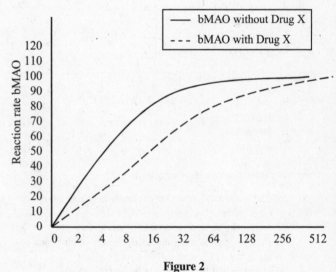

Figure 2

GO ON TO THE NEXT PAGE.

Experiment 2

Heart tissue from the same experimental animal was homogenized and the protein fraction was obtained and purified. Drug X was added in increasing concentrations to hMAO and the reaction rate was measured. The trials were performed using 10 μg/mL of the enzyme. The results are shown in Figure 3.

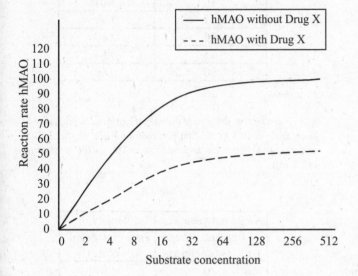

Figure 3

1. In Experiment 1, what is the approximate concentration of K_m for bMAO following treatment by Drug X ?

   A. 5
   B. 20
   C. 50
   D. 100

2. What is the effect of Drug X on the maximum reaction rate of hMAO ?

   F. Drug X increases the maximum reaction rate.
   G. Drug X decreases the maximum reaction rate.
   H. Drug X increases the maximum reaction rate at low concentrations, but decreases it at higher concentrations.
   J. Drug X has no effect on the maximum reaction rate.

3. An important difference between Experiments 1 and 2 is that they:

   A. measured different parameters.
   B. used tissue from different animals.
   C. tested different drugs.
   D. used different enzymes.

4. Which of the following conclusions is most consistent with the results of Experiment 1?

   F. Drug X decreases the K_m but increases V_{max}.
   G. Drug X increases the K_m but decreases V_{max}.
   H. Drug X increases the K_m but does not affect V_{max}.
   J. Drug X does not affect the K_m but increases V_{max}.

5. Based on the results of both experiments, Drug X suppresses:

   A. both hMAO and bMAO, but suppresses hMAO more effectively.
   B. both hMAO and bMAO, but suppresses bMAO more effectively.
   C. hMAO but has no effect on bMAO.
   D. bMAO but has no effect on hMAO.

6. For both experiments, what controlled variable was kept constant?

   F. Enzyme concentration
   G. Reaction rate
   H. Substrate concentration
   J. Drug type

GO ON TO THE NEXT PAGE.

Passage II

An *electromagnetic wave* (or EM wave) is a wave that has oscillating electric and magnetic fields that vary over time and space. The electric and magnetic fields are perpendicular both to each other and to the direction of propagation of the wave. Light is an EM wave, and one can generalize its behavior in most cases to that of all other EM waves. A normal beam of light is made up of a large number of waves emitted by the atoms or molecules of the light source. Each atom produces a randomly directed electric field, and the resulting beam is considered to be *unpolarized*. However, with the use of a *polarizing filter*, it is possible to pick out the components of the electric field point- ing in a particular direction. This direction is called the *axis of polarization* of the filter. A beam of light is called *polarized* if the electric field always vibrates in the same direction at a particular point. In the experiments below, scientists investigated various properties of polarized and unpolarized light.

Experiment 1

The scientists used a laser emitting unpolarized light. The light was directed toward a polarization filter with an axis of polarization pointing straight up, and then through another whose axis of polarization varied. The scientists chose to describe the axis of the second filter by examining the angle between its axis and the axis of the first filter. The intensity of the original beam was 8 W/m² (watts per square meter). Their results are shown in Table 1.

Table 1

Angle between axis of first and second filters (degrees)	Intensity of emerging beam (W/m²)
0	4.00
15	3.73
30	2.99
45	2.01
60	1.00
75	0.27
90	0.00

Experiment 2

The scientists repeated the experimental setup of Experi- ment 1 but used a source of polarized light polarized in the same direction as the axis of the first polarization filter (straight up). The intensity of the original beam was still 8 W/m². The results are shown in Table 2.

Table 2

Angle between axis of first and second filters (degrees)	Intensity of emerging beam (W/m²)
0	8.00
15	7.46
30	6.01
45	3.99
60	2.00
75	0.54
90	0.00

Experiment 3

The scientists decided to polarize the original beam of light at an angle of 30° to the first polarization filter. The intensity of the original beam was kept at 8 W/m². The results are shown in Table 3.

Table 3

Angle between axis of first and second filters (degrees)	Intensity of emerging beam (W/m²)
0	6.01
15	5.60
30	4.49
45	2.99
60	1.50
75	0.41
90	0.00

7. A beam of unpolarized light is shone through two polarizing filters with axes of polarization separated by 20°. The inten- sity of the original beam is 8 W/m². Which of the following could be the intensity of the emerging beam?

   A. 3.53 W/m²
   B. 5.32 W/m²
   C. 6.97 W/m²
   D. 8.00 W/m²

8. The scientists conducted a fourth experiment similar to the first three. The two polarizing filters were placed with their axes 90° apart. Light polarized in the same direction as the axis of the first filter was then shone through the two filters, and the second filter was rotated. As the angle between the axes of the two filters decreased from 90° to 0°, the intensity of the emerging beam:

   F. decreased.
   G. increased, then decreased.
   H. decreased, then increased.
   J. increased.

9. Which of the following graphs best describes the relationship between the angle between the axes of the filters and the intensity of the emerging beam as determined in Experiment 3 ?

A.

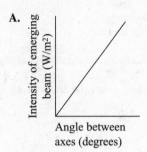

B.

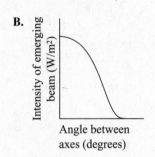

C.

D.

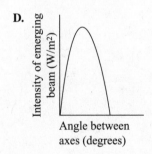

10. How does the setup of Experiment 1 differ from that of Experiment 2 ?

F. In Experiment 1, the original beam was polarized, but in Experiment 2, it was unpolarized.

G. In Experiment 1, the original beam was unpolarized, but in Experiment 2, it was polarized.

H. In Experiment 1, the scientists tested a wider range of angles than they did in Experiment 2.

J. In Experiment 1, the original beam of light was more intense than the one in Experiment 2.

11. The scientists hypothesize that the color of the original beam of light will affect the intensity of the emerging beam. The frequency of a beam of light determines its color. Which of the following would be the best way to test this hypothesis?

A. Repeating the experiments using more than two polarizing filters

B. Repeating the experiments on different planets

C. Repeating the experiments using beams of both high and low frequencies

D. Repeating the experiments using different intensities for the original beam

12. In Experiment 1, if the angle between the axes of polarization increases by 15°, the intensity of the resulting beam:

F. halves.

G. doubles.

H. increases, but not by any constant factor.

J. decreases, but not by any constant factor.

GO ON TO THE NEXT PAGE.

Passage III

Cell division occurs in four stages: gap 1 (G1), synthesis (S), gap 2 (G2), and mitosis (M). Interphase prepares the cell for division and comprises the G1, S, and G2 phases. The physical division of two cells from one cell occurs during mitosis.

Figure 1 represents the amount of time a typical cell spends in each of the four phases of the cell cycle.

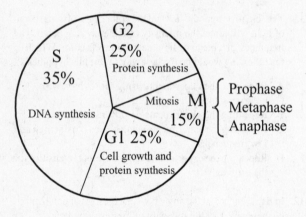

Figure 1

In mammalian cells, cell division is controlled by a class of proteins called cyclins. Figure 2 graphically represents cyclin levels during the cell cycle.

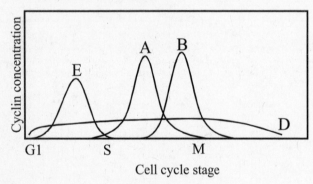

Figure 2

13. A certain mammalian cell, the fibroblast, takes 24 hours to divide. How many hours would such a cell be expected to spend in mitosis?

   A. 3.6
   B. 6.0
   C. 8.4
   D. 12.0

14. Which of the following conclusions can be made regarding the mammalian cell beginning mitosis?

   F. Cyclin A must be at its maximum level.
   G. Cyclin B must be decreasing.
   H. Cyclin D must be increasing.
   J. Cyclin E must be increasing.

15. Suppose that a researcher is adding cyclins to mammalian cells in order to study their effects on the cell cycle. The cyclin that is LEAST likely to have an effect on any phase of the cell cycle is:

   A. Cyclin A.
   B. Cyclin B.
   C. Cyclin D.
   D. Cyclin E.

16. Which cyclin(s) is (are) most likely to initiate the cell cycle in mammalian cells?

   I.   Cyclin A
   II. Cyclin B
   III. Cyclin E

   F. I only
   G. II only
   H. III only
   J. I and II only

17. Which of the following phases is most likely to be triggered by an increase in Cyclin A ?

   A. DNA synthesis
   B. Protein synthesis
   C. Cell growth
   D. Mitosis

GO ON TO THE NEXT PAGE.

Passage IV

A capacitor is a device that stores electromagnetic energy in the form of electric potential energy. The measure of how much energy a capacitor can store is called the *capacitance*, which can (in principle) be determined merely from knowing the geometry of a given capacitor (that is, its shape, the distance between its plates, etc.).

Three common types of capacitor geometries consist of two parallel plates, two coaxial cylinders, and two concentric spherical shells. Another common practice with capacitors is the insertion of a *dielectric*, a material that separates the plates of the capacitor. In the experiments below, scientists set up a potential difference of 9 volts between the plates of different parallel-plate capacitors and measured the capacitance in each case. The results are shown in Table 1.

Table 1

Distance between plates (mm)	Area of plates (m²)	Capacitance (pF)	Dielectric material	Dielectric constant of material
5	0.5	3.11	Paper	3.5
10	0.5	1.57	Paper	3.5
15	0.5	1.02	Paper	3.5
15	1.0	2.07	Paper	3.5
15	2.0	4.13	Paper	3.5
10	0.5	3.09	Porcelain	6.9
10	1.0	6.17	Porcelain	6.9
20	2.0	6.17	Porcelain	6.9
15	0.5	3.50	Silicon	12
20	1.0	5.30	Silicon	12
30	1.0	3.51	Silicon	12

18. According to the data in Table 1, doubling the distance between the plates:

   F. doubles the dielectric constant of material.
   G. halves the area of the plates.
   H. doubles the capacitance.
   J. halves the capacitance.

19. The dielectric constant of ruby mica is approximately the same as that of porcelain. A parallel plate capacitor with a ruby mica dielectric with a distance of 20 millimeters between the plates with area 2 square meters would have a capacitance of approximately:

   A. 3 pF.
   B. 6 pF.
   C. 12 pF.
   D. 24 pF.

20. One of the essential traits of a capacitor is that the plates do not touch. Thus, one benefit of adding a dielectric to a capacitor is that:

   F. the dielectric increases the electric field strength within the capacitor.
   G. the dielectric changes the geometry of the capacitor.
   H. the dielectric makes the capacitor a better conductor of electricity.
   J. the dielectric provides a practical means of separating the plates.

21. According to the data in Table 1, doubling both the area of the plates and the distance between the plates:

   A. quadruples the capacitance.
   B. halves the capacitance.
   C. has no effect on the capacitance.
   D. doubles the capacitance.

22. According to the data in Table 1, the capacitance of a parallel plate capacitor with a paper dielectric and a separation of 15 millimeters between plates of area 1.5 square meters would most nearly be:

   F. 1 pF.
   G. 2 pF.
   H. 3 pF.
   J. 6 pF.

GO ON TO THE NEXT PAGE.

Passage V

The possibility that there may be—or may once have been—life on Mars has been debated intensely for more than a hundred years. Most of these arguments have focused on whether there was ever enough liquid water on Mars to sustain life. Three scientists present their theories concerning Martian life.

Scientist 1

Water is essential for the survival of all known forms of life. There is water on Mars today, in the polar ice caps and the atmosphere. While pools of liquid water may not last long in the frigid climate, they can form under the proper conditions. Salty water has a lower freezing point than pure water, and the soil on Mars contains many salts. Therefore, it is possible that isolated pockets of salty water can be found near the planet's surface. Bacteria found in deserts on Earth can live in extremely salty water, surviving in suspended animation when the water dries up. It is possible that similar bacteria could be living on present-day Mars.

Scientist 2

Two of the arguments against life on Mars are that the atmosphere is too thin and the temperature is too low to support life. Water and carbon dioxide released by past volcanic eruptions could have formed a thick atmosphere, thereby creating a greenhouse effect and warming the planet. Instruments sent to Mars since the late 1990s have sent back pictures of stream gullies and layers of sediment, proof that liquid had once flowed on the surface. In one location, the lowlands have a very smooth surface. The surrounding highlands have a rougher surface, forming a well-defined coastline between the two regions and indicating that an ocean once existed there. Life on Earth began in the ocean; there is no reason to believe that life did not form in a similar fashion on Mars.

The thick Martian atmosphere, which also would have protected the planet from harmful ultraviolet radiation, has long since disappeared. Any forms of Martian life—even those lying dormant—would have died out billions of years ago.

Scientist 3

The gullies on Mars may be the result of some form of liquid, but there is no reason to assume that it was water. It is much more likely that the gullies were formed by liquid carbon dioxide, which forms at very low temperatures; bursting from under the ground, it could have carved paths into the planet's surface before vaporizing. Alternately, these gorges could have been formed by volcanic activity or high winds. Also, the supposed ocean coastline is merely the result of expansion of the planet's crust. Although water plays an important part in the shaping of the Earth's landscape, this does not necessarily mean that similar-looking structures on Mars were formed by water.

More important, the lack of oxygen in the thin Martian atmosphere means that Mars has no protection against the intense ultraviolet radiation from the Sun. Whether or not water is present, the current conditions on the surface of Mars make it impossible for any kind of life to survive.

23. A major difference between the theories of Scientists 1 and 2 is that Scientist 1 believes that life on Mars:

A. is possible only in salty water, whereas Scientist 2 believes that it began in pure water.
B. is currently in a state of suspended animation, whereas Scientist 2 believes that it is dormant.
C. began deep in the ocean, whereas Scientist 2 believes that it began on the planet's surface.
D. may still exist, whereas Scientist 2 believes that it could have existed only in the distant past.

24. A planetary magnetic field helps to protect the planet's atmosphere from solar wind, which can cause the atmosphere to erode and eventually disappear. Mars has an extremely weak magnetic field. How would this information affect the theory of Scientist 2 ?

F. It would strengthen the theory by suggesting that the sediment layers on Mars were caused by strong winds.
G. It would strengthen the theory by raising the possibility that the Martian atmosphere was once thicker.
H. It would weaken the theory by challenging the assumption that volcanic eruptions produced water and carbon dioxide.
J. It would weaken the theory by offering an alternate explanation for the disappearance of the Martian ocean.

25. Scientist 3 mentions all of the following as possible causes of Martian stream gullies EXCEPT:

A. wind.
B. volcanoes.
C. crust deformation.
D. carbon dioxide.

26. Which of the following, if true, could best defend Scientist 1's theory against criticism voiced by Scientist 3 ?

F. Olivine, a mineral that is easily eroded by water, is present in many locations on the Martian surface.
G. The Martian atmospheric pressure is currently too low to allow pure water to remain in a liquid state.
H. Liquid water can collect about a meter below the Martian surface, out of the range of ultraviolet radiation.
J. Martian volcanic rock, almost 2 percent water when formed, currently contains about a hundredth of that amount.

GO ON TO THE NEXT PAGE.

27. A four-billion-year-old Martian meteorite called ALH84001 was discovered in Antarctica in 1984. It contained microscopic crystals of *magnetite*, a compound formed by certain bacteria on Earth. The alignment of the magnetite crystals suggests that they were created by living organisms, and many researchers agree that the meteorite could not have been contaminated by Earth bacteria before its discovery. This discovery supports the theory (theories) of which scientist(s)?

    I.   Scientist 1
   II. Scientist 2
  III. Scientist 3

A. II only
B. I and II only
C. I and III only
D. II and III only

28. Scientists 2 and 3 agree that high levels of which of the following would prevent life from developing on a planet?

F. Ultraviolet radiation
G. Volcanic activity
H. Salt concentration
J. Atmospheric pressure

29. Which of the following statements would be most consistent with the theory of Scientist 3 ?

A. The dried-up ocean bed on Mars may contain dormant bacteria.
B. The crust of Mars is more geologically active than the crust of Earth.
C. Life on Mars will most likely be found near the polar ice caps.
D. There is no evidence that Mars ever had a climate warm enough to support life.

GO ON TO THE NEXT PAGE.

Passage VI

The graph below illustrates the changes that occur in lung volume during respiration. *Total lung capacity* (TLC) is the largest volume of air that the lung can hold and is constant for each individual. However, only a portion of this volume is used for maximal respiration, such as during exercise. An even smaller volume is used for resting respiration, such as while reading. *Vital capacity* (VC) represents maximal respiration and *tidal volume* (TV) represents resting respiration.

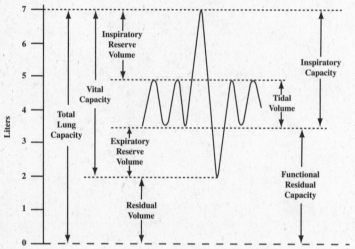

These volumes are theoretical values calculated for a healthy 75-kilogram man.

Figure 1

Forced expiratory volume (FEV) is the maximum volume of air that can be exhaled in one second following maximal inhalation, *forced vital capacity* (FVC). Most patients with lung (or *pulmonary*) disease demonstrate a diminished forced vital capacity. The FEV/ FVC ratio is used clinically to differentiate between *restrictive* and *obstructive* lung disease. Restrictive lung diseases result from a stiffening of lung tissue while obstructive diseases result from fluid or mucus in the lung. The FEV/ FVC ratio for a healthy individual is 0.8. The FEV/ FVC ratio for a patient with restrictive lung disease is normal or elevated while patients with obstructive lung disease demonstrate a reduced FEV/ FVC ratio. A physician tabulated the following data from four of his patients.

Table 1

	Patient 1	Patient 2	Patient 3	Patient 4
FEV	1.58	2.57	1.91	2.27
FVC	2.63	3.16	2.41	2.54
FEV/ FVC Ratio	0.60	0.81	0.80	0.89

30. Based on the information given in Figure 1, what is the volume, in liters, of respiration at rest?

    F. 0.1
    G. 1.5
    H. 3.0
    J. 5.5

31. Patients with restrictive lung diseases, such as emphysema, demonstrate an FEV/ FVC ratio that is 0.8 or higher. The best explanation for this finding is that:

    A. these patients do not have pulmonary disease.
    B. both FEV and FVC are increased proportionally, resulting in a ratio that is normal or elevated.
    C. both FEV and FVC are reduced, resulting in a ratio that is normal or elevated.
    D. emphysema reduces FEV but not FVC.

32. Patients with obstructive lung diseases, such as asthma, demonstrate a reduced FEV/ FVC ratio. Which patient has lung volumes consistent with obstructive lung disease?

    F. Patient 1
    G. Patient 2
    H. Patient 3
    J. Patient 4

33. Based on the information in Figure 1, which of the following conclusions can be made about pulmonary volumes?

    A. Increasing residual volume will reduce vital capacity.
    B. Decreasing tidal volume will increase vital capacity.
    C. Any change in vital capacity will proportionally affect total lung volume.
    D. The sum of the inspiratory reserve volume and the tidal volume equals the vital capacity.

34. Pneumonia, an obstructive lung disease, is commonly caused by a viral infection. If a patient with emphysema (a restrictive pulmonary disease) acquires pneumonia while in the hospital, which of the following is most likely to occur?

    F. The FEV/ FVC ratio will increase because both emphysema and pneumonia will increase the ratio.
    G. The FEV/ FVC ratio will decrease because both emphysema and pneumonia will decrease the ratio.
    H. The FEV/ FVC ratio will be unaffected because pneumonia will not affect respiration.
    J. The FEV/ FVC ratio will decrease because pneumonia will decrease the ratio.

GO ON TO THE NEXT PAGE.

Passage VII

It is well known that applying a force to both ends of a bar will cause the bar to compress or to expand, depending on whether the force pushes or pulls the bar. The *stress* on the bar is defined to be the ratio of the force on the bar to the cross-sectional area, and the *strain* on the bar is the fractional change in length. As long as the force is not too strong, stress is directly proportional to strain, and the constant of proportionality is called *Young's modulus*. If the force on the bar exceeds the yield strength of the material, however, permanent deformation will occur, and the bar will not resume its original shape upon removal of the force. In the experiments below, a scientist investigated these properties.

Experiment 1

Aluminum has a Young's modulus of 70×10^9 newtons per square meter (N/m^2). Using a 2-meter-long bar of cross-sectional area 1 square meter (m^2), a scientist applied different forces to the bar and noted the various changes in length. The bar returned to its original shape after the forces were removed in all trials except the final one. The results are shown in Table 1.

Table 1

Applied Force (10^6 N)	Change in Length (mm)
50	1.4
100	2.8
200	5.6
400	11.2

Experiment 2

The effect of length expansion or compression can be seen in many materials. The scientist performed another experiment in order to determine to what extent a bar made out of each of the materials tested would stretch. The bars under consideration were each 2 meters long with a cross-sectional area of 1 m^2, and compressive forces of 100×10^6 N were applied to each end before the data was recorded. The results are shown in Table 2.

Table 2

Material	Young's Modulus (10^9 N/m^2)	Change in Length (mm)
Steel	200	1.0
Concrete	30	6.6
Wood	13	15.4
Polystyrene	2	66.7

Experiment 3

Finally, the scientist investigated how different aluminum bars stretched when a force of 100×10^6 N was applied to both ends of the bars. The results are shown in Table 3.

Table 3

Length of Bar (m)	Cross-Sectional Area (m^2)	Change in Length (mm)
1.0	2.0	0.7
1.0	4.0	0.4
1.0	8.0	0.2
2.0	2.0	1.4
4.0	2.0	2.8
8.0	4.0	2.8
16.0	4.0	5.6

35. According to the data in the experiments, when both the length and cross-sectional area of an aluminum bar are doubled, the change in length:

A. quadruples.
B. doubles.
C. remains the same.
D. halves.

36. Yield strength is the greatest force that a material can withstand without changing shape permanently. Based on Experiment 1, one can conclude that the yield strengh of aluminum is approximately:

F. 75×10^6 N.
G. 125×10^6 N.
H. 175×10^6 N.
J. 300×10^6 N.

37. The Young's modulus of glass is 65×10^9 N/m^2. A 2-meter-long glass bar with a cross-sectional area of 1 m^2 with a force of 100×10^6 N applied to both ends would experience a change in length of:

A. 3.2 millimeters.
B. 7.3 millimeters.
C. 30.8 millimeters.
D. 133.4 millimeters.

GO ON TO THE NEXT PAGE.

38. Given the results of the experiments, all of the following would be expected to increase the change in the length of a bar EXCEPT:

   F. increasing the applied force.
   G. increasing the cross-sectional area.
   H. increasing the length of the bar.
   J. decreasing the Young's modulus.

39. The scientist suspected that the temperature of the bar may have an effect on the change in length. Which of the following, if true, would best support that hypothesis?

   A. As the temperature of a material changes, so does its Young's modulus.
   B. As the temperature of a material changes, the material becomes less dense.
   C. The Young's modulus of a given material is independent of temperature.
   D. The Young's modulus of steel is greater than that of aluminum.

40. Based on the data in the passage, if a force of 100×10^6 N were applied to an aluminum bar 32 meters long with a cross-sectional area of 4.0 m^2, the change in the length of the bar would most nearly be:

   F. 1.4 millimeters.
   G. 2.8 millimeters.
   H. 11.2 millimeters.
   J. 22.4 millimeters.

END OF TEST 4

STOP! DO NOT TURN THE PAGE UNTIL TOLD TO DO SO.
DO NOT RETURN TO THE PREVIOUS TEST.

NO TEST MATERIAL ON THIS PAGE.

DIRECTIONS

This is a test of your writing skills. You will have thirty (30) minutes to write an essay. Before you begin planning and writing your essay, read the writing prompt carefully to understand exactly what you are being asked to do. Your essay will be evaluated on the evidence it provides of your ability to express judgments by taking a position on the issue in the writing prompt; to maintain a focus on the topic throughout your essay; to develop a position by using logical reasoning and by supporting your ideas; to organize ideas in a logical way; and to use language clearly and effectively according to the conventions of standard written English.

You may use the unlined pages in this test booklet to plan your essay. These pages will not be scored. *You must write your essay on the lined pages in the answer folder.* Your writing on those lined pages will be scored. You may not need all the lined pages, but to ensure you have enough room to finish, do NOT skip lines. You may write corrections or additions neatly between the lines of your essay, but do NOT write in the margins of the lined pages. *Illegible essays cannot be scored, so you must write (or print) clearly.*

If you finish before time is called, you may review your work. Lay your pencil down immediately when time is called.

DO NOT OPEN THIS BOOK UNTIL YOU ARE TOLD TO DO SO.

ACT Assessment Writing Test Prompt

Most schools have established honor codes or other rules to prevent students from cheating on exams and other school assignments. Many students admit to cheating, arguing that the practice has become so common—and is so rarely penalized—that it is the only way to survive in today's competitive academic world. Educators, however, feel that such behaviors only hurt the students, and that cheating in school is just the first step to more academic dishonesty, professional misconduct, and unethical business practices in the future. In your view, should high schools become more tolerant of cheating?

In your essay, take a position on this question. You may write about either one of the two points of view given or you may present a different point of view on this question. Use specific reasons and examples to support your position.

The Princeton Review

ACT Diagnostic Test Form

Use a No. 2 pencil only. Be sure each mark is dark and completely fills the intended oval. Completely erase any errors or stray marks.

1. **YOUR NAME:** _____
(Print)

Last   First   M.I.

SIGNATURE: _____   **DATE:** _____ / _____ / _____

HOME ADDRESS: _____
(Print)   Number and Street

_____
City   State   Zip

E-MAIL: _____

PHONE NO.: _____
(Print)

SCHOOL: _____

CLASS OF: _____

3. TEST CODE

⓪	⓪	⓪	⓪
①	①	①	①
②	②	②	②
③	③	③	③
④	④	④	④
⑤	⑤	⑤	⑤
⑥	⑥	⑥	⑥
⑦	⑦	⑦	⑦
⑧	⑧	⑧	⑧
⑨	⑨	⑨	⑨

IMPORTANT: Please fill in these boxes exactly as shown on the back cover of your tests book.

2. TEST FORM

_____

4. PHONE NUMBER

⓪	⓪	⓪	⓪	⓪	⓪	⓪
①	①	①	①	①	①	①
②	②	②	②	②	②	②
③	③	③	③	③	③	③
④	④	④	④	④	④	④
⑤	⑤	⑤	⑤	⑤	⑤	⑤
⑥	⑥	⑥	⑥	⑥	⑥	⑥
⑦	⑦	⑦	⑦	⑦	⑦	⑦
⑧	⑧	⑧	⑧	⑧	⑧	⑧
⑨	⑨	⑨	⑨	⑨	⑨	⑨

5. YOUR NAME

First 4 letters of last name				FIRST INIT	MID INIT
Ⓐ	Ⓐ	Ⓐ	Ⓐ	Ⓐ	Ⓐ
Ⓑ	Ⓑ	Ⓑ	Ⓑ	Ⓑ	Ⓑ
Ⓒ	Ⓒ	Ⓒ	Ⓒ	Ⓒ	Ⓒ
Ⓓ	Ⓓ	Ⓓ	Ⓓ	Ⓓ	Ⓓ
Ⓔ	Ⓔ	Ⓔ	Ⓔ	Ⓔ	Ⓔ
Ⓕ	Ⓕ	Ⓕ	Ⓕ	Ⓕ	Ⓕ
Ⓖ	Ⓖ	Ⓖ	Ⓖ	Ⓖ	Ⓖ
Ⓗ	Ⓗ	Ⓗ	Ⓗ	Ⓗ	Ⓗ
Ⓘ	Ⓘ	Ⓘ	Ⓘ	Ⓘ	Ⓘ
Ⓙ	Ⓙ	Ⓙ	Ⓙ	Ⓙ	Ⓙ
Ⓚ	Ⓚ	Ⓚ	Ⓚ	Ⓚ	Ⓚ
Ⓛ	Ⓛ	Ⓛ	Ⓛ	Ⓛ	Ⓛ
Ⓜ	Ⓜ	Ⓜ	Ⓜ	Ⓜ	Ⓜ
Ⓝ	Ⓝ	Ⓝ	Ⓝ	Ⓝ	Ⓝ
Ⓞ	Ⓞ	Ⓞ	Ⓞ	Ⓞ	Ⓞ
Ⓟ	Ⓟ	Ⓟ	Ⓟ	Ⓟ	Ⓟ
Ⓠ	Ⓠ	Ⓠ	Ⓠ	Ⓠ	Ⓠ
Ⓡ	Ⓡ	Ⓡ	Ⓡ	Ⓡ	Ⓡ
Ⓢ	Ⓢ	Ⓢ	Ⓢ	Ⓢ	Ⓢ
Ⓣ	Ⓣ	Ⓣ	Ⓣ	Ⓣ	Ⓣ
Ⓤ	Ⓤ	Ⓤ	Ⓤ	Ⓤ	Ⓤ
Ⓥ	Ⓥ	Ⓥ	Ⓥ	Ⓥ	Ⓥ
Ⓦ	Ⓦ	Ⓦ	Ⓦ	Ⓦ	Ⓦ
Ⓧ	Ⓧ	Ⓧ	Ⓧ	Ⓧ	Ⓧ
Ⓨ	Ⓨ	Ⓨ	Ⓨ	Ⓨ	Ⓨ
Ⓩ	Ⓩ	Ⓩ	Ⓩ	Ⓩ	Ⓩ

6. DATE OF BIRTH

MONTH	DAY		YEAR	
◯ JAN				
◯ FEB				
◯ MAR	⓪	⓪	⓪	⓪
◯ APR	①	①	①	①
◯ MAY	②	②	②	②
◯ JUN	③	③	③	③
◯ JUL		④	④	④
◯ AUG		⑤	⑤	⑤
◯ SEP		⑥	⑥	⑥
◯ OCT		⑦	⑦	⑦
◯ NOV		⑧	⑧	⑧
◯ DEC		⑨	⑨	⑨

7. SEX

◯ MALE
◯ FEMALE

8. OTHER

1 Ⓐ Ⓑ Ⓒ Ⓓ Ⓔ
2 Ⓐ Ⓑ Ⓒ Ⓓ Ⓔ
3 Ⓐ Ⓑ Ⓒ Ⓓ Ⓔ

OpScan *i*NSIGHT™ forms by Pearson NCS EM-255315-1:654321   Printed in U.S.A.

THIS PAGE INTENTIONALLY LEFT BLANK

The Princeton Review
Diagnostic ACT Form

ENGLISH

1 Ⓐ Ⓑ Ⓒ Ⓓ   21 Ⓐ Ⓑ Ⓒ Ⓓ   41 Ⓐ Ⓑ Ⓒ Ⓓ   61 Ⓐ Ⓑ Ⓒ Ⓓ
2 Ⓕ Ⓖ Ⓗ Ⓙ   22 Ⓕ Ⓖ Ⓗ Ⓙ   42 Ⓕ Ⓖ Ⓗ Ⓙ   62 Ⓕ Ⓖ Ⓗ Ⓙ
3 Ⓐ Ⓑ Ⓒ Ⓓ   23 Ⓐ Ⓑ Ⓒ Ⓓ   43 Ⓐ Ⓑ Ⓒ Ⓓ   63 Ⓐ Ⓑ Ⓒ Ⓓ
4 Ⓕ Ⓖ Ⓗ Ⓙ   24 Ⓕ Ⓖ Ⓗ Ⓙ   44 Ⓕ Ⓖ Ⓗ Ⓙ   64 Ⓕ Ⓖ Ⓗ Ⓙ
5 Ⓐ Ⓑ Ⓒ Ⓓ   25 Ⓐ Ⓑ Ⓒ Ⓓ   45 Ⓐ Ⓑ Ⓒ Ⓓ   65 Ⓐ Ⓑ Ⓒ Ⓓ
6 Ⓕ Ⓖ Ⓗ Ⓙ   26 Ⓕ Ⓖ Ⓗ Ⓙ   46 Ⓕ Ⓖ Ⓗ Ⓙ   66 Ⓕ Ⓖ Ⓗ Ⓙ
7 Ⓐ Ⓑ Ⓒ Ⓓ   27 Ⓐ Ⓑ Ⓒ Ⓓ   47 Ⓐ Ⓑ Ⓒ Ⓓ   67 Ⓐ Ⓑ Ⓒ Ⓓ
8 Ⓕ Ⓖ Ⓗ Ⓙ   28 Ⓕ Ⓖ Ⓗ Ⓙ   48 Ⓕ Ⓖ Ⓗ Ⓙ   68 Ⓕ Ⓖ Ⓗ Ⓙ
9 Ⓐ Ⓑ Ⓒ Ⓓ   29 Ⓐ Ⓑ Ⓒ Ⓓ   49 Ⓐ Ⓑ Ⓒ Ⓓ   69 Ⓐ Ⓑ Ⓒ Ⓓ
10 Ⓕ Ⓖ Ⓗ Ⓙ   30 Ⓕ Ⓖ Ⓗ Ⓙ   50 Ⓕ Ⓖ Ⓗ Ⓙ   70 Ⓕ Ⓖ Ⓗ Ⓙ
11 Ⓐ Ⓑ Ⓒ Ⓓ   31 Ⓐ Ⓑ Ⓒ Ⓓ   51 Ⓐ Ⓑ Ⓒ Ⓓ   71 Ⓐ Ⓑ Ⓒ Ⓓ
12 Ⓕ Ⓖ Ⓗ Ⓙ   32 Ⓕ Ⓖ Ⓗ Ⓙ   52 Ⓕ Ⓖ Ⓗ Ⓙ   72 Ⓕ Ⓖ Ⓗ Ⓙ
13 Ⓐ Ⓑ Ⓒ Ⓓ   33 Ⓐ Ⓑ Ⓒ Ⓓ   53 Ⓐ Ⓑ Ⓒ Ⓓ   73 Ⓐ Ⓑ Ⓒ Ⓓ
14 Ⓕ Ⓖ Ⓗ Ⓙ   34 Ⓕ Ⓖ Ⓗ Ⓙ   54 Ⓕ Ⓖ Ⓗ Ⓙ   74 Ⓕ Ⓖ Ⓗ Ⓙ
15 Ⓐ Ⓑ Ⓒ Ⓓ   35 Ⓐ Ⓑ Ⓒ Ⓓ   55 Ⓐ Ⓑ Ⓒ Ⓓ   75 Ⓐ Ⓑ Ⓒ Ⓓ
16 Ⓕ Ⓖ Ⓗ Ⓙ   36 Ⓕ Ⓖ Ⓗ Ⓙ   56 Ⓕ Ⓖ Ⓗ Ⓙ
17 Ⓐ Ⓑ Ⓒ Ⓓ   37 Ⓐ Ⓑ Ⓒ Ⓓ   57 Ⓐ Ⓑ Ⓒ Ⓓ
18 Ⓕ Ⓖ Ⓗ Ⓙ   38 Ⓕ Ⓖ Ⓗ Ⓙ   58 Ⓕ Ⓖ Ⓗ Ⓙ
19 Ⓐ Ⓑ Ⓒ Ⓓ   39 Ⓐ Ⓑ Ⓒ Ⓓ   59 Ⓐ Ⓑ Ⓒ Ⓓ
20 Ⓕ Ⓖ Ⓗ Ⓙ   40 Ⓕ Ⓖ Ⓗ Ⓙ   60 Ⓕ Ⓖ Ⓗ Ⓙ

MATHEMATICS

1 Ⓐ Ⓑ Ⓒ Ⓓ Ⓔ   16 Ⓕ Ⓖ Ⓗ Ⓙ Ⓚ   31 Ⓐ Ⓑ Ⓒ Ⓓ Ⓔ   46 Ⓕ Ⓖ Ⓗ Ⓙ Ⓚ
2 Ⓕ Ⓖ Ⓗ Ⓙ Ⓚ   17 Ⓐ Ⓑ Ⓒ Ⓓ Ⓔ   32 Ⓕ Ⓖ Ⓗ Ⓙ Ⓚ   47 Ⓐ Ⓑ Ⓒ Ⓓ Ⓔ
3 Ⓐ Ⓑ Ⓒ Ⓓ Ⓔ   18 Ⓕ Ⓖ Ⓗ Ⓙ Ⓚ   33 Ⓐ Ⓑ Ⓒ Ⓓ Ⓔ   48 Ⓕ Ⓖ Ⓗ Ⓙ Ⓚ
4 Ⓕ Ⓖ Ⓗ Ⓙ Ⓚ   19 Ⓐ Ⓑ Ⓒ Ⓓ Ⓔ   34 Ⓕ Ⓖ Ⓗ Ⓙ Ⓚ   49 Ⓐ Ⓑ Ⓒ Ⓓ Ⓔ
5 Ⓐ Ⓑ Ⓒ Ⓓ Ⓔ   20 Ⓕ Ⓖ Ⓗ Ⓙ Ⓚ   35 Ⓐ Ⓑ Ⓒ Ⓓ Ⓔ   50 Ⓕ Ⓖ Ⓗ Ⓙ Ⓚ
6 Ⓕ Ⓖ Ⓗ Ⓙ Ⓚ   21 Ⓐ Ⓑ Ⓒ Ⓓ Ⓔ   36 Ⓕ Ⓖ Ⓗ Ⓙ Ⓚ   51 Ⓐ Ⓑ Ⓒ Ⓓ Ⓔ
7 Ⓐ Ⓑ Ⓒ Ⓓ Ⓔ   22 Ⓕ Ⓖ Ⓗ Ⓙ Ⓚ   37 Ⓐ Ⓑ Ⓒ Ⓓ Ⓔ   52 Ⓕ Ⓖ Ⓗ Ⓙ Ⓚ
8 Ⓕ Ⓖ Ⓗ Ⓙ Ⓚ   23 Ⓐ Ⓑ Ⓒ Ⓓ Ⓔ   38 Ⓕ Ⓖ Ⓗ Ⓙ Ⓚ   53 Ⓐ Ⓑ Ⓒ Ⓓ Ⓔ
9 Ⓐ Ⓑ Ⓒ Ⓓ Ⓔ   24 Ⓕ Ⓖ Ⓗ Ⓙ Ⓚ   39 Ⓐ Ⓑ Ⓒ Ⓓ Ⓔ   54 Ⓕ Ⓖ Ⓗ Ⓙ Ⓚ
10 Ⓕ Ⓖ Ⓗ Ⓙ Ⓚ   25 Ⓐ Ⓑ Ⓒ Ⓓ Ⓔ   40 Ⓕ Ⓖ Ⓗ Ⓙ Ⓚ   55 Ⓐ Ⓑ Ⓒ Ⓓ Ⓔ
11 Ⓐ Ⓑ Ⓒ Ⓓ Ⓔ   26 Ⓕ Ⓖ Ⓗ Ⓙ Ⓚ   41 Ⓐ Ⓑ Ⓒ Ⓓ Ⓔ   56 Ⓕ Ⓖ Ⓗ Ⓙ Ⓚ
12 Ⓕ Ⓖ Ⓗ Ⓙ Ⓚ   27 Ⓐ Ⓑ Ⓒ Ⓓ Ⓔ   42 Ⓕ Ⓖ Ⓗ Ⓙ Ⓚ   57 Ⓐ Ⓑ Ⓒ Ⓓ Ⓔ
13 Ⓐ Ⓑ Ⓒ Ⓓ Ⓔ   28 Ⓕ Ⓖ Ⓗ Ⓙ Ⓚ   43 Ⓐ Ⓑ Ⓒ Ⓓ Ⓔ   58 Ⓕ Ⓖ Ⓗ Ⓙ Ⓚ
14 Ⓕ Ⓖ Ⓗ Ⓙ Ⓚ   29 Ⓐ Ⓑ Ⓒ Ⓓ Ⓔ   44 Ⓕ Ⓖ Ⓗ Ⓙ Ⓚ   59 Ⓐ Ⓑ Ⓒ Ⓓ Ⓔ
15 Ⓐ Ⓑ Ⓒ Ⓓ Ⓔ   30 Ⓕ Ⓖ Ⓗ Ⓙ Ⓚ   45 Ⓐ Ⓑ Ⓒ Ⓓ Ⓔ   60 Ⓕ Ⓖ Ⓗ Ⓙ Ⓚ

The Princeton Review
Diagnostic ACT Form

Completely darken bubbles with a No. 2 pencil. If you make a mistake, be sure to erase mark completely. Erase all stray marks.

READING

1	Ⓐ	Ⓑ	Ⓒ	Ⓓ	11	Ⓐ	Ⓑ	Ⓒ	Ⓓ	21	Ⓐ	Ⓑ	Ⓒ	Ⓓ	31	Ⓐ	Ⓑ	Ⓒ	Ⓓ
2	Ⓕ	Ⓖ	Ⓗ	Ⓙ	12	Ⓕ	Ⓖ	Ⓗ	Ⓙ	22	Ⓕ	Ⓖ	Ⓗ	Ⓙ	32	Ⓕ	Ⓖ	Ⓗ	Ⓙ
3	Ⓐ	Ⓑ	Ⓒ	Ⓓ	13	Ⓐ	Ⓑ	Ⓒ	Ⓓ	23	Ⓐ	Ⓑ	Ⓒ	Ⓓ	33	Ⓐ	Ⓑ	Ⓒ	Ⓓ
4	Ⓕ	Ⓖ	Ⓗ	Ⓙ	14	Ⓕ	Ⓖ	Ⓗ	Ⓙ	24	Ⓕ	Ⓖ	Ⓗ	Ⓙ	34	Ⓕ	Ⓖ	Ⓗ	Ⓙ
5	Ⓐ	Ⓑ	Ⓒ	Ⓓ	15	Ⓐ	Ⓑ	Ⓒ	Ⓓ	25	Ⓐ	Ⓑ	Ⓒ	Ⓓ	35	Ⓐ	Ⓑ	Ⓒ	Ⓓ
6	Ⓕ	Ⓖ	Ⓗ	Ⓙ	16	Ⓕ	Ⓖ	Ⓗ	Ⓙ	26	Ⓕ	Ⓖ	Ⓗ	Ⓙ	36	Ⓕ	Ⓖ	Ⓗ	Ⓙ
7	Ⓐ	Ⓑ	Ⓒ	Ⓓ	17	Ⓐ	Ⓑ	Ⓒ	Ⓓ	27	Ⓐ	Ⓑ	Ⓒ	Ⓓ	37	Ⓐ	Ⓑ	Ⓒ	Ⓓ
8	Ⓕ	Ⓖ	Ⓗ	Ⓙ	18	Ⓕ	Ⓖ	Ⓗ	Ⓙ	28	Ⓕ	Ⓖ	Ⓗ	Ⓙ	38	Ⓕ	Ⓖ	Ⓗ	Ⓙ
9	Ⓐ	Ⓑ	Ⓒ	Ⓓ	19	Ⓐ	Ⓑ	Ⓒ	Ⓓ	29	Ⓐ	Ⓑ	Ⓒ	Ⓓ	39	Ⓐ	Ⓑ	Ⓒ	Ⓓ
10	Ⓕ	Ⓖ	Ⓗ	Ⓙ	20	Ⓕ	Ⓖ	Ⓗ	Ⓙ	30	Ⓕ	Ⓖ	Ⓗ	Ⓙ	40	Ⓕ	Ⓖ	Ⓗ	Ⓙ

SCIENCE REASONING

1	Ⓐ	Ⓑ	Ⓒ	Ⓓ	11	Ⓐ	Ⓑ	Ⓒ	Ⓓ	21	Ⓐ	Ⓑ	Ⓒ	Ⓓ	31	Ⓐ	Ⓑ	Ⓒ	Ⓓ
2	Ⓕ	Ⓖ	Ⓗ	Ⓙ	12	Ⓕ	Ⓖ	Ⓗ	Ⓙ	22	Ⓕ	Ⓖ	Ⓗ	Ⓙ	32	Ⓕ	Ⓖ	Ⓗ	Ⓙ
3	Ⓐ	Ⓑ	Ⓒ	Ⓓ	13	Ⓐ	Ⓑ	Ⓒ	Ⓓ	23	Ⓐ	Ⓑ	Ⓒ	Ⓓ	33	Ⓐ	Ⓑ	Ⓒ	Ⓓ
4	Ⓕ	Ⓖ	Ⓗ	Ⓙ	14	Ⓕ	Ⓖ	Ⓗ	Ⓙ	24	Ⓕ	Ⓖ	Ⓗ	Ⓙ	34	Ⓕ	Ⓖ	Ⓗ	Ⓙ
5	Ⓐ	Ⓑ	Ⓒ	Ⓓ	15	Ⓐ	Ⓑ	Ⓒ	Ⓓ	25	Ⓐ	Ⓑ	Ⓒ	Ⓓ	35	Ⓐ	Ⓑ	Ⓒ	Ⓓ
6	Ⓕ	Ⓖ	Ⓗ	Ⓙ	16	Ⓕ	Ⓖ	Ⓗ	Ⓙ	26	Ⓕ	Ⓖ	Ⓗ	Ⓙ	36	Ⓕ	Ⓖ	Ⓗ	Ⓙ
7	Ⓐ	Ⓑ	Ⓒ	Ⓓ	17	Ⓐ	Ⓑ	Ⓒ	Ⓓ	27	Ⓐ	Ⓑ	Ⓒ	Ⓓ	37	Ⓐ	Ⓑ	Ⓒ	Ⓓ
8	Ⓕ	Ⓖ	Ⓗ	Ⓙ	18	Ⓕ	Ⓖ	Ⓗ	Ⓙ	28	Ⓕ	Ⓖ	Ⓗ	Ⓙ	38	Ⓕ	Ⓖ	Ⓗ	Ⓙ
9	Ⓐ	Ⓑ	Ⓒ	Ⓓ	19	Ⓐ	Ⓑ	Ⓒ	Ⓓ	29	Ⓐ	Ⓑ	Ⓒ	Ⓓ	39	Ⓐ	Ⓑ	Ⓒ	Ⓓ
10	Ⓕ	Ⓖ	Ⓗ	Ⓙ	20	Ⓕ	Ⓖ	Ⓗ	Ⓙ	30	Ⓕ	Ⓖ	Ⓗ	Ⓙ	40	Ⓕ	Ⓖ	Ⓗ	Ⓙ

I hereby certify that I have truthfully identified myself on this form. I accept the consequences of falsifying my identity.

Your signature

Today's date

The Princeton Review
Diagnostic ACT Form

ESSAY

Begin your essay on this side. If necessary, continue on the opposite side.

Continue on the opposite side if necessary.

The Princeton Review
Diagnostic ACT Form

Continued from previous page.

_____

_____

_____

_____

_____

_____

_____

_____

_____

_____

_____

_____

_____

_____

_____

_____

_____

_____

_____

_____

_____

_____

_____

_____

_____

**PLEASE PRINT
YOUR INITIALS**

First	Middle	Last

The Princeton Review
Diagnostic ACT Form

Continued from previous page.

The Princeton Review
Diagnostic ACT Form

Continued from previous page.

_____

_____

_____

_____

_____

_____

_____

_____

_____

_____

_____

_____

_____

_____

_____

_____

_____

_____

_____

_____

_____

_____

_____

_____

Chapter 28
Practice Exam 2:
Answers and Explanations

EXAM 2 ANSWER KEY

English Test		Mathematics Test		Reading Test		Science Reasoning Test	
1. C	39. C	1. A	31. B	1. D	21. D	1. B	21. C
2. G	40. H	2. K	32. F	2. J	22. G	2. G	22. H
3. D	41. C	3. B	33. E	3. B	23. B	3. D	23. D
4. H	42. J	4. K	34. F	4. J	24. F	4. H	24. G
5. B	43. C	5. A	35. C	5. A	25. C	5. A	25. C
6. G	44. G	6. H	36. J	6. G	26. H	6. F	26. H
7. A	45. B	7. C	37. B	7. B	27. C	7. A	27. B
8. J	46. H	8. G	38. K	8. H	28. F	8. J	28. F
9. C	47. D	9. A	39. D	9. C	29. D	9. B	29. D
10. J	48. H	10. H	40. H	10. F	30. H	10. G	30. G
11. B	49. A	11. B	41. A	11. C	31. C	11. C	31. C
12. H	50. J	12. G	42. J	12. J	32. F	12. J	32. F
13. A	51. D	13. D	43. D	13. B	33. C	13. A	33. A
14. F	52. J	14. K	44. K	14. F	34. G	14. G	34. J
15. C	53. D	15. E	45. E	15. B	35. A	15. C	35. C
16. G	54. H	16. F	46. K	16. J	36. H	16. H	36. J
17. D	55. A	17. C	47. B	17. A	37. B	17. A	37. A
18. J	56. G	18. J	48. J	18. H	38. G	18. J	38. G
19. C	57. B	19. B	49. C	19. A	39. D	19. B	39. A
20. G	58. H	20. K	50. H	20. J	40. G	20. J	40. H
21. D	59. C	21. E	51. A				
22. F	60. H	22. F	52. H				
23. A	61. C	23. B	53. B				
24. G	62. G	24. F	54. H				
25. A	63. C	25. D	55. D				
26. J	64. F	26. G	56. G				
27. A	65. B	27. C	57. A				
28. G	66. J	28. G	58. F				
29. A	67. C	29. A	59. D				
30. H	68. F	30. J	60. H				
31. B	69. A						
32. H	70. J						
33. D	71. B						
34. G	72. F						
35. C	73. C						
36. J	74. H						
37. C	75. D						
38. F							

ENGLISH TEST

Answers and Explanations

Question	Answer	Explanation
1	C	"Destined to become the first successful flight from New York to Paris" is an incomplete sentence. Therefore, it will have to be combined with the sentence that comes before it, and we need something other than a period after the word "journey." This allows us to eliminate (A) and (D). We don't want to separate "embarked" from its object, "on a journey," so we can eliminate (B).
2	G	There is no need for the words "it was" in this sentence, so we can eliminate (F). (J) can be eliminated, because "Flying in his single-engine plane" is an incomplete sentence. Between (G) and (H), (G) is better—try to not use "being" on the ACT unless you really have to.
3	D	As written, the sentence is redundant. Saying that the flight was unique is the same thing as saying that it was different from all other flights, so there's no need for the underlined portion. Choice (B) is also redundant and (C) is awkward, so the best answer is to eliminate the excess and keep it simple.
4	H	In this sentence, what comes before the underlined word ("extremely risky") and what comes after it ("duration of the flight and the exhaustion") are similar ideas; therefore, we need a word that compares similar ideas. "Despite," "except for," and "regardless of" are used to contrast different ideas, not to compare similar ideas, so we can eliminate (F), (G), and (J).
5	B	This is an issue of clumsy—though grammatically correct—English being the wrong answer and concise grammatical English being the right answer. Choices (C) and (D) quickly fall by the wayside: (C) uses regard as a noun in a manner never before seen on this planet, and (D) tosses in however for no good reason. That leaves (A) and (B), both of which are technically acceptable. Choice (B) is more concise, and therefore better on the ACT.
6	G	To answer this question, we should read a little bit of the context. The paragraph says that a "crowd descended" on Lindbergh. We need to choose a word that best describes a great deal of joy and admiration. Does a "trickle" mean a great deal? No. Does an "outpouring" mean a great deal? Yes. Does an "undercurrent" mean a great deal? Not really. Does a "murmur" mean a great deal? No. This will allow us to eliminate (F), (H), and (J).
7	A	Let's look at what follows the punctuation mark in the underlined portion. It's not a complete sentence, so we need punctuation that continues the thought. This will eliminate (B), (C), and (D).
8	J	Because the other verb in this sentence ("was whisked off") is in the past tense, we need another verb in the past tense. This eliminates (F), (G), and (H).
9	C	The other verbs in this sentence and in the sentence that follows are in the past tense: "got back," "were written," and "followed." Therefore, we should pick a verb that is also in the past tense.

ENGLISH TEST

Question	Answer	Explanation
10	J	As written, the sentence is excessively wordy. There is no reason to say "made up of" when "of" will work fine. This eliminates (F). Likewise, (G) can be eliminated because "consisting of" also uses more words than we need. We don't want to put a comma between an adjective and the noun it modifies, so (H) can also be crossed off.
11	B	The "letters" and "proposals of marriage" aren't contrasting ideas, so we don't want to use "even though" or "despite," which are both ways of drawing a contrast. This eliminates (A) and (C). If we omit the underlined portion the sentence won't make any sense, so we can also cross off (D).
12	H	"Becoming" by itself isn't a verb, and "has already become" is in the wrong tense, so we can eliminate (F) and (G). In (J), "remain" is a plural form, but the subject here is Lindbergh, which is singular; for this reason we can eliminate (J) as well.
13	A	If you've been paying attention, you've figured out that parallel structure matters on the ACT. It's the key to this question: "beat...challenged...showed"—that's good. Answer (A) and (C) offer this selection of verbs, but (C) sticks in an extra "and," so (A) is correct.
14	F	The key idea in this question is "Lindbergh is emblematic of the hope and pride of America." We can eliminate (G) and (J) because these choices aren't about America. Further, we can eliminate (H) because this choice doesn't involve Lindbergh. The best choice is the sentence as written.
15	C	The sentence that the author is proposing to add has to do with how the flight affected Lindbergh and how he felt afterward. The best place for this language is in Paragraph 3, which mentions how tired he was after the flight. Therefore, the best answer is (C).
16	G	This is the type of question you can do without reading the passage, because you're told exactly what to look for in the question itself. You want a word that means "appeal to a wide range of viewers." "Deft?" No. "Wordy?" No. "Smart?" No. "Accessible?" Yes!
17	D	The key idea in this question is "sense of the popularity of" the radio hour. Choices (A) and (B) don't really discuss the show's popularity, so we can eliminate them. Although (C) mentions it was "enjoyed by many," it goes on to criticize the show. Therefore, the best answer is (D).
18	J	As written, the sentence has a misplaced comma after the word "material." This eliminates (F). Because the word "serious" is modifying the word "literary," we don't want a comma between the two words. This eliminates (G) and (H), leaving us with (J).

ENGLISH TEST

Question	Answer	Explanation
19	C	"So rising a promising stage director" doesn't make much sense in the sentence as written, so we can eliminate (A). Likewise, "On the promising rise" in (D) is unclear. Deciding between (B) and (C) is difficult—if you're not sure, take the best guess. If you read carefully, you can see that (B) doesn't quite work because it's missing a subject—we'd need to insert "who" before the word "seemed" to make it work.
20	G	Remember when we told you that the non-underlined portion is always perfect and you can use it to guide you in your decisions about the answer choices? Well, this is a great example of that. Because "Martian" is an adjective here, it needs to have "invasion" after it (a noun) or nothing makes sense.
21	D	He? "He" who? That's what should go through your mind every time you see a pronoun. In this case, you can't answer the question "'He' who?" because it could be Wells, and it could be Welles. So (A) and (C) are out the door. (B) is doomed for using a plural to refer to a singular (but you knew that already), so (D) is the lucky winner this time.
22	F	The sentence before the semicolon and the sentence after the semicolon are complete sentences, so we need punctuation that ends the thought here. This eliminates (G), (H), and (J).
23	A	In this case, the broadcast started at a point in time in the past. Therefore, (A) is the best answer.
24	G	The key phrase in this question is "specific detail to convey the panic." We need to look for a choice that gives a specific case of panic. As written, the sentence doesn't give a specific detail, so we should eliminate (F). Likewise, (H) can also be crossed off. Choice (J) states that people jumped to a conclusion, but not that they were panicked.
25	A	The comma and conjunction separate two complete statements so ending punctuation is needed. Choices (B) and (C) are not ending punctuation, and (D) places the comma in the wrong place. That leaves us with (A).
26	J	The sentence, as written, tries to do too much. For this reason we can eliminate (F). (G) and (H) are properly formed, but they add a new idea that doesn't fit with the rest of the paragraph—namely, what is true of other cultures. Therefore, the best option is to leave off this unnecessary information and simply end the sentence.
27	A	The proper idiom is "fooled by."
28	G	We don't need a possessive in this sentence, so choices (H) and (J) can be eliminated. Further, the part of the sentence that begins with "while…" is not a complete sentence, so we need to use punctuation that continues the sentence. For this reason we can eliminate (F).
29	A	The rest of the sentence is in the past tense, with verbs like "did not" and "continued." Therefore, we need a verb in the past tense. This makes (A) the best answer.

ENGLISH TEST

Question	Answer	Explanation
30	H	The key idea in this question is "places the response…in a larger context of other stories of alien invasion." This means that the correct answer must mention other similar stories. Only (H) does this.
31	B	Because the underlined portion follows the preposition "between," we need to use an object pronoun ("me") and not a subject pronoun ("I"). For this reason, we can eliminate (A). Choices (C) and (D) introduce a new verb at the end of the sentence just before the period, which makes the sentence incomplete. This makes (B) the best answer.
32	H	The rest of the sentence doesn't really have anything to do with being "thoughtful," which means being nice or considerate. For this reason, we can eliminate (F), (G), and (J).
33	D	The second half of the sentence shows that "I" is the subject of the sentence. Therefore, (D) is the best answer.
34	G	In this case, the time at which the author expected things to be a certain way was before the time at which the author found out that things were different, so we should use the past perfect in this case. (Remember: Use the past perfect to describe something that happens before another past event.) This makes (G) the best answer.
35	C	This question asks us to link this paragraph to the following paragraph. The following paragraph is about how the author's brother changed his mind and decided to become a doctor instead of a writer or professor. The only sentence that discusses the possibility of the author's brother becoming a doctor is (C).
36	J	The other verbs in this sentence are in the past tense ("told" and "wanted"), so we should use a past tense verb here. This makes (J) the best choice. Don't forget that "of" in (G) is slang and not standard English.
37	C	Sometimes, quotation marks are used not only to show a direct quotation but also to express doubt about the accuracy or truth of a statement. This is supported by the author's slightly sarcastic tone in this paragraph. Therefore both II and III are correct, so (C) is the answer.
38	F	The two sentences on either side of this punctuation mark can stand alone, so we need ending punctuation. Therefore, we can eliminate (H) and (J). (G) doesn't make much sense, so the best answer is (F).
39	C	Because there are only two people in the story, the author and his brother, and the author says that his brother was getting A's, it must be the author who was getting a B+. This means that the pronoun in the underlined portion should be "I." Therefore, (C) must be the answer.
40	H	As written, the sentence has an awkward passive construction. Therefore, we can eliminate (F). The word "it" in (G) is ambiguous, so it can also be eliminated. (J) is also awkward.

ENGLISH TEST

Question	Answer	Explanation
41	C	As written, the comma before "to" is misplaced, so we can eliminate (A) and (B). Because the phrase that begins with "smuggling" and ends with "awake" is purely descriptive and could be removed without affecting the sentence, we will need a comma after the word "awake." This means that we can also eliminate (D). This makes (C) the best answer.
42	J	The author's brother should be compared with other premeds in this sentence, which is not possible by putting "Including my brother" at the beginning of the sentence. For this reason, we can eliminate (F). In (G), the word "soon" is misplaced, and in (H), the words "grade-point average" are repeated, making it extremely wordy. Therefore, the best answer is (J).
43	C	In this sentence, we see two independent clauses joined by the coordinating conjunction "but." In the answers we see that the punctuation and the conjunction are changing. (B) is out because it results in a run-on sentence. Eliminate (A) as well; the semicolon doesn't belong and the "but" is repetitive, showing up later in the same clause. The colon in (D) is incorrect, too. Only (C) connects the clauses with proper punctuation and varies word choice to avoid repetition.
44	G	Sentences 1, 2, and 3 talk about the author's schoolwork. Sentences 4–7 talk about the author's work experience. Because the sentences before number 4 are about one topic and the sentences after number 4 are about another topic, the most logical place to split the paragraph would be at Sentence 4. This makes (G) the best answer.
45	B	The key words in this question are "perspective gained by experience." So we need to pick a choice that shows the benefits of experience. Only (B) discusses the author's experience and what was gained by it.
46	H	The sentence as written is missing a subject, so we can eliminate (F). Choice (G) also leaves out the subject, so we can eliminate it as well. Between (H) and (J) the choice is one of verb tense. In this case, the point at which we left Chicago was "many hours before," so we're talking about a past event that came before another past event. Therefore, we should use the past perfect, which is (H).
47	D	The phrase "embarking on a great adventure" is a verb, and its object should not be interrupted by a comma. For this reason, we can eliminate (B) and (C). Furthermore, a comma should not precede the word "that," so (A) can also be crossed off. This makes (D) correct.
48	H	It's rare that the ACT uses the word "being" correctly, and this isn't one of those cases. Choice (F) is also very wordy, so we should eliminate it. In (G), it's unclear what "having thick accents" modifies, so we can eliminate it as well. If you've got a choice between (H) and (J), you've done very well. In fact, (J) is not quite correct, because "everyone" is singular, but is used here as if it were plural. This makes (H) the best answer.

ENGLISH TEST

Question	Answer	Explanation
49	A	Without a conjunction we're going to have a difficult time making a good sentence. If we have nothing at all, as in (C), we get a run-on sentence. If we simply insert a comma, as in (D), we get two independent sentences spliced together. This means we can eliminate (C) and (D). Starting a sentence with "and" is a bit clumsy, so we should avoid (B). The best choice is (A).
50	J	Because there is no contrast described in this sentence, contrasting words such as "despite" and "nevertheless" don't make any sense. Therefore, we can eliminate (F) and (H). Moreover, to use "in addition" we need something mentioned in the first place to which we are adding something else. But there is no such thing mentioned in the paragraph. For this reason, we can eliminate (G), and the answer is (J).
51	D	The last thing that happens in the sequence of events is putting everything into the car. All the transitions work except for (D).
52	J	Choices (F), (G), and (H) all have misplaced modifiers. The sentence as written makes it sound as if the writer's apprehension was watching the house. This doesn't make sense, so we can eliminate (F). Likewise, in choice (G), the sentence seems to say that it was the apprehension that was "in the distance." Finally, (H) says that the author watched "in the distance" when it was really the house and neighborhood that were distant.
53	D	If we try to put the word "seeming" at the beginning of this sentence, the sentence becomes incomplete. So we can eliminate (B) and (C). Now the only question is: Should we combine Paragraphs 3 and 4? We should, because Paragraph 3 is extremely short, and Paragraph 4 continues the idea started in Paragraph 3. This makes (D) the best answer.
54	H	The sentence as written is extremely wordy. If we can say it in a more concise way, we should. Likewise, (J) is also wordy. Choice (G) makes the sentence incomplete, so (H) is the best answer.
55	A	The key idea in this question is "show she was serious," so we need to look for a choice that shows the author's seriousness about leaving the new house. Only (A) really shows the author doing something that makes it look like she is leaving.
56	G	The phrase "as the first grade was called" is describing the name "P–1." Therefore, this phrase needs to be set off by commas, one on each side. Choices (H) and (J) are each missing one comma and (F) places the first comma in the wrong place, so the answer must be (G).
57	B	Paragraph 5 discusses how the author gets used to life in Ireland. Paragraph 6 suddenly begins with her return to the U.S. To make the transition smoother, we need a sentence that discusses her leaving Ireland and returning to the U.S. Therefore, (B) is the best answer.

ENGLISH TEST

Question	Answer	Explanation
58	H	In the sentence as written, "one at a time," doesn't make sense because it isn't clear what might be going one at a time. Because the author is discussing her feelings at the moment when she returned to the U.S., (G) or (J) don't quite fit, because each of these discusses something that happens over time.
59	C	The key idea in this question is "personal relationships among the writer's family." The passage, in fact, does not mention personal relationship; it talks about the author's feelings when she moves from the U.S. to Ireland. Only one sentence mentions the feelings or views of any other family members. This makes (C) the best answer.
60	H	Putting this sentence at the beginning of Paragraph 4 would not make sense because Paragraph 4 discusses the author's difficulty in adjusting to a new home. Nor would it make sense in Paragraph 6 where the author returns to the U.S. Therefore, we can eliminate (F) and (J). The sentence best fits in Paragraph 5, but it would not work well next to the current first sentence of paragraph 5. Therefore, the best answer is (H).
61	C	The key idea in this question is "without a care in the world." What kind of word best describes this? Something lighthearted and carefree, like skipping, (C).
62	G	In this sentence the author is expressing a contrast between what the others said and what he knew. Therefore we need a contrasting word like "but." Only (G) works.
63	C	In the rest of the sentence, the author uses the pronoun "you" in an impersonal sense. To be consistent, the word "you" should be used throughout the sentence. This makes (C) the best answer.
64	F	This is a great example for POE. Although there may be no immediately obvious reason to pick (F), it's clearly better than the rest, which don't make sense in this sentence.
65	B	Choice (D) leaves an incomplete sentence, so we can eliminate it. We can't use a semicolon, as in (C), because a semicolon requires that a complete phrase follow it. Because the sentence means to introduce a list of customers, the best choice is a colon, (B).
66	J	In this case, the fact that the boy was the same age as the author's sister isn't relevant to the paragraph. Therefore, we can eliminate it and make the paragraph clearer. This makes (J) the best answer.
67	C	In this case, we need the possessive pronoun "their" because the sentence is talking about the behavior of the two boys.
68	F	In the sentence as written, "barely able to remember whose order I had taken" is used to describe the word "man." No conjunction is needed, so (F) is correct.

ENGLISH TEST

Question	Answer	Explanation
69	A	In this case, we need to preserve parallel construction; because the rest of the sentence uses "demanding" and "complaining," we need to use "needing" in the underlined portion. This will eliminate (B) and (D). Choice (C) is awkward, so (A) is the best answer.
70	J	The correct idiom is to "demand something," not to demand about, of, or for something.
71	B	Because the sentence already has the word "but" in it, we don't need another conjunction. This eliminates (A) and (C). Choice (D) leaves the sentence incomplete, so (B) is the answer.
72	F	"Three years of experience" is correct as written.
73	C	It would make more sense if the sentences that mention the manager's questions were kept together: namely, Sentences 3 and 5. This would be accomplished if the positions of Sentences 4 and 5 were reversed.
74	H	The author's tone in this essay is generally lighthearted and humorous. Choices (F), (G), and (J) are much more serious than the rest of the passage warrants. This makes (H) the best answer.
75	D	This sentence introduces irrelevant information and should not be included in the passage.

MATHEMATICS TEST

Question	Answer	Explanation
1	A	To solve for x, we should subtract 2 from each side to get: $4x = 18$. Now we divide each side by 4, which gives us: $x = \dfrac{18}{4}$. So $x = 4.5$, which is (A).
2	K	The easiest way to solve this problem is to draw a number line. If you draw out the line and put point M at 9 and point N at –5, you can simply count the points between the two. Alternately, you can subtract –5 from 9: $9 - (-5) = 14$.
3	B	This is a great example of when you should use Plugging In. If we say the store sold two hats and three shirts, they would make \$40, $x = 2$ and $y = 3$, $2 \times 5 = 10$ and $3 \times 10 = 30$, $10 + 30 = 40$. Plug 2 and 3 into the answer choices to see which one gives you \$40. Plug them into (B) and you get $5(2) + 10(3) = 40$. That's what we were looking for, so (B) is the answer.
4	K	Convert each of the scientific notation numbers into "normal" format by moving the decimal point. Slide the decimal point one notch to the right for each positive power of 10, and one notch to the left for each negative power of 10. Choice (F) becomes 0.000021; (G) becomes 2,100,000; (H) becomes 21,000,000; (J) becomes 210,000; and (K) becomes 210,000,000. Choice (K) is the biggest, so (K) is correct.
5	A	Let's try Plugging In the answer choices and see which one works, starting with (C). If Alice began with 24 marbles and she gave away $\dfrac{2}{3}$ of them, that would leave her with 8. According to the question, she still needs to give $\dfrac{1}{3}$ away and end up with 8, so we need a larger number. Let's plug in (B). If Alice began with 30 marbles and gave $\dfrac{2}{3}$ of them away, that would leave her with 10. If she then gave away $\dfrac{1}{3}$, she would be left with a fraction, which is not an option. Therefore, we can eliminate (B). If she started with 36 marbles, (A), and gave away $\dfrac{2}{3}$ she would have 12 left. If she then gave away $\dfrac{1}{3}$, she would be left with 8, which is the answer. Our answer is (A).
6	H	We know that a is equal to $4y + 2z$, and we know that b is equal to $z - y$, so to figure out the value of $a + b$ we can substitute $4y + 2z$ for a, and substitute $z - y$ for b. So $a + b = (4y + 2z) + (z - y)$. This becomes $4y + 2z + z - y$, which is equal to $3y + 3z$. The choice that says this is (H). You could also plug in for a, b, y, and z.
7	C	To find the average, we add up the numbers to get the sum total $56 + 47 + 43 + 55 + 64 = 265$. Now we divide by the number of days, which is 5, and get $\dfrac{265}{5} = 53$. Therefore, the answer is (C).
8	G	The problem tells us that $x = -2$, so we can replace every value of x with –2 to solve. This means that $x^2 + 3x + 15$ will be equal to $(-2)^2 + 3(-2) + 15$, which is equal to $4 - 6 + 15$, or 13. The answer choice that says 13 is (G).

MATHEMATICS TEST

Question	Answer	Explanation
9	A	To solve this problem, we start by figuring out 8% of 45,000. What is 8% of 45,000? We can write this as $\dfrac{8}{100} \times 45,000$. Put this into your calculator and you will get 3,600. This is the amount of increase in the population of Greenville. The new population will be 45,000 + 3,600, which is 48,600. Which choice says this? (A) does.
10	H	As long as you remember the form of the slope-intercept equation ($y = mx + b$), you should have no problem with this question. Manipulate the equation to isolate y, arriving at $y = -\dfrac{5}{2}x + \dfrac{9}{2}$.
11	B	If we multiply $(x + y)(x + z)$, we get $x^2 + xz + yx + yz$. Now we need to figure out which answer choice is equivalent to this. Factoring out x in the middle terms, we get $x^2 + x(y + z) + yz$, so (B) is the answer.
12	G	In similar triangles, all sides are proportional to each other. We can figure out the ratio of the sides of the triangles by comparing their perimeters. The triangle with sides 4, 7, and 10 has a perimeter of 4 + 7 + 10, which is 21. So the other triangle must be exactly twice its size, and have sides 8, 14, and 20. The question asks for the longest side of the triangle, which is 20. This makes (G) the answer.
13	D	Don't forget to take the absolute value of each term before multiplying! The left term is the absolute value of 2 − 4, which is 2. The right term is the absolute value of −2, which is also 2. Now we multiply 2 times 2 to get 4. This makes (D) the answer.
14	K	The number of different outfits will be the product of the number of things John has to choose from. John can choose from 6 shirts, 4 pants, and 8 pairs of socks, so the number of possible outfits will be $6 \times 4 \times 8$, which is 192. This makes (K) the answer.
15	E	This question gives us the formula $V = \pi r^2 h$, and then gives us the values for r and h. In this case $r = 3$ and $h = 5$, so if we put these values into the formula we get $V = \pi \times 3^2 \times 5$, or $V = 45\pi$. Because π is about 3.14, the volume is about 141 cubic inches.
16	F	To see which function will have the largest value, plug in −10 for x in each of the functions, and solve. Choice (F) becomes $-10^2 - 2(-10)$, which equals 100 + 20, or 120. (G) becomes $-10^2 + 2(-10)$, which equals 120 + −20 = 80. Choice (H) becomes $-(10^2) = -100$. Choice (J) becomes −1,000 − 100, which equals −1,100. Choice (K) becomes -10^0, which equals 1. Therefore, the answer is (F).
17	C	If we translate this into math, we get $50 = \dfrac{20}{100}x$. Now we can reduce $\dfrac{20}{100}$ to $\dfrac{1}{5}$, and we can solve for x: $\dfrac{5}{1} \times 50 = x$, so $x = 250$. This makes (C) the answer.

MATHEMATICS TEST

Question	Answer	Explanation
18	J	For the 24-minute phone call, the first minute will cost 15 cents and the other 23 minutes will cost 3 cents each. So the total cost of the call will be 15 + (3×23). This makes a total of 84 cents. Which choice says this? (J) does.
19	B	To solve the slope, we take $\dfrac{\text{rise}}{\text{run}}$. The rise from 3 to 2 is –1; the run from –1 to 1 is 2. This makes the slope $-\dfrac{1}{2}$, or (B).
20	K	Solve the equation for x. First, distribute the –3 onto each term inside the parentheses: $8 - 3x + 6 = 5$. Note that it's 6, not –6 because the two negative signs cancel. Next, subtract 8 and 6 from each side (subtract 14): $-3x = -9$. Finally, divide both sides by –3: $x = 3$. Alternatively, you could work backward by trying out each possible value for x in the answer choices until you find one that makes the equation true. With (K), use $x = 3$ to get $8 - 3(3 - 2) = 5$, which becomes $8 - 3 = 5$, which is true.
21	E	Be very careful when you simplify a fraction that has addition or subtraction in it. The safest way to reduce this fraction is to remove a factor of 3 from the top of the fraction: $\dfrac{3x + 9y}{6z}$ becomes $\dfrac{3(x + 3y)}{6z}$. Now we can safely reduce top and bottom by a factor of 3, and we get $\dfrac{x + 3y}{2z}$. This makes (E) the correct answer.
22	F	Start by drawing a picture because the question doesn't provide one. Mark the points (–2,2), (2,3), and (3,–1) on a grid and connect them to make the sides of a square. Draw the missing two sides to get a rough idea of where the other corner should be located. You can see that the fourth corner must have a negative x-coordinate and a negative y-coordinate, so eliminate (H), (J), and (K). Opposite sides of a square will be parallel. The side from (2,3) to (3,–1) goes down 4 units and 1 to the right, so the left-hand side will do the same thing. Start at (–2,2) and move down 4 and 1 to the right to get (–1,–2). Choose (F).
23	B	We can find the slope of the line $2y = 10 - 3x$ by first putting it into standard form. First, we rewrite it as $2y = -3x + 10$, then we divide each term by 2, which gives us $y = -\dfrac{3}{2}x + 5$. Whenever you have an equation in the form $y = mx + b$, you know that m is the slope, so the slope of this line is $-\dfrac{3}{2}$. But the question asks for the slope of the line that is perpendicular to this line. The slope of perpendicular lines are the negative reciprocals, so the slope of the line perpendicular to the line $y = -\dfrac{3}{2}x + 5$ will have a slope of $\dfrac{2}{3}$. Therefore, the answer is (B).

MATHEMATICS TEST

Question	Answer	Explanation
24	F	One way to solve this problem is by factoring the equation. Another way to solve it is by plugging in the answer choices. Let's start by plugging in 4; it appears in two answer choices, so POE will be faster. $4^2 + 4(4) = 32$, not 12. Because 4 doesn't work, we can eliminate (H) and (J). Now let's try 6: $6^2 + 4(6)$ is much bigger than 12, so we can eliminate (G) and (K). We could check (F), but because the other four choices don't work, (F) must be correct.
25	D	To solve this question let's set up a proportion: $\dfrac{\text{cups juice}}{\text{quarts lemonade}} \dfrac{3\frac{1}{2}}{4} = \dfrac{x}{10}$. Now we can solve for x, and get $x = \dfrac{35}{4}$, or $8\dfrac{3}{4}$. Therefore, the answer is (D).
26	G	To figure out the hypotenuse of a right triangle, we can use the Pythagorean theorem, but we can also take a shortcut. Remember the 3:4:5 ratio. Because this is a ratio, any multiples of these numbers also work. 12:16:? is a multiple of 3:4:5, with each term increased by a factor of 4. So the hypotenuse must measure 20 inches.
27	C	One of the safest ways to solve this problem is to try each answer choice to see which could be multiplied by something else to get $8x^2 + 22x - 6$. Let's start with (A). What could we multiply $(4x - 3)$ by in order to get $8x^2 + 22x - 6$? We would need to multiply it by $(2x + 2)$ in order to get an $8x^2$ term and a -6 term, but if we multiply $(4x - 3)(2x + 2)$, then our middle term becomes $2x$, not $22x$. So we can eliminate (A). How about (B)? If we were to use $(4x + 3)$, then we'd need to multiply it by $(2x - 2)$ to get an $8x^2$ term and a -6 term. But if we multiply $(4x + 3)(2x - 2)$ then the middle term becomes $-2x$, not $22x$. So we should cross off (B). Now let's try (C). If we were to use $(8x - 2)$, then we'd need to multiply it by $(x + 3)$ to get an $8x^2$ term and a -6 term. When we multiply $(8x - 2)(x + 3)$, the middle term becomes $22x$, exactly as we want. So (C) is the answer.
28	G	Let's start by solving for x in the inequality $2(3x + 4) < 20$. If we multiply out the left side, we get $6x + 8 < 20$. Now let's subtract 8 from each side, and we get $6x < 12$. By dividing each side by 6, we can see that $x < 2$. This makes (G) the answer.
29	A	To solve this question, we need to remember our rules of exponents. Because $(x^y)^z$ is the same as x^{yz}, we know that $(x^{a+1})^3 = x^{3a+3}$. So we can set the exponents equal to each other: $3a + 3 = 9$. Solving this gives us $a = 2$, and the answer is (A).
30	J	To find the cosine of an angle, we solve $\dfrac{\text{adjacent}}{\text{hypotenuse}}$. In this triangle, the adjacent side is $2\sqrt{5}$ (use the Pythagorean theorem), and the hypotenuse is 6, so the cosine is $\dfrac{\sqrt{5}}{3}$. This makes the answer (J).

MATHEMATICS TEST

Question	Answer	Explanation
31	B	The shaded region is a triangle, so use: $A = \frac{1}{2}bh$. The height is 16, because that's the distance from the base to the top of the shaded triangle. It's upside-down, but that's no problem. To find the base, up at the top, we'll have to subtract 8 from the length of the whole top side. The big triangle is a right triangle with a hypotenuse of 20 and one leg of length 16. To find the other leg (the top side), use the Pythagorean theorem ($a^2 + 16^2 = 20^2$), or realize that the triangle fits the 3-4-5 pattern. In either case, the missing side of the big triangle is 12. So the base of the shaded triangle is $12 - 8 = 4$. Plugging that into the area formula, you get $A = \frac{1}{2}(4)(16) = 32$. That's answer choice (B).
32	F	Whenever we have a problem with i in it, all we need to do is replace every i^2 with -1. If we do this with $3i^2 + i^4$ we get $3(-1) + (-1)(-1)$. Multiply this out, and it becomes $-3 + 1$, which equals -2. This makes (F) the answer.
33	E	The problem tells us that the triangle is equilateral and that side BD is 8 units long. Because ABD is a right triangle, we know that this is a 30-60-90 right triangle and that the ratio of its sides must be $x : x\sqrt{3} : 2x$. We know the $x\sqrt{3}$ side, which is 8. So to solve for the x and $2x$ sides, we should solve for x. We know that $x\sqrt{3} = 8$; if we solve for x, we see that $x = \frac{8}{\sqrt{3}}$. This means that $\overline{AD}$ is equal to $\frac{8}{\sqrt{3}}$, and that side AB is equal to twice that, or $\frac{16}{\sqrt{3}}$. It's not good form to leave a root symbol in the denominator of a fraction, so we can rewrite $\frac{16}{\sqrt{3}}$ by multiplying it by $\frac{\sqrt{3}}{\sqrt{3}}$ to get $\frac{16\sqrt{3}}{3}$. As the triangle ABD is equilateral, sides BC and AC must also be equal to $\frac{16\sqrt{3}}{3}$. Therefore, the perimeter is equal to $3 \times \frac{16\sqrt{3}}{3}$ or $16\sqrt{3}$. Therefore, the answer is (E).
34	F	Remember the third side rule for triangles? The rule: Any two sides of a triangle have a sum that is larger than the third side. So if a triangle has sides 4 and 7.5, then the third side plus the side that measures 4 must have a sum larger than 7.5. This means that the third side must be larger than 3.5 inches. So 3.5 inches is NOT a possible length of the third side. This makes (F) the answer. (Don't forget, we were looking for the one that did NOT work this time!)

MATHEMATICS TEST

Question	Answer	Explanation
35	C	Be careful here. The question is asking for the *x*–intercept; what would the value of the *y*-coordinate be where the line crosses the *x*-axis? It must be 0, so you can eliminate (A), (B), and (E). If you ballpark by sketching the line, you'll see that the value of *x* at the *x*-intercept must be negative. Eliminate (D), and choose (C). Alternatively, you could have graphed the line on your TI-83 and used the TRACE function to ballpark.
36	J	One way to figure out whether a point is on a line is to substitute the *x*-coordinate for *x*, and the *y*-coordinate for *y* in the equation, and see whether the equation is true. Let's try this with (F). If we substitute 0 for x and 2 for *y*, is the equation true? Is $2 = \frac{1}{2}(0) - 2$? No, so we can eliminate (F). How about (G)? If we substitute 1 for *x* and 3 for *y*, is the equation true? Is $3 = \frac{1}{2}(1) - 2$? No, so we can eliminate (G). How about (H)? If we substitute 2 for *x* and 4 for *y*, is the equation true? Is $4 = \frac{1}{2}(2) - 2$? No, so we can eliminate (H). Let's look at (J) now. If we substitute 2 for *x* and –1 for *y*, is the equation true? Is $-1 = \frac{1}{2}(2) - 2$? Yes, so (J) is the answer. You can also plug the equation into your calculator and ballpark to save some time—(F), (G), and (H) are way off.
37	B	In this picture, because triangles *ACE* and *BCD* share angle *C*, and because $\overline{BD}$ and $\overline{AE}$ are parallel, we know that these two triangles are similar. This tells us that their sides will be proportional to each other: $\frac{CD}{CE} = \frac{BD}{AE}$. Substituting in the numbers we know, we get $\frac{4}{6} = \frac{6}{x}$. When we solve for *x*, we find that $\overline{AE}$ must equal 9. This makes (B) the answer.
38	K	This is a right triangle, so the Pythagorean theorem will tell us the relationship of the lengths of the sides. This means that if we use *x* for the length of $\overline{AC}$, $8^2 + x^2 = 17^2$. We can transform this into $x^2 = 17^2 - 8^2$. By taking the square root of each side we can solve for $x = \sqrt{17^2 - 8^2}$. This makes (K) the answer.
39	D	Your TI-83 is the best bet for this question. Enter the equation using your Y= key and view the TABLE by hitting 2nd, then GRAPH. Scroll until you find *y* at 0 and you will see that *x* equals 2. Alternatively, you could plug in the points given to you in the answer choices to see which equation checks out.

MATHEMATICS TEST

Question	Answer	Explanation
40	H	We know that sine is the same as $\dfrac{\text{opposite}}{\text{hypotenuse}}$ and that tangent is the same as $\dfrac{\text{opposite}}{\text{adjacent}}$, so now we know that the opposite side to angle θ must be 9, the adjacent side must be 40, and the hypotenuse must be 41. Because cosine is the same as $\dfrac{\text{adjacent}}{\text{hypotenuse}}$, we know that the cosine must be $\dfrac{40}{41}$. Therefore the answer is (H).
41	A	There are several ways to approach this question. If the equations look unfamiliar, think about all the different shapes you might see on an ACT geometry question. Straight lines never have exponents attached to the variables, and we haven't learned any equations for triangles or quadrilaterals. The equations must be circles! If you don't remember, the equation for a circle is $(x - h)^2 + (y - k)^2 = r^2$. Because both of these equations have a center of (0,0), the only difference is the size of the radius in each equation. Use your TI-83 to graph the circles; hit [2nd] [PRGM] to access the [DRAW] menu. Choose option 9 to draw your circles; using the TI-83 format, enter Circle (0,0,3) and Circle (0,0,4). The circles are different, which means they will never intersect.
42	J	Normally two different equations will graph two different lines; however, if the two equations are two versions of the same equation, then they will define a single line. If $b = 9$, then the second equation is the same as the first. $9x + 12y = 45$ is the same equation, simply multiplied by a factor of 3, as the equation $3x + 4y = 15$. This makes (J) the answer.
43	D	We know that ACD is a 30-60-90 right triangle, because it has a right angle and one angle of 30°. We also know that the hypotenuse in a 30-60-90 right triangle will be twice the shorter leg. So the hypotenuse $\overline{AC}$ will measure 12 inches. The problem states that triangle ABC is isosceles, so because $\overline{AC}$ will measure 12 inches, then $\overline{AB}$ will also measure 12 inches. We know that triangle ABC is a 45-45-90 triangle, because it is a right isosceles triangle, and we know that the ratio of the sides of a 45-45-90 right triangle are $x:x:x\sqrt{2}$. This means that the sides must be $12:12:12\sqrt{2}$. Therefore, answer is (D).
44	K	This is a good example of a question for which you should try plugging in the answer choices. Start in the middle with (H); suppose that the width of the rectangle is 6. The problem says that the length is 2 feet less than 4 times the width, so if the width is 6, the length will be 22. Does 22 times 6 make 240? No, it's much smaller, so we can eliminate (H). Now we should try (J). If the width is 7, then the length will be 2 less than 4 times 7, or 26. Does 26 times 7 equal 240? No, it's still too small. So let's try (K). If the width is 8, then the length will be 2 less than 4 times 8, or 30. Does 30 times 8 equal 240? Yes, so (K) is the answer.

MATHEMATICS TEST

Question	Answer	Explanation
45	E	The easiest way to solve this problem is to draw it. Start by drawing a circle with center $(-1,2)$ and the point $(-6,5)$. Now let's draw the lines that would get us from the center to the point $(-6,5)$. To get there we go left 5 units and up 3 units. So to find the opposing point, we start from the center and go right 5 units and down 3 units. This takes us to the point $(4,-1)$. This makes (E) the answer.
46	K	To solve this problem, we need to remember that $x^2 - y^2$ can also be expressed as $(x + y)(x - y)$. We know that $(x + y) = -3$ and that $(x - y) = -4$, so $(x + y)(x - y)$ will be equal to $(-3)(-4)$, or 12. Therefore, (K) is the answer. Remember, you can also plug in for x and y.
47	B	To find the area of the shaded region, we need to take the area of the square and subtract the area of the circle. The area of the square will be length times width. Because the length and width are both 10, the area of the square will be 10^2. The area of the circle will be πr^2, and because the circle's diameter is the same length as one side of the square (10), its radius will be half that length, or 5. So the area of the circle is 52π, and the area of the shaded region will be $102 - 52\pi$. Choice (B) says this and therefore is the answer.
48	J	We can break up this figure into other figures we know. The center of the figure is a rectangle, with length 16 centimeters and height 12 centimeters. We know the height is 12 because it is the third side of a right triangle with hypotenuse 13 and one leg 5. This is one of our 5-12-13 Pythagorean triples. So the area of this part of the figure is 12×16, or 192. Now all we need to do is add the areas of the two triangles on the ends. Each of them has height 12 and base 5, so each of them has an area of 30, because the area of a triangle is $\frac{1}{2}$ (base $\times$ height). $192 + 30 + 30 = 252$, which is (J).

MATHEMATICS TEST

Question	Answer	Explanation
49	C	First draw the figure. If we draw a line from Miko's ending point to her starting point, we get the hypotenuse of a right triangle with base 80 and height 60. This means that the shortest path (the hypotenuse of the triangle) is 100 feet. (Remember your 6-8-10 Pythagorean triple?) Going the long way, Miko actually walked 20 + 70 + 60 + 10, or 160 feet. Therefore, the shortest path, which would have been 100 feet, is 60 feet shorter. The answer is (C).
50	H	If $\log_x 64 = 2$, then we know that $x^2 = 64$. Which value for x makes this true? $8^2 = 64$, so (H) is the answer.
51	A	For $\dfrac{x}{x^2 - 7}$ to be undefined, the denominator must be zero. This means that $x^2 - 7 = 0$, and that $x^2 = 7$. Now we can solve for $x = \sqrt{7}$. Therefore, the value of $x^3 - 7x$ will be equal to $7\sqrt{7} - 7\sqrt{7}$, or zero. This makes (A) the answer.
52	H	Let's plug in on this problem. What would be an easy number to plug in for n? Any small round number will do. Let's try plugging in 10 for n. If Bob drives 3 miles in 10 minutes, how long will it take him to drive 14 miles? We can set up a proportion $\dfrac{3}{10} = \dfrac{14}{x}$. Solving for x, we get $\dfrac{140}{3}$. Which choice also says this? Remembering that n is 10, (H) also reads $\dfrac{140}{3}$.
53	B	Work backward, using numbers that fit the inequality they give you. Then, use POE on the answer choices. If $x = -\dfrac{1}{2}$ and $y = 2$, then $xy = -1$. The only answer choice that includes -1 on its graph is (B).

MATHEMATICS TEST

Question	Answer	Explanation
54	H	Plugging In is a great way to solve this one. What if we try $x = 2$? Choice (F) becomes 4, (G) becomes 12, (H) becomes 9, (J) becomes 13, and (K) becomes 20. Choices (F), (G), and (K) are even numbers in this case, so we can eliminate them. Now let's try $x = 3$. In this case, (H) becomes 19, and (J) becomes 28. Because (J) is an even number, we can eliminate it. The only choice that is always an odd integer is (H).
55	D	The way to think about this question is to ask which of the answers could be plugged in for k and would allow the equation to be factored with one value of x. Let's start with (C) and plug in 12 for k. Can we factor $x^2 - 12x + 12 = 0$? If it doesn't seem like it can be done, let's move on. How about (D)? Let's try assuming that k is 36. Now let's factor $x^2 - 12x + 36 = 0$. We can factor it as $(x - 6)(x - 6) = 0$, which leaves only one possible value for x, which is $x = 6$. Therefore, (D) is the answer.
56	G	Because $\overline{AE} = \frac{1}{2}\overline{BE}$ and the hypotenuse of triangle AEB is $\sqrt{5}$, we can figure out the lengths of $\overline{AE}$ and $\overline{BE}$. The Pythagorean theorem tells us that $\left(\overline{AE}\right)^2 + \left(\overline{BE}\right)^2 = \sqrt{5}^2$. Because $\overline{AE} = \frac{1}{2}\overline{BE}$, we can replace $\overline{AE}$ in the equation by $\frac{1}{2}\overline{BE}$, and get $\left(\frac{1}{2}\overline{BE}\right)^2 + \left(\overline{BE}\right)^2 = \sqrt{5}^2$. If we solve for $\overline{BE}$, we get $\overline{BE} = 2$. Now to find the area of the parallelogram, we take the base (7) times the height (2), which gives us 14, or (G).
57	A	Remember that the tangent of an angle is equal to $\frac{\text{opposite}}{\text{adjacent}}$. In this case, we can say that $\tan 29 = \frac{\text{height of pole}}{40}$. So now we can solve for the height of the pole, which will be equal to $40 \times \tan 29$. This makes (A) the answer.
58	F	The maximum value of the function $\sin x$ is 1. Even if we ask for $\sin 2x$, the maximum value is still 1. Therefore, the maximum value will be $y = -1 + 4(1)$, which is 3.
59	D	If the average of 6 integers is 65, then we can solve for their total, which must be 6×65, or 390. If an average of 7 integers is 66, we can solve for their total, which must be 7×66, or 462. The difference between these two totals is 72, which must be the value of the seventh number.
60	H	This probability problem has two steps. When Jamie pulls out the first sock, there are a total of 28 socks to choose from, 10 of which are black. When she pulls out a black sock on the first draw and goes back in the drawer for another sock, she will be choosing from 27 socks of which 9 are black. Thus, on the second draw she has a $\frac{9}{27}$ chance of drawing a black sock. $\frac{9}{27}$ reduces to $\frac{1}{3}$, making (H) the answer.

READING TEST

Question	Answer	Explanation
1	D	Let's look at how these words are used in context. On the last line of the first paragraph, Mick is wondering whether to climb the ladder, and the passage says that she *screwed up nerve and began to climb*. What word could we put in place of the words *screwed up*? Something like *found* or *gathered*. The choice that comes closest to this idea is (D).
2	J	In the first paragraph, Mick does not find Mr. Singer, so (F) can be eliminated. She doesn't make breakfast for her family, so (G) can also be crossed off. Although the passage says that Bubber goes to Sunday School, it doesn't say that Mick does, so (H) won't be right either. The paragraph does, however, describe how she cares for her younger brothers; this makes (J) the best choice.
3	B	In the third sentence of the third paragraph, Mick is on top of the roof and thinks to herself this is *where everybody wanted to stand*. This supports (B).
4	J	In the first paragraph, we find that Mick cares for Ralph and Bubber, so they aren't her father. The first paragraph also states that her father tells Mick that Mr. Singer came in late the night before. Therefore, we can eliminate (F), (G), and (H), which leaves us with (J) as the answer.
5	A	According to the fourth paragraph, other children also climbed the roof, so we can eliminate (D). Although (B) and (C) might be true, there isn't really any evidence in the paragraph to support them. (A) has some support because the sixth paragraph tells us that Mick was finally somewhere *by herself. No one was around and it was quiet and she could think for a while*. This makes (A) the best answer.
6	G	This is a good example of using POE to solve a problem. There is nothing in line 31 that tells us that Mick felt she had a poor singing voice or that she did not want to scare her brothers, so we can eliminate (F) and (J). While there is some reason from the first paragraph to believe that she was slightly afraid of climbing the ladder, we need to find an answer that has support in this particular line, which doesn't mention fear of heights. Therefore, we should avoid (H) as well. Even if it's not entirely clear what (G) is saying, we should pick it because we're sure that the others aren't correct.
7	B	The first paragraph tells us that Mick *waited for Mister Singer a long time. All the other boarders came down....* This is evidence that Mr. Singer is a boarder in Mick's house.
8	H	In the next-to-last paragraph of this passage, Mick dreams of inventing a tiny radio, a flying machine, and a tunnel through the earth. The passage mentions big balloons but doesn't state that Mick intends to invent them. This makes (H) the best choice.
9	C	Toward the end of the first paragraph, it states that the house was being built, and the fifth paragraph says *soon the work would all be finished*. This tells us that the house is unfinished, so the answer is (C).

READING TEST

Question	Answer	Explanation
10	F	The passage doesn't mention getting good grades in school or wanting to spend more time with parents, so (H) and (J) can be eliminated. Moreover, while Mick does care for her younger brothers, the passage doesn't actually state that she wants to have children of her own. This makes (G) not very promising either. In the seventh paragraph, Mick spends time thinking about what she would do when she was very famous. This makes (F) the most reasonable choice.
11	C	This is another great example of how POE works on the ACT. From the first paragraph we know that the author thinks that television has had a negative effect on news reporting. This will allow us to eliminate (B) and (D); (A) states that he is defending news stations, which also can't be right. This leaves us with (C) as the best answer.
12	J	Let's look at how this word is used in context. The sentence in question states *the world as mapped by the speeded-up electronic media has no order or meaning and is not to be taken seriously.* What word could we put in place of the word *mapped*? Something like *described* or *presented*. The choice that comes closest to this idea is (J).
13	B	Let's try to eliminate what we know is wrong and work our way to the best answer. The question of live television as opposed to recorded television isn't addressed in the passage, so we can eliminate (A). The passage also does not discuss how television brings families together, so we can also eliminate (C). Although the author might believe that television reporters should also write articles, he doesn't actually say that anywhere in this passage, so (D) can also be crossed off. There is evidence to support (B) in lines 29–34, so the best bet is (B).
14	F	The point of the paragraph immediately preceding these lines is that television reporters are chosen based on how they look. Then Christine Craft is cited as an example of someone who was fired because people did not like how she looked. This makes (F) the best answer.
15	B	The author doesn't talk about the future of newspapers, so (C) can be eliminated. Because the passage argues that television has significantly changed the nature of news, (D) isn't likely either. (A) might be something the author thinks, but he doesn't discuss actors in these paragraphs. We can find support for (B) in the third paragraph, where he states that on television *we are presented not only with fragmented news but news without context*...and, therefore, without essential seriousness.
16	J	The author doesn't really discuss the unbiased reporting of facts or informing the public about new products. For this reason we can eliminate (F) and (H). Although (G) might be tempting, nowhere does it actually state that the point of television is to make individuals popular. At the end of the third paragraph, however, the author says that television news has become *pure entertainment*. This makes (J) the best answer.

READING TEST

Question	Answer	Explanation
17	A	Let's look back to the passage where the author mentions "talking hairdos" and re-read just these lines. There the author says that television executives will *exclude women who are not beautiful or who are over the age of 50, men who are bald, all people who are overweight or whose noses are too long...*(lines 42–45) and this best supports (A).
18	H	Let's look back to the beginning of the passage. It says "Now...this" *is commonly used on radio and television newscasts to indicate that what one has just heard or seen has no relevance to what one is about to hear or see.* Answer (H) sounds closest to this.
19	A	At the beginning of the last paragraph, the author claims that *the perception of the truth of a report rests heavily on the acceptability of the newscaster.* This best supports (A).
20	J	In the second paragraph, the author states that *television sells its time in seconds and minutes, that it must use images rather than words,* and that *viewers are rarely required to carry over any thought or feeling from one parcel of time to another.* Therefore, (F), (G), and (H) are cited; the one that is not is (J).
21	D	By reading a few lines above and a few lines below, we can get a better understanding of the context. The author mentions the *photographic motion study* to emphasize the movement being suggested in the painting. The best answer is (D).
22	G	The first paragraph mentions students burning Brancusi in effigy and one of America's more distinguished artists, Kenyon Cox. Line 32 states that Hughes was an art critic. Therefore the answer is (G).
23	B	Lines 12–13 state that Kenyon Cox saw modern art as the *total destruction of the art of painting.* Which choice best paraphrases this idea? (B) does.
24	F	Lines 34–35 discuss Duchamp's painting with the words *to the degree that it looked at all like what it was supposed to be...* The author thereby implies that the painting does not, in fact, look much like a nude person at all. Therefore, (F) is the best answer.
25	C	Let's go back to the passage and re-read the word *abhorrent* in context. The lines in question compare the word *abhorrent* with *absurd* and *unnatural.* The word that best matches these is (C).
26	H	According to lines 49–50, modern artists *saw themselves as articulating an ideology,* that art was not intended to be pretty but instead to be bold and challenging. The choice that best re-states this idea is (H).
27	C	Lines 23–24 say that Roosevelt declared *in a loud voice his disapproval of all but the American entries.* Therefore, we know that he did not like much of it but did like some of it. This best supports (C).
28	F	In line 17, we see that modern art was considered *perverse fantasies of the foreigner.* This implies that the artists were mostly foreign-born. The best paraphrase of this idea is (F).

READING TEST

Question	Answer	Explanation
29	D	The last paragraph states that the organizers took action to encourage viewers to *greet the new art with an open mind*. This tells us that they expected people not to like the art that was displayed, which is (D).
30	H	In the final paragraph, we find that some of the supporters described modern art as art that is *a sign of life. There can be no life without change, as there can be no development without change.* This means that they felt that modern art was associated with change and development. The choice that best paraphrases this idea is (H).
31	C	The point of the first paragraph is contained in the first line: namely, that great discoveries may come from very small beginnings. The choice that best paraphrases this idea is (C).
32	F	According to the final paragraph, it was Berzelius who used the initial of the Latin name of the elements. This makes (F) the best answer.
33	C	The author's attitude toward Dalton is generally positive, so we can eliminate (B) and (D). Evidence for the author's interest in Dalton can be found at the end of the first paragraph, where the author states that Dalton's work was the beginning of the *wonderful theory* of atoms. This makes (C) the best answer.
34	G	Lines 59–60 state that Gay-Lussac was *the rising authority of the French chemical world.* Therefore, the best answer is (G).
35	A	The beginning of the fifth paragraph states that Avogadro discovered the *true explanation of Gay-Lussac's law of combination by volumes.* Even if you're not sure exactly what this says, (A) looks like a close paraphrase.
36	H	While it's true that Berzelius improved upon Dalton's work, the last paragraph doesn't say that he disproved Dalton's view; therefore, we can eliminate (F). Nor does it say that Berzelius was an influence on Avogadro and Gay-Lussac, so we can also eliminate (G). The final paragraph does say that Berzelius's discoveries were facts that *all harmonized with the atomic theory of Dalton.* This makes (H) the best answer.
37	B	Lines 53–55 state that Dalton gives an atomic weight of 5.5 to oxygen, and lines 52–53 say that the unit of weight is based on the hydrogen atom. Therefore, we know that Dalton believed oxygen to weigh 5.5 times as much as hydrogen. Choice (B) is the best paraphrase of this idea.
38	G	Lines 65–70 discuss Gay-Lussac's work. They describe his discovery that gases, when kept at constant temperature and pressure, always combine in definite proportions as to the volume.
39	D	Lines 40–45 describe Dalton's assumption. This caused Dalton to underestimate the weight of oxygen because he thought there was only half as much hydrogen as there really was. This is contradicted in lines 74–76 and 79–80. The answer is (D).
40	G	In lines 80–82, the passage states that Avogadro devised the name of the molecule.

SCIENCE REASONING TEST

Question	Answer	Explanation
1	B	According to the first paragraph, we can figure out K_m by figuring out half the maximum rate of the reaction (V_{max}) and then finding the corresponding substrate concentration. Because this question asks about bMAO, we need to look at Figure 2. In Figure 2 we see that the maximum value of the reaction is at approximately 100. This makes half of it equal to 50. However, 50 is not the answer—we need to find the corresponding substrate value where the reaction rate equals 50. Looking at the line that represents the use of Drug X, we see that it hits 50 where the substrate concentration is about 20. Therefore, the best approximation for K_m is 20.
2	G	Because this question asks about hMAO, we need to look at Figure 3 to find the answer. In Figure 3 we see that without Drug X, the maximum reaction rate is approximately 100. With Drug X, the maximum reaction rate is approximately 50. This means that Drug X cuts the maximum reaction rate in half. The choice that best describes this is (G).
3	D	The paragraphs that describe Experiments 1 and 2 are very similar—they describe the same quantity of enzyme and the same method of increasing the amount of drug used. The significant difference is that Experiment 1 was performed with the enzyme bMAO, while Experiment 2 was performed with the enzyme hMAO. This makes (D) the best answer.
4	H	According to Figure 2, the maximum value of the reaction is about the same whether Drug X is used or whether it is not used. Therefore V_{max} doesn't change. This is enough to get the answer because this will eliminate (F), (G), and (J). We can also see that the curve with Drug X is slightly shifted to the right; this means that K_m will be slightly increased. Therefore (H) is the answer.
5	A	Comparing Figure 2 and Figure 3 shows us that Drug X does have an effect in both cases, but the effect is much more pronounced in the case of hMAO than of bMAO. The choice that best paraphrases this is (A).
6	F	In these experiments, both the type of drugs tested and the reaction rate were variable, so we can eliminate (G). The substrate concentrate was increased steadily, so we can eliminate (H). Both experiments used 10 micrograms per milliliter of enzyme, so the best answer is (F).
7	A	This experiment begins with unpolarized light, so we need to look at Experiment 1. Table 1 shows us that the intensity of the beam at 15° is 3.73 and the intensity at 30° is 2.99. We know that at 20° the intensity will be between these two values. Therefore, the answer is (A).
8	J	In each of the tables, as the angle between the axes of the filters increases, the intensity decreases. Therefore we have good reason to believe that as the angle is decreased from 90° to 0°, the intensity of the resulting beam will steadily increase.

SCIENCE REASONING TEST

Question	Answer	Explanation
9	B	If we look at the values of intensity on Table 3, we see that as the angle goes up, the intensity drops off consistently. In fact, it drops more rapidly as the angle gets greater. The only graph that shows a consistently dropping intensity is graph (B).
10	G	The first line of Experiment 1 states that the scientists were using unpolarized light; the first line of Experiment 2 states that the scientists used the same setup but used polarized light. The choice that best restates this idea is (G).
11	C	The question tells us that the frequency of the beam determines its color, so to know whether color has any effect on the intensity of the emerging beam, we will need to try beams of different frequencies. The choice that paraphrases this idea is (C).
12	J	It's clear from the table that the intensity decreases as the angle of axis increases, so we can eliminate (G) and (H) right away. To choose between (F) and (J) we should first look at the difference between 0° and 15°. According to the table, the intensity changes from 4.00 to 3.73, a difference of 0.27. Now let's look at the difference between 15° and 30°. In this case, the intensity changes from 3.73 to 2.99, a difference of 0.74. Therefore, the difference isn't constant, and the answer is (J).
13	A	From Figure 1, we can deduce that mitosis will take 15% of the time, as the other values add up to 25% + 25% + 35% = 85%. Therefore, the fibroblast should spend 15% of its 24 hours in mitosis, which is 3.6 hours. This makes (A) the best choice.
14	G	According to Figure 2, if we look at the levels of Cyclins A, B, D, and E at the point where the letter M indicates, we see that E has dropped off to zero, D is low and steady, A is dropping off to zero, and B is coming down from its highest point. Therefore, the answer is (G).
15	C	According to Figure 2, Cyclin D is fairly steady throughout every phase. This makes it likely that Cyclin D has the least effect on the phases.
16	H	According to Figure 2, the beginning of the cycle goes along with a rapid increase in Cyclin E. Cyclins A and B change only in the middle of the cycle, so they are probably not responsible for initiating the cycle. This makes (H) the best answer.
17	A	Figure 2 tells us that an increase in Cyclin A comes at the beginning of Stage S. From Figure 1, we know that during Stage S, DNA synthesis takes place. Therefore, the most likely answer is that Cyclin A triggers DNA synthesis.
18	J	If we look just at the first two rows of the table, we see that the distance between similarly sized plates doubles from 5 millimeters to 10 millimeters; at the same time the capacitance is cut in half. This makes (J) the best answer.
19	B	The eighth row of the table shows a 20 millimeters distance between plates of porcelain that are 2 square meters. Its capacitance is given as 6.17 pF. The question tells us that the dielectric constant of mica is similar to that of porcelain, so its capacitance should be about the same as that of porcelain. This makes (B) the answer.
20	J	The question almost answers itself. It mentions that the plates cannot touch, and (J) is the only choice that addresses this issue.

SCIENCE REASONING TEST

Question	Answer	Explanation
21	C	If we look at the seventh and eighth rows of the table, we find a case where both the area of the plates and the distance between them doubles. On these lines we see that the capacitance is, in each case, 6.17. Therefore, we know that doubling the area and the distance between them has no effect on the capacitance, and (C) is the answer.
22	H	The fourth and fifth lines of Table 1 show a paper dielectric with a separation of 15 millimeters and areas of 1.0 and 2.0 square meters. The question asks for the capacitance if the plates measured 1.5 square meters; this will fall somewhere between the values for the capacitance of plates with areas of 1.0 and 2.0 square meters, or between 2.07 and 4.13. The only value that falls in this range is (H).
23	D	In the final sentence of Scientist 1's statement, we see *it is possible that similar bacteria could be living on present-day Mars.* Scientist 2, on the contrary, claims *any forms of Martian life…would have died out billions of years ago.* The choice that best paraphrases this difference is (D).
24	G	Scientist 2 claims that one of the reasons for the extinction of life on Mars is that the *thick Martian atmosphere, which also would have protected the planet…has long since disappeared.* If Mars had a weak magnetic field that allowed the atmosphere to erode, this would support Scientist 2's statement.
25	C	If we re-read the statement of Scientist 3, we can find wind, volcanic activity, and liquid carbon dioxide cited as reasons for the gullies. Although expansion of the planet's crust is mentioned, it is mentioned as an explanation for the appearance of a coastline, not as an explanation for the gullies.
26	H	Scientist 3 claims that whether or not water is present, the harsh ultraviolet radiation would prevent all life from growing on the surface of Mars. But if there were water below the surface, out of range of the ultraviolet rays, then Scientist 1's claim would be stronger. This makes (H) the best answer.
27	B	The bacteria in the meteorite seem to show that there was, at some time in the past, life on Mars. Scientist 1 thinks that there are bacteria on Mars now that are similar to those on Earth. Therefore, the meteorite helps Scientist 1's claim. Scientist 2 claims that there was once water on Mars that could have supported life, so the meteorite also supports Scientist 2's claim. Scientist 3 contends, however, that life does not exist on Mars, so the meteorite does not help Scientist 3's claim.
28	F	Both Scientist 2 and Scientist 3 cite harmful ultraviolet radiation as a factor that would prevent life on Mars today.
29	D	One of Scientist 3's claims is that the gullies were formed by liquid carbon dioxide, which forms at very low temperatures. It would help this claim to know that Mars never had a climate warm enough to support life.
30	G	From the opening paragraph we know that respiration at rest is called tidal volume (TV). In Figure 1, tidal volume is marked out as the region between 3.5 and 5 liters. Therefore, we know that TV, and respiration at rest, is about 1.5 liters.

SCIENCE REASONING TEST

Question	Answer	Explanation
31	C	This is a good case for POE. We know that restrictive lung diseases are pulmonary diseases, so we can eliminate (A). If FEV is reduced, then the ratio will certainly be smaller than 0.8, so we can eliminate (D). FEV and FVC would not be increased in a patient with lung disease, so (B) is out. That leaves us with (C).
32	F	This is a simple look it up question. The passage states that patients with obstructive lung disease tend to have lower FEV/FVC ratios. The lowest one here is Patient 1, (F). If you picked (J), you picked the patient most likely to have restrictive lung disease.
33	A	According to the table, tidal volume has no direct relationship to vital capacity, so (B) can be eliminated. Nor does vital capacity have any relation to total lung volume, so (C) can also be crossed off. The sum of inspiratory reserve volume and the tidal volume makes up only about half of the vital capacity, so (D) can also be eliminated. However, the residual volume is what is left over in the lung aside from vital capacity, so any increase in residual volume will decrease vital capacity. This makes (A) the answer.
34	J	According to the passage, a buildup of fluid in the lungs is characteristic of an obstructive lung disease, which results in a reduced FEV/FVC ratio. This will eliminate (F) and (H). Emphysema will not reduce the ratio because it is a restrictive pulmonary disease and tends to increase the FEV/FVC ratio. Therefore, we can eliminate (G). This leaves us with (J) as the answer.
35	C	If we look at Table 3, and find the entry where the length is equal to 4.0 and the cross-sectional area is equal to 2.0, we see that the change in length is 2.8. If both the length and cross-sectional area are doubled, such that the length is 8.0 and the cross-sectional area is 4.0, the change in length remains 2.8. The change in length has stayed the same so the answer is (C).
36	J	The passage tells us that *if the force on the bar exceeds the yield strength…permanent deformation will occur, and the bar will not resume its original shape.* Under Experiment 1, we see that aluminum returned to its original shape in all trials except in the final one. This means that the yield strength is not as great as 400 but greater than 200. The only value that fits in this range is (J).
37	A	According to Table 2, we see that the Young's modulus of glass will fall somewhere between the Young's modulus of concrete (which is 30×10^9 N/m2) and that of steel (which is 200×10^9 N/m2). This means that the change in length should be somewhere between that of concrete (6.6) and that of steel (1.0). The only answer choice in this range is (A).

SCIENCE REASONING TEST

Question	Answer	Explanation
38	G	From Table 1, we can see that if the applied force increases, so does the change in length. This allows us to eliminate (F). In Table 2, we can see that decreasing the Young's modulus is associated with an increase in the change in length. This allows us to eliminate (J). If we look at the fourth and fifth rows of Table 3, we find a case where the cross-sectional area remains constant but the length of the bar increases. The change in length also increases, so this must be due to the increasing length of the bar. Therefore, we can eliminate (H). We can see from the first two rows of Table 3 that increasing cross-sectional area does not increase the change in length; instead, the change in length decreases from 0.7 to 0.4. This makes (G) the answer.
39	A	We don't know anything about density, so (B) couldn't be the correct answer. Choice (C) actually hurts the hypothesis, as it says that temperature would not affect the Young's modulus, which we know does have an effect on the change in length. Finally, while (D) is a true statement, it would not help the hypothesis that temperature would affect change in length. Therefore, the best answer is (A).
40	H	We can tell from Table 3 that a bar 16 meters long with a 4 meter square cross-section would change about 5.6 millimeters, and that this is double the change from a bar with the same cross-section and half the length. We can, therefore, infer that if we double the length to 32 meters and keep the same cross-section, the bar will change about twice as much, or about 11 millimeters. This makes (H) the best answer.

WRITING TEST

To grade your essay, see the Essay Checklist on the following page. The following is an example of a top-scoring essay for the prompt given in this test. Note that it's not perfect, but it still follows an organized outline and has a strong introductory paragraph, a concluding paragraph, and transitions throughout.

Today's high school student is presented with many opportunities to cheat. The Internet is a ready source of resources for the unscrupulous, even including papers already written on just about any topic imaginable. But the problem of cheating reaches farther than just homework assignments—students today also have chances to cheat during exams in school, as teachers cannot possibly monitor the behavior of every student in a classroom simultaneously. Because the pressure to get great grades and get into a good college is so high, the pressure to cheat is very high. Nevertheless, it is critically important that schools do not give up in the fight against cheating because cheating is unfair to the students who play by the rules, because the consequences of being caught only increase later in life, and because one of the purposes of school is to teach students values.

Contrary to popular belief, not every student cheats. In all likelihood, the percentage of students cheating regularly is much lower than 50 percent. But the damage these students do to the students who don't cheat is very real and very severe. Colleges are choosing students based on their GPA and their class rank (in part—there are obviously other factors). When students cheat, they get higher grades that they don't deserve. As these cheaters move up the class rank, they are pushing down students who deserve to be higher, hurting those students' college opportunities. Cheaters will often say "Who cares if I cheat—it doesn't hurt anyone else's grades." Maybe not, but the damage done is even worse—it's hurting other people's futures.

Because it's hard for teachers in high school to keep an eye on every student, cheaters believe that they won't get caught, and for a while they are probably going to be right. Cheaters learn tricks that work well in the high school environment. The problem is, though, that they will keep on cheating through life and eventually will get caught. Colleges and businesses take this sort of behavior much more seriously, and so the cost of being caught cheating becomes much higher. If the cheater gets caught in high school and learns not to continue this behavior in the future, it will be embarrassing, but the real cost will be much easier for him or her to bear. So, schools should work hard to catch cheating during high school and should treat it seriously.

Finally, schools have a responsibility to set an example to their students. Part of the school's job, whether students like it or not, is to teach them the values of right and wrong. If schools are perceived by the student body to be giving up in the face of cheating, that not only sends us the message that this sort of devious behavior is acceptable (which we know is not true), it also ruins the reputation of the administration in our eyes. We will no longer take the school seriously on any matter, which will have a long-term damaging effect on the school community.

Clearly, cheating is wrong. There is no disagreement on this point, even from those who cheat. Just as clearly, schools have to do their very best to prevent cheating from occurring. Of all the reasons given, the first is the most important: These people are stealing college opportunities from their classmates.

WRITING TEST

1. The Introduction
   Did you
   o   start with a topic sentence that paraphrases or restates the prompt?
   o   clearly state your position on the issue?

2. Body Paragraph 1
   Did you
   o   start with a transition/topic sentence that discusses the opposing side of the argument?
   o   give an example of a reason that one might agree with the opposing side of the argument?
   o   clearly state that the opposing side of the argument is wrong or flawed?
   o   show what is wrong with the opposing side's example or position?

3. Body Paragraphs 2 and 3
   Did you
   o   start with a transition/topic sentence that discusses your position on the prompt?
   o   give one example or reason to support your position?
   o   show the grader how your example supports your position?
   o   end the paragraph by restating your thesis?

4. Conclusion
   Did you
   o   restate your position on the issue?
   o   end with a flourish?

5. Overall
   Did you
   o   write neatly?
   o   avoid multiple spelling and grammar mistakes?
   o   try to vary your sentence structure?
   o   use a few impressive-sounding words?

SCORING YOUR PRACTICE EXAM

Step A

Count the number of correct answers for each section and record the number in the space provided for your raw score on the Score Conversion Worksheet below.

Step B

Using the Score Conversion Chart on the next page, convert your raw scores on each section to scaled scores. Then compute your composite ACT score by averaging the four subject scores. Add them up and divide by four. Don't worry about the essay score; it is not included in your composite score.

Score Conversion Worksheet		
Section	Raw Score	Scaled Score
1	_____/75	_____
2	_____/60	_____
3	_____/40	_____
4	_____/40	_____

SCORE CONVERSION CHART

Scaled Score	Raw Score			
	English	Mathematics	Reading	Science Reasoning
36	75	60	39–40	40
35	74	59	38	39
34	72–73	58	37	38
33	71	57	36	—
32	70	55–56	35	37
31	69	53–54	34	36
30	67–68	52	33	—
29	65–66	50–51	32	35
28	62–64	46–49	30–31	33–34
27	59–61	43–45	28–29	31–32
26	57–58	41–42	27	30
25	55–56	39–40	26	29
24	52–54	37–38	25	28
23	50–51	35–36	24	27–26
22	49	33–34	23	25
21	48	31–32	21–22	24
20	45–47	29–30	20	23
19	43–44	27–28	19	22
18	40–42	24–26	18	20–21
17	38–39	21–23	17	18–19
16	35–37	18–20	16	16–17
15	32–34	16–17	15	15
14	29–31	13–15	14	13–14
13	27–28	11–12	12–13	12
12	24–26	9–10	11	11
11	21–23	7–8	9–10	10
10	18–20	6	8	9
9	15–17	5	7	7–8
8	13–14	4	—	6
7	11–12	—	6	5
6	9–10	3	5	—
5	7–8	2	4	4
4	5–6	—	3	3
3	3–4	1	2	2
2	2	—	1	1
1	0	0	0	0

SCORE CONVERSION CHART

About the Authors

Geoff Martz attended Dartmouth College and Columbia University before joining The Princeton Review in 1985 as a teacher and writer. His first book for The Princeton Review was *Cracking the GMAT*, published in 1989. He is also the author or coauthor of *Cracking the GED* and *Paying for College Without Going Broke*.

Kim Magloire is a graduate of Princeton University with a master's degree from Columbia University where she is currently completing her doctorate in Epidemiology. She joined The Princeton Review in 1984 as an SAT teacher and has since taught SAT, MCAT, GMAT, LSAT, GRE, and science SAT Subject tests.

Ted Silver is a graduate of Yale University, the Yale University School of Medicine, and the law school at the University of Connecticut. He has been intensely involved in the fields of education and testing since 1976 and has written several books and computer tutorials pertaining to those fields. He became affiliated with The Princeton Review in 1988 as the chief architect of The Princeton Review's MCAT course. Dr. Silver's full-time profession is as Associate Professor of Law at Touro College Jacob D. Fuchsberg Law Center.

NOTES

NOTES

NOTES

NOTES

NOTES

NOTES

Our Books Help You Navigate the College Admissions Process

AP Exams

Cracking the AP Biology Exam,
2009 Edition
978-0-375-42884-5 • $18.00/C$21.00

Cracking the AP Calculus AB & BC Exams,
2009 Edition
978-0-375-42885-2 • $19.00/C$22.00

Cracking the AP Chemistry Exam,
2009 Edition
978-0-375-42886-9 • $18.00/C$22.00

Cracking the AP Computer Science A & AB,
2006–2007
978-0-375-76528-5 • $19.00/C$27.00

Cracking the AP Economics Macro & Micro
Exams, 2009 Edition
978-0-375-42887-6 • $18.00/C$21.00

Cracking the AP English Language &
Composition Exam, 2009 Edition
978-0-375-42888-3 • $18.00/C$21.00

Cracking the AP English Literature &
Composition Exam, 2009 Edition
978-0-375-42889-0 • $18.00/C$21.00

Cracking the AP Environmental
Science Exam, 2009 Edition
978-0-375-42890-6 • $18.00/C$21.00

Cracking the AP European History Exam,
2009 Edition
978-0-375-42891-3 • $18.00/C$21.00

Cracking the AP Physics B Exam,
2009 Edition
978-0-375-42892-0 • $18.00/C$21.00

Cracking the AP Physics C Exam,
2009 Edition
978-0-375-42893-7 • $18.00/C$21.00

Cracking the AP Psychology Exam,
2009 Edition
978-0-375-42894-4 • $18.00/C$21.00

Cracking the AP Spanish Exam,
with Audio CD, 2009 Edition
978-0-375-76530-8 • $24.95/$27.95

Cracking the AP Statistics Exam,
2009 Edition
978-0-375-42848-7 • $19.00/C$22.00

Cracking the AP U.S. Government
and Politics Exam, 2009 Edition
978-0-375-42896-8 • $18.00/C$21.00

Cracking the AP U.S. History Exam,
2009 Edition
978-0-375-42897-5 • $18.00/C$21.00

Cracking the AP World History Exam,
2009 Edition
978-0-375-42898-2 • $18.00/C$21.00

SAT Subject Tests

Cracking the SAT Biology E/M Subject Test,
2009–2010 Edition
978-0-375-42905-7 • $19.00/C$22.00

Cracking the SAT Chemistry Subject Test,
2009–2010 Edition
978-0-375-42906-4 • $19.00/C$22.00

Cracking the SAT French Subject Test,
2009–2010 Edition
978-0-375-42907-1 • $19.00/C$22.00

Cracking the SAT U.S. & World History
Subject Tests, 2009–2010 Edition
978-0-375-42908-8 • $19.00/C$22.00

Cracking the SAT Literature Subject Test,
2009–2010 Edition
978-0-375-42909-5 • $19.00/C$22.00

Cracking the SAT Math 1 & 2 Subject Tests,
2009–2010 Edition
978-0-375-42910-1 • $19.00/C$22.00

Cracking the SAT Physics Subject Test,
2009–2010 Edition
978-0-375-42911-8 • $19.00/C$22.00

Cracking the SAT Spanish Subject Test,
2009–2010 Edition
978-0-375-42912-5 • $19.00/C$22.00